History of Multicultural Education, Volume II

Foundations and Stratifications

History of Multicultural Education

Edited by Carl A. Grant and Thandeka K. Chapman

Volume I: Conceptual Frameworks and Curricular Issues

Volume II: Foundations and Stratifications

Volume III: Instruction and Assessment

Volume IV: Policy and Policy Initiatives

Volume V: Students and Student Learning

Volume VI: Teachers and Teacher Education

History of Multicultural Education, Volume II

Foundations and Stratifications

Edited by

Carl A. Grant
University of Wisconsin, Madison

Thandeka K. Chapman
University of Wisconsin, Milwaukee

Routledge
Taylor & Francis Group

NEW YORK AND LONDON

First published 2008
by Routledge
711 Third Avenue, New York, NY 10017

Simultaneously published in the UK
by Routledge
2 Park Square, Milton Park, Abingdon, Oxon OX14 4RN

Routledge is an imprint of the Taylor & Francis Group, an informa business

First issued in paperback 2011

© 2008 Taylor & Francis

Typeset in Sabon by
RefineCatch Limited, Bungay, Suffolk

Library of Congress Cataloging in Publication Data
History of multicultural education / edited by Carl A. Grant and Thandeka K. Chapman.
    p.cm.
Includes bibliographical references and index.

ISBN 978-0-8058-5439-8 (hardback, volume i : alk. paper) – ISBN 978-0-8058-5441-1 (hardback, volume ii : alk. paper) – ISBN 978-0-8058-5443-5 (hardback, volume iii : alk. paper) – ISBN 978-0-8058-5445-9 (hardback, volume iv : alk. paper) – ISBN 978-0-8058-5447-3 (hardback, volume v : alk. paper) – ISBN 978-0-8058-5449-7 (hardback, volume vi : alk. paper)

1. Multicultural education–United States.   I. Grant, Carl A.   II. Chapman, Thandeka K.
LC1099.3.H57 2008
370.1170973–dc22   2008016735

ISBN13: 978-0-415-50484-3 (pbk)
ISBN13: 978-0-8058-5441-1 (hbk)
ISBN13: 978-0-415-98889-6 (set)

CONTENTS

PREFACE TO THE SIX-VOLUME SET

How we came to this work

We were invited by a large publishing house to create a multi-volume set on what we are calling the history of multicultural education. A change within the organizational structure of the publishing house resulted in the discontinuation of the initial project. However, over the course of the last seven years, the project was embraced by a second publishing house that later merged with our first publishing home. Our 360 degree turn has been both a professional challenge and an amazing opportunity. The project has grown and expanded with these changes, and given us the opportunity to work with many different people in the publishing industry.

We relate this series of events for multiple reasons. First we want to encourage new scholars to maintain their course of publication, even when manuscripts are not accepted on the first or second attempt to publish. Second, we would like to publicly thank Naomi Silverman and Lawrence Erlbaum Associates for throwing us a necessary lifeline for the project and for their vision concerning this project. Lastly, we would also like to thank Routledge Press for warmly welcoming us back to their publishing house and providing ample resources to support the publication of the six-volume set.

What we got out of it and what we saw

Over the course of six years, we have worked to complete these volumes. These volumes, separately or as a set, were marketed for libraries and resources rooms that maintain historical collections. For Thandeka it was an opportunity to explore the field of multicultural education in deep and multifaceted ways. For Carl, it was a bittersweet exploration of things past and an opportunity to reflect on and re-conceptualize those events and movements that have shaped multicultural education. Collectively, the time we spent viewing the articles, conceptualizing the volumes, and writing the introductions was also a meaningful chance to discuss, critique, lament, and celebrate the work of past and present scholars who have devoted time to building and expanding the literature on equity and social justice in schools.

Looking across journals and articles we noticed patterns of school reform that are related to political and social ideas that constantly influence and are influenced by the public's perceptions of the state of education and by professionals working in the field of education. We would also like to recognize authors who have made consistent contributions in journals to multicultural education. These authors have cultivated lines of inquiry concerning multicultural education with regard to teachers, students, parents, and classroom events for decades. Although we would like to list these scholars, the fear of missing even one significant name keeps us from making this list.

Moreover, we recognize that a good deal of the significant work in the field was not published in journal articles or that articles were greatly altered (titles, tone, examples, word choice) to suit the editors and perceived constituents of the journal. There are many stories that are told between the lines of these articles that may go unnoticed by readers who are less familiar with the field, such as the difficulty authors had with finding publication outlets, and questions and criticism from colleagues about conducting research and scholarship in the areas of multicultural education. Although these pressures cannot be compared across groups, scholars of color, white scholars, men and women all felt marginalized because they chose to plant their careers in the rich but treacherous soil of multicultural education.

Just as we can see career patterns, we also saw patterns of journals that were willing to publish articles that focused on multicultural education. While many journals have created an *occasional* special issue around topics of equity, social justice, and students of color, there are journals that have consistently provided outlets for the work of multicultural scholars over the past three decades.

Our hopes for the use of the volumes

We began this project with the desire to preserve and recount the work conducted in multicultural education over the past three decades. As scholars rely more heavily on electronic resources, and funding for ERIC and other national data-bases is decreased, we are concerned that older articles (articles from the late 60s thru the early 80s) that may never be placed in this medium would eventually be lost. The volume set is one attempt to provide students, teacher educators, and researchers with a historical memory of debates, conceptualizations, and program accounts that formed and expanded the knowledge-base of multicultural education.

GENERAL INTRODUCTION TO THE VOLUMES

Multicultural education's rich and contested history is more than thirty years old; and is presently having an impact on the field of education, in particular, and society in general. It is time to provide a record of its history in order that the multiple accounts and interpretations which have contributed to the knowledge base, are maintained and documented. Whereas this account is not comprehensive, it nevertheless serves as a historically contextualized view of the development of the field and the people who have contributed to the field of multicultural education.

The paradigm of multicultural education as social reconstruction asserts the need to reform the institutional structures and schooling practices that maintain the societal status quo. These reforms are fashioned by socially reconstructing the ways that educators and politicians approach issues of equity and equality in our public schools. Multicultural education has become the umbrella under which various theoretical frameworks, pedagogical approaches, and policy applications are created, shared, critiqued, and implemented through on-going struggles for social justice in education. These campaigns for educational reform influence and benefit all citizens in the United States.

As a movement, multicultural education has brought forth an awareness of and sensitivity to cultural differences and similarities that continues to permeate the highest institutional infrastructures of our nation. Although the movement is rooted in struggles for racial equality, multicultural education readily includes physical disabilities, sexual orientation, issues of class and power, and other forms of bias affecting students' opportunities for academic and social success. The inclusion of other forms of difference beyond skin color is one way that multicultural education acknowledges diversity in a myriad of forms and dismantles the assumptions of homogeneity within racial groups.

The purpose of this set of volumes on the history of multicultural education is to locate, document, and give voice to the body of research and scholarship in the field. Through published articles spanning the past thirty years, this set of books provides readers with a means for knowing, understanding, and envisioning the ways in which multicultural education has developed; been implemented and resisted; and been interpreted in educational settings. By no means consistent in definition, purpose, or philosophy, multicultural education has influenced policy, pedagogy, and content in schools around the United States and the world. In addition, it has stimulated rigorous debates around the nature and purpose of schooling and how students and teachers should be educated to satisfy those purposes.

This set of volumes draws attention to how scholars, administrators, teachers, students, and parents have interpreted and reacted to various political and social events that have informed school policy and practices. Each volume in the set documents and tells a story of educators' attempts to explicate and advocate for the social and academic needs of heterogeneous and homogeneous communities. Through their struggles to achieve access and equity for all children, different scholars have conceptualized the goals, roles, and participants of multicultural education in numerous ways. Through the academic arena of scholarly publications, and using diverse voices from the past thirty years, the *History of Multicultural Education* acknowledges the challenges and successes distinguished through struggles for equity in education.

Methods for collecting articles and composing the volumes

It is because of the multifaceted nature of multicultural education that we have taken multiple steps in researching and collecting articles for this volume set. Keeping in mind the many ways in which this set of volumes will enrich the study and teaching of education, we have approached the task of creating the texts using various methods. These methods reflect the spirit of inclusion intrinsic to scholarship in multicultural education and respect for diversity in the academic communities that promote and critique multicultural education. This was a multiple step process that included the following stages of data collection.

In the Spring of 2000, we began collecting articles using an electronic data bank called the *Web of Science*. This program allows the Editors to discover the number of times articles have been referenced in a significant number of refereed journals. We submitted proper names, article titles, and subject headings to create lists of articles that have been cited numerous times. The number of citations gave us an initial idea of how frequently the article had been cited in refereed journals. Using the *Web of Science* we established a list of articles, which because of their extensive referencing, have become seminal and historical works in the field of multicultural education. The authors cited in these pieces generated the names of over forty scholars who are both highly recognized or not immediately recognized for their scholarship in the area of multicultural education.

To extend the breadth and depth of these volumes, we returned to the *Web of Science* and used various subject headings to uncover other articles. The articles found in our second round of searching were also highly referenced by various scholars. The two searches were then cross-referenced for articles and authors. Through this process we attempted to reveal as many significant articles that dealt with multicultural education as possible. Some articles are foundational pieces of literature that have been copiously cited since their publication, while other articles represent a specific area of scholarship that has received less attention. For example, articles specific to early childhood and middle school education were not as easily identified as conceptual pieces that articulated various aspects of multicultural education.

The *Web of Science* program has some limitations. Articles that were published in less mainstream or more radical journals may not appear. The creation of a list of articles based solely on this program begs the questions of "What knowledge is of most worth?" and "How do we validate and acknowledge those significant contributions that have been marginalized in educational discourses?"

As multicultural educators, we were cautious not to re-instantiate those very discourses and practices that marginalize academic conversations. Therefore we used other educational and social science databases and traditional library-stack searches to present a more comprehensive set of texts that represent the field of multicultural education. For example, the reference sections in the first two searches were cross-referenced for articles that may not have appeared on-line. These articles were manually located, assessed, and used for their reference pages as well.

The main program limitation that haunted us was the lack of articles from the late 1960s and early 1970s that appeared in the electronic searches. We realized that educational research is lacking a comprehensive knowledge of its history because many scholars only cite articles written in the last ten to fifteen years when reporting their findings in academic journals. The lack of citations from the early years of multicultural education scholarship forced us to take a third approach to researching articles.

Using the ERIC files from 1966–1981 and manually sifting through bounded journals from the 1960s and 1970s, we were able to uncover other significant articles to include in the volumes. The decision to include or exclude certain articles rested primarily on the editors and other scholars who reviewed earlier drafts of the introductions to each volume and the references cited for that volume. We used the feedback from these scholars to complete our search for articles.

The volumes are a reflection of the field of research in multicultural education as well as a reflection of the community of scholars who contribute to the discourse(s) concerning issues of equity and equality in public schools. Our concern with shouldering such an awesome responsibility and our desire to include the voices from the many communities of multicultural education scholarship lead us to the final approach to finding quality articles. We solicited the opinions of over twenty multiculturalists. We asked them to choose the articles they believed belong in the volumes and suggest articles or areas that were not represented. Several scholars such as Sonia Nieto, Carlos Ovando, and Christine Sleeter answered our request and provided us with valuable feedback.

Polling various academic communities made the project a more inclusive effort, but also served as a tool to communicate the work of multicultural scholars. We appreciated the opportunity to engage with other scholars during the creation of these volumes. The multi-step research methodology for this project strengthens and enhances the finished product, making the volumes a valuable contribution to the field of education. This set of volumes, because it represents the voices of many scholars, is a spirited set of articles that reflects the tenets of multicultural education, its history, its present, its ideas for the future, and the people who believe in equity and social justice for all citizenry.

Features of the volumes

Each volume in the set includes a diverse group of authors that have written in the field of multicultural education. The array of work is based on the article's contribution to educational scholarship; they represent well-known and lesser-known points of view and areas of scholarship. The volumes do not promote one scholar's vision of multicultural education, but include conflicting ideals that inform multiple interpretations of the field.

Many of the articles from the early 1970s and 1980s are difficult for students to obtain because technology limits the number of years that volumes can be accessed through web databases. Volumes in the set provide students with access to the foundational articles that remain solely in print. Students and veteran scholars doing historical research may be especially interested in the volumes because of the rich primary sources.

The volumes are delineated by six subject groupings: *Conceptual Frameworks and Curricular Content, Foundations and Stratifications, Instruction and Assessment, Policy and Governance, Students and Student Learning,* and *Teachers and Teacher Education.* These six, broadly defined areas reflect the diversity of scholarship dealing with issues of equity and social justice in schooling. The articles illustrate the progression of research and theory and provide a means for readers to reflect upon the changes in language and thought processes concerning educational scholarship. Readers also will see how language, pedagogical issues, policy reforms, and a variety of proposed solutions for equity attainment have been constructed, assimilated, and mutated over the thirty year time period.

Volume I: Conceptual Frameworks and Curricular Issues

The articles in this volume illustrate the initial and continued debates over the concepts, definitions, meanings, and practices that constitute multicultural education. The authors articulate how best to represent the history and citizens of the United States, what types of content should be covered in public schools, and the types of learning environments that best serve the needs of all students. For example, this volume shows how multicultural education challenged the representations of people of color that are presented or ignored in textbooks. Conversely, articles that challenge conceptions of multicultural education are also included. Content wars over the infusion of authors of color, the inclusion of multiple historical perspectives, and an appreciation for various scientific and social contributions from people of color that reflect challenges to Eurocentric knowledge and perspectives are presented in this volume.

Volume II: Foundations and Stratifications

This volume presents theoretical and empirical articles that discuss the institutional factors that influence schooling. Issues such as the historical configurations of schools, ideologies of reproduction and resistance, and administrative structures that often maintain imbalances of power and equity in schools are discussed. In addition, articles explicating the various ways that students and educational opportunities are racially and socio-economically stratified are present in this volume.

Volume III: Instruction and Assessment

The articles in this volume elucidate general pedagogical approaches and specific instructional approaches with consideration given to content areas and grade level. Diverse instructional practices and the relationships between students and their teachers are discussed. Although content and pedagogy are difficult to separate, the work in this volume addresses the dispositions of the teacher and his/her awareness of learning styles, and his/her ability to incorporate aspects of students' culture and community affiliations into pedagogy. Also included in this volume are theories and models of multicultural assessment tools that reflect the needs of diverse learning communities.

Volume IV: Policy and Policy Initiatives

This volume on policy and governance explores the effects of federal and state mandates on school reforms dealing with equity in education. The articles in this volume show how educational organizations and associations have attempted to influence and guide school policy, instructional practices, and teacher-education programs. In addition, the volume presents articles that discuss how interest groups (e.g., parents and concerned teachers) influence enactments of education policy in schools.

Volume V: Students and Student Learning

This volume on "Students and Student Learning" focuses on students as individuals, scholars, and members of various social and cultural groups. The articles highlight different aspects of students' lives and how they influence their academic behaviors and includes students' affective responses to their schooling and their beliefs about the value of education. The articles also address how schools socially construct student learning through the lenses of race, class, and gender. In addition, the articles show how students act as political agents to structure, direct, and often derail their academic progress. Arguing that multicultural education is necessary for everyone, the articles highlight specific racial and cultural groups as well as offer generalizations about the academic needs of all students.

Volume VI: Teachers and Teacher Education

The teacher education volume addresses issues of multicultural education for preservice and experienced teachers. The articles cover the racial and social demographics of the past and current teaching force in the United States and the impact of these demographics on the structure of multicultural teacher education programs. Several articles speak to the role(s) of the university concerning multicultural preservice and in-service education classes, field placements, and institutional support for veteran teachers. These articles explore the nature of teaching for social justice in higher education, the desire to attract teachers of color, and the juncture between theory and practice for newly licensed teachers.

ACKNOWLEDGEMENTS

There are many who deserve a public thank you for their support of and participation in this project. We would like to thank the many colleagues and graduate students who offered constructive criticism, suggested articles, read drafts of the introductions, and helped to conceptualize the placement of articles in the different volumes. These people include: Barbara Bales, Anthony Brown, Keffrelyn Brown, Nikola Hobbel, Etta Hollins, Gloria Ladson-Billings, Sonia Nieto, Carlos Ovando, Christine Sleeter, and Michael Zambon.

We would like to offer a special thank you to the journals that, because of the nature of the project, reduced or forgave their fees for re-printing.

Thanks to Director JoAnn Carr and the staff in the Center for Instructional Materials and Computing (CIMC) for putting up with our large piles of bound and unbound journals that we pulled from the shelves and made unavailable for others for days at a time. Thank you for re-shelving all the publications (sometimes over and over again) and never reprimanding us for the amount of work we created.

A super big thank you to Jennifer Austin for compiling, organizing, and maintaining our files of publishers' permission requests. Jennifer also contacted and reasonably harassed folks for us until they gave her the answers we needed. Brava!

Thank you to our families for their support and only occasionally asking "Aren't you finished yet?"

STATEMENT CONCERNING ARTICLE AVAILABILITY AND THE CONFLICT WITH REPRINT COST

During this insightful, extensive process, the goal was to share re-printings of all the articles with our readers. However, as we moved to the end of our journey, we discovered that it was financially unfeasible to secure permissions from the publishers of all the articles. We found most publishers more than willing to either donate articles or grant us significant breaks on their re-printing prices. Other publishers were more intractable with their fees. Even if the budget allowed for the purchasing of the 200-plus articles, the price of the books would have become prohibitive for most readers. Therefore, the printed articles found in the volumes do not represent all the articles that met the criteria outlined in the Preface and are discussed in each of the volumes' introductions.

At first we decided not to summarize these articles and use them solely as support for the rest of the volume(s). As we refined our introductions and re-read (and read again) the articles, we could not discount how these pieces continued to provide significant knowledge and historical reflections of the field that are unique and timely. Therefore, if the volumes are to represent the most often referenced examples and keenly situated representations of multicultural education and paint a historically conceptualized picture of the field, we had no choice but to include the works of these scholars in our introductions. Unfortunately, for the reasons explained here, some of these articles are not included in these volumes. In Appendix 2, we have provided a list of all the publishers and publishing houses so that individuals and organizations may access these articles from their local or university libraries or web services free of charge.

LIST OF JOURNALS REPRESENTED IN THE SIX-VOLUME SET

Action in Teacher Education
American Association of Colleges for Teacher Education
American Educational Research Association
American Journal of Education
American Sociological Association
Anthropology and Education
Association for Supervision and Curriculum Development
Comparative Education Review
Curriculum and Teaching
Education
Education and Urban Society
Educational Horizons
Educational Leadership
Educational Research Quarterly
Educators for Urban Minorities
English Journal
Exceptional Children
FOCUS
Harvard Educational Review
Interchange
Journal of Curriculum Studies
Journal of Curriculum and Supervision
Journal of Teacher Education
Journal of Research and Development in Education
Journal of Negro Education
Journal of Literacy Research (formerly Journal of Reading Behavior)
Journal of Educational Thought
Journal of Teacher Education
Language Arts
Momentum
Multicultural Education
National Catholic Educational Association
National Council for the Social Studies
National Educational Service
Negro Educational Review
Peabody Journal of Education

INTRODUCTION TO VOLUME II

We entitled this volume *Foundations and Stratifications* because the articles demonstrate that the emphasis on issues of race, class, gender, and culture during the early days of the movement was the foundation of much, if not most of the discourse surrounding the creation of multicultural education. We define stratification as how schools are structured to privilege and marginalize different groups of students based upon race, class, gender, disability, and language. These institutional stratifications form the basis for inequitable social practices and regulated school procedures that are contested by multicultural education (MCE). The foundations of multicultural education lie within other academic and social movements that continue to evolve with MCE. The foundations of MCE are defined as those academic and social discourses that formed scholars' ideological frameworks and empirical research agendas. The foundations of MCE are not necessarily grouped with the larger body of literature of multicultural education that calls for curricular and pedagogical reforms. However, these frameworks for better understanding the pervasiveness of injustice in schools are well called upon in multicultural education.

In reading the social science and educational literature we note that before MCE there were many ideas dealing with issues of diversity and social justice. The foundations of MCE grow from many of these frameworks such as intercultural/intergroup education, feminism, cultural pluralism, cultural studies, ethnic studies, neo-Marxism, and other ideological frameworks. Other writings such as The Mis-education of the Negro, Dubois' double-consciousness, the tenets of The United Negro Improvement Association, "America as the Great Melting Pot", and "Ain't I A Woman" served as foundational sources and are pivotal to the beginnings of multicultural education. As with multicultural education, these academic and social discourses did not occur in a vacuum. They are deeply tied to social justice movements in the United States that pushed citizens to examine issues of justice and injustice, and called for institutional changes that granted access and opportunity to people who had been historically marginalized through social and legal mandates. Multicultural education is open and willing to acknowledge its ancestry in other academic movements and disciplines; while we do not create a comprehensive list of these roots, we strongly assert the connections between MCE and the greater bodies of literature and history that envelop the paradigm.

Thus, this volume highlights those articles in educational journals that have drawn from various fields to flesh out issues of access and equity in society and in schools. These articles focus upon the ways in which schools and society stratify and institutionalize inequity. Moreover, the authors of these articles are in conversation with multiculturalism by critiquing its limitations through broader concerns of race, class, gender, sexuality, and disability.

Articulations of feminism, cultural studies, and ethnic studies echo in these critiques and create a constant tension between the role(s) of schools and society.

When reading this volume as a text three themes emerge across the four decades of scholarship: (1) society and schools as the targets of change, (2) resistance to assimilation and the melting pot thesis, and (3) debates over deficit and difference models for explaining student achievement. Placing the articles in chronology serves to illuminate the developmental and foundational discussions of multicultural education. That said, we apply our critique of the three themes in the literature across timelines.

Society and Schools as Targets of Change

The context and complexity of the time is reflected in the articles in this volume. Americanization and the melting pot thesis was promoted by many liberal friends of diversity, while cultural pluralism was put forward by more radical friends of diversity. The Krug (1977) and Valverde (1977) articles are representative of scholarship that argued against the "melting pot" theory and advocated for theories of cultural pluralism. Scholars, for example Pacheco (1977), began to discuss the problematic nature of the melting pot in regard to issues of culture, race, and social class, and advocated for the recognition and understanding of different ethnic and racial groups. For such scholars the vision of schooling was that of Intergroup Education. Their writing focused more upon the acceptance of groups and the tolerance of difference, rather than confronting issues of stratification based upon race and social class which permeated the education system.

MCE: 1970s

The 1970s were a very perplexing time for multicultural advocates. They saw some increases in social and economic opportunities for people of color. In addition there was an assertion of: the black is beautiful doctrine and black identity; Latino and Asian American intergroup diversity; advocating for human rights by people living at or below the poverty level; a self-reliant ethic by people with handicaps; women's rights. On the other hand, school desegregation was hampered by violence, racial hostility, and segregated housing patterns. Busing for integration was vigorously opposed in both the North and South. Four Southern governors: Maddox of Georgia, Brewer of Alabama, McKeithen of Louisiana, and Kirk of Florida acted to block the integration of schools. President Nixon argued that *de facto* segregation did not violate the Constitution, but *de jure* desegregation as practice in the South did. Asian Americans were viewed as foreigners, and Latinos were told to learn and speak English. In such an atmosphere, multicultural scholars made a strong case for cultural pluralism and argued that there was "no one model American."

Assimilation and schooling

Articles in this volume by Leyba (1973), Hiraoka (1977), and Valentine (1971) represent scholarship which distinguishes between students' allegiances to the values and norms of their racial and cultural groups and their active participation in the greater society. In different ways, these authors discuss culture as fundamental to the conceptualization and practice of multicultural education. The authors' approaches to the task are to present arguments based upon "rational or logical thinking." There is a "calmness," we could say a nonviolent approach in their efforts, instead of a more passionate cry for equality and social justice which was taking place on college campuses and communities across the United States.

Hiraoka tells his readers that the ". . . concept of multicultural education must be defined and developed in its own right if it is to be effective in removing previous shortcomings."

Hiraoka, Leyba, and Valentine contend that earlier models of cultural identity and the exclusion of people of color are related to academic issues at Preschool/K-12 through college levels. To that end, Valentine proposes "a bi-cultural educational model." He contended that "many blacks are simultaneously committed to both Black culture and mainstream culture, and that these cultures are not mutually exclusive as generally assumed" (1971, p. 137). Early models of double-consciousness, Dubois for example, did not take into account the diversity inherent among groups of people and presented more homogeneous notions of race and culture. For example, gender and sexuality were not a part of the discussions of cultural pluralism. The articles show that the focus remained on the human relations approach to understanding differences between racial and ethnic groups.

Deficit and difference

The articles from the 1970s also illustrate the ongoing debate among scholars concerning cultural deficit and cultural difference models to explain student achievement. Even earlier scholars, such as Hines (1964) advocated that race and socioeconomic status were not indicators of intellectual deficiency, but reflections of group marginalization within the greater society. His writing is an early example of scholarship based on a self-fulfilling prophecy between societal expectations and schools that cyclically reproduces low-achieving students of color and poor students. Theories of social reproduction and debates over difference and deficit models stem from the argument that poor students and students of color do not function in the same ways that white middle-class students are perceived to function. Rist (1970) demonstrates how racism and classism infect all teachers' perceptions of student ability, regardless of the race of the teacher. Privileging students who exhibit more middle-class dispositions can eventually lead to inaccurate student classifications that limit students' access to opportunities.

The article by Barartz and Barartz (1970) received rave attention—some positive and some negative—as it attempted to dispel the deficit model with a theory of cultural difference. Valentine (1971), however, only months later took issue with the Barartz and Barartz's thesis further stimulating the debate. Valentine argued that both the cultural difference and cultural deficit model construct students of color and poor students as inferior to white middle-class students. Thirty years later, Solorzano and Yosso (2001), using a contemporary framework of critical race theory, assert that the deficit paradigm continues to thrive in education, and they re-articulate the need to argue for more egalitarian concepts of difference.

MCE: 1980s

The 1980s presents two distinct areas of scholarship in multicultural education: a focus on the relationships between society and schools and an attempt to more closely define the paradigm of multicultural education. The literature specifically that concerns the foundations of multicultural education becomes very thin in the 1980s. Whereas there was a significant amount of scholars historically situating the field in the 1970s, this focus lags in the 1980s and is replaced by critical theories concerned with embedded contexts of racial and social exclusion. Apple (1980), Apple and Weis (1986), Fine (1987), McCarthy (1988), and Popkewitz (1988) highlight the ways in which school knowledge is conceptualized and also withheld based on racial and socioeconomic stratifications in schools.

It is doubtful that the previously mentioned authors would identify themselves as multiculturalists, however the body of critical work that these authors represent greatly informs the field of multicultural education. Each of these authors makes the argument that society and schools cannot be separated because schools reflect and refract larger relationships of power from the society in which they were created. For example, Anyon (1981) uses theories of cultural reproduction to demonstrate how schools limit students' opportunities to learn from and become invested in their school experiences. Anyon speaks to issues of access and accommodation when she states:

> These working-class children were not offered what for them would be cultural capital-knowledge and skill at manipulating ideas and symbols in their own interests, e.g. historical knowledge and analysis that legitimates their own dissent and furthers their own class in society and in social transformation. (1981, p. 32)

In keeping with other critical theorists, Anyon uses social class as the unit of analysis in her work. In comparison, McCarthy attempts to bring issues of race to neo-Marxist discussions of the nature of schools and society to more strongly reflect of the social complexities endemic to education in the United States. McCarthy's observations on the limitations of neo-Marxism to explain issues of schooling were timely given the heavily attended focus on institutional stratifications in the 1980s. Unfortunately, there have been few scholars who have successfully blended neo-Marxist theories with other issues of "nonsynchrony" (McCarthy, 1988) such as gender, sexuality, and disability.

Whereas Apple, Apple and Weis, McCarthy, and Fine are discussing social reproduction from a curricular perspective and more closely focus upon the school, Popkewitz discusses the limitations of institutional reform as a direct reflection of society. He states:

> Rather, I want to argue against the sciences of change which focus upon particular events without considering relational issues that tie the performance of schooling to questions of history and power. (1988, p. 78)

Popkewitz's less optimistic view of reform exemplifies later critiques of school reform and the gains of multicultural education that are presented in the second group of articles from the 1980s and several articles from the 1990s.

The second area of scholarship from the 1980s largely highlights the construction of a better sense of the gains of multicultural education. Reflecting on little more than a decade of scholarship, these authors (Gay, 1983; Gezi, 1981; Sleeter and Grant, 1987) presented analyses of the themes, approaches, and debates that shaped the formative years of the multicultural education movement. Each of these authors details the evolution of deficit and difference models, the problematic nature of a constantly changing definition for multicultural education, and addresses the anxieties about the lack of consensus in the field. Sleeter and Grant identified five concepts and practices that educators used to define and implement multicultural education near the end of the second decade of the movement. They also recognized that "overall, authors' efforts to show the relationships of these ideas to practice are weak," and that the conceptualizations were limited based on vague goals and insufficient theoretical frameworks.

Additionally, Sleeter (1986) explores the creation of special education categorization. She notes that these categorizations are based on white middle-class norms of behavior and academic success and questions the use of behavior classifications with students of color. Her work frames much of today's interrogations of special education and the placement of African American, Latino, and Asian American students.

MCE: 1990s

The 1980 articles lamenting the lack of boundaries, the water-down focus on race, and the lack of rigorous scholarship foreshadow critiques of the field by Boyle-Baise and McCarthy. As the field of multicultural education moved into its third decade of scholarship, the lack of empirical support for multicultural education became a significant barrier to the growth of the field. Moreover, studies such as Anyon's (1995) and Oakes, Wells, Jones, and Datnow (1997) reported that multicultural education had done little to change the ideologies and practices that continue to stratify students according to their race and socioeconomic status. These unchanged ideologies stem from the deficit models of intelligence for students of color, the limited understandings and acceptance of different cultural groups, and fundamental debates on what/whose knowledge is most valuable.

The less than optimistic attitudes seeping from Anyon (1995) and Oakes, Wells, Jones, and Datnow (1997) mirror the attitudes of Olneck (1990) and McCarthy (1988) and reflect the frustrations of multicultural educators in the field. McCarthy and Olneck detail multiple aspects of the ways in which multicultural education has been conceptualized and practiced in the United States. Their overviews include issues of assimilation, tolerance, and group versus individual identity. They surmised that multicultural education should have a focus on race which would allow it to reconnect with the political roots that gave birth to the movement.

Similarly, Boyle-Baise (1999) questions the breadth of the multicultural paradigm and suggests that a tighter conceptualization of culture would benefit scholars. Yet, she asserts that a common core for multicultural education does exist that consists of "the educational pursuit of cultural dignity, integrity, and equality" (Boyle-Baise, 1999, p. 210). Her chronology of the field through the recollections of long-time scholars is a small-scale example of the types of evaluations currently being completed on the field from a thirty-year standpoint.[1]

Grant's (1994) article was a response to the myths about multicultural education which had resulted from confusion over its definition, purpose, and audience, as well as who was included or not include under the multicultural umbrella. Grant's article seems to act as a turning point in the literature, as MCE scholars stopped spending an overabundance of time responding to critiques, many of which were un-informed.

Articles by Banks (1993) and Payne and Welsh (2000) are more optimistic than the other articles from the 1990s. Banks delineates various types of knowledge (e.g., personal/cultural, popular, mainstream, transformative) and provides historical details about the roles they play in education. His article is not so much a critique of the field, but a response to more conservative groups that sought to disregard multicultural education. Banks seeks "to illustrate how the debate between the multiculturalist and the Western traditionalists is rooted in their conflicting conceptions about the nature of knowledge and their divergent political and social interests" (1993, p. 4). Payne and Welsh discuss the development of multicultural education from the 1960s to the present. Their article is particularly relevant because the authors highlight the various institutions with stated policies on multicultural education.

Discussion

The limited institutionalization of multicultural education is better dealt with in Volume IV, "Policy and Policy Initiatives"; however, the unchanging ideologies that support stratifications of students and continue to push for assimilation in schools is a significant challenge to the foundational elements of diversity and equity in education. Payne and Welsh address this issue by stating:

> Laws and policies alone do not constitute full institutionalization. Full institutionalization does not occur until the idea is reflected in the practices of the people who make-up the institution.
>
> Many of the social and educational changes that people thought were accomplished in the 1960s and 1970s did not succeed over the long term because they did not become fully institutionalized. (2000, p. 45)

In part, the institutionalization of multicultural education remains an elusive goal because scholars still have not come to a consensus on the foundational pillars of multicultural education. This is in part due to on-going debates about not only the place of "race," "class," and "gender" within the field, but the attention and prominence each of these areas should receive. Also, this debate is cloudy over arguments to include "sexuality" and "religion." Furthermore, scholars have only minimally examined the various movements and academic scholarship, such as Black feminism, cultural studies, women's studies, religious studies, etc., that continue to contribute to the field of multicultural education. There continues to be a need for scholarship that clarifies the goals and boundaries of multicultural education within and beyond the field of pre-K-12 education.

This is not to say that multicultural education has not made an impact. As we see in Boyle-Baise's piece and others, the broader scope of research and scholarship under the umbrella of diversity can be attributed to foundations of multicultural education. When one critiques the diffuse nature of the field, the richness of an expanded view of multicultural education can be recognized, particularly when dealing with inter-group diversity and the multiple selves of the individual. A more narrow focus on race and ethnicity becomes extremely problematic as students claim multiple racial, social, political, and sexual allegiances.

The articles seem to argue that multicultural educators must either embrace these multiplicities or continue to define the use of their terminology. In addition, they suggest that authors who use a more limited focus to discuss issues of equity and equality may wish to recognize that the roots of their various branches are connected to the sturdy trunk of the multicultural education paradigm. The connections within and across scholarship are strengths of the field that should be more closely examined.

Points of interest

In this volume we noted the lack of authorial continuity throughout the three decades of scholarship in the realm of multicultural foundations. Scholars such as Baker, Banks, Grant, Sleeter, Bennell, and Gay have greatly contributed to on-going conversations about multicultural education in the areas of teacher education and curriculum. With regard to the documenting of the foundations of the paradigm, it seems there are few authors who have withstood the test of time. Often, as is the case of the previously mentioned scholars, they are borrowed from other areas of multicultural education where the bulk of the scholarship is more fully articulated.

This is not the case with the body of neo-Marxist scholarship that is excerpted in this volume. Apple and Weis, and Fine as well as others who are excerpted in other volumes, such as McLaren (1997) and Giroux (1991), have significant histories of scholarship in critical theory. These rich legacies demonstrate a commitment to the exploration of the continued development of particular ways of knowing and understanding the field of education. As we recognize the areas of need in research, theory, and practice, we cannot help but hypothesize about why those areas remained unfulfilled. Thus we are inclined to believe that multicultural education would greatly benefit from scholars who seek to explore the complex foundations of the paradigm.

Note

1   Several organizations and individual scholars are beginning to evaluate the field. Division K, Teachers and Teacher Education, of the American Education Research Association, is compiling an edition of scholarship reviewing diversity in teacher education. CREDE is compiling several books reviewing empirical work in the field of multicultural education. The second edition of the

Handbook of Multicultural Education, with several chapters providing an in-depth focus on issues of diversity and education, was published in 2003.

References

Anyon, J. (1981). Social class and school knowledge. *Curriculum Inquiry, 11*(1), 3–42.

Anyon, J. (1995). Race, social class, and educational reform in an inner-city school. *Teachers College Record, 97*(1), 69–94.

Apple, M. W. (1980). The other side of the hidden curriculum: Correspondence theories and the labor process. *Interchange, 11*(3), 5–22.

Apple, M. W., & Weis, L. (1986). Seeing educational relationally: The stratification of culture and people in the sociology of school knowledge. *Journal of Education, 168*(1), 7–34.

Banks, J. A. (1993). The canon debate, knowledge construction, and multicultural education. *Educational Researcher, 22*(5), 4–14.

Baratz, S. S., & Baratz, J. C. (1970). Early childhood intervention: The social science base of institutional racism. *Harvard Educational Review, 40*(1), 29–50.

Boyle-Baise, M. (1999). Bleeding boundaries or uncertain center? A historical exploration of multicultural education. *Journal of Curriculum and Supervision, 14*(3), 191–215.

Fine, M. (1987). Silencing in public schools. *Language Arts, 64*(2), 157–173.

Gay, G. (1983). Multiethnic education: Historical developments and future prospects. *Phi Delta Kappan, 64*(8), 560–563.

Gezi, K. (1981). Issues in multicultural education. *Educational Research Quarterly, 6*(3), 5–14.

Giroux, H. (1991). Democracy and the discourse of cultural difference—Towards a politics of border pedagogy. *British Journal of Sociology of Education, 12*(4), 501–519.

Grant, C. (1994). Challenging the myths about multicultural education. *Multicultural Education, 1*, 4–9.

Hines, R. H. (1964). Social expectations and cultural deprivation. *Journal of Negro Education, 33*(2), 136–142.

Hiraoka, J. (1977). The foundations of multicultural education. *Educational Horizons, 55*(4), 177–180.

Krug, M. M. (1977). Cultural pluralism—Its origins and aftermath. *Journal of Teacher Education, 28*(3), 5–9.

Leyba, C. (1973). Cultural identity: Problems and dilemmas. *Journal of Teacher Education, 24*(4), 272–276.

McCarthy, C. (1988). Rethinking liberal and radical perspectives on radical-inequality in schooling: Making the case for nonsynchrony. *Harvard Educational Review, 58*(3), 265–279.

McLaren, P. (1997). Decentering whiteness. *Multicultural Education, 4*, 4–9.

Oakes, J., Wells, A. S., & Jones, M. (1997). Detracking: The social construction of ability politics, and resistance to reform. *Teachers College Record, 98*(3), 482–510.

Olneck, M. R. (1990). The recurring dream: Symbolism and ideology in intercultural and multi-cultural education. *American Journal of Education, 98*(2), 147–174.

Pacheco, A. (1977). Cultural pluralism: A philosophical analysis. *Journal of Teacher Education, 28*(3), 16–20.

Payne, C., & Welsh, B. (2000). The progressive development of multicultural education before and after the 1960s: A theoretical framework. *The Teacher Educator, 36*(1), 29–48.

Popkewitz, T. (1988). Educational reform: Rhetoric, ritual, and social interest. *Educational Theory, 38*(1), 77–94.

Sleeter, C. E. (1986). Learning disability: The social construction of a special education category. *Exceptional Children, 53*(1), 46–54.

Sleeter, C. E., & Grant, C. A. (1987). An analysis of multicultural education in the United States. *Harvard Educational Review, 57*(4), 421–444.

Valentine, C. (1971). Deficit, difference, and bicultural models of Afro-American behavior. *Harvard Educational Review, 41*(2), 137–157.

Valverde, L. A. (1977). Multicultural education: Social and education justice. *Educational Leadership, 35*(3), 196–201.

PART 1

SOCIETY AND SCHOOLS AS TARGETS OF CHANGE

CHAPTER 1

CULTURAL PLURALISM—ITS ORIGINS AND AFTERMATH (1977)

Mark M. Krug

Between the years of 1880 and 1915, the United States faced a serious crisis which has, as yet, been dealt with only sketchily by historians and sociologists. It is estimated, by the best use of only partially reliable statistics kept by the U.S. immigration authorities, and on the basis of more accurate figures supplied by the Census Bureau, that during those 35 years, the United States of America welcomed between 35 and 40 million immigrants. Since the U.S. population in 1880 was about 60 million, the absorption of such a huge number of immigrants, unprecedented in the history of the world, was indeed a most difficult task. It must be remembered that America was a little over 100 years old. The native population contained—in addition to the large and influential groups of descendents of English, Scottish, German, Dutch, and Scandinavian immigrants—large number of Irishmen, Frenchmen, French-Canadians, Chinese, Mexicans, Indians, and Negroes. The American culture, while exhibiting some unique and attractive characteristics in the 1880s, 1890s, and around 1900, was still a culture in the process of formation.

To compound the difficulty, the immigrants were a strikingly heterogenous group. They came from about 40 countries, spoke over 30 languages and dialects, professed a variety of religious beliefs, and belonged to many churches and sects. They exhibited a bewildering variety of cultural habits, customs, and modes of behavior.

The immigrants either came or were brought in by intensive recruiting to provide the needed labor force for the rapidly expanding industrial might of America. Railroads, mines, steel mills, stockyards, garment factories, and other businesses needed millions of workers; Italian, Polish, Jewish, Serbian, Croatian, and Russian immigrants filled the need. When the initial group of immigrants made some money, their letters home brought thousands more relatives to the "Promised Land."

The leaders of American industry were enthusiastic supporters of unrestricted immigration. But many politicians, clergymen, educators, and writers were greatly concerned that the flood of immigrants, unchecked by any legal restrictions, could be dangerous to the United States as a political and cultural entity. It makes no sense, as some spokesmen for new ethnicity occasionally do, to minimize or even to make light of this concern. How was a young country, with a fragile culture, to absorb these millions of immigrants? How were American schools to teach and integrate effectively hundreds of thousands of immigrants' children? This was a dilemma of many dimensions.

Emma Lazarus, in her poem "New Colossus" published in 1883, warmly welcomed the immigrants:

Mother of Exiles, from her beacon-hand
Glows world-side welcome; her mild eyes command
The air-bridged harbor that twin cities frame
"Keep ancient lands, your storied pomp!" cries she
  with silent lips. "Give me your tired, your poor,
Your huddled masses yearning to breathe free,
The wretched refuse of your teeming shore.
Send these, the homeless, tempest-tost to me,
I lift my lamp beside the golden door!"

But a few years later Thomas Bailey Aldrich published a poem in the *Atlantic* which he entitled "Unguarded Gates." It said, in part:

UNGUARDED GATES
Wide open and unguarded stand our gates,
And through them presses a wild motley throng.
Men from the Volga and the Tartar steppes,
Featureless figures of the Hoang-Ho,
Malayan, Scythian, Teuton, Kelt, and Slav,
Flying the Old World's poverty and scorn;
These bringing with them unknown gods and rites,
Those, Tiger passions, here to stretch their claws
In street and alley what strange tongues are these,
Accents of menace alien to our air . . .
O'liberty, white Goddess! is it well to leave the gates
  unguarded? . . . Stay those who to thy sacred
  portals come
To waste the gift of freedom . . .

In the early period of mass immigration, two basic theories were developed on how to deal with the millions of Poles, Italians, Jews, Slovaks, and Greeks. One was the theory of "Americanization" or "Anglo-Saxonization." It postulated that the immigrants must be required to give up their old ways and assimilate into the dominant Anglo-Saxon culture as soon as possible. Madison Grant, a prominent anthropologist and philanthropist, was the most influential spokesman for the "Americanization" approach. In the conclusion to his book, *The Passing of the Great Race*, he wrote that the denial of the superiority of the Anglo-Saxon or Nordic race would mongrelize American society and drive it into a racial and cultural abyss (1). Elwood P. Cubberley, a leading educator, demanded that public schools lead the way in the process of assimilation of the children of the immigrants and teach them "the Anglo-Saxon conceptions of righteousness, law and order and popular government" (2).

When it became clear that millions of immigrants had rejected Anglo-Saxonization, the "Melting Pot" theory was developed by a British writer, Israel Zangwill whose play, *The Melting Pot*, (3) became a great success on Broadway. The melting pot concept denied the supremacy of the Anglo-Saxon culture and rejected the demand that the immigrant cultures assimilate into it. Instead, Zangwill wanted *all* cultures—those of the native population and those of the immigrants—to fuse and melt in order to create a superior new and uniquely American culture.

Throughout the period of this great immigration, most leading American sociologists including Henry Pratt Fairchild, (4) Franz Boas, and later Talcott Parsons, Louis Wirth, Robert Park, and others, predicted that the American industrial and centralized society would inevitably bring an end to the existence of ethnic immigrant groups. They assumed that Blacks, Indians, and Asian-Americans would remain separate entities in the American population.

The ethnic groups found the melting pot concept more attractive than Grant's and Cubberley's and Theodore Roosevelt's "Americanization" scheme, but millions of them still were determined to maintain, to one extent or another, their separate group identity, ties, and loyalties.

Several scholars and writers, particularly the philosopher Horace M. Kallen, saw as early as the 1920s that there was a need for a new theoretical and practical approach to the relationship of the dominant society and the ethnic groups. Kallen developed the theory of "Cultural Pluralism." In contradiction to what the spokesmen for the "new ethnicity" like Michael Novak, Barbara Mikulski, Andrew Greeley, Geno Baroni, and Leonard Fein have written in recent years, in Kallen's conception, cultural pluralism did not mean that America was or would become a multicultural nation or a "mosaic of cultures." Kallen postulated that by the early 1920s there was an "American culture and not an ignoble one . . ." (5). He maintained that the mainstream American culture was rich and attractive. Significant new insight was developed by Kallen. His main thesis was that American culture was historically not monolithic but pluralistic. Its pluralism had its roots in the founding of America, its basic political documents (the Declaration of Independence and the Constitution), the frontier tradition, the way in which the American people settled on this continent, and the values they developed. Cultural pluralism, Kallen maintained, was intrinsic to what he called "the American Idea." Kallen accepted "Americanization" as a powerful and even welcome force in the history of immigration, provided it did not demand the complete assimilation of various ethnic groups. Such as assimilation into nonexistent monolithic Anglo-Saxon culture was contrary to the nature of American culture, whose origins and developmental vigor came from the pluralistic make-up of the American society dating from the Colonial period. Kallen wrote,

> All immigrants and their offspring are by the way undergoing "Americanization" if they remain in one place in the country long enough, say six or seven years. The general notion of "Americanization," appears to signify the adoption of the American variety of English speech, American clothes and manners, the American attitude to politics. "Americanization" signifies, in short, the disappearance of *external* differences upon which so much race prejudice often feeds (6).

Here clearly Kallen underestimated the process of Americanization. Immigrants' adjustment to America included more than acceptance of the *external* values and mores cited by Kallen. First, it included an abiding American patriotism. Immigrants flocked to 4th of July parades in big cities often with greater enthusiasm than native Americans. Poles assimilated, at least in part, by giving up their Polish parochial schools gradually and demanding that their priests preach in English so that their children could understand the sermons. Greeks, in spite of their strong attachment to the Greek Orthodox Church, also insisted that their priests learn and use English in the services. Many Jews, aware that religious observances and the functions of the rabbis could not be transplanted from the "Shtetlech" (towns) of Russia and Poland to New York, Chicago, and Cincinnati, introduced radical changes in their religious observances.

The Jewish Reform movement attempted to make the synagogues fully compatible with the American environment. Prayers in the new Reform prayerbook were predominantly in English, and the rabbi, instead of being the traditional Talmudic scholar, became a spiritual leader of his congregation and its representative to the general community. In 1909, the Union of American Hebrew Congregations adopted a platform which declared "America is our Zion" (7). The process of Americanization was and is evident even in the area of politics, where ethnicity is an important factor. Irish, Jewish, Polish, and Italian congressmen or city and state officials are in many instances elected by their respective ethnic blocs; but once in office they behave as American politicians in the milieu of the congress, city council, or state legislature. As a rule, in these public forums they are indistinguishable from their colleagues.

In a book written a few years after the publication of *Culture and Democracy*, Kallen takes a more comprehensive view. Americanization, Kallen wrote, means the acceptance by all Americans, native and foreign born, of "an over-arching culture based on the 'American Idea.' " That over-arching American culture is pluralistic because it reflects a pluralistic society. Its pluralistic nature is its main attraction and its source of strength. "Cultures," Kallen wrote, "live and grow in and through the individual, and their vitality is a function of individual diversities of interests and associations. Pluralism is the *sine qua non* of their persistence and prosperous growth" (8). An American, Kallen continued, can live in several cultural environments because pluralism is fluid. "Individuals move in and out freely from group to group from home to the business or work or firm, or church, or political organization" (9). With acute insight, Kallen disposes of the idea of a "majority" or "minority" culture by stating that, "Majorities and minorities on any issue in America are not fixed. ... Majorities are minorities in combination; majorities are minorities in division" (10). Students of voting patterns in American elections have long affirmed the soundness of this observation.

Cultural pluralism did not mean to Kallen separatism or tribalization of American society. On the contrary, "Unity in Diversity" was the phrase he often used to answer his nativist critics. It may be important in this period of "new ethnicity" to observe what Kallen had to say about the so called "hyphenated Americans"—Polish-American, Italian-American, and others—terms so despised by the "Americanizers" and Presidents Theodore Roosevelt and Woodrow Wilson. "Culture is nothing more than spiritual hyphenation—it is humanism in the best sense of the word" (11). There is no difference, he added, between an American who calls himself a "British-American" or an "Anglo-Saxon American" and an "Italian-American" or a "Polish-American."

What remains to be said of Kallen's theory is that he too, like the advocates of "Americanization" and the "Melting Pot," did not discuss in his books and essays the place the Blacks, Latinos, and the other racial minorities in the framework of cultural pluralism. In spite of this grave omission, the basic conceptual framework of Kallen's theory of cultural pluralism could be used to great benefit in the present discussion of ethnicity and ethnic group problems. However, there is obviously a need in 1977 to define cultural pluralism in light of the experience of the last 20 years. This experience includes the emergence of new vitality and group awareness among White ethnic groups, the struggles, achievements, and failures of the Black civil rights movement, the militant demands of American Indians (for the redress of their grievances), the social, political and economic demands of Mexican-Americans, Puerto Ricans, and other Spanish-speaking groups for bilingual and bicultural education, and the insistence of Asian-Americans on putting an end to discrimination and isolation imposed on them for many decades by the American society.

Those who today disregard Kallen's original conception of cultural pluralism and suggest that the United States is in the process of becoming a multiethnic society, something similar to the Austro-Hungarian Empire or Switzerland, are subject to challenge. If, in the late 1920s, Kallen assumed the existence of a dominant, attractive, mainstream American culture, there are many who would claim that this is obviously even more true today. To be sure, American society is now in the throes of a deep crisis; its social, political, and religious values are questioned. But there seems to be little doubt that this is a passing stage of periodic malaise.

Clearly, in spite of the predictions of sociologists and political scientists, cultural pluralism is still very much in evidence as a social and political phenomenon in American society. Many ethnic groups, distinguished by skin color, group loyalties, or common aspirations, do exist in our society and will probably continue to exist for a long time. Knowing this, it is regrettable that students in our secondary schools, colleges, and universities are given little or no instruction on how ethnic politics work in our system of government. Ethnicity is an important factor in the political power structure and governance of our larger cities. The same is true in many parts of the country when congressional elections are held. It is a fact of our political life that only a Polish-American like Daniel Rostenkowski can be elected in his Chicago congressional district, only an Italian-American like Peter Rodino can win in Newark, and only a Jewish-American like Elizabeth Holtzman can represent her Brooklyn district in Congress. This, of course, is not true in most congressional districts throughout the country, but ethnic factors are of great importance in the election of at least 50 Congressmen and Congresswomen.

Thousands of American high school and college students must have been baffled by the furor caused by President Ford's remark during the 1976 presidential campaign that the Soviet Union did not dominate Eastern Europe, or the statement made by Governor Carter during his campaign about a hands-off U.S. policy in Yugoslavia in case of Soviet intervention after the death of President Tito. Why, many of them asked, should statements on Eastern Europe or Yugoslavia have such an important bearing on the election of a President of the United States?

They should have known, and should have been taught in social studies, political science, and history courses, that American Poles, Jew, Hungarians, Serbs, and Croats are still deeply concerned about the political situation in their former homelands and that these concerns do often influence their voting in American elections. Whether what happens to Yugoslavia, Poland, and Israel should be a factor in American elections is debatable, but this is a reality in American politics.

The existence, the dynamics of ethnic groups in America, the role of ethnic ties in city, state, and national elections, are mostly ignored or even disdained, not only by secondary schools but in education, history, and political science departments in many institutions of higher learning. For some reason, in our pluralistic society, in a nation of immigrants, concern with ethnicity and ethnic groups is often considered unworthy of scholarly inquiry or is even looked upon as slightly unAmerican. "Black studies," "Chicano studies," "Slavic studies," "Jewish studies"—especially in more elitist universities and colleges—are treated, if not as a necessary evil, then as a passing fad, largely of interest to small parochially-minded groups of students.

That shortsighted attitude can be illustrated by what happened after the death of Chicago Mayor Richard J. Daley, who was also Cook County Democratic party chairman, in December 1976. By design or neglect, during his long tenure of office, no succession procedure in case of his death in office was ever determined. After his sudden death, the leaders of the various ethnic groups began a series of frantic negotiations to choose Daley's successor.

The political compromises that were made and unmade in many closed door caucuses held before the election of Michael Bilandic as Acting Mayor were the results of intense negotiations among the leaders of the "Irish," "Jewish," "Polish," "Italian," "Black," "Croatian," and other blocs of aldermen, all representing their predominantly ethnic wards.

One of the few independent aldermen, Richard Simpson, a professor of political science at the University of Illinois, Chicago Campus, scathingly referred to these negotiations as deals made behind closed doors in smoke-filled rooms. He maintained that the prearranged election of Michael Bilandic was a violation of the democratic process and an attempt to perpetuate the boss rule of Chicago, a division of the ethnic pie which constitutes the city's population. Many Chicagoans undoubtedly agreed with Alderman Simpson. But if one is to understand the realities of Chicago politics, Alderman Roman Pucinski was more accurate. He told a reporter that the final deal which made Michael Bilandic, a Croat, the Acting Mayor; Vito Marzullo, an Italian, the head of the Zoning Committee; Wilson Frost, a Black leader, chairman of the powerful Finance Committee; Edward Vrdolyak, another Croat, President pro-tem; and Casimir Laskowski, a Pole, the Vice-Mayor, simply reflected the ethnic power structure of Chicago. Ignoring the political strength of all the major ethnic groups represented by these men would have made an effective city government impossible.

A previous arrangement or deal, made a few days earlier by a number of power brokers, which excluded William Frost and gave no position of power to a Polish-American politician, was nullified at a combined caucus of Black and Polish aldermen. These groups met not because of any special affection for one another, but because they realized that, in combination, they controlled close to the 25 votes required for the Acting Mayor's election. Thus, they were able to agree on a new arrangement subsequently approved by the City Council by a vote of 45 to 2. Under this final deal, the Black and Polish-American blocs achieved positions, power, and prestige in the new Chicago city government.

These events are not recounted here either with approval or disapproval. They are facts of our pluralistic society and cannot be ignored in American political life. What happened in Chicago is also the political reality in other big cities. Ethnic politics and the use of ethnic blocs and votes in elections are complex. They have potentially positive and negative aspects. Consequently, they must be studied and understood in order to make them positive and beneficial factors in the operation of the American democratic process.

The proceedings of the Chicago City Council, in which Michael Bilandic was elected, were televised by all major television networks in the city and were broadcast by most radio stations. Since it was school vacation time, young people had an opportunity to see the operation of their city's government in action. I wonder how many understood what Alderman Vito Marzullo had to say about the "Italian" support for Bilandic, and what the "Irish" Alderman Edward Burke meant when he told a reporter that he supported the deal in the City Council because it had also been agreed that the Cook County Democratic Committee chairmanship would go to George Dunne, a prominent Irish politician. Dunne's election took place two days later.

One can hope that Chicago's political machinations will convince at least some school administrators, teachers, and professors that intelligent instruction in the ethnic factors and groups which still show great vitality in American pluralistic society is long overdue. The intellectual snobbery on this issue has been, and is, one of the significant obstacles blocking more effective citizenship education in our schools and in the training of better teachers in our teacher preparation programs.

Cultural pluralism and ethnic politics ought to be taught in schools, but the potential pitfalls of such instruction must not be overlooked. The central question to be asked is whether cultural pluralism is a divisive or a uniting factor in American society. In my view, cross-cultural instruction can be a positive force in our pluralistic society, but this position must be backed up by empirical research and factual data.

As we have suggested, the American academic community is not on the whole sympathetic to the concept of cultural pluralism or bilingual education. Let me cite two examples. John Higham, in *Strangers in the Land*, exposed the nativist xenophobia which resulted in the persecution or ridicule of various immigrant groups. He now argues in his new book, *Send These To Me*, that cultural pluralism is "morally objectionable," because it limits the autonomy and freedom of young men and women of the second and third generation of immigrants. Ethnic differences, Higham maintains, are often attractive but can "easily become dangerous and destructive" (12).

The eminent sociologist Gunner Myrdal, author of *An American Dilemma*, states in a recent article that cultural pluralism is reactionary and divisive and that the "new ethnicity" is a romantic aberration (13).

Higham's and Myrdal's attacks on cultural pluralism and their opposition to ethnic cohesiveness of minority groups would indicate that those who advocate cultural pluralism and cross-cultural and bilingual education are called upon to make a convincing case to the scholarly community and to the American public.

Notes

1 Madison Grant, *The Passing of the Great Race* (New York: Charles Scribner and Sons, 1914).
2 Elwood P. Cubberley, *Changing Conceptions of Education* (New York: Riverside Mimographs, 1909), p. 62.
3 Henry Fairchild, *The Melting Pot* (New York: Macmillan, 1910).
4 Henry Fairchild, *The Melting Pot Mistake* (Boston: Little, Brown and Co., 1926).
5 Horace M. Kallen, *Culture and Democracy in the United States* (New York: Boni and Liveright, 1924), p. 41.
6 Ibid., p. 79.
7 Samuel E. Karff, ed., *Jewish Institute of Religion, At One Hundred Years* (Cincinnati: Hebrew Union Press, 1976), p. 80.
8 Horace M. Kallen, *Cultural Pluralism and the American Idea* (Philadelphia: University of Pennsylvania Press, 1956), p. 71.
9 Ibid., p. 55.
10 Ibid., p. 109.
11 Kallen, *Culture and Democracy*, p. 64.
12 John Higham, *Send These to Me: Jews and Other Immigrants in Urban America* (New York: Atheneum, 1975), pp. 283 and 236.
13 Gunnar Myrdal, "The Case Against Romantic Ethnicity," *The Center Magazine* (July-August 1974): 62.

CHAPTER 2

SOCIAL AND EDUCATIONAL JUSTICE (1977)

Leonard A. Valverde

The tumultuous decade of the sixties witnessed a virtual revolution in American social history from the effects of which the multifarious areas of educational theory and practice were not immune. In fact, in certain instances, pedagogy and its attendant concerns were the very arena of activity. The social and intellectual ferment of that period stimulated changes in education along a wide spectrum, encompassing such diverse concepts as the new math and the open classroom to the Head Start program and bilingual education. It is disturbing to note today the extent to which the movement in education now appears to have followed a circular rather than a linear pattern.

In retrospect, it would seem that the majority of changes in traditional educational practices stemmed from one of two basic sources. The first source originated in academic institutions, was led by scholars and educators, and focused on the psychological and ontological nature of the learning process. Discoveries in this field were accountable mainly for such innovations as individualized instruction and the open classroom. The second source of change in educational theory and practice originated in courtrooms and at lunch counters, was led by ministers and social activists, and focused on the social context of the educational process. Progress in the area of social equity was responsible generally for the introduction of such programs as Head Start and bilingual education.

The irony of the seventies and the painful paradox of the contemporary situation for many of us is the degree to which developments of the previous decade have been halted and, in certain cases, are actually being reversed! Note the "Back to Basics" trend that is attempting to solve the novel problems of education's advancement by simply reverting to former practices with their familiar frustrations. Here the reversal is somewhat uncomplicated and comes from troubled citizens seeking to replace a new and slightly suspect set of "experiments" with tried but outdated procedures.

However, in the second area of concern the process is far more complicated and, for those of us committed to the goal of social equity in American education, far more disconcerting. While programs such as Head Start and bilingual education are rather recent facets of the complex institution of public education, they have roots in the broad record of social events, as well as in the specialized history of pedagogy. These programs are a more direct response to demands for social justice than they are a result of breakthroughs in educational psychology and learning theory.

Yet the disturbing irony and paradox of our times is that the very programs that were created to alleviate inequities in public education are now serving to perpetuate the very practices they were devised to eliminate. Specialized enrichment programs are now acting to resegregate students of minority cultures of American society from all other students. In order to clarify the development of this disturbing pattern, it is necessary to examine events that began in the mid-fifties.

In 1954, with the assertion that "separate is unequal," the Supreme Court of the United States outlawed school segregation. This was to be the first in a long series of steps taken in an attempt to equalize the quality of education for all students in the United States, no matter how diverse the culture, income, or race of their family. However, much of the school segregation that was so abhorrent to the Justices of the Warren Court still continues throughout the nation. While some progress has been made in the reduction of the arbitrary segregation of students by race, unfair treatment toward racial and ethnic minority students persists. The public and many educators believe that adverse discrimination continues to plague the house of education because of pervasive patterns of contemporary society: white flight, homogeneous housing patterns, high dropout rates of minority students, and delays in implementing court decisions because of appeal procedures. Furthermore, it appears that major blame is attributable to the harmful intervention of certain parents, real estate entrepreneurs, city officials, lawyers, and school trustees. However, in addition to these blatantly counterproductive forces, there is a more fundamental reason why programs that were originally designed to enhance the quality of educational opportunity for minority students have served to segregate them and thus to defeat the primary goal and intent of the 1954 Supreme Court decision.

Right move wrong philosophy

When school segregation was legally abolished, the prognosis for the success of children who were different racially and ethnically from the dominant culture of the United States still remained poor. The educational philosophy of the nation was unaltered and firmly anchored to the "melting pot" theory. According to this concept, the assimilation of culturally diverse people into the dominant "American" image was stressed through a process of acculturation. Therefore, while the physical integration of students of different racial and ethnic backgrounds was beginning to occur in the late fifties, minority students usually found themselves with teachers emphasizing the images and values of the dominant culture.

Through the next several years, the old, ineffective, and harmful treatment by educators lingered in practice. Educators were virtually wed to the melting pot philosophy and persisted in imposing an alien theory that proved incompatible when instructing culturally different students. During the sixties, as a result of this inappropriate treatment and in concert with the widespread agitation for change, minority peoples demanded changes in the schools. Black college students demonstrated on campuses, Chicano students staged walk-outs, and Native Americans as a community insisted on involvement in their children's education.

Consequently, educators were forced to move in the direction of establishing instructional programs that would accommodate the diverse needs of neglected racial and ethnic minorities. In an effort to meet the special needs of these students, various programs were created, such as compensatory education, ethnic studies, urban studies, Head Start, and others. Unfortunately, while each instructional program was conceived with a pluralistic philosophical base, the actual curriculum predominately included only one minority culture, usually that of the target student population to be served. While the relentless focus of the singular dominant American culture on the melting pot theory was being rejected, its replacement with a genuinely multicultural philosophy was incomplete. As a result, new educational programs founded under the concept of cultural pluralism, promoting diversity among peoples, were restricted in their scope.

Resegregation under cultural pluralism banner

Currently, these specialized programs offer a partial solution to many of the chronic problems of unequal educational opportunity. Programs intended to acknowledge and celebrate cultural diversity are being used by many sincere educators to alleviate long-standing abusive practices, such as distorted curriculum, inferior facilities, inadequate instructional resources, and detrimental teaching by unsympathetic instructors. Regrettably, there is a negative aspect of this phenomenon that fundamentally undercuts and may ultimately outweigh any benefits accrued earlier. In a noticeable number of situations, programs ostensibly advocating cultural pluralism are functioning to resegregate students!

For example, bilingual education was conceived to assist non-English or limited English-speaking students to learn English and their native language concurrently. Also, bilingual instruction would aid students to learn the given curriculum without falling behind. In theory, bilingual education is an instructional approach that not only permits children who speak different languages to learn together, but promotes cross-cultural learning as well. In practice, however, bilingual programs are predominately, if not exclusively, composed of non-English or limited English-speaking students. In the southwestern states, bilingual education is serving to resegregate traditionally segregated Spanish-speaking populations.

The same is true for other instructional programs initiated to encourage cultural diversity or to improve the quality of education for minority students. Students enrolled in compensatory educational programs tend to be as homogeneously isolated on the basis of reading and math scores, as they may have been on the basis of race or ethnicity a generation before. Similarly, most ethnic studies courses are based on voluntary enrollment and have been supported generally by their own populations. Again, education programs designed to promote appreciation of cultural differences and to facilitate integration among various groups are resulting in the resegregation of the nation's school populations.

These categorical models have allowed educators to separate some students from the "mainstream" and have encouraged educators themselves to think in a separatist and discriminatory manner. What is truly needed now is a move to make the mainstream itself culturally diverse. The impulse to integrate the school population must be carried through all aspects of curriculum and instructional practice. Categorical programs may have had some advantages, but they are exceeded by disadvantages. Often rival programs foster competition, with individual groups struggling for limited financial support. In many cases, such programs isolate personnel to work mainly "among their own." These arrangements foster narrow-minded thinking, inhibit cross-cultural communication, hinder cooperative efforts with other groups, and restrict sharing and mutual assistance.

Even worse, documenting need within these specialized programs has imposed an onerous burden on culturally different children. For example, in order for a student to receive Title I assistance, he or she must score low in academic achievement. In essence, educators are condemning the student to remain an underachiever if he or she wishes to receive instruction that is tolerant of his or her culture. For to return the youngster into the regular classroom means to socialize him or her to the white anglo saxon protestant ethic.

A major overhaul

A thoroughly multicultural education must replace what is now considered the regular educational program. Is this possible and if so, is it desirable? The answer to both questions is affirmative. First, multicultural education is wide enough in scope to absorb other existing instructional programs. Second, the core of multicultural education is the study of all people, their customs, history, traditions, values, beliefs, and aspirations. Third, and maybe most important, multicultural education is not only appropriate, but it is necessary for the times facing the various, troubled world societies. As James Banks has written:

> Events of the last decade have dramatically indicated that we live in a world society beset with momentous social and human problems, many of which are related to ethnic hostility and conflict. Effective solutions to these critical problems can be found only by an active, compassionate, and ethnically sensitive citizenry capable of making sound public decisions that will benefit our ethnically diverse world community (1:32).

Multicultural education is imperative for future generations of Americans for a variety of reasons. With a finite amount of world resources, interaction and interdependence among nations are increasing. Also, migration among neighboring and even distant countries is on the rise.

Plan of action

If multicultural education is to replace regular education, so as to serve effectively the needs of all students, what action must be planned for and undertaken by educators? While a truly comprehensive proposal would be a lengthy and detailed *opus*, a few critical steps are presented here (2:270):

1　A humanistic attitude must dominate the curriculum and instruction.
2　Massive staff retraining programs must be launched.
3　Multicultural materials and resources must be developed.
4　Genuine community involvement must be enlisted and maintained.

The humanistic attitude called for in the first consideration has been long absent in this social process we call formal instruction. Teachers should concern themselves with nurturing the psychological identity of their students. Accordingly, administrators must care about their staff, not merely as implementers or performers, but as persons—individual human beings. Instructional supervisors should interact with their specialists in a humane, not merely pragmatic and official manner. Parents, students, and educators should empathize and collaborate with one another. Conflict should be resolved openly and in a positive fashion. Caring for one another should take precedence over fulfilling the requirements of one's duty or role.

Massive staff retraining is mandatory and of high priority, since most public school staffs are culturally limited and thus at a disadvantage when dealing with others. The lack of substantial contact with different lifestyles by most staff members indicates the necessity for sensitivity training and information sharing. However, traditional in-service models will not be enough to compensate for lifelong isolation. Teachers, administrators, and supervisors will need to study in the barrios, work in ghettos, visit across the borders of ethnic communities, and socialize across the tracks of income and class. Retraining our own staffs to function effectively and to teach humanistically may be the educational challenge of the century.

Development of multicultural curricula is essential at a time when knowledge is increasing at a geometrical rate. Therefore, instructors will continue to rely heavily on texts, workbooks, teacher guides, and supplementary resources, such as modules, kits, and others. So, traditional texts and materials will need major revision to eliminate bias and prejudice. Also, new works must be created to present the many hidden and neglected facts about peoples of different cultures and their ways of life. Most crucial is the need for the new curricula to incorporate a multiple perspective, highlighting similarities, acknowledging differences, underscoring positive contributions, capitalizing strengths, and always attempting to foster an enlightened respect for the integrity and worth of diverse cultures.

Authentic community participation must be maintained if decisions in the best interest of the students are to be made and supported. Community involvement will reduce the negative effects of educators who as yet do not accept or respect other cultures and will provide expertise to those educators wanting to provide the best service possible. We must go beyond tokenism if cultural pluralism is to flower in our schools. Parents and community members will have to be relied on as resource persons capable of providing many services in the classrooms with teachers and students. Such community involvement should extend to the principal and other supportive staff. To those inexperienced in community interaction, it is important to remember that communities that have been excluded from their children's schools will need to be encouraged to participate actively. If misunderstanding or hesitancy is encountered, this must not be used as an excuse to abandon the entire effort at community involvement. Patience and a positive attitude are certainly in order here.

Summary

In summary, there are many educational imperatives that need action. High among the list are two: (a) ending the long practice of denying cultural diversity that in turn means stopping all forms of segregation within our public schools; and (b) reorganizing our instructional programs in order to install multicultural education as the core of our schooling and cultural pluralism as our fundamental philosophy.

References

1 James Banks. *Multiethnic Education: Practices and Promises*. Bloomington, Indiana: Phi Delta Kappa Educational Foundation, 1977.
2 Ben M. Harris and Leonard A. Valverde. "Supervisors and Educational Change." *Theory Into Practice* 15(4): 267–73; October 1976.

CHAPTER 3

CULTURAL PLURALISM (1977)
A philosophical analysis
Arturo Pacheco

The call for cultural pluralism

The problems that minority children face in schools now have been heavily researched and documented. Statistics continue to tell a tale of low achievement scores, high drop-out rates and an ever-widening education and income gap between minority poor and middle-class White populations. This gap continues despite a major shift in government attention to the problems of the minority poor, the Great Society programs of the 1960s, and a deluge of scholarly and popular publications calling attention to the problems of the minority poor and the failure of the schools to meet their needs. It is in open recognition of this depressing situation that demands for multicultural education and cultural pluralism are increasingly made.

Since 1969, a wide variety of books, journal articles, conferences, and major policy statements have taken strong positions advocating multicultural education and cultural pluralism as major educational reforms. The 1972 AACTE statement on multicultural education was offered as "a guide for addressing the issue of multicultural education," and it was presented "in the interest of improving the quality of society through an increased social awareness on the part of teachers and teacher educators." (1)

What is almost always clear in each of these position papers is that their authors strongly support the concepts of multicultural education and cultural pluralism and are calling for the massive implementation of these ideas into American educational practice. What is almost never clear is precisely what they mean by "cultural pluralism" or "multicultural education," such discussions generally assume that there is a common understanding of what is meant by those terms.

Where there are attempts at specification, we find a wide variety of definitions offered, some of them quite ambiguous. For example, the statement of the Steering Committee of the National Coalition for Cultural Pluralism defines the concept of cultural pluralism as "the perspective used by different social groups in their attempt to survive as *independent*, yet *interdependent*, segments of society." (2) Alfredo Castaneda suggests that the concept entails the notion that "the child is allowed to explore the mainstream culture freely by using those preferred modes he brings to school from his home and community," (3) while Andrew Kopan declares that cultural pluralism has already become a reality in American life (4). There is widespread confusion between goals and concepts, and more than one author suggests that we implement the *concept* of cultural pluralism with little further specification. Common to the rhetoric of such arguments is a confusion between *descriptions of* American society as culturally pluralistic and *prescriptions for* cultural pluralism as the most desirable form of social organization.

This article focuses on bringing some philosophical analysis and clarification to the language used in discussions about multicultural education and cultural pluralism in American society. Analysis and clarification is necessary if such discussions are to be fruitful; otherwise, we have terms that are only rhetorically useful and function as slogans, serving to call attention to a problem or an issue, while remaining so ambiguous and vague that almost any behavior would seem to fall under their rubric.

Culture and the context of schooling

In a provocative analysis of the relationship of schooling to work, Thomas F. Green, a contemporary philosopher of education, has cited the following as the three major functions of American schooling: (a) socialization, (b) cultural transmission, and (c) the development of self-identity (5). Since these are not very controversial notions and at least two of the three are usually cited in most discussions of schooling, we shall use them as the starting place for our discussion of schooling. We must remember that mass schooling as we know it is a relatively new phenomenon; until very recently the processes of socialization, cultural transmission, and the development of self-identity took place through other institutions (family, church, work guilds, etc.) in the course of daily and routine activities, both within and outside the household. In this context, one might perceive very little difference between socialization and cultural transmission; they occurred in the same context and were under the aegis of roughly the same agents, perhaps differing only in their focus on different aspects. In the United States, mass public schooling is little more than a century old. The institutionalization of schooling seems to coincide with the development of the industrialized nation-state and the introduction and sophistication of the idea of citizenship. (We see dramatic examples of this in our own time in some of the newly-liberated and newly-formed nation-states of Africa and Asia. Mass schooling and the development of loyalty to the newly-formed nation-state via the idea of citizenship seem to go hand-in-hand, especially in those cases where new political boundaries enclose regions marked by tribal, ethnic, and language diversity.)

It is at this point that we can begin to discern some subtle changes in the notions of the socialization and cultural transmission. Both socialization and cultural transmission begin to be defined in the context of the nation-state, as well as the more immediate context of family and community. New elements are introduced into the process by compulsory schooling. With the notion of socialization, the bounds of reference are extended beyond everyday social relations within immediate family and community contexts; and new elements are introduced, such as the development of attitudes about citizenship, occupation groups, and government agencies within the nation-state. With the notion of cultural transmission, two notions of culture begin to emerge: on the one hand, there is the "culture of the community," based on a web of shared values, meanings, language, and life-experiences; on the other hand, there is the culture of the nation-state (in the sense of "civilization"), with its history, heros, structural organization, and values—knowledge of which is perceived as necessary for the cohesiveness and maintenance of the state-society. This second sense of cultural transmission begins to approach in meaning the extended sense of socialization mentioned above.

Given these differences, we can see the very real structural possibilities for cultural conflict and alienation occurring in the schools. The third function of schooling, assisting the development of self-identity, is to a large degree dependent on the integration of the first two functions, that is, on a balanced relationship between socialization and cultural transmission. So long as there is a fairly good mesh between socialization and cultural transmission within one's family and community as well as in the larger context of the state-society, one can expect objective conditions necessary for the development of an integrated and balanced self-identity. However, if there is a major contradiction between socialization (to a state-society) and cultural transmission (of the culture of one's family and community), if these two conflict with one another, the conditions for the development of alienated self-identities are created. Contradictions do develop, because the objective of the state (in the interest of cohesiveness and self-maintenance) is to both subvert local sources of authority, loyalty, and solidarity, and to establish an ideology of uniformity among its citizens (6). Cultural alienation would be far less likely if there were a complete integration between the societal norms and values of the school and those cultural values traditionally transmitted by the family and community. Any attempt to remedy this situation must entail some effort towards reforming the school in order to eliminate the cultural disparity and alienation faced by so many minority students. Calls for multicultural education and cultural pluralism are the next logical step, accompanied by concrete programmatic suggestions including the multiethnic staffing of schools, bilingual education, the employment of community teacher-aides, and more intensive curricular attention paid to cultural minorities' unique contributions to American history. Here we are confronted with two crucial questions: (a) Is this what we mean by multicultural education and cultural pluralism? and (b) Will these programmatic activities in the schools alleviate the problem?

Some necessary analytic distinctions

We begin with the most basic and direct question: what do we mean by cultural pluralism? There are two major and distinct streams of thought about pluralism in the social science literature, and both have long traditions of scholarship centered around theories of society.

Democratic pluralism

The first, usually referred to as *democratic pluralism*, is part of the legacy left by Alexis de Toqueville's analysis of American society and has been one of the dominant models of American society for more than a century. As a descriptive theory, it refers to a model of social organization in which there is a balance of power between competing and overlapping religious, ethnic, economic, and geographical groupings. Each group has some interests which it protects and fosters and each has some say in shaping social decisions which are binding on all groups that make up the society. Common to all groups is a set of political values and beliefs which serve to maintain the entire social system through accommodation and resolution of conflicts via appropriate channels. Democratic pluralism is a more accurate description of actual democracy in America than is classical liberalism, which bases itself on a notion of individual, rather than group, participatory democracy. Modern industrialized societies are considered too large and complex for all individuals to have a direct voice. Democratic pluralism, as the dominant form of the political organization in America, has a long tradition of scholarship, and it has recently been critically attacked as faulty (7).

Theory of the plural society

The second tradition of scholarship on pluralism is nonAmerican in its roots, stemming from early 20th century descriptions of colonized societies in Asia and Africa. This tradition, more generally known as the *theory of the plural society*, deals more exclusively with the phenomenon of culture. In what is now a classic description, J.S. Furnivall, a Dutch social scientist and colonial administrator, described the cultural diversity in the following way:

> In Burma as in Java, probably the first thing that strikes the visitor is the medley of peoples—European, Chinese, Indian, and native. It is in the strictest sense a medley, for they mix but do not combine. Each group holds by its own religion, its own culture and language, its own ideas and ways. As individuals they meet, but only in the market-place, in buying and selling. There is a plural society with different sections of the community living side by side, but separately, within the same political unit. Even in the economic sphere, there is a division of labor along racial lines (8).

This notion of pluralism dominates contemporary discussions of the culturally diverse societies of Africa and the Caribbean, and it has been refined theoretically and extended in the work of the anthropologists Leo Kuper and M.G. Smith (9). Smith, for example, has distinguished between three types of societies: (a) homogeneous, (b) heterogeneous, and (c) plural. *Homogeneous* societies, of which there are few, are those where all the groups within a political unit share the same total institutional system. A *heterogeneous* society, on the other hand, is one in which all groups share the same basic institutions (e.g., economy, education, property relations), but at the same time participate in alternative and exclusive institutions. Alternative institutions are those in which members of groups can freely elect to participate, while exclusive institutions are limited in membership to those who belong to clearly defined groups. Smith sees the United States as a heterogeneous society. The third type, the *plural* society, is different from the other two forms in that groups within a political unit also practice differing basic institutions, as in the description provided by Furnivall. Each group has distinctive educational, religious, and economic institutions, sharing only a common political organization which binds them together. The Union of South Africa could be a paradigm case.

Important analytical points

When we examine recent discussions of cultural pluralism in the light of these two distinctive traditions of scholarship, several important points of analysis immediately present themselves. First, most educationally-related analyses have not drawn on this well-developed tradition of theoretically-oriented scholarship on pluralism. With few exceptions, contemporary educators are either unaware of the theoretical tradition or do not perceive it as relevant and useful. Most discussions, therefore, lack theoretical considerations and are overly programmatic in nature. Second, in being programmatic, they often reveal a fact/value ambiguity, i.e., they confuse prescriptive conceptions of society as it ought to be with descriptive accounts of how it actually is. AACTE lapses into this type of ambiguity in its multicultural statement, calling for the endorsement of cultural pluralism while declaring that "cultural pluralism is so basic a quality of our culture." A clear distinction should be maintained between language which purports to describe society and language which advocates social change to some ideal form of society not yet achieved.

If we assume that most of the discussions of cultural pluralism are prescriptive in nature, then there are four factors that must be specified if those discussions are to be both theoretically and programmatically fruitful. These are: (a) reference-group application, (b) realm of experience, (c) scope of the desired change, and (d) the form that the change is intended to take.

Reference–group application

Reference–group application refers to the notion that we must specify, in our discussions of cultural pluralism, to which groups the plurality is intended to apply. A common ambiguity is to confuse and use interchangeably the concepts "ethnicity" and "culture." Not all members of the same ethnic group share the same culture; for example, a middle-class Mexican-American may culturally identify more with his White counterparts than with lower-class Mexican-Americans. His ability and inclination to do this are greatly affected by the phenomena of class and color, two critical factors usually unspecified and left out of the discussion of cultural pluralism. In addition, there is the question of the recent revival of interest in White ethnicity. In advocating cultural pluralism, are we also advocating some sort of social change on behalf of White ethnics as well? How do we specify characteristic differences between cultural groupings of Italian- and Polish-Americans and the more oppressed minorities, Blacks, Chicanos, Asian- and Native-Americans? Which of these groups have legitimate claims to maintain their language? Sorting out these questions only in the context of the school is extremely difficult while attempting to do so in the context of the larger society is over-whelming.

Realm of experience

The second factor, the realm of experience, refers to the sphere of experience in which cultural pluralism is to take place. It is necessary to be more precise in specifying those realms of lived experience which are to be shared by all, be they political, economic, or socio-cultural, as opposed to those which are to be culturally defined and limited to members of certain groups. Here we gain insight from the institutional analysis in M.G. Smith's work on the theory of the plural society. His distinctions between basic, or compulsory institutions, and alternative and exclusive institutions are useful. We can conceive of a society which has several basic institutions in which all groups participate (for example, schooling), as well as a variety of exclusive institutions that are limited to certain groups (for example, religious groups and fraternal organizations). The criteria for determining a culturally plural society may include the ratio of basic to exclusive institutions in that society.

Scope of intended change

A third and related factor which must be addressed in advocating cultural plural-ism is the scope of the intended social change, both within particular institutions and in the total society at large. For example, what might cultural pluralism mean within the institution of schooling? Is our scope limited to formal aspects of staffing and the curriculum, or will we include more subtle aspects, such as teach-ing and learning styles, friendship patterns, and reward/punishment systems? Do we mean education in all of its aspects, or do we mean formal schooling alone? What about the other institutions in society? While the context of schooling is the appropriate focus for educators who are advocating cultural pluralism, the pro-grammatic suggestions that they make often hinge on the assumption that school reform will bring about corresponding reforms in society. A diverse set of recent historical analyses of schooling strongly suggests that this assumption is no longer tenable, and we must be more clear about the contexts and limitations within which the intended social change is to take place.

Form of change

The fourth and final factor is the form of the change intended by "a move toward cultural pluralism." Some changes treat surface phenomena, while others pene-trate deep into the social structure. For example, many statements about cultural pluralism are replete with calls for awareness, understanding, and tolerance of cultural difference. While these are surely important goals, they must be dis-tinguished in form from changes in the organization of society, such as structur-ally increasing the power that minority groups have to control their own lives. There is an accumulation of evidence that even massive attempts to change people's attitudes about other cultures have had effects of limited value, while few, if any, educational reform efforts have been geared toward the structural change of society. Nor is it clear that educational reform efforts can, in fact, accomplish this.

Multicultural education and cultural pluralism

Most educational reform efforts which are geared toward cultural pluralism also fall under the rubric of "multicultural education." But clearly they are not the same thing and they must be distinguished. The concept of cultural pluralism refers to a theory of society—a particular form of social organization. Multi-cultural education, on the other hand, refers to a form of educational practice—a specific practice within one institution of society which may or may not be congruent with cultural pluralism, depending on how that theory is defined.

As a practice within only one institution of society, multicultural education is clearly more limited in scope and reference than is a theory which takes the entire society as its referent. A brief description of multicultural educational programs will amply illustrate this. There are two major approaches to multicultural pro-grams, each with two variants that can be distinguished by their differing programmatic goals.

The first approach acknowledges the fundamental cultural disparity that minority students experience when they first encounter the institution of school-ing, as outlined in our initial analysis. In contrast to earlier programs based on a notion of cultural deficiency, programmatic attempts are made to make up for the dissonance between the culture of the home and the "mainstream" culture of the school without devaluation of the home culture. Two variants within this approach can be distinguished.

The first, although avoiding derogatory assumptions about the home culture, is still basically compensatory in nature and usually involves the design of alternative programs for the "special needs" of the culturally different student. The assumption is made that if these culturally defined special needs are addressed, the school achievement rates of minority children will be greatly improved. Because such efforts are oriented toward special needs, these alternative programs are designed exclusively for minority students, since they are the ones who "have the problems." This is what distinguishes the second variant in this approach. Here the cultural diversity which is a fact of American life is viewed much more positively and as a valuable resource, and, therefore, multicultural education programs are designed for all students, not just minority group members. The thrust of these programs is heavily psycho-social in nature, stressing awareness, tolerance, understanding, and pride in one's cultural identity, whatever it may be. Both variants of this first approach assume that cultural difference is the problem's root.

The second major approach is much more ambitious in scope, at least within the context of the school. It purports to go beyond either compensatory programs for minority students or programs that stress the overcoming of prejudice through awareness and understanding. This approach treats the school as a place where cultural pluralism can occur. Its goal is to produce students who can function in a culturally plural society, one in which there is parity between various cultural groups. More sensitive to the lack of parity in real life, it attempts, through a variety of structural arrangements in the school, to aggressively support the right of a cultural group to maintain itself, it perceives that parity of power and decision making among groups is crucially important, and it assumes that the school has a critical role to play in bringing cultural pluralism about in the greater society. The major distinction between the two variations in this approach is between those programs which address the problem generally among many cultural groups and those that deal specifically with only two cultures, through programs in bilingual/bicultural education. Ideally intended for all children, these programs, too, are often compensatory in nature, designed for minority children only as a necessary transition to aid their eventual entrance into the mainstream.

In terms of the parameters presented earlier, reference group application, realm of experience, scope, and form of the intended social change, all of the models above are severely limited. We must question the relationship between multicultural education reform efforts in the context of the school and the more ambitious goal of cultural pluralism, which address an alternative social structure.

Cultural pluralism, as an alternative theory of society, also must undergo a radical reanalysis. Like programs in multicultural education, it often assumes that culture is the major factor in addressing the problems. Other sociohistorical factors must be taken into account and integrated into the theory. Most central is the phenomenon of class and its role in the American socioeconomic system. We know that schooling systems are inherently conservative and often reflect the social structure of the greater society, where class stratification continues to play a major role in the maintenance of the present socioeconomic structure. If we neglect or omit these economic factors from our analyses and proposals for change, cultural pluralism may very likely turn out to be, as Thomas R. Lopez, Jr.

suggests (10), a political hoax which diverts us from confronting the history of political-economic oppression and exploitation which has had, perhaps, a more important role than has culture in the structural organization of American society.

Notes

1 AACTE Commission on Multicultural Education, *No One Model American*, AACTE brochure (Washington, D.C.: AACTE, 1973).
2 William R. Hazard and Madelon D. Stent, "Appendix A. Statement by Steering Committee of the National Coalition for Cultural Pluralism," *Cultural Pluralism in Education: A Mandate for Change* (New York: Appleton-Century-Crofts, 1973), p. 150.
3 Alfredo Castañeda, "Persisting Ideological Issues of Assimilation in America," in *Cultural Pluralism*, Edgar G. Epps, ed. (Berkeley: McCutchan, 1974), p. 65.
4 Andrew T. Kopan, "Melting Pot: Myth or Reality?" in *Cultural Pluralism*, p. 51.
5 Thomas F. Green, *Work, Leisure, and the American School* (New York: Random House, 1968), p. 148.
6 Yehudi A. Cohen, "The Shaping of Men's Minds: Adaptations to the Imperatives of Culture," in *Anthropological Perspectives on Education*, Murray Wax, et al., eds. (New York: Basic Books, 1971).
7 See, for example, William E. Connolly, ed., *The Bias of Pluralism* (New York: Lieber-Atherton, 1973). A useful critique is by philosopher Robert Paul Wolff, "Beyond Tolerance," in *A Critique of Pure Tolerance*, Wolff, et al., eds. (Boston: Beacon Press, 1965).
8 J.S. Furnivall, *Colonial Policy and Practice—A Comparative Study of Burma and Netherlands India* (London: Cambridge University Press, 1948), p. 304.
9 See, for example, M.G. Smith, *The Plural Society in the British West Indies* (Berkeley: University of California Press, 1965); Leo Kuper and M.G. Smith, eds., *Pluralism in Africa* (Berkeley: University of California Press, 1971); Leo Kuper, *Race, Class, and Power* (London: Duckworth, 1974).
10 Thomas R. Lopez, Jr., "Cultural Pluralism: Political Hoax? Educational Need?" *The Journal of Teacher Education* (Winter 1973): 277–81.

PART 2

MULTICULTURAL EDUCATION: 1970s
(a) Assimilation and schooling

CHAPTER 4

CULTURAL IDENTITY (1973)
Problems and dilemmas
Charles F. Leyba

The intent of this article is to explore issues that, it is believed, must be faced if institutions of education and ethnic communities are serious in their intent to develop multicultural education.* The article is organized as follows:

1   A description of culture suited to the present analysis will be developed.
2   The description will be applied to the relations between majority and minority ethnic groups. The relations under consideration are those of (a) control and (b) cultural erosion.
3   Finally, two cultural dilemmas will be discussed with some tentative solutions.

Definition of culture

The purpose of the following analysis is to provide a working framework for discussion, not an exploration of various cultural descriptions with a view to developing a definitive statement regarding culture. Accordingly, the data base for the description of culture will be the rather common experiences of people. On this point, then, the description will be of an empirical sort.

In the broadest sense, the phenomenology of culture emerges when one notices that in the billions of actions placed in a single day by members of society, the result is not confusion or chaos but a reasonable approximation of order (1). Just as this is true at the macrocultural or societal level, the same can be said at the stratum of subcultures within a society or nation.

Thus, there appears not only a general patterning of actions, but within this web of interaction clearly identifiable micropatterns emerge. These are the phenomena of institutions, subgroups, etc. For our purpose, however, this is the phenomenon of minority ethnic cultures with their specific organization of life styles. And the extent to which these patterns of action are distinct from one ethnic group to another provides the empirical ground for discerning subcultures from one another. It is this homogeneity (patterning) of action that phenomenologically binds individuals together and identifies them as culturally distinct (2). Because of this homogeneity, there is a predictability in human action within a culture. For example, wherever Mexican Americans are, regardless of geographic distance from the Southwest (e.g., Mexican Americans in Gary, Indiana), characteristic dishes will be prepared at Christmas holidays as they have been from long tradition.

This trans-geographic unity of action has, of course, its inner psychological correlates. These correlates can be described as psycho-inertial mechanisms (cognitive-affective inclinations within the human psyche) that orient human beings within a cultural group (and outside it) to locate fairly identical actions at a given time and place. While the phenomenology of culture is at the action level, its roots are in the cognitive-affective regions of the person (3). As Wirth has said, "A society is possible in the last analysis because the individuals in it carry around in their heads some sort of picture of that society (4)."

As the culture is created in the developing child by the environment, so the environment is the matrix within which a culture sustains itself. A total absence of the ethnically developed environment will gradually undo the psycho-inertial forces referred to. More accurately, new inertial forces will be substituted for the prior ones. When this occurs (at the individual level), the person is no longer culturally bound to his group. Such a person, if he is a Mexican American, will be referred to as a "vendido" (sellout), "Tio Taco" (Uncle Taco, the Chicano version of Uncle Tom), or as a "coconut"—brown on the outside, white on the inside. At the level of the group, cultural distinctness disappears.

Several conclusions derive from the above. First, that cultural preservation is in direct proportion to the presence of an environment including the basic components of the culture sufficient to sustain that culture. Accept for the sake of argument that the vital components of a culture, as described by Dr. John Aragon, are the following: (a) a common language, (b) a common diet, (c) similar costuming, (d) common social patterns, and (e) ethics (common values and beliefs) (5).

Implied in all of these must be a minimal number of enterprises providing the goods and services assumed in these components. More important, in the last analysis, are persons in sufficient numbers to make the provision of these goods and services and especially the sharing of language, social customs and ethics a constant reality. Where these components exist in a marginal fashion, the majority culture will, over time, transform the minority culture which is too diffuse to sustain itself. Group cohesion, then, becomes a sine qua non for sustenance of the culture (e.g., the Amish sect). Even where large concentrations of persons of the same cultural group exist, the larger culture with its almost exclusive control of media and institutions makes deep inroads into the psychosocial life of a minority culture.

This is especially true of the Mexican American. Living largely on the border of the U.S. and Mexico, the Mexican American has a community (communities) powerfully self-sustaining, self-renewed by immigration of Mexicans into these communities, and visits to Mexico. Nonetheless, the Mexican American has a riven conscious life. Being neither Mexican nor American (6) in the sense of full participation in Anglo culture, he suffers a severe loss of identity—if not a loss, certainly a profound confusion as to his identity. Thus, while younger people in the community accept the name *Chicano* as a term to describe Americans of Mexican descent, the same is not always true of the older persons. These latter will vary sometimes vehemently in their opinions as to the correct term. For example, the author has observed lengthy disputes as to whether the correct term should be Mexican American, with or without a hyphen! Other terms are Latino, Hispano, Spanish American and Latin American.

Cultural erosion mechanisms at work

This phenomenon and others like it are evidence that powerful forces in the majority culture are at work to decondition the function of the psycho-social inertial mechanisms referred to above.

Nowhere is this assimilationist, acculturating, inroad-making function more evident than in the school system. Here, apart from marginal (in terms of the quantity of need) efforts to introduce the ethnic language and culture into the curriculum, what exists is a content and methodology developed according to an Anglo cultural Weltanschauung. This means alien, irrelevant content and a demanding competitive-aggressive-noncooperative style of behavior on the part of the students (7). For minority students who continue in the system, they are simply taught to be what they are not. For those forced out, and the majority are, they never become educated and face a confinement-occupational life in the lower-standard job categories.

Not only are content and methodology, in the main, cultural (ethnic) erosion mechanisms, but teachers themselves, completely apart from the education and training they bring to the classroom, being full participants in Anglo culture (are Anglos themselves), bring cultural deficiencies to the classroom. Aragon complains, "The true impediment to cultural pluralism is that we have had culturally deficient educators attempting to teach culturally different children (8)." One immediate consequence of this is that the educators shift their own cultural deficiencies into the children. Again quoting from Dr. Aragon:

> There are cases where educators . . . ranging all the way from professors of liberal arts and education, school administrators, and up to primary teachers, have discounted pluralism by ascribing to culturally different clients (students) all kinds of demeaning terms. We are all familiar with these terms: culturally deficient, culturally disadvantaged, culturally deprived, and in extreme cases even culturally depraved (9).

This last term in the above is not an exaggeration. Consider the following quotation:

> Their (Mexican) general moral conditions are bad when judged by the prevailing standards. It seems just, however, to say that Mexicans are unmoral rather than immoral since they lack a conception of morals as understood in this *country*. Their housing conditions are bad, crime is prevalent, and their morals are a menace to our civilization (10). (Italics are mine.)

School system control

How dominant is the control of school systems by teachers representing the majority culture may be exemplified by the ratio of white teachers to teachers from minority backgrounds in California. The figures are from the latest Racial and Ethnic Survey (11).

Table 4.1 Percentage distribution of teachers in California according to racial/ethnic background

Anglo	89.5
Spanish surname	2.6
Black	5.1
American Indian	.2
Oriental	2.2
Other nonwhite	.4

These figures of course are meaningless unless considered in relationship to the distribution of pupils:

Table 4.2 Teacher/pupil ratio in California by actual numbers

Anglo	1 per 19 students
Spanish surname	1 per 152 students
Black	1 per 46 students
American Indian	1 per 59 students
Oriental	1 per 24 students
Other nonwhite	1 per 63 students

Only the Oriental and Anglo categories show acceptable or better than acceptable ratios. In a condition such as this, most minority children face undoubtedly well-meaning but clearly culturally deficient teachers.

An entirely predictable result is cultural conflict and the tendency of the minority children to face loss of identity and to display what the system describes as "deviant behavior." To the extent that it is Anglo culture they are indoctrinated with, there is also a nonacceptance of school tasks and a diminished sense of respect for parents who embody more fully the ethnic culture and language.

There is, therefore, a fairly complete control by the dominant culture of the institution of education—the institution that is the superdominant and required administrating arm of the rite de passage for all children.

Nor is there any indication that this control is weakening. For instance, a survey of 244 colleges in five southwestern states (with only half showing the interest to respond) indicated that 13 percent had established ethnic departments or degrees (12).

A nationwide study of the Career Opportunities Program which is training minority and poverty-level students for positions in school systems indicates little to no accommodation to these students' special needs other than lowering entrance requirements, some counseling, and establishing noncredit remedial courses.

The message is obvious: Enter, but become like us!

Nor is there any indication that there is even the intent to weaken control. Responding to the fact that there are about 150,000 more teachers receiving credentials yearly than there are jobs for, many teacher training institutions are either no longer producing teachers or are diminishing their enrollments. Furthermore, USOE is cutting back funds for preservice teacher preparation. Apparently satisfied with quantities of teaching personnel unqualified to serve minority youth, federal money may no longer be used to attract and subsidize minorities interested in becoming teachers. Thus for all practical purposes, the only source of sufficient size and influence to produce a growing cadre of teachers representing minority cultures is finally to be denied. Meanwhile, in the case of the Mexican American, community classrooms continue to be woefully short of teachers needed for this ethnic group. In the Southwest as a whole, there are 120 pupils of Mexican-American descent for every Mexican-American teacher (13).

Simply to create an acceptable *mathematical* ratio, the number of Mexican-American teachers would have to be quadrupled.

Not even the ESEA Title VII bilingual program, in the main, has sufficient numbers of teachers for its own programs. To fill the need for bilingual instructional personnel in the classrooms, program directors turn to community persons (usually mothers) to work as aides. Frequently enough, the aides provide better learning experiences than the teachers. Often too, their Anglo counterparts reduce them to the level of academic janitors (roll takers, typists, hall monitors), thus reducing many a bilingual project to the status of a Title I program with an accent. Moreover, because of the undoubtedly respected but inferior economic and academic condition of the aides, they hardly provide role models which stimulate aspirations to high positions, one of the goals of multicultural education. This condition has every prospect of remaining since, as noted, the majority culture through its institutions has expressed its satisfaction that the quantity of teachers produced is more than sufficient.

We turn to the in-service training function as a means of making existing teachers more sympathetic to and cognizant of ethnic cultures. The purpose of this, of course, is to introduce ethnic-cultural subject matter (language, history, art, etc.) into the instructional program. How effective will this training be? Since it has been demonstrated, at least as far as the present state of the art is concerned, that there is no single reliable methodology for increasing teacher effectiveness and thereby improving student performance, the outcomes of in-service training as it relates to students will be predictably nebulous. What is predictable is that teachers who are in complete mastery of their *own* culture will be given an understanding of *another* culture. It is predictable that the teachers will be enriched. The majority culture will have succeeded in equipping itself with a slight overlay of minority culture (and language), a mere *appoggiatura* to its basic themes.

What is predictable is that the "fiesta model"† of academic accommodation to ethnic culture will be incorporated into the school year.

Obviously there is no escape from the need for the presence of teachers from the ethnic cultures, well trained in their own culture, if multicultural education is to be made an abiding reality in classrooms. But that means government subsidized recruitment and preservice training of minority teachers. And we know about that already.

Cultural dilemmas

A point made earlier is that a majority culture has the means to overwhelm minority cultures (14). It is not intended to imply that this will necessarily happen. Nonetheless the means are there. To present courses in the ethnic culture at educational institutions has the effect of using one of the major means employed by the majority culture as an instrument whereby the ethnic culture can center on its own life, values, and interests. Such courses if seriously pursued will have the effect of intensifying and heightening the difference between ethnic cultures and the majority culture.‡

That is, courses in ethnic culture have the effect of prevention against being overwhelmed. To this extent they have a separatist, anti-assimilationist character. Another view is that courses in ethnic studies are like shelters. Such courses are academic holding places where minority persons can develop basic skills which will allow them to survive the performance demands of majority-dominated general education and the major departments—unless the major is itself ethnic studies.

To this extent they are a permeable membrane by which minority persons can be shielded and through which they can make safe passage (assimilation) into the world of success and involvement as defined by majority culture.

Here is the first facet of the dilemma. Are studies in one's ethnic culture to have the effect of centering on that culture, of deepening one's immersion in it, of plunging totally into the unlosable elements of ethnicity, or are these studies to be vehicles for safe passage? Are they separatist or assimilationist?

The next facet concerns the Mexican American in the dilemma.§ There are many characteristics of Mexican Americans that have been identified by writers. For example, there are the structural demographic characteristics identified by Casavantes which may be classified as descriptors, such as educational level of attainment, language, and religious affiliations.

At a deeper level, where the culture forges and casts a personality and with it orients the very roots of one's perception, the author is persuaded that there are at least two primordial elements. These are positive, not negative, characteristics.

1   Mexican-American culture is contractive/centripetal rather than penetrative/centrifugal.
2   Mexican-American culture is philosophico-contemplative in regard to the world rather than managerial/manipulative of it.

1. By describing Mexican-American culture as contractive and centripetal we mean that there is a center of values in the culture that draws its people to them. Thus these values are sufficient in themselves to make life full of meaning and joy. A symbol of this is the geographic location of *la raza*. Whether it be Chicago, Topeka, or the great heartland of the five Southwestern states, Mexican Americans like to be with their people. It is not easy to entice a Mexican American away from the geographic center of his culture. While he does not want to be discriminated against in terms of jobs, or education, or houses or neighborhoods in which to live, or restaurants in which to eat, there is no overpowering interest in penetrating majority-culture neighborhoods, no great value in being bused into other schools. The barrio, unlike the neighborhoods (especially middle-class ones), is not a staging ground for moving on and out. Better housing and better schools where we can be together have higher priority. While there is discrimination in housing and especially in jobs, this is more a sickness in the discriminator than the basis for a universal desire to be in the midst of majority culture. Though we have the right to be and go where we will, we want to be with our own. Contrast this with the mobile, intermingling, move-out and get-better-at-any-cost character of other groups. Like the sea anemone we fold in upon the values and activities that feed our souls and make us who we are.

2. To be managerial and manipulative of the world means to have the Cartesian vision of bodies, from atoms to galaxies, constantly interacting with the

forces and energies each has. It means to be able to quantify and control and change the physical world and ultimately bend its forces, reconstruct it to whatever purpose it can serve. To understand the world in this noological context means to construct hypotheses, prove them—all for the purpose of reconstructing, synthesizing matter into engines, machines, tools, foods, medicines, and so on, to improve the material quality of life. Ideally this should free humans from many everyday cares and free them from the bondage of applying their minds exclusively to these concerns. But it has not. De Tocqueville well understood this character of Anglo culture. (It was really Anglo culture and institutions that he studied under the rubric of democracy.)

In America, the purely practical part of science is admirably understood, and careful attention is paid to the theoretical portion which is immediately requisite to application. On this head, the Americans always display a clear, free, original, and inventive power of mind. But hardly anyone in the United States devotes himself to the essentially theoretical and abstract portions of human knowledge (15).

A philosophico-contemplative view of the world inclines one to a deeper level of understanding. It concerns itself with describing essences, with a quest for inner meaning, with a long and meditative gaze at reality in which the significance of life, beauty, truth and destiny are the goals of intelligence. This character of intelligence leaves the world alone to be what it is and in doing so attempts to know it as it is. From this point of view, to understand life is to see it living, not, as biologists will do to frogs—kill a living thing, dissect it, the better to know life. This becomes an absurdity. The world is, in a philosophico-contemplative view, "the other" with a respectability of its own, and this separateness is at once a recognition of its own respectability, its own inner right to be itself, and the ontological basis for Octavio Paz's *Labyrinth of Solitude*, "the aloneness," that lies at the heart of the philosophico-contemplative attitude in Mexican-American culture.

It is no accident, therefore, that, with this orientation to life, Hispanic culture—of which Mexican-American culture is a variation—has produced world-class painters, musicians, writers and metaphysicians but no one in the manipulative-managerial enterprises whose theorizing center is American science.¶

Here, again, the dilemma is prolonged. If majority culture has as its thrust to master the forces of the material world, to bend them to its purposes, and in effect to restructure the world's meaning, what is the effect of ethnic courses in Mexican-American culture to be? Assimilative? If so, then by entering the "mainstream" will Mexican-American culture lose its philosophico-contemplative nature and, therefore, an essential component? Or will the purposes of these courses be to allow the ethnic culture to do as the human species has done, that is, to center on itself, to heighten and deepen cultural identity and thus to separate itself from majority culture, as man has insistently separated himself as a species from the primate.

It would appear that to retain cultural identity and to instream into majority culture, Mexican Americans will have to develop bicultural identity in the fullest way possible. Is this possible in a single life time, especially in a single academic life? There is no question that it has been accomplished in individuals. But can it be done by the group, or even a majority of the group?

On the other hand, it may be that Mexican-American culture will in time evolve a meaning and accommodation to majority trends. In this process, perhaps, a new culture, not a different one, will emerge. What possible value variables this new culture will have is difficult to imagine. Hopefully, the outcome will not be left to the vagaries of history.

Notes

* Because the author's experience and ethnic relation is within the Mexican-American community of the Southwest, examples drawn from this background related to multi-cultural education will naturally predominate in the themes developed.

† The let's-serve-tacos, break-a-piñata and be-excited-about-another-culture, make-a-field-trip syndrome.

‡ Obviously, this also has the effect of creating an appreciation, respect and understanding of the ethnic culture in those students who are from a different culture.

§ The validity of the succeeding paragraphs is wholly dependent on the clarity and honesty with which the characteristics of the Mexican-American culture are understood by the author. As such, they present points from which a dialogue may proceed. They also are points which can be denied outright.

¶ The author hesitates to say "western" science since the development of (scientific) theory in the strictest sense is the almost exclusive domain of Europeans.

References

1 Ankeles, A. *What is Sociology?* Englewood Cliffs, N.J.: Prentice-Hall, 1964, p. 23.

2 Valencia, Atilano A. *Bilingual-Bicultural Education for the Spanish-English Bilingual.* Las Vegas, New Mexico: New Mexico Highlands University Press, 1972, p. 78.

3 Generatively, of course, the culture is in the environment of the person born into it, in the persons, symbols, etc., that represent the culture.

4 Wirth, Louis in Karl Mannheim's *Ideology and Utopia.* New York: Harcourt, Brace & World, Inc., 1936, Preface xxiii.

5 Stent, Madelon et al., eds. *Cultural Pluralism in Education.* Appleton-Century-Crofts, 1973, p. 79.

6 Valencia, *Bilingual-Bicultural Education*, Appendix A. This citation contains an excellent discussion of the terms *Anglo-American* and *Anglo* as well as other ethnic terms used here.

7 Kagan, S. and M. C. Matlsen. *Cooperation and Competition of Mexican American and Anglo American Children of Two Ages Under Four Instructional Sets* (ERIC No. ED 042 532), 1973.

8 Stent, *Cultural Pluralism*, p. 78.

9 Stent, p. 77.

10 McKuen, W. W. *A Survey of the Mexican in Los Angeles.* Masters thesis. University of Southern California, 1914, p. 100.

11 *Racial and Ethnic Survey of California Public Schools.* Published by the Bureau of Intergroup Relations, State Department of Education, 721 Capitol Mall, Sacramento, California 95814, Fall 1971, revised April 1972.

12 Sanchez, Corinne J. "A Challenge for Colleges and Universities—Chicano Studies," *Civil Rights Digest* III, 4 (Fall 1970).

13 "Title VI Survey." U.S. Department of Health, Education and Welfare. Fall 1968.

14 *Los Angeles Times*, Vol. XCII, Sep. 24, 1973, Part II, p. 10. In the news item Dr. James E. Cheek, President of Howard University, indicates that the current interpretation of Title VI, Civil Rights Act is having the effect (in terms of desegregating black colleges) of turning them into majority-(white) dominated institutions.

15 De Tocqueville, Alexis. *Democracy in America.* Mentor Book, New York: The New American Library, 1961, pp. 164 and 167.

CHAPTER 5

THE FOUNDATIONS OF MULTICULTURAL EDUCATION (1977)

Jesse Hiraoka

In recent years the effort by ethnic groups to establish their own sense of being and place has led to several programmatic concepts useful in education. From these concepts have developed specific ethnic studies courses and programs, bilingual and bicultural training programs, and workshops dealing with a variety of topics on identity, culture and relationships. Multicultural education has been the most general programmatic concept to emerge. It is an easy term to use because it includes several minority groups without specifically naming them, it assumes an opposition to the concept of a single dominant culture, and it addresses the economic and social problems of this country.

Because multicultural education lends itself to ready use, it is important that it be viewed as a developmental concept, rather than an established and complete one. Once viewed in the latter sense, as established and complete, and based principally upon its opposition to monocultural education, there is no significant meaning to the concept of multicultural education. It risks a quick passage into oblivion, similar to other new concepts whose meaning was always dependent on an older concept which it attempted to replace. Such new concepts become only a fashion, ultimately giving way to other fashions. To avoid this fate, the concept of multicultural education must be defined and developed in its own right if it is to be effective in removing previous shortcomings. It is therefore valuable to consider multicultural education within the developmental context and to discuss its foundations within a state of change.

As a concept, multicultural education is significantly affected by the various meanings of the word *culture*. In his "Theoretical Remarks on Afroamerican Cultural Nationalism," Mkalimoto (1974) raised the issue of the meaning of the term "culture":

All of which leads us, as a first step, to focus upon what one conceives "culture" to be. Unfortunately, such a task is complicated by no small amount of confusion engulfing the manifold uses of the term. For that reason, perhaps the worst error one could commit would be to assume any common, *a priori* agreement upon its definition, since one of the first things that strikes us, or *should* strike us, about the notion is its profoundly *equivocal* character: "culture is art, literature, dance, theatre . . .;" "culture is both aim and means of revolutionary struggle;" "culture is the expression of man's relationship to his environment;" "culture is the expression of the *way* in which man lives his relation to his environment;" "culture is everything;" "culture is the way of life of a people, the infinite sum of its thought and behavior;" "culture is not behavior, but an abstraction from that behavior," und so weiter. . . .! [Mkalimoto, pp. 1–2].

In presenting the "culture" of minority groups in America, it becomes crucial to determine within the context of multicultural education exactly what constitutes Afroamerican culture, Native American culture, Asian American culture, Chicano culture, and, as well, majority, minority, and dominant cultures. The very approach to selection and presentation will determine the validity of the concept of multicultural education. The simplest task is to establish multicultural education as a concept in opposition to monocultural education, and to further define it by the specific ways in which each specific minority culture is selected to exemplify the multicultural facts of the American society. For example, note that in utilizing Asian-American studies as a programmatic form, one is faced with several immediate concerns: there are Chinese, Japanese, Korean, Filipino, Vietnamese, Pacific Islanders, and now East Indians to be considered within this cultural context called Asian and Asian American. What aspects of the cultural heritage is one to select? What basic presentation can be made to those of Asian heritage and to those of non-Asian heritage? What references need to be made to specific cultural forms of the Asian heritage? The questions multiply and escape easy intellectual grasp. Yet, the selection and presentation will have to be made for each ethnogroup focus. It should not, therefore, be unexpected that there will be different approaches and diverging views as to what is representative of each culture.

A second dynamic important to the development of the concept of multicultural education is the category of reference points or dimensions of culture that are to be reflective of each of the multicultures. A cultural concept must provide not only knowledge transmission but also, in a more significant sense, it must develop those tools of perception, organization, and action. And this is dependent upon the cultural framework that provides direction as to what one chooses to see, accept, and act upon. The best example of this cultural framework is the view of *time* that so strongly pervades the American culture and creates the conditions for devastating effects upon minority groups. Paz, in *Children of the Mire* (1974) writes:

> As our image of time has changed, so has our relation to tradition. Criticism of a tradition begins with the awareness of belonging to a tradition. Traditionalist peoples live immersed in their past without questioning it. Unaware of their traditions, they live with and in them. Once a man realizes that he belongs to a tradition, he knows implicitly that he is different from that tradition; sooner or later this knowledge impels him to question, examine and sometimes deny it. Our age is distinguished from other epochs and other societies by the image we have made of time. For us time is the substance of history, time unfolds in history. The meaning of "the modern tradition" emerges more clearly! It is an expression of our historic consciousness, it is a criticism of the past, and it is an attempt, repeated several times throughout the last two centuries, to found a tradition on the only principle immune to criticism, because it is the condition and the consequence of criticism; change, history [Paz, pp. 8–9].

If, as Paz observes, time has been linear and progressive within the context of modernity, its effects upon Native American, Afroamericans, Asian Americans, Chicanos, and any groups which can be labeled primitive, ancient and original, should be evident. Again, as Paz has stated:

> Every time the Europeans and their North American descendants have encountered other cultures and civilizations, they have called them backward. This is not the first time a race or a civilization has imposed its forms on others, but it is certainly the first time one has set up as a universal ideal, not a changeless principle, but change itself. The Muslim or Christian based the alien's inferiority on a difference of faith; for the Greeks, Chinese, or Toltecs, he was inferior because he was a barbarian, a Chichimecan. Since the eighteenth century Africans or Asiatics have been inferior because they are not modern. The Western world has identified itself with change and time, and there is no modernity other than that of the West. There are hardly any barbarians, Infidels or Gentiles left; rather, the new Heathen Dogs can be counted in the millions, but they are called "underdeveloped peoples" [ibid., p. 20].

It becomes useful to a "modern people" to focus upon another group as the "other," the pole which furnishes comparison; by having available groups that can be viewed as unchanging or unchangeable (non-assimilable), there is developed a time reference point useful for purposes of comparison. The Afroamerican is linked with an African culture conceived in terms useful to that time progression; the Native American is described to serve that time notion in a similar fashion. And by using those groups as time reference points, the notion of an American people in upward movement is reinforced. The American culture is offered as modern, progressive, rational and practical. And by using certain ethnic groups as time reference verifiers, the relatively new American culture also keeps those very groups from participating advantageously in the American society. That certain ethnic groups were viewed as unchanging reflects a need of the dominant society. As Pearce (1974) has pointed out:

> Let me explicate the idea of savagism: American thinking about the Indian and his relation to White civilization was, until the middle of the eighteenth century, based on the notion that somehow the Indian would absorb, or be absorbed by, White civilization. When the cruelty and rigor of events, White impatience and Indian stubbornness, would not allow for such absorption, American thinking changed its emphasis and direction. It was based more and more on the notion that the gap between Indian and White society was too great to be closed; that corresponding to White civilization there was Indian "savagism"—for which we have no equivalent term now, at least consciously, since we tell ourselves that we no longer subscribe to the notion [Pearce, p. 89].

This distinction between "savage" and "civilized," once drawn, cannot be altered without a change in the concept of culture. The linear and progressive time dimension that requires an original starting point places a group there and maintains that placing. A clear distinction is made as to who can be civilized and who cannot. If this form of cultural bias exists, a change needs to occur at that very basic level. It should be noted that if education also utilizes that linear and progressive time dimension, the gap can never be closed for those who are placed at specific reference points only to serve as a point of comparison for those who have moved on. What does education accomplish, despite all its efforts, if, as an important facet of that culture, there is the view that some changes for some people can never be made. Equality in its real sense never occurs. A different human condition has been posited for a particular group, while another view of the human condition is accepted as valid for others. And it is at this profound level of culture that decisions affecting groups have already been made. This is why the concept of multicultural education requires clarification of the active dimensions that provide the framework of a view of culture. It will not be sufficient to deal with the heritage of each ethnic group, for of equal importance is the development of those large reference points that translate into the human condition and affect all participants.

A third dynamic that is critical to the concept of multicultural education is the nature of change. The recent and specific change that has affected students, teachers, training, and the teaching institutions is the emergence of a society in flux as opposed to an "established" society. Change within an "established" society does not affect the cultural framework. Roles, occupations, goals, manners and morals, and expectations tend to remain intact. Education programs assume their function without necessarily examining their nature, role and effectiveness. Within the context of limited change, the relationship of organizations, groups and individuals are assumed to be clear and distinct, and no clarification of cooperative efforts results. Course content and methodology are assumed to be "correct" in their larger sense, and variety, diversity and differences are discouraged, or simply not tolerated.

In recent years what has occurred is the effect of change at fundamental levels. Change has affected all levels from the individual through the family, the organizations, and the society. The dynamics of change are no longer controlled by the flow of years in measured pace, and even experience itself, normally an ingredient of control, has at times become an obstacle. Multicultural education is itself reflective of this type of change. It sanctions diversity. The individual can be various, the society is multicultural, the interaction of groups is assumed, and the movement toward complementary diversity becomes a desired objective.

Programs in multicultural education in their objectives reflect this substantive change:

1   Acknowledgment of the effects of change on the educational organizations, their participants, processes, and expectations.
2   Acceptance of the presence of a diversity of cultures, each with its specific area of values, of patterns, of attitudes and of behaviors that are sufficiently different so that understanding this very diversity becomes important to the educational process.
3   Development of an awareness on the part of the teachers and interns of the assumptions underlying their basis of knowledge, their own attitudes toward other cultures, and their methods of teaching and learning.
4   Recognition of the interrelationship of participant, process and organization so that the context for content and methods derives from the actual teaching/learning situation in the community and not from assumed or preconceived situations.
5   Acquisition of a variety of skills for teaching and learning relative to different cultural backgrounds within a changing situation.

The challenge of multicultural education as a concept is that, within the dynamics of change, it attempts to include ethnic groups who have been excluded in larger and systematic ways. Where the exclusion was felt to be logical and acceptable in terms of previously established values of individuals, organizations and communities, no significant response needed to be made to the problems and difficulties of excluded groups. Multicultural education stresses inclusion, and, to remain valid, needs to consider the effects of change upon diversity.

If the developmental aspects of multicultural education have been emphasized, it is because the very combination of diversity and culture requires careful and serious consideration. The concept of multicultural education will not suffice in itself and will need to be examined in terms of its functional developments. The immediate replacement of previous forms by multicultural education is not possible since its development remains to be completed. And since we seek to correct previous limitations through the development of multicultural education, there is good advice in Myrdal's words in *An Approach to the Asian Drama* (1970):

> What must be emphasized is that all knowledge, and all ignorance, tends to be opportunistic, and becomes the more so the less it is checked and reconditioned by solid research directed to the empirical facts. Through wide and arduous travelling, which seldom means taking the shortest route, students undoubtedly will be forced gradually to correct their preconceptions, however deeply rooted in opportunism these may be. Until the approach is better tailored to reality, the data fail to fall into place, the facts rebel, and the logic is strained. . . . Inherent in all honest research is a self-correcting, purifying force that in the end will affirm itself [Myrdal, p. 25].

From the efforts of ethnic groups to define themselves, new and different concepts have emerged. Multicultural education is one of them, and, while its function as an alternative to other existing concepts of education is sufficiently clear, its usefulness and validity remain to be established in its development.

References

Mkalimoto, E. Theoretical remarks on Afroamerican cultural nationalism. *The Journal of Ethnic Studies*, 1974, 2, 2, 1–2.

Myrdal, G. *An approach to the Asian drama*. New York: Random House, 1970.

Paz, O. *Children of the mire*. Cambridge: Harvard University Press, 1974.

Pearce, R. H. From the history of ideas to ethnohistory. *The Journal of Ethnic Studies*, 1974, 2, 1, 89.

CHAPTER 6

DEFICIT, DIFFERENCE, AND BICULTURAL MODELS OF AFRO-AMERICAN BEHAVIOR (1971)

Charles A. Valentine

Many writers contend that a psychological-deficit model or normative approach to Afro-Americans rules educational theory and practice, perpetuating both scientifically untenable beliefs and destructive institutional policies. Still others hold that a cultural-difference model or a relativistic anthropological approach, presently absent from the educational scene, should be fostered because it is scientifically more adequate and will produce more constructive results, especially for Afro-American children.

My own somewhat different view of these problems is derived in part from a current ethnographic study of poverty and Afro-American cultures in a large northern city. This ongoing research, which has been in progress for nearly eighteen months, is being carried out by a family team consisting of my wife, our two-year-old son, and me.[1] In order to preserve the confidentiality of our data, protect the interests of local citizens, and safeguard our relationship with people and organizations here, we refer to this community publicly by the pseudonym Blackston.

Deficit model

Anthropological training and experience, plus more than a passing acquaintance with the psychological and sociological literature on Afro-Americans, convince us that the deficit theory is largely undemonstrated. Any theory of class or racial deficits of biological origin is quite undemonstrable, indeed scientifically untestable, in an ethnically plural and structurally discriminatory society. The necessary separation of biological and socio-cultural factors is methodologically impossible in this setting. Writings which put forward bio-chemical genetic determination, or social selection in the evolutionary sense, as explanations for group differences in behavior must therefore be dismissed as pseudo-scientific nonsense.

The "deficit model" of Negro behavior also refers to common psychological assumptions about Black pathology and popular notions of Afro-American speech as a structureless, unexpressive, "incorrect" version of what arrogant cultural elites are pleased to call Standard English. Experience convinces us that to attach labels like "nonverbal" and "linguistically incapable" to a people as adept at, interested in, and expressive through language as Afro-Americans is simply absurd. In these respects the recent critiques of deficit theories are emphatically supported by our findings.

Difference model

Stephen and Joan Baratz, William Stewart, and others have propounded an alternative to the deficit model which they call the "difference model." Their initial premise that Afro-Americans are culturally different from other Americans is a proposition that has lately been gaining attention and acceptance among an increasing number of anthropologists and other specialists. The strongest documentation for this position is in the linguistic demonstration that Afro-Americans have developed structurally differentiated dialectical variants of English and other European languages.[2] Suggestive supporting evidence has also been adduced in folklore and related patterns of oral performance[3] as well as in music.[4] There is nothing in our data to contradict these persuasive demonstrations of ethnic distinctiveness in areas of expressive culture. Indeed we expect to gather much evidence that will confirm and perhaps extend these formulations as the present research develops.

Beyond this, however, the Baratzes and Stewart have over-extended their model into a simplistic portrayal of cultural separation which, our experience persuades us, is an extreme form of earlier unsupported theses about "Negro culture." These writers repeatedly invoke the name of Herskovits as if he had founded their school of thought, while citing that authority's *The Myth of the Negro Past* as if it were their inspiration. There is room for doubt about these implications, just as there is ample basis for debate as to the significance and value of Herskovits' work itself.[5] (At the very least, any formulation which purports to portray a single, homogeneous entity labeled "the Negro subculture" must be a gross oversimplification.)

Indeed, systematic research guided by hypotheses derived in part from a cultural-difference model may reveal unexpectedly rich ethnic variation. Our current field work in a single urban community has so far produced evidence of some fourteen different Afro-American subgroups with more or less distinct cultures, as well as nine other non-Afro-ethnic subgroups.[6] These cultures present distinctive group identities and behavior patterns, including languages and dialects, aesthetic styles, bodies of folklore, religious beliefs and practices, political allegiances, family structures, food and clothing preferences, and other contrasts derived from specific national or regional origins and unique ethnohistories. (It would be absurd to describe any of these cultural systems as differing from mainstream culture only in terms of insufficiency or deficit.)

Nevertheless, a simple model of cultural difference is inadequate to clarify the cultural dynamics of the heterogeneous Blackston community. The notion of a single homogeneous "Negro culture," which is often conveyed by the difference model, will not fit our data except perhaps in certain special senses which await confirmation or disconfirmation as the research continues. Further study of the known cultures may reveal intergroup commonalities that are referable to one or more of three derivations: (1) shared African cultural roots, (2) common influences from the intervening ethnohistory under European domination in the New World, and (3) an emergent Afro-American culture recently influenced by Black Nationalism as a revitalization movement. The last of these three conditions will probably be relatively easy to demonstrate. The other two appear more problematical at the present stage of our research.

The central theoretical weakness of the "difference model" is an implicit assumption that different cultures are necessarily competitive alternatives, that distinct cultural systems can enter human experience only as mutually exclusive alternatives, never as interwined or simultaneously available repertoires.[7] Through the influence of this assumption, the attempt to demonstrate a highly distinctive, minimally variable Negro culture leads to positions which are highly questionable in the light of our evidence. From these premises the argument is made that the misfortunes of Afro-Americans in the contemporary United States are due to "culture conflict" leading to an inability of people brought up in "Negro culture" to understand or practice mainstream behavior. In order to defend these propositions, Stewart first denies that Afro-Americans possess any significant competence in mainstream culture, and then denounces our interest in ethnic subgroup variation as "the tired ploy of attempting to diversify American Negro culture out of existence."[8]

Both the "deficit" and "difference" models neglect and obscure the important concept of "biculturation." Steven Polgar (1960) found that people living on an Indian reservation regularly go through a process which he termed "biculturation."[9] That is, they are simultaneously enculturated and socialized in two different ways of life, a contemporary form of their traditional Amerindian lifeways and mainstream Euro-American culture. Whether or not one accepts an implied analogy between Indian reservations and Black ghettos,[10] the basic idea has very real relevance for Afro-America. This relevance has been partly recognized or at least alluded to by several of the writers already cited. Yet its implications have not been fully appreciated, nor has its interpretive strength been utilized.

In the cases of Ulf Hannerz and Stewart, for example, their own theoretical preoccupations evidently prevent them from making productive use of the concept. Despite a brief recognition by Hannerz that simultaneous enculturation in two sets of lifeways has some relevance to the ghetto,[11] his more general view of mainstream patterns among ghetto people has little in common with the concept of biculturation, either as originally proposed[12] or as used in our work. Hannerz explicitly separates "mainstreamers" from other ghetto people, labels them non-typical, and therefore declares that they are of little interest:

> There are many who are in the ghetto but not of the ghetto in the sense of exhibiting much of a life style peculiar to the community. . . . To their largely mainstream way of life we will devote rather little attention.[13]

Dual socialization thus gets lost in the attempt to establish a single ghetto culture. In a recent paper, Stewart (1969b) refers to his own view of Afro-American language as a "bipolar model of the urban Negro speech community," and he suggests that this is a bicultural concept. Yet he continues, "I know, as Hannerz does, that a biculturalism model is only useful for describing the behavior of total communities, and that virtually no individual in these communities can comfortably manage the entire range."[14] Thus biculturation is transmuted into a concept asserting mutually exclusive ethnic-cultural collectivities—nearly the exact opposite of its original meaning.

Among Afro-Americanists, at any rate, the importance of Polgar's concept seems to have been generally under-estimated or misunderstood. In our view, biculturation is the essence of the divided identity symbolized by the very name Afro-American and celebrated, dramatized, and lamented by every major Black American artist and scholar from DuBois and White through Ellison and Baldwin to Fanon and Cleaver. Indeed it is paradoxical that Hannerz opens his own book with a quotation from *The Souls of Black Folk* in which DuBois remarks upon the "double consciousness" and the "twoness" of Afro-American life—surely a classical statement of biculturation in its original sense. (Neither the quotation nor its source is discussed anywhere in Hannerz' book.)

In any case, biculturation strongly appeals to us as a key concept for making sense out of ethnicity and related matters: the collective behavior and social life of the Black community is bicultural in the sense that each. Afro-American ethnic segment draws upon both a distinctive repertoire of standardized Afro-American group behavior and, simultaneously, patterns derived from the mainstream cultural system of Euro-American derivation. Socialization into both systems begins at an early age, continues throughout life, and is generally of equal importance in most individual lives. The obvious ambiguities and ambivalences of all this are dramatized and sharpened by the fact that mainstream Euro-American culture includes concepts, values, and judgments which categorize Blacks as worthy only of fear, hatred, or contempt because of their supposedly innate characteristics. This is part of what radical and nationalistic Afro-Americans mean when they refer to the "brain-washing" of their people.

The idea of biculturation helps explain how people learn and practice both mainstream culture and ethnic cultures at the same time. Much intra-group socialization is conditioned by ethnically distinct experience, ranging from linguistic and other expressive patterns through exclusive associations like social clubs and recreational establishments to the relatively few commercial products and mass media productions designed for ethnic markets. Yet at the same time, members of all subgroups are thoroughly enculturated in dominant culture patterns by mainstream institutions, including most of the content of the mass media, most products and advertising for mass marketing, the entire experience of public schooling, constant exposure to national fashions, holidays, and heroes. These sources constantly impinge on Afro-American homes which thereby share these enculturation experiences with mainstream America. We also find mainstream socialization in more specialized forms from other institutions which operate particularly, though not always exclusively, within poverty areas. These include the welfare system, the police-courts-prison complex, anti-poverty programs and other forms of petty political patronage, and various types of employment through which middle- and upper-class patterns are commonly communicated, such as domestic service.

Ethnic cultural socialization is focused to some degree within family units and primary groups, with much mainstream enculturation coming more from wider sources. Yet this is by no means a sharp or consistent division of socializing influences. Ghetto homes expose their members from earliest childhood to many mainstream themes, values, and role models. This occurs not only through behavior of parents and others which reflects mainstream as well as ethnic conditioning, but also through external agencies which constantly operate within most households, such as television. Moreover, Afro-American children typically begin, at least during the third year of life, to be exposed outside the home to such mainstream cultural settings as may be available to ghetto dwellers: movies, amusement parks, children's programs of anti-poverty agencies, church activities, retail shopping, public health services, and others. Experience is thus so structured that Afro-Americans become thoroughly bicultural quite early in their lives.

A good deal of the mainstream cultural content Afro-Americans learn remains latent and potential rather than being actively expressed in everyday behavior. One reason for this is that the structural conditions of poverty, discrimination, and segregation prevent people from achieving many mainstream middle-class values, aspirations, and role models to which they nevertheless give psychologically deeprooted allegiance. It seems that for the subordinate strata in plural systems, enculturation in the dominant way of life may often provide great familiarity with mainstream patterns but little opportunity to practice these patterns actively. One result is that Euro-Americans (and sometimes Negroes out of touch with the ghetto) can easily convince themselves that Blacks in poverty areas have no competence in the dominant culture. This conviction in turn becomes a basis or rationalization for continuing discrimination and segregation.

One common pattern of what we call passive enactment of mainstream culture occurs in settings of formalized intergroup contact. Examples include court and commission hearings in which the official personnel are generally middle-class Whites, the proceedings are formally conducted according to mainstream patterns including middle-class American English, sometimes augmented by specialized vocabulary, and the defendants or complainants, or both, are Afro-Americans. Numerous direct observations of such proceedings have convinced us that generally the Black participants understand fully what is being done and said. Yet when called upon to speak they tend to confine themselves to Afro-American English idioms. This often leads to confusion, but it is almost invariably the middle-class Whites who misunderstand. The obvious reason for this is that the Afro-Americans are bicultural and bidialectical, whereas the non-Black mainstreamers are generally limited to a single cultural system. In other words, poor Afro-Americans—far from being either deficient or merely different in culture—often possess a richer repertoire of varied life styles than their ethnically non-descript social superiors.

There is a point of convergence, though, between the difference model and the popular but discredited notions of a so-called "culture of poverty" or "lower-class culture."[15] For example, one proponent of the difference model whose work is otherwise innovative, stimulating, and persuasive has recently published the following remarks. He writes of

> A different culture . . . recurrent throughout the country in lower-class Negroes. And by lower-class here I don't just mean poor; I mean a special culture configuration, what the anthropologist would call a "different" culture . . . The lower-class Negro is certainly in many ways culturally quite different from general middle-class American society. . . .
>
> When Africans came to the United States, they assimilated in part to the white culture but not entirely. African social patterns that were brought to the United States were modified by slavery, were partially conformed to white social patterns, but not entirely. There were innovations . . ., but they were not entirely identical to the white norm of behavior. . . .
>
> The American Negro who hasn't been too much in contact with standard American culture . . . or too assimilated to it, often has a very different kind of family structure, and sometimes the kinship and family relationships are very foreign from any kind of European model.[16]

The author of this quotation is no doubt well aware of the qualifications which need to be added to his seemingly sweeping generalizations. In this quotation we see that the convention of conceptualizing Afro-American culture in terms of acculturation—and especially assimilation—leads to ignoring the bicultural dynamic of Black community life in America. This assimilationist bias—and particularly its key assumption that culture and subcultures are mutually exclusive or inevitably competitive alternatives—becomes vitally important in a practical sense when it is passed on to certain audiences. These include professionals in such service areas as education or psychiatry. However, the quoted passages were presented to a workshop of educators. One can hardly assume that such an audience will make the necessary qualifications on its own.

On the contrary, our present research leads us to believe strongly that most school teachers and other educational specialists working in ghetto schools have well-established cognitive and affective sets into which such portrayals of cultural difference will fit perfectly. Moreover, this perceived consistency will reinforce a complex of attitudes and practices which are injurious to Afro-American pupils, regardless of the intentions of difference-model theorists. On dozens of occasions and in settings ranging from classrooms to counseling sessions to public confrontations with Afro-American parents and children, we have observed white educators expressing highly standardized beliefs and feelings about ghetto children and their families. Key items in this inventory include explicit statements that Afro-Americans are culturally different, that the cultural differences impede or prevent learning, that the school should function to wipe out these differences, but that educators frequently cannot succeed in this aim because the children are psychologically deficient as a result of their cultural difference. The attitude is that such children are "more to be pitied than scorned, but after all. . . ." So the projections by educationists go on around in a self-justification of circular reasoning which rationalizes all the failures of ghetto schools by blaming them on the students and the parents. Particularly when the context is one of intergroup confrontation, it is quite clear that these beliefs are backed by very strong negative emotions which often amount to obvious race hatred and blatant class antagonism.

Of course, all this is superficially disguised by accompanying rhetoric and rituals invoking liberal values, intergroup harmony, and dedication to upward mobility for the so-called "culturally deprived or disadvantaged." Partly because this humane-sounding camouflage is so well developed, it seems most doubtful that these educators will function more constructively after being further exposed to the difference model. On the contrary, we would predict that the respect for subcultural systems as legitimate human creations, which is communicated with the difference model, will be accorded no more than lip service. Meanwhile the descriptive and analytical core of the model will continue to be used as one more excuse for educational failure. It is in these senses that I put forward the thesis that both the deficit model and the difference formulation are already fully established in ghetto schools and that they both are applied to the serious detriment of Afro-American people young and old.

Some illustrative data may now be cited to support the points made so far. Here my text comes from the response by a guidance counselor, made publicly and in our presence, to a question from a long-married Afro-American mother of eleven normal children. The mother had asked why children in our neighborhood public school so often fail to learn. The counselor replied, "We find that children in our school who don't learn either are brain-damaged or don't have a father in their home," and he expanded considerably on this theme. The counselor should have known the normal nature of this woman's household, for he had had a number of private interviews with her concerning one of her sons, who had been doing poorly in the same school. Moreover, the same counselor has been quoted to us by several other community people as advancing the same formula on similar occasions. What is most significant about this example is that this man has the full backing of the school administration in his approach, and the attitudes he expresses are fully typical of his colleagues. In this widespread universe of discourse, "brain damage" is a code phrase for biological deficit, and "no father in the home" is a euphemism for despised cultural differences.

A case history

The case history of a former student at the same neighborhood school becomes relevant. An eight-year-old boy, recently a psychiatric patient, comes from an Afro-American family with roots in a rural seaboard region of the middle South and more recent residence in a port city of the upper South. Our understanding of this boy is based on information from the following sources. (1) Three months of daily observation of the patient's behavior in his present Northern urban home and community, including much contact with his foster family, other local relatives, playmates, and additional neighborhood associates. (2) Weekly or more frequent visits with the patient during a recent psychiatric hospitalization of three and a half months, including observation of most of his daily activities in the hospital. (3) A very full week of interviews and observations in the region of the patient's birth, including intensive contact with all 10 of his most significant surviving relatives, all members of his former foster family, all 14 medical, welfare, law-enforcement, and correctional professionals who had important contact with the patient or his close relatives. At this time we also collected full medical, legal, police, and newspaper records from all sources known to be relevant. (4) Later we were also granted access to the records of the case in two Northern hospitals where the youngster became a psychiatric patient.

The findings from the retrospective evidence can be summarized briefly. All medical and family history data indicate a normal pregnancy and birth, followed by an organically normal early childhood: no serious fevers, no bad falls, no unconsciousness or other obviously pathogenic effects from the physical traumas which it will become clear the boy did receive. With one exception, no other member of the extended family has ever received psychiatric diagnosis or treatment. The exception is the patient's father who experienced a brief psychotic break several months after having been imprisoned for murdering the patient's mother. By the time we talked with this man in May, 1969, he had been returned to the prison as normal, and our impressions accorded with this evaluation.

The boy's early childhood was dominated by an extremely hostile and punitive father and a very passive, indulgent mother. During this period the patient also spent much time in the poor but stable, warm, strict household of his maternal grandparents, spending many long visits there with his mother and his siblings. One of the father's chief impositions, evidently based on intense sexual jealousy, was to keep his wife and children isolated from all other social contacts. Thus the boy had little or no direct experience of the outside world beyond his grandparents' home. Five of the patient's older and younger siblings have lived continuously in this same grandparental household in the South for the last two to three years. All of them appear to be normal and are reported doing well in school. All reliable evidence, including eye-witness testimony from the patient's older adolescent siblings, consistently indicates that the boy was not present when his mother died during his sixth year. Indeed he was shielded by the family from the knowledge of her death until circumstances, including the father's arrest for murder, made this impossible some two months later. On the other hand, the child certainly did both witness and receive many severe beatings from his father during the first 5½ years of his life. From early childhood on, this boy was regarded by all who knew him as decidedly active, highly intelligent, somewhat aggressive and disobedient, but otherwise quite happily related to peers and to adults other than his father. No one in his various family and neighborhood settings regarded him as uncontrollable, and it never occurred to any known relative or associate to label him as mentally ill.

All available family and professional sources directly knowledgeable as to the facts agree that this youngster made a happy adjustment to life in a Southern rural Afro-American foster home during the year following his mother's death. After the initial grief of bereavement, there is no indication of lasting behavioral change in family or neighborhood settings at any time during this year. During this same period, however, the boy received his first exposure to larger social institutions. Here a pattern emerged which appears to represent the roots of the patient's later difficulties. As long as his early experiences with larger institutions were mediated by his guardians or other adults in the foster family, for example in regular church attendance, everything went smoothly.

When the boy was exposed alone to impersonal, bureaucratic, mainstream institutional settings, problems arose immediately. The middle-class and generally White authority figures in these settings saw his hyperactivity and tendency to disobedience as disruptive and uncontrollable. Teachers in a summer Headstart program for pre-schoolers remember this child chiefly as one who would not sit still in his assigned seat and be quiet. When he was taken to a large hospital for minor surgery, he was sent home a day ahead of the post-operative schedule because the nurses could not make him stay in his bed or keep up with his where-abouts within the institution. These institutional problems did not disturb the warm relationships within the foster home. When we met the boy's former guardians some two years later, they were obviously hungry for news of him, spontaneously reminisced about what an appealing child he was, and asked if we could help them get him back.

We interpret this retrospective evidence in the following way. The child suffered considerable emotional deprivation and disturbance of primary object relations during his first six years. This deprivation was substantially compensated by healthy relationships in the grandparents' household and further reduced by nurturance in the first foster family. In this connection, it should be noted that within Afro-American subcultures there appear to be both a structural fact and a socially learned expectation that family attachments are quite diversified and flexible in comparison with the rather narrow and rigid focus on specific parent-figures which is the mainstream norm. (While we do not feel that we fully understand the psychodynamics of this subcultural pattern at the present stage of our research we are gaining the impression that it functions quite positively in the settings of variable household composition which often stem from economic fluctuations and other recurrent stresses of poverty and minority status.) During this period the boy was adjusted, quite within normal limits, to Afro-American family and micro-institutional settings. Here his rambunctious active style was easily tolerated and controlled without difficulty whenever necessary by subcultural standards. Because of the family's social isolation during early years when biculturation normally begins, the child received very little preparation for mainstream macro-institutional settings. His behavior style was not tolerated in these settings. Yet there was neither any close personal relationship nor any subculturally appropriate approach available among the institutional personnel. Under these conditions the already delayed biculturation process again failed to function. So the mainstream educators and health specialists were unable to calm the youngster down and keep him under control within limits acceptable to them. In the patient's history to this point we find no evidence of psychosis, organic deficit, or other serious psychopathology.

We turn now to more current evidence. As we observed this boy during 1969, he showed a continuation of previously noted trends. He was clearly hyperactive, notably aggressive, strongly but never uncontrollably disobedient, and warmly attached to his new urban Northern foster parents, who are also relatives with the same southern Afro-American background. The boy was clearly capable of stable relationships with his neighborhood peers, successful in learning a new physical and social environment, and able to perform such organized activities as periodic work for small payments and participation in small neighborhood institutions like a locally modified cub scout troop.

Nevertheless, the boy was found by the local public school to be incapable of learning and dangerously uncontrollable. Teachers reported that he refused to obey them and that he disrupted classes with various kinds of outbursts, including fights with other youngsters. The same guidance counselor mentioned earlier was called in and decided the boy was deeply disturbed by a tragically unstable family life. This man placed in the record the fatefully erroneous statement that the boy had seen his father murder his mother. Precisely what misunderstanding led to this error is unknown, for none of the patient's kinsmen or associates in the North were acquainted with the circumstances surrounding the mother's death. The boy himself never alleged to us or anyone we know in the community that he had witnessed a killing. Until our trip to the boy's former home, the actual facts were unknown outside the Southern branch of the family and a small circle of professionals in the South. Nevertheless, this non-existent trauma was invoked as the source of deep psychopathology by every educator, psychiatrist, and social worker who subsequently dealt with the child. The counselor and the school principal contrived to have the boy excluded from school without the legally required suspension hearing. By this time the youngster had become a psychiatric out-patient at a nearby hospital. After interviews and tests, the hospital personnel recorded their diagnosis of childhood schizophrenia with mental retardation and probable organic damage. Tranquilizing medication was prescribed. After the expulsion from school, institutional interest in the case dropped away, and nothing further was done.

The boy then spent several months freely and successfully living the life of the ghetto streets each weekday while his foster parents worked literally day and night at minimally remunerative jobs to support the whole family. Over a period of two years in the urban North, the child's adaptation to home and community settings was well within tolerable limits as defined by his Afro-American foster-family and neighborhood associates; no one in these settings saw him as abnormal or impossible to control. Nevertheless, his relationship to home and community became decidedly stressful for obvious reasons as soon as he was excluded from school and defined by external authorities as mentally sick. Among other things, his guardians worried about his safety in the streets, and tried without success to get him back into school.

We first met this youngster after the school expulsion and heard his story from him, his foster parents, and other neighbors. With the permission and encouragement of the guardians, we naively turned to local school and hospital personnel for clarification. Before we knew it, there was suddenly a move afoot at the nearby hospital to have this long-forgotten child involuntarily committed to a state mental hospital immediately. Although there had been no change in the boy's behavior or situation, the plan for commitment was justified by a psychiatrist on the grounds that the patient was an imminent danger to himself and everyone around him. Local community leadership became aware of this plan and prevented it from being carried out. As the compromise among local power-centers worked out, the boy was temporarily hospitalized in another institution for so-called "independent" evaluation. It was soon clear that because of the interlocking professional associations of psychiatrists and others between the two institutions the alleged "independence" of the new evaluation was thoroughly compromised.

After gaining access to the operations and records of the institution, we soon discovered that hospital staff people at all levels felt extremely threatened. Because of the circumstances surrounding this patient's admission, they had concocted an image of the researchers, and even of the little boy himself, as "civil rights agitators" out to expose the institution by accusing it of anti-Black discrimination. This made life for the little boy even more miserable than it would otherwise have been. Lower-echelon staff in particular were openly hostile and punitive, to the extreme of confinement in a straight-jacket for hours at a time. During visits to our friend we found the same child we had known before, with two significant additions. First, it was obvious that the boy actively hated the conditions of enforced confinement. Second, he was so heavily influenced by what the hospital staff referred to as a "chemical straight-jacket" that often he acted like a zombie.

Despite much bureaucratic and professional resistance, we managed to interview and observe all hospital staff with major responsibilities in relation to this patient. We soon found that the staff had projected so much destructive power onto this eight-year-old that they talked about him as if he were about to destroy the hospital. We also found that the middle-class White upper-echelon staff so often misunderstood the youngster's verbalizations that they added "speech pathology" to the many strikes against him. The hospital personnel were largely ignorant of the boy's life before his admission. What little information they had of this nature came from his earlier psychiatric record and a family history composed by hospital social workers. Both these sources were filled with significant errors and distortions.

A clinical psychologist at the hospital found that on the WISC the boy scored a "borderline IQ," but as soon as he was given a chance to learn the arcane secrets of the Benton Visual Retention Test he demonstrated a capacity to learn rapidly. The Rorschach and other projective tests indicated what the psychologist described as good reality testing, normal intelligence, and no evidence of psychosis of any kind. The neurologist reported no hard signs of organic deficit and concluded significant organic pathology must be regarded as unproven.

In spite of all this, two senior psychiatrists insisted that the patient was certainly psychotic, probably brain-damaged, and evidently retarded. The more they insisted, the more the psychologist, neurologist, and lesser staff tended to reinterpret their findings along lines more in accord with the assertion of deep pathology. The proceedings reached such irrational extremes that ordinary experiences described by the young patient, which we know by observation are perfectly real, were presented as evidence of hallucination. The outcome was perhaps even more illogical than the proceedings which led up to it. The patient was to be released to his foster parents with an expressed professional evaluation that he probably could not make it in the outside world and therefore would soon be back in the hospital. It was made clear that wherever this little boy went in the world of macro-institutions he would be followed by a certified record attesting that he is dangerously insane.

Our interpretation of these data can be summarized as follows. The patient received another developmental setback in the object-loss occasioned by his move from the first foster family to his present guardians' household. Fortunately these new parents are warm and responsible people who are devoted to the child's welfare. Beyond these individual characteristics, the culturally-conditioned flexibility of Afro-American domestic relations is again relevant. For these and perhaps other reasons, the boy was able to adjust normally to the family and neighborhood dimensions of a new situation. Associates and intimates in these settings have found him no more than mildly undersocialized or immature, sometimes a nuisance but nothing more.

Yet the earlier difficulties, stemming from circumstantially arrested biculturation, increased to crisis proportions. The personnel of mainstream macro-institutions regarded this patient as essentially without internalized controls. For the same reasons as earlier, these mainstream caretakers were unable to produce any improvement in the patient's behavior. Out of feelings ranging from anxiety over disruption of institutional routines, to fear of racial conflict and stereotyped aversions against ghetto people, they projected upon this small child the image of a powerful monster threatening chaos. They concluded that such a menace should be restrained by custodial and punitive confinement, lest its destructive potential become even more frightening.

Thus the whole mainstream educational and medical apparatus prevented crucial gaps in the child's socialization from being filled. The boy remains illiterate and accustomed to institutional failure and rejection. His guardians are barely resisting mainstream pressure to accept the official diagnosis which their own experience has never supported. Unless the situation changes, these conditions can be expected to injure or sever the parental ties which presently offer the only hope.

Wider implications

During the course of the case history just described, we had occasion to discuss the patient at length with nearly a dozen medical, clinical, and social-work specialists directly or indirectly involved in the case. In fact, we provided them with all our evidence, discussed our interpretations of the data, and made several recommendations. These discussions revealed over and over again that the thinking of these professionals is ruled by highly standardized assumptions embodying both the difference and deficit models of Afro-American psychology. One senior psychiatrist volunteered his considered calculation that within our community and adjacent ghettos there are 30,000 Black children who are just as sick as the patient described earlier. (This statistical opinion casts a depressing light on the question how large a universe of Afro-Americans is represented by our case history.) The implicit assumption evident in all these conversations is that Afro-American culture is not only distinct but pathogenic, thus neatly combining the deficit and difference theories. This is perhaps not surprising, considering the outpouring of both specialized and popular literature campaigning for just this point of view. What has impressed us, however, is the rigidity with which this view is held by relevant professionals and the strength of emotional commitment to it which one senses in such specialists. At no time in these conversations were we able to detect any recognition that a mainstream institution might bear the slightest responsibility for the patient's problems, nor even any interest in the question what effect the various schools and hospitals might have had. On the contrary, the ruling implicit assumption was that all sources of difficulty must lie within the individual, the family, or the non-institutional community.

To those of us who know the patient well in his home milieu of Afro-American subculture, he looks entirely different from the image that institutional specialists have of him. We know that he functions well in his own subcultural world. From this perspective, it seems obvious that, even after months in a punitive custodial institution, the child shows none of the dire pathology attributed to him. The significant professionals in the boy's case, however, have never even seen his home and have no direct experience of Black ghetto life whatever. These men make it clear that they regard themselves as experts on Black children. Yet they make it equally clear, usually without intending to, that they have no understanding of the child's cultural milieu—or even any real interest in it, beyond the derogatory stereotypes carried by the difference and deficit theories. One senior clinician admitted that we might well be right in our contention that the patient was functionally well-adapted to his home environment. This doctor insisted, however, that what goes on in the home or community is totally irrelevant to the problems of diagnosis and disposition: medical diagnosis and therapy are determined strictly within the clinical setting without consideration of extraneous data from the outside world. Such institution-bound professionals have insulated themselves from any understanding of cultural factors, except again the stereotypes in the literature.

Both the theoretical significance and the policy implications of the case history described here now seem clear. This youngster's problems can be understood primarily as a mainstream institutional failure in the process of biculturation. In spite of a stressful and deprived early childhood, the patient succeeded in adapting sufficiently well to his Afro-American subcultural environment. Now the macro-institutional problems are threatening his adaptation to his third Afro-American home and community. The failure of the macro-institutional settings has been manifold. Not only was it in these settings that the patient's difficulties first became evident, but these same institutions have been unable to do anything constructive about his problems. The prognosis appears to be that a basically healthy child will end up being forced into one or more of the delinquent, mentally sick, or functionally illiterate roles defined by the society's major institutions.

This is not to say that the initial home setting played no part in the etiology of this case. Without attempting any psychological analysis of the original parents, it is plain that the father actively inflicted, with the mother's passive complicity, a double disadvantage on their son. Not only was his early maturation compromised by emotional deprivation and injury, but his potential biculturation was initially arrested by parentally imposed or allowed isolation. Yet it is precisely such intra-family problems which the so-called "helping professions" of mainstream culture—social work, guidance counseling, clinical psychology, and psychiatry—are supposed to resolve or at least mitigate. In this case, a long series of these professionals, plus their colleagues in education and hospital management, have done nothing but make the boy's problems worse for so long that they are now the principal source of the present unhappy situation.

The individual aspects of this case are quite enough to make anyone who knows or cares about the people involved both sad and angry. If one contemplates the wider implications, however, one begins to appreciate the dimensions of our society's intergroup tragedy. Reflecting upon a powerful psychiatrist's clear implication that some 30,000 children in one part of a single American city should be treated as this child has been treated, the imagination recoils from the obvious inferences. It seems imperative to recognize that men capable of such projections cannot be made into humanitarians by preaching the difference model to them. When it is remembered that the cultural-difference theory has already been assimilated by these people and made to support their existing approach, the futility, or worse, of communicating with them about cultural contrasts must be apparent.

The practical and policy implications of biculturation theory, at least with respect to Afro-American communities, are radical and stringent in each of the several senses of both terms. Much impairment of Afro-American personalities is directly traceable to the standard operations of mainstream institutions which inhibit or entirely block vital portions of the biculturation process. It therefore appears that no amount of dedication by Afro-Americans to mainstream ideals, and no extremes of assimilationist effort by Negroes, can make these institutions function to the advantage of Black people. The group-destructive tendencies of these settings are too deeply built in to be susceptible to rational reform. Certainly nothing will be accomplished by trying to teach professionals respect for subcultural systems when all their other training and experience has already taught them to regard these same cultures as impersonally pathogenic and personally threatening.

At least two alternatives remain. One is for Afro-Americans to avoid mainstream institutions, as far as possible, and build their own parallel organizations for social services of all kinds. This is essentially the Black Nationalist orientation. For reasons of the existing power relations within our society, this is an approach fraught with problematical practical issues of its own. The other alternative is a radical alteration of the existing dominant institutions with respect to the values, attitudes, and interests which they serve. Nothing like this can be realistically expected short of revolutionary innovations in the national social structure as a whole. This obviously involves equally problematical practical issues and power questions. From these perspectives, everything depends upon the presently unknown potential strength of revolutionary trends as cultural revitalization movements, the rebellion of American youth, and perhaps a few other national tendencies. Some reason for hope may lie in these quarters. Certainly it must be clear that the debate between deficit theorists and difference proponents is of no practical or humane significance.

As is already clear, I believe a biculturation model is preferable to other formulations discussed here. This is not only because a bicultural theory more adequately represents Afro-American realities than the distorting notions of deficit or the oversimplified difference concept. Recognition of bicultural processes is also more congruent with desirable changes in the practice of service institutions operating in Black ghettos. It is important that educators and health specialists not only recognize the legitimacy and creativity of ethnic cultures, but also appreciate that Afro-Americans are already more conversant with, and competent in, mainstream culture than most non-Black Americans believe or admit. Indeed the latter point is more likely to neutralize mainstream ethnocentrism than a simple difference model. The bicultural conception calls attention to a kind of psychocultural adequacy which mainstream Americans can respect *in spite of* their ethnocentrism—if they will only accept its reality. Out of this could perhaps come the beginnings of a more realistic and humane basis for service institutions, changing to serve Afro-American needs and interests.

Finally, however, there must be a word of caution on the relationship between theories and social action. Intensive immersion in ghetto life makes one tend to feel that expecting new concepts in psychology to alter the nitty-gritty practicalities of major institutions may be an extreme form of philosophical idealism.

Let us assume that good scientists who are also real humanitarians can achieve intellectual ascendancy for the difference model, the theory of biculturation, or other better concepts. Let us even assume that this outlook dominates the training of a whole new breed of service professionals. What will happen when this new wave hits the bulwarks of established macro-institutions in the ghetto? We must be prepared for at least three depressing possibilities. Some of the new caretakers will shortly have their idealism shattered against the established stone walls and openly revert to the rationalizations of old hands. A second group may slip into a cynical hypocrisy in which the new ideals are given lip-service but the practitioner acts on his realization that bureaucratized professionals are rewarded for following existing institutionalized routines. Perhaps the remaining group will simply compartmentalize their theoretical training in a separate section of their consciousness from the practical exigencies of institutional practice.

These possibilities seem all too plausible, unless the assumed conceptual changes are accompanied by radical shifts in power relationships and other factors conditioning the present functions of dominant institutions in the context of the class system and race.

Notes

1 Charles A. Valentine and Betty Lou Valentine, "Ghetto Ethnography: A Preliminary Report of Research" (unpublished); "Making the Scene, Digging the Action, and Telling It Like It Is: Anthropologists at Work in a Dark Ghetto," in *Afro-American Anthropology: Contemporary Perspectives*, ed. Norman E. Whitten and John Szwed (New York: Free Press, forthcoming). This research has been supported in part by P. H. S. research grant MH 16866–01 from a division of the National Institute of Mental Health.

2 See the following works written (or edited) by William A. Stewart: "Creole Languages in the Caribbean," in *Study of the Role of Second Languages in Asia, Africa, and Latin America*, ed. Frank A Rice (Washington, D.C.: Center for Applied Linguistics, 1962); *Non-standard Speech and the Teaching of English* (Washington, D.C.: Center for Applied Linguistics, 1964); "Urban Negro Speech: Sociolinguistic Factors Affecting English Teaching," in *Social Dialects and Language Learning*, ed. Roger W. Shuy (Champlain, Ill.: National Council of Teachers of English, 1965); "Observations on the Problems of Defining Negro Dialect," in *Conference on the Language Component in the Training of Teachers of English and Reading: Views and Problems* (Washington, D.C.: Center of Applied Linguistics and the National Council of Teachers of English, 1966); "Nonstandard Speech Patterns," in *Baltimore Bulletin of Education*, 43 (1967), 52–65; "Continuity and Change in American Negro Dialects," *Florida F. L. Reporter*, 6 (Spring 1968); "On the Use of Negro Dialect in the Teaching of Reading" in *Teaching Black Children to Read*, ed. Joan Baratz and Roger Shuy (Washington, D.C.: Center for Applied Linguistics, 1969); "Comments on Valentine's 'It's Either Brain Damage or No Father,' " American Psychological Association Symposium: Deficit or Difference: Negro Culture in the United States, Washington, D.C., September 2, 1969. See also J. L. Dillard, "The Writings of Herskovitz and the Study of the Language of the Negro in the New World," *Caribbean Studies*, 4 (1964), 35–41; J. L. Dillard, "Non-standard Negro Dialects: Convergence or Divergence?" in Whitten and Szwed, *Afro-American Anthropology*; Thomas Kochman, "Black English in the Classroom," Chicago, 1969 (Mimeographed); Thomas Kochman, "Toward an Ethnography of Black American Speech Behavior," in Whitten and Szwed, *Afro-American Anthropology*.

3 Roger D. Abrahams, *Deep Down in the Jungle: Negro Narrative Folklore from the Streets of Philadelphia* (Hatboro, Pa.: Folklore Associates, 1964); Roger D. Abrahams,

Positively Black (Englewood Cliffs, N.J.: Prentice Hall, 1969); Roger D. Abrahams, "Patterns of Performance in the British West Indies," in *Afro-American Anthropology.*

4 Charles Keil, *Urban Blues* (Chicago: University of Chicago Press, 1966); Alan Lomax, *Folksong Style and Culture* (Washington, D.C.: American Association for the Advancement of Science, 1968); Alan Lomax, "The Homogeneity of African-Afro-American Musical Style," in Whitten and Szwed, *Afro-American Anthology.*

5 Whitten and Szwed, *Afro-American Anthropology*, Introduction.

6 Afro-Americans
   A Afro-English speakers:
       1 Northern-urban U.S. Blacks
       2 Southern-rural U.S. Blacks
       3 Anglo-African West Indians
       4 Guyanese
       5 Surinam *Takitaki*-speakers
       *6 West Africans
   B Afro-French speakers:
       7 Haitian Creole-speakers:
       *8 Other French West Indians
       *9 French Guianans
       *10 Louisiana Creoles
   C Afro-Spanish speakers:
       11 Black Cubans
       12 A–B–C Islander *Papiamento*-speakers
       *13 Panamanians
       *14 Black South Americans
   * Groups we have heard about but not yet observed.

7 Valentine, "It's Either Brain Damage or No Father."

8 Stewart, "Comments on Valentine," p. 4.

9 Steven Polgar, "Biculturation of Mesquakie Teenage Boys," *American Anthropologist*, 62 (1960), 217–235.

10 Sidney M. Wilhelm, "Black Man, Red Man and White America: the Constitutional Approach to Genocide," *Catalyst* (Spring 1969), 1–62; Vine Deloria, Jr., *Custer Died for your Sins: an Indian Manifesto* (London: Collier-Macmillan, Ltd., 1969).

11 Ulf Hannerz, *Soulside: Inquiries into Ghetto Culture and Community* (Stockholm: Almquist & Wiksell, 1969), 191–192.

12 Polgar, "Bi-culturation of Mesquakie Teenage Boys."

13 Hannerz, *Soulside*, pp. 15–16.

14 Hannerz, pp. 4–5.

15 See Charles A. Valentine, *Culture and Poverty: Critique and Counterproposals* (Chicago: University of Chicago Press, 1968) and previously cited works.

16 Stewart, "Nonstandard Speech Patterns," pp. 59–60.

MULTICULTURAL EDUCATION: 1970s
(b) Deficit and difference

CHAPTER 7

SOCIAL EXPECTATIONS AND CULTURAL DEPRIVATION (1964)

Ralph H. Hines

Society necessarily makes demands upon its members to conform to certain norms or expectations. It is the norms which give regularity and meaningfulness to behavior and make predictable interaction between members of a group. The absence of these norms would mean chaos and confusion in the normal functioning of the individual with his culture, his sub-cultures and other individuals.

The Negro in America finds himself confronted with two sets of normative patterns which often make confusing and contradictory demands upon him. In the main, the norms affecting Negro behavior represent mutually exclusive expectations. On the one hand, he is inculcated with the ideals of middle class and democratic society, while on the other, he is forced to conform to expectations demanded by a society in which practices of racial inequality permeate almost all levels of his social contact.

Emphasis in the study of cultural deprivation has centered, by and large, around problems of child development, learning situations and school adjustment.[1]

This paper is an attempt to interpret some of the forces affecting behavior of a culturally deprived group which develop out of the normative expectation of the larger society. It is intended to establish, through heuristically expandable hypotheses, some of the causative factors that influence behavior of groups deprived of full scale cultural participation. Further, it is designed to demonstrate that many of these effects, traditionally assumed to be part and parcel of the sub-culture of deprived groups, are, in reality, reactions to and manifestations of the social expectations and definitions of the larger society.

It is of interest to note the manner in which a society, by defining situations and establishing expectations regardless of their truth claims, produces behavior which may be inimical or contradictory to the ideals of that society. And, when such definitions cover a group within the larger society—such as the Negro in America,[2] the "untouchables" in India, the Chinese in many southeast Asian societies, the African in South Africa—the discriminated group will tend to conform to the expectations of the dominant society even though conformity may be diametrically opposed to its own self interests.

W. I. Thomas pointed out long ago that "if men define situations as real they are real in their consequences."[3] Any society which gives special definition to certain of its members will find the consequences of such assignment real for *all* its members.

In a society in which mental inferiority, laziness, incompetency and irresponsibility are part of the definition externally assigned to a group, as is the case with the Negro, the group so defined will tend to confirm this definition. Confirmation does not come about automatically or unassisted. In the first place, the general society sets in motion certain kinds of institutional and cultural forces which reinforce, perpetuate and circulate expectations consonant with this definition. Secondly, the society will reward that behavior which conforms to these expectations and punish that which deviates. A consequent, self-fulfilling prophecy tends to set up response mechanisms which become a part of the social environment of the Negro. The "normal" response is correct to the extent that it conforms to the expectations of the general society.

Embedded in the self-fulfilling prophesy, as both MacIver and Merton point out, is the principle of circularity.[4] In other words, a given condition sets in motion other conditions which in turn keep the first condition going. It is precisely in this way that the social definition of the Negro, for example, contributes to his inferiority. The assertion then becomes a factor which helps to produce its own confirmation.

To pose the same problem in yet another way one might ask: Why in our social system is the Negro considered inferior? The explanation for this question would be found in terms of the self-confirming assessment provided by society. The Negro is inferior, the answer would hold, because he is ignorant. Since ignorance is a matter of not-knowing, the next logical question would be, "Why, then, don't you give him an education?" Answer, "Because he is inferior." And so a vicious circle makes a complete turn which perpetuates the self-confirming definition already built into the social structure of American society. Discrimination by definition means unequal treatment. This unequal treatment results in poverty, which in turn means poor education which produces inferiority which then breeds discrimination. In other words, one might say, that prejudice ultimately becomes one of the causes of prejudice and discrimination causes discrimination.

It will be noted that three elements are involved in the process we have thus far described. In the first instance, the social or cultural definition of the meaning of a characteristic of a group or an element of culture is established by society. Secondly, forces of an institutionalized character are set into motion which enforce behavior conformity to those expectations given by the larger group. In the instance of majority-minority relationship certain forces are set up which act upon the majority and the minority groups and become, in turn, a part of the subculture of each. Lastly, behavior conformity, consequently grows out of these social definitions and expectations.

In most instances, the minority group must accept a lower position in society as a result of vertically imposed definitions. This is the case in the caste system of India where "untouchability" is still prevalent, as well as in the United States. An acquiescence in degradation takes place which becomes internalized and accepted wholly or in part by the discriminated group as a part of its own way of life. This fact is well known and becomes the point of departure for those who would institute social change.[5] The element too often overlooked, however, is the significance of the acquiescence in defining behavior and contributing to the deprivation of a group.

As previously indicated, part of the reason for acquiescing is due to the overwhelming power of the norms set up to ensure the continued subordination of the Negro. The other part of the reason lies in the Negro's acceptance of his status. Recently he has come to recognize that the scope of normative behavior in any society allows alternative patterns which when utilized could provide means of circumventing some of the entanglements of degradation.[6] This facet of the social structure has not readily been perceived because of the preoccupation with and predominance of an inferior status. The inferior status of the Negro in American life has too often been viewed as an inevitable, pre-ordained and insoluble problem.

The social definition of inferiority and its attendant expectations have been major factors contributing to the cultural deprivation of the Negro. He has suffered a form of partial isolation no less real than that experienced by the unwanted and isolated child. The rewards of our society have come to him when he has followed the defined expectations. Psychologically he has tended to be excessively cooperative, submissive, non-verbal, non-competitive, and withdrawing.[7]

One of the arguments frequently used by the segregationist to support his point of view is that Negroes do not want to be integrated. The excepted few are those who have been stirred up by outside agitators. In the larger sense, this evaluation is correct since acceptance of given status in society becomes part of one's own self-image. From childhood, an internalization of basic attitudes and beliefs has taken place which, obviously, has incorporated the societal definition of what being a Negro is in American life. Negroes, particularly in the South, find themselves rewarded for comforming to the norms of isolation and punished when failing to fulfill the required and expected behavior.

It is well known that the acceptance of a status and the resultant life changes of the individual influence his motivation. A person who has learned to behave under a given set of cultural patterns would find it extremely difficult, if not impossible, to be motivated to act otherwise. The first requirement of learning is a drive or motive. Another requirement is the visibility, real or apparent, of a reward. These elements act as limiting factors in effecting changes in the case of the Negro, particularly in the South, since the learner in any situation must be driven or motivated to make a response which will be rewarded as the correct one. If the Negro child is taught that his station will be such that he can expect no higher level of cultural recognition, he will not be motivated to learn some of the skills required for advancement and mobility in a middle class society. He will constantly review his life chances in terms of the social expectations derived from the cultural definition of his status. As a consequence, his level of cultural achievement will be inferior to that of his white contemporaries.[8]

Earl H. Bell cogently articulates some of the facets of this problem in a discussion of life chances and social participation. Bell suggests that when many opportunities are denied a group, there is more pressure within the group to excel in those opportunities which are open to them. The pressure takes the form of more than an average number of individuals working harder for goals in a situation where there are few alternatives.[9]

On the surface it appears that the ability to achieve the permitted goal is more characteristic of the group that is being discriminated against. This represents part of the reason why Negroes appear to be superior and more numerous in the field of entertainment, sports, and the ministry. Negroes are not more gifted in these lines. It is only that more of them devote greater effort in achieving excellence in these fields because there are fewer alternative opportunities open to them.

Shortly after a new field of endeavor is opened to a culturally deprived group, great pressures are brought to bear to take advantage of the new opportunity. In such cases the motivation becomes so strong that other groups may be crowded out of the field. When the motivations of one group are markedly higher than those of another, the former surpasses the latter and may even appear to have "natural" talent for the work.[10] Frequently the majority group may feel that it is necessary to establish quotas which will limit the number of talented persons from such group entering training programs. This fact is often demonstrated, for example, by the quota system operating in a number of medical schools around the country in the admission of Jews.

Here again we see evidence of how the expectations of the society define, limit, and structure those areas within which a particular group may participate. The extent to which the deprived group wholly accepts characterizations of the expected is, however, another matter. If allowed to, social definitions become, in fact, self-definitions which, when pursued to their logical conclusion, would mean that the Negro must always remain a second class citizen. He will remain in an inferior status in our society unless he can utilize the socially prescribed means of circumventing the limitations imposed by social expectations in a manner both effective and normative. In the broader meaning of democracy and liberty, circumvention becomes relatively simple. In the practical affairs of everyday life, the problem is more difficult to cope with.

An acceptance of the social expectations by both the majority and minority groups in America has some of the following consequences:

(1) A double standard of education and cultural achievement is commonplace in America. The double standard not only concerns questions of facilities, differing equipment and pupil-cost-ratios, but also levels of expected achievement. The Negro child, in the North and South, is not presumed by his parents, teachers or the community to be able to achieve as well as his white peers. Even though this expectation is rarely verbalized among Northern educators, it is implicitly understood and assumed as one of the differentials of education in both North and South.

Parents tacitly make this assumption in their admonition to their children to learn "as best as you can." But further, Negro parents fail generally to provide within the home environment those minimal and necessary conditions which act as stimuli to learning, e.g., books, magazines, encyclopedias, journals and other materials.

Teachers make the same assumption in their methods of instruction as well as in their evaluation of pupil achievement. A professor at one of the large state universties in the South, who worked part time with a privately supported Negro college, reported that in lectures and discussions with students, ostensibly taking the same course at these separate institutions, he found himself going at a much slower pace in the Negro college; further, he felt compelled to be more lenient in grading Negro students even though the course followed a more or less standardized form. While the behavior of this professor might be explained in terms of sympathy and understanding, another principle seems to be indicated. Here was, in fact, the principle of differential expectations in operation.[11]

The fact that this professor was white reveals only one portion of this principle. Basically, the Negro teacher or college professor makes the same fundamental assumptions. Expectations of low achievement for the Negro student are built into the social definition and expectations of the majority society.

(2) Up to this point in America's history, the Negro has traditionally held menial status in the economic arena. He has been subjected to the kind of economic conditions in which his talents and motivations have been limited. Socially he has been viewed as one with low economic potentiality, and a burden on the

back of whites. He has more or less accepted this position, having little motivation for becoming an independent economic agent in our society. He has been, in a larger measure, the recipient of what has been left over in the economic field. Where Negroes have entered business for themselves, there has been a timidity of action and a conservativeness of business practice which reflected the social expectations of the larger society. The idea of becoming a millionaire is still somewhat of a foreign notion to the Negro.[12]

(3) The Negro in politics has ventured only into those centered around life that have been considered "safe." These have mostly centered around "race problem" and "race representation." There is, of course, a necessary connection between the political activities of the Negro and the fact that the Negro is a discriminated minority in America.[13]

In terms of the social expectations of the larger society his role in politics has conformed largely to the expected. To some extent it has gone beyond it. But even here there has been an overwhelming acceptance, on the part of the Negro, of his role as a politician. He has conceived this role as one of representing exclusively "his people" and not venturing much beyond these limits. Obviously certain changes are taking place in the structure of America's political life today which are producing alteration. These changes are not, however, so much a consequence of imagination and inventiveness as a question of sheer physical and ecological shifts in the characteristics of certain Northern cities. In the South, the Negro has almost exclusively relegated his affairs in the political arena to those, in terms of the social definition, who are "sophisticated enough to cope with such complex problems." Only recently has the "wind of change" begun to sweep away the traditional role of Negro participation in political affairs.

(4) The creative fields, such as art, literature, music, and drama, have seen also the same kind of fundamental principle in operation. The Negro writer has tended to treat the Negro as if he were his exclusive property; the musician what might be called Negro music. Few have ventured beyond the periphery of limits imposed by a definition which, today, is both archaic and anachronistic.

The shift of the Negro population from the rural South to urban Northern areas may yet bring some consequences which have not been foreseen by the sociologist. Concurrently, the middle-classification of the Negro and the consciousness of achieving those goals that are a part of middle class culture may represent the mainspring by which the Negro will escape the vicious circle of discrimination. One such consequence of these factors is that as societal definitions become realigned and new opportunities requiring educational preparation are opened, Negroes may begin to excel whites in academic endeavors. It is noteworthy that education has become a passion for many segments of the more urbanized Negro population. It is recognized that education can serve as the key to unlock doors of opportunity. If this develops, it will be difficult for those who find in education less of a passion to compete when only this factor is considered.

Time is inevitably on the side of the Negro in his struggle for equality of opportunity. Presumably, changes in other facets of Negro-white relation in America will also mean changes in the social expectations of the general society toward the Negro.

As social expectations are redefined in terms of new evaluations, the cultural achievement of the Negro should show concomitant shifts. These shifts will necessarily set into force the same kind of institutionalized patterns which have in the past tended to deprive the Negro of opportunities to participate fully in his culture.

Notes

1   See F. Reissman, *The Culturally Deprived Child*, Harper Bros, New York 1962; R. J. Havighurst, "Social Class Influences on American Education." *National Society For the Study of Education Yearbook*, vol. 60, April, 1959; A. Davis, *Social Class Influences Upon Learning*, Harvard University Press, Cambridge, 1946; and, J. I. Krugman, "Cultural Deprivation and Child Development," *High Point*, vol. 38; November, 1956, p. 5–20; Reissman, *op. cit.*, uses the term *culturally deprived* interchangeably with educationally deprived, underprivileged, disadvantaged, lower class and lower socio-economic group. Havighurst asserts that the deprived may fall into four groups: (1) affectional deprivation—the person is deprived of an adequate amount of affection, love or emotion support; (2) model-person deprivation—the absence of persons in the child's life who are good examples for the child to imitate as he grows up; (3) intellectual deprivation—books and newspapers are read, where there is little or no discussion of books, politics, music or similar intellectual activities; and (4) nutritional deprivation—the child is not getting adequate food.

2   The term *Negro* is used here as a sociological construct. To suggest that all Negroes are culturally deprived would be an erroneous generalization of the highest order. As a sociologically defined group, however, the Negro, because of prejudice and discrimination, is subjected to limited cultural participation. Culturally deprived groups in America are found in numerous areas and among various racial and ethnic groups and should not be thought of as a phenomenon peculiar to the Negro even though its occurrence among Negroes is probably more general than among other populations. The same basic principles hold true whether we are considering Negroes, American Indians, Smoky Mountain Hillbillies or Harlem dwelling Puerto Ricans. See Reissman, *op. cit.*; D. P. Wolfe, "Curriculum Adaptions for the Culturally Deprived," *Journal of Negro Education*, 31: 139–151, Spring, 1962; and I. D. Reid, "General Characteristics of the Negro Youth Population," JOURNAL OF NEGRO EDUCATION, 9:278–289, July, 1940.

3   W. I. Thomas, *The Unadjusted Girl*. New York; Little Brown, 1923.

4   R. M. MacIver, *A More Perfect Union*. New York: MacMillian Co., 1948, also R. K. Merten, "The Self-fulfilling Prophecy," in *Antioch Review*, Summer, 1948.

5   The acceptance of a certain role and its attendant consequences has been brilliantly portrayed by Bertram Doyle in an analysis of the etiquette of biracial contacts in the Deep South. See B. Doyle, *The Etiquette of Race Relations in the South*. Chicago; University of Chicago Press, 1937.

6   Demonstrations, such as the sit-ins, wade-ins, walk-ins, and pray-ins are examples of the Negro's utilization of the less socially approved methods for reaching what is considered morally, at least, a socially approved goal. The legally sanctioned and socially approved techniques of the lawsuit has proved too slow a process in effecting the changes sought.

7   On this point see E. S. Newton, "Culturally Deprived Child in our Verbal Schools", *Journal of Negro Education* 31: 184–187, Fall, 1962, and M. Krugman, "The Culturally Deprived Child in School", *National Education Association Journal*, vol. 50, April, 1961.

8   J. W. Wrightstone, "Discovering and Stimulating Culturally Deprived Talented: Youth," *Teachers College Record*, 60: 337, October, 1958; On this point see also A. Davis, *op. cit.*

9   E. H. Bell, *Social Foundations of Human Behavior*. New York; Harper Bros., 1961, p. 167–169.

10 *Ibid.*

11 For an additional insight into Negro-White class situations in several college communities see A. T. Hansen "Teaching About Caste in Intra-Caste and in Cross Caste Situations," *Human Organization*, vol. 19, No. 2 Summer, 1960.

12 See E. F. Frazier "The Negro Vested Interest in Segregation" in *Race Prejudice and Discrimination*, edited by A. Rose, New York: A. Knopf, 1951; also R. H. Kinzer, E. Lagarin, *The Negro in America Business*. New York: Greenberg Publisher, 1950 and N. A. Pitts, *The Cooperative Movement in Negro Communities in North Carolina*. Washington, D. C.: Catholic University Press, 1950.

13 H. Gosnell, *Negro Politicians*, Chicago; University of Chicago Press, 1955.

CHAPTER 8

STUDENT SOCIAL CLASS AND TEACHER EXPECTATIONS (1970)
The self-fulfilling prophecy in ghetto education
Ray C. Rist

A dominant aspect of the American ethos is that education is both a necessary and a desirable experience for all children. To that end, compulsory attendance at some type of educational institution is required of all youth until somewhere in the middle teens. Thus on any weekday during the school year, one can expect slightly over 35,000,000 young persons to be distributed among nearly 1,100,000 classrooms throughout the nation (Jackson, 1968).

There is nothing either new or startling in the statement that there exist gross variations in the educational experience of the children involved. The scope of analysis one utilizes in examining these educational variations will reveal different variables of importance. There appear to be at least three levels at which analysis is warranted. The first is a macro-analysis of structural relationships where governmental regulations, federal, state, and local tax support, and the presence or absence of organized political and religious pressure all affect the classroom experience. At this level, study of the policies and politics of the Board of Education within the community is also relevant. The milieu of a particular school appears to be the second area of analysis in which one may examine facilities, pupil-teacher ratios, racial and cultural composition of the faculty and students, community and parental involvement, faculty relationships, the role of the principal, supportive services such as medical care, speech therapy, and library facilities—all of which may have a direct impact on the quality as well as the quantity of education a child receives.

Analysis of an individual classroom and the activities and interactions of a specific group of children with a single teacher is the third level at which there may be profitable analysis of the variations in the educational experience. Such micro-analysis could seek to examine the social organization of the class, the development of norms governing interpersonal behavior, and the variety of roles that both the teacher and students assume. It is on this third level—that of the individual classroom—that this study will focus. Teacher-student relationships and the dynamics of interaction between the teacher and students are far from uniform. For any child within the classroom, variations in the experience of success or failure, praise or ridicule, freedom or control, creativity or docility, comprehension or mystification may ultimately have significance far beyond the boundaries of the classroom situation (Henry, 1955, 1959, 1963).

It is the purpose of this paper to explore what is generally regarded as a crucial aspect of the classroom experience for the children involved—the process whereby expectations and social interactions give rise to the social organization of the class. There occurs within the classroom a social process whereby, out of a large group of children and an adult unknown to one another prior to the beginning of the school year, there emerge patterns of behavior, expectations of performance, and a mutually accepted stratification system delineating those doing well from those doing poorly. Of particular concern will be the relation of the teacher's expectations of potential academic performance to the social status of the student. Emphasis will be placed on the initial presuppositions of the teacher regarding the intellectual ability of certain groups of children and their consequences for the children's socialization into the school system. A major goal of this analysis is to ascertain the importance of the initial expectations of the teacher in relation to the child's chances for success or failure within the public school system. (For previous studies of the significance of student social status to variations in educational experience, cf. Becker, 1952; Hollingshead, 1949; Lynd, 1937; Warner, *et al.*, 1944).

Increasingly, with the concern over intellectual growth of children and the long and close association that children experience with a series of teachers, attention is centering on the role of the teacher within the classroom (Sigel, 1969). A long series of studies have been conducted to determine what effects on children a teacher's values, beliefs, attitudes, and, most crucial to this analysis, a teacher's expectations may have. Asbell (1963), Becker (1952), Clark (1963), Gibson 1965), Harlem Youth Opportunities Unlimited (1964), Katz (1964), Kvaraceus (1965), MacKinnon (1962), Riessman (1962, 1965), Rose (1956), Rosenthal and Jacobson (1968), and Wilson (1963) have all noted that the teacher's expectations of a pupil's academic performance may, in fact, have a strong influence on the actual performance of that pupil. These authors have sought to validate a type of educational self-fulfilling prophecy: if the teacher expects high performance, she receives it, and vice versa. A major criticism that can be directed at much of the research is that although the studies may establish that a teacher has differential expectations and that these influence performance for various pupils, they have not elucidated either the basis upon which such differential expectations are formed or how they are directly manifested within the classroom milieu. It is a goal of this paper to provide an analysis both of the factors that are critical in the teacher's development of expectations for various groups of her pupils and of the process by which such expectations influence the classroom experience for the teacher and the students.

The basic position to be presented in this paper is that the development of expectations by the kindergarten teacher as to the differential academic potential and capability of any student was significantly determined by a series of subjectively interpreted attributes and characteristics of that student. The argument may be succinctly stated in five propositions. First, the kindergarten teacher possessed a roughly constructed "ideal type" as to what characteristics were necessary for any given student to achieve "success" both in the public school and in the larger society. These characteristics appeared to be, in significant part, related to social class criteria. Secondly, upon first meeting her students at the beginning of the school year, subjective evaluations were made of the students as to possession or absence of the desired traits necessary for anticipated "success." On the basis of the evaluation, the class was divided into groups expected to succeed (termed by the teacher "fast learners") and those anticipated to fail (termed "slow learners"). Third, differential treatment was accorded to the two groups in the classroom, with the group designated as "fast learners" receiving the majority of the teaching time, reward-directed behavior, and attention from the teacher. Those designated as "slow learners" were taught infrequently, subjected to more frequent control-oriented behavior, and received little if any supportive behavior from the teacher. Fourth, the interactional patterns between the teacher and the various groups in her class became rigidified, taking on caste-like characteristics, during the course of the school year, with the gap in completion of academic material between the two groups widening as the school year progressed. Fifth, a similar process occurred in later years of schooling, but the teachers no longer relied on subjectively interpreted data as the basis for ascertaining differences in students. Rather, they were able to utilize a variety of informational sources related to past performance as the basis for classroom grouping.

Though the position to be argued in this paper is based on a longitudinal study spanning two and one-half years with a single group of black children, additional studies suggest that the grouping of children both between and within classrooms is a rather prevalent situation within American elementary classrooms. In a report released in 1961 by the National Education Association related to data collected during the 1958–1959 school year, an estimated 77.6% of urban school districts (cities with a population above 2500) indicated that they practiced between-classroom ability grouping in the elementary grades. In a national survey of elementary schools, Austin and Morrison (1963) found that "more than 80% reported that they 'always' or 'often' use readiness tests for pre-reading evaluation [in first grade]." These findings would suggest that within-classroom grouping may be an even more prevalent condition than between-classroom grouping. In evaluating data related to grouping within American elementary classrooms, Smith (1971, in press) concludes, "Thus group assignment on the basis of measured 'ability' or 'readiness' is an accepted and widespread practice."

Two grouping studies which bear particular mention are those by Borg (1964) and Goldberg, Passow, and Justman (1966). Lawrence (1969) summarizes the import of these two studies as "the two most carefully designed and controlled studies done concerning ability grouping during the elementary years. . . ." Two school districts in Utah, adjacent to one another and closely comparable in size, served as the setting for the study conducted by Borg. One of the two districts employed random grouping of students, providing all students with "enrichment," while the second school district adopted a group system with acceleration mechanisms present which sought to adapt curricular materials to ability level and also to enable varying rates of presentation of materials. In summarizing Borg's findings, Lawrence states:

> In general, Borg concluded that the grouping patterns had no consistent, general effects on achievement at any level. . . . Ability grouping may have motivated bright pupils to realize their achievement potential more fully, but it seemed to have little effect on the slow or average pupils. (p. 1)

The second study by Goldberg, Passow, and Justman was conducted in the New York City Public Schools and represents the most comprehensive study to date on elementary school grouping. The findings in general show results similar to those of Borg indicating that narrowing the ability range within a classroom on some basis of academic potential will in itself do little to produce positive academic change. The most significant finding of the study is that "variability in achievement from classroom to classroom was generally greater than the variability resulting from grouping pattern or pupil ability" (Lawrence, 1969). Thus one may tentatively conclude that teacher differences were at least as crucial to academic performance as were the effects of pupil ability or methods of classroom grouping. The study, however, fails to investigate within-class grouping.

Related to the issue of within-class variability are the findings of the Coleman Report (1966) which have shown achievement highly correlated with individual social class. The strong correlation present in the first grade does not decrease during the elementary years, demonstrating, in a sense, that the schools are not able effectively to close the achievement gap initially resulting from student social class (pp. 290–325). What variation the Coleman Report does find in achievement in the elementary years results largely from within-rather than between-school variations. Given that the report demonstrates that important differences in achievement do not arise from variations in facilities, curriculum, or staff, it concludes:

> One implication stands out above all: That schools bring little influence to bear on a child's achievement that is independent of his background and general social context; and that this very lack of independent effect means that the inequalities imposed on children by their home, neighborhood, and peer environment are carried along to become the inequalities with which they confront adult life at the end of school. For equality of educational opportunity through the schools must imply a strong effect of schools that is independent of the child's immediate social environment, and that strong independent effect is not present in American Schools. (p. 325)

It is the goal of this study to describe the manner in which such "inequalities imposed on children" become manifest within an urban ghetto school and the resultant differential educational experience for children from dissimilar social-class backgrounds.

Methodology

Data for this study were collected by means of twice weekly one and one-half hour observations of a single group of black children in an urban ghetto school who began kindergarten in September of 1967. Formal observations were conducted throughout the year while the children were in kindergarten and again in 1969 when these same children were in the first half of their second-grade year. The children were also visited informally four times in the classroom during their first-grade year.[1] The difference between the formal and informal observations consisted in the fact that during formal visits, a continuous handwritten account was taken of classroom interaction and activity as it occurred. Smith and Geoffrey (1968) have labeled this method of classroom observation "microethnography." The informal observations did not include the taking of notes during the classroom visit, but comments were written after the visit. Additionally, a series of interviews were conducted with both the kindergarten and the second-grade teachers. No mechanical devices were utilized to record classroom activities or interviews.

I believe it is methodologically necessary, at this point, to clarify what benefits can be derived from the detailed analysis of a single group of children. The single most apparent weakness of the vast majority of studies of urban education is that they lack any longitudinal perspective. The complexities of the interactional processes which evolve over time within classrooms cannot be discerned with a single two- or three-hour observational period. Secondly, education is a *social process* that cannot be reduced to variations in IQ scores over a period of time. At best, IQ scores merely give indications of potential, not of process. Third, I do not believe that this school and the classrooms within it are atypical from others in urban black neighborhoods (cf. both the popular literature on urban schools: Kohl, 1967; and Kozol, 1967; as well as the academic literature: Eddy, 1967; Fuchs, 1969; Leacock, 1969; and Moore, 1967). The school in which this study occurred was selected by the District Superintendent as one of five available to the research team. All five schools were visited during the course of the study and detailed observations were conducted in four of them. The principal at the school reported upon in this study commented that I was very fortunate in coming to his school since his staff (and kindergarten teacher in particular) were equal to "any in the city." Finally, the utilization of longitudinal study as a research method in a ghetto school will enhance the possibilities of gaining further insight into mechanisms of adaptation utilized by black youth to what appears to be a basically white, middle-class, value-oriented institution.

The school

The particular school which the children attend was built in the early part of the 1960's. It has classes from kindergarten through the eighth grade and a single special education class. The enrollment fluctuates near the 900 level while the teaching staff consists of twenty-six teachers, in addition to a librarian, two physical education instructors, the principal, and an assistant principal. There are also at the school, on a part time basis, a speech therapist, social worker, nurse, and doctor, all employed by the Board of Education. All administrators, teachers, staff, and pupils are black. (The author is caucasian.) The school is located in a blighted urban area that has 98% black population within its census district. Within the school itself, nearly 500 of the 900 pupils (55%) come from families supported by funds from Aid to Dependent Children, a form of public welfare.

The kindergarten class

Prior to the beginning of the school year, the teacher possessed several different kinds of information regarding the children that she would have in her class. The first was the pre-registration form completed by 13 mothers of children who would be in the kindergarten class. On this form, the teacher was supplied with the name of the child, his age, the name of his parents, his home address, his phone number, and whether he had had any pre-school experience. The second source of information for the teacher was supplied two days before the beginning of school by the school social worker who provided a tentative list of all children enrolled in the kindergarten class who lived in homes that received public welfare funds.

The third source of information on the child was gained as a result of the initial interview with the mother and child during the registration period, either in the few days prior to the beginning of school or else during the first days of school. In this interview, a major concern was the gathering of medical information about the child as well as the ascertaining of any specific parental concern related to the child. This latter information was noted on the "Behavioral Questionnaire" where the mother was to indicate her concern, if any, on 28 different items. Such items as thumb-sucking, bed-wetting, loss of bowel control, lying, stealing, fighting, and laziness were included on this questionnaire.

The fourth source of information available to the teacher concerning the children in her class was both her own experiences with older siblings, and those of other teachers in the building related to behavior and academic performance of children in the same family. A rather strong informal norm had developed among teachers in the school such that pertinent information, especially that related to discipline matters, was to be passed on to the next teacher of the student. The teachers' lounge became the location in which they would discuss the performance of individual children as well as make comments concerning the parents and their interests in the student and the school. Frequently, during the first days of the school year, there were admonitions to a specific teacher to "watch out" for a child believed by a teacher to be a "trouble-maker." Teachers would also relate techniques of controlling the behavior of a student who had been disruptive in the class. Thus a variety of information concerning students in the school was shared, whether that information regarded academic performance, behavior in class, or the relation of the home to the school.

It should be noted that not one of these four sources of information to the teacher was related directly to the academic potential of the incoming kindergarten child. Rather, they concerned various types of social information revealing such facts as the financial status of certain families, medical care of the child, presence or absence of a telephone in the home, as well as the structure of the family in which the child lived, *i.e.*, number of siblings, whether the child lived with both, one, or neither of his natural parents.

The teacher's stimulus

When the kindergarten teacher made the permanent seating assignments on the eighth day of school, not only had she the above four sources of information concerning the children, but she had also had time to observe them within the classroom setting. Thus the behavior, degree and type of verbalization, dress, mannerisms, physical appearance, and performance on the early tasks assigned during class were available to her as she began to form opinions concerning the capabilities and potential of the various children. That such evaluation of the children by the teacher was beginning, I believe, there is little doubt. Within a few days, only a certain group of children were continually being called on to lead the class in the Pledge of Allegiance, read the weather calendar each day, come to the front for "show and tell" periods, take messages to the office, count the number of children present in the class, pass out materials for class projects, be in charge of equipment on the playground, and lead the class to the bathroom, library, or on a school tour. This one group of children, that continually were physically close to the teacher and had a high degree of verbal interaction with her, she placed at Table 1.

As one progressed from Table 1 to Table 2 and Table 3, there was an increasing dissimilarity between each group of children at the different tables on at least four major criteria. The first criterion appeared to be the physical appearance of the child. While the children at Table 1 were all dressed in clean clothes that were relatively new and pressed, most of the children at Table 2, and with only one exception at Table 3, were all quite poorly dressed. The clothes were old and often quite dirty. The children at Tables 2 and 3 also had a noticeably different quality and quantity of clothes to wear, especially during the winter months. Whereas the children at Table 1 would come on cold days with heavy coats and sweaters, the children at the other two tables often wore very thin spring coats and summer clothes. The single child at Table 3 who came to school quite nicely dressed came from a home in which the mother was receiving welfare funds, but was supplied with clothing for the children by the families of her brother and sister.

An additional aspect of the physical appearance of the children related to their body odor. While none of the children at Table 1 came to class with an odor of urine on them, there were two children at Table 2 and five children at Table 3 who frequently had such an odor. There was not a clear distinction among the children at the various tables as to the degree of "blackness" of their skin, but there were more children at the third table with very dark skin (five in all) than there were at the first table (three). There was also a noticeable distinction among the various groups of children as to the condition of their hair. While the three boys at Table 1 all had short hair cuts and the six girls at the same table had their hair "processed" and combed, the number of children with either matted or unprocessed hair increased at Table 2 (two boys and three girls) and eight of the children at Table 3 (four boys and four girls). None of the children in the kindergarten class wore their hair in the style of a "natural."

A second major criteria which appeared to differentiate the children at the various tables was their interactional behavior, both among themselves and with the teacher. The several children who began to develop as leaders within the class by giving directions to other members, initiating the division of the class into teams on the playground, and seeking to speak for the class to the teacher ("We want to color now"), all were placed by the teacher at Table 1. This same group of children displayed considerable ease in their interaction with her. Whereas the children at Tables 2 and 3 would often linger on the periphery of groups surrounding the teacher, the children at Table 1 most often crowded close to her.

The use of language within the classroom appeared to be the third major differentiation among the children. While the children placed at the first table were quite verbal with the teacher, the children placed at the remaining two tables spoke much less frequently with her. The children placed at the first table also displayed a greater use of Standard American English within the classroom. Whereas the children placed at the last two tables most often responded to the teacher in black dialect, the children at the first table did so very infrequently. In other words, the children at the first table were much more adept at the use of "school language" than were those at the other tables. The teacher utilized standard American English in the classroom and one group of children were able to respond in a like manner. The frequency of a "no response" to a question from the teacher was recorded at a ratio of nearly three to one for the children at the last two tables as opposed to Table 1. When questions were asked, the children who were placed at the first table most often gave a response.

The final apparent criterion by which the children at the first table were quite noticeably different from those at the other tables consisted of a series of social factors which were known to the teacher prior to her seating the children. Though it is not known to what degree she utilized this particular criterion when she assigned seats, it does contribute to developing a clear profile of the children at the various tables. Table 8.1 gives a summary of the distribution of the children at the three tables on a series of variables related to social and family conditions. Such variables may be considered to give indication of the relative status of the children within the room, based on the income, education and size of the family. (For a discussion of why these three variables of income, education, and family size may be considered as significant indicators of social status, cf. Frazier, 1962; Freeman,

Table 8.1 Distribution of socio-economic status factors by seating arrangement at the three tables in the kindergarten classroom

	Seating arrangement*		
Factors	Table 1	Table 2	Table 3
Income			
1) Families on welfare	0	2	4
2) Families with father employed	6	3	2
3) Families with mother employed	5	5	5
4) Families with both parents employed	5	3	2
5) Total family income below $3,000. /yr**	0	4	7
6) Total family income above $12,000. /yr**	4	0	0
Education			
1) Father ever grade school	6	3	2
2) Father ever high school	5	2	1
3) Father ever college	1	0	0
4) Mother ever grade school	9	10	8
5) Mother ever high school	7	6	5
6) Mother ever college	4	0	0
7) Children with pre-school experience	1	1	0
Family Size			
1) Families with one child	3	1	0
2) Families with six or more children	2	6	7
3) Average number of siblings in family	3–4	5–6	6–7
4) Families with both parents present	6	3	2

* There are nine children at Table 1, eleven at Table 2, and ten children at Table 3.
** Estimated from stated occupation.

et al., 1959; Gebhard, *et al.*, 1958; Kahl, 1957; Notestein, 1953; Reissman, 1959; Rose, 1956; Simpson and Yinger, 1958.)

Believing, as I do, that the teacher did not randomly assign the children to the various tables, it is then necessary to indicate the basis for the seating arrangement. I would contend that the teacher developed, utilizing some combination of the four criteria outlined above, a series of expectations about the potential performance of each child and then grouped the children according to perceived similarities in expected performance. The teacher herself informed me that the first table consisted of her "fast learners" while those at the last two tables "had no idea of what was going on in the classroom." What becomes crucial in this discussion is to ascertain the basis upon which the teacher developed her criteria of "fast learner" since there had been no formal testing of the children as to their academic potential or capacity for cognitive development. She made evaluative judgments of the expected capacities of the children to perform academic tasks after eight days of school.

Certain criteria became indicative of expected success and others became indicative of expected failure. Those children who closely fit the teacher's "ideal type" of the successful child were chosen for seats at Table 1. Those children that had the least "goodness of fit" with her ideal type were placed at the third table.

The criteria upon which a teacher would construct her ideal type of the successful student would rest in her perception of certain attributes in the child that she believed would make for success. To understand what the teacher considered as "success," one would have to examine her perception of the larger society and whom in that larger society she perceived as successful. Thus, in the terms of Merton (1957), one may ask which was the "normative reference group" for Mrs. Caplow that she perceived as being successful.[2] I believe that the reference group utilized by Mrs. Caplow to determine what constituted success was a mixed black-white, well-educated middle class. Those attributes most desired by educated members of the middle class became the basis for her evaluation of the children. Those who possessed these particular characteristics were expected to succeed while those who did not could be expected not to succeed. Highly prized middle-class status for the child in the classroom was attained by demonstrating ease of interaction among adults; high degree of verbalization in Standard American English; the ability to become a leader; a neat and clean appearance; coming from a family that is educated, employed, living together, and interested in the child; and the ability to participate well as a member of a group.

The kindergarten teacher appeared to have been raised in a home where the above values were emphasized as important. Her mother was a college graduate, as were her brother and sisters. The family lived in the same neighborhood for many years, and the father held a responsible position with a public utility company in the city. The family was devoutly religious and those of the family still in the city attend the same church. She and other members of her family were active in a number of civil rights organizations in the city. Thus, it appears that the kindergarten teacher's "normative reference group" coincided quite closely with those groups in which she did participate and belong. There was little discrepancy between the normative values of the mixed black-white educated middle-class and the values of the groups in which she held membership. The attributes indicative of "success" among those of the educated middle class had been attained by the teacher. She was a college graduate, held positions of respect and responsibility in the black community, lived in a comfortable middle-class section of the city in a well-furnished and spacious home, together with her husband earned over $20,000 per year, was active in a number of community organizations, and had parents, brother, and sisters similar in education, income, and occupational positions.

The teacher ascribed high status to a certain group of children within the class who fit her perception of the criteria necessary to be among the "fast learners" at Table 1. With her reference group orientation as to what constitute the qualities essential for "success," she responded favorably to those children who possessed such necessary attributes. Her resultant preferential treatment of a select group of children appeared to be derived from her belief that certain behavioral and cultural characteristics are more crucial to learning in school than are others. In a similar manner, those children who appeared not to possess the criteria essential for success were ascribed low status and described as "failures" by the teacher. They were relegated to positions at Tables 2 and 3. The placement of the children then appeared to result from their possessing or lacking the certain desired cultural characteristics perceived as important by the teacher.

The organization of the kindergarten classroom according to the expectation of success or failure after the eighth day of school became the basis for the differential treatment of the children for the remainder of the school year. From the day that the class was assigned permanent seats, the activities in the classroom were perceivably different from previously. The fundamental division of the class into those expected to learn and those expected not to permeated the teacher's orientation to the class.

The teacher's rationalization for narrowing her attention to selected students was that the majority of the remainder of the class (in her words) "just had no idea of what was going on in the classroom." Her reliance on the few students of ascribed high social status reached such proportions that on occasion, the teacher would use one of these students as an exemplar that the remainder of the class would do well to emulate.

(It is Fire Prevention Week and the teacher is trying to have the children say so. The children make a number of incorrect responses, a few of which follow:) Jim, who had raised his hand, in answer to the question, "Do you know what week it is?" says, "October." The teacher says "No, that's the name of the month. Jane, do you know what special week this is?" and Jane responds, "It cold outside." Teacher says, "No, that is not it either. I guess I will have to call on Pamela. Pamela, come here and stand by me and tell the rest of the boys and girls what special week this is." Pamela leaves her chair, comes and stands by the teacher, turns and faces the rest of the class. The teacher puts her arm around Pamela, and Pamela says, "It fire week." The teacher responds, "Well Pamela, that is close. Actually it is Fire Prevention Week."

On another occasion, the Friday after Hallowe'en, the teacher informed the class that she would allow time for all the students to come to the front of the class and tell of their experiences. She, in reality, called on six students, five of whom sat at Table 1 and the sixth at Table 2. Not only on this occasion, but on others, the teacher focused her attention on the experiences of the higher status students.[3]

(The students are involved in acting out a skit arranged by the teacher on how a family should come together to eat the evening meal.) The students acting the roles of mother, father, and daughter are all from Table 1. The boy playing the son is from Table 2. At the small dinner table set up in the center of the classroom, the four children are supposed to be sharing with each other what they had done during the day—the father at work, the mother at home, and the two children at school. The Table 2 boy makes few comments. (In real life he has no father and his mother is supported by ADC funds.) The teacher comments, "I think that we are going to have to let Milt (Table 1) be the new son. Sam, why don't you go and sit down. Milt, you seem to be one who would know what a son is supposed to do at the dinner table. You come and take Sam's place."

In this instance, the lower-status student was penalized, not only for failing to have verbalized middle-class table talk, but more fundamentally, for lacking middle-class experiences. He had no actual father to whom he could speak at the dinner table, yet he was expected to speak fluently with an imaginary one.

Though the blackboard was long enough to extend parallel to all three tables, the teacher wrote such assignments as arithmetic problems and drew all illustrations on the board in front of the students at Table 1. A rather poignant example of the penalty the children at Table 3 had to pay was that they often could not see the board material.

Lilly stands up out of her seat. Mrs. Caplow asks Lilly what she wants. Lilly makes no verbal response to the question. Mrs. Caplow then says rather firmly to Lilly, "Sit down." Lilly does. However, Lilly sits down sideways in the chair (so she is still facing the teacher). Mrs. Caplow instructs Lilly to put her feet under the table. This Lilly does. Now she is facing directly away from the teacher and the blackboard where the teacher is demonstrating to the students how to print the letter, "O."

The realization of the self-fulfilling prophecy within the classroom was in its final stages by late May of the kindergarten year. Lack of communication with the teacher, lack of involvement in the class activities and infrequent instruction all characterized the situation of the children at Tables 2 and 3. During one observational period of an hour in May, not a single act of communication was directed towards any child at either Table 2 or 3 by the teacher except for twice commanding "sit down." The teacher devoted her attention to teaching those children at Table 1. Attempts by the children at Tables 2 and 3 to elicit the attention of the teacher were much fewer than earlier in the school year.

In June, after school had ended for the year, the teacher was asked to comment on the children in her class. Of the children at the first table, she noted:

I guess the best way to describe it is that very few children in my class are exceptional. I guess you could notice this just from the way the children were seated this year. Those at Table 1 gave consistently the most responses throughout the year and seemed most interested and aware of what was going on in the classroom.

Of those children at the remaining two tables, the teacher commented:

It seems to me that some of the children at Table 2 and most all the children at Table 3 at times seem to have no idea of what is going on in the classroom and were off in another world all by themselves. It just appears that some can do it and some cannot. I don't think that it is the teaching that affects those that cannot do it, but some are just basically low achievers.

The students' response

The students in the kindergarten classroom did not sit passively, internalizing the behavior the teacher directed towards them. Rather, they responded to the stimuli of the teacher, both in internal differentiations within the class itself and also in their response to the teacher. The type of response a student made was highly dependent upon whether he sat at Table 1 or at one of the two other tables. The single classroom of black students did not respond as a homogenous unit to the teacher-inspired social organization of the room.

For the high-status students at Table 1, the response to the track system of the teacher appeared to be at least three-fold. One such response was the directing of ridicule and belittlement towards those children at Tables 2 and 3. At no point during the entire school year was a child from Table 2 or 3 ever observed directing such remarks at the children at Table 1.

Mrs. Caplow says, "Raise your hand if you want me to call on you. I won't call on anyone who calls out." She then says, "All right, now who knows that

> numeral? What is it, Tony?" Tony makes no verbal response but rather walks to the front of the classroom and stands by Mrs. Caplow. Gregory calls out, "He don't know. He scared." Then Ann calls out, "It sixteen, stupid." (Tony sits at Table 3, Gregory and Ann sit at Table 1.)

> Jim starts to say out loud that he is smarter than Tom. He repeats it over and over again, "I smarter than you. I smarter than you." (Jim sits at Table 1, Tom at Table 3.)

> Milt came over to the observer and told him to look at Lilly's shoes. I asked him why I should and he replied, "Because they so ragged and dirty." (Milt is at Table 1, Lilly at Table 3.)

> When I asked Lilly what it was that she was drawing, she replied, "A parachute." Gregory interrupted and said, "She can't draw nothin'."

The problems of those children who were of lower status were compounded, for not only had the teacher indicated her low esteem of them, but their peers had also turned against them. The implications for the future schooling of a child who lacks the desired status credentials in a classroom where the teacher places high value on middle-class "success" values and mannerisms are tragic.

It must not be assumed, however, that though the children at Tables 2 and 3 did not participate in classroom activities and were systematically ignored by the teacher, they did not learn. I contend that in fact they did learn, but in a fundamentally different way from the way in which the high-status children at Table 1 learned. The children at Tables 2 and 3 who were unable to interact with the teacher began to develop patterns of interaction among themselves whereby they would discuss the material that the teacher was presenting to the children at Table 1. Thus I have termed their method of grasping the material "secondary learning" to imply that knowledge was not gained in direct interaction with the teacher, but through the mediation of peers and also through listening to the teacher though she was not speaking to them. That the children were grasping, in part, the material presented in the classroom, was indicated to me in home visits when the children who sat at Table 3 would relate material specifically taught by the teacher to the children at Table 1. *It is not as though the children at Tables 2 and 3 were ignorant of what was being taught in the class, but rather that the patterns of classroom interaction established by the teacher inhibited the low-status children from verbalizing what knowledge they had accumulated.* Thus, from the teacher's terms of reference, those who could not discuss must not know. Her expectations continued to be fulfilled, for though the low-status children had accumulated knowledge, they did not have the opportunity to verbalize it and, consequently, the teacher could not know what they had learned. Children at Tables 2 and 3 had learned material presented in the kindergarten class, but would continue to be defined by the teacher as children who could not or would not learn.

A second response of the higher status students to the differential behavior of the teacher towards them was to seek solidarity and closeness with the teacher and urge Table 2 and 3 children to comply with her wishes.

> The teacher is out of the room. Pamela says to the class, "We all should clean up before the teacher comes." Shortly thereafter the teacher has still not returned and Pamela begins to supervise other children in the class. She says to one girl from Table 3, "Girl, leave that piano alone." The child plays only a short time longer and then leaves.

The teacher has instructed the students to go and take off their coats since they have come in from the playground. Milt says, "Ok y'al, let's go take off our clothes."

At this time Jim says to the teacher, "Mrs. Caplow, they pretty flowers on your desk." Mrs. Caplow responded, "Yes, Jim, those flowers are roses, but we will not have roses much longer. The roses will die and rest until spring because it is getting so cold outside."

When the teacher tells the students to come from their desks and form a semi-circle around her, Gregory scoots up very close to Mrs. Caplow and is practically sitting in her lap.

Gregory has come into the room late. He takes off his coat and goes to the coat room to hang it up. He comes back and sits down in the very front of the group and is now closest to the teacher.

The higher-status students in the class perceived the lower status and esteem the teacher ascribed to those children at Tables 2 and 3. Not only would the Table 1 students attempt to control and ridicule the Table 2 and 3 students, but they also perceived and verbalized that they, the Table 1 students, were better students and were receiving differential treatment from the teacher.

The children are rehearsing a play, Little Red Riding Hood. Pamela tells the observer, "The teacher gave me the best part." The teacher overheard this comment, smiled, and made no verbal response.

The children are preparing to go on a field trip to a local dairy. The teacher has designated Gregory as the "sheriff" for the trip. Mrs. Caplaw stated that for the field trip today Gregory would be the sheriff. Mrs. Caplow simply watched as Gregory would walk up to a student and push him back into line saying, "Boy, stand where you suppose to." Several times he went up to students from Table 3 and showed them the badge that the teacher had given to him and said, "Teacher made me sheriff."

The children seated at the first table were internalizing the attitudes and behavior of the teacher towards those at the remaining two tables. That is, as the teacher responded from her reference group orientation as to which type of children were most likely to succeed and which type most likely to fail, she behaved towards the two groups of children in a significantly different manner. The children from Table 1 were also learning through emulating the teacher how to behave towards other black children who came from low-income and poorly educated homes. The teacher, who came from a well-educated and middle-income family, and the children from Table 1 who came from a background similar to the teacher's, came to respond to the children from poor and uneducated homes in a strikingly similar manner.

The lower-status students in the classroom from Tables 2 and 3 responded in significantly different ways to the stimuli of the teacher. The two major responses of the Table 2 and 3 students were withdrawal and verbal and physical in-group hostility.

The withdrawal of some of the lower-status students as a response to the ridicule of their peers and the isolation from the teacher occasionally took the form of physical withdrawal, but most often it was psychological.

Betty, a very poorly dressed child, had gone outside and hidden behind the door. . . . Mrs. Caplow sees Betty leave and goes outside to bring her back, says in an authoritative and irritated voice, "Betty, come here right now." When the child returns, Mrs. Caplow seizes her by the right arm, brings her over to the group, and pushes her down to the floor. Betty begins to cry. . . . The teacher now shows the group a large posterboard with a picture of a white child going to school.

The teacher is demonstrating how to mount leaves between two pieces of wax paper. Betty leaves the group and goes back to her seat and begins to color.

The teacher is instructing the children in how they can make a "spooky thing" for Hallowe'en. James turns away from the teacher and puts his head on his desk. Mrs. Caplow looks at James and says, "James, sit up and look here."

The children are supposed to make United Nations flags. They have been told that they do not have to make exact replicas of the teacher's flag. They have before them the materials to make the flags. Lilly and James are the only children who have not yet started to work on their flags. Presently, James has his head under his desk and Lilly simply sits and watches the other children. Now they are both staring into space. . . . (5 minutes later) Lilly and James have not yet started, while several other children have already finished. . . . A minute later, with the teacher telling the children to begin to clean up their scraps, Lilly is still staring into space.

The teacher has the children seated on the floor in front of her asking them questions about a story that she had read to them. The teacher says, "June, your back is turned. I want to see your face." (The child had turned completely around and was facing away from the group.)

The teacher told the students to come from their seats and form a semi-circle on the floor in front of her. The girls all sit very close to the piano where the teacher is seated. The boys sit a good distance back away from the girls and away from the teacher. Lilly finishes her work at her desk and comes and sits at the rear of the group of girls, but she is actually in the middle of the open space separating the boys and the girls. She speaks to no one and simply sits staring off.

The verbal and physical hostility that the children at Tables 2 and 3 began to act out among themselves in many ways mirrored what the Table 1 students and the teacher were also saying about them. There are numerous instances in the observations of the children at Tables 2 and 3 calling one another "stupid," "dummy," or "dumb dumb." Racial overtones were noted on two occasions when one boy called another a "nigger," and on another occasion when a girl called a boy an "almond head." Threats of beatings, "whoppins," and even spitting on a child were also recorded among those at Tables 2 and 3. Also at Table 2, two instances were observed in which a single child hoarded all the supplies for the whole table. Similar manifestations of hostility were not observed among those children at the first table. The single incident of strong anger or hostility by one child at Table 1 against another child at the same table occurred when one accused the other of copying from his paper. The second denied it and an argument ensued.

In the organization of hostility within the classroom, there may be at least the tentative basis for the rejection of a popular "folk myth" of American society, which is that children are inherently cruel to one another and that this tendency towards cruelty must be socialized into socially acceptable channels. The evidence from this classroom would indicate that much of the cruelty displayed was a result of the social organization of the class. Those children at Tables 2 and 3 who displayed cruelty appeared to have learned from the teacher that it was acceptable to act in an aggressive manner towards those from low-income and poorly educated backgrounds. Their cruelty was not diffuse, but rather focused on a specific group—the other poor children. Likewise, the incidence of such behavior increased over time. The children at Tables 2 and 3 did not begin the school year ridiculing and belittling each other. This social process began to emerge with the outline of the social organization the teacher imposed upon the class. The children from the first table were also apparently socialized into a pattern of behavior in which they perceived that they could direct hostility and aggression towards those at Tables 2 and 3, but not towards one another. The children in the class learned who was vulnerable to hostility and who was not through the actions of the teacher. She established the patterns of differential behavior which the class adopted.

First grade

Though Mrs. Caplow had anticipated that only twelve of the children from the kindergarten class would attend the first grade in the same school, eighteen of the children were assigned during the summer to the first-grade classroom in the main building. The remaining children either were assigned to a new school a few blocks north, or were assigned to a branch school designed to handle the overflow from the main building, or had moved away. Mrs. Logan, the first-grade teacher, had had more than twenty years of teaching experience in the city public school system, and every school in which she had taught was more than 90 percent black. During the 1968–1969 school year, four informal visits were made to the classroom of Mrs. Logan. No visits were made to either the branch school or the new school to visit children from the kindergarten class who had left their original school. During my visits to the first-grade room, I kept only brief notes of the short conversations that I had with Mrs. Logan; I did not conduct formal observations of the activities of the children in the class.

During the first-grade school year, there were thirty-three children in the classroom. In addition to the eighteen from the kindergarten class, there were nine children repeating the first grade and also six children new to the school. Of the eighteen children who came from the kindergarten class to the first grade in the main building, seven were from the previous year's Table 1, six from Table 2, and five from Table 3.

In the first-grade classroom, Mrs. Logan also divided the children into three groups. Those children whom she placed at "Table A" had all been Table 1 students in kindergarten. No student who had sat at Table 2 or 3 in kindergarten was placed at Table A in the first grade. Instead, all the students from Tables 2 and 3—with one exception—were placed together at "Table B." At the third table which Mrs. Logan called "Table C," she placed the nine children repeating the grade plus Betty who had sat at Table 3 in the kindergarten class. Of the six new students, two were placed at Table A and four at Table C. Thus the totals for the three tables were nine students at Table A, ten at Table B, and fourteen at Table C.

The seating arrangement that began in the kindergarten as a result of the teacher's definition of which children possessed or lacked the perceived necessary characteristics for success in the public school system emerged in the first grade as a caste phenomenon in which there was absolutely no mobility upward. That is, of those children whom Mrs. Caplow had perceived as potential "failures" and thus seated at either Table 2 or 3 in the kindergarten, not one was assigned to the table of the "fast learners" in the first grade.

The initial label given to the children by the kindergarten teacher had been reinforced in her interaction with those students throughout the school year. When the children were ready to pass into the first grade, their ascribed labels from the teacher as either successes or failures assumed objective dimensions. The first-grade teacher no longer had to rely on merely the presence or absence of certain behavioral and attitudinal characteristics to ascertain who would do well and who would do poorly in the class. Objective records of the "readiness" material completed by the children during the kindergarten year were available to her. Thus, upon the basis of what material the various tables in kindergarten had completed, Mrs. Logan could form her first-grade tables for reading and arithmetic.

The kindergarten teacher's disproportionate allocation of her teaching time resulted in the Table 1 students' having completed more material at the end of the school year than the remainder of the class. As a result, the Table 1 group from kindergarten remained intact in the first grade, as they were the only students prepared for the first-grade reading material. Those children from Tables 2 and 3 had not yet completed all the material from kindergarten and had to spend the first weeks of the first-grade school year finishing kindergarten level lessons. The criteria established by the school system as to what constituted the completion of the necessary readiness material to begin first-grade lessons insured that the Table 2 and 3 students could not be placed at Table A. The only children who had completed the material were those from Table 1, defined by the kindergarten teacher as successful students and whom she then taught most often because the remainder of the class "had no idea what was going on."

It would be somewhat misleading, however, to indicate that there was absolutely no mobility for any of the students between the seating assignments in kindergarten and those in the first grade. All of the students save one who had been seated at Table 3 during the kindergarten year were moved "up" to Table B in the first grade. The majority of Table C students were those having to repeat the grade level. As a tentative explanation of Mrs. Logan's rationale for the development of the Table C seating assignments, she may have assumed that within her class there existed one group of students who possessed so very little of the perceived behavioral patterns and attitudes necessary for success that they had to be kept separate from the remainder of the class. (Table C was placed by itself on the opposite side of the room from Tables A and B.) The Table C students were spoken of by the first-grade teacher in a manner reminiscent of the way in which Mrs. Caplow spoke of the Table 3 students the previous year.

Students who were placed at Table A appeared to be perceived by Mrs. Logan as students who not only possessed the criteria necessary for future success, both in the public school system and in the larger society, but who also had proven themselves capable in academic work. These students appeared to possess the characteristics considered most essential for "middle-class" success by the teacher. Though students at Table B lacked many of the "qualities" and characteristics of the Table A students, they were not perceived as lacking them to the same extent as those placed at Table C.

A basic tenet in explaining Mrs. Logan's seating arrangement is, of course, that she shared a similar reference group and set of values as to what constituted "success" with Mrs. Caplow in the kindergarten class. Both women were well educated, were employed in a professional occupation, lived in middle-income neighborhoods, were active in a number of charitable and civil rights organizations, and expressed strong religious convictions and moral standards. Both were educated in the city teachers' college and had also attained graduate degrees. Their backgrounds as well as the manner in which they described the various groups of students in their classes would indicate that they shared a similar reference group and set of expectations as to what constituted the indices of the "successful" student.

Second grade

Of the original thirty students in kindergarten and eighteen in first grade, ten students were assigned to the only second-grade class in the main building. Of the eight original kindergarten students who did not come to the second grade from the first, three were repeating first grade while the remainder had moved. The teacher in the second grade also divided the class into three groups, though she did not give them number or letter designations. Rather, she called the first group the "Tigers." The middle group she labeled the "Cardinals," while the second-grade repeaters plus several new children assigned to the third table were designated by the teacher as "Clowns."[4]

In the second-grade seating scheme, no student from the first grade who had not sat at Table A was moved "up" to the Tigers at the beginning of second grade. All those students who in first grade had been at Table B or Table C and returned to the second grade were placed in the Cardinal group. The Clowns consisted of six second-grade repeaters plus three students who were new to the class. Of the ten original kindergarten students who came from the first grade, six were Tigers and four were Cardinals. Table 8.2 illustrates that the distribution of social economic factors from the kindergarten year remained essentially unchanged in the second grade.

By the time the children came to the second grade, their seating arrangement appeared to be based not on the teacher's expectations of how the child might perform, but rather on the basis of past performance of the child. Available to the teacher when she formulated the seating groups were grade sheets from both kindergarten and first grade, IQ scores from kindergarten, listing of parental occupations for approximately half of the class, reading scores from a test given to all students at the end of first grade, evaluations from the speech teacher and also the informal evaluations from both the kindergarten and first-grade teachers.

The single most important data utilized by the teacher in devising seating groups were the reading scores indicating the performance of the students at the end of the first grade. The second-grade teacher indicated that she attempted to divide the groups primarily on the basis of these scores. The Tigers were designated as the highest reading group and the Cardinals the middle. The Clowns were assigned a first-grade reading level, though they were, for the most part, repeaters from the previous year in second grade. The caste character of the reading groups became clear as the year progressed, in that all three groups were reading in different books and it was school policy that no child could go on to a new book until the previous one had been completed. Thus there was no way for the child, should he have demonstrated competence at a higher reading level, to

Table 8.2 Distribution of socio-economic status factors by seating arrangement in the three reading groups in the second-grade classroom

	Seating Arrangement*		
Factors	Tigers	Cardinals	Clowns
Income			
1) Families on welfare	2	4	7
2) Families with father employed	8	5	1
3) Families with mother employed	7	11	6
4) Families with both parents employed	7	5	1
5) Total family income below $3,000. /yr**	1	5	8
6) Total family income above $12,000. /yr**./	4	0	0
Education			
1) Father ever grade school	8	6	1
2) Father ever high school	7	4	0
3) Father ever college	0	0	0
4) Mother ever grade school	12	13	9
5) Mother ever high school	9	7	4
6) Mother ever college	3	0	0
7) Children with pre-school experience	1	0	0
Family Size			
1) Families with one child	2	0	1
2) Families with six or more children	3	8	5
3) Average number of siblings in family	3–4	6–7	7–8
4) Families with both parents present	8	6	1

* There are twelve children in the Tiger group, fourteen children in the Cardinal group, and nine children in the Clown group.
** Estimated from stated occupation.

advance, since he had to continue at the pace of the rest of his reading group. The teacher never allowed individual reading in order that a child might finish a book on his own and move ahead. *No matter how well a child in the lower reading groups might have read, he was destined to remain in the same reading group. This is, in a sense, another manifestation of the self-fulfilling prophecy in that a "slow learner" had no option but to continue to be a slow learner, regardless of performance or potential.* Initial expectations of the kindergarten teacher two years earlier as to the ability of the child resulted in placement in a reading group, whether high or low, from which there appeared to be no escape. The child's journey through the early grades of school at one reading level and in one social grouping appeared to be pre-ordained from the eighth day of kindergarten.

The expectations of the kindergarten teacher appeared to be fulfilled by late spring. Her description of the academic performance of the children in June had a strong "goodness of fit" with her stated expectations from the previous September. For the first- and second-grade teachers alike, there was no need to rely on intuitive expectations as to what the performance of the child would be. They were in the position of being able to base future expectations upon past performance. At this point, the relevance of the self-fulfilling prophecy again is evident, for the very criteria by which the first- and second-grade teachers established their three reading groups were those manifestations of performance most affected by the previous experience of the child. That is, which reading books were completed, the amount of arithmetic and reading readiness material that had been completed, and the mastery of basic printing skills all became the significant criteria established by the Board of Education to determine the level at which the child would begin the first grade. A similar process of standard evaluation by past performance on criteria established by the Board appears to have been the basis for the arrangement of reading groups within the second grade. Thus, again, the initial patterns of expectations and her acting upon them appeared to place the kindergarten teacher in the position of establishing the parameters of the educational experience for the various children in her class. The parameters, most clearly defined by the seating arrangement at the various tables, remained intact through both the first and second grades.

The phenomenon of teacher expectation based upon a variety of social status criteria did not appear to be limited to the kindergarten teacher alone. When the second-grade teacher was asked to evaluate the children in her class by reading group, she responded in terms reminiscent of the kindergarten teacher. Though such a proposition would be tenuous at best, the high degree of similarity in the responses of both the kindergarten and second-grade teachers suggests that there may be among the teachers in the school a common set of criteria as to what constitutes the successful and promising student. If such is the case, then the particular individual who happens to occupy the role of kindergarten teacher is less crucial. For if the expectations of all staff within the school are highly similar, then with little difficulty there could be an interchange of teachers among the grades with little or no noticeable effect upon the performance of the various groups of students. If all teachers have similar expectations as to which types of students perform well and which types perform poorly, the categories established by the kindergarten teacher could be expected to reflect rather closely the manner in which other teachers would also have grouped the class.

As the indication of the high degree of similarity between the manner in which the kindergarten teacher described the three tables and the manner in which the second-grade teacher discussed the "Tigers, Cardinals, and Clowns," exerpts of an interview with the second-grade teacher are presented, where she stated her opinions of the three groups.

Concerning the Tigers:

Q: Mrs. Benson, how would you describe the Tigers in terms of their learning ability and academic performance?
R: Well, they are my fastest group. They are very smart.
Q: Mrs. Benson, how would you describe the Tigers in terms of discipline matters?
R: Well, the Tigers are very talkative. Susan, Pamela, and Ruth, they are always running their mouths constantly, but they get their work done first. I don't have much trouble with them.
Q: Mrs. Benson, what value do you think the Tigers hold for an education?
R: They all feel an education is important and most of them have goals in life as to what they want to be. They mostly want to go to college.

The same questions were asked of the teacher concerning the Cardinals.

Q: Mrs. Benson, how would you describe the Cardinals in terms of learning ability and academic performance?

R: They are slow to finish their work . . . but they get finished. You know, a lot of them, though, don't care to come to school too much. Rema, Gary, and Toby are absent quite a bit. The Tigers are never absent.

Q: Mrs. Benson, how would you describe the Cardinals in terms of discipline matters?

R: Not too bad. Since they work so slow they don't have time to talk. They are not like the Tigers who finish in a hurry and then just sit and talk with each other.

Q: Mrs. Benson, what value do you think the Cardinals hold for an education?

R: Well, I don't think they have as much interest in education as do the Tigers, but you know it is hard to say. Most will like to come to school, but the parents will keep them from coming. They either have to baby sit, or the clothes are dirty. These are the excuses the parents often give. But I guess most of the Cardinals want to go on and finish and go on to college. A lot of them have ambitions when they grow up. It's mostly the parents' fault that they are not at the school more often.

In the kindergarten class, the teacher appeared to perceive the major ability gap to lie between the students at Table 1 and those at Table 2. That is, those at Tables 2 and 3 were perceived as more similar in potential than were those at Tables 1 and 2. This was not the case in the second-grade classroom. The teacher appeared to perceive the major distinction in ability as lying between the Cardinals and the Clowns. Thus she saw the Tigers and the Cardinals as much closer in performance and potential than the Cardinals and the Clowns. The teacher's responses to the questions concerning the Clowns lends credence to this interpretation.

Q: Mrs. Benson, how would you describe the Clowns in terms of learning ability and academic performance?

R: Well, they are really slow. You know most of them are still doing first-grade work.

Q: Mrs. Benson, how would you describe the Clowns in terms of discipline matters?

R: They are very playful. They like to play a lot. They are not very neat. They like to talk a lot and play a lot. When I read to them, boy, do they have a good time. You know, the Tigers and the Cardinals will sit quietly and listen when I read to them, but the Clowns, they are always so restless. They always want to stand up. When we read, it is really something else. You know— Diane and Pat especially like to stand up. All these children, too, are very aggressive.

Q: Mrs. Benson, what value do you think the Clowns hold for an education?

R: I don't think very much. I don't think education means much to them at this stage. I know it doesn't mean anything to Randy and George. To most of the kids, I don't think it really matters at this stage.

Further notes on the second grade: reward and punishment

Throughout the length of the study in the school, it was evident that both the kindergarten and second-grade teachers were teaching the groups within their classes in a dissimilar manner. Variations were evident, for example, in the amount of time the teachers spent teaching the different groups, in the manner in which certain groups were granted privileges which were denied to others, and in the teacher's proximity to the different groups. Two additional considerations related to the teacher's use of reward and punishment.

Though variations were evident from naturalistic observations in the kindergarten, a systematic evaluation was not attempted of the degree to which such differential behavior was a significant aspect of the classroom interactional patterns. When observations were being conducted in the second grade, it appeared that there was on the part of Mrs. Benson a differentiation of reward and punishment similar to that displayed by Mrs. Caplow. In order to examine more closely the degree to which variations were present over time, three observational periods were totally devoted to the tabulation of each of the individual behavioral units directed by the teacher towards the children. Each observational period was three and one-half hours in length, lasting from 8:30 a.m. to 12:00 noon. The dates of the observations were the Fridays at the end of eight, twelve, and sixteen weeks of school—October 24, November 21, and December 19, 1969, respectively.

A mechanism for evaluating the varieties of teacher behavior was developed. Behavior on the part of the teacher was tabulated as a "behavioral unit" when there was clearly directed towards an individual child some manner of communication, whether it be verbal, non-verbal or physical contact. When, within the interaction of the teacher and the student, there occurred more than one type of behavior, *i.e.,* the teacher spoke to the child and touched him, a count was made of both variations. The following is a list of the nine variations in teacher behavior that were tabulated within the second-grade classroom. Several examples are also included with each of the alternatives displayed by the teacher within the class.

1   Verbal Supportive—"That's a very good job." "You are such a lovely girl." "My, but your work is so neat."
2   Verbal Neutral—"Laura and Tom, let's open our books to page 34." "May, your pencil is on the floor." "Hal, do you have milk money today?"
3   Verbal Control—"Lou, sit on that chair and shut up." "Curt, get up off that floor." "Mary and Laura, quit your talking."
4   Non-verbal Supportive—Teacher nods her head at Rose. Teacher smiles at Liza. Teacher claps when Laura completes her problem at the board.
5   Non-verbal Neutral—Teacher indicates with her arms that she wants Lilly and Shirley to move farther apart in the circle. Teacher motions to Joe and Tom that they should try to snap their fingers to stay in beat with the music.
6   Non-verbal Control—Teacher frowns at Lena. Teacher shakes finger at Amy to quit tapping her pencil. Teacher motions with hand for Rose not to come to her desk.
7   Physical Contact Supportive—Teacher hugs Laura. Teacher places her arm around Mary as she talks to her. Teacher holds Trish's hand as she takes out a splinter.
8   Physical Contact Neutral—Teacher touches head of Nick as she walks past. Teacher leads Rema to new place on the circle.
9   Physical Contact Control—Teacher strikes Lou with stick. Teacher pushes Curt down in his chair. Teacher pushes Hal and Doug to the floor.

Table 8.3 which follows is presented with all forms of control, supportive, and

Table 8.3 Variations in teacher-directed behavior for three second-grade reading groups during three observational periods within a single classroom

| Item | Variations in teacher-directed behavior | | |
	Control	Supportive	Neutral
Observational Period #1*			
Tigers	5%–(6)**	7%–(8)	87%–(95)
Cardinals	10%–(7)	8%–(5)	82%–(58)
Clowns	27%–(27)	6%–(6)	67%–(67)
Observational Period #2			
Tigers	7%–(14)	8%–(16)	85%–(170)
Cardinals	7%–(13)	8%–(16)	85%–(157)
Clowns	14%–(44)	6%–(15)	80%–(180)
Observational Period #3			
Tigers	7%–(15)	6%–(13)	86%–(171)
Cardinals	14%–(20)	10%–(14)	75%–(108)
Clowns	15%–(36)	7%–(16)	78%–(188)

* Forty-eight (48) minutes of unequal teacher access (due to one group of children's being out of the room) was eliminated from the analysis.
** Value within the parentheses indicates total number of units of behavior within that category.

neutral behavior grouped together within each of the three observational periods. As a methodological precaution, since the categorization of the various types of behavior was decided as the interaction occurred and there was no cross-validation checks by another observer, all behavior was placed in the appropriate neutral category which could not be clearly distinguished as belonging to one of the established supportive or control categories. This may explain the large percentage of neutral behavior tabulated in each of the three observational periods.

The picture of the second-grade teacher, Mrs. Benson, that emerges from analysis of these data is of one who distributes rewards quite sparingly and equally, but who utilizes somewhere between two and five times as much control-oriented behavior with the Clowns as with the Tigers. Alternatively, whereas with the Tigers the combination of neutral and supportive behavior never dropped below 93 percent of the total behavior directed towards them by the teacher in the three periods, the lowest figure for the Cardinals was 86 percent and for the Clowns was 73 percent. It may be assumed that neutral and supportive behavior would be conducive to learning while punishment or control-oriented behavior would not. Thus for the Tigers, the learning situation was one with only infrequent units of control, while for the Clowns, control behavior constituted one-fourth of all behavior directed towards them on at least one occasion.

Research related to leadership structure and task performance in voluntary organizations has given strong indications that within an authoritarian setting there occurs a significant decrease in performance on assigned tasks that does not occur with those in a non-authoritative setting (Kelly and Thibaut, 1954; Lewin, Lippitt, and White, 1939). Further investigations have generally confirmed these findings.

Of particular interest within the classroom are the findings of Adams (1945), Anderson (1946), Anderson, *et. al.* (1946), Preston and Heintz (1949), and Robbins (1952). Their findings may be generalized to state that children within an authoritarian classroom display a decrease in both learning retention and performance, while those within the democratic classroom do not. In extrapolating these findings to the second-grade classroom of Mrs. Benson, one cannot say that she was continually "authoritarian" as opposed to "democratic" with her students, but that with one group of students there occurred more control-oriented behavior than with other groups. The group which was the recipient of this control-oriented behavior was that group which she had defined as "slow and disinterested." On at least one occasion Mrs. Benson utilized nearly five times the amount of control-oriented behavior with the Clowns as with her perceived high-interest and high-ability group, the Tigers. For the Clowns, who were most isolated from the teacher and received the least amount of her teaching time, the results noted above would indicate that the substantial control-oriented behavior directed towards them would compound their difficulty in experiencing significant learning and cognitive growth.

Here discussion of the self-fulfilling prophecy is relevant: given the extent to which the teacher utilized control-oriented behavior with the Clowns, data from the leadership and performance studies would indicate that it would be more difficult for that group to experience a positive learning situation. The question remains unanswered, though, as to whether the behavior of uninterested students necessitated the teacher's resorting to extensive use of control-oriented behavior, or whether that to the extent to which the teacher utilized control-oriented behavior, the students responded with uninterest. If the prior experience of the Clowns was in any way similar to that of the students in kindergarten at Table 3 and Table C in the first grade, I am inclined to opt for the latter proposition.

A very serious and, I believe, justifiable consequence of this assumption of student uninterest related to the frequency of the teacher's control-oriented behavior is that the teachers themselves contribute significantly to the creation of the "slow learners" within their classrooms. Over time, this may help to account for the phenomenon noted in the Coleman Report (1966) that the gap between the academic performance of the disadvantaged students and the national norms increased the longer the students remained in the school system. During one of the three and one-half hour observational periods in the second grade, the percentage of control-oriented behavior oriented toward the entire class was about 8 per cent. Of the behavior directed toward the Clowns, however, 27 per cent was control-oriented behavior—more than three times the amount of control-oriented behavior directed to the class as a whole. Deutsch (1968), in a random sampling of New York City Public School classrooms of the fifth through eighth grades, noted that the teachers utilized between 50 and 80 percent of class time in discipline and organization. Unfortunately, he fails to specify the two individual percentages and thus it is unknown whether the classrooms were dominated by either discipline or organization as opposed to their combination. If it is the case, and Deutsch's findings appear to lend indirect support, that the higher the grade level, the greater the discipline and control-oriented behavior by the teacher, some of the unexplained aspects of the "regress phenomenon" may be unlocked.

On another level of analysis, the teacher's use of control-oriented behavior is directly related to the expectations of the ability and willingness of "slow learners" to learn the material she teaches. That is, if the student is uninterested in what goes on in the classroom, he is more apt to engage in activities that the teacher perceives as disruptive. Activities such as talking out loud, coloring when the teacher has not said it to be permissible, attempting to leave the room, calling other students' attention to activities occurring on the street, making comments to the teacher not pertinent to the lesson, dropping books, falling out of the chair, and commenting on how the student cannot wait for recess, all prompt the teacher to employ control-oriented behavior toward that student. The interactional pattern between the uninterested student and the teacher literally becomes a "vicious circle" in which control-oriented behavior is followed by further manifestations of uninterest, followed by further control behavior and so on. The stronger the reciprocity of this pattern of interaction, the greater one may anticipate the strengthening of the teacher's expectation of the "slow learner" as being either unable or unwilling to learn.

The caste system falters

A major objective of this study has been to document the manner in which there emerges within the early grades a stratification system, based both on teacher expectations related to behavioral and attitudinal characteristics of the child and also on a variety of socio-economic status factors related to the background of the child. As noted, when the child begins to move through the grades, the variable of past performance becomes a crucial index of the position of the child within the different classes. The formulation of the system of stratification of the children into various reading groups appears to gain a caste-like character over time in that there was no observed movement into the highest reading group once it had been initially established at the beginning of the kindergarten school year. Likewise, there was no movement out of the highest reading group. There was movement between the second and third reading groups, in that those at the lowest reading table one year are combined with the middle group for a following year, due to the presence of a group of students repeating the grade.

Though formal observations in the second-grade class of Mrs. Benson ended in December of 1969, periodic informal visits to the class continued throughout the remainder of the school year. The organization of the class remained stable save for one notable exception. For the first time during observations in either kindergarten, first or second grade, there had been a reassignment of two students from the highest reading group to the middle reading group. Two students from the Tiger group were moved during the third week of January, 1970 from the Tiger group to the Cardinal group. Two Cardinal group students were assigned to replace those in the Tiger group. Mrs. Benson was asked the reason for the move and she explained that neither of the two former Tiger group students "could keep a clean desk." She noted that both of the students constantly had paper and crayons on the floor beside their desks. She stated that the Tigers "are a very clean group" and the two could no longer remain with the highest reading group because they were "not neat." The two Cardinals who were moved into the Tiger reading group were both described as "extremely neat with their desk and floor."

Poor kids and public schools

It has been a major goal of this paper to demonstrate the impact of teacher expectations, based upon a series of subjectively interpreted social criteria, on both the anticipated academic potential and subsequent differential treatment accorded to those students perceived as having dissimilar social status. For the kindergarten teacher, expectations as to what type of child may be anticipated as a "fast learner" appear to be grounded in her reference group of a mixed white-black educated middle class. That is, students within her classroom who displayed those attributes which a number of studies have indicated are highly desired in children by middle-class educated adults as being necessary for future success were selected by her as possessing the potential to be a "fast learner." On the other hand, those children who did not possess the desired qualities were defined by the teacher as "slow learners." None of the criteria upon which the teacher appeared to base her evaluation of the children were directly related to measurable aspects of academic potential. Given that the I.Q. test was administered to the children in the last week of their kindergarten year, the results could not have been of any benefit to the teacher as she established patterns of organization within the class.[5] The I.Q. scores may have been significant factors for the first- and second-grade teachers, but I assume that consideration of past performance was the major determinant for the seating arrangements which they established.[6]

For the first-grade teacher, Mrs. Logan, and the second-grade teacher, Mrs. Benson, the process of dividing the class into various reading groups, apparently on the basis of past performance, maintained the original patterns of differential treatment and expectations established in the kindergarten class. Those initially defined as "fast learners" by the kindergarten teacher in subsequent years continued to have that position in the first group, regardless of the label or name given to it.

It was evident throughout the length of the study that the teachers made clear the distinctions they perceived between the children who were defined as fast learners and those defined as slow learners. It would not appear incorrect to state that within the classroom there was established by the various teachers a clear system of segregation between the two established groups of children. In the one group were all the children who appeared clean and interested, sought inter-actions with adults, displayed leadership within the class, and came from homes which displayed various status criteria valued in the middle class. In the other were children who were dirty, smelled of urine, did not actively participate in class, spoke a linguistic dialect other than that spoken by the teacher and students at Table 1, did not display leadership behavior, and came from poor homes often supported by public welfare. I would contend that within the system of segregation established by the teachers, the group perceived as slow learners were ascribed a caste position that sought to keep them apart from the other students.

The placement of the children within the various classrooms into different reading groups was ostensibly done on the promise of future performance in the kindergarten and on differentials of past performance in later grades. However, the placement may rather have been done from purely irrational reasons that had nothing to do with academic performance. The utilization of academic criteria may have served as the rationalization for a more fundamental process occurring with the class whereby the teacher served as the agent of the larger society to ensure that proper "social distance" was maintained between the various strata of the society as represented by the children.

Within the context of this analysis there appear to be at least two interactional processes that may be identified as having occurred simultaneously within the kindergarten classroom. The first was the relation of the teacher to the students placed at Table 1. The process appeared to occur in at least four stages. The initial stage involved the kindergarten teacher's developing expectations regarding certain students as possessing a series of characteristics that she considered essential for future academic "success." Second, the teacher reinforced through her mechanisms of "positive" differential behavior those characteristics of the children that she considered important and desirable.

Third, the children responded with more of the behavior that initially gained them the attention and support of the teacher. Perceiving that verbalization, for example, was a quality that the teacher appeared to admire, the Table 1 children increased their level of verbalization throughout the school year. Fourth, the cycle was complete as the teacher focused even more specifically on the children at Table 1 who continued to manifest the behavior she desired. A positive interactional scheme arose whereby initial behavioral patterns of the student were reinforced into apparent permanent behavioral patterns, once he had received support and differential treatment from the teacher.

Within this framework, the actual academic potential of the students was not objectively measured prior to the kindergarten teacher's evaluation of expected performance. The students may be assumed to have had mixed potential. However, the common positive treatment accorded to all within the group by the teacher may have served as the necessary catalyst for the self-fulfilling prophecy whereby those expected to do well did so.

A concurrent behavioral process appeared to occur between the teacher and those students placed at Tables 2 and 3. The student came into the class possessing a series of behavioral and attitudinal characteristics that within the frame of reference of the teacher were perceived as indicative of "failure." Second, through mechanisms of reinforcement of her initial expectations as to the future performance of the student, it was made evident that he was not perceived as similar or equal to those at the table of fast learners. In the third stage, the student responded to both the definition and actual treatment given to him by the teacher which emphasized his characteristics of being an educational "failure." Given the high degree of control-oriented behavior directed toward the "slower" learner, the lack of verbal interaction and encouragement, the disproportionally small amount of teaching time given to him, and the ridicule and hostility, the child withdrew from class participation. The fourth stage was the cyclical repetition of behavioral and attitudinal characteristics that led to the initial labeling as an educational failure.

As with those perceived as having high probability of future success, the academic potential of the failure group was not objectively determined prior to evaluation by the kindergarten teacher. This group also may be assumed to have come into the class with mixed potential. Some within the group may have had the capacity to perform academic tasks quite well, while others perhaps did not. Yet the reinforcement by the teacher of the characteristics in the children that she had perceived as leading to academic failure may, in fact, have created the very conditions of student failure. With the "negative" treatment accorded to the perceived failure group, the teacher's definition of the situation may have ensured its emergence. What the teacher perceived in the children may have served as the catalyst for a series of interactions, with the result that the child came to act out within the class the very expectations defined for him by the teacher.

As an alternative explanation, however, the teacher may have developed the system of caste segregation within the classroom, not because the groups of children were so dissimilar they had to be handled in an entirely different manner, but because they were, in fact, so very close to one another. The teacher may have believed quite strongly that the ghetto community inhibited the development of middle-class success models. Thus, it was her duty to "save" at least one group of children from the "streets." Those children had to be kept separate who could have had a "bad" influence on the children who appeared to have a chance to "make it" in the middle class of the larger society. Within this framework, the teacher's actions may be understood not only as an attempt to keep the slow learners away from those fast learners, but to ensure that the fast learners would not so be influenced that they themselves become enticed with the "streets" and lose their apparent opportunity for future middle-class status.

In addition to the formal separation of the groups within the classroom, there was also the persistence of mechanisms utilized by the teacher to socialize the children in the high reading group with feelings of aversion, revulsion, and rejection towards those of the lower reading groups. Through ridicule, belittlement, physical punishment, and merely ignoring them, the teacher was continually giving clues to those in the high reading group as to how one with high status and a high probability of future success treats those of low status and low probability of future success. To maintain within the larger society the caste aspects of the position of the poor *vis a vis* the remainder of the society, there has to occur the transmission from one generation to another the attitudes and values necessary to legitimate and continue such a form of social organization.

Given the extreme intercomplexity of the organizational structure of this society, the institutions that both create and sustain social organization can neither be held singularly responsible for perpetuating the inequalities nor for eradicating them (cf. Leacock, 1969). The public school system, I believe, is justifiably responsible for contributing to the present structure of the society, but the responsibility is not its alone. The picture that emerges from this study is that the school strongly shares in the complicity of maintaining the organizational perpetuation of poverty and unequal opportunity. This, of course, is in contrast to the formal doctrine of education in this country to ameliorate rather than aggravate the conditions of the poor.

The teachers' reliance on a mixed black-white educated middle class for their normative reference group appeared to contain assumptions of superiority over those of lower-class and status positions. For they and those members of their reference group, comfortable affluence, education, community participation, and possession of professional status may have afforded a rather stable view of the social order. The treatment of those from lower socio-economic backgrounds within the classrooms by the teachers may have indicated that the values highly esteemed by them were not open to members of the lower groups. Thus the lower groups were in numerous ways informed of their lower status and were socialized for a role of lower self expectations and also for respect and deference towards those of higher status. The social distance between the groups within the classrooms was manifested in its extreme form by the maintenance of patterns of caste segregation whereby those of lower positions were not allowed to become a part of the peer group at the highest level. The value system of the teachers appeared to necessitate that a certain group be ostracized due to "unworthiness" or inherent inferiority. The very beliefs which legitimated exclusion were maintained among those of the higher social group which then contributed to the continuation of the pattern of social organization itself.

It has not been a contention of this study that the teachers observed could not or would not teach their students. They did, I believe, teach quite well. But the high quality teaching was not made equally accessible to all students in the class. For the students of high socio-economic background who were perceived by the teachers as possessing desirable behavioral and attitudinal characteristics, the classroom experience was one where the teachers displayed interest in them, spent a large proportion of teaching time with them, directed little control-oriented behavior towards them, held them as models for the remainder of the class and continually reinforced statements that they were "special" students. Hypothetically, if the classrooms observed had contained only those students perceived by the teachers as having a desirable social status and a high probability of future success outside the confines of the ghetto community, the teachers could be assumed to have continued to teach well, and under these circumstances, to the entire class.

Though the analysis has focused on the early years of schooling for a single group of black children attending a ghetto school, the implications are far-reaching for those situations where there are children from different status backgrounds within the same classroom. When a teacher bases her expectations of performance on the social status of the student and assumes that the higher the social status, the higher the potential of the child, those children of low social status suffer a stigmatization outside of their own choice or will. Yet there is a greater tragedy than being labeled as a slow learner, and that is being treated as one. The differential amounts of control-oriented behavior, the lack of interaction with the teacher, the ridicule from one's peers, and the caste aspects of being placed in lower reading groups all have implications for the future life style and value of education for the child.

Though it may be argued from the above that the solution to the existence of differential treatment for students is the establishment of schools catering to only a single segment of the population, I regard this as being antithetical to the goals of education—if one views the ultimate value of an education as providing insights and experience with thoughts and persons different from oneself. The thrust of the educational experience should be towards diversity, not homogeneity. It may be utopian to suggest that education should seek to encompass as wide a variety of individuals as possible within the same setting, but it is no mean goal to pursue.

The success of an educational institution and any individual teacher should not be measured by the treatment of the high-achieving students, but rather by the treatment of those not achieving. As is the case with a chain, ultimate value is based on the weakest member. So long as the lower-status students are treated differently in both quality and quantity of education, there will exist an imperative for change.

It should be apparent, of course, that if one desires this society to retain its present social class configuration and the disproportional access to wealth, power, social and economic mobility, medical care, and choice of life styles, one should not disturb the methods of education as presented in this study. This contention is made because what develops a "caste" within the classrooms appears to emerge in the larger society as "class." The low-income children segregated as a caste of "unclean and intellectually inferior" persons may very well be those who in their adult years become the car washers, dishwashers, welfare recipients, and participants in numerous other un- or underemployed roles within this society. The question may quite honestly be asked, "Given the treatment of low-income children from the beginning of their kindergarten experience, for what class strata are they being prepared other than that of the lower class?" It appears that the public school system not only mirrors the configurations of the larger society, but also significantly contributes to maintaining them. Thus the system of public education in reality perpetuates what it is ideologically committed to eradicate—class barriers which result in inequality in the social and economic life of the citizenry.

Notes

1 The author, due to a teaching appointment out of the city, was unable to conduct formal observations of the children during their first-grade year.
2 The names of all staff and students are pseudonyms. Names are provided to indicate that the discussion relates to living persons, and not to fictional characters developed by the author.
3 Through the remainder of the paper, reference to "high" or "low" status students refers to status ascribed to the student by the teacher. Her ascription appeared to be based on perceptions of valued behavioral and cultural characteristics present or absent in any individual student.
4 The names were not given to the groups until the third week of school, though the seating arrangement was established on the third day.
5 The results of the I.Q. Test for the kindergarten class indicated that, though there were no statistically significant differences among the children at the three tables, the scores were skewed slightly higher for the children at Table 1. There were, however, children at Tables 2 and 3 who did score higher than several students at Table 1. The highest score came from a student at Table 1 (124) while the lowest came from a student at Table 3 (78). There appear to be at least three alternative explanations for the slightly higher scores by students at Table 1. First, the scores may represent the result of differential treatment in the classroom by Mrs. Caplow, thus contributing to the validation of the self-fulfilling prophecy. That is, the teacher by the predominance of teaching time spent with the Table 1 students, better prepared the students to do well on the examination than was the case for those students who received less teaching time. Secondly, the tests themselves may have reflected strong biases towards the knowledge and experience of middle-class children. Thus, students from higher-status families at Table 1 could be expected to perform better than did the low-status students from Table 3. The test resulted not in a "value free" measure of cognitive capacity, but in an index of family background. Third, of course, would be the fact that the children at the first table did possess a higher degree of academic potential than those at the other tables, and the teacher was intuitively able to discern these differences. This third alternative, however, is least susceptible to empirical verification.
6 When the second-grade teacher was questioned as to what significance she placed in the results of I.Q. tests, she replied that "They merely confirm what I already know about the student."

References

Adams, R. G. "The Behavior of Pupils in Democratic and Autocratic Social Climates." Abstracts of Dissertations, Stanford University, 1945.

Anderson, H. *Studies in Teachers' Classroom Personalities*. Stanford: Stanford University Press, 1946.

Anderson, H.; Brewer, J.; and Reed, M. "Studies of Teachers' Classroom Personalities, III. Follow-up Studies of the Effects of Dominative and Integrative Contacts on Children's Behavior." *Applied Psychology Monograph*. Stanford: Stanford University Press, 1946.

Asbell, B. "Not Like Other Children." *Redbook*, 65 (October, 1963), pp. 114–118.

Austin, Mary C. and Morrison, Coleman. *The First R: The Harvard Report on Reading in Elementary Schools*. New York: Macmillan, 1963.

Becker, H. S. "Social Class Variation in Teacher-Pupil Relationship." *Journal of Educational Sociology*, 1952, 25, 451–465.

Borg, W. "Ability Grouping in the Public Schools." Cooperative Research Project 557. Salt Lake City: Utah State University, 1964.

Clark, K. B. "Educational Stimulation of Racially Disadvantaged Children." *Education in Depressed Areas*. Edited by A. H. Passow. New York: Columbia University Press, 1963.

Coleman, J. S., *et al. Equality of Educational Opportunity.* Washington, D. C.: United States Government Printing Office, 1966.

Deutsch, M. "Minority Groups and Class Status as Related to Social and Personality Factors in Scholastic Achievement." *The Disadvantaged Child.* Edited by M. Deutsch, *et al.* New York: Basic Books, 1967.

Eddy, E. *Walk the White Line.* Garden City, N. Y.: Doubleday, 1967.

Frazier, E. F. *Black Bourgeoisie.* New York: The Free Press, 1957.

Freeman, R.; Whelpton, P.; and Campbell, A. *Family Planning, Sterility and Population Growth.* New York: McGraw-Hill, 1959.

Fuchs, E. *Teachers Talk.* Garden City, N. Y.: Doubleday, 1967.

Gebhard, P.; Pomeroy, W.; Martin, C.; and Christenson, C. *Pregnancy, Birth and Abortion.* New York: Harper & Row, 1958.

Gibson, G. "Aptitude Tests." *Science,* 1965, *149,* 583.

Goldberg, M.; Passow, A.; and Justman, J. *The Effects of Ability Grouping.* New York: Teachers College Press, Columbia University, 1966.

Harlem Youth Opportunities Unlimited. *Youth in the Ghetto.* New York: HARYOU, 1964.

Henry, J. "Docility, or Giving the Teacher What She Wants." *Journal of Social Issues,* 1955, *11,* 2.

———. "The Problem of Spontaneity, Initiative and Creativity in Suburban Classrooms." *American Journal of Orthopsychiatry,* 1959, *29,* 1.

———. "Golden Rule Days: American Schoolrooms." *Culture Against Man.* New York: Random House, 1963.

Hollingshead, A. *Elmtown's Youth.* New York: John Wiley & Sons, 1949.

Jackson, P. *Life in Classrooms.* New York: Holt, Rinehart & Winston, 1968.

Kahl, J. A. *The American Class Structure.* New York: Holt, Rinehart & Winston, 1957.

Katz, I. "Review of Evidence Relating to Effects of Desegregation on Intellectual Performance of Negroes." *American Psychologist,* 1964, *19,* 381–399.

Kelly, H. and Thibaut, J. "Experimental Studies of Group Problem Solving and Process." *Handbook of Social Psychology,* Vol. 2. Edited by G. Lindzey. Reading, Mass.: Addison-Wesley, 1954.

Kohl, H. *36 Children.* New York: New American Library, 1967.

Kozol, J. *Death at an Early Age.* Boston: Houghton Mifflin, 1967.

Kvaraceus, W. C. "Disadvantaged Children and Youth: Programs of Promise or Pretense?" Burlingame: California Teachers Association, 1965. (Mimeographed.)

Lawrence, S. "Ability Grouping." Unpublished manuscript prepared for Center for Educational Policy Research, Harvard Graduate School of Education, Cambridge, Mass., 1969.

Leacock, E. *Teaching and Learning in City Schools.* New York: Basic Books, 1969.

Lewin, K.; Lippitt, R.; and White, R. "Patterns of Aggressive Behavior in Experimentally Created Social Climates." *Journal of Social Psychology,* 1939, *10,* 271–299.

Lynd, H. and Lynd, R. *Middletown in Transition.* New York: Harcourt, Brace & World, 1937.

Mackinnon, D. W. "The Nature and Nurture of Creative Talent." *American Psychologist,* 1962, *17,* 484–495.

Merton, R. K. *Social Theory and Social Structure.* Revised and enlarged. New York: The Free Press, 1957.

Moore, A. *Realities of the Urban Classroom.* Garden City, N. Y.: Doubleday, 1967.

Notestein, F. "Class Differences in Fertility." *Class, Status and Power.* Edited by R. Bendix and S. Lipset. New York: The Free Press, 1953.

Preston, M. and Heintz, R. "Effects of Participatory Versus Supervisory Leadership on Group Judgment." *Journal of Abnormal Social Psychology,* 1949, *44,* 345–355.

Reissman, L. *Class in American Society.* New York: The Free Press, 1959.

Riessman, F. *The Culturally Deprived Child.* New York: Harper and Row, 1962.

———. "Teachers of the Poor: A Five Point Program." Burlingame: California Teachers Association, 1965. (Mimeographed.)

Robbins, F. "The Impact of Social Climate upon a College Class." *School Review,* 1952, *60,* 275–284.

Rose, A. *The Negro in America.* Boston: Beacon Press, 1956.

Rosenthal, R. and Jacobson, Lenore. *Pygmalion in the Classroom.* New York: Holt, Rinehart & Winston, 1968.

Sigel, I. "The Piagetian System and the World of Education." *Studies in Cognitive Development.* Edited by D. Elkind and J. Flavell. New York: Oxford University Press, 1969.

Simpson, G. and Yinger, J. M. *Racial and Cultural Minorities.* New York: Harper and Row, 1958.

Smith, L. and Geoffrey, W. *The Complexities of an Urban Classroom.* New York: Holt, Rinehart & Winston, 1968.

Smith, M. "Equality of Educational Opportunity: The Basic Findings Reconsidered." *On Equality of Educational Opportunity.* Edited by F. Mosteller and D. P. Moynihan. New York: Random House, 1971 (In Press).

Warner, W. L.; Havighurst, R.; and Loeb, M. *Who Shall Be Educated?* New York: Harper and Row, 1944.

Wilson, A. B. "Social Stratification and Academic Achievement." *Education in Depressed Areas.* Edited by A. H. Passow. New York: Teachers College Press, Columbia University, 1963.

CHAPTER 9

EARLY CHILDHOOD INTERVENTION (1970)
The social science base of institutional racism
Stephen S. Baratz and Joan C. Baratz

To understand the present political and academic furor over the efficacy—and therefore the future—of such early-intervention programs as Head Start, it is necessary first to examine the basic concepts and assumptions upon which these programs are founded and then to determine whether existing data can support such an approach to the problem of educating children from black ghettoes.

This paper attempts (1) to present an overview of the interventionist literature with particular emphasis on the role of the social pathology model in interpreting the behavior of the ghetto mother, and (2) to illustrate how the predominant ethnocentric view of the Negro community by social science produces a distorted image of the life patterns of that community. The importance of this distortion is that, when converted into the rationale of social action programs, it is a subtle but pernicious example of institutional racism.

This paper is concerned with the goals of intervention programs that deal with altering the child's home environment, with improving his language and cognitive skills, and most particularly with changing the patterns of child-rearing within the Negro home. These goals are, at best, unrealistic in terms of current linguistic and anthropological data and, at worst, ethnocentric and racist. We do not question the legitimacy of early childhood programs when they are described solely as nursery school situations and are not based on the need for remediation or intervention; nor do we question such programs when they increase chances for the employment of economically deprived Negroes. Finally, we do not question such programs when they are described as opportunities to screen youngsters for possible physical disorders, even though follow-up treatment of such diagnostic screening is often unavailable.

We wish to examine in more detail, however, the social pathology model of behavior and intelligence in Head Start[1] projects. We shall attempt to demonstrate that the theoretical base of the deficit model employed by Head Start programs denies obvious strengths within the Negro community and may inadvertently advocate the annihilation of a cultural system which is barely considered or understood by most social scientists. Some thirty years ago, Melville Herskovits (1938–39) made the following insightful observation when talking about culturally related behavioral differences:

> [We need to recognize the existence of] . . . the historical background of the . . . behavioral differences . . . being studied and those factors which make for . . . their . . . existence, and perpetuation. When, for instance, one sees vast

programs of Negro education undertaken without the slightest consideration given even to the possibility of some retention of African habits of thought and speech that might influence the Negroes' reception of the instruction thus offered—one cannot but ask how we hope to reach the desired objectives. When we are confronted with psychological studies of race relations made in utter ignorance of characteristic African patterns of motivation and behavior or with sociological analyses of Negro family life which make not the slightest attempt to take into account even the chance that the phenomenon being studied might in some way have been influenced by the carry-over of certain African traditions, we can but wonder about the value of such work. (Herskovits, 1938–39, p. 121)

It is one of the main contentions of this paper that most, if not all, of the research on the Negro has sorely missed the implications of Herskovits' statement. Rather, research on the Negro has been guided by an ethnocentric liberal ideology which denies cultural differences and thus acts against the best interests of the people it wishes to understand and eventually help.

Socio-political ideology and studies of the Negro

Though it has seldom been recognized by investigators, it has been virtually impossible for social science to divorce itself from ideological considerations when discussing contemporary race relations. As Killian (1968) has pointed out with reference to the social science role after the 1954 Supreme Court Decision:

Because of their professional judgment that the theories were valid and because of the egalitarian and humanitarian ethos of the social sciences, many sociologists, psychologists, and anthropologists played the dual role of scientist and ideologist with force and conviction. Without gainsaying the validity of the conclusions that segregation is psychologically harmful to its victims, it must be recognized that the typically skeptical, even querulous attitude of scientists toward each other's work was largely suspended in this case. (Killian, 1968, p. 54)

Social science research with Negro groups has been postulated on an idealized norm of "American behavior" against which all behavior is measured.

This norm is defined operationally in terms of the way white middle-class America is supposed to behave. The normative view coincides with current social ideology—the egalitarian principle—which asserts that all people are created equal under the law and must be treated as such from a moral and political point of view. The normative view, however, wrongly equates equality with sameness. The application of this misinterpreted egalitarian principle to social science data has often left the investigator with the unwelcome task of describing Negro behavior not as it is, but rather as it deviates from the normative system defined by the white middle class. The postulation of such a norm in place of legitimate Negro values or life ways has gained ascendance because of the pervasive assumptions (1) that to be different from whites is to be inferior and (2) that there is no such thing as Negro culture. Thus we find Glazer and Moynihan (1963) stating: "The Negro is only an American and nothing else. He has no values and culture to guard and protect" (Glazer, N. and Moynihan, D., 1963).

Billingsley (1968) has taken sharp objection to the Glazer and Moynihan statement, pointing out:

> The implications of the Glazer-Moynihan view of the Negro experience is far-reaching. To say that a people have no culture is to say that they have no common history which has shaped and taught them. And to deny the history of a people is to deny their humanity. (Billingsley, 1968, p. 37)

However, the total denial of Negro culture is consonant with the melting-pot mythology and it stems from a very narrow conceptualization of culture by non-anthropologists (Baratz and Baratz, 1969). Social science has refused to look beyond the surface similarities between Negro and white behavior and, therefore, has dismissed the idea of subtle yet enduring differences. In the absence of an ethno-historical perspective, when differences appear in behavior, intelligence, or cognition, they are explained as evidence of genetic defects or as evidence of the negative effects of slavery, poverty, and discrimination. Thus, the social scientist interprets differences in behavior as genetic pathology or as the alleged pathology of the environment; he therefore fails to understand the distortion of the Negro culture that his ethnocentric assumptions and measuring devices have created. The picture that emerges from such an interpretive schema may be seen as culturally biased and as a distortion of the Negro experience.

Liberals have eagerly seized upon the social pathology model as a replacement for the genetic inferiority model. But both the genetic model and the social pathology model postulate that something is wrong with the black American. For the traditional racists, that something is transmitted by the genetic code; for the ethnocentric social pathologists, that something is transmitted by the family. The major difference between the genetic model and the social pathology model lies in the attribution of causality, *not* in the analysis of the behaviors observed as sick, pathological, deviant, or underdeveloped. An example of the marked similarity between the genetic and the social pathology perspectives can be found in the literature concerning language abilities of Negroes.

Language abilities of Negroes

Language proficiency is considered at length in both the social and the genetic pathology models. This concern is not accidental, but is the result of a basic assumption shared by both the social pathologists and the genetic racists that one's linguistic competence is a measure of one's intellectual capacity.

Thus we find Shaler (1890), who believed in the genetic inferiority of the Negro, writing:

> His inherited habits of mind, framed on a very limited language—where the terms were well tied together and where the thought found in the words a bridge of easy passage—gave him much trouble when he came to employ our speech where the words are like widely separated steppingstones which require nimble wits in those who use them. (Shaler, 1890, p. 23)

And later, Gonzales (1922) describes the language of the Carolina coastal Negroes called Gullahs in a similar manner:

> Slovenly and careless of speech, these Gullahs seized upon peasant English

used by some of the early settlers and by the white servants of the wealthier colonists, wrapped their clumsy tongues about it as well as they could, and, enriched with certain expressive African words, it issued through their flat noses and thick lips as so workable a form of speech that it was gradually adopted by other slaves and became in time the accepted Negro speech of the lower districts of South Carolina and Georgia. With characteristic laziness, these Gullah Negroes took short cuts to the ears of their auditors, using as few words as possible, sometimes making one gender serve for three, one tense for several, and totally disregarding singular and plural numbers. (Gonzales, 1922, p. 10)

Hunt (1968) provides a similar description, but from the social pathology perspective, when he writes of the parents of Negro children:

These parents themselves have often failed to utilize prepositional relationships with precision, and their syntax is confused. Thus, they serve as poor linguistic models for their young children. (Hunt, 1968, p. 31)

And Deutsch (1963), writing on the same subject, states:

In observations of lower-class homes, it appears that speech sequences seem to be temporally very limited and poorly structured syntactically. It is thus not surprising to find that a major focus of deficit in the children's language development is syntactical organization and subject continuity. (Deutsch, 1963, p. 174)

Green (1964) gives us another example of the deficit orientation of social pathology thinkers:

The very inadequate speech that is used in the home is also used in the neighborhood, in the play group, and in the classroom. Since these poor English patterns are reconstructed constantly by the associations that these young people have, the school has to play a strong role in bringing about a change in order that these young people can communicate more adequately in our society. (Green, 1964, p. 123)

Finally, Hurst (1965) categorizes the speech of many Negro college freshmen as:

. . . [involving] such specific oral aberrations as phonemic and sub-phonemic replacements, segmental phonemes, phonetic distortions, defective syntax, misarticulations, mispronunciations, limited or poor vocabulary, and faulty phonology. These variables exist most commonly in unsystematic, multifarious combinations.

Because of their ethnocentric bias, both the social pathologists and the genetic racists have wrongly presumed that linguistic competence is synonymous with the development of standard English and, thus, they incorrectly interpret the different, yet highly abstract and complex, non-standard vernacular used by Negroes as evidence of linguistic incompetence or underdevelopment (Baratz, J., 1969). Both share the view that to speak any linguistic system other than standard English is to be deficient and inferior.

Since as early as 1859, when Müller (1859) wrote the *History of Ancient Sanskrit Literature*, the racist contention has been that languages (and their cognitive components) could be hierarchically ordered. Müller himself offered German as the "best" language for conceptualization, but it will not surprise anyone to learn that at various times and according to various writers, the "best" language has been the language of the particular person doing the thinking about the matter. Thus, the ethnocentrism of the social pathology model, which defines a difference as a deficit, forces the misguided egalitarian into testing a racist assumption that some languages are better than others.

The logic of intervention

It is important, then, to understand that the entire intervention model of Head Start rests on an assumption of linguistic and cognitive deficits which must be remedied if the child is to succeed in school. The current linguistic data, however, do not support the assumption of a linguistic deficit. The linguistic competence of black children has been well documented in a number of recent investigations (Stewart, 1968; Labov and Cohen, 1967; Labov, 1969; Dillard, 1969; Baratz, 1969; Wolfram, 1969). Many lower-class Negro children speak a well ordered, highly structured, but different, dialect from that of standard English. These children have developed a language. Thus one of the basic rationales for intervention, that of developing language and cognitive skills in "defective" children, cannot be supported by the current linguistic data.

Nonetheless, the first intervention programs assumed that the causes of a Negro child's failure in school could be counteracted in those months prior to his entrance into school. Data soon became available concerning the effects of Head Start, indicating that three months was not enough time for intervention to be effective (Wolff and Stein, 1967). The social pathologists reasoned that the supposedly progressive deleterious effects of the early environment of the Negro child were so great they could not be overcome in a few months. This argument provided the basis for the extension of Head Start to a full year before school—and by extension into intervention programs which begin earlier and earlier in the child's life and which eventually call for interference with existent family and child-rearing activities.

This expanding web of concern is consistent with the deficit model. Postulation of one deficit which is unsuccessfully dealt with by intervention programs then leads to the discovery of more basic and fundamental deficits. Remediation or enrichment gradually broadens its scope of concern from the fostering of language competence to a broad-based restructuring of the entire cultural system. The end result of this line of argument occurs when investigators such as Deutsch and Deutsch (1968) postulate that "some environments are better than others."

With the recognition of failures and limitations within Head Start and like programs with a social pathology base, proponents of intervention call for earlier and earlier intervention in the child's life. This follows from an interlocking set of assumptions which they frequently make:

1   that, upon entering school, the Negro disadvantaged child is unable to learn in the standard educational environment;
2   that this inability to learn is due to inadequate mothering;
3   that the ghetto environment does not provide adequate sensory stimulation for cognitive growth.

The first premise is buttressed by the continued reports of failure of black children in our schools. Indeed, they do not benefit from the standard educational environment. (That does not, however, say anything about whether they are capable of learning generally.) The second premise is an extension of the earlier work on mothering of institutionalized children as reported by Spitz (1945), Goldfarb (1955), Rheingold (1956), and Skeels and Dye (1939). Much of this literature, however, is predicated on the total absence of a mother or mothering agent. Indeed, the Skeels follow-up study (1960) indicates that a moronic mother is better than no mother at all. The difficulty in extending this logic to the ghetto child is that *he has a mother*, and his behavior derives precisely from her presence rather than her absence.

Then too, the sensory stimulation assumption was an over-extension of the earlier work of Kretch *et al.* (1962), where animals were raised in cages with either considerable sensory stimulation or *none* at all. Again, the model was that of absence of stimulation rather than difference in type and presentation of stimulation.

The inadequate mother hypothesis

It is important to understand that the inadequate mother hypothesis rests essentially on the grounds that the mother's behavior produces deficit children. It was created to account for a deficit that in actuality does not exist—that is, that ghetto mothers produce linguistically and cognitively impaired children who cannot learn. Black children are neither linguistically impoverished nor cognitively underdeveloped. Although their language system is different and, therefore, presents a handicap to the child attempting to negotiate with the standard English-speaking mainstream, it is nonetheless a fully developed, highly structured system that is more than adequate for aiding in abstract thinking. French children attempting to speak standard English are at a linguistic disadvantage; they are not linguistically deficient. Speaking standard English is a linguistic disadvantage for the black youth on the streets of Harlem. A disadvantage created by a difference is not the same thing as a deficit!

In addition, before reviewing some of the notions of the inadequate mother hypothesis, it is necessary to stress that the data presented in that literature fail to show anything more than correlations between child-rearing behaviors and school achievement. As has been discussed elsewhere (Baratz, S., 1968), these correlations cannot be utilized as if they are statements of cause and effect. Although available data do indeed indicate that these culturally different Negro children are not being educated by the public school system, the data fail to show (1) that such children have been unable to learn to think and (2) that, because of specific child-rearing practices and parental attitudes, these children are not able (and, presumably, will never be able) to read, write, and cipher—the prime teaching responsibilities of the public school system.

Nevertheless, the inadequate mother hypothesis has proliferated in the literature of educational psychology. Of chief concern in this literature is the mother-child interaction patterns of lower-class Negroes. Despite the insistence that these patterns are the chief cause of the child's deficits, the supporting data consist almost entirely of either (1) responses to sociological survey-type questionnaires or (2) interaction situations contrived in educational laboratories. There is almost no anthropologically-oriented field work that offers a description of what actually does happen *in the home* wherein the deficit is alleged to arise.

One of the chief complaints leveled against the black mother is that she is not a teacher. Thus one finds programs such as Caldwell's (1968) which call for the "professionalization of motherhood," or Gordon's (1968) which attempts to teach the mother how to talk to her child and how to teach him to think.

The first assumption of such programs is that the ghetto mother does not provide her child with adequate social and sensory stimulation (Hunt, 1961). However, further research into the ghetto environment has revealed that it is far from a vacuum; in fact, there is so much sensory stimulation (at least in the eyes and ears of the middle-class researcher) that a contrary thesis was necessarily espoused which argues that the ghetto sensory stimulation is excessive and therefore causes the child to inwardly tune it all out, thus creating a vacuum for himself (Deutsch, C., 1968).

More recently, studies of social interaction suggest that the amount of social stimulation may be quantitatively similar for lower-class and middle-class children. Thus, the quantitative deficit explanation now appears, of necessity, to be evolving into a qualitative explanation; that is, the child receives as much or even more stimulation as does the middle-class child, but the researchers feel this stimulation is not as "distinctive" for the lower-class child as it is for the middle-class child (Kagan, 1968). Of course, it is interesting to note here that, except for those environments where social and sensory deprivation are extremely severe or total, a condition which is certainly not characteristic of the ghetto environment, there is not evidence to suggest that the ghetto child is cognitively impaired by his mother's sensory social interactions with him.

It has further been suggested that the ghetto mother manages her home in such a manner that the child has difficulty developing a proper sense of time and space—i.e. the organization of the house is not ordered around regularly occurring mealtimes and is not ruled by the White Anglo-Saxon Protestant maxim "everything in its place, and a place for everything." To the middle-class observer, such a home appears to be disorganized and chaotic, while it is merely organized differently. Thus we have data which tell what the mother does not do, but we are missing the data which describe what she does do and explain how the household manages to stay intact. Again, there is no extant research that indicates that the development of a concept of time is either helped or hindered by a child's growing up in an environment where there are regularly occurring meal and bedtimes. There is, however, a considerable literature concerning cultural differences in the concept of time (Henry, 1965).

Further, it is continually asserted that the ghetto mother does not talk or read to her child, thus supposedly hindering his intellectual growth and language development. Despite the fact that no study has ever indicated the minimal amount of stimulation necessary for the child to learn language, and despite the fact that *the child has in fact developed language*, the ghetto mother is still accused of causing language retardation in her infant.

The mother's involvement in reading activities is also presumed to be extremely important to the child's development and future school success. The conclusions of many studies of the black ghetto home stress the absence of books and the fact that ghetto mothers rarely read to their children. Although the presence of books in the home may be quite indicative of middle-class life styles, and stories when read may very well give pleasure to all children, there appears to be no evidence which demonstrates that reading to children is essential for their learning to read, or that such reading will enhance their real language development. Although Irwin's (1960) landmark study indicates that children who are systematically read to babble more, it does not demonstrate that they are linguistically more proficient than those children who are not read to systematically.

A further factor in the mother's behavior which is continually blamed for deficits in the child is her lack of communication to him of the importance of school achievement. Although the literature presents a great many cases which illustrate that the lower-class mother verbalizes great achievement motivations concerning her children, these verbalizations are largely discredited in the eyes of some psychologists (Katz, 1968) who see little action—e.g., helping with homework, joining the PTA—underlying her statement of achievement motivation for her child. (Here, ironically, the supposedly non-verbal mother is now being penalized for her verbal behavior.) Indeed, her verbalizations tend to exhort the child to behave and achieve in class in relation to some assumed behavioral norm rather than to some educational reward; e.g., learn to read because the teacher says so, not because there are many things that one can learn from books (Hess, *et al.*, 1968). Nonetheless, there do not appear to be any data which show that preschool children resist learning, avoid schooling, or generally do not wish to achieve in the classroom; nor are there data to suggest that intrinsic motivations (learn for learning's sake) are effective for teaching reading, or that extrinsic ones (do it because I tell you) are not. In fact, the behaviorist literature tends to indicate that different sub-groups (i.e. lower-class versus middle-class) respond differently to various reinforcements (for instance, food versus praise).

The recent work of Hess, Shipman, Brophy, and Bear (1968) is sure to add considerable fuel to the inadequate mother hypothesis. Hess and his colleagues collected data on 163 black mothers and their four-year-old children. The mothers were divided into four groups: professional, skilled, unskilled-family intact, and unskilled-father absent. Social workers collected data in two extensive home interviews. Later, the mothers and children came to the university where IQ and other formal tests were administered. The mothers were also presented with theoretical situations and asked what they would do or say—e.g., what would you say to your child on his first day of school. In addition, the mothers were asked to teach their children a block-sorting task and to replicate a design on an etch-a-sketch box with their children. The Hess *et al.* data furnished a good deal of information concerning teaching styles of lower- and middle-class black women. These data, however, were undoubtedly influenced by the fact that the situations in which they were elicited (i.e., interviewing and a laboratory task) are much more typical of middle-class experiences. Nevertheless, many differences in maternal language and teaching styles appeared. It would be a mistake, however, to conclude that these differences in language and teaching style cause the child to be uneducable. What makes him appear "uneducable" is his failure in an educational system that is insensitive to the culturally different linguistic and cognitive styles that he brings to the classroom setting. The school, therefore, fails to use the child's distinct cultural patterns as the vehicle for teaching new skills and additional cultural styles.

One of the major difficulties with the work of Hess *et al.* lies in their concept of "educability." Superficially this refers to those skills which every child potentially possesses but which presumably are not developed if the mother's behavior is "restricted" and not similar to that of those middle-class mothers who produce children who succeed in school. Those skills which the child potentially possesses, however, are not defined by Hess *et al.* simply as language development, but rather more subtly as the use of standard English. Concept development is not seen as the development of language for thought (There are, of course, no languages that one cannot think in!) but rather, it is defined in terms of performance on standardized tasks or measures of verbal elaboration. Again, motivation is described not in terms of wanting to read, but rather in terms of books around the house and the use of the public library. "Educability" then, is really defined as specific middle-class mainstream behaviors rather than as the possession of universal processes through which specific behaviors can be channeled. The lower-class mother is *a priori* defined as inadequate because she is not middle-class.

In their discussions of the mothers' language behavior, Hess *et al.* rely heavily on the concepts of Basil Bernstein, who describes two different communicative styles generally used by lower- and middle-class English children. That the language and teaching behaviors of lower-class Negro mothers are different from those of middle-class mothers is beyond question. That the different behavior leads to cognitive defects has yet to be demonstrated. Carroll (1964) has discussed the methodological issue of the relationship of language style to cognition. To say that a particular language has a deleterious effect on cognitive performance, speakers of that language must be tested for cognitive ability on a non-linguistic task—such a task has yet to be developed or tested.

The Hess data, while providing considerable information on maternal behavior differences in lower- and middle-class black women, do not indicate that the children from lower-class homes are any less ready to learn than are the middle-class children, nor do they demonstrate that these children will be less able— especially if they are placed in a school that takes advantage of their experiences, as the present school curriculum does in certain crucial regards for the middle-class child. The Hess data do show, however, that the behaviors of the middle-class Negro mothers are more typically mainstream and that what these mothers teach their children is more typically within mainstream expectations; therefore, such children tend to perform better in a testing situation—and subsequently in a school situation—which requires mainstream behaviors and heuristic styles than do lower-class children, who have learned something else.

There is much to be learned about maternal teaching styles and how they can be used to help the child function better in interactions with the mainstream culture. Research has indicated how unlike the middle-class mother the lower-class mother is, but there is very little description of who the lower-class mother is and what she does.

The failure of intervention

Intervention programs postulated on the inadequacy of the mother or the lack of environmental stimulation (Shaefer, 1969; Gordon, 1968; Klaus and Gray, 1968) fail after an initial spurt in IQ scores. This appears to be an artifact of the methodology, for the first contact with mainstream educational patterns (an agent intervening in the home, a Head Start Program, kindergarten or first grade in the public school) appears automatically to cause an increase in IQ for these children. This artifact is clearly evidenced in the "catch-up" phenomenon where non-Head Start children gain in IQ apparently as a result of exposure to a school environment. The additional observation, that increases in IQ of both Head Start *and* non-Head Start children decrease after second or third grade, is a further indication that early childhood intervention is not where the answer to the failure of children in public school lies.

Interventionists argue that what is needed are school-based programs (Project

Follow-Through) which maintain the "gains" of Head Start by changing the nature of the school environment. In effect, this argument is a specious one since it was the intervention program itself which was supposed to insure the child's success in the schools as they are presently constituted. For the early childhood interventionists then to turn around and say that the schools do not do their job in maintaining the increases which the school itself has generated in non-Head Start children (as well as the increases of Head Start children) is indeed to point to the crux of the matter: the failure lies in the schools, not the parents, to educate these children. This clearly indicates that critical intervention must be done, but on the procedures and materials used in the schools rather than on the children those schools service. Intervention which works to eliminate archaic and inappropriate procedures for teaching these children and which substitutes procedures and materials that are culturally relevant is critically needed. It is important to note here that such intervention procedures—e.g. the use of Negro dialect in the teaching of reading (Baratz and Baratz, 1969)—are not ends in themselves. The goal of such procedures is to have the children perform adequately on standardized achievement tests. It is the process, not the goals, of education that must be changed for these children. *The educational problems of lower-class culturally different Negro children, as of other groups of culturally different children, are not so much related to inappropriate educational goals as to inadequate means for meeting these goals.*

It is not, therefore, a particular program for early childhood intervention at a critical period which affects IQ scores. Rather it is the initial contact with mainstream middle-class behaviors that tends to raise temporarily the scores of young children. As the test items, however, begin to rely more and more heavily on the language style and usage of the middle-class, these culturally different dialect-speaking children tend to decrease in test performance. Unlike the behaviors which initially raise IQ scores and which the child learns simply from contact with the middle-class system, fluency in a new language style and usage must be taught formally and systematically for it to be mastered. Indeed, this failure to teach the mainstream language styles and usage by means of the child's already existing system may well explain why the initial test gains of these children are not maintained.

The early childhood programs, as well as public schools, fail in the long run because they define educability in terms of a child's ability to perform within an alien culture; yet they make no attempt to teach him systematically new cultural patterns so that the initial spurt in test scores can be maintained. Educability, for culturally different children, should be defined primarily as the ability to learn new cultural patterns within the experience base and the culture with which the child is already familiar. The initial test scores of culturally different children must not be misevaluated as evidence of "educability," but rather should be viewed as evidence of the degree to which the child is familiar with the mainstream system upon which the tests are based both in content and presentation.

Because of the misconception of educability and the misevaluation of the test data, interventionists and educators create programs that are designed (1) to destroy an already functionally adequate system of behavior because it is viewed as pathological and (2) to impose a system of behavior without recognizing the existence of a functionally adequate system of behavior already in place. (Thus it is comparable to attempting to pour water into an already wine-filled pitcher.) Education for culturally different children should not attempt to destroy functionally viable processes of the sub-culture, but rather should use these processes to teach additional cultural forms. The goal of such education should be to pro-duce a bicultural child who is capable of functioning both in his sub-culture and in the mainstream.

However, since Head Start has disregarded or attempted unknowingly to des-troy that which is a viable cultural system, we should not have been surprised by its failure in attempting to "correct" these behaviors. Head Start has failed because its goal is to correct a deficit that simply does not exist. The idea that the Negro child has a defective linguistic and conceptual system has been challenged by the findings of Stewart (1964, 1967, 1968, 1969), Baratz, J. (1969), Labov (1969), and by Lesser and his colleagues (1965, 1967), who point to the structur-ally coherent but different linguistic and cognitive systems of these children. Indeed, the deficit model of Head Start forces the interventionist closer and closer to the moment of conception and to the possibility of genetic determination of the behavior now attributed to a negative environment. This position is plaintively described by Caldwell (1968):

> Most of us in enrichment . . . efforts—no matter how much lip service we pay to the genetic potential of the child—are passionate believers in the plasticity of the human organism. We need desperately to believe that we are born equalizable. With any failure to demonstrate the effectiveness of compensa-tory experiences offered to children of any given age, one is entitled to conclude parsimoniously that perhaps the enrichment was not offered at the proper time. (Caldwell, 1968, p. 81)

Elsewhere Caldwell refers to what she calls the Inevitable Hypothesis which we interpret as backing up further and further (intervene at four, at three, at one, at three months) until we are face to face with the possibility of genetic differences between Negroes and whites which forever preclude the possibility of remediation or enrichment. We are in Caldwell's debt for such a passionate statement of the real issue at hand. All educators concerned with intervention of any kind and unaware of the culture (and the alternative conceptual framework it offers) respond at a gut level to the implications which the failure of early childhood programs has for the overtly racist genetic model. The frustration due to the failure of intervention programs proposed by the social pathologists could lead to three possible lines of responses from those watching and participating in the unfolding of events. They are:

1   an increased preoccupation with very early intervention, at birth or shortly thereafter, to offset the allegedly "vicious" effects of the inadequate environment of the Negro child;
2   the complete rejection of the possibility of intervention effects unless the child is totally removed from his environment to be cared for and educated by specialists;
3   the total rejection of the environmentalist-egalitarian position in favor of a program of selective eugenics for those who seem to be totally unable to meet the demands of a technological environment—scientific racism.

Suffice it to say that recently we have seen an articulation of all three of these unfeasible positions.

The clearest line of thought currently evident comes from people such as Shaefer (1969a), Gordon (1968), and Caldwell (1967) advocating the introduction of specialists into the home who would not only provide the missing stimulation to the child, but also teach the mother how to raise her children properly. Thus, the new input is an intensive attempt to change totally the child's environment and the parent's child-rearing patterns.

But the fear is that even such a massive attempt will still fail to innoculate the child against failure in the schools. Recognizing this, Caldwell (1967) provides the model for intervention programs which take the child completely out of the home for short periods of time for the purpose of providing him with the experiences unavailable to him during his first three years of life. It is only a short distance from this position to Bettelheim's statement (*New York Times*, March 1969) advocating total removal of Negro children to kibbutz-like controlled environments in order to overcome the effects of the allegedly negative values and practices of the ghetto—in short, the annihilation of distinctive Afro-American cultural styles.

Finally, the appearance of the scholarly article recently published by Arthur Jensen (1969) in the *Harvard Educational Review* represents the attempt of a former social pathologist to deal with the failure of the intervention programs. He may find his position politically distasteful but, for a scientist who lacks a cross-cultural perspective and a historical frame of reference, it is the only way to maintain his scientific integrity. Like most scholars who come to advocate an unpopular thesis, Jensen has done his homework. His familiarity with the data indicates to him the futility of denying (1) that Negro children perform less well on intelligence tests than whites and (2) that Head Start has failed in its intent to produce permanent shifts in IQ which lead to success in the educational system. Since Jensen rejects the social pathology model but retains a concept that describes Negro behavior as defective, it is not at all surprising that he has no alternative other than a model of genetic inferiority.

However, like the social pathologists who had to create an explanation (i.e., inadequate mothering) for a non-existent deficit, Jensen is also called upon to explain the reasons for a relative theory of genetic inferiority in the American Negro. His argument, similar to those of earlier genetic racists, states that the Negroes who were brought over as slaves "were selected for docility and strength and not mental ability, and that through selective mating the mental qualities present never had a chance to flourish." (Edson, 1969). Interestingly enough, this contention was decimated almost thirty years ago by Melville Herskovits (1941) in his book, *The Myth of the Negro Past*, in which he presents historical and anthropological data to reject the notion of selective enslavement and breeding. It is precisely the absence of a sophisticated knowledge and perspective of cultural continuity and cultural change which has forced both the social pathologists and the genetic pathologists to feel that they have dealt with "culture" if they acknowledge that certain test items are "culture-bound." Such changes represent very surface knowledge of the concept of culture and, in particular, do not deal with subtle yet significant cultural differences. Many social scientists believe that they are dealing with the culture when they describe the physical and social environment of these children. One must not confuse a description of the environment in which a particular culture thrives for the culture itself.

Because historical and political factors have combined to deny the existence of a Negro culture (Baratz and Baratz, 1969), social scientists have found themselves having to choose between either a genetic deficit model or a deficit model built on an inadequate environment (the "culture" of poverty). However, our view of the current status of research on the Negro in the United States indicates that we are on the brink of a major scientific revolution with respect to American studies of the Negro and the social action programs that derive from them. This revolution began with Herskovits and is being forwarded by the linguistic and anthropological studies of Stewart (1964–1969), Szwed (1969), Abrahams (1967), Hannerz (1969), and others. The basic assumption of this research is that the behavior of Negroes is not pathological, but can be explained within a coherent, structured, distinct, American-Negro culture which represents a synthesis of African culture in contact with American European culture from the time of slavery to the present day.

Since the pathology model of the language and thought of Negroes as it is used in intervention programs has been created by the superimposition of a standard English template on a non-standard dialect system, producing a view of that non-standard system as defective and deviant, then the data gathered in support of that pathology view must be totally re-evaluated and old conclusions dismissed, not solely because they are non-productive, but also because they are ethnocentric and distorted and do not recognize the cultural perspective. The great impact of the misuse of the egalitarian model on social science studies of the Negro must be re-examined.

As long as the social pathology and genetic models of Negro behavior remain the sole alternatives for theory construction and social action, our science and our society are doomed to the kind of cyclical (environment to genes) thinking presently evident in race relations research. Fortunately, at this critical point in our history, we do have a third model available, capable of explaining both the genetic and social pathology views with greater economy and capable of offering viable research and societal alternatives.

The major support for the assertion of a revolution in scientific thinking about the Negro comes from the discovery that the urban Negro has a consistent, though different, linguistic system. This discovery is an anomaly in that it could not have been predicted from the social pathology paradigm. This finding, if we can judge from the incredulity expressed about it by our colleagues, violates many of the perceptions and expectations about Negro behavior which are built into the assumptive base of the social pathology model. This assumptive base, it is argued, has restricted our phenomenological field to deviations from normative behavior rather than to descriptions of different normative configurations. In the present case, it would appear that the defect and difference models of Negro behavior cannot exist side by side without a growing awareness of the need for change and radical reconstruction of our modes of theorizing and conceptualizing about Negro behavior.

However, there may be resistance to adopting the cultural difference model which stems not only from the inherent methodologies of the social pathology theory, but also from the much more vague, and often unexpressed socio-political view of the particular investigator seeking to support his view of our current racial situation—views which are unarticulated and therefore unexamined. Thus, the resistance we anticipate may be intensified by the fear that talking about differences in Negro behavior may automatically produce in the social pathologist the postulation of genetic differences. This fear, so often expressed, is related to the real fact that the genetic model itself relied on behavioral differences as the basis for its conclusions about genetic determination. Three points can be made here to deal with this concern: (1) it has not and should not be the role of rational scholarly discourse to dismiss data and knowledge simply because it does not fit a particular ideological position extant at a particular moment in history; (2)

differences, which indicate that learning has taken place, are not deficits; and (3) the view of the current social pathology position is in many ways prone to the same criticisms leveled at the genetic pathology model. The current scientific crisis will resolve itself solely on the basis of scholarly research and not ideology or polemic. The basic assumptions of scholarly research must be examined and models tried out that offer more successful and economical explanations.

In summary, the social pathology model has led social science to establish programs to prevent deficits which are simply not there. The failure of intervention reflects the ethnocentrism of methodologies and theories which do not give credence to the cognitive and intellectual skills of the child. A research program on the same scale as that mounted to support the social pathology model must be launched in order to discover the different, but not pathological, forms of Negro behavior. Then and only then can programs be created that utilize the child's differences as a means of furthering his acculturation to the mainstream while maintaining his individual identity and cultural heritage.

Note

1   We recognize that no two Head Start projects are exactly alike. Head Start is used here as a generic term for intervention programs designed for under-privileged pre-school children.

References

Abrahams, R. *Deep Down in the Jungle*, Revised edition, Hatboro, Pa.: Folklore Associates, 1967.

Baratz, J. Language development in the economically disadvantaged child: A perspective. *ASHA*, 1968, March.

Baratz, J. Linguistic and cultural factors in teaching English to ghetto children. *Elementary English*, 46, 1969, 199–203.

Baratz, J. Language and cognitive assessment of Negro children: Assumptions and research needs. *ASHA*, March, 1969.

Baratz, J. and Shuy, R. (Eds.) *Teaching Black Children To Read*. Washington, D.C.: Center for Applied Linguistics, 1969.

Baratz, S. and J. Negro ghetto children and urban education: A cultural solution, *Bulletin of the Minnesota Council for the Social Studies*, Fall, 1968, Reprinted in *Social Education*, 33, 4, 1969, 401–404.

Baratz, S. and J. The social pathology model: Historical Bases for psychology's denial of the existence of Negro culture. APA Paper, Washington, D.C., 1969.

Baratz, S. Social science research strategies for the Afro-American. In J. Szwed (Ed.), *Black America*. New York: Basic Books, in press.

Bettelheim, B. Psychologist questions value of Head Start program. *New York Times*, March 17, 1969.

Billingsley, A. *Black Families in White America*. Englewood Cliffs, New Jersey: Prentice-Hall, Inc., 1968.

Caldwell, B. The fourth dimension in early childhood education. In R. Hess and R. Bear (Eds.), *Early Education: Current Theory, Research and Action*. Chicago: Aldine Publishing Co., 1968.

Caldwell, B. What is the optimal learning environment for the young child? *American Journal of Orthopsychiatry*, 37, 1967, 9–21.

Carroll, J. *Language and Thought*. Englewood Cliffs, New Jersey: Prentice-Hall, 1964.

Deutsch, C. Auditory discrimination and learning social factors. *Merrill-Palmer Quarterly*, 10, 1964, 277–296.

Deutsch, M. The disadvantaged child and the learning process. In A. Passow (Ed.), *Education in Depressed Areas*. New York: Columbia University Teachers College, 1963.

Deutsch, C. and Deutsch, M. Theory of early childhood environment programs. In R. Hess and R. Bear, Eds., *Early Education: Current Theory, Research and Action.* Chicago: Aldine Publishing Co., 1968.

Dillard, J. L. *Black English in the United States.* New York: Random House, in press.

Dye, H. B. A study of the effects of differential stimulation on mentally retarded children. The Procedures of the American Association of the Mentally Deficient, Vol. 44, 1939, 114–136.

Edson, L. Jensenism, n. The theory that I.Q. is largely determined by the genes. *New York Times*, August 31, 1969. 10ff.

Glazer, N. and Moynihan, D. *Beyond the Melting Pot.* Cambridge, Massachusetts: MIT Press and the Harvard University Press, 1963.

Goldfarb, W. Emotional and intellectual consequences of psychological deprivation in infancy: A re-evaluation. In P. H. Hoch and J. Zobin (Eds.), *Psychopathology of Childhood.* New York: Grune and Stratton, 1955.

Gonzales, A. *The Black Border: Gullah Stories of the Carolina Coast.* South Carolina: The State Company, 1922.

Gordon, I. Research Report: Infant performance. Gainesville, Florida: Institute for Development of Human Resources, University of Florida, 1968.

Green, R. Dialect sampling and language values. In R. Shuy (Ed.), *Social Dialects and Language Learning.* Champaign; Ill.: NCTE, 1964, 120–123.

Hannerz, U. *Soulside Inquiries into Ghetto Children and Community.* Stockholm, Sweden: Almquist & Wiksele, 1969.

Henry, J. White people's time, colored people's time. *Transaction*, March-April, 1965.

Herskovits, M. The ancestry of the American Negro. *American Scholar*, 1938–39, reprinted in *The New World Negro.* Bloomington, Indiana University Press, 1966. 114–122.

Herskovits, M. *The Myth of the Negro Past.* New York: Harper and Brothers, 1941.

Hess, R., Shipman, V., Brophy, J. & Bear, R. *The Cognitive Environments of Urban Preschool Children.* The Graduate School of Education, University of Chicago, 1968.

Hunt, J. McV. *Intelligence and Experience.* New York: The Ronald Press Company, 1961.

Hunt, J. McV. Towards the prevention of incompetence. In J. W. Carter (Ed.), *Research Contributions from Psychology to Community Health.* New York: Behavioral Publications, 1968.

Hurst, C. G., Jr. *Psychological Correlates in Dialectolalia*, Washington, D.C., Howard University: Communities Research Center, 1965.

Irwin, D. C. Infant speech: Effect of systematic reading of stories. *Journal of Speech and Hearing Research*, 1960, 3, 187–190.

Jensen, A. How much can we boost IQ and scholastic achievement? *Harvard Educational Review*, 39, 1969, 1–123.

Kagan, J. His struggle for identity, *Saturday Review*, December, 1968.

Katz, I. Research issue on evaluation of educational opportunity: Academic motivation, *Harvard Educational Review*, 38, 1968, 57–65.

Killian, L. M. *The Impossible Revolution?* New York: Random House, 1968.

Klaus R. A. and Gray, S.W. The early training project for disadvantaged children: A report after five years. *Monograph, SRCD*, 33, 1968.

Kretch, D., Rosenzweig, M. & Bennet, E. L. Relations between brain chemistry and problem solving among rats raised in enriched and impoverished environments. *Journal of Comparative Physiological Psychology*, 55, 1962, 801–807.

Labov, W. The logic of nonstandard dialect. In J. Alatis (Ed.), *School of Languages and Linguistics Monograph Series, No. 22.* Georgetown University, 1969, 1–43.

Labov, W. and Cohen, P. Systematic relations of standard rules in grammar of Negro speakers. Project Literacy #7, 1967.

Lesser, G., Fifer, G. & Clark, D. H. Mental abilities of children from different social class and cultural groups. *Monograph of Society for Research in Child Development*, 1965, 30, 647.

Malone, C. A. Developmental deviations considered in the light of environmental forces. In Pavenstedt, E. (Ed.), *The Drifters: Children of Disorganized Lower Class Families.* Boston: Little, Brown and Co., 1967.

Müller, F. M. *History of Ancient Sanskrit Literature, so far as it illustrates the primitive religion of the Brahmans.* London: Williams and Norgate, 1859.

Rheingold, H. The modification of social responsiveness in institutional babies, *Monograph of Society for Research and Child Development*, 21, (2), Serial No. 63, 1956.

Shaefer, E. Tutoring the "disadvantaged." *The Washington Post*, February 9, 1969.

Shaefer, E. Home tutoring, maternal behavior and infant intellectual development, APA Paper, Washington, D.C., 1969.

Shaler, N. S. The nature of the Negro, *Arena*, 3, 1890, 23–35.

Skeels, H. Adult status of children with contrasting early life experiences. *Monograph Society for Research in Child Development*, 31, 3, 1960, 1–65.

Skeels, H. and Dye, H. A study of the effects of differential stimulation on mentally retarded children. Proceeding of the American Association for Mental Deficiency, 44, 1939, 114–136.

Spitz, R. Hospitalism: An inquiry into the genesis of psychiatric conditions in early childhood. *Psychoanalytic Study of the Child*, 1945, 1, 53–74.

Stewart, W. Urban Negro speech: Sociolinguistic factors affecting English teaching. In R. Shuy (Ed.), *Social Dialects and Language Learning*, NCTE, Champaign, Ill., 1964.

Stewart, W. Social dialects. In E. Gordon (Ed.), *Research Planning Conference on Language Development in Disadvantaged Children*, Yeshiva University, 1966.

Stewart, W. Sociolinguistic factors in the history of American Negro dialects, *The Florida FL Reporter*, 5, 2, Spring, 1967.

Stewart, W. Sociopolitical issues in the linguistic treatment of Negro dialect. *School of Languages and Linguistics Monograph Series, No. 22*. Georgetown University, 1969, 215–223.

Stewart, W. Historical and structural bases for the recognition of Negro dialect. *School of Languages and Linguistics Monograph Series, No. 22*. Georgetown University, 1969, 239–247.

Stewart, W. Continuity and change in American Negro dialects, *The Florida FL Reporter*, Spring, 1968.

Stewart, W. On the use of Negro dialect in the teaching of reading. In J. Baratz and R. Shuy (Eds.), *Teaching Black Children To Read*. Washington, D.C.: Center for Applied Linguistics, 1969.

Stewart, W. Teaching black language: A forum lecture for Voice of America, Washington, D.C., May 1969.

Stodolsky, S. and Lesser, G. Learning patterns in the disadvantaged. *Harvard Educational Review*, 1967, 37, 546–593.

Szwed, J. Ethnohistory of the Afro-American in the United States, APA Paper, Washington, D.C., 1969.

Szwed, J. *Black America*. New York: Basic Books, in press.

Wolff, M. and Stein, A. Head Start six months later. *Phi Delta Kappan*, March, 1967. Reprinted in J. Frost (Ed.), *Early Childhood Education Rediscovered*. New York: Holt, Rinehart & Winston, Inc., 293–297.

Wolfram, W. *Sociolinguistic description of Detroit Negro speech*. Washington, D.C.: Center for Applied Linguistics, 1969.

CHAPTER 10

FROM RACIAL STEREOTYPING AND DEFICIT DISCOURSE TOWARD A CRITICAL RACE THEORY IN TEACHER EDUCATION (2001)

Daniel G. Solorzano and Tara J. Yosso

Introduction

> The sad and simple fact is that while there are some excellent black students . . . on average, black students do not try as hard as other students. The reason they do not try as hard is not because they are inherently lazy, nor is it because they are stupid . . . these students belong to a culture infected with an Anti-intellectual strain, which subtly but decisively teaches them from birth not to embrace school-work too whole heartedly.
>
> —p. E3, *George*, 2000, quoting John McWhorter

> . . . it is to "get real" about race and the persistence of racism in America.
> —Derrick Bell, *Faces at the Bottom of the Well*, 1992, p. 5

The two epigraphs above exemplify two distinct methods of addressing teacher education in the United States today. While John McWhorter explains the status of African American students in stereotypical, deficit terms, Derrick Bell offers a reminder of the lingering significance of racism and our inability to eliminate it from U.S. society. In this essay, we examine the linkages between a theoretical framework—critical race theory (CRT)—and its relation and application to the concepts of race, racism, and racial stereotyping in teacher education.

Critical race theory

Critical race theory (CRT) challenges the dominant discourse on race and racism as it relates to education by examining how educational theory and practice are used to subordinate certain racial and ethnic groups (Bell, 1995; Calmore, 1992; Crenshaw, Gotanda, Peller, & Thomas, 1995; Delgado, 1995a&b, 1996; Harris, 1994; Matsuda, Lawrence, Delgado, & Crenshaw, 1993).[1] A CRT of education has at least five themes that form its basic perspectives, research methods, and pedagogy:

1   **The Centrality and Intersectionality of Race and Racism:** A CRT of education recognizes the central role racism has played in the structuring of schools and schooling practices, and that racism intersects with other forms of subordination including sexism and classism. In this, a CRT acknowledges how notions of objectivity, neutrality, and meritocracy, as

well as curricular practices, such as tracking, teacher expectations, and intelligence testing, have historically been used to subordinate students of color.[2] Critical race theorists also take the position that racism has at least four dimensions: (1) it has micro and macro components; (2) it takes on institutional and individual forms; (3) it has conscious and unconscious elements; and (4) it has a cumulative impact on both the individual and group (Davis, 1989; Lawrence, 1987).

2   **The Challenge to Dominant Ideology:** CRT examines the system of education as part of a critique of societal inequality. In this, critical race educators challenge dominant social and cultural assumptions regarding culture and intelligence, language and capability, through research, pedagogy, and praxis. Critical race theorists argue that traditional claims of objectivity and meritocracy camouflage the self-interest, power, and privilege of dominant groups in U.S. society (Calmore, 1992).

3   **The Commitment to Social Justice:** A critical race framework is committed to social justice and offers a liberatory or transformative response to racial, gender, and class oppression (Matsuda, 1991). We envision a social justice research agenda that leads toward the elimination of racism, sexism, and poverty, and the empowering of underrepresented minority groups.

4   **The Centrality of Experiential Knowledge:** CRT recognizes that the experiential knowledge of women and men of color is legitimate, appropriate, and critical to understanding, analyzing, practicing, and teaching about racial subordination (Calmore, 1992). Just as "issues of experience, culture, and identity are not the subject of explicit legal reasoning" (Caldwell, 1995, p. 270), lived experiences of students of color are generally marginalized, if not silenced from educational discourse. Critical race educators can utilize methods such as: storytelling, narratives, chronicles, family history, scenarios, biographies, and parables to draw on the strength of the lived experiences students bring to the classroom (Bell, 1987; Delgado, 1989, 1995a&b, 1996; Olivas, 1990; Solorzano, 1998).

5   **The Interdisciplinary Perspective:** CRT challenges ahistoricism and the unidisciplinary focus of most traditional analyses and insists on analyzing race and racism by placing them in both an historical and contemporary context using interdisciplinary methods (Delgado, 1984, 1992; Garcia, 1995; Harris, 1994; Olivas, 1990). Critical race educators also look to such frameworks as Chicana/o, African American, Asian American, Native American, and Women's Studies in examining the educational experiences of students of color.

While not static or uniform, these five themes lead us toward an overall goal of a CRT in teacher education. This goal is to develop a pedagogy, curriculum, and research agenda that accounts for the role of race and racism in U.S. education and to work toward the elimination of racism as part of a larger goal of eliminating all forms of subordination in education.

We define a CRT in teacher education as a framework that can be used to theorize and examine the ways in which race and racism impact on the structures, processes, and discourses within a teacher education context. This framework challenges dominant ideology, which supports deficit notions about students of color. Utilizing the experiences of students of color, a CRT in teacher education also theorizes and examines that place where racism intersects with other forms of subordination such as sexism and classism. Critical race scholars in teacher education acknowledge that schools operate in contradictory ways with their potential to oppress and marginalize co-existing with their potential to emancipate and empower. CRT is conceived as a social justice project that attempts to link theory with practice, scholarship with teaching, and the academy with the community. CRT is transdisciplinary and draws on many other schools of progressive scholarship.[3]

A CRT in teacher education asks the following questions:

1   How do educational institutions function to maintain racism, sexism, and classism?

   • How do educational structures function to maintain racism, sexism, and classism?
   • How do educational processes function to maintain racism, sexism, and classism?
   • How do educational discourses function to maintain racism, sexism, and classism?

2   How do Students of Color resist racism, sexism, and classism in educational structures, processes, and discourses?
3   How can educational reforms help end racism, sexism, and classism?

Utilizing the five themes, our working definition, and related questions in CRT, we can begin to identify, analyze, and transform the use of racial stereotypes and deficit-based theories in education, which help maintain the subordination of students of color. We first define race, racism, and racial stereotypes, and then examine how racial stereotypes in the media and professional environments are based on deficit theoretical models and are used to justify certain teacher attitudes and behaviors toward students of color.

Race, racism, and racial stereotyping

In 1903, W.E.B. DuBois (1989) commented that "the problem of the 20th century is the problem of the color-line" (p. 29). When we examine popular and professional literature, and political debates around immigration, welfare, crime, and affirmative action, it appears that DuBois's prophecy has continued into the 21st century. In dealing with the issue of the "color-line" or race, history has shown that the United State has never been a "color-blind" society (Gotanda, 1991). The United States is very color conscious and color affects the way people view their separate and interrelated worlds (Dalton, 1987, 1995; Duster, 1993).

United States history reveals that race is a socially constructed category, created to differentiate racial groups, and to show the superiority or dominance of one race over another (Banks, 1995). Indeed, race can be viewed as an "objective" phenomenon until human beings provide the social meaning. The social meaning applied to race is based upon and justified by an ideology of racial superiority and white privilege. That ideology is called racism. Audre Lorde (1992) concisely defines racism as, "the belief in the inherent superiority of one race over all others and thereby the right to dominance" (p. 496). Manning Marable (1992) also defined racism as "a system of ignorance, exploitation, and power used to oppress

African-Americans, Latinos, Asians, Pacific Americans, American Indians and other people on the basis of ethnicity, culture, mannerisms, and color" (p. 5).

Embedded in Lorde and Marable's definitions of racism are at least three important points: (1) one group believes itself to be superior, (2) the group which believes itself to be superior has the power to carry out the racist behavior, and (3) racism effects multiple racial/ethnic groups. These two definitions take the position that racism is about institutional power, and people of color in the United States have never possessed this form of power. By merely having a "conversations about race," without talking about racism, we decontextualize those places where race and racism enters our lives in macro and micro ways (Solorzano, 1998).

Racial stereotyping and students of color

A critical race theory in teacher education seeks to identify, analyze, and transform subtle and overt forms of racism in education in order to transform society. Therefore, how does racism shape the education of Latina/o, African American, Asian, Pacific Islander, Native American, and other Students of Color differently than the education of White students?

To answer this question, we first define and examine racial stereotypes. Gordon Allport (1979) defines a stereotype as "an exaggerated belief associated with a category. Its function is to justify (rationalize) our conduct in relation to that category" (p. 191). This definition provides a valuable tool for teacher educators to examine how racial stereotypes function to justify certain attitudes and behaviors toward students of color.

Racial stereotypes in media and students of color

Figure 10.1 shows how racial and ethnic stereotypes can be placed into at least three general categories: (1) intelligence and educational stereotypes; (2) personality or character stereotypes; and (3) physical appearance stereotypes. Indeed, these racial stereotypes and related conduct toward Blacks, Chicanas/os, and Native Americans are often times interchangeable between the groups. The fact that Blacks, Chicanas/os, and Native Americans have been and are often still seen on television, film, and in print media as "dumb," "violent," "lazy," "irresponsible," or "dirty" may often be used to rationalize their subordinate position in society (Berkeley Art Center, 1982; Bonilla & Girling, 1973).

In educational settings, these stereotypic traits can be used to justify: (1) having low educational and occupational expectations for students of color, (2) placing students of color in separate schools and in separate classrooms within schools, (3) remediating or "dumbing down" the curriculum and pedagogy for students of color, and (4) expecting students of color to one day occupy lower status and levels of occupations. Too often, the social issues of welfare, crime, drugs, immigrants, and educational problems are given a racial face or are racialized through stereotypical media depictions of people of color (Omi & Winant, 1994).

Racial stereotypes in professional environments and students of color

Racial stereotypes often take on different forms at the professional level. Indeed, it would be unprofessional for teachers and teacher educators to describe students of color as "dumb," "dirty," or "lazy." Instead, some educators and scholars

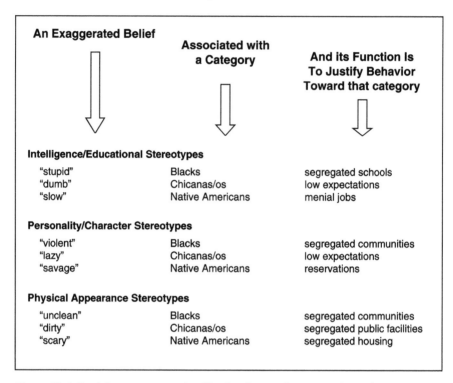

Figure 10.1 Racial stereotypes as justification for conduct toward people

might use different terminology, such as "uneducable," "lack hygiene," or "lack motivation." For example, around the turn of the century, Lewis Terman (1916), the major importer and translator of the Alfred Binet's intelligence, or IQ, test, commented that:

> high grade or border-line deficiency ... is very, very common among Spanish-Indian and Mexican families of the Southwest and also among Negroes. Their dullness seems to be racial, or at least inherent in the family stocks from which they come. ... Children of this group should be segregated into separate classes. ... They cannot master abstractions but they can often be made efficient workers. ... There is no possibility at the present of convincing society that they should not be allowed to reproduce, although from a eugenic point of view they constitute a grave problem because of their unusually prolific breeding. (pp. 91–92)

In the 1960s, Cecilia Heller (1966), in theorizing why Mexican Americans lack social mobility, stated:

> The kind of socialization that Mexican American children generally receive at home is not conducive to the development of the capacities needed for advancement in a dynamic industrialized society. This type of upbringing creates stumbling blocks to future advancement by stressing values that hinder mobility—family ties, honor, masculinity, and living in the present—and

by neglecting the values that are conducive to it—achievement, independence, and deferred gratification. (p. 34)

In addition, Heller stated that Mexican American "[p]arents, as a whole, neither impose standards of excellence for tasks performed by their children nor do they expect evidence of high achievement" (p. 37).

In the 1980s, Thomas Sowell (1981) claimed that "the goals and values of Mexican Americans have never centered on education" (p. 266) and that many Mexican Americans find the process of education "distasteful" (p. 267). Also, in the 1990s, former United States Secretary of Education Lauro Cavazos stated that Latino parents deserve much of the blame for the high dropout rate among their children because, "Hispanics have always valued education ... but somewhere along the line we've lost that. I really believe that, today, there is not that emphasis" (Snider, 1990, p. 1). Moreover, John Ogbu (1990) commented that, "involuntary minorities [Blacks and Chicanos] have not developed a widespread effort optimism or a strong cultural ethic of hard work and perseverance in the pursuit of education" (p. 53). Indeed, the first epigraph by John McWhorter in this essay offers a recent addition to this list of professional racial stereotypes.

Can these comments be interpreted as "professional" ways of stating that Blacks and Latinos are socially and culturally inferior to Whites? Can racial stereotypes, illustrated here in the media and professional settings, serve the purpose of rationalizing and keeping communities and students of color in poor and unequal conditions? These questions are important because the answers can theoretically guide the policy recommendations and educational reforms needed to solve educational inequities.

At least four general theoretical models are used to explain the lower educational attainment of minority students: (1) genetic determinist, (2) cultural determinist, (3) school determinist, and (4) societal determinist. Each model begins with a specific unit of analysis and draws upon particular concepts for explaining how and why students of color experience lower educational attainment compared to Whites. It is important to note that more specific models exist within these general theoretical frameworks, and these specific models may bridge two or more general frameworks. Figure 10.2 presents, in simplified form, each general model's underlying theoretical perspective, each model's attribution of responsibility for school failure, and each model's primary policy solutions.

Whether through media or professional venues, racial stereotyping blames unequal outcomes on the students of color themselves rather than on society and its institutions. Racial stereotypes find their theoretical foundations from two traditions of deficit thinking—genetic and cultural deficit models. The genetic determinist model reflects the position that the low educational attainment of minority students can be traced to deficiencies in their genetic structure (Jensen, 1969; Kamin, 1974; Terman, 1916). In this scenario, there are few social policy options—lacking genetic transformation or total neglect—to raise the educational attainment of minority students. While seemingly out of favor in educational research and policy circles, there is a resurgence in interest in the genetic model resulting from the works of Lloyd Dunn (1987; see Fernandez 1988), the Minnesota Twin Studies (Bouchard, Lykken, McGue, Segal, & Tellegen, 1990), Frederick Goodwin (see Breggin & Breggin, 1993), and Richard Herrnstein and Charles Murray (1994).

The second and more widely used model in this deficit tradition is the cultural deficit model. The cultural deficit model contends that minority cultural values, as

Theoretical Perspectives	Attribution of Responsibility	Primary Policy Solutions
Genetic Determinist— The minority fails because they are genetically inferior. Traces inequality to the minority genes.	The minority genetic makeup is responsible.	No solution is possible because nothing can be done to change the minority genetic makeup. Segregation or incarceration deemed most viable policy solutions.
Cultural Determinist— The minority fails because their culture is viewed as deficient. Traces inequality to minority culture.	The minority cultural values and related behaviors are responsible.	Acculturate minorities to the values and behaviors of the dominant group.
School Determinist— The minority fails because of the unequal conditions (e.g. structures and processes) at the schools they attend. Traces inequality to social institutions.	The unequal conditions at the schools that minorities attend are responsible.	Change the unequal conditions at the schools that minority students attend to that of majority students.
Societal Determinist— The minority fails because schools reinforce and reproduce societal inequalities. Traces inequality to the overall social system.	The socioeconomic structure is ultimately responsible. Institutions, such as schools, serve primarily to reinforce the unequal social structure.	Change the socioeconomic system to one that is more equitable, then social institutions, such as schools, will reflect that equality.

(*) Within these general theoretical categories are specific hypotheses that focus on specific constructs.

Figure 10.2 Theoretical perspectives on minority education inequality

Sources: Adapted from Alfred Alschuler, *School Discipline: A Socially Literate Solution* (New York: McGraw-Hill, 1980); and Stanley Sue & Amado Padilla, "Ethnic Minority Issues in the United States: Challenges for the Educational System," in California State Department of Education, *Beyond Language: Social and Cultural Factors in Schooling Language Minority Students* (Los Angeles, CA: Evaluation, Dissemination and Assessment Center, California State University, Los Angeles, 1986).

transmitted through the family, are dysfunctional, and therefore cause low educational and occupational attainment. The model explains that deficient cultural values include: present versus future time orientation, immediate instead of deferred gratification, an emphasis on cooperation rather than competition, and placing less value on education and upward mobility (see Carter & Segura, 1979). These cultural deficit models also name the internal social structure of families of color as deficient. They cite that such deficiency is caused by large, disorganized, female-headed families; Spanish or non-standard English spoken in the home; and patriarchal or matriarchal family structures. Cultural deficiency models argue that since parents of color fail to assimilate and embrace the educational values of the dominant group, and continue to transmit or socialize their children with values that inhibit educational mobility, then they are to blame if low educational attainment continues into succeeding generations.

This cultural deficit discourse about people of color has become the "norm" in social scientific research, despite insufficient empirical evidence to support it (Kretovics & Nussel, 1994; Persell, 1977; Solorzano, 1991, 1992a&b; Solorzano & Solorzano, 1995; Valencia, 1998; Valencia & Solorzano, 1998). In practice, the deficit model is applied in the classroom, and to students of color, by teachers who are professionally trained in colleges, and specifically in teacher education programs that utilize an individualistic and cultural deficit explanation of low minority educational attainment (Kretovics & Nussel, 1994; Persell, 1977). Often, schools of education seek to solve the issues emerging from this model through a teacher training focus on the acculturation of minority students to the values and behaviors of the culturally dominant group, while criticizing, downplaying, or ignoring the values and behaviors of marginalized minority cultures.

Claims that the cultural deficit model is no longer widely used seem premature. In fact, the 1980s and 1990s have seen a revival of the cultural deficit model, under the rubric of the cultural "underclass" (Baca Zinn, 1989; Valencia & Solorzano, 1998). Indeed, Joseph Kretovics and Edward Nussel (1994) have stated, "[a]t the highest levels of educational policy, we have moved from deficiency theory to theories of difference, back to deficiency theory" (p. x). The cultural deficit model, with its related racial stereotypes in the media and in professional environments, remains the hidden theory of choice at many elementary and secondary schools, teacher education departments, professional meetings, and settings where the topic of minority educational inequality is discussed (Chavez, 1992; McWhorter, 2000).

It is important to note that unconscious and subtle forms of racial stereotyping are pervasive in the public and private discourse and are usually not socially condoned (Delgado & Stefancic, 1992; Lawrence, 1987; Pierce, 1974, 1978). Harlon Dalton (1995) has argued that it is important for Whites "to conceive of themselves as members of a race and to recognize the advantages that attach to simply having white skin" (p. 6). Andrew Hacker (1992) has raised the question: Can we place a price on being White in the United States? (see pp. 31–32).

However, Dalton (1995) goes on to state that most Whites do not see themselves in racial terms because being White "is like the tick of a familiar clock, part of the easily tuned-out background noise" (p. 6). In the teacher education classroom, the racial/ethnic experiences of Whites can be an important part of the discussion and analysis of the advantages and privileges of being White in the United States (see Allen, 1993; Dalton, 1995; Hacker, 1992; Halewood, 1995; Scheurich, 1993a&b; Sleeter, 1993; Sleeter, 1994).

Occasionally, people of color get a glimpse into this world of subtle and unconscious racism and racial stereotyping (Lawrence, 1987). For instance, people of color often hear the following remarks:

"When I talk about those Blacks, I really wasn't talking about you."

"You're not like the rest of them. You're different."

"I don't think of you as a Mexican."

"You speak such good English."

"Aren't all Asians good in math?"

"If only there were more of them like you."

"All Native Americans are such spiritual people."

"But you speak without an accent."

Taken individually, these comments are viewed by most people of color as insults. However, many Whites see these statements differently and respond to people of color with such retorts as "you're being too sensitive about race," or "why does everything have to go back to race?" In fact, Charles Lawrence (1987) has commented that through "selective perception, whites are unlikely to hear many of the inadvertent racial slights that are made in their presence" (pp. 340–341). Similarly, Richard Delgado (1988) has stated that "White people rarely see acts of blatant racism, while minority people experience them all the time" (p. 407).

In dealing with racial stereotypes in our teacher education classrooms, we need to hear about, discuss, and analyze those racial experiences that People of Color and Whites encounter in their public and private worlds. Not only do we need to discuss overt or blatant racial stereotypes, attitudes, and behaviors, but we also need to listen, understand, and analyze racial microaggressions: those "subtle, stunning, often automatic, and non-verbal exchanges which are 'put downs' of blacks by offenders" (Pierce, Carew, Pierce-Gonzalez, & Wills, 1978, p. 66; Solorzano, 1998). Richard Delgado and Jean Stefancic (1992) describe how:

> Racism's victims become sensitized to its subtle nuances and codewords—the body language, averted gazes, exasperated looks, terms such as "you people," "innocent whites," "highly qualified black," "articulate" and so on—that, whether intended or not, convey racially charged meanings. (p. 1283)

One might add other coded language to this list such as "quotas," "preferences," "affirmative action," "reverse discrimination," and "illegal aliens" (Williams, 1991). In our teacher education classrooms, we need to closely and thoroughly examine the cumulative effect of these racial microaggressions on both minority and non-minority students and teachers (Solorzano, 1998; Solorzano & Villalpando, 1998; Solorzano & Yosso, 2000; Yosso, 2000).

Conclusion

Critical race theory in teacher education provides a framework to challenge genetic and cultural deficit theories. In fact, using the five themes of CRT, we can engage in the following four exercises to better understand and challenge race, racism, and racial stereotypes in our classrooms.

(1) Define, analyze, and give examples for the concepts of race, racism, and racial stereotypes. Engaging in a discussion, analysis, and debate around these concepts is a critical first step. Students can examine and give examples of racism in its institutional and individual forms, its macro and micro forms, conscious and unconscious elements, and its cumulative effects on both minority and non-minority students.

(2) Identify racial stereotypes in film, television, and print forms of media, which are used to justify attitudes and behavior toward students of color. For example, students can conduct a comparative analysis of three high school genre

films, *Stand and Deliver* (1988), *Lean on Me* (1989), and *Dangerous Minds* (1995), looking for the quantity and quality of Black and Latina/o characters. A discussion of these images can lead to the development of alternative story lines and scripts for the portrayal of students of color in film. This same content analysis and alternative portrayals can be performed on television programs and news broadcasts.

Documentary films on the historical and contemporary condition of the Black and Chicano communities can provide an invaluable resource for developing an anti-racist and anti-sexist curriculum. For instance, such Public Broadcasting Service film series as the *Eyes on the Prize I: America's Civil Rights Years* (1986), *Eyes on the Prize II: America at the Racial Crossroads* (1990), and *Chicano: History of the Mexican American Civil Rights Movement* (1996) can serve as an important filmic base to challenge some of the racial and gender stereotypes related to Communities of Color. This visual curriculum can also be supplemented by the work of other artists who use their talents to challenge racial stereotypes and deficit discourse, as evidenced in the CD *Music for The Native Americans* by Robbie Robertson and The Red Road Ensemble (1994) and the comedy CD *Alien Nation* by George Lopez (1996).

(3) Identify racial stereotypes in professional settings, show their relationship to media stereotypes, and then examine how both are used to justify the unequal treatment of students of color. For example, using the current state mandated language arts and social science elementary and secondary textbooks, students can conduct a content analysis of the quantity and quality of portrayals of Blacks, Chicanas/os, Native Americans, and Asian Americans (Council on Interracial Books for Children, 1977). As a follow-up, students can use contemporary and historical ethnic studies texts about People of Color to re-create alternative depictions to those found in the state mandated textbooks.

(4) Find examples within and about communities of color that challenge and transform racial stereotypes. In many communities of color, students can find and analyze street murals that artistically portray the positive and negative conditions in these communities. Also, in many of these communities, elders keep some of the history and traditions of the community alive. Both street murals and elders can be invaluable resources to dispel the myths of an "uneducated" minority community. Additionally, information gathered by interviewing day laborers, who congregate in the mornings on certain street corners, can challenge the stereotype of the "lazy" minority worker (Valenzuela, 1999). Moreover, rich sources of material include individual and family oral and pictorial histories, institutional and community studies, and artistic and cultural artifacts and ideologies, which can challenge popular and professional racial stereotypes.

Racial stereotypes, whether in popular or professional literature, continue to impact our students and communities. As educators, we must critically analyze their source, rationale, and impact on the people who perpetuate the stereotyping and on those being stereotyped. The discussion of race, racism, and racial stereotypes must be a continuing part of our teacher education discourse. In our classrooms, we must seek out media, professional, and artistic images that depict people of color in multiple contexts. As educators, we need to identify the resources and strengths of students of color and place them at the center of our research, curriculum, and teaching.

The five elements of critical race theory provide a framework for teacher education faculty and students to create, recreate, and recover knowledge and art in communities of color. In turn, CRT can empower teachers and students to better understand and challenge racially stereotypical portrayals. CRT challenges us to look for the many strengths within students and communities of color in order to combat and eliminate negative racial stereotypes.

Notes

1   See Richard Delgado and Jean Stefancic (1993, 1994) for two comprehensive annotated bibliographies on critical race theory.
2   For this essay, students and people of color are defined as those persons of African American, Chicana/o, Asian American, and Native American ancestry. We sometimes use this term synonymously with minority. Chicanas and Chicanos are defined as female and male persons of Mexican-origin living in the United States. Latinas and Latinos are persons of Latin American origin living in the United States.
3   Our definition of Critical Race Theory is adapted from the LatCrit Primer (1999).

References

Allen, W. (1993). A Response to a "White Discourse on White Racism." *Educational Researcher*, 22, 11–13.

Allport, G. (1979). *The Nature of Prejudice. 25th Anniversary Edition*. Reading, MA: Addison-Wesley.

Baca Zinn, M. (1989). Family, Race, and Poverty in the Eighties. *Signs: Journal of Woman in Culture and Society*, 14, 856–874.

Banks, J. (1995). The Historical Reconstruction of Knowledge about Race: Implications for Transformative Teaching. *Educational Researcher*, 24, 15–25.

Bell, D. (1987). *And We Will Not Be Saved: The Elusive Quest for Racial Justice*. New York: Basic Books.

Bell, D. (1992). *Faces at the Bottom of the Well: The Permanence of Racism*. New York: Basic Books.

Bell, D. (1995). Who's Afraid of Critical Race Theory? *University of Illinois Law Review*, 1995, 893–910.

Berkeley Art Center. (1982). *Ethnic Notions: Black Images in the White Mind*. Berkeley, CA: Berkeley Art Center (There is also an accompanying film/video of the same name).

Bonilla, F. & Girling, R. (Eds.). (1973). *Structures of Dependency*. Stanford, CA: Stanford Institute of Politics.

Bouchard, T., Lykken, D., McGue, M., Segal, N., & Tellegen, A. (1990). Sources of Human Psychological Differences: The Minnesota Study of Twins Reared Apart. *Science*, 250, 223–250.

Breggin, P. & Breggin, G. (1993). The Federal Violence Initiative: Threats to Black Children (and Others). *Psych Discourse*, 24, 8–11.

Caldwell, P. (1995). A Hair Piece: Perspectives on the Intersection of Race and Gender. In R. Delgado (Ed.). *Critical Race Theory: The Cutting Edge* (pp. 267–277). Philadelphia, PA: Temple University Press.

Calmore, J. (1992). Critical Race Theory, Archie Shepp, and Fire Music: Securing an Authentic Intellectual Life in a Multicultural World. *Southern California Law Review*, 65, 2129–2231.

Carter, T. & Segura, R. (1979). *The Mexican Americans in School: A Decade of Change*. New York: College Entrance Examination Board.

Chavez, Linda. (1992). *Out of the Barrio: Toward a New Politics of Hispanic Assimilation*. New York: Basic Books.

Crenshaw, K., Gotanda, N., Peller, G., & Thomas, K. (Eds.). (1995). *Critical Race Theory: The Key Writings That Formed the Movement*. New York: The New Press.

Council on Interracial Books for Children. (1977). *Stereotypes, Distortions and Omissions in U.S. History Textbooks*. New York: Council on Interracial Books for Children.

Dalton, H. (1987). The Clouded Prism. *Harvard Civil Rights-Civil Liberties Law Review*, 22, 435–447.

Dalton, H. (1995). *Racial Healing: Confronting the Fear Between Blacks and Whites*. New York: Doubleday.

Davis, P. (1989). Law as Microaggression. *Yale Law Journal*, 98, 1559–1577.

Delgado, R. (1984). The Imperial Scholar: Reflections on a Review of Civil Rights Literature. *University of Pennsylvania Law Review*, 132, 561–578.

Delgado, R. (1988). Critical Legal Studies and the Realities of Race: Does the Fundamental Contradiction Have a Corollary? *Harvard Civil Rights-Civil Liberties Law Review*, 23, 407–413.

Delgado, R. (1989). Storytelling for Oppositionists and Others: A Plea for Narrative. *Michigan Law Review*, 87, 2411–2441.

Delgado, R. (1992). The Imperial Scholar Revisited: How to Marginalize Outsider Writing, Ten Years Later. *University of Pennsylvania Law Review*, 140, 1349–1372.

Delgado, R. (1995a). *The Rodrigo Chronicles: Conversations About America and Race*. New York: New York University Press.

Delgado, R. (Ed.). (1995b). *Critical Race Theory: The Cutting Edge*. Philadelphia, PA: Temple University Press.

Delgado, R. (1996). *The Coming Race War?: and Other Apocalyptic Tales of American After Affirmative Action and Welfare*. New York: New York University Press.

Delgado, R. & Stefancic, J. (1992). Images of the Outsider in American Law and Culture: Can Free Expression Remedy Systemic Social Ills? *Cornell Law Review*, 77, 1258–1297.

Delgado, R. & Stefancic, J. (1993). Critical Race Theory: An Annotated Bibliography. *Virginia Law Review*, 79, 461–516.

Delgado, R. & Stefancic, J. (1994). Critical Race Theory: An Annotated Bibliography 1993, A Year of Transition. *University of Colorado Law Review*, 66, 159–193.

DuBois, W.E.B. (1989). *The Soul of Black Folks*. New York: Bantam. (Originally published in 1903).

Dunn, L. (1987). *Bilingual Hispanic Children on the Mainland: A Review of Research on their Cognitive, Linguistic, and Scholastic Development*. Circle Pines, MN: American Guidance Service.

Duster, T. (1993). The Diversity of California at Berkeley: An Emerging Reformulation of "Competence" in an Increasingly Multicultural World. In B. Thompson and S. Tyagi, *Beyond a Dream Deferred: Multicultural Education and the Politics of Excellence* (pp. 231–255). Minneapolis, MN: University of Minnesota Press.

Fernandez, R. (Ed.). (1988). Special Issue, Achievement Testing: Science vs Ideology (Response to Lloyd Dunn). *Hispanic Journal of Behavioral Sciences*, 10, 179–323.

Garcia, R. (1995). Critical Race Theory and Proposition 187: The Racial Politics of Immigration Law. *Chicano-Latino Law Review*, 17, 118–148.

George, L. (2000, October 17). Stirring Up a Rage in Black America. *Los Angeles Times*, E1, E3.

Gotanda, N. (1991). A Critique of "Our Constitution is Color-Blind". *Stanford Law Review*, 44, 1–68.

Hacker, A. (1992). *Two Nations: Black and White, Separate, Hostile, Unequal*. New York: Ballantine.

Halewood, P. (1995). White Men Can't Jump: Critical Epistemologies, and the Praxis of Legal Scholarship. *Yale Journal of Law and Feminism*, 7, 1–36.

Harris, A. (1994). Forward: The Jurisprudence of Reconstruction. *California Law Review*, 82, 741–785.

Heller, C. (1966). *Mexican American Youth*. New York: Random House.

Herrnstein, R. & Murray, C. (1994). *The Bell Curve: Intelligence and Class Structure in American Life*. New York: Free Press.

Jensen, A. (1969). How Much Can We Boost I.Q. and Scholastic Achievement? *Harvard Educational Review*, 39, 1–123.

Kamin, L. (1974). *The Science and Politics of I.Q.* New York: John Wiley & Sons.

Kretovics, J. & Nussel, E. (Eds.). (1994). *Transforming Urban Education*. Boston, MA: Allyn & Bacon.

LatCrit Primer. (1999). Fact Sheet: LatCrit. Presented to the 4th Annual LatCrit Conference, "Rotating Centers, Expanding Frontiers: LatCrit Theory and Marginal

Intersection." Stanford Sierra Conference Center, Lake Tahoe, NV, April 29–May 5, 1999.

Lawrence, C. (1987). The Id, the Ego, and Equal Protection: Reckoning with Unconscious Racism. *Stanford Law Review*, 39, 317–388.

Lopez, G. (1996). CD. *Alien Nation*. Lake Village, CA: Uproar Entertainment.

Lorde, A. (1992). Age, Race, Class, and Sex: Women Redefining Difference. In M. Andersen & P. Hill Collins, *Race, Class, and Gender: An Anthology* (pp. 495–502). Belmont, CA: Wadsworth.

Marable, M. (1992). *Black America*. Westfield, NJ: Open Media.

Matsuda, M. (1991). Voices of America: Accent, Antidiscrimination Law, and a Jurisprudence for the Last Reconstruction. *Yale Law Journal*, 100, 1329–1407.

Matsuda, M., Lawrence, C., Delgado, R., & Crenshaw, K. (1993). *Words That Wound: Critical Race Theory, Assaultive Speech, and the First Amendment*. Boulder, CO: Westview Press.

McWhorter, J. (2000). *Losing the Race: Self-Sabotage in Black America*. New York: Free Press.

Ogbu, J. (1990). Minority Education in Comparative Perspective. *Journal of Negro Education*, 59, 45–57.

Olivas, M. (1990). The Chronicles, My Grandfather's Stories, and Immigration Law: The Slave Traders Chronicle as Racial History. *Saint Louis University Law Journal*, 34, 425–441.

Omi, M. & Winant, H. (1994). *Racial Formation in the United States: From the 1960s to the 1990s*. Second Edition. New York: Routledge.

Persell, C. (1977). *Education and Inequality: The Roots and Results of Stratification in America's Schools*. New York: Free Press.

Pierce, C. (1974). Psychiatric Problems of the Black Minority. In S. Arieti (Ed.), *American Handbook of Psychiatry* (pp. 512–523). New York: Basic Books.

Pierce, C., Carew, J., Pierce-Gonzalez, D., & Wills, D. (1978). An Experiment in Racism: TV Commercials. In C. Pierce (Ed.), *Television and Education* (pp. 62–88). Beverly Hills, CA: Sage.

Robertson, R. & The Red Road Ensemble. (1994). CD. *Music for The Native Americans*. Hollywood, CA: Capitol Records.

Scheurich, J. (1993a). Toward a White Discourse on White Racism. *Educational Researcher*, 22, 5–10.

Scheurich, J. (1993b). A Difficult, Confusing, Painful Problem That Requires Many Voices, Many Perspectives. *Educational Researcher*, 22, 15–16.

Sleeter, C. (1993). Advancing a White Discourse: A Response to Scheurich. *Educational Researcher*, 22, 13–15.

Sleeter, C. (1994, Spring). White Racism. *Multicultural Education*, pp. 5–8, 39.

Snider, W. (1990, April 18). Outcry Follows Cavazos Comments on the Values of Hispanic Parents. *Education Week*, p. 1.

Solorzano, D. (1991). Mobility Aspirations Among Racial Minorities, Controlling For SES. *Sociology and Social Research*, 75, 182–188.

Solorzano, D. (1992a). An Exploratory Analysis of the Effect of Race, Class, and Gender on Student and Parent Mobility Aspirations. *Journal of Negro Education*, 61, 30–44.

Solorzano, D. (1992b). Chicano Mobility Aspirations: A Theoretical and Empirical Note. *Latino Studies Journal*, 3, 48–66.

Solorzano, D. (1998). Critical Race Theory, Racial and Gender Microaggressions, and the Experiences of Chicana and Chicano Scholars. *International Journal of Qualitative Studies in Education*, 11, 121–136.

Solorzano, D. & Solorzano, R. (1995). The Chicano Educational Experience: A Proposed Framework For Effective Schools in Chicano Communities. *Educational Policy*, 9, 293–314.

Solorzano, D. & Villapando, O. (1998). Critical Race Theory: Marginality and the Experiences of Students of Color in Higher Education. In C. Torres & T. Mitchell (Eds.), *Sociology of Education: Emerging Perspectives* (pp. 211–224). Albany, NY: State University of New York Press.

Solorzano, D. & Yosso, T. (2000). Toward a Critical Race Theory of Chicana and Chicano

Education. In Tejeda, C., Martinez, C., & Leonardo, Z. (Eds.), *Charting New Terrains of Chicana(o)/Latina(o) Education* (pp. 35–65). Cresskill, NJ: Hampton Press.

Sowell, T. (1981). *Ethnic America: A History*. New York: Basic Books.

Terman, L. (1916). *The Measurement of Intelligence*. Boston, MA: Houghton Mifflin.

Valencia, R. (Ed.). (1998). *The Evolution of Deficit Thinking in Educational Thought and Practice*. Bristol, PA: Taylor & Francis.

Valencia, R. & Solorzano, D. (1998). Contemporary Deficit Thinking. In R. Valencia (Ed.), *The Evolution of Deficit Thinking in Educational Thought and Practice*. Bristol, PA: Taylor & Francis.

Valenzuela, A. (1999). *Day Laborers in Southern California: Preliminary Findings from the Day Labor Survey*. Los Angeles, CA: Center for the Study of Urban Poverty, University of California, Los Angeles.

Williams, P. (1991). *The Alchemy of Race and Rights: Diary of a Law Professor*. Cambridge, MA: Harvard University Press.

Yosso, T. (2000). A Critical Race and LatCrit Approach to Media Literacy: Chicana/o Resistance to Visual Microagressions. Unpublished doctoral dissertation, University of California, Los Angeles.

PART 3

MULTICULTURAL EDUCATION: 1980s

CHAPTER 11

THE OTHER SIDE OF THE HIDDEN CURRICULUM (1980)

Correspondence theories and the labor process

Michael W. Apple

Beyond simple reproduction

The laws of physics determine the shape any object will take in an ordinary mirror. The image may be distorted by imperfections in the glass, but by and large, what you see is what you get. The internal composition of the mirror reproduces the external object standing before it. This set of laws may be good for thinking about optics, but it is questionable whether it is adequate for thinking about schools. We, especially many of us on the left side of the political spectrum, tend to act as if it is adequate, however. We see schools as a mirror of society, especially in the school's hidden curriculum. A "society" needs docile workers; schools, through their social relations and covert teaching, roughly guarantee the production of such docility. Obedient workers in the labor market are mirrored in the "marketplace of ideas" in the school. As I shall try to show in this article, though, such mirror image analogies are a bit too simple *both* in the school and in the supposedly mirrored external object, the workplace.

The assumptions behind most recent analyses of the hidden curriculum can generally be grouped around a theory of correspondence. Broadly, correspondence theories simply that there are specific characteristics, behavioral traits, skills, and dispositions that an economy requires of its workers. These economic needs are so powerful as to "determine"[1] what goes on in other sectors of a society, particularly the school. Thus, if we look at our educational institutions, we should expect to find that the tacit things taught to students roughly mirror the personality and dispositional traits that these students will "require" later on when they join the labor market.

One of the most recent explications of this kind of analysis is, of course, found in Bowles and Gintis's *Schooling in Capitalist America*. Here the hidden curriculum is differentiated by economic class and by one's expected economic trajectory. The arguments presented by Bowles and Gintis have led a number of investigators to argue that his differential hidden curriculum can be seen in the fact that lower-class students are taught punctuality, neatness, respect for authority, and other elements of habit formation. The students of more advanced classes are taught intellectual openmindedness, problem solving, flexibility, and so on—skills and dispositions that will enable them to function as managers and professionals, not as unskilled or semiskilled laborers. Though the socioeconomic causes of this differentiated hidden curriculum are seen as quite complex, still the fundamental role of the school is seen as the rough reproduction of the division of labor outside of it. The school is a determined institution.

Now, social phenomenologists, philosophers of science, critical social theorists, and others have maintained that how we act on the world, be it the educational, economic, or political world, is in part determined by the way we perceive it. While this point can be so general as to be relatively inconsequential, it is important that the ties between perception and action not be ignored. This is especially true in any serious analysis of schooling that wishes to go beyond correspondence theories. Correspondence theories tend to "cause" us to see the school only in reproductive terms. Their logic sees the institution as acting only to reproduce a social order. Both the form and content of the formal corpus of school knowledge and the hidden curriculum help create the conditions for the cultural and economic reproduction of class relations in our society.

There certainly is evidence to support this kind of assertion, some of which I have contributed myself (Bernstein, 1977; Karabel and Halsey, 1977; Bourdieu and Passeron, 1977; Tapper and Salter, 1978; Apple, 1979a). However, by seeing the school in only reproductive terms, in essence as a passive function of an external unequal social order, it is hard to generate any serious educational action whatsoever. For if schools are *wholly* determined and can do no more than mirror economic relations outside of them, then nothing can be done within the educational sphere. This is pessimistic, of course, and is an argument to which I shall return later. Yet there is something besides its pessimistic perspective that we must point to. It is, in some very important ways, also inadequate as a theory of the relationship both among all social institutions and between the school and other powerful socioeconomic forces. For the concept of reproduction does not exhaust the nexus of relationships that ties institutions and people to each other. It may be an important element; however, there will be constitutive aspects of day-to-day life that can best be described not as mirror images of what larger economic and social forces require, but as genuinely contradictory. Thus, by focusing on schools only as reproductive institutions, we may miss the dynamic interplay between education and an economy and be in danger of reducing the complexity of this relationship to a bare parody of what actually exists at the level of practice.

In order to go beyond this, we need to think more clearly about the range of ways institutions and people may be "determined." What "modes of determination" actually exist, modes which go beyond "mere" reproduction? While these are actually heuristic devices which might enable us to see how the institutions of a society are dialectically interrelated, we can distinguish at least six modes of determination which represent the structural constraints and contradictions present in a given society. These include: structural limitations, selection, reproduction–nonreproduction, limits of functional compatibility, transformation, and mediation.[2] Given this set of relationships, ones that enable us to go well beyond mirror image analogies, in this essay I shall take two of these— mediation and transformation—and use them to begin to unpack some of the possible complexities associated with the hidden curriculum.

Elsewhere, I have argued that the traditional literature on the hidden curriculum has been guided by an overly restricted view of socialization (Apple, 1979c). It has pictured not just schools, but students as well, as passive recipients of the norms and values embodied in the curricular and social environment of the school. The conceptual weaknesses of this approach (Is a one-way perspective on socialization an adequate metaphor for illuminating what happens in schools?) make its continued dominance questionable. Yet just as important is an empirical issue. Is it accurate? Do students always internalize these norms and dispositions unquestioningly? There is evidence to suggest that not all students simply "take in" this hidden curriculum; that students often creatively act to control their school environments; and that, at least for certain segments of the working class, they in fact expressly *reject* the norms of obedience, respect for authority, and so on (Willis, 1977; Mehan, 1978; Mehan, in press). In essence these norms are mediated by the day-to-day life of schools and, at least in part, transformed by the activity of many working-class students.

For example, as Paul Williams has documented in his ethnography of working-class students in an urban high school, many students reject the hidden curriculum. They spend their days learning how to "work the system," to get out of classes, to gain some measure of control over their time and activity in schools (Willis, 1977). At the same time, however, as Willis also shows, their actions are contradictory. For while the students react against the overt and hidden curriculum of the school, they also reproduce in subtle ways the ideological distinctions (e.g., that between mental and manual labor) that lie at the heart of our economy (Braverman, 1974). Thus, at least for these high school students, two things are going on. They are both reproducing the ideological forms that are "required" in the workplace (by rejecting the mental labor of the school and glorifying physicality) *and* learning skills and values about working the system to give them some semblance of real power in the very same workplace. Because of this complexity, obviously, no simple model of reproduction can fully describe what is going on. Any analysis that wishes to be complete must account for the elements of situations like these that do not "merely" reproduce themselves, that mediate and transform social pressures, tensions, and contradictions.

The hidden curriculum and the norms of the workplace

The status of theories of the hidden curriculum does not only depend on the accuracy of their perception of what actually occurs in classrooms. There is another end to the rope which binds schools to outside agencies. Here I am talking about the workplace itself. For one could describe the reality of what is taught to students with exceptional clarity and still be wrong about the actual effects this hidden teaching has, if the norms and values which organize and guide the day-to-day subjective lives of workers are *not the same* as those found in schools.

In the rest of this essay, hence, I want to give a portion of the other side of this picture. I want to claim that the hidden curriculum literature, because of its overly deterministic model of socialization and its exclusive focus on reproduction to the exclusion of other things that may be happening, has a tendency to portray workers as something like automatons who are *wholly* controlled by the modes of production and ideological forms of our society. In more theoretical terms, agents exist (as abstract social roles), but they have no agency. In a real sense, then, structures exist, actors do not (Poulantzas, 1975; Bridges, 1974).

I also want to claim something else. I want to argue that such overly deterministic and economistic accounts of the hidden curriculum are themselves elements of the subtle reproduction, at an ideological level, of perspectives required for the legitimation of inequality. What I mean to say is simply this. The analyses recently produced by a number of leftist scholars and educators are themselves reproductions of the ideological vision of corporate domination. By seeing schools as total reflections of an unequal "labor market," a market where workers simply do what they are told and passively acquiesce to the norms and authority relations of the workplace, these analyses accept as empirically accurate the ideology of management.

In order to unpack these issues, we shall have to examine the labor process itself. A good many of the recent writings on the relationship between the hidden curriculum and the labor process have been strongly influenced by work such as Harry Braverman's exceptionally important historical investigation of the growth of corporate procedures for ensuring management control of the production process (Braverman, 1974).

Braverman makes a powerful case for the relentless penetration of corporate logic into the organization and control of day-to-day life in the workplace. In his portrayal, workers are continually deskilled (and, of course, some are "reskilled"). The skills they once had—skills of planning, of understanding and acting on an entire phase of production—are ultimately taken from them by management and housed elsewhere in a planning department controlled by management (Montgomery, 1976). In order for corporate accumulation to proceed, planning must be separated from execution, mental labor separated from manual labor, and this separation needs to be institutionalized in a systematic and formal manner. The archetypal example of this is, of course, Taylorism and its many variants. In plain words, management plans, workers merely execute. Thus, a major organizing principle of the workplace must be "taking the managers' brains from under the workman's cap." (Burawoy, 1979, p. 5).

This kind of analysis is a major contribution, not the least in its "demystification" of a number of assumptions held by many educators, policy analysts, and others. In particular, it serves to raise serious questions about our assumption that there is a widespread historical tendency toward increasing the skill level in industrial occupations throughout our economy. It is just as correct, Braverman maintains, to see the opposite of this. One can see the corporate expropriation of skill and knowledge, the rationalization of the workplace, and the increasing centralization of control of work so that all important decisions are made away from the point of production (Burawoy, 1979, p. 89).

Braverman also sees something else, though, to complete this story. As the process of deskilling—or what can be called the degradation of work—proceeds, workers also continuously lose power. While it is never totally successful, as corporate logic and power enter ever more aspects of their lives and institutions, workers become appendages to the production process. They are ultimately confronted by the uses of Taylorism and scientific management, by human relations management techniques, or finally by the threat of authority. In the face of all this, workers can do little. Caught in management's web, they are relatively passive, obedient, and hardworking. The cash nexus replaces craft and worker control.

While Braverman does not expressly point to this, the differentiated hidden curriculum in school has served to prepare them well, for if this is what the inexorable logic of corporate control is like, then we should expect that workers will need particular norms and dispositions to function within a hierarchical labor market. They will need habits that contribute to the smooth and rational flow of production. They will need to acquiesce to "expert" authority. They will not need collective commitment, a sense of craft, creativity, or control.

However, just as there are serious weaknesses in looking at schools in only reproductive terms (and thereby missing the possible ways day-to-day life and the internal history of schools mediate and often provide the possibility for some students to act against powerful social messages), so too can this view, so powerfully put by Braverman, cause us to neglect similar things that may occur in the workplace. Let us look at this much more closely.

What do we find at the level of execution, on the shop floor itself? Does the inexorable logic of capital call forth the lessons learned (or at least taught) in the hidden curriculum in school? Here, an examination of the separation of conception or planning from execution may be helpful. Recent research on the history of the relations between management and labor, especially of Taylorism, paints a somewhat different picture than Braverman does. It is becoming increasingly clear that what is missing in this account is the actual response of workers to these expected norms and organizational strategies and their ability to resist them. This general point is clearly documented by Burawoy (1979).

> It is one thing for management to appropriate knowledge, it is another thing to monopolize it. Braverman himself says "... since the workers are not destroyed as human beings but are simply utilized in inhuman ways, their critical intelligent, conceptual faculties, no matter how deadened or diminished, always remain in some degree a threat to capital."
>
> Rather than a separation of conception and execution, we find a separation of workers' conception and management's conception, of workers' knowledge and management's knowledge. The attempt to enforce Taylorism leads workers to recreate the unity of conception and execution but in opposition to management rulings. Workers show much ingenuity in defeating and outwitting the agents of scientific management before, during and after the "appropriation of knowledge." In any shop there are "official" or "management approved" ways of performing tasks and there is the workers' lore devised and revised in response to any management offensive. (pp. 33–34)

In essence, study after study has confirmed the fact that a large proportion of working adults have been able to continue their own collective setting of informal production norms and their ability to "defy" the supervisor and the "expert" (Burawoy, 1979, p. 34). In fact, one of the major results of the attempts to totally separate conception from execution and to emphasize worker compliance and obedience to management in the pursuit of management's expanding production goals was exactly the opposite of what managers intended. Rather than always creating a "compliant workforce," it quite often *promoted* resistance, conflict, and struggle. It heightened collective action by workers at the point of production and in so doing also often undermined both management control and the norms that were "required" in the work place (Burawoy, 1979, p. 40).[3]

Partial support for my claims here—that workers at a variety of levels often subtly resist, that they are not as truly and fully socialized to be obedient operatives as correspondence theories would suggest—can be found in the literature on bureaucratic control. This is summarized in a recent investigation of the growth of bureaucratic mechanisms in the workplace by Daniel Clawson. He argues, after a thorough review of research on the topic, that the rapid growth of bureaucratic controls is evidence of the struggle by blue- and white-collar workers. For if all workers could be counted upon to be obedient and respect authority, if they continued to work as hard as they could, if they didn't "take materials that didn't belong to them," and if they always followed what management wanted them to do, then the enormous cost of bureaucratic and hierarchical supervision and control would not have to be paid (Clawson, 1978, pp. 45–46).[4]

While there is clearly a danger in overstating this case, it is largely confirmed by other investigators. For example, a number of writers argue that not only is the growing bureaucratization of the workplace a response to workers' attempts to maintain some serious element of control, but bureaucratic control has itself often engendered even more conflict.

Richard Edwards (1978) makes this point rather well.

> Thus bureaucratic control has created among American workers vast discontent, dissatisfaction, resentment, frustration, and boredom with their work. We do not need to recount here the many studies measuring alienation: the famous HEW-commissioned report, *Work in America*, among other summaries, has already done that. It argued, for example, that the best index of job satisfaction or dissatisfaction is a worker's response to the question: "What type of work would you try to get into if you could start all over again?" A majority of both blue and white-collar workers—and an increasing proportion of them over time—indicated that they would choose some different type of work. This overall result is consistent with a very large literature on the topic. Rising dissatisfaction and alienation among workers, made exigent by their greater job security and expectations of continuing employment with one enterprise, directly create problems for employers (most prominently reduced productivity) (p. 123).

This very conflict has forced employers to introduce plans for job enrichment, job enlargement, worker self-management, worker-employer comanagement, and so on. Yet we should not forget that these very plans may ultimately threaten the control of employers over the workplace. Thus, as Edwards (1978) contends, "The trouble is that a little is never enough. Just as some job security leads to demands for guaranteed lifetime wages, so some control over workplace decisions raises the demand for industrial democracy" (p. 124).[5]

How are we to understand all of this? Correspondence theories would have it that schools are exceptionally successful in teaching specific norms that are lived out at the workplace. Yet at best, if these recent investigators of the actual working out of the labor process are correct, this supposed correspondence can only partially describe what *is* lived out at the workplace. We shall need to go into this in somewhat more detail.

If we are to understand the actual lives of workers at a variety of levels of the "occupational ladder," an important key is what has been called *"work culture."* Work culture is not easily visible to the outsider and, like studies of the hidden curriculum, requires living within it to come close to comprehending its subtleties and organization. However, even with its subtle character, informal practices, and clear variations, it can generally be defined as "a relatively autonomous sphere of action on the job, a realm of informal, customary values and rules which *mediates* the formal authority structure of the work place and distances workers from its impact" (Benson, 1978, p. 41, emphasis mine). In essence, work culture, as a "relatively autonomous sphere of action," is not necessarily only a reproductive form. It constitutes a realm of action that in part provides both strength and the possibility of transformative activity.

This very work culture provides a ground for the development of alternative norms, norms which are quite a bit richer than those pictured by theories of bare correspondence. These norms provide a locus for workers resistance, at least partial control of skills, pacing, and knowledge, collectively rather than complete fragmentation of tasks, and some degree of autonomy from management.

On close examination, there are a number of norms that pervade the work-place in many industries, norms which give more than a mere semblance of autonomy and which "are manifested every day in the forms of interaction that reproduce the work culture." Among the strongest of these is cooperation as exemplified in work-sharing arrangements. An instance of this is the practice of workers saving finished pieces in the wood- and metal-working industries. These pieces are lent to other workers so that the daily completion rate can be met by one's fellow workers "who have had a hard day (because of machine breakdown, because they do not feel good, etc.)" (Aronowitz, 1978, p. 142).

Significant counterexamples to passive acquiescence, deskilling, and loss of control are found elsewhere as well. Industrial workers in, say, steel mills in particular, have maintained a significant degree of worker autonomy by develop-ing and redeveloping a shop floor culture that allows them a very real role in production. Even within highly mechanized industries, worker "militancy" to protect what is not mislabeled as "solidarity" is clear. Steve Packard's account of day-to-day life in the steel mills documents this rather well. Here is one example.

> One day a white craneman was assigned to a good crane that should have gone to a black. Black cranemen decided to sabotage production until this bullshit was straightened out. They had mild support from most white cranemen, who also thought the foreman was wrong.
>
> Nothing can operate without the cranes bringing and taking steel, so blacks quietly stopped the whole mill. They kept the cranes in lowest gear and worked in super slow motion. Foremen soon began hatching out of their offices, looking around, rubbing their eyes in disbelief. It was like the whole building popped LSD or the air had turned into some kind of thick jelly: everything but the foremen moved at one tenth of normal speed. (Quoted in Aronowitz, 1978, p. 142. See also Packard, 1978; Theriault, 1978).

Here is a prime example of how the control of workers by management is less than total, to say the least. The unspoken cultural life within the mill, the power of workers' cooperation, provides a substantial check to the norms of profit, author-ity, and productivity sought by the employers (Aronowitz, 1978, p. 143).

This resistance, as we know, has often been turned into avenues that are overly economistic. We strike and bargain over wages and benefits, less often over con-trol and power (see Aronowitz, 1973). In certain industries, of course—coal mines provide one example—the tradition of overt resistance is still very visible. Yet, overt and formally organized resistance (or even the relative lack of it at times) is not as significant to my argument as the fact of informal resistance to control at the point of production.[6]

For rather than being left, as Noble puts it, with a corporate juggernaut on one side and impotence and total despair on the other, we find evidence to the contrary again at the level of informal practices. Thus, in the metal-working industry, new technologies have been developed over the years with the express purpose of increasing production and deskilling occupations. They, thereby, would increase the rate of capital accumulation in two ways—more goods sold and less salary paid to workers who were mere "button pushers." Among the most significant of these technologies was the development in recent decades of numerical control. In brief, numerical control entails the specifications of a part that is to be produced on the machine being broken down into a mathematical representation of that part. These representations are then themselves translated into a mathematical description of the desired path of the cutting machine that will make the part. This leads, finally, to a system of control in which hundreds or thousands of discrete instructions are translated into a numerical code which is automatically read by the machinery. Numerical control, hence, is a means of totally separating conception from execution, of "circumventing [the worker's] role as a source of the intelligence in production *(in theory)*" and of management getting greater control over and compliance from its employees (Noble, 1979, p. 11).

The stress on "in theory" is important here. The introduction of numerical control has not been uneventful. Let me be specific here. Overt and covert resistance was and is quite common. Strikes and work stoppages have not been unusual. At the Lynn, Massachusetts General Electric plant, the introduction of numerical controls caused a strike which shut down the factory for a month. Workers saw the issue clearly. As one machine operator put it:

> The introduction of automation means that our skills are being down-graded and instead of having the prospect of moving up to a more interesting job we now have the prospect of either unemployment or a dead-end job. But there are alternatives that unions can explore. We have to establish the position that the fruits of technical change can be divided up—some to the workers, not all to management as is the case today. We must demand that the machinist rise with the complexity of the machine. Thus, rather than dividing his job up, the machinist should be trained to program and repair his equipment—a task well within the grasp of most people in industry.
>
> Demands such as this strike at the heart of most management prerogative clauses which are in many collective bargaining contracts. Thus, to deal with automation effectively, one has to strike at another prime ingredient of business unionism: the idea of "let the management run the business." The introduction of [numerical control] equipment makes it imperative that we fight such ideas (Noble, 1979, p. 48).

This is clearly overt and organized resistance and struggle. But what about the informal norms of the work culture on the shop floor? What happens there? Do workers there embody the norms of obedience to authority, punctuality, etc. When there is not a strike? While in theory under numerical control all that a machine operator must do is to press buttons to stop or start the machine and continue to load and unload it, this rarely happens. Here too the actual process of work at the point of production does not necessarily correspond to the norms "required." On the shop floor, one often finds workers engaged in what is called "pacing" or "the 70 percent syndrome"—the collective restriction of output on the floor by workers cooperating to set the speed at which the machine is fed at 70 to 80 percent of capacity. One can again often find workers running the machine harder to get enough products to help each other out. And, finally, there are the more subtle forms of resistance in terms of negative and uncooperative attitudes and the lack of "willing acceptance of authority." As some managers note: "When you put a guy on a N.C. machine, he gets temperamental . . . And then, through a process of osmosis, the machine gets temperamental" (Noble, 1979, pp. 45–46).

Women at work

So far I have painted a picture of workers who were predominantly male and industrial in my attempt to uncover whether the hidden curriculum literature is correct in seeing a correspondence between what is supposed to be taught to working-class children in schools and what is "required" in their later participation in a stratified labor market. Yet what about women? If male workers often showed serious signs of collective commitment, struggle, and attempts to maintain control of their skills and knowledge (though often informally)—and hence act against and not necessarily reproduce the expected norms of the labor market—can we say the same for other groups of workers?

The large body of research on women's day-to-day work is relatively recent, but nevertheless, a number of striking points emerge from the literature. Women were often quite effective in resisting the production requirements and norms handed down by management in factories. In the shoe and garment industries, "the effective unionization of women operatives was likely to have a remarkably radicalizing impact on the organization." Sharing, mutual respect, resistance to management control, all of these counterbalancing norms came to the fore even more noticeably when, say, women shoe workers were organized along with men. Here, at least, women workers were quite aggressive in their relationships with their employers (Montgomery, 1976, pp. 500–501).

Much the same situation is found in areas of employment which for a variety of economic and ideological reasons have consciously sought to hire women, such as clerical and sales work (see Rothman, 1978; Altbach, 1974). Perhaps the most interesting aspect of this can be seen in the latter areas, that of working in retail stores.

Examples of subtle resistance among saleswomen abound. For instance, when management directives designed to tighten to obedience on the sales floor interfered with the established informal rules which maintained the work culture, they were often quite effectively sabotaged or altered. If these directives included extra duties, they were often merely refused or fought informally. Saleswomen would engage in sloppy or "eccentric" work when setting up new displays. As a group, they might take back the time management had extracted from them for these extra duties by unilaterally extending the lunch hour. Or, they could visibly insult the authority of management by, say, purposely ignoring the requirements of the store's dress code (Benson, 1978, p. 49).

The countervailing norms of the work culture frequently went further. Since so much of a saleswoman's work was public, since it was carried out on the sales floor, many employees developed rather clever ways of turning back management harassment and abuse of authority. Saleswomen could easily embarrass a buyer or a floor manager in front of his or her superiors or an important customer. Further, solidarity against management directives and control was repeatedly enforced by informal sanctions. A saleswoman who transgressed the work culture could find her stock mysteriously messed up. Shins could be banged into by drawers. And like floor managers, the transgressor could be embarrassed before customers and higher management (Benson, 1978, p. 49). All of this does not leave one with a sense of total worker internalization of and acquiescence in the face of the imperatives of the norms and values of management ideology.

The resistance and collective commitment went further in many stores. The work culture on the sales floor also developed important ways of controlling the pacing and meaning of work, ways which mirror those found in my earlier discussion of day-to-day life on the shop floor. Just as in the factory, where workers found ways to effectively transform, mute, or work against the demands of management, so too did clerks develop a work culture that could effectively set limits on output and dampen competitiveness among departments in sales. These tactics are nicely illustrated in the following discussion.

> Each department had a concept of the total sales that constituted a good day's work. Saleswomen used various tactics to keep their "books" (sales tallies) within acceptable limits: running usually low books would imperil a worker's status with management just as extraordinarily high books would put her in the bad graces of her peers. Individual clerks would avoid customers late in the day when their books were running high, or call other clerks to help them. Saleswomen managed to approximate the informal quota with impressive regularity, ironing out the fluctuations in customers' buying habits in ways the management never dreamed of. They adjusted the number of transactions they completed to compensate for the size of the purchases; if they made a few large sales early in the day, they might then retire to do stockwork. During the slow summer season or during inclement weather, they were more aggressive with the smaller volume of customers; at peak seasons, they ignored customers who might put them over their quota (Benson, 1978, p. 50).

Managers were not the only recipients of these kinds of informal practices. Customers came in for their share too, a share that naturally arises since, unlike the factory, the sales floor involves not just the production of goods but the "production of customers." Through subtle ways—picking and choosing among waiting customers, pretending not to notice customers while doing stockwork or having a conversation with one's peers, disappearing into the storeroom, rudeness, and so on—sales-women communicated a hidden message to both management and the customer. We take customers on our terms not yours. While you might have a superior class position, we have the upper hand here—we control the merchandise (Benson, 1978, p. 51).

There are, of course, other possible examples. One would expect similar informal "culture" practices to be found in secretarial work, for instance. However, the major point to be kept in mind brings into serious question the myth—and it may be just that—of the passive woman worker. As we have seen, men and women do have some agency. It may be informal and relatively disorganized, and hence may be at a cultural, not a political level. But it exists in ways which are not simply reproductive. To speak metaphorically, the reproductive mirror has some serious cracks in it.

A note of caution

In this essay, I have sought to bring together a set of counterexamples to illuminate the partial quality of the research being done on the hidden curriculum in schools. I have argued that correspondence theories—even if they develop the ethnographic and statistical sophistication required to unpack what schools actually teach—are *dependent upon* the accuracy of their view of the labor process. The exclusive use of the metaphor of reproduction, however, leads them to accept the ideology of management (i.e., workers at all times are guided by the cash nexus, by authority, by expert planning, by the norms of punctuality and productivity) as a real description of what goes on outside the school. When the metaphor of reproduction is complemented by metaphors describing other modes of determination such as mediation and transformation, among others, and when one examines the actual organization and control of the labor process, one finds a somewhat different picture of important aspects of the day-to-day life than one might expect.

Rather than the labor process being totally controlled by management, rather than hard-and-fast structures of authority and norms of punctuality and compliance, one sees a complex work culture. This very work culture provides important grounds for worker resistance, collective action, informal control of pacing and skill, and reasserting one's humanity. In the counterexamples I have given here, men and women workers seem engaged in overt and informal activity that is somehow missed when we talk only in reproductive terms. These terms make us see the school and the workplace as black boxes.[7]

These are not unimportant points, for the organization and control of work in corporate economics *cannot* be understood without reference to the overt and covert attempts of workers to resist the rationalizing control of employers (Brecher, 1978, p. 3). A theory of the hidden curriculum that loses sight of this risks losing its conceptual vitality, to say nothing of its empirical accuracy.

When all this is said, however, we still must be very careful of appropriating an overly romantic outlook. I have focused on the other side of the norms and dispositions that guide the workplace, norms, and dispositions signifying struggle, resistence, conflict, and aspects of collective action which counterbalance the obedience, compliance, bureaucratic authority structure, and relations to the experts that management seeks to impose. Yet, while we need to see how the actual lived conditions at the workplace both mediate ideological and economic "requirements" and have transformative potential, we need to remember at all times that power *is* often unequal in factories, offices, shops, and stores. Struggle and conflict may indeed exist; but that does not mean that they will be successful. The success is determined by the structural limitations and selection processes that occur in our day-to-day lives.

There are powerful features within and outside the productive process that militate against a sense of collectivity and which exacerbate a sense of isolation and passivity. The "serial organization of production," where assembly lines spread workers out over the vast interior landscapes of factories (and now many offices), provides one obvious example (Ehrenreich and Ehrenreich, 1976, p. 13). This is coupled with status and rank distinctions within the work place so that even in areas not overtly like the factory—in the hospital, for instance—"there are often injunctions against fraternizing with workers of marginally different ranks and penalties against workers who seek to exercise initiative in the interests of good patient care" (Ehrenreich and Ehrenreich, 1976, p. 14). These are obviously not exhaustive examples. (My earlier discussion of Taylorism and even newer time and motion measurement and control systems such as numerical control documents this.) However, they do point to how what might be called atomization or the creation of the abstract individual can and does go on.[8]

Any honest appraisal must not ignore Braverman's analysis quoted earlier. Management *has* historically attempted to incorporate resistance and to extend its dominion over the workplace. While, as we have seen, it has met with varying degrees of success, it is also clear that many management techniques developed in response to worker knowledge and informal control and resistance have been relatively fruitful. Among these techniques are some I have already mentioned: the rationalization of production (cost accounting systems, centralization of authority, formalization of bureaucratic and supervisory structures and procedures), the redivision of labor (transforming skilled into less-skilled and standardized jobs, differential training and knowledge for management and workers, a strong division between mental and manual labor), and the design of technology (numerical control devices to eliminate worker knowledge and control, assembly line production where the pace of the line regulates the pace of the work). Other techniques include: hiring practices (a battery of tests given to prospective employees, selection of employees by economic background for low-paying work, exclusion or inclusion by race or sex), corporate welfare policies (human relations training added to Taylorism, "high" raises in times of expanding economy, bonuses, health and pension plans often granted "in trade for" more management control and no-strike provisions), union policies (unions used to discipline militant workers and to standardize grievance procedures, thereby eliminating wildcat strikes), and workplace location (the runaway shop where corporations move their factories and offices to locations where abundant and more compliant labor is available, threats of plant closings) (Brecher, 1978, pp. 7–14).

There clearly may be many more. And even here these do not account for the ideological and economic pressures outside of the workplace which may "cause" men and women to accept both their work and their social life as pregiven and natural.[9]

More could be said about the informal work culture. Many of these informal "attempts" at transformation, and the ways the work culture may mediate management ideology and pressures, may be turned back against the workers themselves. This is a critical point. The situation may be similar to that of the students studied by Willis. These "lads" rejected the credentials, the book learning, the norms and habits of the school and thereby rejected many of the hidden and overt messages of the surrounding institutions as well. In the process, though, they ultimately reproduced at a deeper level the ideological distinction between mental and manual labor which lies near the heart of the economy. The same may be true of life on the shop floor and elsewhere. A question we must ask is, if, as I have maintained, these countervailing and relatively autonomous norms and practices exist, where, when, and how *specifically* may they ultimately lend partial support to ideological and economic rubrics of control at an even deeper level?[10] It is a question that will not be easy to answer; but we cannot understand either the hidden curriculum or the labor process without asking it.

Educational action

These arguments may seem a long way from the reality of classroom practice and curricular activity. After all, the academic debate about the conceptual issues and the empirical justification surrounding the hidden curriculum is, in part, just that—an academic debate about how we are to interpret what goes on in schools. However, besides the comparison between what happens in schools and its supposed effect on (or correspondence to) what occurs outside these institutions, a number of things need to be realized about this discussion. As I maintained previously, there are very real ties between conception and action. As I argued, a vision of the successful degradation of work unwittingly accepts on a conceptual level a management ideology, one which on a political level can lead to a cynicism or pessimism about the possibilities of any successful action in both the socioeconomic arena and in the school. Or, it can cause us to wait for some cataclysmic event that will suddenly alter everything. Either one can ultimately lead to inactivity.

With this in mind, let us return to the pessimistic posture I pointed to earlier in this article. Schools can be no more than reproductive mirrors. Therefore, any action within them is doomed to failure. If I have been correct in my analysis here—that in nearly every real work situation, there will be elements of contradiction, of resistance, of relative autonomy that have transformative potential, then the same should be true in schools. If we ignore these situations we ignore, first, the elemental fact that millions of people *work* in them. Because of their structural position as state employees, the conditions of their work can lead them to the beginnings of a serious appraisal of power and control in society. As the fiscal crisis of the state deepens, as the conditions of state employees become less secure because of the "crisis of accumulation," as educational work enters more and more into the political and economic arena, as I predict it will, this increases the possibility of self-conscious organization (see O'Connor, 1973; Wright, 1978). Even on the level of informal work, the work culture of teachers (which undoubtedly exists, as I know from personal experience) can be used for educative purposes. It can be employed in a process of political education by using elements of it as exemplars of the very possibility of regaining at least partial control over the conditions of one's work and for clarifying the structural determinations that set limits on progressive pedagogic activity.[11]

But action can be taken not only in the long slow process of enabling teachers to understand their situation. There is a great need for curricular action as well. Here I will not say much beyond what has been said by others who have struggled long and hard to introduce honest, controversial, and racially, sexually, and economically controversial material into schools.[12] If resistance is found, even if only on an informal level, we find men and women in our businesses, factories, and elsewhere struggling to maintain their knowledge, humanity, and pride, then curricular action may be *more* important than we realize. Students need to see the history and legitimacy of these struggles. The teaching of serious labor history, organized around the countervailing norms generated by men and women who have resisted living out the hidden curriculum, could be one effective strategy for educational action here. As Raymond Williams reminds us, the overcoming of what he has called the "selective tradition" is essential for current emancipatory practice (Williams, 1977).

This will require not only theoretical analyses, but the ongoing production of viable curricular materials and teaching strategies that can be used in classrooms and elsewhere (see Rydlberg, 1974 and Quebec Education Federation). Local political and organizational activity to provide the conditions necessary for even attempting to use new or previously prepared documentary material obviously needs to be considered. The selective tradition has operated in such a way that the most widely employed curricular materials now provide a less than significant sense of the heritage of a sizable portion of the population. Significant aspects of the labor movement are often systematically neglected, defined as outside the boundaries of "responsible" labor activity, or subject to editorial commentary that manages to disparage them (Fantasia, 1979). It is evident that concrete educational and political work could be done here.

But what about our understanding of the hidden, not the overt, curriculum? If simple models of reproduction and correspondence cannot adequately account for the complexity of day-to-day life in either schools or where people work, this has important implications for future research on the hidden curriculum. Again being careful about romanticizing the resistence to ideological and economic "determinations," we should want to see if patterns of mediation, resistance, and partial transformation similar to those found in the workplace are found in the school. With the increasing encroachment of procedures for rationalization and management ideologies into schools (e.g., systems management, management by objectives, competency-based instruction, the growth of national testing, and so on), do teachers respond in ways like those of the workers I have examined here? Do students, like those found in the study by Willis also act against, partially transform, or somehow engage in activity which goes beyond mere socialization to and reproduction of the norms and values considered legitimate in the hidden curriculum? Does this ultimately turn back against them at a deeper ideological level? Which students—by race, sex, and class—do what?[13]

We may find that much more is going on than meets the eye or than some of the more deterministic hidden curriculum theorists would have us believe. If determinations are seen not as producing mirror images, but as setting contra-dictory limits (Apple, 1979a), limits which at the level of practice are often medi-ated by (and can *potentially* transform) the informal (and sometimes conscious) action of groups of people, then we can explore ways these limits are now being contested. In the process, we might find spaces where limits dissolve. There are few things more worthy of effort.

Notes

1   The concept of determination is systematically ambiguous in this literature. For a discussion of its use, see Apple (1979a) and Williams (1977).
2   I am indebted to Erik Olin Wright's (1978, pp. 15–29) articulation of these six modes of determination. Aside from reproduction, we may define Wright's categories gener-ally in the following ways: to what extent any institutional structure like the school can vary (an example of structural limitation); the mechanisms such as funding patterns and state intervention which exclude certain possible decisions (an example of selec-tion); what aspects of institutional structures are *not* merely reproductive but are con-tradictory (an example of the limits of functional compatibility); and, finally, what concrete actions and struggles inside and outside schools may now be altering these institutions and processes (an example of transformation).
3   See also the analysis of the "failure" of Taylorism in Noble (1977).
4   The relationship between the growth of bureaucratic management and the control of labor is nicely documented by Clawson (1978) in chapter 8 of his analysis. See also Edwards (1979).
5   Edwards (1978) distinguishes between three types of control—simple, technical, and bureaucratic. Each of these lends itself to and in part is a result of specific kinds of resistance.
6   However, we should not forget that even such resistance can be "incorporated" by management (and our more conservative unions), so that resistance turns toward paths that do not threaten production. See, e.g., Burawoy (in press).
7   I have discussed the problems of seeing institutions as if they were black boxes in Apple (1978b) and Apple (1979a).
8   On the creation of an abstract individual as an ideological form, see Apple (1978a), Apple (1979a), Williams (1961), and Lukes (1973).
9   The literature on the creation and reaction of ideological hegemony is becoming quite extensive and is obviously helpful in unpacking this issue. Among the most recent analyses which might be helpful are Williams (1977), Williams (1975), W. Wright (1975), Connell (1977), Center for Contemporary Cultural Studies (1977), Brenkman (1979), Aronowitz (1979), and Jameson (1979).
10 I am indebted to a discussion with Paul Willis for my basic point here.
11 Hinton's (1966) discussion of "fanshen" is interesting here.
12 Within mainstream curriculum work, Newmann's continuing emphasis on public issues and community action programs deserves mention here. See also my discussion with Newmann in Weller (1977).
13 I have purposely *undertheorized* my arguments in this essay for ease of readability. On a theoretical level, my points here constitute part of a larger debate within the analysis

of the relationship between economic and cultural reproduction. In essence, I want to claim that it is not only an epistemological possibility, but an actual accomplishment that large numbers of working people can create alternative and "relatively autonomous" forms of knowledge that are not merely representations of "bourgeois social categories." This is done even in the face of both the power of the economic and cultural capital of dominant classes and the state apparatus in its various forms. My position here is similar to Willis and Aronowitz, who argue strongly against both traditional base–superstructure formulas, and the overly deterministic theories of Althusser, the capitalistic logic school, and others. See, for example, Willis (1977), Willis (1979), and Aronowitz (1978).

References

Altbach, E. *Women in America*. Lexington, Mass.: D. C. Heath, 1974.

Apple, M. W. Ideology and form in curriculum evaluation. In G. Willis (Ed.), Qualitative evaluation. Berkeley, Calif.: McCutchan, 1978(a).

Apple, M. W. The new sociology of education: analyzing cultural and economic reproduction. *Harvard Educational Review*, 1978, 48, 495–503(b).

Apple, M. W. *Ideology and curriculum*. Boston: Routledge and Kegan Paul, 1979(a).

Apple, M. W. The production of knowledge and the production of deviance in schools. In L. Barton and R. Meighan (Eds.), *Schools, pupils and deviance*. Nafferton, England: Nafferton Books, 1979(b).

Apple, M. W. What correspondence theories of the hidden curriculum miss. *The Review of Education*, 1979, 5, 101–112(c).

Aronowitz, S. *False promises*. New York: McGraw-Hill, 1973.

Aronowitz, S. Marx, Braverman, and the logic of capital. *The Insurgent Sociologist*, 1978, 8, 126–146.

Aronowitz, S. Film—the art form of late capitalism. *Social Text*, 1979, 1, 110–129.

Benson, S. P. The clerking sisterhood: rationalization and the work culture of saleswomen in American department stores, 1890–1960. *Radical America*, 1978, 12, 41–55.

Bernstein, B. *Class, codes and control, Vol. 3*, Towards a theory of educational transmission. 2nd ed. London: Routledge and Kegan Paul, 1977.

Bourdieu, P., and Passeron, J. *Reproduction in education, society and culture*. Beverly Hills, Calif.: Sage, 1977.

Bowles, S. & Gintis, H. *Schooling in capitalist America*. New York: Basic Books, 1976.

Braverman, H. *Labor and monopoly capital*: the degradation of work in the twentieth century. New York: Monthly Review Press, 1974.

Brecher, J. Uncovering the hidden history of the American workplace. *The Review of Radical Political Economics*, 1978, 10, 1–23.

Brenkman, J. Mass media: from collective experience to the culture of privatization. *Social Text*, 1979, 1, 94–109.

Bridges, A. B. Nicos Poulantzas and the Marxist theory of the state. *Politics and Society*, 1974, 4, 161–190.

Burawoy, M. The politics of production and the production of politics: a comparative analysis of piecework machine shops in the United States and Hungary. *Political Power and Social Theory* (in press).

Burawoy, M. Toward a Marxist theory of the labor process. *Politics and Society*, 1979, 8, (3–4).

Center for Contemporary Cultural Studies. On ideology. *Working Papers in Cultural Studies*, 1977, 10.

Clawson, D. *Class struggle and the rise of bureaucracy*. Unpublished doctoral dissertation, State University of New York at Stony Brook, 1978.

Connell, R. W. *Ruling class, ruling culture*. New York: Cambridge University Press, 1977.

Edwards, R. C. *Contested terrain: the transformation of the workplace in the 20th century*. New York: Basic Books, 1979.

Edwards, R. C. The social relations of production at the point of production. *The Insurgent Sociologist*, 1978, 8, 109–125.

Ehrenreich, J., & Ehrenreich, B. Work and consciousness. In R. Baxandall et al. (Eds.),

Technology, the labor process and the working class. New York: Monthly Review Press, 1976.

Fantasia, R. The treatment of labor in social studies textbooks. Unpublished paper, Department of Sociology, University of Massachusetts, 1979.

Hinton, W. *Fanshen.* New York: Vintage, 1966.

Jameson, F. Reification and utopia in mass culture. *Social Text,* 1979, *1,* 130–148.

Karabel, J., & Halsey, A. H. (Eds.). *Power and ideology in education.* New York: Oxford University Press, 1977.

Lukes, S. *Individualism.* Oxford: Basil Blackwell, 1973.

Mehan, H. Structuring school structure. *Harvard Educational Review,* 1978, *48,* 32–64.

Mehan, H. The structure of classroom events and their consequences for students' performance. In P. Gilmore (Ed.), *Children in and out of school.* Philadelphia: University of Pennsylvania Press (in press).

Montgomery, D. Workers' control of machine production in the nineteenth century. *Labor History,* 1976, *17,* 485–509.

Noble, D. *America by design:* science, technology, and the rise of corporate capitalism. New York: Knopf, 1977.

Noble, D. Social choice in machine design. Unpublished paper, University of Minnesota, 1979.

O'Connor, J. *The fiscal crisis of the state.* New York: St. Martin's Press, 1973.

Packard, S. *Steelmill blues.* San Pedro, Calif.: Singlejack Books, 1978.

Poulantzas, N. *Classes in contemporary capitalism.* London: New Left Books, 1975.

Quebec Education Federation. *Pour une journée au service de la class ouvrière.* Toronto: New Hogtown Press, no date.

Rothman, S. *Woman's proper place.* New York: Basic Books, 1978.

Rydlberg, P. *The history book.* Culver City, Calif.: Peace Press, 1974.

Tapper, T., & Salter, B. *Education and the political order.* New York: Macmillan, 1978.

Theriault, R. *Longshoring on the San Francisco waterfront.* San Pedro, Calif.: Singlejack Books, 1978.

Weller, R. (Ed.). *Humanistic education.* Berkeley, Calif: McCutchan, 1977.

Williams, R. *The long revolution.* London: Chatto & Windus, 1961.

Williams, R. *Television: technology and cultural form.* New York: Schocken, 1975.

Williams, R. *Marxism and literature.* New York: Oxford University Press, 1977.

Willis, P. *Class struggle, symbol and discourse.* Unpublished paper, The University of Birmingham, 1979.

Willis, Paul. *Learning to labour: how working class kids get working class jobs.* England: Saxon House, Teakfield Ltd., 1977.

Wright, E. O. *Class, crisis and the state.* London: New Left Books, 1978.

Wright, W. *Sixguns and society.* Berkeley: University of California Press, 1975.

CHAPTER 12

SEEING EDUCATION RELATIONALLY (1980)

The stratification of culture and people in the sociology of school knowledge

Michael W. Apple and Lois Weis

The daily life of teachers, administrators, parents, and students in our schools is filled with political and ideological pressures and tensions. Budget cuts and lay-offs, class, race, and gender antagonisms, and the internal politics of complex bureaucratic institutions—all of these are part of the turmoil experienced by those working within the schools. At a time of fiscal crisis and, often, severe ideological differences about what schools should do, it is hard *not* to think about education as part of a larger framework of institutions and values. While this has been recognized for years by many people who work in schools and/or write about them, the mainstream of educational research has been overly psychological. By focusing primarily on how to get students to learn more mathematics, science, history, and so forth (surely not an unimportant problem), it has neglected to inquire into the larger context in which schools exist, a context that may actually make it very difficult for them to succeed.

Actually, this dominant research model—what has been called the "achievement tradition"—has been weakened by its neglect of two things. First, because of its positivistic emphasis and its overreliance on statistical approaches, it has been unable to unravel the complexities of everyday interaction in schools. Its focus on product has led to a thoroughgoing naivete about the very process of education, about the internal dynamics of the institution. Second, its tendency toward a-theoreticism has made it difficult for us to link these internal dynamics to that larger ideological, economic, and political context.[1] In this research model, schools sit isolated from the structurally unequal (and conflict-ridden) society of which they are—in real life—fully a part.

In their exceptionally clear discussion of the major approaches to research in education, Karabel and Halsey (1977, p. 61) state that one of the most important research programs required at this time is to connect "interpretive" studies of schools with "structural" analyses. That is, to move forward we need an approach which combines an investigation of the day-to-day curricular, peda-gogic, and evaluative activities of schools with generative theories of the school's role in society. This essay reviews some of the arguments that have led to this recognition and have carried it forward.

What schools do

As Hogan (1982) notes, it is difficult to separate educational issues from larger "political" issues. He identifies four categories into which these issues have fallen:

structural politics centered upon the nature and strength of the alignment of the school with the economy (for example, conflicts over differentiated and vocational education) and conflicts over the structure of authority relations within schools (for example, conflicts over the centralization of administrative authority, unionization and professionalism); *human capital politics* generated by the efforts of parents or communities to enhance the rates of return to their children or school population relative to other children or school populations; *cultural capital politics* created by conflicts over competing definitions of legitimate knowledge, that is, conflicts over the distribution of symbolic authority in the society (for example, conflicts over curricula content or textbooks); and finally, *displacement politics*, in which educational issues (often, though not always, conflicts of a cultural capital kind) become proxies for other non-educational conflicts in the community. (pp. 52–53) (italics added)

Hogan's categories are ideal types but still useful. Conflicts over knowledge, over economic goods and services, and over power relations within and outside the school are all of considerable moment. In order to understand these complex issues, we need to step back from thinking about schools as places that seek only to maximize the achievement of individual students. Instead of this more psychological and individualistic perspective, we need to interpret the school more socially, culturally, and structurally. A number of questions organize these interpretations. What is it that education does in this larger context? When it does this, who benefits?

In general, recent research on the social, ideological, and economic role of our educational apparatus has pointed to three activities schools engage in. Though these are clearly interrelated, we can label these "functions" as assisting in (a) accumulation, (b) legitimation, and (c) production.[2] Each deserves some elaboration.

Accumulation. Schools assist in the process of capital accumulation by providing some of the necessary conditions for re creating an unequally responsive economy. They do this in part through their internal sorting and selecting of students by "talent." By integrating students into a credential market and a system of urban segregation, they roughly reproduce a hierarchically organized labor force (see, e.g., Castells, 1980; Collins, 1979; Ogbu, 1978). It has been argued that, as students are hierarchically ordered—an ordering generally based on the cultural forms of dominant groups (Bernstein, 1977; Bourdieu & Passeron, 1977)—different groups of students are taught different norms, skills, values, knowledge, and dispositions by race, class, and sex. In this way, schools help meet the economy's need for a stratified and at least partially socialized body of employees (see, e.g., Bowles & Gintis, 1976; but cf. Apple, 1982c; Olneck & Bills, 1980).

We have to be quite cautious here. One can easily make it seem as if everything pertaining to education can be reduced to the needs of the division of labor or economic forces outside the school. Such a perspective—commonly called a "base/superstructure" model—is much too simplistic and mechanistic (see Apple, 1982b, 1982c; Hall, 1977). Avoiding such reductionism, however, does not mean that we can ignore the very real ties between an economy and the sorting and selecting activity of education.

Legitimation. Schools are an important part of a complex structure through which social groups are given legitimacy and through which social and cultural ideologies are re-created, maintained, and continuously built. That is, they are agencies of legitimation (Meyer, 1977). Thus, schools tend to describe both themselves and society as meritocratic and as inexorably moving toward greater social and economic justice. In this way, they foster a social belief that the major institutions of our society are equally responsive to all regardless of race, class, and sex. Unfortunately, the available data suggest that this is less the case than we might like to think. In fact, as a number of investigators have demonstrated, slogans of pluralism aside, in almost every social arena from health care to anti-inflation policy, one can see a pattern in which the top 20% of the population consistently benefit much more than the bottom 80% (e.g. Navarro, 1976; O'Connor, 1973). Given the emerging politics of rightist regimes in advanced capitalist societies this disparity may be exacerbated even further (Castells, 1980). In essence, while "late capitalist society" does have some measure of pluralism, the amount of it has been greatly exaggerated, and its character has changed markedly, as both the corporate-managed and the state-operated sectors have increasingly gained power over our lives (Macpherson, 1981, p. 65).

Yet the school's role in legitimation is not limited to making our socioeconomic system seem natural and just or demarcating groups from one another. Since schools are also part of the political institutions of our society, part of the *state*, they must legitimate *themselves* as well. That is, not just the economy, but the educational apparatus and the state bureaucracy and government in general have their own needs for legitimacy. They too must generate consent from the governed. Thus, the need for political legitimacy may not always resonate with the requirements of the economy. This complicates matters considerably.

Production. Finally, the educational apparatus as a whole constitutes an important set of agencies for production. This is quite complex, but basically what it implies is the following. Our mode of production, distribution, and consumption requires high levels of technical/administrative knowledge for the expansion of markets, "defense," the artificial creation and stimulation of new consumer needs, the control and division of labor, communicative and technical innovations to increase or hold one's share of a market or increase profit margins, and, just as importantly, cultural control.[3] Schools and universities ultimately help in the production of such knowledge. As research and development centers whose costs are socialized (i.e., spread among all of us so that capital need not pay the bulk of the cost) and as training grounds for future employees of industry, universities, for example, play an essential role in making available the technically utilizable knowledge on which so much of our science-based industries depend and on which the culture industry is based.

At the same time, technical/administrative knowledge plays another, less economic, role in education. Schools themselves are dominated increasingly by technicist ideologies. The major curricular, teaching, and testing programs in use in, say, the United States are nearly all strikingly behavioral and reductive in orientation. Yet, by attempting to reduce all knowledge to atomistic behaviors, many school practices also reduce the cultural sphere (the sphere of democratic discourse and shared understandings) to the application of technical rules and procedures. In essence, questions of "why" are transformed into questions of "how to." When this is combined with the fact that serious conflict is usually absent from the curriculum itself, it substitutes instrumental ideologies for ethical and political awareness and debate (Apple, 1979). Here, the ideological and economic roles of schools often intersect.

When this is said, though, we need again to be quite careful of falling into the trap of economism. The very notion of the educational system as assisting in the production of economically and ideologically useful knowledge points to the fact that schools are *cultural* as well as economic institutions. By defining certain groups' knowledge as legitimate for production and/or distribution, while other groups' knowledge and traditions are considered inappropriate as school knowledge, schools help not only in the production of useful technical/ administrative knowledge but in the reproduction of the culture and ideological forms of dominant groups.

Even here, however, as research such as Willis's (1977) analysis of working-class youth culture demonstrates, students in schools may often reject dominant knowledge and ideologies. The school can serve as a site for the production of alternative and/or oppositional cultural practices which do not serve (at least in any straightforward way) the accumulation, legitimation, or production needs of the state or capital. There is no simple one-to-one correspondence between economics and culture. Thus, just as when we alluded to the relatively autonomous needs for legitimacy on the part of institutions of the state, there is a partially autonomous cultural dynamic at work in schools also, one that is not necessarily reducible to the results and pressures of the capital accumulation process.

This brief description does not exhaust what schools do, of course. However, our major claims are these: We cannot fully understand the way our educational institutions are situated within a larger configuration of economic, cultural, and political power unless we attempt to examine the *different* functions they perform in our unequal social formation. Further, while we need to unpack the various roles schools perform, we should not necessarily assume that educational institutions will always be successful in carrying out these three functions. Accumulation, legitimation, and production represent structural pressure on schools, not foregone conclusions. In part, the possibility that education may be unable to carry out what is "required" by these pressures is strengthened by the fact that these three functions are often *contradictory*. They may work against each other at times.

Perhaps a current example will be helpful here. In a time of fiscal crisis, industry requires fewer highly paid and highly credentialed employees. The declining need for credentialed employees and the problems of declining revenues brought about by the current economic crisis are creating a concomitant crisis in educational institutions and the government. Powerful classes and industry have begun to question the need for so many liberally trained students. The very basis of the acceptance of education's usual modes of operating is threatened. In order to cope with the problems of falling monetary support and the questioning of its operations, the state bureaucracy and its educational apparatus (stimulated by economic pressures and by higher officials in the government itself) have introduced highly centralized cost–benefit and accountability mechanisms, tightened "standards," reduced funding for higher education and "frills," reintroduced "basics," and so forth. In the process, however, other elements of the public may lose faith in the authority and legitimacy of the government if they see the tightening up as actually creating inequality and reducing the avenues they need to get ahead. Here, two of the functions of schools clash. Educational policy is truly caught in a contradictory situation. It must assist in re-creating a relatively tight economic and ideological ship, while keeping its legitimacy in the eyes of others. The state's need for consent, therefore, is sometimes at odds with the pressures being placed upon it by changing economic conditions (Apple, 1982c).

While this is a relatively simple example, it does serve to highlight the fact that the educational apparatus is often caught between a number of potentially competing imperatives. "Solving" one set of problems may exacerbate others. Responding overtly to the problems of economic inequality may create tensions due to the other functions education "must" perform.

Therefore, focusing on a single dominant requirement that the educational system supposedly performs—such as, say, its ideological and economic role in helping to reproduce the social division of labor—cannot provide an adequate account of its position as a site for other activity. As Roger Dale (1982, p. 137) has persuasively argued, any one demand being placed upon education can only be fully comprehended by seeing the *relationship* between it and the other structurally generated demands on the school. And these relationships are often fundamentally contradictory. Returning to our previous quote from Hogan, we can see that economic forces and conflicts do not totally cover how we should see what education does. Conflicts over knowledge and power, over culture and politics, intersect with economic determinations. Gaining a measure of theoretical insight on how these forces and conflicts both reproduce and contradict the larger relations of inequality outside the school is important, to say the least.

Status attainment and class

While the issue of the contradictory roles schools perform has not been a primary focus among those who study education, the question of the relationship between schooling and the amelioration or re-creation of inequality has not been ignored. The sociology of education in particular has had a long tradition of dealing with exactly this area, both through its work on status attainment and the more recent ethnographic investigations of school culture that have grown in response to some of the weaknesses of status attainment research.

Unfortunately, both of these areas of the sociology of education have been less structurally inclined than they might be. They too have been challenged for some of the same reasons that the dominant, more psychological, "achievement" model has been. And while they have taken some of Hogan's points about the political/economic nature of the institution seriously (in, for instance, the persistent attempts by status attainment researchers to link achievement in school to the occupational structure outside of it), they have been less successful in recognizing the other conflicts about and functions of our educational system. "Inequality" cannot be seen as a proxy for relations of structural domination and exploitation. Occupational choice by individuals underrepresents class dynamics and class structure. In fact, the occupational structure is *not* the same as class structure (Wright, 1980). And, finally, as we have argued, schools do more than link one to an occupational status in the first place.

Let us examine the status attainment research in more detail, since its conceptual and empirical strengths and weaknesses provide the context for a good deal of the impetus for the arguments we shall make here. Perhaps the best way of seeing these issues is to counterpose the status attainment and ethnographic research programs against each other and examine the arguments about each one. As we shall see, there is often a relatively large divide between, and within, these two approaches.

Though it is unfortunate, the division between a sociology of education concerned with large-scale and statistically complex studies of status attainment on the one hand and smaller-scale, more intense, studies of the internal characteristics on the other is currently rather large. It is almost as if the "soft" folks never read the "number crunchers" and vice versa. One need only read, say, two journals to find evidence of this split: *Sociology of Education* here in the United States and a new English publication that promises to be quite interesting, the *British Journal of Sociology of Education*. The former is filled with relatively a-theoretical but statistically sophisticated studies; the latter mainly contains theoretical, historical, and ethnographic papers.

Of course, there are other divisions within this literature, ones that are just as significant as we shall see. The debate between Marxist and more usual stratification approaches to the study of the benefits one might get from education is beginning in earnest. The argument between symbolic interactionism and more Marxist, structural analyses of the internal characteristics of schools is continuing and is still rather intense (Apple, 1978). Many of our comments in this section will have to do with these multiple divisions and how they have led to a substantive and fruitful program of research on the more general problem of the relationship between education and the economic and cultural reproduction of class relations.

The basic question that research on status attainment seeks to answer is this: What is the balance between ascribed and achieved characteristics in the determination of someone's future educational and occupational success (Wright, 1979, p. 77)? Status attainment researchers also investigate this question with respect to adult income. Many of the longitudinal studies that have emerged from this approach have sought to investigate the relationship between differential educational attainment and social stratification. The underlying idea on which such studies are based is that longitudinal investigations of the relationship between academic attainment and, say, future occupation or income level "will help us understand not only 'who ends up where' but 'how they get there?' " (Kerckhoff, 1980, p. viii).

The tradition on which this research is based should be applauded for its statistical sophistication, a sophistication that has grown markedly in the last decade or so. It should be commended for both its emphasis on reanalysis of its prior work in the light of new methodological advances and its practitioners' attempt to build upon one another's research.[4] Finally, it should be recognized as having played quite an important part (though perhaps less than it might like) in policy deliberation at a national level. However, when all of this is said, and it should be, it is just as clear that the research is undertheorized in important ways. What it all *means* is opaque since its theoretical grounding remains problematic. Whether it fully answers the question of "how they got there," or how we are to think about who "they" are, remains open to question.

For example, the relationship between educational attainment and occupational structure, even when treated elegantly, relies on a particular unarticulated vision of our economy. It underrepresents and undertheorizes class as an essential variable. Here we mean class not as where you stand on a particular occupational scale (such as the widely known Duncan scale), but class as a complex assemblage of cultural and economic relationships which help constitute the production, consumption, and control of labor and of economic and cultural capital.[5]

The significance of these kinds of questions about class and the control of labor and production is partly documented by Wright (1979) in his interesting criticism of the tradition of status attainment research. He argues that the theoretical underpinnings of this program rest on a particular unit of analysis. This is the atomistic individual. That is, "outcomes which are attached to individuals are the essential objects of investigation, and the causes of these outcomes are largely seen as operating through individuals" (p. 70).

Wright goes on, arguing that:

> [While] the metric for discussing occupational positions [in status attainment theory] is based on social evaluations of positions, and thus has a supraindividual character ... the essential dynamic of the theory, however, is conceived almost entirely at the level of atomistic individuals. Social structures have their consequences because they are embodied in individuals, in the form of personal characteristics. The class structure is seen as relevant in the analysis ... only insofar as it constitutes one of the factors which shape the individual's own achievements and motivations. The preoccupation of the theory is with ascription vs. achievement as determinants of individual outcomes, *not* with the structure of the outcomes themselves. ... The point is that in ... status attainment theories ... social structures are viewed as interesting largely as determinants or constraints on individual actions and outcomes. With few exceptions, they have little theoretical relevance in their own right. (p. 70)

Thus, Wright claims that the lack of an adequate theory of social structure and political economy, one that is specific to our kind of economic formation, makes it difficult for stratification researchers to fully understand the relationship between education and differential benefits. To do otherwise would require a different unit of analysis, a fully developed perspective on social class rather than the atomistic individual.

In sum, it has been argued that this kind of research is fundamentally weakened by its underdeveloped notion of class, its choice of the individual rather than social structure and classes as the basic unit of analysis, and its a-theoretical assumptions about occupations and the division of labor (Wright, 1980).

These are not "merely" theoretical points. They have provided the background for an interesting and more structurally oriented empirical program as well. Recent research summarized by Wright (1979) has documented some rather important conclusions here. For example, class compares favorably with status in predicting even individual success (p. 126). When class is a major unit of analysis, it is clear that in the current class structure of the United States, managers receive greater income returns from their education than do workers (p. 165). Furthermore, some data indicate that "class position is at least as powerful an explanatory variable in predicting income as occupational status" (p. 225).

But what about advantages by race and gender? While it would be historically inaccurate and conceptually naive to reduce all gender and racial issues to those of class, research suggests that when class (defined more fully and adequately than in most of the stratification and status attainment literature) is controlled, other differences in the benefits gotten from education are flattened out. This is true of the differences between blacks and whites (p. 195) and, to a somewhat lesser extent, between women and men (p. 216). The real issue here is to begin to inquire into why there is such a large concentration of women and minority members within the working class and even more specifically within particular fractions of that class. How do gender, race, and class interpenetrate each other in contemporary capitalism?[6] It is difficult to fully understand given the theoretical gaps in much of the current literature.

This is *not* to say that the results of this tradition of research are inconsequential. Indeed, many of the results, and the technical procedures employed to generate them, are quite interesting. An example is found in the recent report by Jencks and his colleagues, *Who Gets Ahead?* (1979). The findings there (largely by Michael Olneck in his analysis of the effects of education) are often quite provocative. Olneck argues, for instance, that there are few substantial returns to blacks if they complete only high school, and that relatively higher returns accrue only to those blacks who make it through college. Such data can (and should) make us raise rather important questions about our attempts at ameliorative curricular reform. Added to this is the fact that high school graduation seems to have greater payoff for those people who already come from relatively advantaged backgrounds. "Men who come from disadvantaged backgrounds must attend college to reap large occupational benefits from their education."[7] Surely these findings are interesting. But, again, without a more serious analysis of the political economy of our kind of social formation, they lack a coherent framework that would enable us to put these and other data together into a viable structural program. Their meaning is, in fact, unclear.

Status attainment research, even in its more interesting empirical work, has been subject to at least one other serious criticism that is quite important to our arguments in this essay. It has tended to treat schools as black boxes. It relies largely on questionnaires, tests of various kinds, official records, occasionally interviews, and so on, but it almost never enters into schools to find out how the results that appear on these records are actually produced. The flesh and blood of real students, teachers, and administrators accomplishing all this is never seen. Even those researchers who—like Bowles and Gintis (1976)—are critical of existing research in that tradition and who are on the political left, fall into the same trap. They still treat schools as if the internal characteristics of these institutions are relatively unimportant sociologically or, even when discussed, not to be probed first hand. In Bowles and Gintis's case, this proved to be a particular problem since as recent Marxist ethnographies have demonstrated, the correspondence between what is purported to be taught in schools and the needs of a hierarchical labor market are not that clear. As we noted earlier, working-class students, for instance, often expressly reject the credentials, the overt and hidden curriculum, and the norms that are purportedly taught in schools (Apple, 1982c). The reliance on "external" and "objective" data made it hard for Bowles and Gintis, like other stratification researchers before them, to do other than treat the school like a black box. Unfortunately, in this approach we miss out on what is actually taught, what is actually learned, what is rejected, and how the lived experience of class, race, and gender actors mediates the outcomes so well studied by stratification researchers.

To be sure, the need for such research has not gone unrecognized within the status attainment tradition. Two of the most empirically sophisticated investigators within it have recently argued, quite strongly in fact, that in order to go substantially further in our understanding of what schools actually do, we need to know much more about what goes on within the walls of that institution itself (Kerckhoff, 1976; Sewell & Hauser, 1980; Weis, 1982). They are clearly suggesting an ethnographic program of analysis.

Inside the black box

By examining one side of the divisions in sociology of education and by exploring some of the debates within that side, we do not want to give the impression that ethnographic analyses can answer all of our questions (they can't); nor do we want the reader to assume that there is no division within this side that is equally as contentious (there is).

Theoretically a good deal of ethnographic research is indebted more to phenomenologically inclined sociology than the procedures and linguistic styles of stratification research. Rather than focusing on large-scale sampling techniques, one acts as a participant observer. Rather than occupational and income results, one examines cultural practices within the school itself. The researcher spends long periods of time within the school, examining the "negotiated" informal and implicit social rules and meanings that actors in the particular setting apply. Woods (1979) puts it:

> The sociological approach which informs [this] work derives from symbolic interactionism. This concentrates on how the social world is constructed by people, how they are continually striving to make sense of the world, and assigning meanings and interpretations to events, and on the symbols used to represent them. It puts emphasis on pupils' and teachers' own subjective constructions of events, rather than sociologists' assumptions of them, and elevates the process of meaning-assignation and situation-defining to prime importance. Hence the emphasis on "perspectives," the frameworks through which we make sense of the world, and on different "contexts" which influence the formation and operation of these perspectives. These perceptual frameworks are then linked to action. The action is thus impregnated with the meanings assigned to it by the participants, and is revealed as a mixture of strategies, adaptations and accommodations. Wherever they go in the school, pupils and teachers are continually adjusting, reckoning, bargaining, acting, and changing. (p. 2)

Such adjusting, reckoning, bargaining, acting, and changing does go on, of course. And it is important to know how it occurs, how the reality of school life is continuously produced by our meaningful interaction. Yet the mere fact that reality is socially constructed does not indicate "how and why reality comes to be constructed in particular ways and how and why particular constructions of reality seem to have the power to resist subversion" (Whitty, 1974, p. 125). Thus, ethnographic studies too often fall short of achieving something that Karabel and Halsey realized was essential: a recognition of *and* a structural theory which *accounts for* the differential power of economic and cultural capital within the schools.

This is not to say that all activity in institutions such as schools should be reduced to abstract theoretical formulations. It is to say, though, that one important weakness of such research is that it does not take seriously enough the fact that class and culture, reproduction, contestation and resistance, and contradiction *are* found in the everyday lives of teachers, children, and parents. They *are* all class, gender, and racial actors, not simply individual actors. Contradictions and tensions between and within classes, between the country and the city (and hence within particular local political economies), between sexes and races, and so on are all lived out in local communities and schools like the ones investigated by most participant observers. With all of the richness and value of these ethnographic descriptions, with all of their help in enabling us to get inside the black box of the institution, they too often leave us wondering what it all means. How can we understand elementary schools in the United States, for example, without placing them in the dynamics of class and gender? A huge majority of elementary school teachers are women, an overwhelming number of the principals are men, and these employment patterns are part of the sexual and social divisions of labor. This situation is structural, yet it is not abstract—it is lived out in schools every day (Kelly & Nihlen, 1982b; Apple, in press).

Much ethnographic research in education falls prey to problems that are strikingly similar to those found in the literature on social stratification. One often finds an underdeveloped notion of social class, insufficiently linked to the political economy of the areas being studied. Appraisals of the cultural form and content of the students and the school, whatever their advances beyond most status attainment research, are still less strongly linked to the literature on class, race, and gender cultures than they should be (Clarke, Critcher, & Johnson, 1979; Women's Studies Group, 1978). And, finally, the approach—and this is true of many ethnographies and many studies of education and stratification—lacks an important historical element. It is not connected fully enough to changes over time in the division and control of labor, to ongoing alterations in class composition, and to the historically changing functions of the state in education. This latter point, as we saw in our earlier example, is especially critical in times of what has been called the fiscal crisis of the state. As in the dominant psychological tradition of research on education, schools still too often are not consciously situated within the historically changing dynamics of the society of which they are a part.

We are left here with an interesting predicament. Status attainment research has been strongly criticized for not getting within the black box of the school. A tradition of ethnographic investigation has grown rapidly, one which offers an important counter-balance to these more statistically oriented studies. Yet, while both complement each other in this way, they are equally subject to other important criticisms. Neither has rigorously pursued the connections between their questions and data and structural issues related to the organization and control of the particular kind of social formation in which we live. In the same way, both have employed undertheorized notions of economy, class, and culture. And, finally, each of them has systematically neglected the complex dynamics and interrelationships *among* class, economy, and culture. It is this nexus—the dialectical interconnections among relations of domination and exploitation, cultural form and content, and dominant modes of production—that has become the focus of "culturalist" research on the reproductive role of education. This has come to be called the "sociology of school knowledge."

The sociology of school knowledge

These issues surrounding economy, class, and culture within the school did not spring fully blown upon the scene. More than a decade of investigations—some conceptual, others empirical—have preceded them and have now firmly established what might be called a critical culturalist problematic within sociological studies of the school.

There has been a dual focus in these culturalist studies. Culture has been analyzed both as *lived experience* and as *commodity*. The first examines culture as it is produced in ongoing interaction and as a terrain in which class, gender, and racial meanings and antagonisms are lived out. The second looks at culture as a product, as a set of artifacts produced for use. Both are necessary, and both have been present in the scholarship that has evolved. We shall not present a detailed history of the growth of the traditions these studies represent. Such analyses are available elsewhere (Apple, 1976, 1978, 1979; Grierson, 1978; Karabel & Halsey, 1977, esp. chapter 1). We shall, however, briefly lay out some of the historical, conceptual, and political foundations upon which they have rested.

In the late 1960s and early 1970s, at a time when a structural analysis of the actual cultural form and content inside schools remained relatively unexplored in the sociology of education in the United States, perceptible inroads were being made into this area elsewhere. In England, for instance, the publication of Michael F.D. Young's collection *Knowledge and Control* (1971) signaled the growing interest in the social origins and effects of the organization and selection of curricular knowledge. Young, Bernstein (1977), Bourdieu and Passeron (1977), and others in Europe argued that the organization of knowledge, the form of its transmission, and the assessment of its acquisition are crucial factors in the cultural reproduction of class relationships in industrial societies.

In the United States, often in reaction to the positivistic and technical orientation (what we earlier called the "achievement" tradition) which dominated the field, similar kinds of questions emerged. Yet they emerged less from the sociology of education than from the curriculum field itself. Strongly influenced by critical theory and the sociology of knowledge, as well as the rebirth of Marxist and neo-Marxist dialogue, attempts were made to link the actual knowledge—both hidden and overt—found in schools to the relations of domination and subordination outside the institution (Apple, 1979).

In the United States, England, and France, it was argued that the questions which most sociologists of education and curriculum researchers asked covered the fact that real relations of power were already embedded in their research models and the approaches from which they drew. As Young (1971) put it, sociologists were apt to "take" as their research problems those questions which were generated out of the existing administrative apparatus, rather than "make" them themselves. In curriculum studies, it was claimed that issues of efficiency and increasing meritocratic achievement had almost totally depoliticized the field. Questions of "technique" had replaced the more potent and essential political and ethical issues of what we should teach and why (Apple, 1974).

The interests that guided this research program as it emerged in the prior decade were threefold: (a) to replace the "individualistic, meritocratic analysis of the relationship between education and social inequality" with a more historical and structural appraisal; (b) "to displace the objectivist, psychologized" approaches to research on academic achievement and school curriculum with a "socio-political analysis" of what counts as legitimate school knowledge; and (c) to raise challenges to the managerial, efficiency- and technique-oriented approaches to the organization and control of classrooms and schools and replace them with a "socially interactive and culturally based critical view" (Wexler, 1981b, p. 2).

Schools were seen not only as places that "processed people," but as institutions that "processed knowledge" as well (Young, 1971). One of the primary foci, in fact, was the complex relationship between these two kinds of "processing." In terms of the concepts we previously introduced, it was recognized that school practices needed to be related not only to problems of individual achievement, occupational choice, and mobility, but to the processes of capital accumulation, legitimation, and production as well. Taking a key concept from Gramsci, this research sought to determine how "ideological hegemony" was maintained. How was the control of culture and meaning related to the reproduction of (and, later, resistance to) our socio/economic order? The intellectual work of this period was primarily devoted to ideology critique (Wexler, 1981a, p. 259).[8]

Ideology was usually understood in an Althusserian manner. As Mouffe (1979) put it, the individual person was not "the originating source of consciousness, the irruption of a subjective principle into objective historical process." Instead, consciousness and meaning are made up of ("constituted by") ideological practices that pre-exist human subjects and which actually "produce subjectivity." Thus, "ideology is a practice producing subjects."[9]

For critical researchers on both sides of the Atlantic, then, the symbolic resources organized and transmitted in the school were not neutral. Instead, they were conceptualized in *ideological* terms, as the cultural capital of specific groups which—though this culture did have a life of its own—functioned to re-create relations of domination and subordination by "positioning" subjects within larger ideological discourses and relations. The culture of the school, hence, was a terrain of ideological conflict, not merely a set of facts, skills, dispositions, and social relationships that were to be taught in the most efficient and effective way possible.

For Bernstein, for example, the emphasis was on how a particular segment of the middle class reproduced itself by controlling the curricular and pedagogical apparatus of the school. In Bourdieu and Passeron's work, one saw how the cultural capital of elite groups worked in schools and universities to reproduce class boundaries both within and outside of ruling groups. This was accomplished in part *because* the educational system was relatively autonomous from the needs of production. It was this very autonomy that enabled it to do its ideological work.[10] Other investigators pursued similar paths, examining how the major forms of curriculum, pedagogy, and evaluation contributed to the re-creation of the ideological hegemony of dominant classes in equally subtle and complex ways. What bound these researchers together, though, was a persistent concern with *culture*, not only economy, and with the relationship between what actually happened within the educational system and the structures of exploitation and domination outside it. The attempt—one which grew in sophistication over the years—was to begin to blend together serious structural analysis with studies of the lived and commodified culture of the school. The problem was to integrate micro and macro in a coherent way.

This integrative intent is summarized by one of us in a passage from an earlier volume. There it was suggested that three areas needed to be interrogated if we were to go further than previous research into what schools do and who benefits from their current organization and content.

> We need to examine critically not just "how a student [can] acquire more knowledge" (the dominant question in our efficiency minded field) but "why and how particular aspects of the collective culture are presented in school as objective, factual knowledge?" How, *concretely*, may official knowledge represent ideological configurations of the dominant interests in a society? How do schools legitimate these limited and partial standards of knowing as unquestioned truths? These questions must be asked of at least three areas of school life: (1) how the basic day to day regularities of schools contribute to students learning these ideologies; (2) how the specific forms of curricular

knowledge ... reflect these configurations; (3) how these ideologies are reflected in the fundamental perspectives educators themselves employ to order, guide, and give meaning to their own activity.

The first of these questions refers to the hidden curriculum in schools—the tacit teaching to students of norms, values, and dispositions that goes on simply by their living in and coping with the institutional expectations and routines of schools day in and day out for a number of years. The second question asks us to make educational knowledge itself problematic, to pay much greater attention to the "stuff" of the curriculum, where knowledge comes from, whose knowledge it is, what social groups it supports, and so on. The final query seeks to make educators more aware of the ideological and epistemological commitments they tacitly accept and promote by using certain models and traditions—say, a vulgar positivism, systems management, structural-functionalism, a process of social labeling, or behavior modification—in their own work. Without an understanding of these aspects of school life, one that connects them seriously to the distribution, quality, and control of work, power, ideology, and cultural knowledge outside our educational institutions, educational theory and policy making may have less of an impact than we might hope. (Apple, 1979, p. 14)

While such a critical interrogation of knowledge, social relations, and ideological commitments would not by itself alter either education or society, such a program of criticism was seen as an essential first step in generating more emancipatory research and practice. It was felt necessary to keep in mind the interests both of ethnographers in day-to-day life inside the school and of stratification researchers in the institutions beyond the school. However, instead of mere description of the way actors socially construct and interpret reality, that reality was itself seen critically, as an ideological construction related to class, race, and gender hegemony. And instead of individual occupational selection, the major organizing concept was the reproduction of class relations.[11] As Wexler (1983) put it, such criticism involved "removing the cloak of neutrality by reversing the cognitive social process of converting values to facts." Without reversing this process, we would have nowhere to begin.

There were problems, of course, with some of these early critical formulations. They assumed that it was relatively simple to "read" a text ideologically, that social interests were always "represented" in curriculum and teaching in some straightforward fashion much as a mirror reflects an image. Sometimes this is the case; often it is decidedly not.[12] They too at times embodied a position that schools were necessarily successful in teaching a hidden curriculum, one which "reflects" (again the mirror analogy) the requirements of the division of labor in society. And, finally, they neglected the reality of contradictions and struggle. They posited too passive a model. As has become much clearer over the past few years, people—including teachers and students—may act against dominant ideological forms. The ultimate results may not be either what schools "intended" or what a simple "ideological reading" might imply. Ideological hegemony wasn't something that either existed or didn't exist at any particular moment. It was (and is) a constant struggle, the conclusion of which cannot be known in advance.[13]

This is a crucial point. Because hegemony requires the "consent" of the dominated majority in society, it can never be something that is permanent, universal, or simply given. It needs to be won continually. Whatever stability it possesses is a "moving equilibrium containing relations of forces favorable or unfavorable to this or that tendency."[14] If hegemony is neither fixed nor guaranteed, it can be fractured and challenged. These challenges, in fact, would have to arise because of the tensions, contradictions, and increasingly visible inequalities produced from our dominant mode of production, distribution, and consumption. Resistance to it, even when the resistance is less than conscious, cannot always be automatically incorporated back into dominant ideological forms.[15] Thus, even the educational system itself, in terms of its internal culture and its relations to the wider society, is *not* simply an instrument of domination in which powerful groups control less powerful ones. It is the *result* of an ongoing struggle between and within dominant and dominated groups.[16]

Such internal criticism was not without impact. Wexler, a participant in the debates over the past decade, describes part of the changes in outlook in the following way:

> The dominant theoretical tendency in the critical social theory of education . . . stressed the extent to which education is social structurally determined, the depth of the operation of cultural domination through schooling, and the ways in which the culture and the microstructure of the school enable perpetuation of the macrostructural functions of capital accumulation and social legitimation. These initial insights [were] then modified. The central tenets in the model of political economy of schooling and of class cultural rule by the transmission of ideology as educational knowledge [were] significantly qualified. The concept of [economic] totality [was] replaced by an awareness of relative institutional autonomy. Structural integration [gave] way to the description of internal contradictions. Domination [was] mitigated by study of class conflict and student resistance within the school.[17]

Let us examine Wexler's historical points in somewhat more detail. While the history of this kind of critical work in the sociology of school knowledge has not necessarily been linear, it has in essence gone through a number of phases. The first was the introduction of the importance of studying the role of ideas and consciousness, not only the occupational outcomes of the school. In England in particular, some of the more extreme versions of what was then called the "new sociology of education" seemed to assume that such "questioning of teachers' and others' taken for granted assumptions about prevailing curricular arrangements and pedagogical practices would not only transform education but also lead to wide-ranging changes in the wider society" (SESCT, 1981). Though they were a bit naive politically, the impact of their position should not be dismissed. By legitimating the study of knowledge and consciousness—of culture—they set the stage for much that followed.

Stimulated in part by criticisms of such a "naive possibilitarian" stand (e.g., Bernbaum, 1977; Demaine, 1977; Grierson, 1978; Sharp & Green, 1974; Whitty, 1974), a broader social theory was incorporated into the research program. This tended to be a relatively crude correspondence theory, one often based on or similar to that posited by Bowles and Gintis in *Schooling in Capitalist America*. Here the emphasis was on the "determining effects of capitalist production relations on the nature of schooling and consciousness in capitalist societies" (SESCT, 1981, p. 3). As a consequence, somewhat less attention was paid to the power of cultural forms within the schools. Such a mechanistic theory was clearly untenable for long and in its place a more structuralist Marxist orientation developed.[18] Rather than seeing the economy as determining everything else, with schools having little autonomy, a social formation was described as being made up of a *complex totality* of economic, political, and cultural/ideological practices. Instead of a base/superstructure model—in which "superstructural" institutions such as schools are seen as wholly dependent upon and controlled by the economy—these three sets of interrelated practices *jointly* create the conditions of existence for each other. Thus, the cultural sphere, for instance, has "relative autonomy" and has a "specific and crucial role in the functioning of the whole" (SESCT, 1981, p. 3). Theories of "over-determination," then, became much more visible.

This may seem quite abstract, but its implications proved to be quite consequential. It once again engendered a rapid increase in the study of cultural production and reproduction. For if ideology and culture are "conceived of as having a more real autonomy than merely that which is required for the reproduction of the relations of production," then the school curriculum and the day-to-day social relations in schools, as sets of ideological practices, become very significant both theoretically and in terms of possibilities for action, once again (SESCT, 1981, p. 4; see also Nash, 1984).

However, in recognition of the arguments made earlier about the possibly contradictory nature of the "functions" schools perform and the nature of the conflicts within and over the institution, there was (and is) now a distinct difference. Whereas before one simply assumed a correspondence between economy and ideology, now it was realized that there might be disjunctions between the two. Reproduction was not all that was going on. Culture could, say, both reproduce *and* contradict economic needs. Ideologies might be inherently contradictory in and of themselves.

We want to stress the importance of the fact that there has been a rapid movement away from earlier dogmatic formulations (see Apple, 1982b, on this point). As economism has been increasingly questioned, as simple base/superstructure models have come under closer scrutiny, this has brought about a considerable degree of flexibility. This has been important in a number of ways. It has brought an element of serious self-criticism into the debate over the relationship among education, culture, and economy. By showing the relatively autonomous nature of culture (and the state), and by rejecting reductive approaches which merge everything back into "functions" of a mode of production, we can much more easily unpack the specificities of each area we are studying. Finally, and perhaps most important for educators, these theoretical debates have had a crucial impact on what is seen as the efficacy of practical efforts.[19]

Let us be specific here. If education can be no more than an epiphenomenon tied directly to the requirements of an economy, then little can be done within education itself. It is a totally determined institution. However, if schools (and people) are not passive mirrors of an economy, but instead are active agents in reproducing and contesting dominant social relations, then understanding what they do and acting upon them becomes of no small moment. For if schools are part of a "contested terrain," if they are part of a much larger set of political, economic, and cultural conflicts the outcomes of which are *not* naturally preordained to favor capital, then the hard and continuous day-to-day struggle at the level of curriculum and teaching practice in schools is part of these larger conflicts as well. The key is linking those day-to-day struggles within the school to other action for a more progressive society in that wider arena.

This is notable tonic for the cynicism or the sense that nothing can be done in schools that has pervaded a significant portion of the critically oriented educational community over the past decade or so. Instead, the very sense of the school's active role in re-creating hegemonic relations that are constantly being threatened—and, hence, are in constant need of being rebuilt—opens up a whole arena for joint action with other progressive educators, parents, students, labor groups, women, people of color, and so on. Culture—commodified and lived— within the black box, then, takes an even more critical place. Investigating the role it plays—and struggling over it—becomes quite consequential.

Therefore, there has been even greater interest in culturalist studies. A large number of studies have begun again to pay considerable attention to how ideology "works" in cultural materials. This research focuses on commodified culture, on the "things" of culture such as films, texts, novels, art, and so forth in an attempt to illuminate the ideological tensions, commitments, and contradictions in the material. Some of these investigations have been much more sophisticated than earlier approaches to ideological analysis, enhancing their cultural examination by drawing on the work in semiotics and literary structuralism that has grown out of European work on ideology.[20]

However, while certainly better than what preceded them, we need to remember that these approaches do only study one half of the cultural dynamic. As we argued, a thoroughgoing analysis of the relation between ideology and the knowledge and social relations of schooling must involve investigating not only the material of culture, but subjectivity as well. Process must complement product. Without this dual focus, we run the risk of forgetting something very important: the concrete activity of people.

Whitty (1981) directs our attention to some of these dangers:

> Many post-Althusserian writers, engaged in an attempt to elucidate more clearly the specific characteristics of ideological practice, have drawn heavily on work in linguistics and semiotics and this has led to a variety of "structuralist" approaches to reading ideology, which focus on the ways in which texts produce meaning and position human subjects through their internal structures and rules rather than their overt content. . . . Such studies often concern the ways in which texts address and position "ideal subjects," whereas [Richard] Johnson reminds us that the actual significance of the ideological work they do depends on their relationship to "attitudes and beliefs already lived. Ideologies never address ('interpellate') a 'naked subject'. . . . Concrete social individuals are always already constructed as culturally classed and sexed agents, already having a complexly formed subjectivity". . . . In structuralist analysis, there is always a danger of "remaining locked in the ideological forms themselves and *inferring* effects" [and] of underplaying the significance of the *"moment* of self creation, of the *affirmation* of belief or of the *giving* of consent." As such, they are in danger of producing too mechanistic a model of the formation of subjectivities.[21]

Thus, the active agent must take its place beside the subject who is "produced" by ideology. The tension between the two positions is constant. There is a strong relationship between ideology and the knowledge and practices of education. Ideology does have power, through both what it includes *and* what it excludes. It does position people within wider relations of domination and exploitation. Yet, when lived out, it also often has elements of a "good" as well as a "bad" sense in it (Johnson, 1979, p. 43). Side by side with beliefs and actions that maintain the dominance of powerful classes and groups, there are elements of serious (though perhaps incomplete) understanding: elements that see differential benefits, power, and control and penetrate close to the heart of an unequal reality. Thus, while we must continue that part of our program that analyzes the ideological content of education, we should also remember that real people with real and complex histories interact with that content. The ideological outcome is always the result of that interaction, not an act of imposition.

This is a more dynamic way of looking at the question of ideological reproduction than the one that has prevailed in the literature on ideology and schooling in the past. It provides the foundations for a more complete theory of how ideology functions. In the next section of this article we will provide a concrete model which will synthesize the theoretical points we have just made.

Analyzing the dynamics of ideology

In the previous sections we pointed out the growing sophistication of our concepts of what schools do socially. We argued that approaches that focused only on economy and not on culture, or that dealt only with cultural products and not lived cultural processes, were incomplete. We also claimed that education is not a stable enterprise dominated by consensus, but instead is riven with ideological conflicts. These political, cultural, and economic conflicts are dynamic. They are in something like constant motion, each often acting on the others and each stemming from structurally generated antagonisms, compromises, and struggles. Given our increasingly deep understanding of the complex relationship between culture and the formation of, and/or resistance to, ideological hegemony, what does it mean for our more specific problem of ideology and education?

First, rather than a unidimensional theory in which economic form is determinate, society is conceived of as being made up of *three interrelated spheres*: the economic, the cultural/ideological, and the political.

Second, we need to be cautious about assuming that ideologies are only ideas held in one's head. They are better thought of less as things than as social processes (Therborn, 1980, p. vii). Nor are ideologies linear configurations, simple processes that all necessarily work in the same direction or reinforce each other. Instead, these processes sometimes overlap, compete, drown out, and even clash with each other. They are better pictured perhaps as the "cacophany of sounds and signs of a big city street than by a text serenely communicating with the solitary reader, or the teacher or TV-personality addressing a quiet domesticated audience" (Therborn, 1980, p. viii).

That there may not be "a quiet domesticated audience" points to the dialectical character of ideology. This is brought out clearly if we think about the two opposite meanings of the word "subject." Persons can be both subjects of a ruler and the subjects of history. Each connotes a different sense—the first passive, the second active. Thus, ideologies not only subject people to a pre-existing social order, they also qualify members of that order for social action and change. In this way, ideologies function as much more than the cement that holds society together. *They empower as well as depower* (Therborn, 1980, p. vii).

This process of empowering is partly the result of the fact that a number of elements or *dynamics* are usually present at the same time in any one instance. This is important. Ideological form is not reducible to class. Processes of gender, age, and race enter directly into the ideological moment.[22] It is actually out of the articulation with, clash among, or contradictions among and within, say, class, race, and sex that ideologies are lived in one's day-to-day life.

In order to unpack how ideology works, then, we have to consider each of the spheres and the dynamics which operate within them. It may be helpful to conceptualize the intricate connections among these elements with the use of the following figure:

Spheres

	Economic	Cultural	Political
Class			
Race			
Gender			

(Dynamics)

As the figure shows, each sphere of social life is constituted by the dynamics of class, race, and gender. Each of these dynamics, and each of these spheres, has its own internal history *in relation to* the others. Each dynamic is found in each of the spheres. Thus, to give an example, it is impossible to completely comprehend class relations in capitalism without seeing how capital uses patriarchal social relations in its organization. The current deskilling of women clerical workers through the introduction of word processing technology and the overall loss of jobs that will result among working-class women offers one instance where class and gender interact in the economy. In schools, the aforementioned fact that elementary school teachers are mostly women who historically have come from a particular segment of the population illuminates the dual dynamics of class and gender at work again (Apple, in press). Likewise, the rejection of schooling by many black and brown youth in our urban centers, along with the sense of pride felt by many unmarried minority high school girls in their ability to bear a child, is a result of the complex interconnections among class, race, and gender oppressions and struggles at the level of the lived culture of these youth.[23]

Examples like these could be multiplied. Our major point is to document the relational quality of ideology. Schools are part of the economic, political, and cultural spheres. The needs of each may not always fully overlap. The dynamics which make these spheres up, therefore, also interact in everyday activity in schools. They, too, may not always reinforce each other. This makes ideological analyses a complicated endeavor since unpacking even one ideological process like that of gender is quite difficult. Integrating the others into it may be exceptionally hard.

The recognition of this difficulty is important. We must not assume that simple formulations will enable us to understand the real life of our educational institutions. As we have shown here, the theories currently being debated have themselves changed markedly over time as such complications have arisen. We have no reason to believe that they will be static now, nor do we think such stasis would be helpful. We do believe, however, that only through their use in the analysis of concrete practices in concrete institutions and of the concrete stratifying processes of culture and people in schools will the field progress.

Notes

1 For more extensive analysis of this and other research approaches, see Apple (1979).
2 Apple and Taxel (1982). We have purposely set off the word "functions," given the debate over the utility of the concept of functionality itself, since it often implies an endlessly reproductive process that is relatively conflict free with little chance of change. As will be seen later in this article, we have fundamental disagreements with this position. For criticisms of functionalist logic in education, see Apple (1982). A sophisticated version of functionalist analysis is defended, however, in Cohen (1978).
3 I am indebted to Walter Feinberg for part of this argument. See also Noble (1977) and Apple (1979, 1982c, chapter 2).
4 Much of the recent work is summarized in Kerckhoff (1980), a valuable book within the context of this research program.
5 While this is a very complex issue, the interested reader might want to follow up the argument about how one interprets class by looking at the work of, say, recent Marxist critics of status attainment research such as that of Erik Olin Wright or some of the historical and empirical work on class formation, culture, and the labor process in Europe and the United States. See, for example, Poulantzas (1975), Edwards (1979), and Clarke, Critcher, and Johnson (1979). For a historical analysis of the role of education in class formation in the United States, see Hogan (1982).
6 Wright (1979), p. 201. See also Women's Studies Group (1978), Reich (1981), and Omi and Winant (in press).
7 Jencks, et al. (1979), pp. 174–175. It is very important to note that nearly all of these studies have been of *men*. They, thus, underrepresent and in part reproduce the structure of patriarchal domination in society.
8 Green (1980) makes a similar point.
9 Mouffe (1979), p. 171. See also Althusser (1971). As we shall see later, this position has been strongly criticized both politically and conceptually.
10 See especially final chapter in Bernstein (1977). Bernstein (1982) is an even more ambitious attempt to develop a theory that would link class, culture, and ideology together.
11 We shall argue later, though, that ideology is *not* reducible to class dynamics. This neglects the impressive contributions made by feminist criticisms of orthodox Marxist research and theories. See Women's Studies Group (1978) and Arnot (1981).
12 For further discussion of the complicated issue of ideological "representation" in a text, see Barrett, Corrigan, Kuhn, and Wolff (1979) and Sumner (1979).
13 These criticisms have been discussed at much greater length in Apple (1982c) and Wexler (1982). See also Giroux (1981, 1983).
14 Hebdige (1980), p. 16. See also the well-known work of Connell, Ashendon, Kessler, & Dowsett (1982).
15 We do *not* mean to imply that such challenges will always be progressive. The possibility that they will not be is raised by Plotke (1980, 1981).
16 It is important to stress the fact that educational policies and practices are often the outcomes of conflict between segments of dominant classes. The way the state is currently acting to rebuild hegemonic control given the current economic, political, and cultural crisis is examined in Apple (1982a, 1982c).
17 Wexler (1981a), p. 248. While Wexler has been involved in this tradition of critical culturalist analysis, he is critical of a number of tendencies within it and argues that they must be superseded given current economic, political, and cultural conditions. See also Wexler and Whitson (1981).
18 Bowles and Gintis themselves have since criticized their initial work. See Gintis and Bowles (1981).
19 See Apple (1982c), especially chapters 1 and 6, and the discussions of the state in Carnoy and Levin (1985).
20 For further analysis and examples of this work, see Apple and Weis (1983). For further discussion of the text as a particular constellation of political, cultural, and economic practices, see Apple (1985, in press).
21 Whitty (1981), p. 16. See also Wexler (1982) and Apple and Weis (1983).
22 Therborn (1980), p. 26. See also Therborn's interesting discussion of the necessity of

linking analysis of class ideologies with those of male chauvinism on p. 38 and the more extensive analysis of the relationship among class and, especially, gender, in Apple (in press).
23 For an empirical analysis of some of these interconnections, particularly those associated with racial dynamics, see Weis (1985).

References

Althusser, L. (1971). Ideology and ideological state apparatuses. In L. Althusser, *Lenin and philosophy and other essays*. London: New Left Books.
Apple, M. W. (1974). The process and ideology of valuing in educational settings. In M. W. Apple, M. Subkoviak, & H. Lufler, Jr. (Eds.), *Educational evaluation: Analysis and responsibility* (pp. 3–34). Berkeley: McCutchan.
Apple, M. W. (1976). Curriculum as ideological selection. *Comparative Education Review, 20,* 209–215.
Apple, M. W. (1978). The new sociology of education: Analyzing cultural and economic reproduction. *Harvard Educational Review, 48,* 495–503.
Apple, M. W. (1979). *Ideology and curriculum.* Boston: Routledge and Kegan Paul.
Apple, M. W. (1982a). Common Curriculum and state control. *Discourse, 2,* 1–10.
Apple, M. W. (Ed.). (1982b). *Cultural and economic reproduction in education: Essays on class, ideology and the state.* Boston: Routledge and Kegan Paul.
Apple, M. W. (1982c). *Education and power.* Boston: Routledge and Kegan Paul.
Apple, M. W. (1985) The culture and commerce of the textbook. *Journal of Curriculum Studies, 17,* 147–162.
Apple, M. W. (in press). *Teachers and texts: A political economy of class and gender relations in education.* Boston: Routledge and Kegan Paul.
Apple, M. W., & Taxel, J. (1982). Ideology and the curriculum. In A. Hartnett (Ed.), *The social sciences and education* (pp. 166–178). London: Heinemann.
Apple, M. W., & Weis, L. (Eds.). (1983). *Ideology and practice in schooling.* Philadelphia: Temple University Press.
Arnot, M. (1981). *Class, gender and education.* Milton Keynes: The Open University Press.
Barrett, M., Corrigan, P. Kuhn, A., & Wolff, J. (Eds.). (1979). *Ideology and cultural production.* New York: St. Martin's Press.
Bernbaum, G. (1977), *Knowledge and ideology in the sociology of education.* New York: Macmillan.
Bernstein, B. (1977). *Class, codes and control, Vol. 3.* Boston: Routledge and Kegan Paul.
Bernstein, B. (1982). Codes, modalities and the process of cultural reproduction. In M. W. Apple (Ed.), *Cultural and economic reproduction in education: Essays on class, ideology and the state* (pp. 304–355). Boston: Routledge and Kegan Paul.
Bourdieu, P., & Passeron, J. C. (1977). *Reproduction in education, society and culture.* Beverly Hills: Sage.
Bowles, S., & Gintis, H. (1976). *Schooling in capitalist America.* New York: Basic Books.
Carnoy, M., & Levin, H. (1985). *Schooling and work in the democratic state.* Stanford: Stanford University Press.
Castells, M. (1980). *The economic crisis and American society.* Princeton: Princeton University Press.
Clarke, J., Critcher, C., & Johnson, R. (Eds.). (1979). *Working class culture.* London: Hutchinson.
Cohen, G. A. (1978). *Karl Marx's theory of history: A defense.* Princeton: Princeton University Press.
Collins, R. (1979). *The credential society.* New York: Academic Press.
Connell, R. W., Ashendon, D., Kessler, S., & Dowsett, G. W. (1982). *Making the difference.* Sydney: George Allen and Unwin.
Dale, R. (1982). Education and the capitalist state. In M. W. Apple (Ed.), *Cultural and economic reproduction in education: Essays on class, ideology and the state* (pp. 127–161). Boston: Routledge and Kegan Paul.
Demaine, J. (1977). On the new sociology of education. *Economy and Society, 6,* 111–144.
Edwards, R. (1979). *Contested terrain.* New York: Basic Books.

Gintis, H., & Bowles, S. (1981). Contradiction and reproduction in educational theory. In L. Barton, R. Meighan, & S. Walker (Eds.), *Schooling, ideology and curriculum* (pp. 51–65). Barcombe: Falmer Press.

Giroux, H. (1981). *Ideology, culture and process of schooling.* Philadelphia: Temple University Press.

Giroux, H. (1983). *Theory and resistance in education.* South Hadley: Bergin and Garvey.

Green, A. (1980). Extended review. *British Journal of Sociology of Education, 1,* 121–128.

Grierson, P. C. (1978). An extended review of *Knowledge and control, Explorations in the politics of school knowledge,* and *Society, state and schooling. Educational Studies, 4,* 67–84.

Hall, S. (1977). Rethinking the "base and superstructure" metaphor. In J. Bloomfield (Ed.), *Class, hegemony and party* (pp. 43–72). London: Lawrence and Wishart.

Hebdige, D. (1980). *Subculture: The meaning of style,* London: Methuen.

Hogan, D. (1982). Education and class formation: The peculiarity of the Americans. In M. W. Apple (Ed.), *Cultural and economic reproduction in education. Essays on class, ideology and the state* (pp. 32–78). Boston: Routledge and Kegan Paul.

Jencks, C., et al. (Eds.). (1979). *Who gets ahead?* New York: Basic Books.

Johnson, R. (1979). Histories of culture/theories of ideology. In M. Barrett, P. Corrigan, A. Kuhn, & J. Wolff (Eds.), *Ideology and cultural production* (pp. 49–77). New York: St. Martin's Press.

Karabel, J., & Halsey, A. H. (Eds.). (1977). *Power and ideology in education.* New York: Oxford University Press.

Kelly, G., & Nihlen, A. (1982). Schooling and the reproduction of patriarchy. In M. Apple (Ed.), *Cultural and economic reproduction in education: Essays on class, ideology and the state* (pp. 162–180). Boston: Routledge and Kegan Paul.

Kerckhoff, A. C. (1976). The status attainment process: Socialization or allocation? *Social Forces, 55,* 368–381.

Kerckhoff, A. C. (Ed.). (1980). *Research in sociology of education and socialization: Longitudinal perspectives on educational attainment.* Greenwich: JAI Press.

Macpherson, C. B. (1981). Do we need a theory of the state? In R. Dale, G. Esland, R. Fergusson, & M. MacDonald (Eds.), *Education and the state, Vol. 1* (pp. 61–75). Sussex: Falmer Press.

Meyer, J. (1977). The effects of education as an institution. *American Journal of Sociology, 83,* 55–77.

Mouffe, C. (1979). Hegemony and ideology in Gramsci. In C. Mouffe (Ed.), *Gramsci and Marxist theory* (pp. 168–204). Boston: Routledge and Kegan Paul.

Nash, R. (1984). On two critiques of the Marxist sociology of education. *British Journal of Sociology of Education, 5,* 19–31.

Navarro, V. (1976). *Medicine under capitalism.* New York: Neale Watson.

Noble, D. (1977). *America by design.* New York: Knopf.

O'Connor, J. (1973). *The fiscal crisis of the state.* New York: St. Martin's Press.

Ogbu, J. (1978). *Minority education and caste.* New York: Academic Press.

Olneck, M. R., & Bills, D. B. (1980). What makes Sammy run: An empirical assessment of the Bowles-Gintis correspondence theory. *American Journal of Education, 89,* 27–61.

Omi, M., & Winant, H. (in press). *Racial formation in the United States.* Boston: Routledge and Kegan Paul.

Plotke, D. (1980). The United States in transition: Toward a new order? *Socialist Review, 10,* 71–123.

Plotke, D. (1981). The politics of transition: The United States in transition, II. *Socialist Review, 11,* 21–72.

Poulantzas, N. (1975). *Classes in contemporary capitalism.* London: New Left Books.

Reich, M. (1981). *Racial inequality.* Princeton: Princeton University Press.

Sewell, W., & Hauser, R. (1980). The Wisconsin longitudinal study of social and psychological factors in aspirations and achievements. In A. C. Kerckhoff (Ed.), *Research in sociology of education and socialization: Longitudinal perspectives on educational attainment* (pp. 59–99). Greenwich: JAI Press.

Sharp, R., & Green, A. (1974). *Education and social control.* Boston: Routledge and Kegan Paul.

SESCT [Society, Education and the State Course Team]. (Eds.) (1981). *The politics of cultural production*. Milton Keynes: The Open University Press.

Summer, C. (1979). *Reading ideologies*. New York: Macmillan.

Therborn, G. (1980). *The ideology of power and the power of ideology*. London: New Left Books.

Weis, L. (1982). Educational outcomes and school processes. In P. Altbach, R. Arnove, & G. Kelly (Eds.), *Comparative education*. New York: Macmillan.

Weis, L. (1982). *Between two worlds*. Boston: Routledge and Kegan Paul.

Wexler, P. (1981a). Body and soul: Sources of social change and strategies for education. *British Journal of Sociology of Education, 2,* 247–267.

Wexler, P. (1981b). Change: Social, cultural, educational. In *New directions in education: Critical perspectives* (Occasional paper #8). Buffalo: Department of Social Foundations and Comparative Education Center, State University of New York at Buffalo.

Wexler, P. (1982). Structure, text and subject. In M. W. Apple (Ed.), *Cultural and economic reproduction in education: Essays on class, ideology and the state* (pp. 275–303). Boston: Routledge and Kegan Paul.

Wexler, P. (1983). *Critical social psychology*. Boston: Routledge and Kegan Paul.

Wexler, P., and Whitson, T. (1981). *Hegemony and education*. Unpublished manuscript, University of Rochester, Rochester, New York.

Whitty, G. (1974). Sociology and the problem of radical educational change. In M. Flude & J. Ahier (Eds.), *Educability, schools and ideology* (pp. 2–137). London: Croom Helm.

Whitty, G. (1981). Ideology, politics and curriculum. In Society, Education and the State Course Team (Eds.), *The politics of cultural production*. Milton Keynes: The Open University Press.

Willis, P. (1977). *Learning to labour*. Westmead: Saxon House.

Women's Studies Group. (1978). *Women take issue*. London: Hutchinson.

Woods, P. (1979). *The divided school*. Boston: Routledge and Kegan Paul.

Wright, E. O. (1979). *Class structure and income determination*. New York: Academic Press.

Wright, E. O. (1980). Class and occupation. *Theory and Society, 9,* 177–214.

Young, M. F. D. (Ed.). (1971). *Knowledge and control*. London: Macmillan.

CHAPTER 13

SILENCING IN PUBLIC SCHOOLS (1987)

Michelle Fine

> Lying is done with words and also with silence.
> Adrienne Rich, *On Lies, Secrets and Silence.*

Demands for silencing signify a terror of words, a fear of talk. This essay examines these demands as they echoed through a comprehensive public high school in New York City. The silencing resounded in words and in their absence; the demands emanated from the New York City Board of Education, book publishers, corporate sponsors, religious institutions, administrators, teachers, parents, and students. In the odd study of *what's not said* in public schools, one must be curious about whom silencing protects, but vigilant about how silencing students and their communities undermines fundamentally the vision of education as empowerment (Freire 1985; Shor 1980).

This essay examines what doesn't get talked about in schools and how "undesirable" talk is subverted, appropriated, and exported. In this essay silencing constitutes a process of institutionalized policies and practices which obscure the very social, economic, and therefore experiential conditions of students' daily lives, and which expel from written, oral, and nonverbal expression substantive and critical "talk" about these conditions. Silencing orchestrates the paradoxical life of institutions such as schools, which are marked as *the* opportunity for mobility when indeed groups are unevenly "mobilized" by the same educational credential, and even more unevenly disabled by its absence. Further, in a city such as New York, dropouts from the wealthiest neighborhoods are systematically more likely to be employed than high school graduates from the poorest neighborhoods (Tobier 1984). Yet simple, seamless pronouncements of equal opportunity and educational credentials as the primary mode of mobility are woven through the curriculum and pedagogy of urban high school classes. Silencing constitutes the process by which contradictory evidence, ideologies, and experiences find themselves buried, camouflaged, and discredited.

While schools are replete with countertensions, including the voices of exposure and critique, the press for silencing pervades low income urban schools. The centralized and tiered structure of educational administration, books used, curriculum generated, pedagogy applied, administrative withholding of data, "objective" mechanisms for evaluating teachers and students, and strategies for excluding parents/guardians and community activists compromise the means by which schools establish themselves as fortresse against low-income communities;

students are subverted in their attempts to merge school and home, and conversations are aborted.

Silencing, I would guess, more intimately informs low-income, public schooling than relatively privileged situations. To question from above holds intellectual promise; to question from below forebodes danger. In low-income schools both the process of inquiry into students' lived experience, and the content to be unearthed are assumed to be, a priori, unsafe territory.

Silencing sustains the belief in schooling as the mechanism for social mobility, with contradictory evidence barred. And silencing diverts critique away from the economic, social, and educational institutions which organize class, race, and gender hierarchies. But the silencing process bears not only ideological or cosmetic consequence. These very demands permeate classroom life so primitively as to make irrelevant the lived experiences, passions, concerns, communities, and biographies of low-income, minority students. In the process the very voices of students and their communities that public education claims to nurture, shut down.

This essay focuses on silencing primarily at the level of classroom and school talk in a low-income, "low-skill" school. The corporate, institutional, and bureaucratic mandates from which demands for silencing derive, while acknowledged, remain relatively immune from the present analysis. This is not to locate blame inside classrooms nor with individual teachers, but merely to extract from these interactions the raw material for a critical view of silencing. The data derive from a year-long ethnography of a high school in Manhattan, attended by 3,200 students, predominantly low-income blacks and Hispanics from Central Harlem, and run primarily by black paraprofessionals and aides, white administrators and teachers, with some Hispanic paraprofessionals and teachers (see Fine 1985, 1986).

The analysis seems important for two reasons. First, there is substantial evidence that many students in this school, considered low in skill and motivation, were eager to choreograph their own learning, to generate a curriculum of lived experience and to engage in a participatory pedagogy. Every attempt, intended or not, to undermine their educational autobiographizing, by teachers or administrators, sacrificed another chance to connect with students and their communities (Bastian, Fruchter, Gittell, Greer & Haskins 1985; Connell, Ashenden, Kessler & Dowsett 1984; Lightfoot 1978). While not overstating the academic energy spontaneously displayed by these adolescents, I would stress that those administrators, teachers, and paraprofessionals sufficiently interested and patient did generate classrooms of relatively "alive" participants. More overwhelming to the observer, however, silencing engulfed life inside the classrooms and administrative offices.

This loss of connection bears significant consequence for low-income, minority students who are fundamentally ambivalent about the educational process and its credentials (Carnoy & Levin 1985). As confident as they were that "you can't get nowhere without a diploma," most were also mindful that "the richest man in my neighborhood didn't graduate but from eighth grade." And, of course, they were not wrong. Each of these two beliefs withstands tests of empirical validity, measured in labor force statistics, as well as experiential validity, confirmed daily on their streets. "Within democratic society, . . . contradictions between the rhetoric of equality and the reality of domination must be obscured" (Cummins 1986, p. 25). And so the process of silencing camouflaged such contradictions, advancing ironically the cynicism of the latter student belief, eroding the idealism of the former.

The silencing process is but one aspect of what is often, for low-income students, an impoverished educational tradition. Infiltrating administrative "talk," curriculum development, and pedagogical technique, the means of silencing establish impenetrable barriers between the worlds of school and community life.

The impulse to silence: fears of naming

In June of 1984 I decided to spend the following fall and spring conducting an ethnography inside this high school, watching specifically for the production and reproduction of high school graduates and dropouts, not yet interested in anything I would later consider silencing (see Fine 1985, 1986).[1] To my request for entree to his school, the principal greeted me as follows:

Field Note, June 1984.

Mr. Stein: Sure you can do your research on dropouts at this school. With one provision. You can not mention the words "dropping out" to the students.
MF: Why not?
Stein: I firmly believe that if you say it, you encourage them to do it.

My field notes continue, "When he said this, I thought, adults should be so lucky, that adolescents wait for us *to name* dropping out, or sex, for them to do it." From September through June I witnessed daily life inside classrooms, deans' and nurses' offices, the attendance room, and the lunchroom. Over time it struck me as even more naive that the school administrator would believe that what adults say engenders teenage compliance. With so little evidence that adult talk promotes any adolescent compliance, how could one continue to believe that if an authority says it, students will conform; that naming is dangerous and not naming is safe?

As the year transpired, what became apparent was not naivete but a systematic, school-based fear of talk; a special kind of talk which might be called *naming*. Naming gives license to critical conversation about social and economic arrangements, particularly inequitable distributions of power and resources, by which these students and their kin suffer disproportionately. The fear of naming provoked the move to silence.

One can only speculate on this inferred fear of naming. By no means universal, it was, by every measure, commonplace. Let us assume that urban teachers and administrators seek to believe that schooling can make a significant difference, collectively or individually, in the lives of these adolescents. Given that they have little authority to create what they might consider the necessary conditions (see Carnegie Forum on Education and the Economy 1986; Holmes Group 1986), "choices" are undoubtedly made about how to make sense of their work and their presumably limited effectiveness. Not naming fits essentially with how one structures meaning of the work of public education.

With one strategy administrators and teachers viewed most of these students as unteachable, following the logic of social studies teacher Mr. Rosaldo, "If I reach 20 percent, if we save 20 percent, that's a miracle. Most of these kids don't have a chance." While the incidence of this belief remains to be documented, compelling correlational evidence suggests that those teachers who feel most disempowered in their institutions are also most likely to subscribe to such a notion, to agree that "These kids can't be helped." (Fine 1983). Perhaps these teachers have themselves been silenced over time. For them, *naming* social equities in the classroom could only expose social circumstances they believed to be basically self-imposed and diminish the distance between "them" and "us." When I presented the data to the faculty at the end of the year and suggested, for example, that the level of involuntary "discharges" processed through this school would never be tolerated in the schools attended by the faculty's children, I was reminded by a faculty member, "That's an absurd comparison. The schools my kids go to are nothing like this— the comparison is itself sensationalism!" The social distance between "them" and "us" was reified and naturalized.

Other teachers subscribed loyally to beliefs in a color-blind meritocracy. They merely dismissed the empirical data which would have had to inform the process of naming. Here they followed the logic of science teacher Ms. Tannenbaum, "If these students work hard, they can really become something. Especially today with Affirmative Action." They rejected or avoided counterevidence: e.g., that black high school graduates living in Harlem are still far less likely to be employed than white high school dropouts living in more elite sections of New York (Tobier 1984). Enormous energy must be required to sustain beliefs in equal opportunity and the color-blind power of credentials, and to silence nagging losses of faith when evidence to the contrary compels on a daily basis. Naming in such a case would only unmask, fundamentally disrupting or contradicting one's belief system.

But some educators did actively engage their students in lively, critical discourse about the complexities and inequities of prevailing economic and social relations. Often importing politics from other spheres of their lives, the feminist English teacher, the community activist who taught grammar, or the Marxist historian wove critical analysis into their classrooms with little effort. These classrooms were permeated with the openness of naming, free of the musty tension which derives from conversations-not-had.

Most educators at this school, however, seemed to survive by not naming or analyzing social problems. They taught the curricula and pedagogical techniques they hoped would soothe students and smooth social contradictions. Many would probably have not considered conversation about social class, gender, or race politics relevant to their courses, or easily integrated into their curricula. One could have assumed, therefore, that they had benignly neglected these topics.

Evidence of *fear*, however, rather than neglect, grew salient when students (activated by curiosity or rebellion) raised topics which were rapidly shut down. A systemic expulsion of dangerous topics permeated the room. I would posit that, to examine power differentials, the very conditions which contribute to insidious social class, racial, ethnic, and gender divisions in the U.S., when the teacher is relatively privileged by class usually and race often, introduces for educators fantasies of danger. Such conversations *problematize* what seem like "natural" social distinctions, such as the distinction between where one teaches and where one sends one's children to be taught. Such conversations threaten to erode teachers' authority. While usually not by conscious choice, teachers and administrators engaged in diverse strategies to preempt, detour, or ghettoize such conversations. *Not naming*, as a particular form of silencing, was accomplished creatively. Often with good intentions, not naming bore equally devastating consequences.

Naming may indeed be dangerous to beliefs often promoted in public schools; it is for that very reason *essential* to the creation of an empowered and critical constituency of educated social participants (Aronowitz & Giroux 1985). To *not name* bears consequences for all students, but more so for low-income, minority youths. To not name is to systematically alienate, cut off from home, from heritage and from lived experience, and ultimately to sever from their educational process. Following the lead of Adrienne Rich in the opening quote, silencing is examined below through what was said and what was not said in this public school across the academic year 1984–1985, beginning with the obvious, if redundant occurrence of administrative silencing.

Administrative silencing: white noise

Field Note: September 1985

We are proud to say that 80 percent of our high school graduates go on to college.
                                        Principal, Parents' Association meeting, September 1985

At the first Parents' Association meeting, Mr. Stein, the principal, boasted an 80 percent "college-bound" rate. Almost all graduates of this inner city high school head for college; a comforting claim oft repeated by urban school administrators in the 1980s. While accurate, this pronouncement fundamentally detoured the conversation away from the fact that in this school, as in others, only 20 percent of incoming ninth graders *ever* graduated. In other words, *16 percent* of the 1220 ninth graders of 1978–1979 were headed for college by 1985. The "white noise" promoted by the administration reverberated silence in the audience. Not named, and therefore not problematized, was retention. No questions were asked.

Not naming signifies an administrative craft. The New York City Board of Education, for example, refuses to monitor retention, promotion, and educational achievement statistics by race and ethnicity for fear of "appearing racist" (Personal Communication 1984).[2] As a result huge discrepancies in educational advancement, by race and ethnicity, remain undocumented in Board publications. Likewise dropout calculations may include students on register when they have not been seen for months; may presume that students who enroll in GED programs are not dropouts, or that those who produce "working papers" are about to embark on careers (which involves a letter, for example, from a Chicken Delight clerk assuring that José has a job, so that he can leave school at sixteen). Such procedures insidiously contribute to not naming the density of the dropout problem.

While administrative silencing is unfortunately almost a redundant notion, the concerns of this essay are primarily focused on classroom- and school-based activities of silencing. Examining the processes of not naming pedagogically and within the public school curriculum, the essay ends with the most dramatic embodiment of silencing, the academically mute bodies of those young black teenage girls who say nothing all day, who have perfected the mask of being silenced, who are never identified as a problem.

The remainder of the essay moves from pedagogy to curriculum to discipline as discrete moments in the silencing process.

Closing down conversations

Field Note: October 17, Business Class

| *White teacher:* | What's EOE? |
| *Black male student:* | Equal over time. |

White teacher:	Not quite. Anyone else?
Black female student:	Equal Opportunity Employer.
Teacher:	That's right.
Black male student (2):	What does that mean?
Teacher:	That means that an employer can't discriminate on the basis of sex, age, marital status, or race.
Black male student (2):	But wait, sometimes white people only hire white people.
Teacher:	No, they're not supposed to if they say EOE in their ads. Now take out your homework.

Later that day:

| *MF:* | Why don't you discuss racism in your class? |
| *Teacher:* | It would demoralize the students, they need to feel positive and optimistic—like they have a chance. Racism is just an excuse they use not to try harder. |

What enables some teachers to act as if students benefit from such smoothing over (Wexler 1983)? For whose good are the roots, the scars and the structures of class, race, and gender inequity obscured by teachers, texts and tests (Anyon 1983)? Are not the "fears of demoralizing" a projection by teachers of their own silenced loss of faith in public education, and their own fears of unmasking or freeing a conversation about social inequities?

At the level of curriculum, texts, and conversation in classrooms, school talk and knowledge were radically severed from the daily realities of adolescents' lives and more systematically allied with the lives of teachers (McNeil 1981). Routinely discouraged from critically examining the conditions of their lives, dissuaded from creating their own curriculum, built of what they know, students were often encouraged to disparage the circumstances in which they live, warned by their teachers: "You act like that, and you'll end up on welfare!" Most were or have been surviving on some form of federal, state or city assistance.

"Good students" managed these dual/duel worlds by learning to speak standard English dialect, whether they originally spoke black English, Spanish, or Creole. And more poignant still, they trained themselves to speak and produce in two voices. One's "own" voice alternated with an "academic" voice which denied class, gender, and race conflict; reproduced ideologies about hard work, success, and their "natural" sequence; and stifled the desire to disrupt.

In a study conducted in 1981, it was found that the group of South Bronx students who were "successes"—those who remained in high school—when compared to dropouts, were significantly *more* depressed, *less* politically aware, *less* likely to be assertive in the classroom if they were undergraded, and *more* conformist (Fine 1983)! A moderate level of depression, an absence of political awareness, the presence of self-blame, low-assertiveness, and high conformity may tragically have constituted evidence of the "good" urban student at this high school. They learned not to raise, and indeed to help shut down, "dangerous" conversation. The price of "success" may have been muting one's own voice.

Other students from this school resolved the "two voices" tension with creative, if ultimately self-defeating, strategies. Cheray reflected on this moment of hegemony after she dropped out: "In school we learned Columbus Avenue stuff and *I* had to translate it into Harlem. They think livin' up here is unsafe and our lives are so bad. That we should want to move out and get away. That's what you're supposed to learn."[3]

Tony thoroughly challenged the academic voice as ineffective pedagogy: "I never got math when I was in school. Then I started sellin' dope and runnin' numbers and I picked it up right away. They should teach the way it matters."

Alicia accepted the academic voice as the standard, while disparaging with faint praise what *she* knew: "I'm *wise*, not *smart*. There's a difference. I can walk into a room and I knows what people be thinkin' and what's goin' down. But not what he be talkin' about in history."

Finally many saw the academic voice as exclusively legitimate, if inaccessible. Monique, after two months out of school, admitted, "I'm scared to go out lookin' for a job. They be usin' words in the interview like in school. Words I don't know. I can't be askin' them for a dictionary. It's like in school. You ask and you feel like a dummy."

By segregating the academic voice from one's own, schools contribute to controversy not only linguistic in form (Zorn 1982). The intellectual, social, and emotional substance which constitutes minority students' lives was routinely treated as irrelevant, to be displaced and silenced. Their responses, spanning acquiesence to resistance, bore serious consequence.

Contradictions folded: the pedagogical creation of dichotomies

If "lived talk" was actively expelled on the basis of content, contradictory talk was basically rendered impossible. Social contradictions were folded into dichotomous choices. Again, one can only speculate on whom this accommodates, but the creation of dichotomies and the reification of single truths does much to bolster educators' control, enforcing an explicit distance between those who *know* and those who don't; discrediting often those who *think* (McNeil 1981).

In early spring, a social studies teacher structured an in-class debate on Bernard Goetz—New York City's "subway vigilante." She invited "those students who agree with Goetz to sit on one side of the room, and those who think he was wrong to sit on the other side." To the large residual group who remained mid-room the teacher remarked, "Don't be lazy. You have to make a decision. Like at work, you can't be passive." A few wandered over to the "pro-Goetz" side. About six remained in the center. Somewhat angry, the teacher continued: "Ok, first we'll hear the pro-Goetz side and then the anti-Goetz side. Those of you who have no opinions, who haven't even thought about the issue, you won't get to talk unless we have time."

Deidre, a black senior, bright and always quick to raise contradictions otherwise obscured, advocated the legitimacy of the middle group. "It's not that I have no opinions. I don't like Goetz shootin' up people who look like my brother, but I don't like feelin' unsafe in the projects or in my neighborhood either. I got lots of opinions. I ain't bein' quiet 'cause I can't decide if he's right or wrong. I'm talkin'."

Deidre's comment legitimized for herself and others the right to hold complex, perhaps even contradictory positions on a complex situation. Such legitimacy was rarely granted by faculty—with clear and important exceptions including activist faculty and paraprofessionals who lived in central Harlem with the kids, who understood and respected much about their lives.

Among the chorus of voices heard within this high school, then, lay little room for Gramsci's (1971) contradictory consciousness. Artificial dichotomies were understood as received and natural: right and wrong answers, good and bad behavior, moral and immoral people, dumb and smart students, responsible and irresponsible parents, good and bad neighborhoods. Contradiction and ambivalence, forced underground, were experienced often, if only expressed rarely.

I asked Ronald, a student in remedial reading class, why he stayed in school. He responded with the sophistication and complexity the question deserved, "Reason I stay in school is 'cause every time I get on the subway I see this drunk and I think 'not me.' But then I think 'bet he has a high school degree.' " The power of his statement lies in its honesty, as well as the infrequency with which such comments were voiced. Ronald explained that he expected support for this position neither on the street nor in the school. School talk filled youths with promises that few believed, but many repeated: the promises of hard work, education, and success; warnings about welfare. Street talk belied another reality, described by Shondra, "They be sayin', 'What you doin' in school? Could be out here scramblin' [selling drugs] and makin' money now. That degree ain't gonna get you nothing better.' "

When black adolescent high school graduates, in the October following graduation, suffered a 56 percent unemployment rate and black adolescent high school dropouts suffered a 70 percent unemployment rate, the very contradictions which remained unspoken within school were amplified in the minds and worries of these young men and women (Young 1983).

Conversations psychologized: the curriculum splits the personal and the social

Some conversations within schools were closed; others were dichotomized. Yet a few conversations, indeed those most relevant to socioeconomic arrangements and inequities, remained psychologized. The topics were managed exclusively as personal problems inside the offices of school psychologists or counselors. The lived experiences of *all* adolescents, and particularly those surviving city life in poverty, place their physical and mental well being as well as that of their kin in constant jeopardy. And yet conversations about these were conditions of life, about alcoholism, drug abuse, domestic violence, environmental hazards, gentrification, and poor health—to the extent that they happened at all—remained confined to individual sessions with counselors (for those lucky enough to gain hearing with a counselor in the 800–1 ratio, and gutsy enough to raise the issue) or, if made academic, were raised in hygiene class (for those fortunate enough to have made it to twelfth grade when hygiene was offered). A biology teacher, one of the few black teachers in the school, actually integrated creative writing assignments such as "My life as an alcoholic" and "My life as the child of an alcoholic" into her biology class curriculum. Her department chairman reprimanded her severely for introducing "extraneous materials" into her classroom. Teachers, too, were silenced.

The prevalence of health and social problems experienced by these adolescents, and their curricular marginalization, exemplified a rigid academic unwillingness to address these concerns, in social studies, science, English, or even math. A harsh resistance to name the lived experiences of these teens paralleled the unwillingness to integrate these experiences as the substance of learning. Issues to be avoided at all costs, they were addressed only once they dramatically pierced the life of an adolescent who sought help.

The offices of school psychologists or counselors therefore became the primary sites for addressing what were indeed social concerns, should have been academic concerns, and were most likely to be managed as personal and private concerns. The curricular privatizing and psychologizing of public and political issues served to reinforce the alienation of students' lives from their educational experiences, made worse only by those conversations never had.

Conversations never had

A mechanistic view of teachers terrorized of naming and students passively accommodating could not be further from the daily realities of life inside a public high school. Many teachers name and critique, although most don't. Some students passively shut down, but most remain alive and even resistant. Classrooms are filled with students wearing Walkmans, conversing among themselves and with friends in the halls, and some even persistently challenging the experiences and expertise of their teachers. But the typical classroom still values silence, control, and quiet, as John Goodlad (1984), Theodore Sizer (1985), Jean Anyon (1983), and others have documented. The insidious push toward silence in low-income schools became most clear sometime after my interview with Eartha, a sixteen-year-old high school dropout.

> MF: Eartha, when you were a kid, did you participate a lot in school?
> *Eartha:* Not me, I was a good kid. Made no trouble.

I asked this question of fifty-five high school dropouts. After the third responded as Eartha did, I realized that for me, participation was encouraged, delighted in, and a measure of the "good student." For these adolescents, given their contexts of schooling, "participation" signified poor discipline and rude classroom behavior.

Students learned the dangers of talk, the codes of participating and not, and they learned, in more nuanced ways, which conversations were never to be initiated. In Philadelphia a young high school student explained to me: "We ain't allowed to talk about abortion. They tell us we can't discuss it no way." When I asked a School District Administrator about this policy, she qualified: "It's not that they can't talk about it. The teacher, if the topic is raised by a student, can define abortion, just not discuss it beyond that." This distinction between *define* and *discuss* makes sense only if education signifies teacher authority, and control implies silence. Perhaps this is why classroom control often feels so fragile. Control through omission *is* fragile, fully contingent on students' willingness to collude and "play" at not naming. While it ostensibly postures teacher authority, it actually betrays a plea for student compliance.

Silence comes in many forms. Conversations can be closed by teachers, or forestalled by student compliance. But other conversations are expressly subverted, never had. A policy of enforced silencing was applied to information about the severe economic and social consequences of dropping out of high school. This information was systematically withheld from students who were being discharged. When students were discharged in New York State—a "choice" available to few middle-class, particularly white students—they were guaranteed an exit interview, which, in most cases, involved an attendance officer who asked students what they planned to do, and then requested a meeting with a parent/guardian to sign official documents. The officer handed the student a list of GED/outreach programs. The student left, often eager to find work, get a GED, go to a private business school, or join the military. Informed conversations about the consequences of the students' decision are not legally mandated. As they left, these adolescents *did not learn*:

- that over 50 percent of black high school dropouts suffer unemployment in cities like New York City (U.S. Commission on Civil Rights 1982);
- that 48 percent of New Yorkers who sit for the Graduate Equivalency Diploma test fail (New York State Department of Education 1985);
- that private trade schools, including cosmetology, beautician, and business schools have been charged with unethical recruitment practices, exploitation of students, earning more from students who drop out than those who stay, not providing promised jobs and having, on average, a 70 percent dropout rate (see Fine 1986);
- that the military, during "peacetime," refuses to accept females with no high school degree, and only reluctantly accepts such males, who suffer an extremely high rate of less-than-honorable discharge within six months of enlistment (Militarism Resource Project 1985).

Students were thereby denied informed consent if they left high school prior to graduation. These conversations-not-had failed to correct and therefore nurtured powerful beliefs that "the GED is no sweat, a piece of cake"; that "you can get jobs, they promise, after goin' to Sutton or ABI"; or that "in the Army I can get me a GED, skills, travel, benefits. . . ."

Maintaining silence through democracy and discipline

Means of maintaining silences and assuring no dangerous disruptions know few bounds. One institutionalized strategy involves the appropriation of internal dissent, framed as democracy for parents and students. This strategy is increasingly popular in this era of rhetorical "empowerment."

At this school the Parents' Association executive board was comprised of ten parents: eight black women, one black man, and one white woman. Eight no longer had children attending the school. At about midyear teachers were demanding smaller class size. So too was the President of the Parents' Association at this Executive meeting with the Principal.

President: I'm concerned about class size. Carol Bellamy (City Council President) notified us that you received monies earmarked to reduce class size and yet what have you done?

Mr. Stein: Quinones (Schools Chancellor) promised no high school class greater than 34 by February. That's impossible! What he is asking I can't guarantee unless *you* tell me how to do it. If I reduce class size, I must eliminate all specialized classes, all electives. Even then I can't guarantee. To accede to Quinones, that classes be less than 34, we must eliminate the elective in English, in social studies, all art classes, eleventh year math, physics, accounting, wordprocessing. We were going to offer a Haitian Patois bilingual program, fourth year French, a museums program, bio-pre-med, health careers, coop and pre-coop, choreography and advanced ballet. The nature of the school will be changed fundamentally.

> We won't be able to call this an academic high school, only a program for slow learners.
>
> *Woman (1):* Those are very important classes.
>
> *Stein:* I am willing to keep these classes. Parents want me to keep these classes. That's where I'm at.
>
> *Woman (2):* What is the average?
>
> *Stein:* Thirty-three.
>
> *Woman (1):* Are any classes over forty?
>
> *Stein:* No, except if it's a *Singleton* class—the only one offered. If these courses weren't important, we wouldn't keep them. You know we always work together. If it's your feeling we should not eliminate all electives and maintain things, OK! Any comments?
>
> *Woman (1):* I think continue. Youngsters aren't getting enough now. And the teachers will not any more.
>
> *Woman (3):* You have our unanimous consent and support.
>
> *Stein:* When I talk to the Board of Education, I'll say I'm talking for the parents.
>
> *Woman (4):* I think it's impossible to teach forty.
>
> *Stein:* We have a space problem. Any other issues?

An equally conciliatory student council was constituted to decide on student activities, prom arrangements, and student fees. They were largely pleased to meet in the principal's office.

At the level of critique, silence was guaranteed by the selection of and then democratic participation of individuals within "constituency-based groups."

If dissent was appropriated through mechanisms of democracy, it was exported through mechanisms of discipline. The most effective procedure for silencing was to banish the source of dissent, tallied in the school's dropout rate. As indicated by the South Bronx study referred to above (Fine 1983), and the research of others (Elliott, Voss & Wendling 1966; Felice 1981; Fine & Rosenberg 1983), it is often the academic critic resisting the intellectual and verbal girdles of schooling who "drops out" or is pushed out of low-income schools. Extraordinary rates of suspensions, expulsions, and discharges experienced by black and Hispanic youths speak to this form of silencing (Advocates for Children 1985). Estimates of urban dropout rates range from approximately 42 percent for New York City, Boston, and Chicago Boards of Education to 68–80 percent from Aspira, an educational advocacy organization (1983).

At the school which served as the site for this ethnographic research, a 66 percent dropout rate was calculated. Two-thirds of the students who began ninth grade in 1978–79 did not receive diplomas nor degrees by June 1985. I presented these findings to a collection of deans, advisors, counselors, administrators, and teachers, many of whom were the sponsors and executors of the discharge process. At first I met with total silence. A dean then explained, These kids need to be out. It's unfair to the rest. My job is like a pilot on a hijacked plane. My job is to throw the hijacker overboard." The one black woman in the room, a guidance counselor, followed: "What Michelle is saying is true. We do throw students out of here and deny them their education. Black kids especially." Two white male administrators interrupted, chiding the "liberal tendencies" of guidance counselors, who, as they put it, "don't see how really dangerous these kids are." The meeting ended.

Dissent was institutionally "democraticized," exported, trivialized, or bureaucratized. These mechanisms made it unlikely for change or challenge to be given a serious hearing.

Whispers of resistance: the silenced speak

In nonelite public high schools organized around control through silence, the student, teacher, or paraprofessional who talks, who tells or who wants to speak, transforms rapidly into the subversive, the trouble maker. The speaking student, unless she or he spoke in an honors class or affected the academic mode of imputing nondangerous topics and benign words, unless protected by wealth, influential parents, or an unusual capacity to be both critic *and* good student, emerged as provocateur. Depending on school, circumstance, and style, the students' response to silence varied. She may have buried herself in mute isolation. He may have been promoted to resist or organize other students. But most of these youths, for complex reasons, were ultimately propelled to flee prior to graduation. Some then sought "alternative contexts" in which their strengths, their competencies, and their voices could flourish on their own terms:

> [*Hector's a subway graffiti artist:*] It's like an experience you never get. You're on the subway tracks. It's 3:00 A.M., dark, cold and scary. You're trying to create your best. The cops can come to bust you, or you could fall on the electric third rail. My friend died when he dropped his spray paint on that rail. It exploded. He died and I watched. It's awesome, intense. A peak moment when you can't concentrate on nothin', no problems, just creation. And it's like a family. When Michael Stewart [graffiti artist] was killed by cops, you know he was a graffiti man, we all came out of retirement to mourn him. Even me, I stopped 'cause my girl said it was dangerous. We came out and painted funeral scenes and cemeteries on the #1 and the N [subway lines]. For Michael. We know each other, you know an artist when you see him: It's a family. Belonging. They want me in, not out like at school.
>
> *Carmen pursued the Job Corps when she left school:* You ever try plastering, Michelle? It's great. You see holes in walls. You see a problem and you fix it. Job Corps lost its money when I was in it, in Albany. I had to come home, back to Harlem. I felt better there than ever in my school. Now I do nothin'. It's a shame. Never felt as good as then.
>
> *Monique got pregnant and then dropped out:* I wasn't never good at nothing. In school I felt stupid and older than the rest. But I'm a great mother to Chita. Catholic schools for my baby, and maybe a house in New Jersey.
>
> *Carlos, who left school at age twenty, after a frustrating five years since he and his parents exiled illegally from Mexico hopes to join the military:* I don't want to kill nobody. Just, you know how they advertise, the Marines. I never been one of the Few and the Proud. I'm always 'shamed of myself. So I'd like to try it.

In an uninviting economy, these adolescents responded to the silences transmitted through public schooling by pursuing what they considered to be creative alternatives. But let us understand that for such low-income youths, these alternatives generally *replaced* formal schooling. Creative alternatives for middle-class adolescents, an after-school art class or music lessons, privately afforded by parents, generally *supplement* formal schooling.

Whereas school-imposed silence may be an *initiation* to adulthood for the middle-class adolescent about to embark on a life of participation and agency, school-imposed silence more typically represents the *orientation* to adulthood for the low-income or working-class adolescent about to embark on a life of work at McDonald's, in a factory, as a domestic or clerk, or on Aid to Families with Dependent Children. For the low-income student, the imposed silence of high school cannot be ignored as a necessary means to an end. They are the present *and* they are likely to be the future (Ogbu 1978).

Some teachers, paraprofessionals, and students expressly devoted their time, energy, and classes to exposing silences institutionally imposed. One reading teacher prepared original grammar worksheets, including items such as "Most women in Puerto Rico (is, are) oppressed." A history teacher dramatically presented his autobiography to his class, woven with details on the life of Paul Robeson. An English teacher formed a writers' collective of her multilingual "remedial" writing students. A paraprofessional spoke openly with students who decided not to report the prime suspect in a local murder to the police, but to clergy instead. She recognized that their lives would be in jeopardy, despite "what the administrators who go home to the suburbs preach." But these voices of naming were weak, individual, and isolated.

What if these voices, along with the chorus of dropouts, were allowed expression? If they were not whispered, isolated, or drowned out in disparagement, what would happen if these stories were solicited, celebrated, and woven into a curriculum? What if the history of schooling were written by those high school critics who remained in school and those who dropped out? What if the "dropout problem" were studied in school as a collective critique by consumers of public education?

Dropping out instead is viewed by educators, policy makers, teachers, and often students as an individual act, an expression of incompetence or self-sabotage. As alive, motivated, and critical as they were at age seventeen, most of the interviewed dropouts were silenced, withdrawn, and depressed by age twenty-two. They had tried the private trade schools, been in and out of the military, failed the GED exam once or more, had too many children to care for, too many bills to pay, and only self-blaming regrets, seeking private solutions to public problems. Muting, by the larger society, had ultimately succeeded, even for those who fled initially with resistance, energy, and vision (Apple 1982).

I'll end with an image which occurred throughout the year, repeated across classrooms and across urban public high schools. As familiar as it is haunting, the portrait most dramatically captures the physical embodiment of silencing in urban schools.

Field Note: February 16

Patrice is a young black female, in eleventh grade. She says nothing all day in school. She sits perfectly mute. No need to coerce her into silence. She often wears her coat in class. Sometimes she lays her head on her desk. She never disrupts. Never disobeys. Never speaks. And is never identified as a problem. Is she the student who couldn't develop two voices and so silenced both? Is she so filled with anger, she fears to speak? Or so filled with depression she knows not what to say?

Whose problem is Patrice?

Postscript on research as exposing

The process of conducting research within schools to identify words that could have seen said, talk that should have been nurtured, and information that needed to be announced, suffers from voyeurism and perhaps the worst of post hoc arrogance. The researcher's sadistic pleasure of spotting another teacher's collapsed contradiction, aborted analysis, or silencing sentence was moderated only by the ever-present knowledge that similar analytic surgery could easily be performed on my own classes.

And yet it is the very "naturalness" of not naming, of shutting down or marginalizing conversations for the "sake of getting on with learning" that demands educators' attention. Particularly so for low-income youths highly ambivalent about the worth of a diploma, desperately desirous of and at the same time discouraged from its achievement.

If the process of education is to allow children, adolescents, and adults their voices—to read, write, create, critique, and transform—how can we justify the institutionalizing of silence at the level of policies which obscure systemic problems behind a rhetoric of "excellence" and "progress," a curriculum bereft of the lived experiences of students themselves, a pedagogy organized around control and not conversation, and a thoroughgoing psychologizing of social issues which enables Patrice to bury herself in silence and not be noticed?

A self-critical analysis of the fundamental ways in which we teach children to betray their own voices is crucial.

Notes

1   This research was made possible by a grant from the W.T. Grant Foundation, New York City, 1984 through 1985.
2   Personal communication with employee in the High Schools' Division, New York City Board of Education, in response to inquiry about why New York City does not maintain race/ethnicity-sensitive statistics on dropping out and school achievement.
3   Columbus Avenue, on the upper West Side, has recently become a rapidly gentrified, elite neighborhood in Manhattan, displacing many low-income, particularly black and Hispanic residents.

References

Advocates for Children. *Report of the New York Hearings on the Crisis in Public Education.* New York, 1985.
Anyon, J. "Intersections of Gender and Class: Accommodation and Resistance by Working Class and Affluent Females to Contradictory Sex Role Ideologies." In *Gender, Class and Education,* edited by S. Walker and L. Barton. London: Falmer Press.
Anyon, J. "School Curriculum: Political and Economic Structure and Social Change." *Social Practice,* (1980): 96–108.
Apple, M. *Cultural and Economic Reproduction in Education.* Boston: Routledge & Kegan Paul, 1982.
Aronowitz, S., & Giroux, H. *Education under Siege.* South Hadley, Massachusetts: Bergin & Garvey, Inc., 1985.
Aspira, *Racial and Ethnic High School Dropout Rates in New York City: A Summary Report.* New York, New York, 1983.
Bastian, A., Fruchter, N., Gittell, M., Greer, C., & Haskins, K. "Choosing Equality: The Case for Democratic Schooling." *Social Policy,* (1985): 35–51.
Carnegie Forum on Education and the Economy. *A Nation Prepared: Teachers for the 21st Century.* New York: Carnegie Foundation, 1986.

Carnoy, M., & Levin, H. *Schooling and Work in the Democratic State.* Stanford: Standford University Press, 1985.

Connell, R., Ashenden, D., Kessler, S., & Dawsett, G. *Making the Difference.* Sydney, Australia: George Allen & Unwin, 1982.

Cummins, J. "Empowering Minority Students: A Framework for Intervention." *Harvard Education Review, 56* (1986).

Elliott, D., Voss, H., & Wendling, A. "Capable Dropouts and the Social Milieu of High School." *Journal of Educational Research*, 60 (1966): 180–186.

Felice, L. "Black Student Dropout Behaviours: Disengagement from School Rejection and Racial Discrimination," *Journal of Negro Education*, 50 (1981): 415–424.

Fine, M. "Perspectives on Inequity: Voices from Urban Schools." In *Applied Social Psychology Annual IV*, edited by L. Bickman. Beverly Hills: Sage, 1983.

Fine, M. "Dropping out of High School: An Inside Look." *Social Policy*, (1985): 43–50.

Fine, M. "Why Urban Adolescents Drop into and out of Public High School." *Teachers College Record*, 87 (1986).

Fine, M., & Rosenberg, P. "Dropping Out of High School: The Ideology of School and Work." *Journal of Education*, 165 (1983): 257–272.

Freire, P. *The Politics of Education.* South Hadley, Massachusetts: Bergin & Garvey Publishers, 1985.

Goodlad, J. *A Place called School: Prospects for the Future.* New York: McGraw Hill, 1984.

Gramsci, A. *Selections from Prison Notebooks.* New York: International, 1971.

Holmes Group. *Tomorrow's Teachers.* East Lansing, Michigan, 1986.

Lightfoot, S. *Worlds Apart.* New York. Basic Books, 1978.

McNeil, L. "Negotiating Classroom Knowledge: Beyond Achievement and Socialization." *Curriculum Studies*, 13 (1981): 313–328.

Militarism Resource Project, *High School Military Recruiting: Recent Developments.* Philadelphia, PA, 1985.

New York State Department of Education. Memo from Dennis Hughes, State Administrator on High School Equivalency Programs. December 4, 1985. Albany, NY.

Ogbu, J. *Minority Education and Caste: The American System in Cross-cultural Perspective.* New York: Academic Press, 1978.

Rich, A. *On Lies, Secrets and Silence.* New York. Norton Books, 1979.

Shor, I. *Critical Teaching and Everyday Life.* Boston: South End Press, 1980.

Sizer, T. *Horace's Compromise: The Dilemma of the American High School.* Boston: Houghton Mifflin, 1985.

Tobier, E. *The Changing Face of Poverty: Trends in New York City's Population in Poverty, 1960–1990.* New York, New York: Community Service Society, 1984.

U.S. Commission on Civil Rights. *Unemployment and Underemployment among Blacks, Hispanics and Women.* Washington, DC., 1982.

U.S. Department of Labor. *Time of Change: 1983 Handbook of Women Workers.* Washington, DC., 1983.

Wexler, P. *Critical Social Psychology.* Boston: Routledge & Kegan Paul, 1983.

Young, A. Youth Labor Force Marked Turning Point in 1982. U.S. Department of Labor. Bureau of Labor Statistics, Washington, DC., 1983.

Zorn, J. "Black English and the King Decision." *College English*, 44 (1982).

CHAPTER 14

RETHINKING LIBERAL AND RADICAL PERSPECTIVES ON RACIAL INEQUALITY IN SCHOOLING (1988)

Making the case for nonsynchrony

Cameron McCarthy

> It is not altogether surprising to find a certain uneven development within the various branches of the social science disciplines. . . . It could be argued that race analysis is surprisingly backward in this respect, far more so, for instance, than recent debates within the feminist movement. (*Ben-Tovim, Gabriel, Law, & Stredder, 1981, p. 155*)

> Marxist and other progressive writers on Africa generally approach the issue of "tribalism" as one would approach a minefield. (*Saul, 1979, p. 391*)

Despite comprehensive evidence of glaring disparities in education in the United States, rigorous, durable, and compelling explanations of the reproduction and persistence of racial inequality in schooling have been slow in coming. In sharp contrast, American curriculum theorists and sociologists of education have been far more forthcoming in their examination of how the variables of class and, more recently, those of gender, have informed the organization and selection of school knowledge and the production and reproduction of subcultures among school youth (Anyon, 1979; Apple, 1982; Apple & Weis, 1983; Bowles & Gintis, 1976; Everhart, 1983). As Black sociologists such as Mullard (1985) and Sarup (1986) have pointed out, both mainstream and radical educational researchers have tended to under-theorize and marginalize phenomena associated with racial inequality.

This essay seeks to fulfill three objectives. First, I situate the issue of racial inequality within the context of current data on the status of racial minorities vis-à-vis Whites in American schools and society. Second, I examine how the topic of race is treated in contemporary mainstream and neo-Marxist curriculum and educational research, paying particular attention to the limits and possibilities of the value-oriented thesis of multiculturalism that mainstream liberal educators have championed over the last fifteen years or so as a panacea for racial inequality in schooling. I also offer a critique of neo-Marxist subordination of racial inequality in education to working-class exploitation and the structural requirements of the economy. Third, I present an alternative approach, what I call a nonsynchronous theory of race relations in schooling, in which I argue against the "essentialist" or single-cause explanations of the persistence of racial inequality in education currently offered in both mainstream and radical curriculum and educational literatures. Instead, I direct attention to the complex and contradictory nature of race relations in the institutional life of social organizations such as schools. In addition, this nonsynchronous approach attempts to dissolve the unwarranted separation of "values" from considerations of structural constraints on human actions in current accounts of the race/education couplet. I emphasize the materiality of ideology and argue for the codetermination of culture and politics, along with the economy, in radical accounts of the elaboration of the racial character of schooling. Ideology, culture, and politics are as important determinants in shaping race relations in schooling as is the economy. Typically, neo-Marxists emphasize the last of these realms. Racist ideology as a specific set of linked but contradictory ideas manifests itself unevenly in educational structures and the formal and informal practices of school life. In this sense, curricula and programs that seek to address racial antagonism in schooling must take into account, for example, the discriminatory effects of what Kevin Brown (1985) calls "White non-racism" (p. 670). "Non-racism" refers to the covert use of racial evaluation, "apparently" neutral but coded rhetoric or criteria to discuss minorities—for example, the use of code words such as "over-crowding," "welfare mothers," "the lack of experience," or "strain on current resources."

Mounting statistical evidence supplied in government commission reports, census data, and academic journals documents persistent and glaring disparities in the relative economic, social, and educational status of racial minorities and Whites in the United States (Editors, 1986). For instance, unemployment among Black women and men is currently more than twice the level of that among Whites. For Black families, the median income remains at about 56 percent of White families' median income—roughly what it was three decades ago. The Alliance Against Women's Oppression (1983) contends that Black mothers are four times as likely to die in childbirth as White mothers. Black and Native American infant mortality rates are currently higher than those of such Third World countries as Trinidad and Tobago and Costa Rica.

Current data on schooling also present an alarming picture of minority disadvantage. Data from a 1979 Census Bureau study showed that 35 percent of Hispanic and 26 percent of Black youth, ages 18 through 21, had dropped out of school, compared with 15 percent of all Whites of similar ages. Black and Hispanic youth who graduate from high school are less likely than White graduates to enroll in college. At the university level, the percentage of degrees awarded to minority students is also declining. Black students earned only 6.5 percent of all bachelor's degrees awarded in 1981 compared with 10 percent in 1976 (Editors, 1986). These statistics trenchantly underscore the intractability of racial inequality in school and society in the United States. But racial inequality of this sort is by no means peculiar to America; in other urban industrialized societies, such as England, Japan, Canada, and Australia, research has shown that minority youth fare poorly in school and in the labor market (Ogbu, 1978).

Over the years, mainstream and radical sociologists of curriculum and education have provided contrasting explanations for the persistence of racial inequality in schooling. Neo-Marxist sociologists of education such as Berlowitz (1984), Bowles and Gintis (1976), Carnoy (1974), Jakubowicz (1985), and Nkomo (1984) locate the roots of racial domination within the structural properties of capitalism and its elaboration as a world system. In these accounts, racial antagonism is seen as a by-product of the major class contradiction between labor and capital. These radical critics of schooling subsume the problem of racial inequality under the general rubric of working-class oppression. They argue that there is a structural relationship between a racially differentiated school curriculum and a discontinuous labor market. Schools in this view follow the pattern of the economy and serve a narrow reproductive function. As a result, neo-Marxist sociologists of education offer no satisfactory theoretical explanation and no programmatic solution to the problem of racial inequality—the racial dimension is seen as of secondary import, and the inequality is expected to disappear with the abolition of capitalism.

Conversely, mainstream sociologists of schooling reduce the complexities associated with racial inequality to one overwhelming theoretical and programmatic concern: *the issue of the educability of minorities.* Their central task has been to explain perceived differences between Black and White students as reflected in differential achievement scores on standardized tests, high school dropout rates, and so on. Their explanations of Black "underachievement" consequently depend upon pathological constructions of minority cognitive capacities (Jensen, 1981), child-rearing practices (Bell, 1975), family structures (Moynihan, 1965), and linguistic styles (Hess & Shipman, 1975). (For an extended discussion of these constructions see Henriques, 1984.) Mainstream theorists have in this sense tended to "blame the victim." Interventions and curriculum practices predicated on these approaches attempt to improve minority school performance through the manipulation of specific school variables, such as teacher behavior, methods of testing, placement, and so on (Atkinson, Morten, & Sue, 1979; Banks, 1981; Ogbu, 1978). As we shall see, multiculturalism represents an important but contradictory inflection on mainstream approaches to racial inequality in schooling.

The multicultural solution

Multiculturalism is a body of thought which originates in the liberal pluralist approaches to education and society. Multicultural education, specifically, must be understood as part of a curricular truce, the fallout of a political project to deluge and neutralize Black rejection of the conformist and assimilationist curriculum models solidly in place in the 1960s. Gwendolyn Baker (1977), for instance, cites Black "discontent" as the "catalyst" for the multicultural education movement in the United States: "The school district in Ann Arbor, Michigan, was much like other school districts throughout the country in the late 60s. Students, particularly Black students, were involved in and responded to the civil rights and ethnic awareness activities of that decade" (p. 163). Barry Troyna (1984) makes similar claims with respect to the origins of multicultural education policies in England: "It is no coincidence that this flurry of [multicultural] activity has taken place in the period since the civil disturbances rocked virtually every major English city in the summer of 1981. . . . Broadly speaking, this educational response parallels what took place in the U.S.A. after the 1965 riots" (p. 76).

Multicultural education as a "new" curricular form attempted to absorb Black radical demands for the restructuring of school knowledge and pedagogical practices and rearticulated them into a reformist discourse of "nonracism." The discourse of nonracism was explicitly aimed at sensitizing White teachers and school administrators to minority "differences" as part of the plurality of differences that percolated throughout the educational system. At the same time, multiculturalism represented an ameliorative advance over rigidly coercive policies and Anglo conformity that had stabilized in American education during the first half of the century. The early twentieth-century educator Ellwood P. Cubberley summarized the curriculum and policy objectives of the American education system in these terms:

> Our task is to assimilate these people [racial minorities and immigrants] as part of the American race, and to implant in their children so far as can be done the Anglo-Saxon conceptions of righteousness, law, order, and popular government, and to awaken in them reverence for our democratic institutions and for those things which we as a people hold to be of abiding worth. (quoted in Grant, Boyle, & Sleeter, 1980, p. 11)

Proponents of multicultural education explicitly challenge this assimilationist stance, and urge that we draw more closely to the democratic pulse of egalitarianism and pluralism (Banks, 1981). Grant (1975), for example, argues that "multicultural education assigns a positive value to pluralism" (p. 4). The ideological and professional stance of multiculturalism therefore espouses an emancipatory program with respect to racial inequality in school. First, proponents of multicultural education suggest that the fostering of universal respect for the various ethnic histories, cultures, and languages of the students in American schools will have a positive effect on individual minority student self-concepts. Positive self-concepts should in turn help to boost academic achievement among minority youth. Second, proponents suggest that through achieving, minority students could break the cycle of "missed opportunity" created by a previous biography of cultural deprivation. The labor market is expected to verify multicultural programs by absorbing large numbers of qualified minority youth. This thesis of a "tightening bond" between multicultural education and the economy is suggested in the following claim by James Rushton (1981):

> The curriculum in the multicultural school should encourage each pupil to succeed wherever he or she can and strive for competence in what he or she tries. Cultural taboos should be lessened by mutual experience and understandings. The curriculum in the multicultural school should allow these experiences to happen. If it does, it need have no fear about the future careers of its pupils. (p. 169)

But, as asserted by Rushton and other multicultural proponents, this linear connection between educational credentials and the economy is problematic. The assumption that a more sensitive curriculum will necessarily lead to higher educational attainment and achievement and to jobs for Black and minority youth, is frustrated by the existence of racial practices in the job market itself. Troyna (1984) and Blackburn and Mann (1979), in their incisive analyses of the British job market, explode the myth of a necessary "tightening bond" between education and the economy. In his investigation of the fortunes of "educated" Black and White youth in the job market, Troyna concludes that racial and social connections, rather than educational qualifications per se, "determined" the phenomenon of better job chances for White youth even when Black youth had higher qualifications than their White counterparts (1984). The tendency of employers to rely on informal channels or "word of mouth" networks, and the greater likelihood that White youth will be in a position to exploit such networks, together represent some of the systematic ways in which the potential for success of qualified Black youth in the labor market is undermined. Carmichael and Hamilton (1967) and Marable (1983) have made a similar argument with respect to the racial obstacles to the employment of qualified Black youth in the job market in the United States. In an analysis of Black unemployment in the 1980s, Chrichlow (1985) concludes that there is no "good fit" between Black educational achievement and the job market. Expanding this argument, he makes the following claim:

> In combination with subtle forms of discrimination, job relocation, and increasing competition among workers for smaller numbers of "good" jobs, rising entry level job requirements clearly underscore the present employment difficulties experienced by young Black workers. Whether they possess a high school diploma or not. Blacks, in this instance, continue to experience high rates of unemployment despite possessing sound educational backgrounds and potential (capital) to be productive workers. (p. 6)

Besides this particular naiveté about the racial character of the job market, a further criticism can be made of the multicultural reformist thesis. As Berlowitz (1984), Carby (1982), and Mullard (1985) have all contended, the underlying assumptions of multicultural education are fundamentally idealistic. As such, the structural and material relations in which racial domination is embedded are underemphasized. This has a costly result. By focusing on sensitivity training and on individual differences, multicultural proponents typically skirt the very problem which multicultural education seeks to address: WHITE RACISM. The A.L.T.A.R.F. (All London Teachers Against Racism and Fascism), in their volume *Challenging Racism* (1984), berate the multicultural education program in London on precisely these grounds:

> These years have witnessed the growing acceptance by LEAs [local educational agencies] of a bland and totally depoliticized form of multicultural education alongside the intensification of state racism in the form of ever increasing deportations, police brutality against Black people, discrimination in employment and harassment in unemployment. (p. 1)

Despite these problems, multicultural education offers a range of ameliorative possibilities to the school curriculum that are not present within an assimilationist framework of Anglo-conformity. For example, in terms of what should be included in the school curriculum, multiculturalism raises the possibility that the plurality of experiences of racial minorities, women, and the socially disadvantaged classes would be taken seriously within a new core curriculum (Banks, 1981). In this sense, multicultural proponents strain their relationship to more mainstream notions of "what every American school child ought to know." This strategic challenge to liberal frameworks over what should constitute the core curriculum represents an important political space within current educational discourses—a political space that must be used to develop more creative and sustained challenges to racial inequality in schooling.

Neo-Marxist approaches to race and education

> Left critics provided theoretical arguments and enormous amounts of empirical evidence to suggest that schools were in fact, agencies of social, economic and cultural reproduction. (Giroux, 1985, p. xv)

On the subject of racial inequality in schooling neo-Marxist and radical formulations stand in sharp relief to the formulations of mainstream educational theorists. Neo-Marxist sociologists of education critique mainstream frameworks which depict the relationship between education and social differences and inequality. These radical theorists maintain that attempts to cast the problem of racial oppression in American schooling in terms of attitudes, values, and psychological differences are grossly inadequate. They argue further that liberal emphasis on the domain of values serves to divert our attention from the relationship of schooling to political economy and political power.

Radical educational theorists such as Berlowitz (1984), Bowles and Gintis (1976), and Nkomo (1984) have asserted instead that problems of social difference and inequality are more firmly rooted in the socioeconomic relations and structures generated within capitalist societies such as the United States. Education plays an essentially reproductive role in this story, insofar as it functions to legitimize social disparity and social differences through its selection process and its propagation of dominant values. But in these analyses, racial domination occurs as a tangential distraction to the main drama of class conflict. The whole structure of this radical theoretical framework ultimately rests upon an economic base, from which class relations are derived. All that is non-economic exists in the firmament of the superstructures, namely, the arenas of ideology, culture, consciousness, and so on. Schooling and ethnicity or race are thus dependent variables—epiphenomena relegated to the superstructures.

As C. L. R. James (1980) maintains, neo-Marxist sociologists and educational theorists tend to conceptualize race and racial struggles as episodic rather than determinant. Race, defined as the "otherness" of subordinate groups, manifests itself in neo-Marxist sociological theories only through a proliferation of negatives—"superexploitation" (Blauner, 1972), "split/labor market" (Bonacich, 1980), and the "divide and conquer" strategies of individual capitalist employers (Roemer, 1979). This emphasis on the negative features of racial dynamics is reproduced in neo-Marxist theories of education. Berlowitz (1984) and Edari (1984), for example, explore the relationship of race to schooling through such taken-for-granted concepts as "minority failure," "underachievement," and "drop-out" rates. But for Berlowitz (1984), Jakubowicz (1985), and others, racial inequality in schooling is at best symptomatic of more powerful class-related dynamics operating within the economy. Edari (1984) summarizes the structuralist definition of race within the neo-Marxist framework: "For this purpose, ethnicity, racism and sexism must be understood in the proper perspective as forms of ideological mystification designed to facilitate exploitation and weaken the collective power of the laboring classes" (p. 8).

In summary, then, neo-Marxist educational theorists explain the specificity of racial domination within the evolution of capitalism in terms of a "structurally convenient form of ideology" (Mullard, 1985, p. 66). Racism as an ideology fulfills capitalism's economic requirements for superexploitation and the creation of a vast reserve army of labor. Racial strife disorganizes the working class and hence weakens working-class resistance to capitalist domination. Schools, as apparatuses of the state, both legitimize racial differences in society and reproduce the kind of racially subordinate subjects who are tracked into the secondary labor market.

But there are significant weaknesses in neo-Marxist theories of racial inequality in general and racial inequality in schooling in particular. First, the specification of the origins of racism within the origins of capitalism seems theoretically and empirically dubious. As both West (1982) and Mullard (1985) have noted, forms of racism existed prior to capitalism in pre-Columbian Latin America, ancient Greece, and elsewhere.

Second, there appears to be neither historical nor contemporary evidence to substantiate that relations established and legitimized on the basis of race were or are identical to those established and legitimized on the basis of class. Historically, for instance, slave labor was constituted by fundamentally different forms of economic, political, and ideological relations from those of wage labor (West, 1982). Slavery involved the exploitation of unfree and politically disenfranchised labor (the slave was the property of her or his employer). On the other hand, the wage-earning worker has the "freedom" within the capitalistic society to sell her or his labor power and the political civil right of mobility—the right to choose employers. It would be very difficult to explain the current incidences of racism against minorities on college campuses across the United States as an effect solely of class differences between different groups of students (Lord, 1987). These examples underscore the fact that the logic and fortunes of race relations are not at all coterminous with those of capitalism, as the persistence of racial antagonism in post-capitalist societies demonstrates (Greenberg, 1980).

Third, the neo-Marxist overemphasis on structural factors associated with the economy underrates the school's role in the production and reproduction of cultural identities and social differences. As such, these formulations trivialize the role of schooling in their accounts of the reproduction and transformation of race relations. In this sense, too, these school critics have ignored or minimized the importance of Black struggles, particularly those struggles conducted on the terrain of education. Black struggles have encouraged and intensified similar efforts with respect to class and gender struggles for political participation and inclusion, and for social and economic amelioration within the United States and in the Third World (McCarthy & Apple, 1988).

Fourth, both neo-Marxist and mainstream educational theorists treat racial groups as monolithic entities, disregarding both differences within groups and the interrelated dynamics of class and gender. As Marable (1985) has insisted, with respect to class dynamics among Black Americans, and Fuller (1980) has maintained, in relation to gender-based forms of resistance within West Indian subcultures in England, the characterization of minority groups in monolithic terms leads to unwarranted generalizations about the social, political, and cultural behavior of racially oppressed groups.

Parallelism and nonsynchrony: toward an alternative approach to race and education

The traditional literature on race and education has failed to reconcile an unwarranted bifurcation. On the one hand, mainstream educational theories assign racial phenomena to the realm of values, beliefs, individual preferences, tastes, and so on; thereby forfeiting a consideration of the structural constraints that limit and regulate human action, and denying the power and materiality of ideology. On the other hand, orthodox and neo-Marxist formulations customarily subordinate human agency and consciousness in their discussion of racial inequality. In significant ways, then, both mainstream and neo-Marxist approaches to racial inequality are "essentialist" in that they eliminate the "noise" of multidimensionality, historical variability, and subjectivity from their explanations of educational differences (Omi & Winant, 1986). The theoretical and practical insights gained from a more relational analysis of racial domination in schooling – one that attempts to show the links between existing social structures (whether economic, political, or ideological) and what real people such as teachers do—have been forfeited.

In recent years, we have witnessed the appearance of more subtle cultural theories and ethnographies of inequality and schooling within Marxist sociology of education paradigms. The work of Apple and Weis (1983), Carby (1982), Giroux (1985), Omi and Winant (1986), Troyna and Williams (1986), and Weis (1985) represents the emergence of a culturalist Marxism that has begun to awaken the radical and liberal school theories with respect to racial and sexual inequality. These educators have drawn attention to the autonomous logics and effects of racial and sexual dynamics in schooling, and to their necessary interaction with class, in lived social and cultural practices in the organization, reproduction, and transformation of social life. These cultural-studies approaches to schooling also call into question the base-superstructure model of society traditionally used by neo-Marxist theorists to explain the relationship between education and the economy and between race and class.

Marxist cultural theorists have therefore argued for a more integrated and synthetic conceptual framework as the basis for researching inequality in schooling. This framework—one that directs our attention to the interrelationships among a number of dynamics and that attempts to illuminate complexity, not with it away—is known as the *parallelist* position. The case for the parallelist approach to race and schooling is very effectively presented by Michael W. Apple and Lois Weis (1983). Apple and Weis criticize the tendency of mainstream and radical theorists to divide society into separate domains of structure and culture. They argue that this arbitrary bifurcation directly promotes tendencies toward essentialism (single-cause explanations) in contemporary thinking about race. Researchers often "locate the fundamental elements of race, not surprisingly, on their home ground" (Omi & Winant, 1986, p. 52). For neo-Marxists, then, one must first understand the class basis of racial inequality; and for liberal theorists, cultural and social values and prejudices are the primary sources of racial antagonism. In contrast, Apple and Weis contend that race is not a "category" or a "thing-in-itself" (Thompson, 1966) but a vital social process which is integrally linked to other social processes and dynamics operating in education and society. These proponents of the parallelist position therefore hold that at least *three* dynamics – race, class, and gender – are essential in understanding schools and other institutions. None are reducible to the others, and class is not necessarily primary:

> [A] number of elements or *dynamics* are usually present at the same time in any one instance. This is important. Ideological form is not reducible to class. Processes of gender, age, and race enter directly into the ideological moment. . . . It is actually out of the articulation with, clash among, or contradictions among and within, say, class, race, and sex that ideologies are lived in one's day-to-day life. (Apple & Weis, 1983, p. 24)

In addition to this critique of class essentialism, these writers also offer a reevaluation of economically reductive explanations of unequal social relations. It is acknowledged that the economy plays a powerful role in determining the structure of opportunities and positions in capitalist society. But "the" economy does not exhaust all existing social relations in society. Rather than using the economy to explain everything, theorists of the parallelist position have argued for an expanded view of the social formation in which the role of ideology and culture is recognized as integral to the shaping of unequal social relations and life chances. Apple and Weis (1983) maintain that there are three spheres of social life: economic, political, and cultural. The dynamics of class, race, and gender operate within each sphere while the spheres themselves continually interact. Unlike base-superstructure models, proponents of parallelist theory assume that action in one sphere can have an effect on action in another (Omi & Winant, 1986). The parallelist position therefore presents us with a theory of *overdetermination* in which the unequal processes and outcomes of teaching and learning and of schooling in general are produced by the constant interactions among three dynamics (race, gender, and class) and in three spheres (economic, political, and cultural). The parallelist model is presented in Figure 14.1.

The proposition that "each sphere of social life is constituted by the dynamics of class, race, and gender" (Apple & Weis, 1983, p. 25) has broad theoretical and practical merit. For example, it is impossible to understand fully the problem of the phenomenal high dropout rate among Black and Hispanic school youth without taking into account the interrelated race, class, and gender oppressions in U.S. urban centers and the ways in which the intersections of these social dynamics work to systematically "disqualify" innercity minority youth in educational institutions and in the job market. In a similar manner, theoretical emphasis on gender dynamics complements our understanding of the unequal division of labor in schools and society and directs our attention to the way in which capitalism uses patriarchal relations to depress the wage scale and the social value of women's labor.

At a time when class and economic reductionism still play important roles in our explanations, the thesis of parallelism holds promise. This does not mean, however, that the movement toward a parallelist position is without problems. Its basic drawback is that parallelism has been construed in terms of static, additive models of double and triple oppression in which racial oppression is simply added to class and gender oppression.

Attempts to specify the dynamics of race, class, and gender phenomena in education have often been formulated in terms of a system of linear "additions" or gradations of oppression. Thus, for example, Spencer (1984), in her insightful case study of women schoolteachers, draws attention to their double oppression. Simply stated, these women perform onerous tasks with respect to both their domestic and emotional labor in the home and their instructional labor in the classroom (pp. 283–296). In Spencer's analysis, the oppression of these women in

		Spheres		
		Economic	Cultural	Political
	Class			
Dynamics	Race			
	Gender			

Figure 14.1 The Parallelist Position

Taken from Michael W. Apple and Lois Weis, eds., *Ideology and Practice In Schooling* (Philadelphia: Temple University Press, 1983), p. 25. Reprinted with permission.

the home is "added" to their oppression as teachers working in the classroom. No attempt is made here to represent the *qualitatively* different experiences of Black women both in the context of the domestic sphere and within the teaching profession itself. In this essentially incremental model of oppression, patriarchal and class forms of oppression unproblematically reproduce each other. Accounts of the intersection of race, class, and gender such as these overlook instances of tension, contradiction, and discontinuity in the institutional life of the school setting (McCarthy & Apple, 1988). Dynamics of race, class, and gender are thus conceptualized as having individual and uninterrupted effects.

Notions of double and triple oppression are not wholly inaccurate. Nevertheless, we need to see these relations as far more complex, problematic, and contradictory than parallelist theory suggests. One of the most useful attempts to conceptualize the interconnections between race, class, and gender has been formulated by Emily Hicks (1981). She cautions critical researchers against the tendency to theorize about the interrelations between social dynamics as "parallel," "reciprocal," or "symmetrical." Instead, Hicks offers the thesis that the operation of race, class, and gender relations at the level of daily practices in schools, workplaces, and so forth, is systematically *contradictory or nonsynchronous*. Hicks's emphasis on nonsynchrony (the production of difference) helps to lay the basis for an alternative approach to thinking about the operation of these social relations and dynamics at the institutional level.

By invoking the concept of nonsynchrony, I wish to advance the position that individuals or groups in their relation to economic, political, and cultural institutions such as schools do not share an identical consciousness and express the same interests, needs, or desires "at the same point in time" (Hicks, 1982, p. 221). In this connection, it is also necessary to attach great importance to the organizing principles of selection, inclusion, and exclusion. These principles operate in ways that affect how marginalized minority youth are positioned in dominant social and educational policies and agendas. Schooling, in this sense, constitutes a site for the production of the politics of difference. The politics of difference or nonsynchrony in the material context of the school expresses "culturally sanctioned, rational responses to struggles over scarce [or unequal] resources" (Wellman, 1977, p. 4).

The concept of nonsynchrony begins to untangle the complexity of causal motion and effects "on the ground," as it were. It also raises questions about the nature, exercise, and multiple determination of power within the middle ground of everyday practices in schooling. The fact is that, as Hicks (1981) suggests, dynamic relations of race, class, or gender do not unproblematically reproduce each other. These relations are complex and often have contradictory effects even in similar institutional settings. It is, therefore, important that we begin to understand the dynamics of the interaction of race, class, and gender in settings inside and outside of schools. The patterns of the social stratification by race, class, and gender emerge not as static variables but as efficacious structuring principles that shape minority/majority relations in everyday life.

In their discussion of educational and political institutions, Gilroy (1982), Omi and Winant (1986), and Sarup (1986) have emphasized the fact that racial and sexual antagonism can, at times, "cut at right angles" to class solidarity. The work of Gilroy (1982) and others directs our attention to the issues of nonsynchrony and contradiction in minority/majority relations in institutional settings, and suggests not only their complexity, but the impossibility of predicting these dynamics in any formulaic way based on a monolithic view of race. For instance, both Omi and Winant (1986) and Sarup (1986) point to examples of the diminution of working-class solidarity outside education, in the context of racial antagonism within North American and British White-dominated labor unions. These unions have had a long history of hostility to minorities and minority causes. On the other hand, Nkomo (1984), in his discussion of the dynamics of race/class relations in South African educational institutions, cites examples of the augmentation of racial solidarity across class lines. He argues that the high levels of cultural alienation experienced in South African Bantu universities by both Black students from urban, professional, middle-class backgrounds and working-class students from the Bantustans heightens the bonds of racial solidarity between these youth of different class backgrounds. Burawoy (1981) has identified the opposite effect of the intersection of race and class in the South African context. In this case, the operation of class contradictions as expressed in the differing material interests and aspirations of middle-class Black teachers, nurses, state bureaucrats, and their racial counterparts—the Black proletariat from the Bantustans—undermines racial solidarity between these radically opposed socioeconomic groups. Mary Fuller (1980) points to other contradictions in her study of the subculture of West Indian girls at a British working-class high school. These students exist in a nonsynchronous relationship with both their West Indian male counterparts and White working-class girls. While West Indian male youth reject the British school curriculum, the West Indian girls in Fuller's study were among the school's high achievers. However, their apparent compliance with school values of academic success paradoxically constituted the ideological basis for their assertion of their "independence" from West Indian boys as well as their rejection of the racial "underachievement" label that the British school system applies to West Indian youth as a whole.

It is to this literature—literature on the tensions and contradictions among raced, classed, and gendered forms of domination both inside and outside education—that critical scholarship in education should now turn. The key concepts of nonsynchrony and contradiction need to be fully integrated into current research on racial domination in schooling. At the same time, though, we need to be careful not to revert to a totally structural reading of these issues. That is, we need to emphasize the symbolic, signifying, and language dimensions of social interactions and their integral relationship both to systems of control and to strategies for emancipation.

This emphasis on symbols, signs, and representations has been particularly important for advancing our theoretical understanding of the ways racial and sexual antagonisms operate within cultural, political, and economic institutions such as schools (Carby, 1982). Indeed, we must remember that for a long time Black and feminist writers have argued (much against the tide of dominant research) that racial antagonism and sexual oppression are mediated through ideology, culture, politics, and social theories themselves. While neo-Marxist researchers maintained that it was economic exploitation and capitalist need for surplus value that explained the oppression of the socially disadvantaged, Black and feminist writers drew attention to modes of devaluation of self-image, culture, and identity. For writers such as James Baldwin (1986), Ntozake Shange (1983), June Jordan (1980), and Audre Lorde (1982), American schools are principal sites for the production and naturalization of myths and ideologies that systematically disorganize and neutralize minority cultural identities. With the full acknowledgment of the persuasiveness of these claims, race relations theorists such as Cornel West (1982) have argued that it is precisely in these "non-economic" sites of self-production and identity formation, such as the school and the church, that Afro-Americans have sought to struggle against White oppression.

The issues of culture and identity must be seriously incorporated into a non-synchronous approach to racial domination in schooling—not in the sense of an easy reduction to beliefs and values or the benign pluralism ("We are all the same because we are different.") of the multicultural paradigm, but in terms of a politic that recognizes the strategic importance of the historical struggles over the production of knowledge and the positioning of minorities in social theories and educational policies. Only by taking these issues seriously can we overcome the past and present tendencies in radical scholarship, which, as cultural critics such as Edward Said (1986) argue, obliterate the specific histories and struggles of the oppressed. This, of course, must be done with a full recognition that culture and identity are produced in a material context—one that is complexly racial, gendered, and class-defined. The fact that the principles of selection, inclusion, and exclusion that inform the organization of school life have been hitherto understood primarily through class and socioeconomic paradigms says more about the biographies of mainstream and radical neo-Marxist school theorists than about the necessary character of schooling. Critical analysis of inequality in schooling must involve some sober reflection on the racist and sexist character of the production and reproduction of curriculum research itself.

Theories of how race, class, and gender interact, and of how economic, political, and cultural power act in education, need to become increasingly subtle. A nonsynchronous theoretical framework remains to be fully articulated. But we need to remember what all of this theoretical labor is about—the political, economic, and cultural lives of real people. Oppressed women and men and children of color are subject to relations of differential power. These relations are not abstract, but are experienced in ways that now help or hurt identifiable groups of people in all-too visible ways.

References

All London Teachers Against Racism and Fascism. (1984). *Challenging racism*. London: A.L.T.A.R.F.

Alliance Against Women's Oppression. (September, 1983). Poverty not for women only: A critique of the "feminization of poverty." AAWO *Discussion Paper 3*. San Francisco.

Anyon, J. (1979). Ideology and the United States history textbooks. *Harvard Educational Review, 49*, 361–386.

Apple, M. (1982). *Cultural and economic reproduction in education*. Boston: Routledge & Kegan Paul.

Apple, M., & Weis, L. (Eds.). (1983). *Ideology and practice in schooling*. Philadelphia: Temple University Press.

Atkinson, D., Morten, G., & Sue, D. W. (Eds.). (1979). *Counseling American minorities: A cross-cultural perspective*. Dubuque, IA: William C. Brown.

Baker, G. (1977). Development of the multicultural program: School of Education, University of Michigan. In F. H. Klassen & D. M. Gollnick (Eds.), *Pluralism and the American teacher: Issues and case studies* (pp. 163–169). Washington, DC: Ethnic Heritage Center for Teacher Education of the American Association of Colleges for Teacher Education.

Baldwin, J. (1961). *Nobody knows my name*. New York: Dial.

Banks, J. (1981). *Multiethnic education: Theory and practice*. Boston: Allyn & Bacon.

Bell, R. (1975). Lower class Negro mothers' aspirations for their children. In H. R. Stub (Ed.), *The sociology of education: A sourcebook* (pp. 125–136). Homewood, IL: The Dorsey Press.

Ben-Tovim, G., Gabriel, J., Law, I., & Stredder, K. (1981). Race, left strategies and the state. In D. Adlam et al. (Eds.), *Politics and power three: Sexual politics, feminism, and socialism* (pp. 153–181). London: Routledge & Kegan Paul.

Berlowitz, M. (1984). Multicultural education: Fallacies and alternatives. In M. Berlowitz & R. Edari (Eds.), *Racism and the denial of human rights: Beyond ethnicity* (pp. 129–136). Minneapolis: Marxist Educational Press.

Blackburn, R. M., & Mann, M. (1979). *The working class in the labour market.* London: Macmillan.

Blauner, R. (1972). *Racial oppression in America.* New York: Harper & Row.

Bonacich, E. (1980). Class approaches to ethnicity and race. *Insurgent Sociologist, 10,* 9–24.

Bowles, S., & Gintis, H. (1976). *Schooling in capitalist America.* New York: Basic Books.

Brown, K. (1985). Turning a blind eye: Racial oppression and the unintended consequences of white "non-racism." *Sociological Review, 33,* 670–690.

Burawoy, M. (1981). The capitalist state in South Africa: Marxist and sociological perspectives on race and class. In M. Zeitlin (Ed.), *Political power and social theory* (Vol. 2, pp. 279–335). Greenwich, CT: JAI Press.

Carby, H. (1982). Schooling in Babylon. In Centre for Contemporary Cultural Studies (Ed.), *The empire strikes back: Race and racism in 70s Britain* (pp. 183–211). London: Hutchinson.

Carmichael, S., & Hamilton, C. (1967). *Black power.* New York: Vintage.

Carnoy, M. (1974). *Education as cultural imperialism.* New York: Longman.

Carnoy, M., & Levin, H. (1985). *Schooling and work in the democratic state.* Stanford: Stanford University Press.

Chrichlow, W. (1985). *Urban crisis, schooling, and black youth unemployment: Case study.* Unpublished manuscript.

Edari, R. (1984). Racial minorities and forms of ideological mystification. In M. Berlowitz & R. Edari (Eds.), *Racism and the denial of human rights: Beyond ethnicity* (pp. 7–18). Minneapolis: Marxist Educational Press.

Editors. (1986, May 14). Here they come ready or not: An *Education Week* special report on the ways in which America's population in motion is changing the outlook for schools and society. *Education Week,* p. 28.

Everhart, R. (1983). *Reading, writing and resistance.* London: Routledge & Kegan Paul.

Fuller, M. (1980). Black girls in a London comprehensive school. In R. Deem (Ed.), *Schooling for women's work* (pp. 52–65). London: Routledge & Kegan Paul.

Gilroy, P. (1982). Steppin' out of Babylon: Race, class, and autonomy. In Centre for Contemporary Cultural Studies (Ed.), *The empire strikes back: Race and racism in 70s Britain* (pp. 278–314). London: Hutchinson.

Giroux, H. A. (1985). Introduction to P. Freire's *The politics of education.* South Hadley, MA: Bergin & Garvey.

Grant, C. (1975). Exploring the contours of a multicultural education. In C. Grant (Ed.), *Sifting and winnowing: An exploration of the relationship between CBTE and multicultural education* (pp. 1–11). Madison: Teacher Corps Associates, University of Wisconsin–Madison.

Grant, C., Boyle, M., & Sleeter, C. (1980). *The public school and the challenge of ethnic pluralism.* New York: The Pilgrim Press.

Greenberg, S. (1980). *Race and state in capitalist development: Comparative perspectives.* New Haven: Yale University Press.

Henriques, J. (1984). Social psychology and the politics of racism. In J. Henriques (Ed.), *Changing the subject* (pp. 60–89). London: Methuen.

Hess, R., & Shipman, V. (1975). Early experience and socialization of cognitive modes in children. In H. R. Stub (Ed.), *The sociology of education: A source book* (pp. 96–113). Homewood, IL: The Dorsey Press.

Hicks, E. (1981). Cultural Marxism: Non-synchrony and feminist practice. In L. Sargeant (Ed.), *Women and revolution* (pp. 219–238). Boston: South End Press.

Jakubowicz, A. (1985). State and ethnicity: Multiculturalism as ideology. In F. Rizvi (Ed.), *Multiculturalism as an educational policy.* Geelong, Victoria: Deakin University Press.

James, C. L. R. (1980). *Spheres of existence: Selected writings.* Westport, CT: Hill & Co.

Jensen, A. (1981). *Straight talk about mental tests.* New York: Free Press.

Jordan, J. (1980). *Passion*. Boston: Beacon Press.

Lamar, J. V., Jr. (1986, December 1). Today's native sons. *Time*, p. 27.

Lord, M. (1987). Frats and sororities: The Greek rites of exclusion. *The Nation, 245* (1).

Lorde, A. (1982). *Zami: A new spelling of my name*. New York: Crossing Press.

Marable, M. (1985). *Black American politics*. London: Verso.

McCarthy, C. *Beyond intervention: Neo-Marxist theories of racial domination and the state*. Unpublished manuscript.

McCarthy, C., & Apple, M. W. (1988). *Race, class, and gender in American educational research: Toward a Nonsynchronous Parallelist Position*. In L. Weis (Ed.), *Class, Race, and Gender in American Education*. Albany: State University of New York Press.

Moynihan, D. (1965). *The Negro family: The case for national action*. Washington, DC: United States Department of Labor, Office of Policy, Planning, and Research.

Mullard, C. (1985). Racism in society and schools: History, policy, and practice. In F. Rizvi (Ed.), *Multiculturalism as an educational policy* (pp. 64–81). Geelong, Victoria: Deakin University Press.

Nkomo, M. (1984). *Student culture and activism in black South African universities*. Westport, CT: Greenwood Press.

Ogbu, J. (1978). *Minority education and caste*. New York: Academic Press.

Omi, M., & Winant, H. (1986). *Racial formation in the United States*. New York: Routledge & Kegan Paul.

Roemer, J. (1979, Autumn). Divide and conquer: Microfoundations of Marxian theory of wage discrimination. *Bell Journal of Economics, 10,* 695–705.

Rushton, J. (1981). Careers and the multicultural curriculum. In J. Lynch (Ed.), *Teaching in the multicultural school* (pp. 163–170). London: Ward Lock.

Said, E. (1986). Intellectuals in the post-colonial world. *Salmagundi, 70/71,* 44–64.

Sarup, M. (1986). *The politics of multiracial education*. London: Routledge & Kegan Paul.

Saul, J. (1979). *The state and revolution in Eastern Africa*. New York: Monthly Review Press.

Shange, N. (1983). *A daughter's geography*. New York: St. Martin's Press.

Spencer, D. (1984). The home and school lives of women teachers. *The Elementary School Journal, 84,* 283–298.

Thompson, E. P. (1966). *The making of the English working class*. New York: Vintage Books.

Troyna, B. (1984). Multicultural education: Emancipation or containment? In L. Barton & S. Walker (Eds.), *Social crisis and educational research* (pp. 75–97). London: Croom Helm.

Troyna, B., & Williams, J. (1986). *Racism, education and the state*. London: Croom Helm.

Weis, L. (1985). *Between two worlds*. Boston: Routledge & Kegan Paul.

Wellman, D. (1977). *Portraits of white racism*. Cambridge: Cambridge University Press.

West, C. (1982). *Prophesy and deliverance! Toward a revolutionary Afro-American Christianity*. Philadelphia: Westminster.

CHAPTER 15

MULTIETHNIC EDUCATION (1983)
Historical developments and future prospects
Geneva Gay

What began in the late 1960s with the political demands of racial minority groups—that their heritages and experiences be reflected accurately in school curricula—has now extended to other ethnic groups and to all aspects of the education enterprise. As the idea of ethnic education continues to mature, other expansions are evident, too.

Today, the arguments in favor of multiethnic education have become more pedagogical than political, and its espoused objectives, goals, and functions have broadened in scope. Whereas multiethnic education was at one time regarded as strictly compensatory, today its aim is to help improve the overall quality of general education. The mission of multiethnic education is no longer seen simply as the transmission to minority students only of cultural information about ethnic minority groups. It has moved from the correction of errors of omission and commission in portrayals of ethnic experiences to the promotion of ethnic pluralism as a social value at all grade levels. Thus multiethnic education today requires more than mere tinkering with the curriculum.

Although the years since its inception have been productive, the progress of multiethnic education has been uneven—especially in moving from theory to practice. Most theoreticians and scholars of multiethnic education have come to view it as comprehensive and multidimensional, but many school-based practitioners continue to view it in rather narrow, simplistic, and rudimentary ways. Decision makers at one level of schooling establish policies that encourage multiethnic education, while their colleagues at another level institute rules and regulations that discourage it. Mandates for minimum competency testing often include objectives that are directly related to a familiarity with various ethnic groups, but most colleges of education are still reluctant to require multiethnic education in the preparation of teachers. Some educational planners and practitioners have been quick to endorse the notion of infusing multiethnic education into the entire curriculum without first having a sufficient understanding of its characteristics and components.

As we approach the midpoint of the 1980s, it is appropriate to think about where multiethnic education has come from and to chart future directions. We are indeed at a crossroads. The concept, though still relatively young, is old enough for the novelty to have worn off and for authentic commitment to the idea to surface. Those who remain loyal to multiethnic education do so because they believe deeply in its merits and validity—not because it is the fashionable thing to do.

Multiethnic education is facing difficult times—perhaps even more difficult than it faced in its early, formative years. Multiethnic education emerged from the turmoil of the late 1960s, but in the 1980s it will face its trial by combat. To understand why this is so and how some of the challenges to multiethnic education will take shape requires us to reflect on the development of the movement.

The beginnings

Multiethnic education was not conceived in a vacuum. Like other educational innovations, it originated in a sociopolitical milieu and is to some extent a product of its times. Concerns about the treatment of ethnic groups in school curricula and instructional materials directly reflected concerns about their social, political, and economic plight in the society at large. In the mid-1960s three distinct forces converged to set the scene for the inception of multiethnic education and to shape its philosophical and programmatic contours: new directions in the civil rights movement, the criticisms expressed by textbook analysts, and the reassessment of the psychological premises on which compensatory education programs of the late 1950s and early 1960s had been founded.

The civil rights movement had begun to change its character and tone by the mid-Sixties. Whereas the middle-aged leaders of the movement had previously tried to change laws through passive non-violence, the movement began to attract a younger following and to advance a more assertive agenda. The arenas of activity moved from courtrooms and the southern states to the northern ghettoes and the campuses of colleges and schools. The ideological and strategic focus of the movement shifted from passivity and perseverance in the face of adversity to aggression, self-determination, cultural consciousness, and political power. Along the way, marching and singing were backed up by burning and rioting. Newly formed student activist organizations, as well as the older established civil rights groups, began to demand restitution for generations of oppression, racism, and cultural imperialism. The shifting ideological focus of the movement was captured in such slogans as "Black is beautiful," "Yellow is mellow," "Black power," and "Power to the people." Moreover, as these slogans suggest, the civil rights movement for Afro-Americans gradually became a movement for recognition of the rights of *all* minority groups, including Mexican-Americans, Native Americans, Asian-Americans, and Puerto Ricans. Poets, writers, musicians, and revisionist scholars joined politicians and philosophers in speaking for the movement.

It is not surprising, then, that, when campuses became centers of civil rights activities in the late Sixties, their instructional programs became targets of criticism. After all, these sources of oppression and racism were what the young activists knew most intimately. Whereas other activists could speak passionately and from personal knowledge about racist practices in employment and housing, many of the students could not. But they did know from personal experience what it was like to spend 12 or more years in school without ever seeing their ethnic peoples and experiences portrayed except in stereotypic, derogatory ways. These educational practices became the targets of their protests.

From within the ranks of the education community itself some new developments complemented the students' activism and reinforced their demands. Two particularly significant ones were the emergence of new philosophies about the learning potential of minority youths and the continuing analyses of instructional materials. Many educators and social scientists who had endorsed the deprivation theory that undergirded compensatory education in the 1950s began to rethink their premises. Some completely abandoned the idea that the poor academic achievement of racial minority youths was caused by some lack in their backgrounds or some dysfunction in their families. Others argued vehemently that the academic failure of minority youths was due more to the conflicting expectations of school and home and to the school's devaluation of minority group cultures than to any inherent failing in the cultures of racial minorities. William Ryan argues the point eloquently in *Blaming the Victim*. Ryan writes:

> We are dealing, it would seem, not so much with culturally deprived children as with culturally depriving schools. And the task to be accomplished is not to revise, and amend, and repair deficient children but to alter and transform the atmosphere and operations of the schools to which we commit these children. Only by changing the nature of the educational experience can we change its product. To continue to define the difficulty as inherent in the raw materials—the children—is plainly to blame the victim and to acquiesce in the continuation of educational inequity in America.[1]

Another noteworthy defense of the abilities that ethnic minority youths brought to classrooms was *The Study of Nonstandard English*, by William Labov. He concluded:

> [T]he principal problem in reading failure for speakers of nonstandard English dialects is not dialect or grammatical differences but rather a cultural conflict between the vernacular culture and the schoolroom. . . . Some of this conflict proceeds from the pluralistic ignorance which prevails in the classroom: the teacher does not know that the student's dialect is different from his own, and the students do not know just how the teacher's system differs from theirs.[2]

Textbook analysts provided additional support to minority demands for an accurate depiction of their heritages and experiences in the school curriculum. Textbook critics had been actively pursuing the question of how racial minorities were treated in instructional materials since the 1980s. Edward Johnson observed that the earliest criticisms—that white textbook authors committed sins of omission and commission against Afro-Americans, that books seemed to be written exclusively for white children, and that they either ignored the creditable deeds of Afro-Americans or taught that Afro-Americans were innately inferior—remained as pertinent as ever 70 years later.[3]

The textbook analyses that appeared from the 1930s through the 1960s reported similar results for Afro-Americans, Hispanics, Native Americans, and Asians. In fact, textbooks continued to report ethnic distortions, stereotypes, omissions, and misinformation as recently as the mid-1970s. In 1970 Juanita Roderick reported that, although the most blatant derogatory stereotypes of Afro-Americans had been eliminated, textbooks still tended to "type" Afro-Americans negatively by habitually showing them in occupational uniform, by not naming them, and by not giving them speaking roles in stories.[4] In 1971 a state task force in California found that the books it reviewed were ignorant of the bilingual/bicultural realities of minority children, provided inadequate portrayals of minorities, and were written chiefly from a white middle-class point of view.[5] Jeannette Henry's analysis of 300 books led her to conclude that "not one could be approved as a dependable source of knowledge about the history and culture of the Indian people in America. Most . . . were . . . derogatory . . ., [and] contained misinformation, distortions, and omissions of important history."[6]

Since 1968 the state department of education in Michigan has sponsored biennial studies of instructional materials, especially in social studies, to determine how accurately they portray America's pluralistic society. A study released in 1980 of four elementary social studies programs concluded:

> The programs deal with minority groups in some context and make an effort to present with accuracy and honesty the pluralistic character of the American society, historically and in contemporary context. The degree of effectiveness differs with each of the programs reviewed. Minority groups are discussed with sympathy and respect. The characteristics which are universally shared and differences from one culture to another are presented in a positive style, although generally only through Western eyes and with ethnocentric attitudes.[7]

The student activists, abetted by the efforts of textbook analysts and by the new thinking about cultural differences, provided the stimulus for the first multiethnic education programs. They employed many of the strategies pioneered by the first civil rights activists. They, too, marched, boycotted, sat-in, locked-out, and issued lists of demands. Instead of demanding direct social change, however, they demanded that educational institutions stop their racists, oppressive practices of ignoring and distorting the cultural heritages and contributions to society of ethnic minorities.

As a result of these charges, claims, and demands, a bevy of minority studies programs were launched. Some were as simple as supplementary lessons or units on heroic deeds and "ethnic firsts," on the virtues of ethnic cuisine, and on the festivities of ethnic celebrations. Others were as complex as a series of courses that constituted a program of ethnic studies. Most were poorly conceived and hastily designed; they overlooked some necessary and basic principles of pedagogy, learning, and curriculum design. The first ethnic studies courses aimed to correct distortions of existing programs about ethnic experiences. They concentrated on racial minorities and had their greatest impact on the humanities, the social sciences, and the language arts. They were "crisis programs" in that they arose in response to a need to placate pressure groups rather than from pedagogical foresight.

The goals and priorities of these early programs were justifiable because of the ideological premises on which they were founded. As early as 1964 Milton Gordon had proclaimed the vitality and perseverance of ethnicity in shaping human behavior and attitudes.[8] He argued that networks of organizations and interpersonal relationships develop within an ethnic group, which encourages an individual to look first to the group for the fulfillment of fundamental needs throughout life. The persistence and significance of the ethnic factor in the lives of individuals (and by extension the social character of American society) make it imperative that ethnic pluralism be included in the education of young people—if schools hope to realize their goals of maximizing human potential, improving the quality of life for students, and advancing such values as freedom, justice, and dignity.

Prime times

The first seven or eight years of the movement—roughly the middle of the 1970s—were "prime times" for multiethnic education. This was an era of growth and expansion, both quantitative and qualitative. The educational and sociopolitical climates were receptive to innovation and change; a wave of exploration and experimentation swept the nation and the schools. Traditional American values were reassessed. The youth counterculture, the anti-war movement generated by Vietnam, and experimentation with alternative lifestyles flourished. Such critics of education as Charles Silberman, Paul Goodman, Jonathan Kozol, John Holt, and Nat Hentoff were publishing exposés of the crises and chaos that seemed to be pandemic in urban schools. Ethnic groups celebrated their heritages, experiences, and cultures in movies, books, plays, films, concerts, classrooms, and pulpits. This era, tagged the "me generation," committed its intellectual, personal, and ideological resources to achieving self-understanding and human liberation and to improving the overall quality of life.

Everyone got into the ethnic act. White ethnics (Poles, Slavs, Germans, Greeks, Italians, etc.) began to rediscover their heritages and joined racial minorities in demanding that their cultures and experiences be included under the umbrella of multiethnic education. An avalanche of revisionist materials—including pedagogies, psychologies, ethnographies, histories, and sociologies—appeared. A wide variety of ethnic books, films and filmstrips, recordings, audio-visual packets, course outlines, and study guides were readily available.

At the same time, legal precedents and changing practices established the legitimacy of multiethnic education. The *Lau* decision and the Bilingual Education Act legitimated bilingualism. The Ethnic Heritage Act made federal funds available to support research, curriculum design, and dissemination projects that dealt with cultural studies of ethnic groups, particularly those of European ancestry. State legislatures and departments of education adopted goal statements and endorsed minimum competency testing plans that included competence in areas directly related to ethnic pluralism. School districts and professional associations sponsored conferences, workshops, seminars, and publications to help educators learn about ethnic groups, their cultures, heritages, lifestyles, and experiences. Commercial publishers established policies to govern the production of instructional materials, so that the ethnic and cultural diversity of America would be clearly reflected. The National Council for Accreditation of Teacher Education included multiethnic education among its new set of requirements for the certification of teacher education programs.

Advocates of multiethnic education enjoined policy makers, diagnosticians, evaluators, administrators, and teacher educators, as well as classroom teachers and curriculum developers, to implement ethnic pluralism in schools. High-quality programs involved systemic and systematic reform; they were designed to influence all aspects of schooling for all students, at all grade levels, kindergarten through graduate school. Rather than merely adding on separate and supplementary techniques, the new models of educational change were integrative and inclusive.

The goals of multiethnic education expanded, too. Conceptual mastery replaced factual information as the primary objective. Clarifying attitudes and values became standard procedure, and promoting ethnic pluralism as necessary to the health and vitality of society gained prominence. Thus, as the idea grew to conceptual maturity, multicultural education came to mean both content and

process, curriculum and pedagogy, ideology and policy. Three essential ideological orientations emerged: teaching ethnically different students differently,
using insights into ethnic pluralism to improve all educational decision making,
and teaching content about ethnic groups to all students.

Yet even during these "good times," multiethnic education had its problems.
Many skeptics expressed fears that emphasizing differences among ethnic groups
would balkanize American society. Others felt (and some of them said) that
multiethnic education was a self-indulgent fad, an excuse for people not to exert
the efforts necessary to succeed according to the standards set by society and its
institutions. The revival of ethnic interest among whites was labeled a backlash
intended to weaken the cause of racial minorities. Others saw this "new ethnicity"
as the romanticized delusions of aimless white middle-class young adults who
were trying to authenticate something that was long since lost. Many of the efforts
to implement multiethnic programs lacked sufficient conceptual understanding,
clearly defined goals, long-range planning, adequate diagnoses of needs, and the
necessary pool of professionally prepared and committed personnel. Hence, the
theory was advancing, emerging, and evolving with apparent continuity, but
multiethnic practice remained largely fragmentary, sporadic, unarticulated, and
unsystematic.

Future prospects

Before the 1970s ended, it was clear that multiethnic education would face perilous prospects in the near future. The challenge for the 1980s will be to survive.
Multiethnic education must be vital enough to weather the skepticism and
retrenchment of a chilly educational climate. Many of the new priorities in education—vocationalism, the worship of technology, and an insistence on quantifiable
criteria of success—are antithetical to the essential goals of multiethnic education.
Multiethnic education is fundamentally an affective, experiential, and qualitative
phenomenon that requires, if it is to be effective, a commitment to imagination,
innovation, and change.

The survival of multiethnic education is in jeopardy on several fronts. Two
of the most potentially devastating challenges are economic and ideological.
Even under the best of circumstances, multiethnic education has never been
totally accepted, nor has its legitimacy gone unquestioned in the education
community. Moreover, fiscal allocations have always been minimal and have
usually fallen into the categories of "soft money" and "discretionary funds."
The current budgetary cutbacks in education will threaten even the minimal
financing that multiethnic education has received. Economic hard times necessitate fiscal reductions and programmatic streamlining. As educational practices
go, multiethnic education is still relatively new and has yet to be fully absorbed
into the mainstream of U.S. education. Thus, when program reductions occur
because of fiscal constraints, multiethnic education tends to be one of the first
casualties.

Such reductions are now evident across the board. The number of visible multiethnic programs, courses, units, and lessons now in existence is a mere fraction of
those that existed a decade ago. Many centers of ethnic culture at universities now
operate on shoestring budgets; others no longer exist at all. The attrition rate of
ethnic student organizations (e.g., black student unions) and the declining enrollments in ethnic studies courses are staggering. All of these signs point to a lean
time ahead for multiethnic education. Advocates of multiethnic education must

find creative and unorthodox ways to achieve their objectives in the absence of adequate financial resources.

Changing ideologies and shifting values are as threatening to the future of multiethnic education as are economic constraints. The current societal and educational emphases on basics, conservatism, fundamentalism, and the cost-effectiveness of human services are not conducive to educational ideas that run counter to the status quo. Given its history of struggle for legitimacy and acceptance (even in the 1970s when American society and education were more open to innovation), we can expect the 1980s to be unreceptive to multiethnic education.

Therefore, it seems unwise for proponents of ethnic pluralism to squander their energies in advocating multiethnic education as an entity separated from other aspects of education. A more pedagogically plausible and politically expedient strategy is to demonstrate, conceptually and programmatically, that multiethnic education can improve the overall quality of general education. One way to do this is to show how multiethnic education can be infused into all other aspects of education without compromising the integrity of either. This demonstration must convey the message that it is virtually impossible to teach or learn any subject, lead a school or a district, diagnose and assess students' potential and actual performances, and create school and classroom climates conducive to learning without simultaneously teaching, learning, and responding to ethnic pluralism. More attention must be paid to modeling ways to make educational programs ethnically diverse and to providing empirical evidence of the effectiveness of multiethnic education. These efforts represent a major change in strategy for supporters of multiethnic education, much of whose energy has, up to now, been devoted to conceptual clarification.

Another potential threat to multiethnic education comes from within. Although any educational idea must grow and change if it is to stand the test of time, such growth must remain within reasonable boundaries and retain a certain degree of continuity. If many new dimensions are added to an idea too rapidly, the original idea may be distorted beyond recognition. This may be beginning to happen to multiethnic education.

The original aim of multiethnic education was to include information about the lifestyles and the heritages of American ethnic groups in school programs. But this notion has expanded considerably since the late 1960s. Now, discussions of multiethnic or multicultural education frequently include the diversities, dilemmas, and experiences of women, the handicapped, the aged, and the poor. Donna Gollnick and Philip Chinn exemplify this eclectic view of multiethnic/multicultural education. They write:

> Our approach to multicultural education is based on a broad definition of culture. By using *culture* as the basis of understanding multicultural education . . . we focus on the complex nature of pluralism in this country. An individual's cultural identity is based not only on ethnicity but also on such factors as socioeconomic level, religion, and sex. . . .[9]

These issues are legitimate areas of study, and they are clearly intertwined with ethnicity. But including them under the conceptual rubric of multiethnic or multicultural education may tend to divert attention away from ethnicity.

The fact that the initial dimensions of multiethnic education have matured conceptually is also a source of strength. These broader dimensions can make the concept more acceptable to a variety of constituents in a variety of educational circumstances. However, this very growth may cause multiethnic education to become a synonym for "pluralism" in its broadest sense. Should this happen, there may be so many "pluralities" vying for attention in educational programs and policies that ethnic pluralism will be lost in the shuffle. Add to this the tendency of educators to extol any idea that is in vogue or politically expedient to the virtual exclusion of all others, and the threat that these tendencies pose to the authentic survival and further development of multiethnic education is clear. Multiethnic education is definitely not in vogue now, although the need for it is as great in 1983 as it was a decade ago. Supporters must find ways to protect the integrity of multiethnic education. One way to do so is to reaffirm its original intentions and to insist on reasonable demarcations of its conceptual boundaries.

The future of multiethnic education is in some ways more uncertain and challenging than it was when this discipline emerged. One kind of political expediency gave it birth; another, coupled with economic and ideological constraints, threatens its existence. Whereas much of the history of multiethnic education to date has been devoted to its justification and conceptual clarification, its future will require long-range pragmatic planning, practical models for implementing ideas, and demonstrations of its effectiveness (both in terms of student performance and of fiscal expenditures). The major challenges for the future of multiethnic education are to translate theory into practice, to institutionalize the concept, and to provide hard evidence of its efficacy.

Notes

1 William Ryan, *Blaming the Victim* (New York: Pantheon, 1971), p. 60.
2 William Labov, *The Study of Nonstandard English* (Urbana, Ill.: National Council of Teachers of English, 1970), p. 43.
3 Edward A. Johnson, *A School History of the Negro Race in America from 1619 to 1890* (Chicago: W.B. Conkey, 1891).
4 Juanita Roderick, "Minority Groups in Textbooks," *Improving College and University Teaching*, Spring 1970, pp. 129–32.
5 California State Board of Education, "Task Force to Re-evaluate Social Studies Textbooks, Grades Five Through Eight," mimeographed, December 1971.
6 Jeannette Henry, *Textbooks and the American Indian* (San Francisco: Indian Historian Press, 1970), p. 11.
7 *1978–79 Michigan Social Studies Textbook Study*, Vol. I (Lansing: Michigan State Department of Education, 1980), p. 103.
8 Milton M. Gordon, *Assimilation in American Life: The Role of Race, Religion, and National Origins* (New York: Oxford University Press, 1964).
9 Donna M. Gollnick and Philip C. Chinn, *Multicultural Education in a Pluralistic Society* (St. Louis: C.V. Mosley, 1983), p. viii.

CHAPTER 16

ISSUES IN MULTICULTURAL EDUCATION (1981)

Kal Gezi

Several scholars, such as Cordianni and Tipple (1980) and Gordon (1964), have observed the historical change in emphasis in American society from Anglo conformity and the melting pot to the notions of cultural mosaic and cultural pluralism. In addition, ethnic groups have moved to assert their right to maintain their cultural identity and to demand their share of power and resources in American society.

As a result, multicultural and bilingual programs were introduced into the curriculum of many American schools. According to Giles (1978), most of our states have established legislation, regulations, guidelines and/or policies in "curriculum, instructional materials, teacher certification and education, staff development and resource centers" (p. 82) relevant to multicultural education.

Furthermore, Gollnick (1977) reported, on the basis of a survey of 395 teacher education institutions, that most institutions provided for study of intergroup communications and classroom dynamics and student teaching experience in schools with culturally diverse students. A large number of institutions offered studies of ethnicity, racism, cultural differences, value clarification and experience in teaching from a multicultural perspective.

What is multicultural education

Many writers, such as Banks (1979), Grambs (1979) and Suzuki (1979), have underscored the confusion in defining the term "multicultural education." Gibson (1976) identifies the following five major approaches to multicultural education: 1) education for the culturally-different helping to equalize educational opportunities for such students; 2) education about cultural differences leading to cultural understanding; 3) education to preserve cultural pluralism; 4) education to help students function in two cultures; and, 5) education to develop competencies in multiple systems.

The term "multicultural education" is used in this article to denote the kind of instruction which provides knowledge about different cultures which forms attitudes toward various peoples and which develops patterns of behaviors and skills appropriate to diverse cultural settings. In the following section, the major issues in multicultural education will be discussed.

Cultural deprivation vs. cultural democracy

Should children from different cultures be given remedial education to alleviate their cultural and educational deficit? Those who respond affirmatively to this question point out that persons from different cultures are culturally deprived and, hence, need to be helped to overcome their deprivation by offering them special classes. When these children are brought up to the level of the Anglo children, they will then be able to benefit from the instruction normally offered in American schools. The concept of cultural deprivation is based on the supposition that the host culture is superior to others and that a culturally different group should abandon its culture and assimilate into the majority culture in order for that group to live and work successfully in its new environment.

There are others, such as Ramirez and Castaneda (1974), who believe that in a cultural democracy, every group should be free to maintain its cultural heritage and to contribute in its own way to American society. The notion of cultural deprivation and deficit should be replaced by the commitment for cultural pluralism and enrichment. The school should not treat children from other cultures as handicapped or inferior. American society should provide through its public schools equal opportunities to have a good education without the sacrificing of native skills, language or culture. Education should begin where the child is.

Campbell (1980) points out that compensatory approaches have had little success because they placed the blame on the deficits in their target population and not on the educational and governmental approaches dealing with this population. He stresses the need for a high quality multicultural curriculum which helps all children understand concepts such as race, culture and ethnicity and their own cultures as well as the cultures of others. Quality education is needed which, according to Carter and Segura (1979), accomplishes the following:

> (1) equalizes benefits—the poor are not recycled; (2) improves school holding power and academic performance; (3) involves all elements of a school or school system; (4) effects radical improvements in the total school social climate; (5) demands the total elimination of all institutional racism and bias; and (6) creates an environment where participation provides its own reward. (p. 386)

Bilingualism: transition or maintenance?

Should Spanish-speaking children be taught in Spanish and English until their English is improved enough for them to make the "transition" to English or should they be taught in Spanish and English throughout their schooling to help them maintain their native language as well as to learn English?

Those who believe in the transitional notion usually subscribe to the idea that children who speak another language have a language deficit and need to be given remedial English as soon as possible. On the other hand, those who support the language maintenance model usually hold the belief that children have a right to be proficient in their native language as well as in the language of the majority.

Persons who may be considered linguistically deprived could be fluent in their own language whether Spanish, Portuguese, Punjabi, Filipino, Cantonese or non-standard English. Learning about the child's language and culture is a prerequisite for understanding the child. Otherwise, how could the teacher begin to communicate with the students, work with them and guide them to learn without knowing their basic skills, cultural background and value system.

The 1974 Supreme Court decision in Lau v. Nichols declared that the failure of the San Francisco school district to provide Chinese non-English speakers with instruction in English or other suitable means had denied these students equal opportunity to education. As a consequence, a greater awareness of the need to provide adequate instructional programs to children who do not speak English occurred. However, districts were faced with compliance with the Lau decision without a corresponding federal allocation of additional resources to them.

Is multicultural education divisive or enriching?

Freedman (1977) urges caution in implementing multicultural education because of its potential as a divisive force. Dolce (1973) questions how the schools could foster unity while being asked to preserve and encourage cultural diversity. Rudman (1977) believes that ethnicity destroys national unity and cohesiveness. Patterson (1975) argues that the emphasis on ethnic identification and cultural pluralism leads to increasing individual autonomy.

On the other hand, Banks (1974) sees the role of the school as that of helping all students to develop ethnic literacy and of allowing students to maximize their cultural options. Banks (1977a) also points out that when excluded minorities are allowed to take part in the various institutions in society, the thrust will change from alienation to national cohesion and mutual interests. Ramirez and Castaneda (1974) underscore the right of all American citizens, according to the Civil Rights Act of 1964, to be free to identify with their own ethnic culture and language. In a cultural democracy, Ramirez and Castaneda point out, one could be multicultural, multi-lingual and still be loyal to American ideals.

The politics of multicultural education

Different views abound in the literature as to why schools should offer multicultural education. One view identifies the push for multicultural and bilingual education as emanating from certain minority groups in their quest for establishing group cohesiveness, for more jobs, for greater resources and increased power. Such programs are seen as self-serving and power building.

A second view considers multicultural education as not only offering minority groups equal educational opportunities but also as providing all students with cultural alternatives (Banks, 1977b). Multicultural education is seen by the ASCD Multicultural Education Commission (1979) as:

> (a) recognizing and prizing diversity; (b) developing greater understanding of other cultural patterns; (c) respecting individuals of all cultures; and (d) developing positive and productive interaction among people *and* among experiences of diverse cultural groups. (p. 3)

A third view conceives of such programs as a form of concession by the majority to placate specific minorities with no real intention for these programs to be permanent or far-reaching.

Hourihan and Chapin (1976) believe that multicultural programs actually perpetuate the political and economic domination of the society over ethnic groups. Labelle (1979) states that the dominant groups are likely to permit school programs to reflect greater cultural rather than structural diversity, as long as the existing social structure and balance of power among groups are not threatened.

St. Lawrence and Singleton (1976) agree that the debate about multiculturalism is really a debate about issues of social structure and stratification and not about culture.

Therefore, is multicultural education used as a means of encouraging students to maintain their ethnic identity and their satisfaction with the limited economic, social and political avenues available to them? Or is multiculturalism a way of increasing options, stimulating mobility and increasing opportunities for all children? The answer depends on our philosophy and commitment in what we do in our schools.

Multicultural education and marginality

How do culturally diverse children deal with the clash between their own native cultures and the dominant culture? Functional marginalism occurs when a person from a specific minority group is alienated from his group because of education, behavior or status and is not totally accepted as equal by members in the dominant culture. How does multicultural education assist in the resolution of cultural clash and value conflict? How could it help each individual maintain a balance between native and dominant values?

How should multicultural education be taught?

Should multicultural education become another subject added to the curriculum? Should it be a series of designated topics to be covered in social studies? Or should it permeate the whole school curriculum? Let us examine the approach suggested by the California State Department of Education as an example.

According to the California State Board of Education policy, adopted in 1979, "multicultural education is an interdisciplinary process rather than a single program or a series of activities." (p. 23) The California State Department of Education suggests that a multicultural program should be cross cultural, interdisciplinary and an integral part of the total curriculum. Program instructional materials and approaches should be unbiased, mindful of student languages, varied and appropriate to the maturity level of the students. Further, the program should avail itself of the people of the community as a valuable resource in understanding similarities and differences among cultures. Staffing should reflect the pluralistic nature of society and staff development and student assessment should be continued and culturally appropriate. Each school district in California is encouraged to provide multicultural instruction for all students (California State Department of Education, 1979).

Along these same lines, ASCD (Grant, 1977) asserts that multicultural education should include curricular, instructional, administrative, and environmental efforts to help students learn from all cultures. It insists that we treat multicultural education as "a continuous, systematic process that will broaden and diversify as it develops."

So, while ethnic studies, special programs and community courses are helpful, McDonald (1977) advocates "the enlargement of human potential by the actual living in multi cultural situations in the classrooms." (p. 8) The classroom becomes a living laboratory for cross-cultural interaction and learning.

Alternative models of curriculum are urgently needed. Textbooks and instructional materials are beginning to portray various ethnic groups and to use greater care in avoiding sexual and cultural stereotypes. Gezi and Bradford (1976, 1978, 1980), for example, developed a series of children's books depicting girls and boys from different ethnic groups working together to solve mysteries or dealing with unfinished stories relating to cultural awareness. God examples of alternative curriculum models are presented by ASCD (Grant, 1979) and Campbell (1980).

The place of multicultural education in teacher preparation

Arciniega (1977) points out that schools of education have tended to follow three approaches in planning and designing new teacher preparation programs:

1   The single "redo" method which presents a bandaid approach
2   A needs assessment based approach which defines the problem of educating minorities in terms of ethnic, and/or linguistic deficiencies—such an approach is doomed to failure
3   A role-derived approach which identifies the desirable competencies we need to develop in our teachers in order to prepare them to work successfully in our multicultural schools.

Hilliard (1974) suggests that teachers should be made aware of the facts that teaching, the classroom and their own backgrounds are culturally oriented; consequently as teachers they need to understand the culture of their students and how such students could have been victimized by oppressive societal conditions. He implores teachers to be cognizant of the achievement of many minority children despite such oppressive conditions and of their increased achievement when proper environmental assistance and adequate opportunities are provided.

The National Council for the Accreditation of Teacher Education (NCATE) has adopted a new multicultural standard in the evaluation and accreditation of teacher education institutions requiring them to plan for and incorporate multicultural education in their programs. How well such institutions are preparing teachers who are culturally aware, sensitive and able to function in multicultural classrooms has been a criterion in the accreditation process since January 1979.

Throughout the nation there is a noticeable emphasis on multicultural instruction, materials, approaches, experiences, in-service activities and research in programs for the preparation of educational personnel. One such program is CUTE, which Houston (1979) describes with respect to its impact on her, as a student teacher, in understanding inner-city schools and children from diverse cultural programs. Yet, there is a long way to go in terms of extent of commitments to multicultural education, agreement on its purposes, its scope, strategies and evaluation and degree of its financial support.

Financial support

The federal government has supported several programs related to bilingual and multicultural education. The states have varied in terms of extending their financial support to these programs while some private and public foundations have allocated monies to such programs on a limited basis.

But with recent and current federal and state budget cuts, the future expansion or even of the continued support for multicultural education is in doubt. For instance, the California State Board of Education policy on multicultural education "is not a mandate and hence cannot generate reimbursable costs." (California State Department of Education, 1979, p. 25) School districts are merely encouraged to implement the various guidelines on multicultural education for all students without the appropriate financial support to do so from the state or the federal government.

This situation has led some educators to be pessimistic about the prospect of a vigorous and comprehensive implementation of bilingual and multicultural education by schools and colleges. It has led some to seek private funding and others to operate limited programs on drastically reduced budgets beset by competing demands from various educational interests. While there seems to be a great need to implement multicultural programs, less resources seem to be on the horizon for the foreseeable future.

Evaluating children from diverse cultures

The controversy about the I.Q. differences among various cultural groups is still with us. While some researchers have concluded that the I.Q. of certain minorities tended to be lower than that of their Anglo counterparts, others believe that no marked I.Q. differences distinguish whites from non-whites. The culprit is seen as the inappropriateness of the I.Q. tests used. Standardized tests normed on one group may be biased when used with a different cultural group.

Chinn (1980) points out that cross cultural assessment may be addressed through: (1) culture-free tests, (2) culture-fair tests, (3) development of culture-specific tests, (4) modification of existing tests with new norms and test sample, and (5) differential weighing of verbal and non-verbal portions of intelligence and achievement tests. (p. 50)

She suggests that teachers use the diagnostic-prescriptive kind of evaluation which would permit them to determine which type of test is more appropriate to use with their particular students.

Several assessment scales have been developed by local districts and state agencies to be used in multicultural education. For instance, the California State Department of Education (n.d.) offers a scale for such an evaluation serving also as a means for self-study, systematic reporting, program development and review. This scale deals with examining the needs assessment process, goals and objectives, instruction, staff, leadership development, materials and facilities, community involvement, environment and background and program evaluation, auditing and reporting.

Another example is the System of Multicultural Pluralistic Assessment (SOMPA) which utilizes medical, social and pluralistic components to assess the achievement of children from diverse cultural backgrounds and identify the health and sociocultural impediments to the full realization of their potentials. This approach was developed by Mercer (1977) who believes that the failure of recognizing culture differences among students in evaluation and cultural bias in testing has resulted in unjustifiably labeling many Mexican-American children as mentally retarded.

To evaluate, educators should: 1) specify reasonable objectives in multicultural education; 2) develop sound and relevant multicultural strategies; 3) provide appropriate materials and experiences; and, 4) evaluate the effectiveness of curricula in terms of specific objectives, using the results to improve future instruction.

What can schools and universities do?

In order to enhance the effectiveness of multicultural education, some steps should be taken by the education community. Colleges and universities should include in their teacher education curricula the content and experiences which are relevant to developing culturally sensitive, aware and skillful teachers who are able to understand, appreciate and work effectively with children from various cultural backgrounds. School districts should strive to provide an ongoing program of multicultural inservice training for all of their teachers. Furthermore, programs for the training of counselors and administrators should likewise emphasize courses, activities and experiences aimed at producing skillful, aware and sensitive professionals who could exert educational leadership in planning, developing, implementing and evaluating multicultural education in their local settings. Teachers, counselors and administrators must become aware of the different cognitive learning styles of children from various cultural backgrounds. For instance, Anglo children tend to be more field-independent while Mexican-American children tend to be more field-dependent in their learning styles (Ramirez & Castaneda, 1974).

Multicultural and bilingual programs should be integrated in the mainstream curriculum of the school. In the past, there has been a tendency to label such programs as remedial or compensatory and to grant them unequal importance in the total curriculum hierarchy of the school. Consequently, less and less attention is paid to them by teachers, counselors and administrators, rendering these programs to be of little real value. We need a major commitment on the part of the school.

School districts should encourage teachers and publishers to provide a variety of multicultural and bilingual materials to be used at different classes and levels of instruction. When the schools make the commitment to multicultural and bilingual education, school funds and efforts as well as commercial resources are likely to be committed to them too.

Above all, schools and university faculty and administrators should develop and foster a living laboratory where students study, work and interact in cross-cultural settings and where one learns to appreciate the human heritage and achieve Paulo Friere's "critical consciousness" of the world in a climate reflecting and supporting the reality of cross cultural education.

References

Arciniega, T. Planning and organizational issues involved in operationalizing the multi-cultural education standard. Washington, D.C.: American Association of Colleges for Teacher Education, December 1977. Mimeo.

ASCD Multicultural Education Commission. Encouraging multicultural education. In C. Grant (Ed.), *Multicultural education: Commitments issues and applications*. Washington D.C.: ASCD, 1979.

Banks, J. Shaping the future of multicultural education. *Journal of Negro Education*, 1979, *48*, 237–252.

Banks, J. A response to Phillip Freedman. *Phi Delta Kappan*, 1977(a), *58*, 695–697.

Banks, J. The implications of multicultural education for teacher education. In F.H. Klassen & D.M. Gollnick (Eds.), *Pluralism and the American teachers: Issues and case studies*. Washington, D.C.: American Association of Colleges for Teacher Education, 1977(b).

Banks, J. Cultural pluralism and the schools. *Educational Leadership*, 1974, *32*(3), 163–66.

California State Department of Education. *An assessment scale for use in examining a multicultural program.* Mimeo, n.d.

California State Department of Education. *Planning for multicultural education as a part of school improvement.* Sacramento: The Office of State Printing, 1979.

Campbell, D. *Education for a democratic society: Curriculum ideas for teachers.* Cambridge, Mass.: Schenkman Publishing Co., 1980.

Carter, T. & Segura, R. *Mexican Americans in school: A decade of change.* New York: College Entrance Examinations Board, 1979.

Chinn, K. Assessment of culturally diverse children. *Viewpoints in Teaching and Learning,* 1980, *56,* 50.

Cordianni, A., & Tipple, B. Conceptual changes in ethnic studies. *Viewpoints in Teaching and Learning,* 1980, *56,* 26–37.

Dolce, C.J. Multicultural education—some issues. *The Journal of Teacher Education,* 1973, *24*(4), 282–284.

Freedman, P. Multi ethnic studies: Proceed with caution. *Phi Delta Kappan,* 1977, *58,* 401–403.

Gezi, K., & Bradford, A. *Beebi, the little blue bell.* Elgin, Ill.: The Child's World, 1976.

Gezi, K., & Bradford, A. *The maple street five series* (9 books). Elgin, Ill.: The Child's World, 1978 & 1980.

Gezi, K., & Bradford, A. *One little white shoe.* Elgin, Ill.: The Child's World, 1976.

Giles, R. *State legislation, provisions and practices related to multicultural education.* Washington, D.C.: American Association of Colleges for Teacher Education, 1978. Mimeo.

Gibson, M. Approaches to multicultural education in the United States: Some concepts and assumptions. *Anthropology and Education Quarterly,* 1976, *7*(4), 7–18.

Gollnick, D. *Multicultural education—preliminary findings of three surveys.* Washington, D.C.: American Association of Colleges for Teacher Education, 1977. Mimeo.

Gordon, M. *Assimilation in American life: The role of race, religion and national origins.* New York: Oxford University Press, 1964.

Grambs, J.D. Multicultural education: Issues without answers. *Education Digest,* 1979, *45,* 45–47.

Grant, C. (Ed.). *Multicultural education: Commitments, issues and application.* Washington, D.C.: ASCD, 1977.

Hilliard, A.G. Restructuring teacher education for multicultural imperatives. In W.A. Hunter (Ed.), *Multicultural education through competency-based teacher education.* Washington, D.C.: American Association of Colleges for Teacher Education, 1974.

Hourihan, J. & Chapin, D. Multicultural education in a pluralistic society: Group vs. individual. *Anthropology and Education Quarterly,* 1976, *7*(4), 23–26.

Houston, D. CUTE: A training program for inner-city teachers. *The Journal of Teacher Education,* 1979, *24,* 302–303.

LaBelle, T. Schooling and intergroup relations: A comparative analysis. *Anthropology and Education Quarterly,* 1979, *10*(1), 43–60.

MacDonald, J. Living democratically in schools: Cultural pluralism. In C. Grant (Ed.), *Multicultural education: Commitments, issues and applications.* Washington, D.C.: ASCD, 1977.

Mercer, J. *Implications of current assessment procedures for Mexican-American children.* Los Angeles: National Dissemination and Assessment Center, 1977, *1,* 1. Occasional paper.

Patterson, O. Ethnicity and the pluralist fallacy. *Change Magazine,* 1975, *7*(2), 10–11.

Ramirez, M. & Castaneda, A. *Cultural democracy, biocognitive development and education.* New York: Academic Press, 1974.

Rudman, H. Multi-ethnicity: Regression or progression? *Educational Administration Quarterly,* 1977, *13*(3), 1–16.

St. Lawrence, T. & Singleton, J. Multiculturalism in social context: Conceptual problems raised by educational policy issues. *Anthropology and Education Quarterly,* 1976, *7*(4), 19–22.

Suzuki, B. Multicultural education: What's it all about? *Integrated Education,* 1979, *17,* 43–50.

CHAPTER 17

AN ANALYSIS OF MULTICULTURAL EDUCATION IN THE UNITED STATES (1987)

Christine E. Sleeter and Carl A. Grant

The Civil Rights movement of the late 1960s and early 1970s spawned several related movements to make education more equitable for various groups. Movements such as desegregation, bilingual education, special needs education, and the use of mainstreaming attempted to make schools more accessible to more students by removing barriers to schooling in general and to particular programs within schools. Multicultural education has been a reform movement aimed at changing the content and processes within schools. Originally linked only to concerns about racism in schooling, it has expanded to address sexism, classism, and handicappism. Like many other such movements, it began with a few people articulating concerns and recommendations and grew as these first voices were joined by many others who shared similar concerns. A few books and articles on multicultural education in the United States began to appear in the early 1970s; they were soon followed by a broad array of writing which addressed related concerns, theoretical formulations, and recommendations. To date, no one has synthesized and analyzed this body of literature. We do so here, with two main purposes.

One purpose is to bring conceptual clarity to the field by examining what multicultural education means. Over the years it has become clear that it means different things to different people (Dolce, 1973; Hiraoka, 1977; Tesconi, 1984). To address this problem, both Gibson (1976) and Pratte (1983) developed typologies of approaches to multicultural education. Each presented four existing approaches differentiated by target population, long-term goals, and assumptions about cultural differences. While we found these typologies helpful, we also found that each failed to distinguish between related but different approaches. We refined their typologies, distinguishing among five approaches, all of which are called "multicultural education."

A second purpose is to evaluate the literature for its contributions to both the theory and the practice of multicultural education, including a critical examination of its limitations. Some topics and themes have been discussed thoroughly and repeatedly, to the point where new articles rehash old ideas, while other ideas have been virtually ignored.

Method

We limited our review to books and articles published in the United States, about American schools, for grades K-12. To locate journal articles, we conducted a search in the Educational Resources Information Center, using the descriptors *multicultural education, multiethnic education, multiracial education,* and *bicultural education.* To locate books we conducted a Library of Congress search, using the same descriptors as well as *biracial education* and *ethnic education.* We excluded literature on multicultural pre-service and in-service teacher education, chapters in books unless the entire book focused on multicultural education, and literature that discussed the education of only one ethnic group or discussed bilingual education without referring to culture. As a result, we were able to identify a total of 89 articles and 38 books for review.

Our analysis examines five approaches to multicultural education which emerge from the literature. "Teaching the Culturally Different" is an approach used to assimilate students of color into the cultural mainstream and existing social structure by offering transitional bridges within the existing school program. A "Human Relations" approach is used to help students of different backgrounds get along better and appreciate each other. "Single Group Studies" fosters cultural pluralism by teaching courses about the experiences, contributions, and concerns of distinct ethnic, gender, and social class groups. The "Multicultural Education" approach promotes cultural pluralism and social equality by reforming the school program for all students to make it reflect diversity. These reforms include school staffing patterns that reflect the pluralistic nature of American society; unbiased curricula that incorporate the contributions of different social groups, women, and the handicapped; the affirmation of the languages of non-English-speaking minorities; and instructional materials that are appropriate and relevant for the students and which are integrated rather than supplementary. Finally, "Education That Is Multicultural and Social Reconstructionist" prepares students to challenge social structural inequality and to promote cultural diversity.

For each approach we analyzed the literature according to fourteen categories (see Table 17.1–17.5). The first category addresses the goals of each approach. The next eight categories refer to scope and theoretical foundations. All authors addressed the issue of race or ethnicity, but varied in the extent to which they addressed culture, language, and social stratification, gender, social class, and handicap. In addition, a few writers incorporated discussions of history and policy/legal issues. The tenth category consists of instructional models—conceptual frameworks for thinking about and organizing both the content and the process of instruction. Literature covering the eleventh and twelfth categories, curriculum and instruction, focuses primarily on recommendations for these areas. The last two categories deal with implementation: teaching guides that include practical "how-to's" and project descriptions that report actual implementation efforts. In our tabulations, we counted a book or article as addressing one of these categories if it was central to the work, or at least received sufficient attention that one could profitably read it to learn more about the topic.

Teaching the culturally different

We examined seventeen articles and eleven books that conceptualize multicultural education as something one does mainly with students who are of color (see Table 17.1).* Thirteen of these use the word "multicultural" in the title, seven use the word "bicultural," and one uses "multiethnic." Three state their purpose as helping teachers teach "culturally different" students.

There is considerable agreement on goals. Lewis (1976) states the goals succinctly: Multicultural education should help "minority students ... develop

Table 17.1 Teaching the culturally different

	Goals	Language/bilingual	Culture	Social stratification	Gender	Social class	Handicap	History	Policy/legal issues	Instructional models	Curriculum	Instruction	Teaching guides	Project description
Abrahams & Troike (1972) B		X	X					X						
Arenas (1980) J		X	X											X
Baker (1983a) J											X			
Barnhardt (1977) B		X	X	X						X	X			
Brembeck & Hill (1973) B			X					X	X				X	X
Carlson (1976) J			X											
Carter (1983) J											X			
Epstein (1977) B	X	X	X					X						
Garcia (1984) J			X					X						
Irving (1984) J	X	X	X											
Laosa (1977) J			X									X		
Lewis (1976) J	X			X										
Myers (1980) J	X	X						X						
Ornstein & Levin (1982) J		X										X		
Payne (1977) J													X	
Pulte (1978) J	X	X	X											
Ramirez & Castaneda (1974) B	X		X							X		X		
Reyes (1976) J			X								X			
Sancho (1977) J		X	X									X		
Saville-Troike (1976) B	X	X	X									X		
Sims & de Martinez (1981) B	X			X				X			X		X	
Stone & DeNevi (1971) B	X		X	X			X	X						
Uhlig & Vasquez (1982) J			X											
Valencia (1976) B		X	X											
Von Maltitz (1975) B	X	X						X	X					X
Wagner (1981) J			X									X		
Wolfgang (1977) J			X									X		
Zintz (1963) B		X	X					X	X			X		

Note: See reference list for bibliographic data on these studies.
B = Book.
J = Journal article.

competence in the public culture of the dominant group" and at the same time help them develop "a positive group identity" which builds on their home cultures (p. 35). In bilingual education, for example, students should be taught English as well as the knowledge, skills, and attitudes needed to participate in mainstream society, and they should also be encouraged to develop competence in and knowledge of their own cultural background.

As Table 17.1 shows, most of this literature treats various aspects of culture or language. Its main purposes are to challenge the cultural deficiency orientation, to establish the importance of maintaining one's own cultural identity, and to describe aspects of culture a teacher can build on. Cultural and language differences among groups are addressed much more frequently than unequal social relationships. Authors advocating this approach emphasize building bridges between cultures to facilitate individual achievement and social mobility, rather than combating unequal distribution of goods and power among racial groups.

Most authors discuss race and ethnicity without mentioning other forms of human diversity. In their discussions of history and policy/legal issues they focus on establishing the extent to which schools have either failed to serve or have underserved children of color, and on providing a moral and legal basis for reforming education in order to help students of color maintain their ethnic cultures and languages. Of all the aspects of classroom teaching found in the literature, instruction receives the greatest attention. Most authors describe ways to modify instructional practices to make them more compatible with students' learning and communication styles.

As a whole, we found this segment of the literature strong in its commitment to and interest in the welfare and educational achievement of children of color, but weak in its development of recommendations for practice. First, all but a few authors tend to lump several distinct cultural groups together. For example, while a few authors specify which Hispanic group they are discussing, others refer loosely to the "child of Spanish heritage" (Reyes, 1976, p. 57). There are differences among Hispanic groups, and for some instructional purposes these differences matter; a fair-skinned child whose parents are from Spain is less likely to experience the school-based discrimination directed toward a dark-skinned child whose parents are Mexican-American. Authors need to be clearer in their recommendations, or at least indicate whether they are referring to specific Hispanic, Asian, or Native American groups. They must make sure, for example, that the instructional practices they suggest for Asian-American students differentiate, where appropriate, between Hmong-American and Japanese-American students. The previous learning experiences of many Southeast Asian refugees, for instance, were likely to have been by rote; students listened, and then repeated on tests verbatim what had been presented in classes. Hmong-American students, therefore, may well need to learn to ask questions, to use creative thinking skills, and to participate in the class. By contrast, many Japanese-American students, whose families have lived in this country for longer amounts of time, are more likely to be familiar with these classroom routines and expectations.

Second, many of the articles provided little specific information about how to teach children of color. For example, Laosa (1977) points out that "childhood socialization practices that are characteristic of certain cultures tend to foster the development of particular cognitive styles" (p. 28), but gives only a few examples contrasting Mexican-American and Anglo-American children. One would need to research other descriptors and titles (such as learning styles) to find specific information on teaching children of color, since not much of it is to be found in the "multicultural education" literature.

Third, there is little discussion of goals. Most authors evaluate transitional versus maintenance approaches to bilingual education thoughtfully and informatively. But only one offers a substantive discussion of the goals of Teaching the Culturally Different as one among the several approaches to multicultural education (Lewis, 1976). The other articles and books do not explain that other approaches to multicultural education exist; they simply seem to assume that most people would agree that multicultural or bicultural education is for students of color only, and proceed to provide either a rationale for it or information on its implementation.

A fourth weakness is that suggestions for curricula are even less well developed than are suggestions for instruction. The former are very short and superficial, reducing curriculum to materials rather than considering the entire spectrum of planned school experiences. What to teach, aside from the English language, is addressed only marginally. For example, Carlson (1976) points out that cultural similarities outweigh cultural differences between most children, but no one mentions which differences are important in adapting curricula.

We share the authors' commitment to improving education for children of color, and doing so in ways that build on, rather than replace, the language, values, and experiences children bring with them. But this approach is too limited, primarily because it puts the burden of eliminating racism on people of color and their teachers rather than on the general population and especially on Whites. For example, the income of Hispanic families has ranged from between 65 and 70 percent of that for White families for the past fifteen years (U.S. Department of Commerce, 1987, p. 436). In 1984, the median income for Whites with four or more years of college was $43,753, while the median income for Hispanics with equivalent education was only $36,728. (In addition, the proportion of Hispanics with this level of education is much smaller than that of Whites.) These facts stem from several features of society, including the inability of our current economy to employ all who seek jobs, the existence of many low-wage jobs, racist hiring practices, and the unequal geographic distribution of higher-wage employment opportunities. The Teaching-the-Culturally-Different approach addresses these problems primarily by trying to equip people of color more successfully with the knowledge and skills to compete with Whites. It does not imply that Whites should be taught anything more than they are now about racism, classism, or other cultural groups.

Human relations

We examined nine articles and five books that conceptualize multicultural education as a way to help students of different backgrounds communicate, get along better with each other, and feel good about themselves (see Table 17.2). Ten of these use the word *multicultural* in the title, and two of these ten also use the term *human relations*.

As Table 17.2 shows, four of these works discuss the goals of the Human Relations approach. Perry (1975), for example, in discussing a multicultural literature program, describes its purpose as the promotion of good human relations among students of different races. He writes that "serving as a vehicle to foster conversation, the literature selected should afford an opportunity for a variety of viewpoints. What the students do with these ideas and perceptions gained is really the most important aspect of a reading program in developing positive human relationships" (p. 8). Advocates of the Human Relations approach to multicultural education emphasize improving communication between people of different cultural backgrounds. These books and articles all dwell much more on how to apply the approach than on providing a theoretical foundation for it. Colangelo, Foxley, and Dustin (1979) provide short and rather superficial developments of theory. They suggest a potentially useful model for nonsexist, multicultural human relations in the first chapter, while subsequent chapters provide information about topics not directly connected to the model. A second

Table 17.2 Human relations

	Goals	Language/bilingual	Culture	Social stratification	Gender	Social class	Handicap	History	Policy/legal issues	Instructional models	Curriculum	Instruction	Teaching guides	Project description
Bernstein (1984) J		X	X											
Berry (1979) J			X											
Colangelo, Dustin, & Foxley (1982) B		X		X						X			X	
Colangelo, Foxley, & Dustin (1979) B		X	X	X	X					X	X	X		
Cole (1984) J														
Deyoe (1977) J										X				
Ethnic Cultural Heritage Program (1977) B			X										X	
Forman & Mitchell (1977) J														X
Kendall (1983b) J										X				
Mortenson (1975) B				X									X	
Perry (1975) J	X									X				
Skinner (1977) J														
Tiedt & Tiedt (1986) B			X	X									X	
Velez (1981) J			X	X										

Note: See reference list for bibliographic data on these studies.
B = Book.
J = Journal article.

book (Colangelo, Dustin, & Foxley, 1982) provides some limited theory within the lesson plans presented for the teacher. Books and articles in this approach that focus on applications instruct teachers on the importance of using non-stereotypic materials and provide human relations activities mainly for elementary school students.

Much of the literature that uses a Human Relations approach seems to have been written by educators involved directly with schools and especially with problems accompanying desegregation. Accordingly, these materials offer teachers practical ideas in clear language for improving their students' understanding of culturally different peers, and include features which maximize usefulness (such as workbook pages, illustrations, and the like).

This approach, however, has produced almost no literature that links practical application theoretically and conceptually with social psychology and theory on intergroup conflict and prejudice formation, although such connections are evident in other human relations literature (Johnson, 1972). Nor is there conceptual linkage with research on crosscultural differences, as exists in the anthropological literature: Are there, for example, cultural differences between Asian-Americans and Euro-Americans that interfere with communication? Such theoretical connections would enrich the Human Relations approach to multicultural education by promoting better development of practical applications. For example, cognitive development theory suggests that humans progress through stages in their tendency to stereotype phenomena; knowing this, could educators follow a developmental sequence when they plan teaching activities for reducing the stereotyping of different groups?

Perhaps few multicultural education theorists advocate the human relations approach because its development of long-term goals is lacking. If conflict among racial groups in a desegregated school has been reduced, are there additional social goals to be addressed? None of the books and articles adopting a Human Relations approach addresses concerns about social stratification. This approach seems to suggest that people should get along, communicate, and appreciate each other within the existing stratified social system. Advocates may hope that eventually better communication will lead, for example, to cooperation between Blacks and Whites to reduce the incidence of poverty among Blacks. But issues such as poverty, institutional discrimination, and powerlessness are addressed little or not at all in the Human Relations literature.

Single group studies

Two books and nine articles adopt a Single Group Studies approach to multi-cultural education; a third book by Tiedt and Tiedt (1986) combines this approach with Human Relations (see Table 17.3). By Single Group Studies, we mean lessons or units that focus on the experiences and cultures of a specific group, such as an ethnic group. Only one source addresses gender and class as

Table 17.3 Single group studies

	Goals	Language/bilingual	Culture	Social stratification	Gender	Social class	Handicap	History	Policy/legal issues	Instructional models	Curriculum	Instruction	Teaching guides	Project description
Anderson (1980) J											X			
Banks (1973) B		X	X	X	X	X					X			
Christian (1977) J			X											
Garcia & Denton (1980) J												X		
Heller (1983) J								X						
Houston (1975) J														X
King (1980) B		X											X	
Krug (1977) J								X						
O'Brien (1980) J											X			
Santos (1980) J														X
Tiedt & Tiedt (1986) B											X	X	X	
Wilson (1979) J												X		

Note: See reference list for bibliographic data on these studies.
B = Book.
J = Journal article.

well as race and ethnicity. Thus, in this body of literature, Single Group Studies means ethnic studies. Of these twelve books and articles, five use *multicultural education* in the title, two use *ethnic*, and most of the others include a form of the word *culture*.

This approach pays least attention to goals, perhaps because the authors assume that the goals are understood and require little elaboration. Two authors who do discuss goals suggest somewhat different ones: King (1980) writes that ethnic education should "develop an acceptance, appreciation and empathy for the rich cultural and linguistic diversity in America" (p. 7), while Banks (1973) writes that it should "help students develop the ability to make reflective decisions so that they can resolve personal problems, and through social action, influence public policy and develop a sense of political efficacy" (p. 116).

Language is a major topic in one article, and one book provides a substantive discussion of culture. Only one author discusses social stratification and social class. Otherwise, curriculum and instruction receive more attention than any other topic.

Like the literature adopting a Human Relations approach, the Single Group Studies literature focuses on prescription and application much more than on goals or theory. Although all twelve books and articles discuss a broad array of topics, such as music, leadership, human resources, and stages of thinking, only Banks (1973) has developed a conceptual foundation for this approach. No one discusses more than one application in any of these areas.

The lack of attention to goals and social stratification presents a rather serious problem. Most scholars who write about Black studies, Chicano studies, Indian studies, Asian-American studies, and women's studies very explicitly advocate social change as the major long-term goal. Specific groups are studied to sensitize students to a group's victimization as well as to its accomplishments, and to mobilize student participation in current attempts to improve social conditions for the group (Blassingame, 1976; Bowles & Klein, 1983). Although Banks (1973) clearly articulates these goals, authors of the other books and articles emphasize teaching about the contributions and experiences of a group without necessarily raising awareness of racial oppression or mobilizing for social action. We are concerned that teachers, especially many White teachers, may not view social change as a goal of Single Group Studies. For example, a teacher might teach about traditional American Indian cultural practices but not even mention their oppression today. Although there is value in teaching about cultures, the failure to address issues of current social stratification and social action ignores a major component of what many scholars deem essential to Single Group Studies. Those who see multicultural education as Single Group Studies need to discuss its goals more clearly and in so doing, should draw on discussions by advocates of Black studies, women's studies, Chicano studies, Asian-American studies, Native American studies, and so on.

One additional problem is prevalent: The tendency to ignore multiple forms of human diversity. Single Group Studies attempts to deal with racism in the curriculum by developing units or courses of study about ethnic groups. But such units can still be sexist and classist, replacing, for example, the study of White middle-class men with the study of Black men (many of whom had lower class origins as a result of racism). Thus Cortes's (1973) chapter, "Teaching the Chicano Experience," in Banks's (1973) book, names several events and Chicano people and recommends several books—most of which feature males. Banks's chapter on women does not directly correct this imbalance, because it focuses on White women.

Multicultural education

We examined forty-seven articles and nineteen books that adopt a Multicultural Education approach (see Table 17.4). We termed this approach *Multicultural Education*, because, even though advocates of the previous approaches used the same phrase, these authors do emphasize education that is truly multicultural and that focuses on common goals.

Goals are discussed in nineteen articles and ten books, with considerable agreement. Gollnick (1980) summarizes the five major goals of this approach as promoting "strength and value of cultural diversity. . . . Human rights and respect for cultural diversity. . . . Alternative life choices for people. . . . Social justice and equal opportunity for all people . . . and Equity distribution of power among members of all ethnic groups" (p. 9). Authors emphasize and elaborate on different goals, but most accept all five.

Treatments of culture and language are complementary and provide conceptual support for and clarification of Gollnick's (1980) first three goals. Some authors provide information about the cultures of American racial groups (Banks, 1984; Gold, Grant & Rivlin, 1977), other about culture as an anthropological concept (Gibson, 1976; Gollnick & Chinn, 1986; Goodenough, 1976), and still others discuss bilingualism and cultural pluralism as goals for society (Epps, 1974; Stent, Hazard, & Rivlin, 1973). Social stratification receives somewhat less attention than culture. The main issues addressed are institutional racism in society and schools, unequal power relationships among racial groups, and economic stratification and social class. These discussions develop the ideas presented in Gollnick's fourth and fifth goals.

Most of the literature focuses on race and ethnicity. Gender is included mainly in the form of separate chapters in books, and social class is included primarily in discussions of the social class characteristics of ethnic groups. There is some disagreement over whether multicultural education should deal only with ethnicity or should include additional forms of human diversity. Gay (1983b) cautions that the initial intent of multicultural education, which is "concern for the study of ethnic cultures, experiences, and issues, especially those of racial minorities, may be shortchanged" if the concept becomes too elastic (p. 7).

Treatments of history in this approach are essentially limited to histories of multicultural education, in some cases contextualized within the Civil Rights movement. Most discussions of policy and legal matters center on state and national policy regarding ethnicity, language, and issues of school reform.

Several authors offer models to help teachers implement multicultural education. Some describe stages of development in either the teacher or the students (Baker, 1978; Baker, 1983b; Banks, 1981; Cross, Long, & Ziajka, 1978; Kendall, 1983); some offer several different approaches to implementing multicultural education in the classroom and invite teachers to choose among them (Banks, 1984; Gay, 1975; Garcia, 1979); and some provide schemes for examining several different aspects of one's instructional program, such as visual displays, curriculum materials, and tests, as well as suggestions for making each aspect multicultural (Baptiste, 1979; Clasen, 1979; Grant, 1977a; Payne, 1983, 1984; Sizemore, 1979). All of these models are well developed and appear useful; none, however, expands work on curriculum and instruction or on teaching guides.

Table 17.4 Multicultural education

	Goals	Language/bilingual	Culture	Social stratification	Gender	Social class	Handicap	History	Policy/legal issues	Instructional models	Curriculum	Instruction	Teaching guides	Project description
Adachi (1975) J											X			
Baker (1976) J	X													
Baker (1978) J									X					
Baker (1979) J					X			X	X					
Baker (1983b) B	X										X	X	X	
Banks (1979) J	X		X		X			X						
Banks (1981) B	X	X	X	X							X	X	X	
Banks (1983) J			X		X				X					
Banks (1984) B	X		X								X	X	X	
Baptiste (1979) B	X	X							X	X				
Baptiste & Baptiste (1977) J													X	
Baptiste & Baptiste (1979) B	X		X		X			X			X	X		
Barnes (1979) J				X										
Barnhardt (1977) B		X	X	X					X					
Bennett (1986) B	X		X										X	
Butterfield et al. (1979) J					X	X	X				X			
Cheng, Brizendine, & Oaks (1979) J	X			X					X					
Clasen (1979) J									X					
Commission on Multicultural Education (1973) J	X													
Cortes (1976) J											X			
Cortes (1980) J											X			
Cox & Fundis (1982) J	X													
Cross, Baker, & Stiles (1977) B	X								X		X	X		
Cross, Long, & Zlajka (1978) J										X				
DeCosta (1984) J						X								X
Dodds (1983) J											X			
Ehlers & Crawford (1983) J	X			X										
Epps (1974) B	X		X											
Foerster (1982) J	X													
Garcia (1979) B		X	X	X							X	X		
Gay (1975) J											X			
Gay (1977) J	X								X			X		
Gay (1981) J													X	
Gay (1983a) J						X			X					
Gay (1983b) J						X			X					
Gezi (1981) J	X													
Gibson (1976) J	X		X											
Gold, Grant, & Rivlin (1977) B			X	X	X									

(Continued)

Table 17.4 (continued)

	Goals	Language/bilingual	Culture	Social stratification	Gender	Social class	Handicap	History	Policy/legal issues	Instructional models	Curriculum	Instruction	Teaching guides	Project description
Gollnick (1980) *J*	X													
Gollnick & Chinn (1986) *B*		X	X	X	X	X	X				X	X		
Goodenough (1976) *J*	X		X	X										
Grant (1977a) *J*				X						X				
Grant (1977b) *B*	X	X	X		X						X			
Grant (1979) *J*			X						X					
Grant, Boyle, & Sleeter (1980) *B*	X		X											
G. Grant (1977) *B*				X		X	X						X	
Hernandez (1977) *J*									X					
Hollins (1982) *J*												X		
Hourthan & Chapin (1976) *J*	X													
Kendall (1983a) *B*				X							X		X	X
Lee (1983) *J*		X												
Levy (1980) *J*		X												
McCormick (1984) *J*		X												
Nagtalon-Miller (1977) *J*			X	X										
Ovando (1983) *J*		X							X					
Pasternak (1977) *B*				X									X	
Payne (1983) *J*										X				
Payne (1984) *J*					X			X	X					
Poster (1979) *J*		X										X		
Ramsey (1982) *J*													X	
Sims & de Martinez (1981) *B*	X								X				X	X
Sizemore (1979) *J*									X					
Stent, Hazard, & Rivlin (1973) *B*		X	X											
Stewart (1978) *J*												X		
Trueba (1976) *J*		X	X	X										
Valverde (1977) *J*		X												

Note: See reference list for bibliographic data on these studies.
B = Book.
J = Journal article.

Authors discuss curriculum much more than instruction; they critique materials, recommend specific materials for teaching about ethnic groups, and suggest approaches to multicultural curriculum design and curriculum revision. Teaching guides are more plentiful than discussions of curriculum or instruction. Two of the nine guides are written exclusively for elementary teachers (Kendall, 1983a; Ramsey, 1982). The other seven are written for both elementary and secondary teachers although they direct more attention to the elementary teachers (Baker, 1983b; Banks, 1984; Bennett, 1986; Gay, 1981; Grant, 1977; Pasternak, 1977;

Sims & de Martinez, 1981). Most of the guides—Baker (1983b) is the main exception—offer examples of lesson plans rather than entire units; it is likely that the authors hope that teachers will use them as models for developing or modifying their own courses of study.

Clearly, the Multicultural Education approach is the most popular, although the absence of project descriptions showing it in operation suggests it is not the main approach implemented. Goals are the points most frequently discussed, and there is so much agreement on these that the material became repetitious. There are, however, issues related to goals and scope that remain to be addressed.

One issue is the relative emphasis that should be given to culture as opposed to social stratification. Culture is discussed chiefly in textbooks, where the purpose is to help students understand what culture is and why cultural assimilation is undesirable. Authors present these concepts clearly, drawing upon anthropological studies to provide a sound counterargument to the notion of cultural deprivation. Social stratification, by contrast, is discussed mainly in short articles and usually in little detail. Although both can be attended to simultaneously (for example, by fighting institutional racism while promoting the cultures of minority groups), few authors emphasize both or discuss their relative importance. This inadequate coverage is significant because social stratification, as well as racial oppression, has provided much of the impetus for recognizing the need for multicultural education. The desire not to have to assimilate culturally has been only part of the concern; the desire to have power and economic resources equal to Whites has also been a concern. Emphasizing culture at the expense of social stratification may suggest to those Whites who prefer not to confront racism that maintaining and valuing cultural differences is *the* main goal of multicultural education.

A second unresolved issue is the extent to which the topics of social class, gender, and handicap are included and/or discussed. Those writers who include one or more of these topics tend not to explain why they do so or why they exclude others. Gollnick and Chinn (1986) and Gay (1983b) are exceptions to this particular criticism. Gollnick and Chinn (1986) argue that the "overall goal of multicultural education is to help all students reach their potential. Educational and vocational options should not be limited by sex, age, ethnicity, native language, religion, socio-economic level, or exceptionality" (p. vii). Gay's position, by contrast, is that attention to groups identified by other than ethnic status will hamper the development of multicultural education by rendering it too diffuse (1983b, p. 7). There needs to be more discussion about whether multicultural education should deal with other status groupings in addition to race and ethnicity, and such discussions should recognize the interrelationships among status groupings so that, for example, Blacks and women are not viewed as discrete and separate groups.

Only a few authors present language and bilingualism from a multicultural perspective; most of those who write about multicultural education do not examine language. Language is usually addressed with the purpose of discussing how or what to teach linguistic minority children, and thus adopts the Teaching-the-Culturally-Different approach. Most who write about cultural diversity tend to ignore language, probably unintentionally. This suggests the need for more dialogue between advocates of bilingual education and multicultural education.

A few authors present the short history of multicultural education, yet none provides a broader history of education from a multicultural perspective. Several revisionist historians, including Tyack (1974) and Katz (1975), have written provocative histories that examine how social class has permeated the development of education. An examination of the history of education from the perspective of race, social class, and gender would be a welcome addition.

The fact that there is little discussion of policy is another weakness in the Multicultural Education literature. Educators in countries such as England and Australia debate much more about national policy in relation to multiculturalism than do educators in the United States. Should the U.S. government establish more policies related to multicultural education, such as mandating the use of nonracist materials in schools that receive federal funding? One way, for example, that the federal government might demonstrate its support of multicultural education is through the explicit funding of research and development in this area. Are there areas in which existing policies need to be enforced more vigorously? Those educators involved in desegregation, for example, actively debate policy at the federal and state levels, whereas those educators involved in multicultural education rarely write about issues beyond the individual classroom or school level.

The writings about curriculum and instruction have both strengths and weaknesses. The models of instruction seem worthwhile and well conceptualized. A few authors, such as Banks (1981, 1983, 1984) and Baker (1979, 1983a, 1983b), elaborate on their own models, but there is little carryover from the models to the teaching guides. This may be because advocates of the Multicultural Education approach have needed to concentrate so much on clarifying goals and providing a rationale that they have considered implementation less systematically. Models that have been proposed should be refined, tested in the classroom, and researched.

Discussions of both curriculum and instruction could be developed much further. The instructional process is virtually overlooked in this literature. We doubt that Multicultural Education advocates wish to see a multicultural curriculum taught via lectures and textbooks, and with students occupying a passive role. By failing to address pedagogy, Multicultural Education can remain trapped in those instructional patterns that predominate in our schools. The literature that discusses curriculum tends to prescribe what should be included; few authors examine or develop curriculum theory. No one, for example, discusses connections between models of curriculum and multiculturalism, examines the hidden curriculum from a multicultural perspective, or analyzes existing multicultural curricula.

The teaching guides provide a wealth of ideas for the elementary teacher but much less for the secondary teacher, where the need may be greater. Goodlad (1984), for example, has found that teachers from the fourth grade up individualize instruction and vary their teaching strategies less and less. Our own experience suggests that elementary teachers are more likely to work with multicultural education than are secondary teachers, who seem compelled to cover only the standard curriculum. There remains a critical absence of teaching guides appropriate for use by secondary teachers, guides which integrate multicultural education into the curriculum while recognizing the instructional demands placed upon them.

The great majority of the teaching guides and discussions of implementation are written for the individual classroom teacher. There is little discussion of school- or system-wide practices that need change. Ability grouping and tracking, standardized intelligence and achievement testing, and the declining numbers of minority staff members are widespread realities that often place students of color at a disadvantage. Failure to discuss such issues may suggest that they are separate from multicultural education. We do not believe they are, nor do we believe most advocates see them as separate.

In sum, the Multicultural Education approach has well-developed statements of goals, several promising models of curriculum and instruction, and many teaching guides. In order to progress, however, the literature should grapple more with the relationship of social stratification to culture, as well as consider the integration of race, class, and gender factors when examining oppression. Authors should also endeavor to connect the approach more directly with established bodies of inquiry on educational history and social policy, curriculum theory, the hidden curriculum, and the sorting function of schools.

Education that is multicultural and social reconstructionist

Seven articles and three books conceptualize multicultural education as an approach to education that prepares young people to take social action against social structural inequality (see Table 17.5). Eight titles include the term *cultural*, and five use the term *multicultural*. Grant's (1978) earlier phrase "education that is multicultural" has been modified to read ". . . and social reconstructionist" to underscore its emphasis on social action (Sleeter & Grant, 1986).

Goals are discussed in one book and six articles. Essentially, authors extend the goals of the Multicultural Education approach. They suggest more emphasis on helping students "gain a better understanding of the causes of oppression and inequality and ways in which these social problems might be eliminated" (Suzuki, 1984, p. 308). They argue that teachers can accomplish this by "changing their teaching practices in ways that will make their classrooms more democratic"

Table 17.5 Education that is multicultural and social reconstructionist

	Goals	Language/bilingual	Culture	Social stratification	Gender	Social class	Handicap	History	Policy/legal issues	Instructional models	Curriculum	Instruction	Teaching guides	Project description
Appleton (1983) B	X	X						X	X		X	X		
Grant (1978) J	X				X									
Hernandez-Chavez (1977) J		X	X							X				
Myers, Banfield, & Colon (1983) B					X	X	X							X
Pacheco (1977) J	X		X											
St. Lawrence & Singleton (1976) J	X		X											
Schniedewind & Davidson (1983) B					X	X	X							X
Suzuki (1979) J	X		X		X			X						
Suzuki (1984) J	X		X		X					X	X			
Williams (1982) J	X													

Note: See reference list for bibliographic data on these studies.
B = Book.
J = Journal article.

(Suzuki, 1984, p. 312). Students should learn to use power for collective betterment, rather than learning mainly obedience.

In their discussions of culture and bilingualism authors criticize the emphasis of other approaches on culture. Pacheco (1977), for example, argues that cultural pluralism theory "often assumes that culture is the major factor," when in fact class is a more central factor (p. 20). Suzuki (1979) warns that "the social realities of racism, sexism, and inequality are often overlooked or conveniently forgotten" when culture is overemphasized (p. 45). Two books, both teacher guides, deal directly with social stratification by providing lessons to help children learn to analyze and take action against social inequality. It seems strange that so few works advocating this approach elaborate on social structural inequality, since its central goal is preparing future citizens to make social structural changes that will uphold equality. Footnotes and references suggest that the authors themselves are familiar with the literature on social stratification; so little, however, has been written specifically about this approach that they should not assume readers have a working understanding of it.

The categories of gender and social class receive more consistent attention from literature in this approach than from other approaches. Both of the teaching guides give as much attention to gender and almost as much attention to social class as to race. As in the Multicultural Education approach, some authors provide short histories of multicultural education. Two of the policy discussions are substantive; Hernandez-Chavez (1977) critiques bilingual education policy, and Appleton (1983) describes and evaluates federal policy on ethnicity and schooling.

No instructional models are provided, and little is written about curriculum and instruction. The two teaching guides offer different but compatible resources, one to assist elementary teachers and the other to assist both elementary and secondary teachers help students deal with social inequalities engendered by racism, sexism, and classism.

This approach to multicultural education is, at present, the least developed. We view it as an outgrowth of the Multicultural Education approach, which includes among its goals the objectives of reducing racism and building a more just society. Some Multicultural Education authors, such as Banks (1981, 1983, 1984), discuss developing social action for this purpose but give greater attention to other goals, while other authors do not address this goal at all. Advocates of Education That Is Multicultural and Social Reconstructionist assume this is the leading goal. In doing so, they expend much energy criticizing shortcomings of the Multicultural Education approach. In fact, there is less consensus about what to call this approach than there is about the others. Some, such as Suzuki (1984), call it multicultural education; we are aware that other authors concerned with race, class, and gender issues call their approaches emancipatory education (Gordon, 1985), transformative education (Giroux, 1985), and critical teaching (Shor, 1980). Agreement on a term will help advance the approach by fostering dialogue. Much more needs to be developed for this approach in all the categories shown in Table 17.5. Particularly lacking is material on achieving the goals in schools; without this material the approach runs the risk of being passed off as a good, but impractical or unrealistic, idea.

Discussion

Clearly, the term *multicultural education* means different things to different people. The only common meaning is that it refers to changes in education that are supposed to benefit people of color. The typology we have presented here provides a way of differentiating among various meanings. It is important for readers to be aware of these differences because authors do not necessarily spell out their goals and assumptions. Readers need to consider for themselves, for example, whether better education for Hispanic children should aim chiefly to teach them more successfully what White children are taught—without changing what White children are taught (Teaching the Culturally Different), help them develop better self-concepts and friendships with White children (Human Relations), or help them learn to fight racism alongside White children (Education That Is Multicultural and Social Reconstructionist). Then readers should examine what they read that is called *multicultural education* accordingly.

The literature we reviewed addresses race and ethnicity as the main form of human diversity. Some of the books and articles include language or gender, fewer include social class, and very few include handicap. All five approaches will serve children better when they acknowledge other factors in addition to race.

Overall, authors' efforts to show the relationships of these ideas to practice are weak. They do not provide a thorough discussion of the theoretical frameworks supporting their goals. Statements concerning goals are often vague, and clear connections between what authors expect of the approach and what they recommend as practices for educators are either ambiguous or missing altogether. Goals for several areas, including curricula, instruction, and school policy, for example, are listed, while the recommended practices are limited to curricula. The chief such link for Teaching the Culturally Different is in translating information on culture and learning styles into suggestions for instruction. Literature for both the Human Relations and the Single Group Studies approaches is prescriptive without necessarily being grounded in theory or even in clear discussions of goals and assumptions. The Education-That-Is-Multicultural-and-Social-Reconstructionist approach offers very little on curriculum and instruction; it also offers little theory about changing social stratification. The Multicultural Education approach is the most successful at demonstrating relationships between goals, theory, and practice. Writers such as Baker, Banks, Gay, Gollnick, and Grant all develop a considerable body of literature on similar goals and theories, elaborate on their own ideas, and provide practical illustrations for teachers. Many recent articles, however, have failed to provide new ideas while they continue simply to rehash old ones.

As a whole, these books and articles focus heavily on the individual classroom teacher as the agent of school change. While classroom teachers are necessary participants in school reform, individual classroom teachers alone tend not to be successful agents of such large-scale school reforms as multicultural education. Research on program implementation suggests that most teachers perpetuate "business as usual," even when constraints on their doing otherwise are weak (Grant & Sleeter, 1985). Other agents in the education system—administrators, governmental policymakers, and teacher educators—have more power than the teacher, can provide help and support to her or him, and can help determine who will teach. Of these three groups, only teacher educators receive specific attention in the literature. Moreover, no recommendations are directed specifically to those community groups who may have a stake in school reform.

Additionally, focusing on the classroom teacher implies that schools are fine as they are—except for classroom teaching. Issues outside the classroom, however, that are directly related to multicultural education must be addressed. One example is tracking: Can a school provide multicultural education and simultaneously channel some students (who tend to be disproportionately lower class and of color) toward low-paying, low-status labor and others toward professional occupations? Another example, although only briefly mentioned in a few books, is staffing: Should a school which is attempting to provide multicultural education seek staff members with distinct characteristics (ethnic diversity being an obvious one)? These are not issues for teachers alone to resolve in their classrooms, but they do involve multicultural education.

The teaching guides themselves have two main limitations. First, most are written for the elementary teacher. It appears that authors perceive the elementary curriculum as more fluid and more easily altered than the secondary curriculum, and elementary children as more impressionable targets of attitudinal change. These perceptions may be accurate, but if so, they suggest even more strongly the need to address teachers at the secondary level. For example, what would an algebra class or a senior economics class be like when taught from a multicultural perspective? Since colleges expect high schools to teach content that generally does not reflect multiculturalism (anyone who doubts this should examine an SAT test), how should the teacher address both college preparation and multicultural education?

Second, most examples of practice in teaching guides take the form of single lessons. How should one design a unit or an entire course of study from a multicultural perspective? By providing examples of individual lessons, most authors implicitly suggest that teachers can do what needs to be done with occasional multicultural lessons, or that teachers have less autonomy to determine entire units or courses of study and are change agents only in isolated classrooms. We are quite sure authors do not intend to imply this, yet we have observed that teachers interpret the message this way (Grant & Sleeter, 1986).

We perceive one particularly disturbing gap in the literature we reviewed: There are virtually no research studies on multicultural education. Some authors draw on related areas of research, such as bias in materials, effects of bilingual education, desegregated schooling, teacher attitudes toward diverse students, and student friendships across race, gender, and handicap lines. But we have not been able to locate research studies of any kind on multicultural education in the classroom for grades K-12. So far, most of the literature in this category stresses advocacy, discusses issues, and recommends courses of action. It must move beyond this. There needs to be research on what happens when teachers work with multicultural education in their classrooms, what forms it takes and why, how students respond, and what barriers are encountered.

The fulfillment of two central and related needs would further develop the field of multicultural education: funding and a journal. Multicultural education has never been targeted for federal funding; its development has been subsidized from related areas such as Ethnic Studies, bilingual education, and Teacher Corps. The 1980s may not be an auspicious decade in which to seek funding, but at least the need should be recognized. Perhaps lack of funding explains why the literature tends to remain at the advocacy level. A journal for multicultural education in the United States would provide a central forum for dialogue. Authors have had to seek publication outlets where they could, and readers have had to hunt about to locate the existing literature. This may account for the large number of recent articles that rehash issues discussed in other disciplines' journal articles. Although funding for multicultural education may be difficult to obtain at present, a journal is a more immediate possibility. Nonetheless, the field of multicultural education has been established without either of these, and it shows no signs of disappearing. In fact, there are a few small positive signs. "Multicultural education" is becoming an accepted and articulated concept among teacher educators and teachers, in part because of the increased attendance of students of color in our schools. Teachers are explicitly requesting help in the forms of materials and information about multicultural education. Textbook publishers have become more assertive in efforts to identify and publish multicultural materials for teacher training as well as staff development. Additionally, during the summer of 1987, several leading advocates of multicultural education met to discuss the feasibility of establishing a journal in the field. These efforts parallel those in Australia and England, for example, where a small but growing group of scholars and practitioners is trying to develop the field. These scholars are beginning to organize a network with their North American counterparts. Finally, whether it will be necessary for critics or scholars to undertake a comparable review and analysis of multicultural education ten or fifteen years into the future will depend largely upon the extent to which the field enjoys both excellent scholarship and financial support.

Note

* We did not include, but wish to note, a thematic issue of the *Journal of Research and Development in Education, 4* (1971), titled "MultiEthnic and MultiCulture Classrooms." This thematic issue conceptualizes multicultural education as Teaching the Culturally Different. The title of the issue suggests it should be included in this review, but none of the articles uses terms we use as descriptors in their titles. All the articles discuss the education of single racial minority groups, and thus do not qualify for inclusion here.

References

Abrahams, R. D., & Troike, R. C. (Eds.). (1972). *Language and cultural diversity in American education*. Englewood Cliffs: Prentice-Hall.

Adachi, M. (1975). Living use: Example of a multicultural approach. *Educational Leadership, 33*, 189–191.

Anderson, W. H. (1980). Teaching musics of the world: A renewed commitment. *Music Education Journal, 67*, 39–42.

Appleton, N. (1983). *Cultural pluralism in education*. New York: Longman.

Arenas, S. (1980). Innovation in bilingual/multicultural curriculum development. *Children Today, 9*, 17–21.

Baker, G. C. (1975). Cultural diversity: Strength of the nation. *Educational Leadership, 33*, 257–260.

Baker, G. C. (1978). The role of the school in transmitting the culture of all learners in a free and democratic society. *Educational Leadership, 36*, 134–138.

Baker, G. C. (1979). Policy issues in multicultural education in the United States. *Journal of Negro Education, 48*, 253–266.

Baker, G. C. (1983a). Motivating the culturally different student. *Momentum, 14*, 44–45.

Baker, G. C. (1983b). *Planning and organizing for multicultural instruction*. Reading, MA: Addison-Wesley.

Banks, J. A. (Ed.). (1973). *Teaching ethnic studies*. Washington, DC: National Council for the Social Studies.

Banks, J. A. (1979). Shaping the future of multicultural education. *Journal of Negro Education, 48*, 237–252.

Banks, J. A. (1981). *Multiethnic education: Theory and practice.* Boston: Allyn & Bacon.

Banks, J. A. (1983). Multiethnic education and the quest for equality. *Phi Delta Kappan, 64*, 582–585.

Banks, J. A. (1984). *Teaching strategies for ethnic studies* (3rd ed.). Boston: Allyn & Bacon.

Baptiste, H. P., Jr. (1979). *Multicultural education: A synopsis.* Washington, DC: University Press of America.

Baptiste, H. P., Jr., & Baptiste, M. L. (1977). Multicultural education: Knowing me and you. *Educational Perspectives, 16*, 23–25.

Baptiste, H. P., Jr., & Baptiste, M. L. (1979). *Developing the multicultural process in classroom instruction.* Washington, DC: University Press of America.

Barnes, W. J. (1979). Developing a culturally pluralistic perspective: A community involvement task. *Journal of Negro Education, 48*, 419–430.

Barnhardt, R. (Ed.). (1977). *Cross-cultural issues in Alaskan education.* Fairbanks: Center for Northern Educational Research.

Bennett, C. I. (1986). *Comprehensive multicultural education.* Boston: Allyn & Bacon.

Bernstein, G. (1984). Ethnicity: The search for characteristics and context. *Theory into Practice, 23*, 98–103.

Berry, G. L. (1979). The multicultural principle: Missing from the seven cardinal principles of 1918 and 1978. *Phi Delta Kappan, 60*, 745.

Blassingame, J. E. (Ed.). (1976). *New perspectives on Black studies.* Urbana: University of Illinois Press.

Bowles, G., & Klein, R. D. (Eds.). (1983). *Theories of women's studies.* London: Routledge & Kegan Paul.

Brembeck, C., & Hill, W. (Eds.). (1973). *Cultural challenges to education.* Boston: Allen & Unwin.

Butterfield, R. A., Demos, E. S., Grant, G. W., Moy, P. S., & Perez, A. L. (1979). A multi-cultural analysis of a popular basal reading series in the International Year of the Child. *Journal of Negro Education, 48*, 382–389.

Carlson, P. E. (1976). Toward a definition of local-level multicultural education. *Anthropology and Education Quarterly, 7*, 26–30.

Carter, D. A. (1983). Selecting resources for the multicultural classroom. *Momentum, 14*, 46–48.

Cheng, C. W., Brizendine, E., & Oakes, J. (1979). What is "an equal chance" for minority children? *Journal of Negro Education, 48*, 267–287.

Christian, C. C., Jr. (1977). The role of language in multicultural education. *Education Horizons, 55*, 184–188.

Clasen, R. E. (1979). Models for the educational needs of gifted children in a multicultural context. *Journal of Negro Education, 48*, 357–363.

Colangelo, N., Dustin, D., & Foxley, C. H. (Eds.). (1982). *The human relations experience.* Monterey, CA: Brooks/Cole.

Colangelo, N., Foxley, C. H., & Dustin, D. (Eds.), (1979). *Multicultural nonsexist education: A human relations approach.* Dubuque: Kendall/Hunt.

Cole, D. J. (1984). Multicultural education and global education: A possible merger. *Theory into Practice, 23*, 151–154.

Commission on Multicultural Education. (1973). No one model American. *Journal of Teacher Education, 24*, 264–265.

Cortes, C. E. (1973). Teaching the Chicano experience. In Banks, J. A. (Ed.), *Teaching ethnic studies* (pp. 181–200). Washington, DC: National Council for the Social Studies.

Cortes, C. E. (1976). Need for a geo-cultural perspective in the Bicentennial. *Educational Leadership, 33*, 290–292.

Cortes, C. E. (1980). The role of media in multicultural education. *Viewpoints in Teaching and Learning, 56*, 38–49.

Cox, G. R., & Fundis, R. J. (1982). Multicultural education: Issues, a model and recommendations. *Action in Teacher Education, 4*, 33–39.

Cross, D. E., Baker, G., & Stiles, L. (1977). *Teaching in a multicultural society.* New York: The Free Press.

Cross, D. E., Long, M. A., & Ziajka, A. (1978). Minority cultures and education in the United States. *Education and Urban Society, 10*, 263–276.

DeCosta, S. B. (1984). Not all children are Anglo and middle class: A practical beginning for the elementary teacher. *Theory into Practice, 23,* 154–155.

Deyoe, R. M. (1977). Theory as practice in multicultural education. *Educational Horizons, 55,* 181–183.

Dodds, J. B. P. (1983). Music as a multicultural education. *Music Educators Journal, 69,* 33–34.

Dolce, C. J. (1973). Multicultural education—Some issues. *Journal of Teacher Education, 24,* 282–284.

Ehlers, H., & Crawford, D. (1983). Multicultural education and national unity. *Educational Forum, 47,* 263–277.

Epps, E. (1974). *Cultural pluralism.* Berkeley: McCutchan.

Epstein, N. (1977). *Language, ethnicity, and the schools.* Washington, DC: George Washington University.

Ethnic Cultural Heritage Program. (1977). *Rainbow activities.* South El Monte, CA: Creative Teaching Press.

Foerster, L. (1982). Moving from ethnic studies to multicultural education. *The Urban Review, 14,* 121–126.

Forman, S., & Mitchell, R. (1977). The Hawaii Multicultural Awareness Pilot Project (HMAP). *Educational Perspectives, 16,* 26–28.

Garcia, J. (1984). Multiethnic education: Past, present, and future. *Texas Tech Journal of Education, 11,* 13–30.

Garcia, J., & Denton, J. J. (1980). Instruction strategies for multiethnic materials. *The High School Journal, 63,* 293–298.

Garcia, R. (1979). *Teaching in a pluralistic society.* New York: Harper & Row.

Gay, G. (1975). *Organizing and designing culturally pluralistic curriculum. Educational Leadership, 33,* 176–183.

Gay, G. (1977). Changing conceptions of multicultural education. *Educational Perspectives, 16,* 4–9.

Gay, G. (1981). What is your school's MEQ? *Educational Leadership, 39,* 187–189.

Gay, G. (1983a). Multiethnic education: Historical developments and future prospects. *Phi Delta Kappan, 64,* 560–563.

Gay, G. (1983b). Retrospects and prospects of multicultural education. *Momentum, 14,* 4–8.

Gezi, K. (1981). Issues in multicultural education. *Educational Research Quarterly, 6,* 5–13.

Gibson, M. A. (1976). Approaches to multicultural education in the United States: Some concepts and assumptions. *Anthropology and Education Quarterly, 7,* 7–18.

Giroux, H. A. (1985). *Theory and resistance in education.* South Hadley, MA: Bergin & Garvey.

Gold, M., Grant, C. A., & Rivlin, H. (Eds.). (1977). *In praise of diversity: A resource book for multicultural education.* Washington, DC: Teacher Corps and Association of Teacher Educators.

Gollnick, D. M. (1980). Multicultural education. *Viewpoints in Teaching and Learning, 56,* 1–17.

Gollnick, D. M., & Chinn, P. (1986). *Multicultural education* (2nd ed.). Columbus, OH: Charles E. Merrill.

Goodenough, W. H. (1976). Multiculturalism as the normal human experience. *Anthropology and Education Quarterly, 7,* 4–7.

Goodlad, J. I. (1984). *A place called school.* New York: McGraw-Hill.

Gordon, B. M. (1985). Toward emancipation in citizenship education: The case of African American cultural knowledge. *Theory and Research in Social Education, 12,* 1–23.

Grant, C. A. (1977a). The mediator of culture: A teacher role revisited. *Journal of Research and Development in Education, 11,* 102–117.

Grant, C. A. (Ed.). (1977b). *Multicultural education: Commitments, issues, and applications.* Washington, DC: ASCD.

Grant, C. A. (1978). Education that is multicultural—Isn't that what we mean? *Journal of Teacher Education, 29,* 45–48.

Grant, C. A. (1979). Education that is multicultural as a change agent: Organizing for effectiveness. *Journal of Negro Education, 48,* 253–266.

Grant, C. A., Boyle, M., & Sleeter, C. E. (1980). *The public school and the challenge of ethnic pluralism.* New York: The Pilgrim Press.

Grant, C. A., & Sleeter, C. E. (1985). Who determines teacher work: The teacher, the organization, or both? *Teaching and Teacher Education, 1,* 209–220.

Grant, C. A., & Sleeter, C. E. (1986). *After the school bell rings.* Barcombe, Eng.: Falmer Press.

Grant, G. W. (Ed.). (1977). *In praise of diversity: Multicultural classroom applications.* Omaha: University of Nebraska Press.

Heller, G. N. (1983). Retrospective of multicultural music education in the United States. *Music Education Journal, 69,* 35–36.

Hernandez, N. G. (1977). Another look at multicultural education today. *Journal of Research and Development in Education, 11,* 4–9.

Hernandez-Chavez, E. (1977). Meaningful bilingual bicultural education: A fairytale. *NABE Journal, 1,* 49–54.

Hiraoka, J. (1977). The foundations of multicultural education. *Educational Horizons, 55,* 177–180.

Hollins, E. R. (1982). Beyond multicultural education. *Negro Educational Review, 33,* 140–145.

Hourihan, J. J., & Chapin, D. (1976). Multicultural education in a pluralistic society: Group vs. individual. *Anthropology and Education Quarterly, 7,* 23–26.

Houston, A. V. (1975). Leadership for multicultural experiences. *Educational Leadership, 33,* 199–202.

Irving, K. J. (1984). Cross-cultural awareness and the English-as-a-second-language classroom. *Theory into Practice, 23,* 138–143.

Johnson, D. W. (1972). *Reaching out: Interpersonal effectiveness and self-actualization.* Englewood Cliffs, NJ: Prentice-Hall.

Katz, M.B. (1975). *Class bureaucracy and schools: The illusion of educational change in America.* New York: Praeger.

Kendall, F. E. (1983a). *Diversity in the classroom.* New York: Teachers College Press.

Kendall, F. E. (1983b). Presenting multicultural education to parents. *Momentum, 14,* 11–12.

King, E. W. (1980). *Teaching ethnic awareness.* Santa Monica: Goodyear.

Krug, M. M. (1977). Cultural pluralism—Its origins and aftermath. *Journal of Teacher Education, 27,* 5–9.

Laosa, L. (1977). Multicultural education—How psychology can contribute. *Journal of Teacher Education, 28,* 26–30.

Lee, M. K. (1983). Multiculturalism: Educational perspectives for the 1980's. *Education, 103,* 405–409.

Levy, J. (1980). Multicultural education and intercultural communication: A family affair. *Viewpoints in Teaching and Learning, 56,* 64–76.

Lewis, D. K. (1976). Commentary: The multi-cultural education model and minorities: Some reservations. *Anthropology and Education Quarterly, 7,* 32–37.

McCormick, T. E. (1984). Multiculturalism: Some principles and issues. *Theory into Practice, 23,* 93–97.

Mortenson, R. A. (1975). *Prejudice project.* New York: Anti-Defamation League of B'nai B'rith.

Myers, M. (1980). Going back to Hollister: Conflict in bilingual/bicultural education. *Phi Delta Kappan, 62,* 189–192.

Myers, R. A., Banfield, B., & Colon, J. J. (1983). *Embers: Stories for a changing world.* Westbury, NY: Feminist Press, and New York City: Council on Interracial Books for Children.

Nagtalon-Miller, H. (1977). Pluralism and bilingual/multicultural education in Hawaii. *Educational Perspectives, 16,* 14–17.

O'Brien, J. P. (1980). Integrating world music in the music "appreciation" course. *Music Education Journal, 67,* 39–42.

Ornstein, A. C., & and Levin, D. U. (1982). Multicultural education: Trends and issues. *Childhood Education, 58,* 241–245.

Ovando, C. J. (1983). Bilingual/bicultural education: Its legacy and its future. *Phi Delta Kappan, 64,* 564–567.

Pacheco, A. (1977). Cultural pluralism: A philosophical analysis. *Journal of Teacher Education, 28*, 16–20.

Pasternak, M. (1977). *Helping kids learn multicultural concepts.* Nashville: Nashville Consortium Teacher Corps.

Payne, C.R. (1977). A rationale for including multicultural education and its implementation in the daily lesson plan. *Journal of Research and Development in Education, 11*, 31–45.

Payne, C. R. (1983). Multicultural education: A natural way to teach. *Contemporary Education, 54*, 98–104.

Payne, C. R. (1984). Multicultural education and racism in American schools. *Theory into Practice, 23*, 124–131.

Perry, J. (1975). Notes toward a multi-cultural curriculum. *English Journal, 64*, 8–9.

Poster, J. B. (1979). Bilingual-multicultural education: Towards collaboration between bilingual education and the social studies. *Social Education, 43*, 112.

Pratte, R. (1983) Multicultural education: Four normative arguments. *Educational Theory, 33*, 21–32.

Pulte, W. (1978). Are bilingual bicultural programs socially divisive? *Integrateducation, 16*, 31–33.

Ramirez, M., & Castaneda, A. (1974). *Cultural democracy, and bicognitive development, and education.* New York: Academic Press.

Ramsey, P. G. (1982). Multicultural education in early childhood. *Young Children, 37*, 13–24.

Reyes, V. H. (1976). Self-concept and the bicultural child. *NABE Journal, 1*, 57–59.

St. Lawrence, T. J., & Singleton, J. (1976). Multiculturalism in social context: Conceptual problems raised by educational policy issues. *Anthropology and Education Quarterly, 7*, 19–23.

Sancho, A. R. (1977). Culture and the bilingual-bicultural curriculum. *NABE Journal, 1*, 55–58.

Santos, S. L. (1980). Cultural crossroads center helps Dallas students celebrate cultural diversity. *Phi Delta Kappan, 62*, 211–212.

Saville-Troike, M. (1976). *Foundations for teaching English as a second language: Theory and method for multicultural education.* Englewood Cliffs, NJ: Prentice-Hall.

Schniedewind, N., & Davidson, E. (1983). *Open minds to equality.* Englewood Cliffs, NJ: Prentice-Hall.

Shor, I. (1980). *Critical teaching in everyday life.* Boston: South End Press.

Sims, W., & de Martinez, B. (Eds.). (1981). *Perspectives in multicultural education.* Washington, DC: University Press of America.

Sizemore, B. A. (1979). The four M curriculum: A way to shape the future. *Journal of Negro Education, 48*, 341–356.

Skinner, L. (1977). Multicultural Education: A Challenge for the Future. *Educational Horizons, 55*, 189–190.

Sleeter, C. E., & Grant, C. A. (1986). Educational equity, education that is multicultural and social reconstructionism. *Journal of Educational Equity and Leadership, 6*, 105–118.

Stent, M., Hazard, W., & Rivlin, H. (Eds.). (1973). *Cultural pluralism in education: A mandate for change.* New York: Appleton-Century Crofts.

Stewart, W. J. (1978). Infusing multiculturalism into the curriculum through broad themes. *Education, 98*, 334–336.

Stone, J. C., & DeNevi, D. P. (Eds.). (1971). *Teaching multi-cultural populations.* New York: Van Nostrand Reinhold.

Suzuki, B. H. (1979). Multicultural education: What's it all about? *Integrateducation, 97*, 43–50.

Suzuki, B. H. (1984). Curriculum transformation for multicultural education. *Education and Urban Society, 16*, 294–322.

Tesconi, C. A. (1984). Multicultural education: A valued but problematic ideal. *Theory into Practice, 23*, 87–92.

Tiedt, P., & Tiedt, I. (1986). *Multicultural teaching: A handbook of activities, information, and resources.* Boston: Allyn & Bacon.

Trueba, E. T. (1976). Issues and problems in bilingual bicultural education today. *NABE Journal, 1*, 11–19.

Tyack, D. B. (1974). *The one best system.* Cambridge, MA: Harvard University Press.

Uhlig, G. E., & Vasquez, A. G. (1982). Cross-cultural research and multicultural education: 1970–1980. *Journal of Teacher Education, 33,* 45–48.

U.S. Department of Commerce, Bureau of the Census. (1987). *Statistical Abstract of the United States* (107th ed.), Washington, DC: U.S. Government Printing Office.

Valencia, A. (1976). *Bilingual bicultural education for the Spanish-English bilingual.* Berkeley: BABEL Productions.

Valverde, L. A. (1977). Multicultural education: Social and educational justice. *Educational Leadership, 35,* 196–201.

Velez, J. F. (1981). Understanding bilingual-bicultural education in the eighties. *Baylor Educator, 6,* 13–17.

Von Maltitz, S. (1975). *Living and learning in two language.* New York: McGraw-Hill.

Wagner, H. (1981). Working with the culturally different student. *Education, 101,* 353–358.

Williams, M. (1982). Multicultural/pluralistic education: Public education in America "the way it's 'spoze to be." *Clearinghouse,* 131–135;

Wilson, A. H. (1979). People, the forgotten resource in intercultural education. *The Social Studies, 70,* 258–264.

Wolfgang, A. (1977). The silent language in the multicultural classroom. *Theory into Practice, 16,* 145–152.

Zintz, M. V. (1963). *Education across cultures.* Dubuque: Wm. C. Brown.

CHAPTER 18

LEARNING DISABILITIES (1986)
The social construction of a special education category
Christine E. Sleeter

Current reports of education reform advocate that schools raise standards for achievement and test students according to those standards more regularly and more rigorously. For example, *A Nation at Risk* (National Commission on Excellence and Education, 1983) recommends that "schools, colleges, and universities adopt more rigorous and measurable standards, and higher expectations, for academic performance and student conduct" (p. 27). It goes on to advocate that "standardized tests of achievement . . . should be administered at major transition points from one level of schooling to another" (p. 28). Similarly, *Action for Excellence* (Task Force on Education for Economic Growth, 1983) recommends that we "raise both the floor and the ceiling of achievement in America" (p. 18).

These reports have been criticized for their failure to address substantively the needs of handicapped students. For example, the CEC Ad Hoc Committee to Study and Respond to the 1983 Report of the National Commission on Excellence in Education (1984) applauded *A Nation at Risk* for its "efforts to improve curricula and methods to assess the acquisition of required skills and knowledge" (p. 488) but criticized it for its failure to address the diverse capabilities and needs of students. The Committee noted that special education has expanded over the past several decades and advocated its continuing development and provision of services. Implicitly, the CEC reply accepted existing categories of exceptionality and saw reform attempts as delinquent mainly in their failure to address the needs of students who occupy or should occupy those categories. In this article it will be argued that the problem in today's reform movement is more than merely overlooking those who are handicapped. Rather, reforms such as those just cited help create handicapped children, and the main category for which this has been true historically is learning disabilities.

Many educators suggest that learning disabilities always has been and continues to be an ill-defined special education category. A full 20 years after the founding of the Association for Children with Learning Disabilities (ACLD), the 1983 *Annual Review of Learning Disabilities* featured a series of articles by prominent scholars in the field still debating its definition and criteria for identification. Recently Ysseldyke, Algozzine, Shinn and McGue (1982) found little difference between students classified as learning disabled (LD) and non-LD low-achievers on several psychometric tests commonly used to classify students as LD. They concluded that "we must begin to evaluate very carefully the purposes and needs being served by identifying certain students as LD while not identifying others (who are very much their twins)" (p. 84).

Why did the category come about in the first place, and whose interests has it served? This article addresses these questions by briefly critiquing the prevailing interpretation of why the category emerged when it did and who it has served, and then by showing that learning disabilities is in part an artifact of past school reform efforts that have escalated standards for literacy. In so doing, this article shows the implications of the emergence of the LD category during the early 1960s for debates about school reform in the 1980s.

Prevailing interpretation of the emergence of LD

To investigate how the history of the LD field is usually interpreted, I examined 15 learning disabilities textbooks published between 1980 and 1985 in the U.S. Textbooks were examined because they typically present the field's history in a manner conventionally accepted by professionals in the field. (Several authors drew on the interpretation of the field's history offered by J. L. Wiederholt, Historical perspectives on the education of the learning disabled, in L. Mann & D. Sabatino (Eds.), *The second review of special education*, Philadelphia: Journal of Special Education Press, 1974.) The average learning disabilities textbook, which was 403 pages long, devoted 10 pages to explaining how and why the field emerged when it did (range = 6–34 pages). Five did not discuss its history. (See end of article for complete list of textbooks reviewed.)

The LD field usually is presented as having developed on the basis of medical research beginning in the 1800s. This research documented links between brain damage and subsequent behavior. More recent advances in our understanding of learning disabilities are presented as having been made by psychologists, neurologists, and physicians studying children who displayed difficulties acquiring language and reading skills, and by educators who experimented with methods for teaching them. These children were believed to have suffered minimal brain dysfunction. Once sufficient research had been conducted and publicized, parents, educators, and physicians began to organize and press for appropriate educational services. Since then, schools have with growing vigor developed and provided these services.

The ideology underlying this interpretation is that schools, supported by medical and psychological research, are involved in a historic pattern of progress. Problems that have always existed are one by one being discovered, researched, and solved. Learning disabilities is essentially a medical problem; it is thought to reside within the child. Progress is brought about mainly by individual thinkers involved in medical and psychological research, and at times by pressure groups who use that research to advance the interests of the underdogs. Once alerted to problems, the American public tends to support their amelioration, and the main beneficiaries are those whose needs are finally recognized and met.

Missing from this interpretation is much analysis of the social context that created conditions favorable to the category's emergence. A sizable body of literature outside special education links school structures and processes with needs of dominant economic and political groups in society (e.g., Apple, 1981; Spring, 1976). This literature suggests that changes in schools are instituted mainly to serve more efficiently existing social and economic structures, although changes may also offer some benefit to students whom schools had previously disserved most. One school structure this literature has examined, which is closely related to special education, is tracking.

While many people see tracking as a way of homogenizing students in classrooms so teachers can teach them better, research studies have found that lower track students consistently fare worse than their nontracked counterparts (Persell, 1977) and rarely achieve upward mobility (Rosenbaum, 1976). Furthermore, those in the upper track are disproportionately from white middle class backgrounds; lower track students disproportionately represent minority and lower social class backgrounds (Shafer & Olexa, 1971). This literature argues that tracking is widely practiced largely for the purpose of sorting and preparing students for a stratified labor market: Students are rank-ordered and classified for instruction such that those from advantaged social groups tend to be prepared for the better jobs, while those from disadvantaged backgrounds tend to be channeled into low pay, low status work.

With a few exceptions (e.g., Coles, 1978; Farber, 1968; Sarason & Doris, 1979; Ysseldyke & Algozzine, 1982), special education usually is not examined with relationship to social competition for power, wealth, and prestige. Rather, it usually is presented as a school structure instituted solely to benefit students unable to profit from school because of handicapping conditions. The textbook interpretation of the emergence of learning disabilities is an example. While there is merit to this interpretation for children with obvious handicaps (e.g., severely retarded and physically impaired), it must be questioned for children whose handicaps are not obvious. The remainder of this article does that.

Schooling in the late 1950s and early 1960s

Learning disabilities was officially founded with the birth of ACLD in 1963. Learning disabled children suffer chiefly from an inability to achieve certain standards for literacy. These standards have changed historically as requirements of the American economy and the race for international supremacy have changed. Let us examine how the raising of reading standards, coupled with social expectations that schools help America's cold war effort and also sort students for future work roles in a stratified economy, led to the creation of learning disabilities.

Before the twentieth century, most information could be exchanged face to face and records were relatively simple. At that time, children with reading difficulties did not present a great social problem because most Americans did not need to be able to acquire new information through reading. Industrial expansion escalated literacy standards, requiring more and more people who could keep and understand increasingly complex records, pursue advanced professional training, and follow written directions in the workplace. As literacy standards in society escalated, schools responded by emphasizing reading more and by expecting students to attain increasingly higher levels of literacy (Chall, 1983; Resnick & Resnick, 1977).

Before the 1980s, the most recent major escalation of reading standards followed the Soviet Union's launching of Sputnik in 1957. Americans reacted to Sputnik by charging schools with failing to produce scientists and technicians needed for the U.S. to remain ahead internationally in technological development. This charge was widely publicized in numerous popular magazines (e.g., *Good Housekeeping, Time*). American schools were compared with Russian schools and found deficient. The chief problem, critics believed, was lax standards. For example, in March of 1958, *Life* magazine compared the schooling of two boys; one in Moscow and one in Chicago. It reported that in the Soviet Union, "The laggards are forced out [of school] by tough periodic examinations and shunted to less demanding trade schools and apprenticeships. Only a third—1.4 million in

1957—survive all 10 years and finish the course"("School Boys," p. 27). In contrast, American students lounge in classrooms that are "relaxed and enlivened by banter," and in which the "intellectual application expected of [students] is moderate" (p. 33).

Recommendations for reforming American education included (a) toughening elementary reading instruction (Trace, 1961); (b) introducing uniform standards for promotion and graduation and testing students' mastery of those standards through a regular, nation-wide examination system ("Back to the 3 R's?", 1957; Bestor, 1958); (c) grouping students by ability so the bright students can move more quickly through school and then go on to college and professional careers, while the slower students move into unskilled or semiskilled labor ("Famous Educator's Plan," 1958; "Harder Work for Students," 1961; Woodring, 1957); and (d) assigning the most intellectually capable teachers to the top group of students (Rickover, 1957). To some extent, all these reforms were implemented in the late 1950s and early 1960s.

In reading, elementary textbooks were toughened and some tests were renormed. Chall (1977) analyzed the readability levels of widely used textbooks published between 1930 and 1973. She found elementary readers to offer progressively less challenge from 1944 until 1962; in 1962 first grade readers appearing on the market were more difficult, a trend that continued into the 1970s. There is also evidence that some widely used achievement tests were renormed shortly after Sputnik to reflect escalated standards for literacy. The 1958 version of the Metropolitan Achievement Tests were renormed in 1964; the new norms reflected average reading levels 2 to 13 months higher for students in grades 2 through 9 (no gain was found for first grade) (Special Report No. 7, 1971). Similarly, the 1957 version of the Iowa Tests of Basic Skills was renormed in 1964. Hieronymus and Lindquist (1974) reported that the average gain in reading was 1.9 months at the 90th percentile, 2.6 months at the 50th, and 1.0 months at the 10th.

Many children were unable to keep up, but few blamed the raising of standards. Instead, students who scored low on reading achievement tests were personally blamed for their failure. By the early 1960s, children who failed in reading were divided into five categories, differentiated by whether the cause of the problem was presumed to be organic, emotional, or environmental, and whether the child was deemed intellectually normal or subnormal. They were called slow learners, mentally retarded, emotionally disturbed, culturally deprived, and learning disabled.

Slow learners and the mentally retarded were distinguished mainly on the basis of IQ: Those scoring between 75 and 90 were considered slow learners, and those scoring below were considered retarded. Both categories included disproportionate numbers of low-income children and children of color. As adults, slow learners were expected to occupy semi-skilled and unskilled occupations, and retarded individuals were expected to occupy unskilled occupations or work in sheltered workshops (Goldstein, 1962). The emotionally disturbed also included large numbers from low-income backgrounds (Dunn, 1963). A subcategory was the "socially maladjusted," who were concentrated in Black, Puerto Rican, and immigrant neighborhoods (Shaw & McKay, 1942). A fourth category, which overlapped considerably with the previous three, was referred to as the culturally deprived. The National Conference on Education and Cultural Deprivation held in 1964 identified them as Puerto Ricans, Mexicans, southern Blacks and whites who moved to urban areas; and the poor already living in inner cities and rural areas (Bloom, Davis, & Hess, 1965). They were believed severely handicapped by home environments that lacked environmental stimuli; systematic ordering of stimuli sequences; language training; and training in the value of intellectual work, delayed gratification, individuality, and the belief that hard work brings success (e.g., Deutsch, 1963; Riessman, 1962).

A fifth category came to be known as the learning disabled. Of the five categories, this is the only one for which descriptions of the kinds of neighborhoods most likely to produce them were virtually absent from literature. The closest statement one finds is that they are essentially "normal" or come from "normal family stock" (Strauss & Lehtinen, 1963, p. 112), whatever that means (Strauss and Lehtinen, reknown pioneers in learning disabilities research, reported 12 case studies that give some indication of what "normal family stock" meant to them. Of the eight whose race was specified, all were white, and of the four whose race was not specified, two were of "above average" social standing or home environment. (No data were given for the other two.)

The cause of LD reading retardation was believed to be organic. Hypothesized causes included minimal brain damage (e.g., Strauss & Kephart, 1955), a maturational lag in general neurological development (e.g., Bender, 1957; Rabinovitch, 1962), a failure of the brain to establish cerebral dominance (Orton, 1937), or a failure to achieve certain stages of neurological development (Delcato, 1959).

Who was classified as learning disabled?

National-level statistics were not collected on the student composition of LD classes until the late 1970s. While the category was in name open to children of any background, I suspected it would be populated by a select group during the early years of its existence. To estimate the student composition of LD classes, I examined descriptions of samples of LD students used in research studies published between 1963 and 1973 in the *Journal of Learning Disabilities, Exceptional Children*, and the *Journal of Special Education*. To be included in my analysis, the study had to specify either that sample students were in LD classes, were identified by the school district as learning disabled although they may not yet have been assigned to LD classes, attended a private clinic for LD students, or attended a private reading clinic and were suspected by the clinic or the researcher as being learning disabled. Not included were samples of low achievers in general, retarded readers in general, or samples from programs that combined LD students with students in other special education categories.

A total of 61 studies with LD samples were located. Of these, 12 reported the racial composition of their samples; this made a total of 460 subjects whose race was known. These subjects were overwhelmingly white: 98.5% were white, only 1.5% were of color. In 10 of the 12 studies, samples were all white. Sixteen studies reported the social class composition of their samples, totalling 588 subjects whose social class background was known. There was more balance with respect to social class than race: 69% of the subjects were middle class or higher, 31% were lower middle class or lower. Of the 16 studies, 12 had samples that were at least 90% middle class or above.

The literature offers additional evidence that students in LD classes were overwhelmingly white and middle class during the category's first 10 years. White and Charry (1966) studied characteristics of children in special programs in Westchester County, New York, and found those labeled "brain damaged" to have no significant IQ or achievement differences from those labeled "culturally deprived," but to be from significantly higher social class backgrounds. Franks (1971) surveyed Missouri school districts that received state reimbursement for LD and educable mentally retarded (EMR) services during school year 1969–1970. He found the LD classes to be almost 97% white and 3% Black, while the EMR classes were only 66% white and 34% Black. Furthermore, the professional literature during the 1960s and early 1970s discussed failing children of the white middle class and those of lower class and minority families as if they were distinct. For example, volumes 1 and 3 of the *Journal of Learning Disabilities* (1968, 1970) contained 12 articles about culturally "deprived" or "disadvantaged" children. Most of these reported studies; none of the subjects were reported to be in LD classes (many were in Head Start programs), and only two authors suggested they could or should be (Grotberg, 1970; Tarnopol, 1970).

The learning disabilities category probably was not consciously established just for white middle class children, even though it was populated mainly by them. It was established for children who, given the prevailing categories used to describe failing children, did not seem to fit any other category. Since most educators explained the failures of children of color and lower socioeconomic backgrounds with reference to the other four categories, such children tended not to have been placed in LD classes. White middle class parents and educators who saw their failing children as different from poor or minority children pressed for the creation and use of this category. By defining the category in terms of organic causality and IQ score, the white middle class preserved for itself some benefits.

First, the use of IQ to help distinguish LD students from other categories of failing children suggested its members "really" belonged in the middle or upper tracks or ability groups. As proponents of tracking during the late 1950s clearly pointed out, students were to be sorted for differentiated education based on ability, and members of each track were destined to hold different kinds of jobs in the labor market (e.g., Woodring, 1957). White children tend to score about 15 points higher on IQ tests than children of color, ensuring a greater likelihood that they would be seen as intellectually "normal" and thus potentially able to fill higher status positions. The intent of defining the category partly on the basis of IQ score was probably not to disadvantage the "disadvantaged" further, but to provide failing children whom educators saw as intellectually normal their best chance for moving ahead as rapidly and as far as possible.

Second, distinguishing between environmental and organic causes of failure helped legitimate the "superiority" of white middle class culture. The literature during the early 1960s contains much about the failings of low-income homes, and especially those of people of color. For example, readers of *Saturday Review* in 1962 were told that "slow learners appear most frequently in groups whose home environment affords restricted opportunity for intellectual development" ("Slow Learners," p. 53), and that "culturally deprived children" learn "ways of living [that] are not attuned to the spirit and practice of modern life" ("Education and the Disadvantaged American," p. 58). One does not find similar condemnations of the average white middle class home. If one were to accept such homes as normal, organic explanations for failure would seem plausible. One must view this as peculiar, since the main proponents of raising school standards to help America retain economic and political international supremacy were members of the white middle class. Yet rather than questioning the culture that viewed children as raw material for international competition, most educators questioned the organic integrity of members of that culture who could not meet the higher demands.

Third, some viewed minimal brain dysfunction as an organ deficiency that could potentially be cured in the same way diseases can be cured. The cure was hypothesized as involving the training of healthy brain cells to take over functions of damaged cells (e.g., Cruickshank et al., 1961; Frostig & Horne, 1964; Strauss & Lehtinen, 1963), the promoting of overall neurological development (e.g., Doman, Delcato, & Doman, 1964), the training of the brain to assume greater hemispheric dominance (Orton, 1937), or the altering of chemical balances through diet or drugs (e.g., Feingold, 1975; Sroufe & Stewart, 1973). Professionals may have cautioned against overoptimism, but the popular press did not. For example, in 1959, *Newsweek* readers were told about "Johnnies" with "very high IQ's" who can't read due to inherited neurological conditions. These "Johnnies" were described as educationally treatable using the Gillingham reading method; "Of the 79 Parker students taught under the method so far, 96 per cent have become average or above average readers" ("Learning to Read," p. 110). In 1964, *Reader's Digest* provided case descriptions of children who were brain-injured at birth and experienced difficulty learning language, physical movements, and reading. A new program for motor development by Delcato and the Doman brothers was reported to "activate the millions of surviving [brain] cells to take over the functions of the dead ones" (Maisel, 1964, p. 137). Prognosis was reported excellent, and readers were told that it even helped affected children learn to read.

Probably due to these optimistic perceptions, students in LD classes seem to have suffered lesser negative teacher attitudes than other categories of failing students. Research studies have found that regular teachers see the LD student as less different from the "norm" than the ED or EMR student, and as demanding less of their time and patience (Moore & Fine, 1978; Shotel, Iano, & McGettigan, 1972; Williams & Algozzine, 1979), even when they observe behavior that contradicts their expectations for the label (Foster & Ysseldyke, 1976; Salvia, Clark, & Ysseldyke, 1973; Ysseldyke & Foster, 1978). Studies have not compared teacher attitudes toward LD and "culturally deprived" students, but there is evidence that teachers have more negative attitudes toward and lower expectation of children of color and lower class children than white or middle class children (e.g., Anyon, 1981; Jackson & Cosca, 1974; Rist, 1970).

Whether teacher attitudes toward various categories of exceptionality actually affected how students were taught in school has not been reported in the literature. However, there is evidence from outside special education that teacher attitudes toward children based on social class or presumed intellectual ability do affect the quality and amount of instruction they give (e.g., Brookover et al., 1979; Rosenthal & Jacobson, 1968; Rist, 1970). Thus, it is reasonable to assume that teachers gave more and better instruction to low-achieving students labeled as learning disabled than to low-achieving students bearing other labels, even if actual behavioral differences among such students would not in itself warrant differential treatment.

Learning disabilities in the 1970s

Since the early 1970s, there has been a shift in who has been classified as learning disabled and how the category has been used politically. That shift was propelled by a decline in the late 1960s in school standards for achievement, the civil rights movement and subsequent school responses, and a redefinition of mental retardation.

Although standards for school achievement were raised immediately after Sputnik, student test scores have caused many to believe standards were not maintained, for a variety of reasons (Goodlad, 1984). Declines in SAT scores, beginning in about 1966, have been widely publicized, and some state achievement tests also have shown declines (Boyer, 1983). One would think that if standards for achievement dropped during the late 1960s, fewer students would have been seen as failures and interest in classifying students as learning disabled would have waned. What happened was the reverse, due to other social developments.

During the late 1960s and early 1970s, minority groups pressured schools to discard the notion of cultural deprivation and stop classifying disproportionate numbers of minority children as mentally retarded. In 1973, the category of mental retardation was redefined, lowering the maximum IQ score from one standard deviation below the mean to two (Grossman, 1973), which dissolved the category of slow learner. The intent of these moves was to pressure schools to teach a wider diversity of students more effectively. Instead, many students who previously were or would have been classified as retarded, slow, or culturally deprived were now classified as learning disabled.

For example, based on a study of the racial composition of LD and MR classes in over 50 school districts between 1970 and 1977, Tucker (1980) found Black students overrepresented in MR classes but underrepresented in LD classes until 1972. After 1972, the proportion of the total school population in MR classes declined and Blacks lost some overrepresentation in that category, but they rapidly gained representation in LD classes, where they were overrepresented by 1974. Thus, even though pressure may have subsided during the late 1960s and early 1970s to provide a protected placement for failing white middle class children, learning disabilities has been used increasingly as a more palatable substitute for other categories to "explain" the failure of lower class children and children of color.

Learning disabilities and today's reform movement

In the 1980s, educators and the public are again viewing children as raw material for international competition, very much like during the late 1950s. Standards for achievement are again seen as too low, and schools are again being called upon to raise standards for reading, math, science, and computer literacy, and to test students more rigorously based on those raised standards. What will be done with those who do not measure up to the new standards? When standards were raised previously, failing children were defined as handicapped and segregated. Learning disabilities was created to explain the failure of children from advantaged social groups, and to do so in such a way that it suggested their eventual ability to attain relatively higher status occupations than other low achievers.

Schools need to focus much greater attention on how to teach children rather than on how to categorize those who do not learn well when offered "business-as-usual." But it is not enough to search for better ways to remediate those who have the greatest difficulty achieving standards for school success *as long as society* still expects schools to produce "products" with certain kinds of skills developed to certain levels of competence, and to rank-order those "products" based on their achievement of those skills. Those who come out on the bottom will still be destined for the lowest paying jobs or the reserve labor force and will still experience the pain of failure when compared to their peers. And members of advantaged social groups will still advocate treating their failing children in ways that maintain their advantaged status as much as possible. We need to shift our perspective from the failings of individuals or the inefficiencies of schools to the social context of schooling. Rather than attempting to remake children to fit social needs, we must first give greater consideration to the possibility that society's expectations for children and society's reward structure for their performance may need remaking.

References

Anyon, J. (1981). Elementary schooling and distinctions of social class. *Interchange, 12,* 118–132.

Apple, M. W. (Ed.). (1981). *Cultural and economic reproduction in education.* Boston: Routledge and Kegan Paul.

Back to the 3 R's? (1957, March 15). *U.S. News and World Report,* pp. 38–44.

Bender, L. (1957). Specific reading disability as a maturational lag. *Bulletin of the Orton Society, 7,* 9–18.

Bloom, B. S., Davis, A., & Hess, R. (1965). *Compensatory education for the culturally deprived.* New York: Holt, Rinehart, and Winston.

Boyer, E. L. (1983). *High school.* New York: Harper and Row.

Brookover, W. B., Beady, C., Flood, P., Schweitzer, J., & Wisenbaker, J. (1979). *School social systems and student achievement: Schools can make a difference.* New York: Praeger.

CEC (Council for Exceptional Children) Ad Hoc Committee to Study and Respond to the 1983 Report of the National Commission on Excellence in Education. (1984). Reply to "A Nation at Risk". *Exceptional Children, 52,* 484–494.

Chall, J. S. (1977). *An analysis of textbooks in relation to declining SAT scores.* Princeton, NJ: College Entrance Examination Board.

Chall, J. S. (1983). *Stages of reading development,* New York: McGraw-Hill.

Coles, G. S. (1978). The learning disabilities test battery: Empirical and social issues. *Harvard Educational Review, 48,* 313–340.

Cruickshank, W. M., Bentzen, F. A., Ratzeburg, F. H., & Tannhauser, M. T. (1961). *A teaching method for brain-injured and hyperactive children.* Syracuse, NY: Syracuse University Press.

Delcato, C. H. (1959). *The treatment and prevention of reading problems.* Springfield, IL: Charles C. Thomas.

Deutsch, M. (1963). The disadvantaged child and the learning process. In A. H. Passow (Ed.), *Education in depressed areas,* (pp. 163–179). New York: Teachers College Press.

Doman, G., Delcato, C., & Doman, R. (1964). *The Doman-Delcato developmental profile.* Philadelphia: Institutes for the Achievement of Human Potential.

Dunn, L. M. (1963). *Exceptional children in the schools.* New York: Holt, Rinehart, and Winston.

Education and the disadvantaged American. (1962, May 19). *Saturday Review,* p. 58.

Famous educator's plan for a school that will advance students according to ability. (1958, April 14). *Life,* pp. 120–121.

Farber, B. (1968). *Mental retardation: Its social context and social consequences.* Boston, MA: Houghton Mifflin.

Feingold, B. F. (1975). *Why your child is hyperactive.* New York: Random House.

Foster, G., & Ysseldyke, J. (1976). Expectancy and halo effects as a result of artifically induced teacher bias. *Contemporary Education Psychology, 1,* 37–45.

Franks, D. J. (1971). Ethnic and social status characteristics of children in EMR and LD classes. *Exceptional Children, 37,* 537–538.

Frostig, M., & Horne, D. (1964). *The Frostig program for the development of visual perception.* Chicago: Follett.

Goldstein, H. (1962). *The educable mentally retarded child in the elementary school.* Washington, DC: National Education Association.

Goodlad, J. I. (1984). *A place called school.* New York: McGraw-Hill.

Grossman, H., Ed. (1973). *Manual on terminology and classification in mental retardation* (rev. ed.). Washington, DC: American Association on Mental Deficiency.

Grotberg, E. H. (1970). Neurological aspects of learning disabilities: A case for the disadvantaged. *Journal of Learning Disabilities, 3*, 25–31.

Harder work for students. (1961, Sept. 4). *U.S. News and World Report*, p. 45.

Hieronymus, A. N., & Lindquist, E. G. (1974). *Manual for administrators, supervisors, and counselors, Forms 5&6, Iowa tests of basic skills*. Boston: Houghton Mifflin.

Jackson, G., & Cosca, C. (1974). The inequality of educational opportunity in the Southwest: An observational study of ethnically mixed classrooms. *American Educational Research Journal, 11*, 219–229.

Learning to Read. (1959). *Newsweek*, p. 110.

Maisel, A. Q. (1964). Hope for brain-injured children. *The Reader's Digest, 11*, 219–229.

Moore, J., & Fine, M. J. (1978). Regular and special class teachers' perceptions of normal and exceptional children and their attitudes toward mainstreaming. *Psychology in the Schools, 15*, 253–259.

National Commission on Excellence in Education. (1983). *A nation at risk*. Washington, DC: U.S. Government Printing Office.

Orton, S. T. (1937). *Reading, writing, and speech problems in children*. New York: W. W. Norton.

Persell, C. A. (1977). *Education and inequality*. New York: The Free Press.

Rabinovitch, R. D. (1962). Dyslexia: Psychiatric considerations. In J. Money (Ed.), *Reading disability: Progress and research needs in dyslexia*. Baltimore: Johns Hopkins Press.

Resnick, D. P., & Resnick, L. B. (1977). The nature of literacy: An historical exploration. *Harvard Educational Review, 47*, 370–385.

Rickover, H. G. (1957, March 2). Let's stop wasting our greatest resources. *Saturday Evening Post*, p. 19, 108–111.

Riessman, F. (1962). *The culturally deprived child*. New York: Harper and Row.

Rist, R. C. (1970). Student social class and teacher expectations in ghetto education. *Harvard Educational Review, 40*, 411–451.

Rosenbaum, J. E. (1976). *Making inequality*. New York: John Wiley and Sons.

Rosenthal, R., & Jacobson, L. (1968). *Pygmalion in the classroom*. NYC: Holt, Rinehart, & Winston.

Salvia, J., Clark, G., & Ysseldyke, J. (1973). Teacher retention of stereotypes of exceptionality. *Exceptional Children, 39*, 651–652.

Sarason, S. B., & Doris, J. (1979). *Educational handicap, public policy, and social history*. New York: The Free Press.

Schoolboys point up a U.S. weakness. (1958, March 24), *Life*, pp. 26–37.

Shafer, W. E., & Olexa, C. (1971). *Tracking and opportunity*, Scranton, PA: Chandler.

Shaw, C. R., & Mckay, H. D. (1942). *Juvenile delinquency and urban areas*. Chicago: University of Chicago Press.

Shotel, J. R., Iano, R. P. & McGettigan, J. F. (1972). Teacher attitudes associated with the integration of handicapped children. *Exceptional Children, 38*, 677–683.

Slow Learners. (1962, Feb. 17) *Saturday Review*, pp. 53–54.

Special Report No. 7. (1971). Guidelines for standardization sampling *Metropolitan achievement tests special report*. New York: Harcourt Brace Jovanovich.

Spring, J. (1976). *The sorting machine*. New York: Longman.

Sroufe, L. A., & Stewart, M. A. (1973). Treating problem children with stimulant drugs. *New England Journal of Medicine, 289*, 407–413.

Strauss, A. A., & Kephart, N. C. (1955). *Psychopathology and education of the brain-injured child*. New York: Grune and Stratton.

Strauss, A. A., & Lehtinen, L. E. (1963). *Psychology and education of the brain-injured child*. New York: Grune and Stratton.

Tarnopol, L. (1970). Delinquency and minimal brain dysfunction. *Journal of Learning Disabilities, 3*, 200–207.

Task Force on Education for Economic Growth. (1983). *Action for excellence*. Denver: Education Commission of the States.

Trace, A. S., Jr. (1961, May 27). Can Ivan read better than Johnny? *Saturday Evening Post*, pp. 30+.

Tucker, J. A. (1980). Ethnic proportions in classes for the learning disabled: Issues in nonbiased assessment. *Journal of Special Education, 14*, 93–105.

What went wrong with U.S. schools: An interview with Professor Arthur Bestor, University of Illinois. (1958, January 24). *U.S. News and World Report, 44,* 68–80.

White, M. A., & Charry, J. (1966). *School disorder, intelligence, and social class.* New York: Teachers College Press.

Williams, R. J., & Algozzine, B. (1979). Teachers' attitudes toward mainstreaming. *Elementary School Journal, 80,* 63–67.

Woodring, P. (1957, Sept. 2). Reform plan for schools. *Life,* pp. 123–136.

Ysseldyke, J. E., & Algozzine, B. (1982). *Critical issues in special and remedial education.* Boston: Houghton Mifflin.

Ysseldyke, J. E., Algozzine, B., Shinn, M. R., & McGue, M. (1982). Similarities and differences between low achievers and students classified as learning disabled. *Journal of Special Education, 16,* 73–85.

Ysseldyke, J. E., & Foster, G. G. (1978). Bias in teachers' observations of emotionally disturbed and learning disabled children. *Exceptional Children, 44,* 613–615.

PART 4

MULTICULTURAL EDUCATION: 1990s

CHAPTER 19

RACE, SOCIAL CLASS, AND EDUCATIONAL REFORM IN AN INNER-CITY SCHOOL (1995)

Jean Anyon

It has become increasingly clear that several decades of educational reform have failed to bring substantial improvement to schools in America's inner cities.[1] Most recent analyses of unsuccessful school reform (and prescriptions for change) have isolated educational, regulatory, or financial aspects of reform from the social context of poverty and race in which inner-city schools are located.[2] This article will discuss failed school reform from a somewhat different perspective. Drawing on an assessment of reform efforts in one school in an urban ghetto in a large district in the Northeast, the article describes processes and events that illustrate how social manifestations of racial and social class status can combine to vitiate efforts at school reform.[3]

I will first describe how sociocultural differences between reformers and the parents and teachers, and between reforms and the student population, created distrust among participants as well as inappropriate curriculum and instruction for the students. These sociocultural disjunctions made the successful implementation of change extremely difficult. A second factor I will discuss is the relationship between educators and students in the school. The lived professional culture of many teachers and the administrators in this school (for thirty years one of the poorest in the city) has deteriorated into a dehumanizing, abusive stance toward the student population, whose families lack the clout to ensure better treatment. This professional culture, and the students' active opposition to it, also contributed to the failure of attempted improvement projects. The final phenomenon to be discussed is the expectation of school staff that educational reform was not going to succeed. Almost all staff members felt that reform efforts were futile; most also felt that even if the reforms could be made to work, the resulting changes would have very little impact on the children's lives or futures.

I will argue that these three factors—sociocultural differences among participants in reform, an abusive school environment, and educator expectations of failed reform—occurring in a minority ghetto where the school population is racially and economically isolated constitute some of the powerful and devastating ways that concomitants of race and social class can intervene to determine what happens in inner-city schools, and in attempts to improve them.

Background

During the first two decades of the twentieth century, the schools in the city in which the research site is located (Newark, N.J.) were nationally recognized for their innovative attempts to serve an urban clientele, which included children of the industrial working class, the middle class, and the business elite as well as the poor.[4] However, in the early 1920s wealthy families began moving to the suburbs, followed in the next forty years by most of the city's middle class. Between 1917 and the early 1960s rural blacks, most of them with no financial resources and little formal schooling, moved up from the South and into the city. By 1961, the district schools were majority black and poor.

Until 1971, with the election of a black mayor and a black city council, the schools continued to be staffed by white administrators and teachers, and the city government was composed primarily of white ethnic personnel. No major educational initiatives were taken by government or educational leaders between 1922 and the 1971 election of the first black mayor. The system deteriorated. A 1940 assessment of the district schools noted that low achievement and dilapidated schools were common, and that measures to meet the needs of the city's poor (most of whom in 1940 were still white working-class ethnics) must be taken.[5] By 1968, a state-sponsored citizens' report found that the school system was in "an advanced state of decay," and advised that the state run the city schools and provide massive assistance.[6] No such action by the state was undertaken.

The state did, however, begin to closely monitor the continuing decline of the schools in its largest city. A series of state-sponsored evaluations was undertaken, and in 1984 the state mandated that the district administration take action or the district would lose its accreditation.[7] In 1989, in response to a state threat of takeover, the district's leaders initiated a four-year program of reform in eight schools in the central section of the city, including the school that was the focus of the research to be reported here.

There were reasons to hope that this reform effort would bring some success: Millions of dollars had been donated by major corporations and foundations for projects in the eight schools (seven feeder schools and one high school). Twenty-five corporate, higher education, and local citizen groups provided plans and personnel.

Moreover, the reforms were organized and directed by representatives of the city's majority black population. In 1989 (as now), the superintendent was African-American, and the board of education was African-American and Hispanic; the assistant superintendent with responsibility for the reform initiatives (who is no longer with the district) was black, and her staff consisted of two blacks and a Hispanic. Then as now, African Americans were the majority of significant players at most levels of the school system and in the city government.

It was possible that local control by blacks would be a catalyst of change, making the schools more responsive to black students: The administration could, for example, choose reforms that empowered members of their own constituency—significant parent involvement if not community control could be a focus. A celebration of minority cultures could infuse the curriculum. Or the district could, given the studies that show black students' difficulty with standardized tests, present a serious challenge to government reliance on these tests as measures of achievement and funding.

The majority of classroom teachers in the district are African-American.[8] Perhaps these black educators could reverse commonly held low expectations for minority students from low-income households; perhaps they could understand and nurture their charges, laying the educational groundwork for academic success.[9]

However, and conversely, it was also possible that, as Edward Said, Albert Memmi, Frantz Fanon, and others studying oppressed minorities have shown, victims of race and class exploitation sometimes grow to mimic the behavior and attitudes of their oppressors, and themselves victimize others of their own group over whom they have power.[10] It becomes important, then, to note here that some black educators, as products of past racial (and perhaps class) discrimination and exploitation, may have internalized beliefs about their students that mimic attitudes held by the white dominant society but that work to the detriment of children of color from poverty backgrounds.

Before proceeding further, I want to acknowledge the potentially controversial nature of statements by a white middle-class researcher concerning race and the possible effects of race on teaching, learning, and school reform. Perhaps it appears that I am stereotyping black teachers by asserting that some could excel with their students because they are black. Perhaps to expect a black administration to challenge the white power structure is to misplace the burden and is unfair. It is possible that these and other statements will be seen as racist.

It is important to remember, however, that the meanings or attributions of such terms as *race* (or gender, sexuality, or social class, for that matter) are not absolute. They are socially constructed. Groups and individuals develop from their experience and points of view denotations of these terms that make sense to them. I—as a white professional—discuss race in this paper in ways that may differ from the constructs others with other experiences might use. My interpretation of events, therefore, may differ from those of others: Where I will describe a black teacher, for example, as abusive of black students, others might see culturally sanctioned "strict discipline."

Moreover, I do not intend to disparage "all black teachers," "all white principals (or white teachers) in inner-city schools," "all low-income parents," "all middle-class consultants," or any other group, by inferring that all members of any group act in the manner to be described here. I report behaviors that I observed.

Marcy School

The research site, a K–8 school, will be called Marcy School.[11] Marcy was considered by some personnel to be a good school ("It's a happening school" [assistant superintendent]; "It's a very good school—there aren't drugs all over it like in some of the other schools" [drug counselor]). Others considered it to be "in the middle—not great, not terrible; right at the mean" [school psychologist]. No teacher or administrator considered it among the worst schools. As the principal said. "We may have problems, but we're no way the worst."

The student body is 71 percent black, 27 percent Hispanic, and 2 percent Asian and white. All but 3 of the 500 students in the school are from families with incomes below the poverty line, and qualify for free lunch. (In the district as a whole, 63 percent of the students are African-American, 26 percent are Hispanic, and most [78 percent] are poor, and qualify for free lunch.)

The majority of the students at Marcy School live in nearby housing projects. During the period of this study, the school had an official homeless rate that fluctuated between 5 and 20 percent. A recent psychological assessment of a random sample of forty-five Marcy students found that they were plagued by the problems that result from extreme poverty: chaotic lives, neglect and/or abuse, poor health histories and chronic health problems, emotional stress, anxiety, and anger.[12] Drug use and AIDS have claimed the parents of a large (but uncatalogued) number of the students, and teachers comment that many of their students are being raised by relatives and friends or, as a recent newspaper article stated, are growing up "without any apparent adult supervision."[13]

During the period of this study, the principal of Marcy School was a white Italian male (a former shop teacher) and the assistant principal was a Hispanic woman. Sixteen (64 percent) of the twenty-five classroom teachers were black and a sizable minority of these stated in interviews they had grown up in poor or working-class neighborhoods of this or other cities. Six classroom teachers (24 percent) were Hispanic, and three (12 percent) were white (almost all of both groups are from working-class backgrounds; all but two now live in the suburbs).

Most (61 percent) of the specialists and nonclassroom teachers in the school (basic-skills teachers, special education teachers, art and gym teachers, psychologist, social worker, learning disabilities specialist, etc.) were white. The rest were African-American. All the teacher aides in the buildings were black (with the exception of several Hispanic) women, and were parents of students or former students; all lived in the neighborhood, most in nearby housing projects. Perhaps half of the aides had themselves attended Marcy School. Almost all janitors and kitchen workers were black long-time residents of the city.[14]

Sociocultural differences between reformers, parents, and school personnel

The following portions of the article discuss ways in which I see the racial-class histories and characteristics of participants in the reform process affecting attempts to change Marcy School. This section describes ways in which the sociocultural distances between reformers and parents and school personnel interfered with the implementation of several projects.

The assistant superintendent in charge of the reform, a black female Ph.D., called occasional meetings of her "collaborators"—twenty-five representatives from groups or agencies with projects in the eight schools. The collaborators included administrators and professors from three area colleges and universities (including me); executive directors of two regional philanthropic foundations; representatives of three statewide special-interest groups (Educate America, Cities in Schools, and One to One—a mentoring program started by a black congressman); the assistant director of a coalition of church groups; members of the city's chamber of commerce; an activist minister; representatives of three national financial corporations with headquarters in the city; the president and vice-president of a large consulting firm from a highly affluent suburb; and the director and representatives of the National Executive Service Corps, a group of retired white business executives who volunteer their services in city schools.

All who attended these meetings, and who took part in projects in the schools, were professionals; five (in addition to the assistant superintendent) were African-American and the other twenty were white. The field notes that follow are excerpted from a meeting that suggests how sociocultural differences between two of these reformers and low-income minority parents at Marcy School manifested themselves.

> Two retired white executives from the National Executive Service Corps have been brought in by the assistant superintendent to advise parents at Marcy School on how to collaborate. The men are meeting with the Parent Corps in

the library. Mrs. Betty Williams, a black woman of about sixty, former parent and student at Marcy, head of the Parent Corps, and a community leader in the housing projects where she and the four other parents (four black women and one Hispanic male) live, are sitting around a rectangular table. On the other, far side of the room, around a smaller table, sit the two executives, wearing expensive-looking suits, smiling across the room at the parents, and holding pencils above long yellow pads.

The five parents are seated so that only Mrs. Williams faces the two men across the room. At no time during the discussion does she or any of the other parents look at the executives.

One executive smiles broadly and asks the group: "We each had our own company. We've had a good deal of experience. What problems do you have that we—with our background—could help you with?"

Mrs. Williams responds, "Maintenance are our only problems. We've gotten everything done except the bathrooms. And we're fighting for equipment. I fought for two years to get a gym floor. I went to this school. We had all kind of equipment here. Now the kids don't have nothing to do in the gym. [Several parents nod.] We're going to send letters to parents so kids'll wear uniforms for gym. We go to the board meetings. The eighth graders don't know how to play kickball! We got taught that in gym. We were so amazed. They didn't know how to play kickball, so we teach them."

Retired white executive, "But [pause]—if there's anything we can do for you, we'd like your suggestions."

Mrs. Williams ignores his question and says to the parents, "I'm going to the dentist—to get me some teeth. And then I'm *really* going to eat!" (She then talks to the parents about an upcoming assembly in which she will give certificates to parent volunteers.)

Retired white executive intercedes: "What are your plans for getting more parents [referring to the fact that the Parent Corp has only eight parents]?"

Mrs. Williams says, "We *have* a lot of parents. We found that this is the way we get parents: In the morning I stand by the door and tell them they can talk to me about anything." [She again speaks to the group at her table about the upcoming assembly.]

The retired executives look at each other, smile again at the parents, and stop asking questions. They sit quietly at the back of the room during the rest of the meeting and Mrs. Williams does not acknowledge them again.

The social gulf between the parents and the reformers that appeared to me to impair communication and joint planning at this meeting was never breached. During the subsequent months neither the white executives from the corporate world nor the black and Hispanic parents from the projects were able to utilize each others' skills. Commentators have long pointed to the fact that differences between social backgrounds and language can impair interaction and trust.[15] Other factors (such as inexperience) certainly contributed to the executives' lack of expertise in working with the parents, but even this lack of experience can be attributed in part to the enormous social and cultural gulf separating the two groups. Nothing came of the executives' attempted involvement in the parent group, and they terminated their visits after several months.

A similar social distance separated many teachers (most of whom, as noted above, were African-American, and who stated in interviews they had grown up in poor or working-class families) from the two consultants directing the largest reform project, "Training in Shared Decision Making" for school-based management. This project was run by two blond, expensively dressed consultants based in an exclusive suburb twenty-five miles away. In part because of their blond, suburban "look," the consultants were called by teachers "the all-American kids."

On several occasions these consultants complained to me that the teachers and administrators in this district "are just like the kids. They don't even know how to *talk* about collaboration. And they want immediate gratification. If they don't get it, they want to quit." The teachers also complained to me that they thought the two consultants were "too suburban": "They have no idea what city schools are like. They don't know what we're up against." "They don't know the kids!" A number of teachers complained to the assistant superintendent that the consultants were racist, and had made racist comments. The assistant superintendent told me she had agreed with the teachers, but that she had counseled the teachers, "We have to work with them despite the racism. They have a lot to teach us [about cooperation]."

The professional development project was resisted by both teachers and administrators as "too abstract," and "not geared to city schools."[16] In part because of teacher complaints of racism and the perceived inappropriateness of the consultants for the city's schools, the board of education rescinded permission for the consultants to continue the project in shared decision making after the second year, and it was never fully implemented in the eight schools.

Middle-level management employees (both black and white) from the nearby headquarters of two national corporations in town participated in a tutoring program at Marcy and two other elementary schools. In two schools the administration refused to cooperate with them, saying they were not equipped "to deal with the kids." In Marcy School the tutors quit because they said "nobody was interested in the students getting any tutoring" from them. Referring to middle- and upper-middle-class helpers in the reform effort (such as the groups of executives, as well as graduate students from a university in New York City), a Marcy teacher stated: "They come in the schools and they can't handle the kids. We have to train them and monitor them. It takes too much time." Another said, "They have no idea of the *situation* we have here! They just get in the way."

As these examples indicate, social distance arising in part from lack of mutual experience and knowledge of each other in people of different class and racial backgrounds can impair communication, trust, and joint action between reformers and school personnel, can foster an incompetence that arises in part from this lack of knowledge, and can in these and other ways hamper the implementation of educational improvement projects. In the examples presented here, teachers and parents resisted the efforts of reformers, and several improvement projects were vitiated.

Sociocultural differences between reforms and the student population

I asked the assistant superintendent who had decided which projects would be part of this reform effort. She said that she, members of the board of education, a union representative, and a parent representative had taken a weekend retreat together in June of 1989 and had chosen the projects that would be attempted. I asked whether what she and they chose differed in any way from what the state had mandated in recent regulations. "No, we chose the exact same things," she said. "We chose what is raising scores across the country: school-based management, ungraded primary, all-day kindergarten, departmentalization of the middle grades, programs like whole language and cooperative learning. We ordered all new textbooks in math, science, reading, phonics, and a whole language series."

I asked if any of the reforms responded to the fact that most of the school children were African-American. "No," she said, "although the superintendent and I are black nationalists—well, I was a pan-Africanist, but we chose what was fundable." I asked if any of the reforms responded to the poverty of the children. "No," she stated again, "just the parent forums [informational meetings]. A lot of our parents are young, and disenfranchised." I then inquired if any of the reforms had anything to do with the students' black dialect (or, more accurately, "inner-city dialect," since all the students seem to speak it—blacks, Hispanics, and the few poor whites as well). "No—but that does get in the way. They can't express themselves."

I press, "Why not choose reforms that respond in some way to the children—at the least a multicultural focus to curriculum, for example?" She responds, "It wouldn't be politically do-able. Education is as much about politics as it is about kids. You have to be aware of the larger bureaucratic system you're working in. The old-boy network, they're white men, and that's where the money is! You have to go to them for money to do things. What you do has to be acceptable to them."

What I would like to suggest is that these and other reforms that were chosen (see below) have little if anything to do with this district's students and the cultural and economic realities of their lives, and in part because of this sociocultural inappropriateness, the reforms actually impede the students' academic progress and thereby preclude reform success.

One of the reforms initiated by the board of education in 1989 was an attempt to enforce teacher accountability by mandating that instruction be based on the new textbooks, and that these texts were to be used "on grade level"—for example, fifth-grade texts used with all fifth-graders, despite the fact that the majority of students in most classrooms are reading and computing well below grade level. A recent state report directed district teachers to adhere closely to those texts. Both state and district mandates include directives that teachers are to reteach and retest students on any skills not passed on the quarterly tests devised by the publishers of the reading and math series.[17]

Teachers complain bitterly about the "on-grade-level" policy, stating that it is impossible to teach students from textbooks they cannot understand. "They can't read the books and they're labeled failures before they even try!" was a typical complaint.

There are additional ways in which this reliance on mainstream texts and workbooks to teach students marginalized by poverty and race interferes with their achievement. An examination of the texts revealed that despite an occasional story featuring a minority character, the texts are a microcosm of white middle-class interests and situations. Teachers state that the stories in the reading and language series, for example, "have nothing to do with the kids, they hate them, they think they're boring and stupid." Exclusive use of these texts and the continual testing and retesting of the skills in them mean that there is no room for (for example) curriculum about black and Latino history (although the district has produced excellent curriculum guides in this area). No teacher of the twenty-four in the school I queried supplements the written curriculum with black studies in a systematic way except—to varying degrees—during black history month. Two years ago high school students at two city high schools demonstrated (unsuccessfully) to get a black studies curriculum in use at their schools.

The children I interviewed at Marcy School knew very little about black history. I interviewed twenty-five nine- to thirteen-year-olds at the school, and only eight knew who Martin Luther King, Jr., was. Of these, five stated they had heard about him or other figures in black history from family members. More knew about Malcolm X because of the recent movie ("they have T-shirts and hats about that," said one twelve-year-old).

However alienating a curriculum that does not concern them may be to students, and however frustrating trying to study a book that is too difficult for them may be, there is another way in which the curriculum impedes the progress of the students. This is the fact that the texts are written in standard English, a dialect that, because of their extreme marginalization and isolation from the mainstream, almost none of the students speak.[18] As Joan Baratz argued in 1970, the fact that the texts continually reject nonstandard dialect as inferior provides a continual insult to nondialect speakers.[19]

Not only is the standard English in written materials an insult to non-standard dialect speakers; according to a large body of research it also interferes in important ways with reading achievement.[20] This interference is caused in part by the subtlety of the differences between standard English and nonstandard English. Joan Baratz and others demonstrated that it is extremely difficult to learn to read a language you do not speak, and that reading achievement can be significantly retarded by a reliance on texts whose syntax and phonetic structure differ from the structures of one's own language. Conversely, reading comprehension increases significantly when one learns to read from texts printed in one's native tongue.[21]

In 1987, Eleanor Orr demonstrated fundamental ways black dialect can interfere with mathematical thinking in educational contexts, where mathematical thinking is governed, in textbook and in most pedagogy, by standard English language and forms of thought.[22] She argues that not only do the subtlety of differences and the lack of familiarity with terms impede mathematical understanding, but that outright conflicts of black dialect terms with standard English terms also interfere. Orr demonstrates that the grammars are distinct, the lexicons overlap; and—significantly—the unconscious rules that govern syntax in black dialect often conflict with and cause interference with standard English, which uses different rules.

One of the many kinds of mathematical problems encountered by the black dialect speaker involves the conflicts among standard and nonstandard English expressions used to compare parts of objects or amounts (partitive comparative expressions):

Standard English	*Nonstandard English phrases used to express the standard English expression*
half of	two times less than
half as large as	two times smaller than twice as small as half as small as
half as much as	half less than

half as fast as   twice as slow as
                       half as slow as

In some cases, the terms in which black dialect speakers think are the inverse of what they read in the math textbooks. For example, in an expression like "half as much as," the expression is in the vocabulary of both languages—the students' language and the language of the texts—but with opposite meanings. The confusion that can occur is substantial. Orr demonstrates how such confusion over the meanings of standard English mathematical expressions can also affect scientific reasoning:

> In a chemistry class a student [who speaks nonstandard dialect] stated that if the pressure was doubled with the temperature remaining constant, the volume of a gas would be "half more than it was." When I asked her if she meant that the volume would get larger, she said, "No, smaller." When I then explained that "half more than" would mean larger, one and a half times larger, indicating the increase with my hands, she said she meant "twice" and with her hands indicated a decrease. When I then said, "But 'twice' means larger, two times larger," again indicating the increase with my hands, she said, "I guess I mean 'half less than.' It always confuses me."[23]

When the teacher attempting to teach speakers of nonstandard dialect from books written in standard English is also a speaker of nonstandard dialect, as many teachers are in the district under discussion here, the confusion can be compounded.[24]

Despite the curricular reforms—new textbooks, departmentalization, mandated instructional changes, and state and district regulations that attempt to align instruction with basals and other textbooks—the children's achievement scores have not increased. The standardized scores of the students at Marcy School (and at the other seven schools in this, one of the poorest wards of the city) are (as they have traditionally been) among the lowest in the district, and they declined between 1988 and 1992. District achievement scores are among the lowest in the state, and are considerably below national medians.[25]

The teachers, black and white, are in the unenviable position of being asked to impart a white, middle-class curriculum, written in a language that differs from and interferes with the students' (and many teachers') own language and that in most cases is presented to students in textbooks that are too difficult for them to fully comprehend. The situation certainly fosters student failure, and—consequently—the failure of reform to raise achievement. Moreover, the frustration engendered by the students' low achievement has the potential to worsen classroom relations between teachers and students.

Relations between teachers and students

Teachers face an extremely difficult pedagogical situation at Marcy School. In addition to the curricular and instructional mandates and circumstances discussed above, teachers confront classrooms full of anxious and angry students. The desperate lives most of the children lead make many of them become restless and confrontational; many are difficult to teach, and to love. This section first discusses interactions I observed between black personnel and students, and then those of white staff.

It was apparent to me that some black teachers care deeply about their students: For example, one young teacher at Marcy School prays over her class every morning and evening, and prays each day for each of her students. Another teacher in the building takes homeless students home to live with her whenever she can. Another coordinates a clothing drive in the spring, and food baskets at Thanksgiving.

Most African-American teachers I interacted with during my work in the school also, however, expressed deep frustration in dealing with their students. Perhaps fueled by this frustration, these black teachers are—to varying degrees—abusive of their students. (I will argue below that most white teachers also exhibit—to varying degrees—systematically abusive behavior toward their students.)

During the ten months in which I spent a full day each week working with teachers and their classes, I heard a tirade from black teachers of what seemed to me to be verbal humiliation and degradation, directed at students. For example: "Shut up!" "Get your fat head in there!" "Did I tell you to move [talk; smile]?" "I'm sick of you." "He's not worth us wasting our time waiting for." "Act like a human being." "I'm going to get rid of you!" and "Excuse me!" said with what sounds like withering contempt. I heard one particularly abusive black male teacher tell a girl her breath "smelled like dog shit," and her clothes "smelled like stale dust." A sampling of other, not atypical, comments I overheard includes:

You're disgusting; you remind me of children I would see in a jail or something. (Black teacher to her class of black and Hispanic first-graders.)

Shut up and push those pencils. Push those pencils—you borderline people! (Black teacher to his class of black and Hispanic sixth-graders.)

Your mother's pussy smells like fish. *That's* what stinks around here. (Black teacher to black fourth-grade girl whose mother is a prostitute.)

Janice Hale-Benson argues that a cultural norm of harsh discipline exists among African-Americans, and thus verbal expressions that a white observer might perceive as abusive are not so perceived by African-American teachers or students.[26] As one black teacher explained to me, "It's what they're used to. They wouldn't listen to us if we didn't yell and put on a mean face. They know it's only our school voice." An older black teacher explained, "You can't treat these kids nice. They don't deserve it." Then, referring to a beginning teacher who had taken her class to the museum and had been asked to leave because the students were "touching everything," the older teacher said, "Why did she take them on a trip? They don't deserve to go to the museum! They don't know how to act!"

On eight occasions when I was working with teachers in their classrooms I saw black teachers, none of whom was considered an unusually harsh disciplinarian, smack a student with some force on the head, chest, or arm as if it were a routine occurrence. On numerous occasions I saw teachers grab students by the arm and shake them. No one reacted to these actions. I also witnessed two severe beatings by parents or guardians while a teacher or the school disciplinarian was present and did nothing to stop the beating.

My experience at Marcy School leads me to believe that the treatment of students by many black adults at this school goes beyond any tradition of harsh discipline that would be culturally sanctioned among African Americans, and represents, instead, aspects of a lived professional culture that characterizes the behavior of both black and white teachers, and that systematically degrades the children.

Thus, I found many white personnel to be just as verbally abusive as the black teachers discussed above. The following comment is from the white male gym teacher, who refused to give a fourth grade their scheduled gym class because "they're too rough. They throw the ball, it could kill you!": "If I had a gun I'd kill you. You're all hoodlums." Other white staff:

> Stop picking in your ear. Go home and get a bath. (White basic-skills teacher to a black boy.)

> Why are you so stupid! I'm going to throw you in the garbage. (Other white basic-skills teacher to a black boy.)

> Don't you have *any* attention span? You have the attention span of cheerios! (White principal trying to quiet a class of black and Hispanic fourth-graders.)

> This ain't no restaurant, you know—where you go in and get what you *want*! [pause] You have no sense! You have no sense! (White teacher reprimanding three African-American girls in the hall outside his door.)

As if in explanation for the way he treated his students, a white teacher stated during a meeting, "When you realize who they [the students] are, you laugh, and you can't take it [teaching] seriously." Two white teachers expressed fear of confronting their students. One stated: "I don't talk to them like I used to. They'll challenge you now, and you might not win." I did not see any white teacher strike a student, perhaps out of cultural norms that do not sanction it, or perhaps out of fear of retaliation. As one white male teacher said, "They all have social workers, and the social workers tell the girls don't let any man touch you. One girl accused me of touching her on the knee—her mother told her to do it, to get [her] out of my class. And it worked."

The school psychologist alleged that abuse by teachers is "common" in this school. The school social worker told me that she thinks there is less teacher abuse in the last four to five years because the Department of Social Services is "more diligent." However, the district—which serves only 4 percent of the state's students, but which itself is 89 percent minority and 78 percent poor—reports over 40 percent of the institutional child abuse reported by school systems to the state.[27]

Each school is required by the board to post "inspirational sayings" on walls and bulletin boards around the building. The purpose of the sayings is to motivate the students. The following are sayings the principal and a teacher posted:

> If you have an open mind, chances are something will fall into it.

> The lazier we are today, the more we have to do tomorrow.

> The way to avoid lieing [sic] is not to do anything that involves deception.

> It is easier to think you are right than to be right.

> Don't pretend to be what you don't intend to be.

> If you can't think of anything to be thankful for, you have a poor memory.

These "motivational" sayings are also instantiations of a lived professional culture that degrades the students at Marcy School. The school staff's abusive, implicitly sanctioned attitudes and behaviors have evolved over time in a situation in which the student population is extremely poor, racially marginalized, of low academic achievement, difficult to motivate educationally, and from families that have little or no social power. The lived culture of the teachers combines with the alien curriculum described above to create a hostile, rejecting situation for the students.

The students in turn describe their reactions. Following are representative quotes from eight of the twenty-five students I interviewed. The students are African-American, unless otherwise noted.

"Tell me about your class," I say to a fifth-grade girl during her interview. "My class stupid. They mentally depressed. They don't want to learn." "Why not?" "They don't like the teachers." "Why not?" "Well, Miss Washington, she assigns all this homework, and she never collect it. Lots of parents puts in complaints about Mr. D., but they don't do nothin." "Do you have many friends in your class?" I ask. "No," she responds, "I'm lonely. I'm a nerd." When asked to explain why her teachers and the principal act the way they do, this girl said, "When they need a low place to come to [teachers and principals] they come here. That the only place they get a job." (Eleven-year-old girl who attempted suicide twice during the year I knew her.)

During another interview a boy tells me, "Teachers throw kids out, say 'I don't want you in my class.' They throw us on the floor and be grabbin us. Teachers too mean. They lie on people." "So what do you do?" I ask. "We make him mad." "How?" "Talk, laugh and have fun." (Eleven-year-old boy)

I ask a boy to "tell me about the teachers in this school." He responds, "Most teachers here don't teach us." "Why not"? "Because of the kids. They runs the halls and makes the teachers upset." "Why do they do that?" "Um, they think [teachers] just doin the job for money, they don't care." [Ten-year-old boy]

A boy tells me, "Most of the kids here don't do well." "Why?" I ask. "They fight too much and they don't feel like going to school." "Why not?" "They don't like school. They want to hang out." "And then?" "Then they'll drop out." (Eleven-year-old boy)

When I ask a girl why some kids don't do well at school, she says, "Kids don't want to learn. They be playin in the halls. They don't study." "Why not?" "It's boring and they get mad at the teachers." "How do you think the teachers feel about that?" "They don't care. [pause] If we don't learn, the teachers still gets their paycheck." (Thirteen-year-old girl, one of the three white students in the school)

I ask a ten-year-old girl, "Why don't some kids here do well at school?" "It's they fault. Because Mr. Thompson—you saw him teach—he's crazy, but he's a good teacher. The kids that don't learn don't want to learn." "Why not?" "They don't like school. They don't like Mr. Thompson. They playin so much in school they don't have time to learn." [At this point the principal comes over, and pinches her hard on her cheek leaving a red mark. He says, "Mr. Thompson knows what to do with *you*, doesn't he?"] (Ten-year-old Hispanic girl)

"Tell me about your teacher," I request of a boy. "He says we're animals. Hooligans. He said we should be in a zoo. I feel bad when he say that. I get kinda sad." "So what do you do?" "I put my head down." (Nine-year-old boy)

A boy walking past us as we sat talking in the hall added, "He treats us like we're toys. So we make him mad." "What do you do?" "We run around. [pause] Watch!" This ten-year-old boy proceeded to do forward and backward cartwheels, flipping high in the air off a desk that was in the hall. Several other boys who were wandering the halls gathered around and cheered him on.

Almost all of the students I interviewed seemed to be in an oppositional stance to their teachers; most were aware that they are in a situation in school that is hostile and aggressively rejecting of them.

McDermott argued several years ago that black children who have white teachers may "achieve" failure by rejecting the oppressive definition of them they perceive their teachers to hold, and concomitantly rejecting the teachers' and schools' definition of success.[28] The black and Hispanic children I interviewed apparently feel oppressive rejection on the part of both black and white teachers. In this regard, almost all of the interviewees said it did not matter whether you had white or black teachers ("They all the same"). One student stated that his aunt told him, when he complained about his teacher, "Just be glad you got a black teacher," but another black child said it was better to have a white teacher, "as long as it's a lady."

It may be that the hostile social situation in which teaching, learning, and testing occur in this school has important consequences for achievement on the standardized tests given the students every quarter and every spring, which are the benchmark of success in educational reform. Ernest Haggard demonstrated in 1954 that the social situation made a significant difference in how the 671 black inner-city children he studied performed on IQ tests. The attitude of the student to the tester was the most important aspect in determining how students did on these tests. Significantly, the attitude of the student toward the tester was more important than the content—for example, identifiable cultural bias—of the test items.[29]

Teachers and administrators at Marcy School wonder aloud why the students "can do all the things in the street they won't do for us. Did you ever see a drug dealer who couldn't make change? They're walking spread sheets!" In the face of intense district pressure on teachers to "get the scores up," teachers convey to their students angry, desperate hopes that students will perform well on the tests. I suspect that, although some children may not be intellectually capable of learning what the school asks, one effect of the hostile atmosphere in the school is that many students may simply refuse to comply. The assistant superintendent told me that one of her biggest problems in the high school was "to get the students to take the [standardized] tests seriously."[30]

The result of student opposition to the academic demands of the school could be devastating for reform. Standardized tests are almost always the criterion that defines success in inner-city schools. As long as testing takes place in a hostile, oppressive situation, and measures a curriculum that is culturally and linguistically unsuited to the students, I suspect the scores will not rise.

Expectations for reform

Most school personnel appear resigned to the failure of current reform efforts in the eight schools. The principal of Marcy School stated that "nothing will happen. This school was built over a hundred years ago. They just replaced the [original] windows five years ago! With the decades of neglect in this ward, it'll take years to fix it up." Teachers agree: "Nothing will be left when the money goes home." "The first year was nice—we were treated like professionals; the second and third year? Nothing." One teacher stated, when asked what she thought would come from the reform projects: "Maybe I'll get them [her students] from 'very low' to 'low' on the [achievement] tests." Then she added, "But even if they do learn to read and write, there are no jobs."

A consequence of this resignation is that it is much harder to garner the enthusiasm and energy to carry out improvement projects that most people are convinced will fail. Indeed, most personnel imply that they accept the present situation as "the best that can be expected." I heard over and over again, "We're doing the best we can" and "This is the best that can be done with what we have."

Many of the district's administrators, teachers, and principals, as well as the majority of the participating parents (e.g., classroom aides), grew up in the city. They and their children attended the city's schools. Due in large part to a diminished industrial base (and resulting insufficient employment opportunity) and nine decades of political patronage in the city bureaucracies, the board of education is the largest employer in the city. For the people who work in the schools, this is "their" system; the system provides their jobs, and despite the system's faults, they defend and support it.

Even I, an outsider, after several months of intense work with the students and teachers, began to think of the school as a good urban school, and I hoped the state evaluators in an upcoming evaluation would see it that way also. From my field notes:

> I was very negative about the school when I arrived. Now I find myself thinking, "This is a good urban school," and hoping the state people will feel that way too. I feel many of the teachers work very hard, and actually teach. I go through the halls—with the doors slamming, adults going in and out of classes, kids roaming the halls, the intercom blaring and crackling, and the teachers shouting and angry—and I have to remind myself that this is an incredibly noisy and distracting place for studying. It is beginning to sound normal to me. So is what goes on in the classrooms. ("Good" is, of course, relative. If I were in [an affluent district in which I have done several district evaluations] what happens here would signal crisis/breakdown of the system. It would never be considered "good." I must be part of the system now; those who are in an institution have a hard time seeing it from the outside.

Several days later I write in my field notes:

> After being in Marcy yesterday where chaos filled the halls, and teachers tried angrily and in vain to get the children to go back in their rooms, I went into my daughter's class today. [She is in third grade, in a public school in another city in a "model" school. The parents are, for the most part, professionals;

40 percent of the students are minority, but only 10 percent of them are low-income students. It is widely known as a very good school, occasionally being written up in the *New York Times*.]

The contrast was overwhelming. The kids were sitting, doing various activities, all over the room, on the floor, at tables—one black boy was curled up on top of a low book shelf, reading a book. The children were reading, making Father's Day presents from brightly colored materials; they were working with manipulables of various kinds. Materials, books, and supplies were everywhere, and in abundance; the children's work was on display on the walls, hanging from the ceiling, and in the hall. Murals and papier-mâché projects decorated the back of the room. The T-shirts they had tie-dyed and silk-screened for their "Olympics" day the next day were hanging from rope across the room drying. The children were working easily, absorbed, in little clusters. Chatter filled the air, and smiles; and—most importantly—they seemed involved and interested in what they were doing. They seemed happy to be there!

It seemed unbelievable to me, how wonderful it was. It made me realize how far I had gone toward accepting the starkness of Marcy's bare and vacant rooms, the angry, wounded-looking children, and the resentful, hostile teachers—as acceptable.

Conclusion

The foregoing discussion delineates some of the ways blackness and whiteness, extreme poverty and relative affluence, cultural marginalization and social legitimacy, come together—and conflict—within a school to affect educational reform. The events and behaviors I have described take place when people of low social status—for example, impoverished people of color—comprise the student and parent population and do not have the power to prevent them. Such events occur when the rage and resignation of those in a community and school are so great that no good deeds can overcome them.

Such tragedies occur in a school and district when administrators from an oppressed group (for example) mimic, in educational policy choices, their oppressors, and when teachers from an oppressed group (for example) devalue students of their own group, as does the dominant culture and teachers of that culture. Perhaps most of all, such tragedy occurs when people in a community and a school confront the workings of a racist, class-biased system without sufficient resources and without hope.

What is to be done? Are the children in our ghettos doomed? I predict that educational change in schools like Marcy will require fundamental alteration of the social situation. First, we must create an alliance of blacks and whites in political struggle to eliminate poverty. A broad redistribution of social and economic resources must take place. In this city, an arts center whose initial cost is estimated at over $104 million is under construction downtown, less than a mile from Marcy school.[31] The art center is touted as destined to draw suburban residents to its performances and nearby businesses, thus "revitalizing" the downtown area. However, if the history of Detroit, Philadelphia, Boston, and Baltimore (among other cities that attempted "revitalized" downtown areas) is any indication, this art center will do little if anything for the residents of the surrounding ghettos.[32] It would be better to spend money to create meaningful long-term jobs in the locality, to train people for those and other well-paying jobs that may already exist in the locality, to provide adequate health care and housing, and, ultimately, to improve the schools.

Adequate health, personal finance, and social resources bring people a freedom of choice that poverty denies, and bring an end to the debilitating dependency that poverty enforces. A population can then feel hope; and people can feel a sense of agency, rather than unproductive rage and resignation. Students who are less oppressed are easier to teach, and teachers can then more easily excel.

I am suggesting that the structural basis for failure in inner-city schools is political, economic, and cultural, and must be changed before meaningful school improvement projects can be successfully implemented. Educational reforms cannot compensate for the ravages of society.

In the interim, before poverty and racial marginalization can be eliminated, I foresee three possible courses of action, none of which appears to me particularly viable. One possibility is metropolitan-area desegregation, as Gary Orfield and Jonathon Kozol have recommended.[33] For example, schools in this city could be closed, and students and teachers integrated into wealthier nearby suburban school systems—the students to get a better education, the teachers to participate in a professional culture that does not systematically devalue children. Such a solution, however, although it might provide an educational alternative, would not by itself overcome the deleterious effects of the students' returning each night to the ghetto—to poverty and desperate situations. Unless metropolitan-area school desegregation were accompanied by (at a minimum) substantial housing and job desegregation, metropolitan-area school desegregation would be a partial and ultimately unsuccessful solution.

A second possibility is that the state "take over" and run the city district (as it runs two other districts). Given the fact that many of the reforms attempted by the district in Marcy and the other pilot schools were actually mandated by the state department of education, it is not likely that the reforms the state would attempt in the district's other schools would be different. Moreover, the reforms described in this article, as well as other, administrative, reforms, have already been introduced by the state in two nearby low-income minority urban districts when state personnel took control of those districts in 1989 and 1991. So far, little if any academic progress has been made in these cities' schools, and insufficient numbers of students have passed recent state standardized tests to certify the districts.[34] According to news reports concerning the two districts under state control, some administrative mismanagement of funds by prior officials has been stopped, so that more classrooms have textbooks, paper, and other supplies, but several state personnel administering the larger district are themselves under indictment for misuse of school funds.[35]

A third eventuality that should be considered is that personnel in the district described here will themselves ultimately effect significant improvements in the schools—with time, perhaps, and with larger infusions of money and more or better assistance. It should be noted in this regard that the district has unsuccessfully attempted continual reform initiatives since 1984. Moreover, the numerous improvement projects of the 1970s also failed to raise students' achievement.[36] While poverty and racial despair have escalated in this city since the 1970s—as in other cities—so has educational alienation and failure.[37]

Given the persistent historical correlation between poverty and school failure; given the resiliency of lived professional cultures such as that of school personnel described in this study; and acknowledging the power of the social and cultural distances between racially/economically marginalized school populations and the educational "help" they receive, it is unlikely that educators in ghetto schools will be successful in making substantial, long-term changes in their schools.

Thus, I think the only solution to educational resignation and failure in the inner city is the ultimate elimination of poverty and racial degradation. The solution to educational failure in the ghetto is elimination of the ghetto. This prescription seems extremely difficult to implement. I acknowledge this, but urge you to view its assumed improbability differently. As James Baldwin suggests in *The Fire Next Time*,

> I know that what I am asking is impossible. But in our time, as in every time, the impossible is the least that one can demand—and one is, after all, emboldened by the spectacle of human history in general, and American Negro history in particular, for it testifies to nothing less than the perpetual achievement of the impossible. ... If we do not now dare everything, the fulfillment of that prophecy, recreated from the Bible in song by a slave, is upon us: GOD GAVE NOAH THE RAINBOW SIGN, NO MORE WATER, THE FIRE NEXT TIME![38]

Acknowledgments

I would like to acknowledge the valuable comments by Janet Miller, Lois Weis, and Julia Wrigley on earlier versions of this paper. I could not have completed the article without the crucial advice given to me by Roslyn Arlin Mickelson.

Notes

1 See, for example, Jonathan Kozol, *Savage Inequalities: Children in America's Schools* (New York: Crown Publishers, 1991); and Gary Orfield and Carole Ashkinaze, *The Closing Door: Conservative Policy and Black Opportunity* (Chicago; The University of Chicago Press, 1991). See also, among others, Lauro Cavazos, "National Assessment of Educational Progress," *Education Week* 7 (1990): 1, 21; Seymour B. Sarason, *The Predictable Failure of Educational Reform: Can We Change Course Before It's Too Late?* (San Francisco: Jossey-Bass, 1990); and Robert Rothman, "Obstacle Course: Barriers to Change Thwart Reformers at Every Twist and Turn," *Education Week* 10 (February 1993): 9–12.

2 See, among others, Sarason, *Predictable Failure*; Richard F. Elmore and Associates, *Restructuring Schools: The Next Generation of Educational Reform* (San Francisco: Jossey-Bass, 1990); Michael Fullan (with Suzanne Steigelbauer), *The New Meaning of Educational Change* (New York: Teachers College Press, 1991); George A. Goens and Sharon I. R. Clover, *Mastering School Reform* (Boston: Allyn and Bacon, 1991); Dwight W. Allen, *Schools for a New Century: A Conservative Approach to Radical School Reform* (New York: Praeger, 1992); Ann Bradley, "Education for Equality," *Education Week* 11 (1994): 28–32; Peter Schmidt, "Urban School Results Linked to Funding Woes," *Education Week* 11 (1994): 3; Patricia Wasley, *Stirring the Chalkdust: Tales of Teachers Changing Classroom Practice* (New York: Teachers College Press, 1994); and Ann Lieberman, ed., *The Work of Restructuring Schools: Building from the Ground Up* (New York: Teachers College Press, 1995). But see Kozol, *Savage Inequalities*, and James Comer, *School Power* (New York: Free Press, 1980), who consider more than most the contributions of race and poverty to the success or failure of educational reform.

3 I will call on the concept of "ghetto" to highlight the extreme poverty and destitution of children in America's inner cities. The definition of ghetto that I will use throughout the article is that recently proposed by William Julius Wilson: A ghetto is an inner-city neighborhood in which more than 40 percent of the inhabitants are poor. Most inhabitants of such neighborhoods are black (with increasing percentages of Hispanics)

and are economically, culturally, and politically isolated from the mainstream, despite their usual proximity to city hall and downtown shopping districts. The school that is to be discussed in this article exists in such a neighborhood, or ghetto. Census data from 1990 show that, in the census tract in which the school is located, 45 percent of all persons have incomes below the poverty level; of female-headed householder families with related children under eighteen years, 66 percent are below the poverty level; of female-headed householder families with related children under five years, 82 percent are below the poverty level. According to the 1990 census, the per capita income in the census tract in which the research site is located was $7,647. (The per capita income in 1990 in the city was $9,437. Per capita income in the state was $24,936, which was 33 percent higher than the national average. New Jersey, the state in which the school is located, was in 1990 the nation's second wealthiest state.)

(See William Julius Wilson, "Public Policy Research and 'The Truly Disadvantaged,' " in *The Urban Underclass*, ed. Christopher Jencks and Paul E. Peterson [Washington, D.C.: The Brookings Institution, 1991], pp. 460–82; and idem, *The Truly Disadvantaged: The Inner City, the Underclass, and Public Policy* [Chicago: University of Chicago Press, 1987].)

4 David B. Corson, "Some Ideals and Accomplishments of the Newark School System," National Education Association Proceedings and Addresses (1921): 707–13; and idem, "Leading School Systems of New Jersey: The Newark System," *New Jersey Journal of Education* 13 (March 1924): 1 ff.

5 George D. Strayer et al., *The Report of a Survey of the Public Schools of Newark, New Jersey* (New York: Bureau of Publications, Teachers College, Columbia University, 1942).

6 State of New Jersey Governor's Select Commission of Civil Disorder, *Report for Action: An Investigation into the Causes and Events of the 1967 Newark Race Riots, February, 1968* (New York: Lemma Publishing Corporation, 1972), pp. 170–71.

7 *Report to the Acting Executive Superintendent, Newark School District*, from the State of New Jersey Department of Education and the Commissioner of Education, Trenton, August 13, 1984.

8 According to New Jersey Department of Education data, in 1992–1993, 51 percent of the certificated full-time teachers in the city were black, and 8.5 percent were Hispanic (*New Jersey Department of Education, 1992–93 Certificated Full-Time Staff Report by District, Position and Race* [Trenton: Department of Education, 1994]), p. 1374. According to an informant in the Bureau of Research at the city's Board of Education, the percentage of African-American teachers cited in the state statistics is low. According to this informant, the percent of African-American teachers in the city is much higher, due to the relatively high number of teachers in the district who are not certified, and who are part-time (long- or short-term substitutes). Almost all part-time teachers in the district are African-American.

Although statistics could not be obtained from the district, observation reveals that in schools (such as the research site) where black children are the majority, there are more black teachers than at district schools where the majority of the children are Italian or Portuguese. As noted below, 64 percent of the classroom teachers at the site were African-American.

According to state figures, in 1992–1993, 43.3 and 7.7 percent of district administrators were black and Hispanic, respectively. Fifty percent and 5.8 percent of special-services personnel in the schools were black and Hispanic, respectively (p. 1374).

9 Sabrina Hope King, "The Limited Presence of African-American Teachers," *Review of Educational Research* 63 (1993): 115–50.

10 Albert Memmi, *The Colonizer and the Colonized* (Boston: Beacon Press, 1965 and 1991); idem, *Dominated Man* (Boston: Beacon Press, 1968); Frantz Fanon, *Black Skin, White Masks* (New York: Grove, 1967); Paulo Freire, *Pedagogy of the Oppressed* (New York: Herder and Herder, 1970); and Edward Said, *Orientalism* (New York: Pantheon, 1978).

11 I participated in the reform during 1991–1993 primarily as staff developer. I carried out workshops in cooperative learning in several of the eight target schools and subsequently assisted teachers in their classrooms. I carried out the workshops at Marcy School between January 1992 and February 1993, and worked at least one full day a

week during the ten school months in teachers' classrooms, providing coaching in the new methods (see Jean Anyon, "Teacher Development and Reform in an Inner-City School," *Teachers College Record* 96 [1994]: 14–31, for further description of one portion of this work).

In addition to the more than 200 hours spent with teachers in their classrooms, I also attended reform team meetings during school years 1991–1992 and 1992–1993, and spent numerous hours talking with teachers at these meetings. In my year at Marcy School I spent approximately half (21) of the lunch periods "hanging out" with the students in the cafeteria and on the asphalt yard; I also chatted with them frequently in classrooms and halls. I became well acquainted with the assistant superintendent responsible for the reform, commuted on the train with her on numerous occasions, and often discussed the reform efforts with her, and with members of her staff. Between 1991 and 1993 I formally interviewed the assistant superintendent, her staff, twenty-four of the twenty-five classroom teachers at Marcy School, the members of Marcy School's school-based support team, both Marcy School administrators, the school's drug counselor, fifteen parents, and twenty-five students. I read numerous school and district reports and other documents (such as state reports) pertaining to the schools and the reform initiative. I examined all curriculum materials—those in use and those prepared by the district but not much used.

12 Mun Wong et al., "Under Seige: Children's Perception of Stress" (Paper presented at the annual meeting of the American Psychological Association, Washington, D.C., August 1992).

13 "For Idle Young in Newark, Pride in a Theft Done Right," *New York Times*, August 11, 1992, p. A1.

14 The analysis of adults in the school reported in this article is based on my observations and interactions with African-American and white employees, and statements about teachers are confined to members of these groups. As far as I could tell, the relatively few Hispanic employees (six classroom teachers, several aides, and the vice-principal) did not differ in substantive ways from their white and black colleagues. However, with the exception of one teacher and the vice-principal, the Hispanic staff were (unofficially) isolated from the rest of the school in a bilingual program, and the time I spent with them was limited.

15 See David D. Laitin, *Hegemony and Culture* (Chicago: University of Chicago Press, 1986); and Russell Hardin, *Collective Action* (Baltimore: Johns Hopkins University Press, 1982).

16 See Jean Anyon, "Inner City School Reform: Toward Useful Theory," *Urban Education* (in press), for further description of the Professional Development Project. See also idem, "The Retreat of Marxism and Socialist Feminism: Postmodern and Poststructural Theories in Education," *Curriculum Inquiry* 24 (1994): 115–34, for a discussion of the theoretical import of this and other reforms.

17 New Jersey Department of Education, *Newark Public Schools, Level III Exterial Review* (Trenton: Author, April 16, 1993: Education Programs, pp. 13, 15.

18 Examples of black dialect (gathered in classrooms of Marcy School) follow. (See also Geneva Smitherman, *Black Language and Culture: Sounds of Soul* [New York, Harper & Row, 1975].)

STUDENTS: "They lookin at us paper." [at our paper]
            "He ain't ax you." [didn't ask you].
            "I'm is the girl you want." [I am]
            "When my sister take my baby sister toys she be in school."

19 Joan C. Baratz, "Beginning Readers for Speakers of Divergent Dialects," in *Reading Goals for the Disadvantaged*, ed. J. Allen Figurel (Newark, Del.: International Reading Association, 1970), pp. 77–83.

20 Ibid.; Morton Wiener and Ward Cromer, "Reading and Reading Difficulty: A Conceptual Analysis," *Harvard Educational Review* 37 (1967): 620–43; William Labov, "Some Sources of Reading Problems for Negro Speakers of Non-standard English," in *Teaching Black Children to Read*, ed. Joan Baratz and Roger Shuy (Washington, D.C.: Center for Applied Linguistics, 1969); Joan Baratz, "Teaching Reading in an Urban Negro School System," in *Teaching Black Children*, pp. 92–116; and Bernice E.

Cullinan, *Black Dialects and Reading* (Urbana, Ill.: National Council for Teachers of English, 1974).

21 See Cullinan, *Black Dialects and Reading*, Figurel, *Reading Goals for the Disadvantaged*; and Baratz, "Beginning Readers." For studies of children speaking other nonstandard dialects (Native American, Appalachian, Hawaiian), see, among others, Barbara Z. Kiefer and Johanna S. DeStefano, "Cultures Together in the Classroom: 'What You Saying"? in *Observing the Language Learner*, ed. Angela Jaggar and M. Trika Smith-Burke (Urbana, Ill.: National Council of Teachers of English, 1985).

22 Eleanor Wilson Orr, *Twice as Less: Black English and the Performance of Black Students in Mathematics and Science* (New York: W. W. Norton, 1987).

23 Ibid., p. 171.

24 I estimate that most of the African-American teachers at Marcy use dialect with their students at least some of the time (mixing it with standard English). I estimate that approximately one-third use dialect all the time with their students. Examples follow:

TEACHERS: "What does a sentence begins with?"
"When I be out they has a good time!"
"You didn't do nothin' yet."
"You wrong!"
"Take care your crayons—we can't get no more."
"Have anyone seen Shawana?"

I estimate that approximately the same fraction, one-third, of the principals I talked with at reform team meetings also consistently spoke black dialect. According to the assistant superintendent, these men speak dialect "most of the time."

PRINCIPALS: "He have a parent who . . ."
"Many people have came here."
"He don't never come to school."

25 Newark Board of Education, *Restructuring Urban Schools in Newark, NJ: An Evaluation of the Cluster Program*, Newark, N.J.: Author, 1992.

26 Janice E. Hale-Benson, *Black Children: Their Roots, Culture, and Learning Styles*, rev. ed. (Baltimore, Md.: Johns Hopkins University Press, 1986).

27 New Jersey Department of Education, *Newark Public Schools*, Education Programs, p. 68. The phrase "institutional abuse" as used by the New Jersey Department of Education refers to emotional, physical, or sexual abuse of students by public school employees.
A conversation I had early in my work at Marcy School is of interest here. During one of my first few weeks in the building, the child study team (psychologist, social worker, learning disabilities specialist) invited me to lunch. They seemed eager to tell me about the school. The following is from my field notes:

We are discussing the enormous problem the team sees "getting anything done" at Marcy School. "We're part of the problem, you know," the psychologist says, "I mean, jailors and prisoners are the same." The social worker adds, "This district has enormous problems—the mayhem of the system itself is a big problem. But the children's lives are the biggest problem." "Yes," agrees the psychologist, "We should be teaching them [the students] who they are in the system, and what the system does to them. We need a diagnosis like they have in Europe—of economic and social victimization—that's what these kids are—victims."

"What about the teachers," I ask. "What are they like?" The psychologist states, "There is a lot of teacher abuse of the students—it's common here. The children have desperate lives, and the teachers distance themselves from that by abusing them, by separating themselves from the children, even though they're [the teachers are] black, too. But you know, most of these teachers are one paycheck away from welfare themselves."

"And you," I ask, "how do you deal with the children and the system?" They say they blame the system. "Contradictory initiatives on the part of the board; disarray at the board," says the learning disabilities specialist. And he blamed the state. "The state is weak; it has no money to monitor the system, and couldn't afford to take over [the city's schools]." "Even your project," says the psychologist, referring to my work teaching the teachers to use cooperative learning. "We've seen it all before. We did cooperative learning in the early 1970's—the open classroom, curriculum integration, there's nothing new being done now, it's all been tried before." "Yes," I say. "But maybe this is how *we* distance ourselves from the problems. We say, "there's nothing we can do, it's all been tried before.' " "Maybe," said the psychologist.

28 Ray McDermott, "Achieving School Failure: An Anthropological Approach to Literacy and Social Stratification," in *Education and Cultural Process: Anthropological Approaches*, 2nd ed., ed. George Spindler (Prospect Heights, Ill.: Waveland, 1987), pp. 82–118.

29 Ernest A. Haggard, "Social Status and Intelligence: An Experimental Study of Certain Cultural Determinants of Measured Intelligence," *Genetic Psychology Monographs* 49 (1954): 141–86. See also, among others, Courtney Cazden, "The Neglected Situation in Child Language Research and Education," in *Language and Poverty: Perspectives on a Theme*, ed. Frederick Williams (Chicago: Markham, 1970); and Geneva Smitherman, *Talking and Testifying: The Language of Black America* (Boston: Houghton-Mifflin, 1977).

30 See also Herbert Kohl, *"I Won't Learn from You": The Role of Assent in Learning* (Minneapolis: Milkweed Editions, 1991).

31 "In Newark, a Prologue to a Performing Arts Center," *New York Times*, January 1, 1995, p. A9.

32 Orfield and Ashkinaze, *The Closing Door*; Norman Fainstein and Susan Fainstein, *Urban Policy under Capitalism* (Beverly Hills: Sage, 1982); and Dennis R. Judd and Todd Swanstrom, *City Politics: Private Power and Public Policy* (New York: Harper Collins, 1994).

33 Orfield and Ashkinaze, *The Closing Door*; and Kozol, *Savage Inequalities*.

34 Mathew Reilly, "Report Says Jersey City Schools Need Two More Years under State Control," *The Star Ledger*, June 21, 1994, p. 19. See also Kimberly J. McLarin, "Education Board Extends Takeover of Jersey City Schools," *New York Times*, September 8, 1994, p. B6; and idem, "Schools in Paterson Lagging on Standards, Report Says," *New York Times*, November 4, 1994, p. B6.

35 Robert J. Braun, "Top School Officials Fired in Jersey City," *The Star Ledger*, July 6, 1994, p. 1; and idem, "Klagholz Details 'Loose' Fiscal Policies Found in Jersey City Audit," *The Star Ledger*, July 7, 1994, p. 16.

36 An assessment detailing the fact that the city's student achievement scores were well below national levels in the late 1970s stated, "In both reading and mathematics Newark has attempted to improve pupil performance during the past ten years by resort to a staggering variety of new programs. Indeed, one of the consistent criticisms voiced is that too many programs have been tried with too little effective evaluation of them" (Paul Trachtenberg. "Pupil Performance in Basic Skills in the Newark School System since 1967," in *1967–1977: An Assessment*, ed. Stanley B. Winters (Newark, N.J.: New Jersey Institute of Technology, 1978), pp. 235–43.

37 Orfield and Ashkinaze, *The Closing Door*; idem, "Public Policy Research"; and Andrew Hacker, *Two Nations: Black and White, Separate, Hostile, Unequal* (New York: Charles Scribner's Sons, 1992).

38 James Baldwin, *The Fire Next Time* (London: Michael Joseph, 1963 [Reprinted: Random House, 1992]), pp. 119–20.

CHAPTER 20

BLEEDING BOUNDARIES OR UNCERTAIN CENTER? (1999)

A historical exploration of multicultural education

Marilynne Boyle-Baise

> It takes some time for a field to reach a degree of maturity where it can be self-reflective or self-monitoring. And keep in mind that multicultural education is a very young field . . . I think that the field is approaching the point where someone needs to do . . . a reflective analysis of where the field is. Because I think that there are some messages or some movement that are kind of in between the lines, sort of underneath the message, that haven't been addressed because so many of us are so busy trying to persuade folks that this is a legitimate endeavor.
>
> —Geneva Gay, 10/8/96

Recently symposium participants at the annual meeting of the American Educational Research Association (AERA) debated the boundaries of multicultural education.[1] One participant, James Sears, speaking on behalf of gay and lesbian concerns, noted that if the boundaries of multicultural education narrowed to focus on ethnic minority concerns, he believed it unlikely that his views would be heard in the future. Geneva Gay, another participant, argued that without firm boundaries, multicultural education suffered as a discipline of study. She urged reconsideration of the field's roots in ethnic minority studies. A third participant, Carl Grant, encouraged coalition among the field's diverse constituents. To Grant, grappling with ways to work together was the utmost challenge for multicultural education.

I could not help but hear echoes of this conversation that reached back to the early days of the field. Multicultural education is a young domain of studies, only about 25 years old. As with most new areas of study, multicultural education is emerging and struggling with its identity.

This article explores historical trends in multicultural education that relate to its definition as a field of study. Primary sources of information were interviews with scholars who were central to founding the field. I asked these scholars to recommend research that each considered consequential to multicultural education, and I read that body of work. From these sources, I constructed an early portrait of the field. The first section of the article traces the genesis of multicultural education, based largely on memories of founding scholars. In the second part, I interpret their remarks in relation to disciplinary parameters for the field. I was especially concerned with the following questions: What concerns mark conversations about boundaries? Does a common core to this multifaceted domain of study exist? Should issues of race and racism stand as central to the field? Should interactive studies of race, social class, gender, disability, and sexuality shape multicultural education? Should issues of sexual orientation be included in the field, and, if so, in what manner? These issues merged into the following guiding questions:

- What conceptual arguments characterize multicultural education discourse?
- What is the common core for multicultural education?
- What are the boundaries for multicultural education?

Methodology

This study used methods associated with interpretive case studies to collect and analyze data.[2] Eight scholars, most of whom are generally considered the first generation of scholars within the field of multicultural education, constituted the case studied. I interviewed them, mainly by telephone, using a standard, open-ended interview with a liberal use of probing. As part of each interview, scholars identified benchmark literature for the field (see Appendix A). Information from this literature buttressed interview data.

This case study used oral history procedures. Interview questions tended to generate rich, detailed responses based on personal recollections that spanned 25 years, although respondents certainly did not reveal all that they knew about multicultural education.

Centered around personal recollections, the collective account glossed over some of the historical context that influenced the emergence of multicultural education. For example, the post-World War II Intergroup Education Movement, which preceded the rise of multicultural education and engendered commitment to interracial understanding, was discussed minimally.[3] Although this movement pioneered studies of prejudice and racial attitudes and contributed curriculums that fostered positive intergroup relations, its legacy remains mixed. As a tolerance-oriented approach to cultural diversity, its orientation skirted concerns about power and equality that are central to contemporary multicultural education. Additionally, this study paid scant attention to the impact of the Ethnic Heritage Studies Program of 1972. This program responded to interest in ethnicity generated by the civil rights movement.[4] It supported a multiethnic approach to curriculum that benefited multicultural education. However, its aims to be broadly inclusive tended to dilute ethnic studies to uncritical celebrations of ethnic roots. Heritage studies were a mixed blessing: they promoted ethnic study, but they avoided issues of racism and ethnocentrism significant to struggles for educational equality.

Respondents

The selection of scholar-respondents was based on "connoisseurship" born of long association with the field.[5] The selected scholars were among the first to study and advance multicultural education and are known widely for their seminal contributions to the field. These scholars also contributed to the selection process. Each encouraged me to talk with different individuals in order to reveal more fulsome sources of the story. Finally, seven scholars were identified: James Banks, Christine Bennett, Carlos Cortes, Geneva Gay, Donna Gollnick, Carl Grant, and Wilma Longstreet. Additionally, Christine Sleeter, who worked in partnership with Carl Grant and who has become a major voice in the field, agreed to participate. Although most of these scholars are well known, their standpoints within multicultural education discourse are less apparent. To make their positions more visible, I wrote profiles of each scholar, drawing information from their remarks during interviews. Respondents reviewed and in many cases modified what I wrote. As a result, the following profiles are not parallel.

James Banks taught 5th grade before pursuing doctoral work at Michigan State University, where he specialized in social studies education, sociology, and anthropology. He wrote the first major textbook about ethnic studies for teachers, *Teaching Strategies for Ethnic Studies*.[6] Banks developed several major theoretical frameworks for the field, including "approaches to multicultural curriculum reform" and "dimensions of multicultural education."[7] Additionally, he did historical research about the field. Currently Banks acknowledges inter-relationships among race, social class, and gender, but he writes primarily about race, ethnicity, and culture.

Christine Bennett pursued studies in sociology and social studies education as an undergraduate and master's degree student. While teaching in California, she became aware of the dearth of information about African American students. She took courses in African and African American history and wrote curricular materials that incorporated these perspectives. Bennett pursued her interests in racism, culture, and curriculum in her doctoral studies at The University of Texas at Austin. There she began to work with Geneva Gay, a classmate. She developed a multifaceted model for multicultural education that included understanding multiple historical perspectives, developing cultural consciousness and competence, combating racism, and taking social action.[8] Currently, Bennett continues to focus on ways multicultural education can assist teachers in understanding their students.

Carlos Cortes is a historian drawn to education from the field of Chicano studies. Cortes brought understandings about ethnicity developed outside of education to his work in multicultural education. He studied the impact of "societal curriculum"—socializing forces such as families, churches, and mass media—on multicultural understandings. Cortes met James Banks when both served on a textbook reform committee in California in the early 1970s. The discussions of this committee helped Cortes to connect Chicano studies to other ethnic movements. Shortly thereafter he developed a framework for history that challenged normative, Eurocentric views and included multiethnic perspectives.[9] Currently Cortes considers race and ethnicity as central to multicultural education.

Geneva Gay was a secondary teacher in Ohio before pursuing doctoral studies in curriculum and social studies education at The University of Texas at Austin. Immediately following graduate school, she became a staff member of the Association for Supervision and Curriculum Development (ASCD). Among her responsibilities was the organization of institutes focused on ethnic and multi-ethnic studies. These institutes became meeting places for many early scholars. Gay furthered discussions of multicultural education as curriculum reform.[10] She focused her work on educational equality for ethnic minority students and resisted the expansion of the field to include gender and disability.[11] At present, she is concerned that multicultural education suffers as a discipline from ever-expanding boundaries.

Donna Gollnick has worked at the national level to promote multicultural education since the mid-1970s. As a staff member of the American Association of Colleges for Teacher Education (AACTE) and, later, the National Council for

Accreditation of Teacher Education (NCATE), she promoted the integration of multicultural education into standards for teacher education programs. Gollnick thought of multicultural education as a broad-based battle against discrimination. Her work with Phillip Chinn, whose background was in special education, expanded her concern for multiple forms of diversity. Their text was one of the first to include disability issues within multicultural education.[12] Currently, Gollnick is interested in the impact of multiple-group membership on personal identity.

Carl Grant was a teacher and administrator in Chicago before pursuing doctoral studies in the areas of educational studies and black studies at the University of Wisconsin. Early in his career, he focused on community participation in education. In the 1970s Grant directed a national Teacher Corps Associates Program that prepared a broad range of people for community leadership. He perceived his efforts as being within multicultural education rather than ethnic or multiethnic studies. Early on he included race, social class, gender, and ageism within multicultural education.[13] His work with Christine Sleeter, a former teacher of students with learning disabilities, deepened his understanding of multiplicity. At present, Grant seeks to find common ground among the diverse groups that embrace multicultural education.

Wilma Longstreet came from a multiethnic, urban background. Arriving at Indiana University for her doctoral studies in curriculum and social studies education, she realized that she differed from other students, many of whom held small-town, Midwestern norms. Longstreet sought to understand this difference within the framework of ethnicity. As she worked with high school students in Gary, Indiana, her interest in ethnicity increased. Longstreet studied a broad range of students to discover aspects of ethnicity.[14] Also, she developed a framework to conduct action research about ethnicity. To Longstreet, the inclusive nature of multicultural education retarded the scholarly study of race and ethnicity. Currently Longstreet is working to develop a theory of ethnicity for education.

Christine Sleeter entered the field after teaching urban high school youth with learning disabilities. She wondered about interrelationships between discrimination based on race and disability. As a doctoral student at the University of Wisconsin, she studied social class oppression and interacted with women who advocated for gender equality. Sleeter began to view multiple forms of difference as interlocking systems of oppression. In the mid-1980s, she and Carl Grant assessed multicultural education and perceived a need to reorient the field toward social reconstruction. They argued that the entire educational process should reflect concerns of diverse cultural groups, emphasize critique of inequality, and prepare students as social activists.[15] At present, Sleeter is concerned that multicultural education be understood as a social movement.

Data collection

During the summer of 1996 I developed a general time line for the field from historical overviews written by Banks and Gollnick.[16] I used this time line to formulate interview questions that would reveal the field's conceptual development. During the late summer and fall, I interviewed the target group of scholar-respondents. Interviews lasted from 30 minutes to an hour. I asked respondents the following five questions:

1   What factors influenced the movement of the field from multiethnic to

multicultural studies? What do you think was gained and lost by this movement?

2   As the boundaries expanded to include studies of gender, disability, and sexual orientation, what do you think happened to studies of race and ethnicity?

3   In your opinion, what understandings or tensions resulted from including multiple forms of difference under the multicultural tent?

4   In your opinion, has the emphasis on oppression as an aspect of the field changed over time?

5   In your opinion, what does the emphasis on multicultural education as social reconstruction or critical multicultural education mean for the development of the field?

In recognition of their contributions to shifts in the field, I asked Donna Gollnick to explain her inclusion of disability, and I asked Carl Grant and Christine Sleeter to share their thinking about multicultural education as social reconstruction.

Almost all of the respondents noted that my first question should have been preceded by another. That prior question should have inquired about the impact of ethnic studies on multicultural education. Several scholars began their commentary with recollections about ethnic studies related to the civil rights movement. They also nominated what they considered to be benchmark literature in the field. Many nominated publications that, in their opinions, changed the direction of discourse in the field (see Appendix A).

Data analysis

The interviews were audiotape-recorded and transcribed. I collated the responses by interview question, read and reread the data, and searched for themes and trends. I used constant comparison analysis to search for diversity within responses.[17] Then I read the benchmark literature suggested by the respondents, reviewing it for trends and discrepant claims. I considered this literature as written documentation of the interview data. I recalled my own early involvement in the field as a reality check on emerging concerns. When the data were unclear, I telephoned respondents for further clarification.

A modified Delphi technique helped refine my interpretations.[18] Respondents reviewed an early draft of the paper. They assessed my identification of critical trends and reconsidered their interview responses. In this way, I constructed this conceptual history of the field.

Conceptual history

According to Banks, early African American scholarship about ethnicity provided an important foundation for multicultural education.[19] He considered first-generation scholars—Grant, Gay, and himself among them—as strongly influenced by this scholarship. For example, both Banks's and Grant's dissertations centered on black studies topics. Gay published research on African American culture and identity.[20] Further, Grant served as professor in Afro-American Studies at the University of Wisconsin-Madison. Banks argued that Carter G. Woodson and W. E. B. Dubois served as early models for researching black history and culture and improving education for African Americans.

Banks also acknowledged the legacy of the Intergroup Education Movement on multicultural education.[21] However, he claimed important differences between early ethnic and intergroup studies. Early ethnic studies emphasized empowerment, whereas intergroup studies emphasized cooperation within the American mainstream. Sleeter and Grant considered the influence of the Intergroup Education Movement slightly differently.[22] They identified this movement as the antecedent of human relations, an approach to multicultural education focused on interracial tolerance.

The civil rights movement provided the direct social impetus for multicultural education. It revived interest in studies of ethnic minority groups that aimed toward radical social change.[23] At the college level, the institution of black studies soon was followed by Chicano, Asian American, and Native American studies.[24] Later, the idea of single-group studies extended to women's studies, disability studies, and gay and lesbian studies. Although these studies differed by group, they commonly challenged the neutrality of knowledge and the centrality of white men in curriculum, and sought to develop a sense of group pride and to teach about discrimination against minority groups.

A quest for ethnic content

The first generation of scholars in multicultural education came to the field from ethnic studies. James Banks recalled this time as a "quest for ethnic content" (8/28/96), part of a biographical journey that included a search for self in curriculum content. According to Banks, "We simply wanted blacks in the school curriculum" (8/28/96). Banks, Gay, and Grant also were interested in strengthening educational access and achievement for children of color. "We really started out as kind of a children's civil rights movement" (J. Banks, 8/28/96). Grant, however, held a broader view:

> I believe I have always ... looked upon the field as multicultural ... The reason is that, to me, it has always been larger than black and white issues. We needed to include other groups like women and those who are disabled ... (8/30/96)

To Grant, multicultural education went beyond cultural studies to affirm the intrinsic worth of all people. Grant believed that "all people must be accorded respect regardless of their racial, social, ethnic, cultural, or religious backgrounds; age; sex; or physical differences."[25] To endorse this fundamental belief, schools should "affirm the racial and cultural diversity and individual differences" of all children.[26]

Many early scholars moved in an evolutionary fashion from ethnic to multiethnic to multicultural studies. Some, like Geneva Gay, barely paused at ethnic studies on the way to a more comparative multiethnic view. Others, like Carlos Cortes, questioned the extent to which multiethnic studies were conceptualized as something more than a collection of ethnic studies. Carl Grant and others, on the other hand, moved directly to the development of multicultural education. Cortes's recollections exemplify an evolutionary development.

In 1971 Cortes participated on a textbook evaluation task force for California. There he met James Banks and was introduced to the curricular viewpoints of other ethnic groups.

> Every person there was coming at it from the particular point of view of their group. I began to realize that I simply couldn't look at this thing to improve my group's place in the curriculum, but had to take in consideration how other groups were perceiving things. I began to make the shift from . . . ethnic studies to multiethnic, without ethnic studies disappearing because they are still in existence. (9/3/96)

Subsequently, Banks invited scholars from the task force to write chapters for a teachers guide to ethnic studies. In the introduction to *Teaching Ethnic Studies*, Banks described ethnic studies as a commitment to bringing about social justice.[27] He called upon teachers to act as change agents in schools.

> This is a hard-hitting book written by a group of fighters who have an unrelenting commitment to social justice. . . . They believe that change is possible and that what teachers do in classrooms, or don't do, can make a difference . . . [the book] is bound to help every teacher who reads it sense the urgency of the racial crisis in our nation, and to develop a commitment to act to resolve it.[28]

In the book, ethnicity was considered the primary determinant of social stratification.[29] The book took a group-by-group approach, in which racism and social oppression were significant factors.[30] Attention to women within these ethnic studies was fairly minimal. Women stood alone, included as a separate chapter.[31] At this point, interrelationships among groups appeared to be a peripheral consideration.

Movement from multiethnic to multicultural education

After the publication of *Teaching Ethnic Studies*, Cortes accepted an invitation to speak about curriculum reform from a multiethnic perspective. As he remembered it, this occasion was the first time that he heard the term "multiethnic." He used the occasion to develop his own understanding of the concept and to find ways to compare ethnic group experiences. "The idea of looking at multiple perspectives is now accepted, but at that point it was . . . a new way of doing things" (9/3/96).

Cortes used the idea of multiple perspectives to view history through a comparative lens. He developed a new frame of reference that criticized the east-west, Eurocentric focus for U.S. history. In an article in *Educational Leadership*, Cortes argued that U.S. history developed from northwesterly slave trade, south-to-north colonization, and east-to-west immigration.[32] The article provided a novel way to view history from the perspectives of different ethnic groups.

As scholars made comparisons across ethnic groups, the rise of women's studies motivated the examination of intragroup diversity. According to Cortes, "You had cross-cutting factors of gender, class, religion . . . you simply couldn't look at any particular group as a model . . . you had to look at some of these cross-cutting dimensions" (9/3/96). Reference to cultural dynamics as ethnic was insufficient. "People just started using the word 'multicultural' rather than 'multiethnic.' I don't think 'multiethnic' was ever used that long" (9/3/96).

In 1976 Banks chaired the Task Force on Ethnic Studies Curriculum Guidelines for the National Council for the Social Studies.[33] Gay and Cortes also served as members of this project. The task force used the term "multiethnic" rather than "multicultural" education in order to focus its concerns on race and ethnicity.[34]

Its ideal multiethnic school acknowledged ethnicity as a vital factor in all students' lives, stressed community involvement and project work, and envisioned a multiethnic faculty.[35]

Carl Grant disagreed about the importance of several terms. He remembered that the term "ethnicity" appealed to publishers, and its usage likely expedited the publication of research. Sometimes the term "ethnicity" was used in titles of articles that were actually about multicultural education. Additionally, "ethnic studies," "multiethnic studies," and "multicultural education" were used interchangeably. As an example, Grant, Sleeter, and Boyle's monograph, *The Public School and the Challenge of Ethnic Pluralism*, discussed multicultural education but offered meager treatment of ethnic pluralism.[36]

In the late 1970s, Christine Bennett developed a model for comprehensive multicultural education. She sought to help preservice teachers connect with all their students.

> Most of them [the teachers] were white . . . teaching in predominately African American and Latino schools. . . . I was concerned with helping them transform the curriculum and understand the world views and cultural backgrounds of their students. (9/3/96)

Bennett conducted an extensive literature search for information about race relations, multicultural education, and ethnic studies. She discovered that most research dealt with ethnic perspectives of history. She concluded that some of this literature confronted racism, but most of it did not. A small body of literature focused on cultural styles and institutional racism. Bennett linked the ideas gleaned from this research to her doctoral studies on political efficacy in action.[37] She generated a comprehensive view of multicultural education that included four dimensions: movement toward educational equity, curricular reform, becoming an intercultural person, and combating prejudice and discrimination.

The concept of cultural pluralism added another dimension to multicultural education. Bennett recalled two conferences in the mid-1970s, organized by the Anti-Defamation League and the National Council for the Social Studies, that focused on cultural pluralism. Scholars discussed "potential drawbacks of it . . . how people can have a sense of their cultural identity and still be open to others" (9/3/96). These discussions helped Bennett to relate her ideas about culture to issues of power:

> Even with the concept of culture as worldviews of different groups, the understanding was still missing that social structures of our society were racist. It seemed like nothing was adequate; it needed to be pulled together. (9/3/96)

In 1978 Carl Grant furthered discussion about the nature of multicultural education. He argued against the term "multicultural education" and in favor of the phrase "an education that is multicultural."[38] To Grant, the first term modified education, whereas the second phrase suggested the entire transformation of schooling. Like Banks, Grant defined an education that is multicultural as all-encompassing. Faculty, curriculum, language, and instructional materials should reflect regard for cultural diversity. Regardless of the term used, by the late 1970s multicultural education was perceived as pluralistic, comprehensive, and transformative.

The move to greater inclusion

During the late 1970s and early 1980s, the thrust of civil rights advocacy expanded to include rights for women and people with disabling conditions. Following a path similar to that of early scholars, advocates for gender and disability rights challenged biased school policies, procedures, and curriculum content. Although gender and disability issues were distinct from racial and ethnic concerns, the confrontations with discriminatory school practices were similar. To support struggles against inequality, yet avoid the complications of multiple, separate group agendas, national associations, such as NCATE, addressed race, gender, and disability under the mantle of multicultural education (D. Gollnick, personal communication, 8/5/97).

For some scholars, such as Christine Sleeter, the expanded discussion of educational rights motivated theoretical connections across race, gender, social class, and disability. As a teacher of youth with disabilities, she questioned these connections. Then, in graduate school,

> sitting in Mike Apple's classes, grappling with social class, then talking with other women students, grappling with issues of gender . . . I started looking at connections between race, class, and gender . . . eventually, I saw connections with disability. Not as multiple forms of difference, but as interlocking systems of oppression. (9/26/96)

Carl Grant and Donna Gollnick made similar linkages. To them, distinctive demands of ethnic minority groups, women, and those with disabilities blurred and blended in efforts to bring about equality, and equity, in education. Gollnick recalled this stance:

> We don't make many gains if we take care of one group and then let inequality remain against other groups. As you study race or gender you also study discrimination and inequality related to all of the other groups. . . . I think it's worth the battle to fight discrimination broadly rather than for one group. (9/16/96)

The coalition of distinct social and cultural groups around themes of injustice emphasized similar educational and political needs. Yet, inclusion was justified by the definition of ethnic, gender, and disability groups as microcultural groups.[39] Carl Grant realized this view might be questioned: "The cultural aspects are contested. A number of people ask, 'Are women or gay men and lesbians a cultural group?' " However, his primary concern was that "all of these groups need to be accepted. Issues of social justice need to be taken into consideration through schooling as we think about all of these groups" (8/30/96).

For some of these early scholars, the emphasis on social justice came at the expense of cultural understandings. Bennett considered Gollnick and Chinn's text[40] an "erroneous conception of culture" (9/9/96). Gay and Longstreet took the same position. According to Bennett, "When you talk about gender, disabilities, and age, these are attributes that transgress cultures . . . it's not the same thing as having a pervasive worldview" (9/6/96). To these scholars, perceptions of gender and disability were influenced by ethnic attitudes, values, and worldviews.[41] To consider gender or disability as a cultural group took the field off track. It blurred reasons for inclusion in or exclusion from multicultural education.

Gay argued that the experiences of women, those with disabilities, the aged, and the poor

> . . . are legitimate areas of study, and they are clearly intertwined with ethnicity, but including them under the rubric of multiethnic or multicultural education may tend to divert attention away from ethnicity.[42]

Gay suggested that inclusiveness might make the field acceptable to a wider audience, but multicultural education could become a "synonym for pluralism in its broadest sense."[43] Gay encouraged the field to "reaffirm its original intentions and to insist on reasonable demarcations of its conceptual boundaries."[44]

Bennett agreed with Gay. Particularly, she worried about the linkage of disability and cultural diversity. Bennett feared that multicultural education might be perceived as remedial education and reference to children of color as disadvantaged might be strengthened. On the other hand, Bennett, like Grant, considered support for human dignity a core value for multicultural education. This value disallowed a neutral stance toward the devaluation of human beings. According to Bennett, "Sympathy to the intrinsic worth of all people was more appropriate [as an inclusive criteria] for multicultural education than justifying each form of diversity as a cultural group" (9/9/96).

Cortes did not consider culture to be of much help to the delimitation of the field. To him, culture was "protean" (in reference to the Greek god Proteus):

> It is formless and can take on new boundaries, and, therefore, it allows the field to move and expand. The name "multicultural education" is protean enough to allow us the flexibility to move ahead. (9/3/96)

Cortes cautioned that an expanding field should continually reevaluate and reassert its common core.

Politics of the 1980s

At the outset of the 1980s, the United States moved into a conservative period. Educational interest in ethnicity shifted to concerns about accountability. Geneva Gay gauged the winds of the times and considered ways to achieve the aims of the field in an unreceptive atmosphere.[45] To Gay, multiethnic education as a separate entity was no longer feasible. A more "pedagogically plausible and politically expedient strategy is to demonstrate, conceptually and programmatically, that multiethnic education can improve the overall quality of general education."[46] She proposed the infusion of multiethnic education into general education. Gay realized that infusion might confuse a field still focused on conceptual clarification but considered this strategy necessary for its survival.

Simultaneously, in federal policies, race, national origin, and gender issues were merged into one "delivery group" (D. Gollnick, 9/16/96). Also, NCATE issued standards for teacher accreditation that specified preparation to confront racism and sexism as part of multicultural education. By the mid 1980s, the standards included competency with students with disabilities as part of multicultural teacher preparation. Social and economic forces operated to define disparate groups as a collective.

What was gained and lost by this conceptual and political jockeying? To some of these scholars, expansion of the field diverted attention from racism and eroded the original intentions of the field. In their view, trying to mean everything to everybody put the field in danger of meaning nothing to anybody. From an alternative viewpoint, expansion enhanced the field by providing multiple lenses through which to understand culture and power. Additionally, the political prowess of the field was strengthened through coalition among marginalized groups.

Searching for conceptual clarity

By the latter 1980s, multicultural education meant different things to different people. In search of conceptual clarity, Sleeter and Grant reviewed the literature about multicultural education.[47] They found five approaches operative within the field. They examined each approach and suggested limitations and strengths of each. They did not endorse any approach or try to delineate the common core for multicultural education. Rather, they settled for a vague common foundation: "the only common meaning is that it refers to changes in education that are supposed to benefit people of color."[48] While illuminating the range of practices called multicultural education, the authors trod lightly on core understandings for the field.

Subsequently, Sleeter and Grant took a stronger stance.[49] In *Making Choices for Multicultural Education*, they supported an approach called "education that is multicultural and social reconstructionist." This approach emphasized educational responsiveness to social/structural inequality. Sleeter recalled the rationale for this move in the following way:

> I view multicultural education . . . as having gotten its start in challenges to racial oppression. Saying the word "oppression" isn't comfortable in this country. As a result, a lot of discussions about multicultural education get couched in more comfortable terms. . . . So for me, multicultural education as social reconstruction tries to keep people focused on what the big issues are and the hard issues of oppression. (9/29/96)

Recently, Sleeter and others in the field joined critical theorists in calling for "critical multiculturalism," which focuses on the dynamics of oppression in contrast to "mainstream multiculturalism," which sidesteps such issues.[50] According to Sleeter, this critique was not directed at longtime multicultural education theorists, like the first-generation scholars in this study, who tended to situate racism at the heart of the field. Rather, people "using 'comfy' ideas to talk about multicultural education are some of the newer people in the field, probably largely white" (C. E. Sleeter, personal communication, 5/97).

Not surprisingly, Banks, Gay, Cortes, and Bennett considered critical multiculturalism unnecessary. To Gay, "by nature cultural education is a critical field. As far as I am concerned, it is redundant to talk about critical multiculturalism and social reform. That's endemic to the movement" (10/8/96). For Banks, social reconstruction was not new to multicultural education:

> Reconstruction goes back to Carter G. Woodson. Clearly that was not a new focus at all. . . . One tension that I have about critical multiculturalism is it is . . . a kind of appropriation of what we've had there without them knowing it . . . (8/28/96)

For these scholars, concern with critique and activism permeated the field and reached back to its earliest days.

Carlos Cortes expressed a different concern with critical multiculturalism. He perceived oppression as a theme in cultural studies that should neither be lost nor become the whole story:

> I don't think the study of race, ethnicity, gender, etc., are equal to the study of oppression. Oppression is an element within those stories. To make it the equivalent ... is to miss a point. ... You are saying that experience is monodimensional, being oppressed. (9/3/96)

Life cycles of new groups

Longstreet and Gay expressed concerns that the continual inclusion of new groups in multicultural education repoliticized the field and diverted attention from pedagogical research. According to Gay,

> One segment of the field is trying to push forward into . . . deeper pedagogical conceptualization, analysis, reform, and transformation. The other groups are giving primary attention to those aspects of multicultural education that deal with oppression and discrimination. (10/8/96)

Gay proposed that the cyclical nature of the field increased inner tensions. She wondered whether or not the field was ready to divide into subfields oriented toward study of different cultural concerns. Longstreet interpreted this tension somewhat differently. To her, multicultural education faced a continual struggle between the search for ethnic, cultural understandings and the championship of political, equality goals.

Currently, the inclusion of gay and lesbian issues in multicultural education is debated. Banks recognized "absolutely no consensus" about this concern (8/28/96). For Banks, further clarification of the field was needed. Cortes agreed. He noted that the field "is not *too* big, but is *so big* that it makes it difficult to define a common core" (9/3/96). The question raised by Gay in 1983 remained pertinent: Can you expand the boundaries of a field indefinitely and still protect its integrity?

Bleeding boundaries or uncertain center: toward clearer disciplinary parameters

What is central to the integrity of the field? What characterizes its common core? What types of boundaries make sense? This historical commentary captured a field in the process of development. Growth was marked by consensus, controversy, and conceptual differences.

What conceptual arguments characterize multicultural education discourse?

The central focus of multicultural education was debated in the commentary reported here. Longstreet suggests a framework that clarifies ideological stances in this debate.[51] She differentiates between a biological/cultural perspective and a political perspective. From the biological/cultural perspective, all groups are ethnic, ethnicity is embedded in one's earliest learning, and multicultural education is coming to understand and respond affirmatively to ethnicity within schooling. From a political perspective, equal education is a civil right that transcends group boundaries, recognition of underrepresented groups is a just cause, and multicultural education is the advancement of cultural pluralism, particularly within the realm of schooling. Significantly, Longstreet notes that these orientations are not mutually exclusive. Rather, they need to be delineated carefully in order for the field to firm disciplinary parameters.

This study revealed some ideological splintering along cultural/political lines. Gay, Bennett, and Longstreet were oriented toward understanding the manner in which ethnicity—understood as early, family-based learning—influences attitudes, behaviors, and approaches to learning. Cortes was attuned to ethnicity as one's cultural story, affected by societal factors such as the media. Grant, Gollnick, and Sleeter were directed toward political projects that challenge discrimination and oppression. Banks claimed a middle ground. He described the genesis of the field culturally, as a "biographical journey" or "search for self." Alternatively, he referred to multicultural education as a "children's civil rights movement."

Still, the allure of cultural/political divisions is too simplistic. Commitments to culturally relevant and responsive teaching "crossed the board" of respondents. Additionally, the transformation of schooling to assist marginalized groups was recognized collectively as a significant struggle. Perhaps philosophical differences occur as a function of emphasis. On the other hand, perhaps the argument comes down to how much one field can fight for with integrity. For some scholars interviewed in this study, cultural misunderstanding and denigration, often based on different ethnic frames of reference or the stratification of ethnic groups, were paramount. A boundary line might be drawn here to delimit the field. For other scholars, identity was complicated to such an extent by interactive forces of race, disability, gender, and the like that there was no stopping place. Confrontations with multiplicity and complexity were inevitable and even desirable.

A strand of continual questioning about who's "in" or "out" ran through this commentary. Perhaps division cannot be avoided; educational responsiveness to sociocultural difference is a vast, complicated, ambitious undertaking. Boundaries must be drawn, at least for a discipline of study. Conversely, boundaries are not necessary for an expanding vision of equitable education. This debate is of long standing, yet in need of further discussion. These early scholars easily could reformulate and remount this discussion for those newer to the field.

What is the common core of multicultural education?

The educational pursuit of cultural dignity, integrity, and equality resonated through these recollections. However, the notion of culture was bandied about to justify the reduction or expansion of interests central to the field. Multicultural educators probably could benefit from attention to anthropological debates about culture, especially those that ponder relationships between culture and multicultural education.[52] Increasingly, culture is viewed as fluid, contested, and multivocal. Ethnic boundaries are blurred. Struggles for equality engender new coalitions among varied sociocultural groups. These perceptions of culture are marked by perplexity and boundary crossing. They do not make it any easier to ascertain why youth do well or poorly in school. Yet, the supposed distinctions between cultural/political "camps" within multicultural discourse might recede through closer examinations of cultural complexity.

As a corollary to this point, the interpretation of cultural difference simply may change over time. To explore this assertion, feminist perspectives on difference can be instructive. Fraser, for example, describes three phases of feminist debate about the concept of gender difference.[53] In the first phase, from the 1960s to the 1980s, the focus of argument was gender difference: meanings, causes of injustice, and appropriate remedies. In the second phase, from the mid-1980s to the 1990s, the focus shifted to differences among women. During this time, lesbians and feminists of color argued that mainstream American feminism did not represent all women. The third phase of debate currently is underway. Its focus is the development of a viable approach to multiple, intersecting differences; advocates argue that no single way of being a woman exists that is not raced, classed, and sexed.

Perhaps the comprehension of cultural difference is not a matter of determining who's "in" or "out" but rather a recognition of on-going reinterpretations of this concept. Shifts from a focus on ethnic difference, to multiethnic comparisons, to interrelated aspects of identity can be interpreted as conceptual gains. Fraser cautioned that conceptual gains need not overshadow the original debate.[54] For multicultural educators, the original debate centered around ways in which the denigration of cultural difference related to the perpetuation of educational inequality and what should be done to disrupt and alter this negative relationship. The perception of cultural difference with increased nuance should assist the struggle to improve educational experiences and outcomes for all youth.

Efforts to achieve educational quality and equality, especially for youth historically ill-served by schools, is terra firma for multicultural education. Some scholars, like Christine Sleeter, worried that reconstructive endeavors already have been forgotten and need a reemphasis. Others, such as Geneva Gay and James Banks, assumed critical, reconstructive underpinnings for the field. Perhaps this common purpose needs to be reasserted; many multicultural educators likely have not read of these early scholars' commitment to being "fighters for social justice."[55]

What are the boundaries for multicultural education?

As a reform movement, multicultural education is bound by an educational platform that calls for the total transformation of schooling in ways that affirm cultural diversity, support human dignity, and foster educational accomplishment for all youth. The constituency for multicultural education may expand as more groups demand equal educational opportunities, but the coalition of these groups centers around this platform. Of course, as cultural diversity and human dignity are interpreted in increasingly complex and contested ways, the meaning of educational equality and equity alters. The field may have to rely on its central purpose as a primary boundary.

Alternatively, as a discipline of study, the integrity of multicultural education is threatened by an increasingly inclusive field. Different groups tend to have varied and, possibly, conflicting purposes. A coalition of interest groups may be politically viable but conceptually confusing. Carl Grant held out the possibility that various groups can find ways of handling multiplicity. What it means to confront multiplicity remains an issue of long standing for the field. Certainly, central concepts, common beliefs, and general purposes need further clarification. The following questions seem pertinent to the process of clarification: Should ethnicity be studied with increased complexity, as the result of multifaceted messages about gender, sexuality, and the like? Should ethnicity, gender, disability, and/or sexuality be studied as interacting aspects of identity? Should the field divide into subfields to focus on pedagogical issues affected by distinctive aspects of one's personhood?

Conclusions

Notions of culture and cultural difference are not strong delimiters for multicultural education. The cultural aspects of "multicultural" have been construed broadly in ways that support impressions about "bleeding boundaries." Several questions arise. Should scholars declare the field to be about some things and merely sympathetic to others? Should scholars emphasize core aims and values and embrace multiple, marginalized groups within the field? Reasonably, discussion of such questions should heed the original intentions for the field.

A solid, yet debated, center seems to exist. Fundamentally, respect for cultural diversity is connected to commitment to social justice. The major arena for struggle toward equality and equity is the school. Although boundaries may be flexible, a "certain center" can strongly structure the field. Common grounds for multicultural education deserve heightened discussion.

These historical recollections indicate that debate about core ideas, purposes, and parameters for multicultural education endures. Awareness of the serious nature of this debate offers insights and clarification to multicultural education as a field of study.

Appendix A: benchmark literature in multicultural education

James Banks, *Teaching Ethnic Studies: Concepts and Strategies* (Washington, DC: National Council for the Social Studies, 1973).

    Connects ethnic studies to teaching. Provides theoretical foundations, ethnic histories, and teaching strategies. Takes a group-by-group approach and focuses on ethnic minority experiences. Attends to the experiences of women and white ethnic groups in separate chapters. Considers intersections among ethnicity, social class, and gender minimally.

James Banks, *Teaching Strategies for Ethnic Studies*, 6th ed. (Boston: Allyn & Bacon, 1997).

    Provides theoretical grounding for a multiethnic curriculum. Develops a curricular framework for teaching multiethnic studies, including key concepts and generalizations for the study of ethnic pluralism. Includes concepts, strategies, and materials for teaching about major ethnic groups within the United States.

James Banks and Cherry McGee Banks, eds., *Handbook of Research on Multicultural Education* (New York: Macmillan, 1995).

    Explores the current state of multicultural education. Describes the nature, history, goals, and key issues in the field. Includes major research related to multicultural education since its emergence in the 1960s and 1970s and suggests future research issues. Examines the nature of knowledge construction that is at the heart of the field. Provides current research on major ethnic groups in the United States. Examines the relationship of immigration issues to multicultural education. Considers research on teaching various ethnic and language minority groups and suggests policies to increase the academic achievement of students from diverse groups.

James Banks, Carlos Cortes, Geneva Gay, Ricardo Garcia, and Anna Ochoa, *Curriculum Guidelines for Multiethnic Education* (Arlington, VA: National Council for the Social Studies, 1976).

Presents a rationale for ethnic pluralism and multiethnic education. Provides guidelines for creating multiethnic school environments. Includes an educational program evaluation checklist. Adopted as a position statement by the National Council for the Social Studies.

Christine Bennett, "Teaching Students as They Would Be Taught: The Importance of Cultural Perspective," *Educational Leadership* 36 (January 1979): 259–268.

Makes a case for teaching students in ways that attend to cultural and individual differences. Describes culture as worldview. Proposes that groups tend to share similar values, assumptions, ideas, beliefs, and modes of thought. Encourages teachers to respond to cultural patterns in their teaching. Provides examples of culturally sensitive teaching.

Christine Bennett, *Comprehensive Multicultural Education: Theory and Practice*, 3rd ed. (Boston: Allyn & Bacon, 1995).

Provides a model for comprehensive multicultural education that includes six interactive dimensions: developing multiple historical perspectives, strengthening cultural consciousness and intercultural competence, combating racism and other forms of prejudice, increasing awareness of global dynamics, and building social action skills. Argues for delimiting multicultural education to concerns with race and culture.

Carlos Cortes, "Need for a Geo-cultural Perspective in the Bicentennial," *Educational Leadership* 33 (January 1976): 290–292.

Argues against teaching American civilization with a unidirectional, east-west orientation. From this perspective, ethnic groups appear as obstacles to westward-moving civilization or problems that must be controlled. Proposes a geo-cultural alternative that attends to all multiple civilizations and flow of culture into what ultimately became the United States.

Geneva Gay, "Multiethnic Education: Historical Developments and Future Prospects," *Phi Delta Kappan* 64 (April 1983): 560–563.

Traces the roots of multiethnic studies to the civil rights movement. Describes the history of curriculum reform motivated by multiethnic studies, including textbook reform, ethnic studies programs, and movement toward more systemic reform. Warns against lean times in the politically conservative 1980s. Suggests the infusion of multiethnic studies into general education. Argues against the expansion of multiethnic/multicultural education to include experiences of women, those with disabilities, and the poor.

Donna Gollnick and Philip Chinn, *Multicultural Education in a Pluralistic Society*, 4th ed. (New York: Merrill, 1994).

Considers U.S. society as composed of the macroculture and various microcultures. Describes a microcultural group as one that shares distinctive cultural patterns. Considers ethnic, religion, gender, age, social class, and language groups as microcultural groups. Explains that individuals may be members of several microcultural groups. Argues that schools should respond to all these forms of diversity.

Carl Grant, "Education That Is Multicultural—Isn't That What We Mean?" *Journal of Teacher Education* 29 (September–October 1978): 45–49.

Argues that the term "multicultural education" indicates modification rather than transformation of education. Proposes usage of "education that is multi-cultural" to promote comprehensive school change. Includes men, women, people of color, those living in poverty, and those with disabilities as part of multicultural education. Defines an education that is multicultural as attentive to staffing patterns, curriculum, language, and instructional materials.

Wilma Longstreet, *Aspects of Ethnicity: Understanding Differences in Pluralistic Classrooms* (New York: Teachers College, 1978).

Defines ethnicity as that portion of cultural development that occurs before an individual is in complete command of his/her abstract powers and that is formed through contact with family, neighbors, and others in his/her immediate environment. Describes five aspects of ethnicity: verbal communication, nonverbal communication, orientation modes, social value patterns, and intellectual modes. Suggests teachers use action research to discover aspects of ethnicity in operation in their classrooms.

Christine Sleeter and Carl Grant, "An Analysis of Multicultural Education in the United States," *Harvard Educational Review* 57 (November 1987): 421–444.

Analyzes literature related to multicultural education to determine what the field means and to describe multicultural education theory and practice. Develops a topology of five operational approaches to the field: teaching the culturally different, human relations, single group studies, multicultural education, and education that is multicultural and social reconstructionist. Proposes the last approach as more attentive to concern for social/structural equality than other forms. Encourages attention to relationship of social stratification to culture.

Notes

1 Geneva Gay, Maureen Gillette, Carl Grant, Valerie Pang, James Sears, Juan Rivera, and Russell Young, "Asking Tough Questions: Who Should Be Included in Multicultural Education? Which Group(s) Should We Focus On? What United Position Can We Take?" (symposium presented at the annual meeting of the American Educational Research Association, San Diego, April 1998).
2 Margaret LeCompte and Judith Preissle, *Ethnography and Qualitative Design in Educational Research*, 2nd ed. (New York: Academic Press, 1993).
3 James Banks, "Multicultural Education: Historical Development, Dimensions, and Practice," in *Handbook of Research on Multicultural Education*, ed. James Banks and Cherry McGee Banks (New York: Macmillan, 1995), pp. 3–24; Cherry McGee Banks, "The Intergroup Education Movement," in *Multicultural Education, Transformative Knowledge, and Action: Historical and Contemporary Perspective*, ed. James Banks (New York: Teachers College, 1996), pp. 251–277; Christine Sleeter and Carl Grant, *Making Choices for Multicultural Education: Five Approaches to Race, Class, and Gender*, 2nd ed. (New York: Merrill, 1994).
4 Christine Sleeter and Carl Grant, *Making Choices for Multicultural Education: Five Approaches to Race, Class, and Gender*, 2nd ed. (New York: Merrill, 1994).
5 Elliot Eisner, *The Educational Imagination: On the Design and Evaluation of School Programs* (New York: Macmillan, 1994).
6 James Banks, *Teaching Strategies for Ethnic Studies*, 6th ed. (Boston: Allyn & Bacon, 1997).
7 James Banks, "Multicultural Education: Historical Development, Dimensions, and Practice," in *Handbook of Research on Multicultural Education*, ed. James Banks and Cherry McGee Banks (New York: Macmillan, 1995), pp. 3–24.
8 Christine Bennett, *Comprehensive Multicultural Education: Theory and Practice*, 3rd ed. (Boston: Allyn & Bacon, 1995).

9   Carlos Cortes, "Need for a Geo-cultural Perspective in the Bicentennial," *Educational Leadership 33* (January 1976): 290–292.
10 Geneva Gay, "Designing Relevant Curricula for Diverse Learners," *Education and Urban Society* 20 (August 1988): 327–340.
11 Geneva Gay, "Multiethnic Education: Historical Developments and Future Prospects," *Phi Delta Kappan* 64 (April 1983): 560–563; Geneva Gay, "Educational Equality for Students of Color," in *Multicultural Education: Issues and Perspectives*, ed. James Banks and Cherry McGee Banks (Boston: Allyn & Bacon, 1997), pp. 195–228.
12 Donna Gollnick and Philip Chinn, *Multicultural Education in a Pluralistic Society*, 4th ed. (New York: Merrill, 1994).
13 Carl Grant, "Education That Is Multicultural—Isn't That What We Mean?" *Journal of Teacher Education* 29 (September–October 1978): 45–49.
14 Wilma Longstreet, *Aspects of Ethnicity: Understanding Differences in Pluralistic Classrooms* (New York: Teachers College, 1978).
15 Christine Sleeter and Carl Grant, *Making Choices for Multicultural Education: Five Approaches to Race, Class, and Gender*, 2nd ed. (New York: Merrill, 1994).
16 James Banks, *Multiethnic Education: Theory and Practice*, 2nd ed. (Boston: Allyn & Bacon, 1988); James Banks, "Multicultural Education: Historical Development, Dimensions, and Practice," in *Handbook of Research on Multicultural Education*, ed. James Banks and Cherry McGee Banks (New York: Macmillan, 1995), pp. 3–24; Donna Gollnick, "Multicultural Education: Policies and Practices in Teacher Education," in *Research and Multicultural Education: From the Margins to the Mainstream*, ed. Carl Grant (London: Falmer, 1992), pp. 218–239.
17 Barney Glaser and Anselm Strauss, *The Discovery of Grounded Theory: Strategies for Qualitative Research* (Chicago: Aldine, 1967).
18 Andrea Fontana and James Frey, "Interviewing: The Art of Science," in *Handbook of Qualitative Research*, ed. Norman Denzin and Yvonna Lincoln (Thousand Oaks, CA: Sage, 1994), pp. 361–376.
19 James Banks, "The African American Roots of Multicultural Education," in *Multicultural Education, Transformative Knowledge, and Action: Historical and Contemporary Perspectives*, ed. James Banks (New York: Teachers College, 1996), pp. 30–45.
20 See, for example, Geneva Gay and Willie Baber, *Expressively Black: The Cultural Basis of Ethnic Identity* (New York: Praeger, 1987).
21 James Banks, "Multicultural Education: Historical Development, Dimensions, and Practice," in *Handbook of Research on Multicultural Education*, ed. James Banks and Cherry McGee Banks (New York: Macmillan, 1995), pp. 3–24.
22 Christine Sleeter and Carl Grant, *Making Choices for Multicultural Education: Five Approaches to Race, Class, and Gender*, 2nd ed. (New York: Merrill, 1994).
23 Stokely Carmichael and Charles Hamilton, *Black Power: The Politics of Liberation in America* (New York: Vintage, 1967).
24 Christine Sleeter and Carl Grant, *Making Choices for Multicultural Education: Five Approaches to Race, Class and Gender*, 2nd ed. (New York: Merrill, 1994).
25 Carl Grant, "Education That Is Multicultural—Isn't That What We Mean?" *Journal of Teacher Education* 29 (September–October 1978): 47.
26 Ibid.
27 James Banks, ed., *Teaching Ethnic Studies: Concepts and Strategies* (Washington, DC: National Council for the Social Studies, 1973).
28 Ibid., p. xi.
29 Mildred Dickeman, "Teaching Cultural Pluralism," in *Teaching Ethnic Studies: Concepts and Strategies*, ed. James Banks (Washington, DC: National Council for the Social Studies, 1973), pp. 5–25.
30 See, for example, Lowell Chun-Hoon, "Teaching the Asian Experience," in *Teaching Ethnic Studies: Concepts and Strategies*, ed. James Banks (Washington, DC: National Council for the Social Studies, 1973), pp. 119–147.
31 Janice Law Trecker, "Teaching the Role of Women in American History," in *Teaching Ethnic Studies: Concepts and Strategies*, ed. James Banks (Washington, DC: National Council for the Social Studies, 1973), pp. 279–297.

32 Carlos Cortes, "Need for a Geo-cultural Perspective in the Bicentennial," *Educational Leadership* 33 (January 1976): 290–292.
33 James Banks, Carlos Cortes, Geneva Gay, Ricardo Garcia, and Anna Ochoa, *Curriculum Guidelines for Multiethnic Education* (Arlington, VA: National Council for the Social Studies, 1976).
34 James Banks, "Curriculum Guidelines for Multicultural Education," *Social Education* 56 (September 1992): 274–294.
35 James Banks, *Multiethnic Education: Practices and Promises* (Bloomington, IN: Phi Delta Kappa Educational Foundation, 1977).
36 Carl Grant, Marilynne Boyle, and Christine Sleeter, *The Public School and the Challenge of Ethnic Pluralism* (New York: Pilgrim Press, 1980).
37 Christine Bennett, "The Development of an Experimental Curriculum in Government to Effect the Political Socialization of Anglo, Black, and Mexican American Adolescents" (doctoral dissertation, University of Texas, Austin, 1972).
38 Carl Grant, "Education That Is Multicultural—Isn't That What We Mean?" *Journal of Teacher Education* 29 (September–October 1978): 45–49.
39 Donna Gollnick and Philip Chinn, *Multicultural Education in a Pluralistic Society*, 4th ed. (New York: Merrill, 1994).
40 Ibid.
41 See, for example, Christine Bennett, "Teaching Students as They Would Be Taught: The Importance of Cultural Perspective," *Educational Leadership* 36 (January 1979): 259–268.
42 Geneva Gay, "Multiethnic Education: Historical Developments and Future Prospects," *Phi Delta Kappan* 64 (April 1983): 563.
43 Ibid.
44 Ibid.
45 Ibid.: 560–563.
46 Ibid.: 563.
47 Christine Sleeter and Carl Grant, "An Analysis of Multicultural Education in the United States," *Harvard Educational Review* 57 (November 1987): 421–444.
48 Ibid.: 436.
49 Christine Sleeter and Carl Grant, *Making Choices for Multicultural Education: Five Approaches to Race, Class, and Gender*, 2nd ed. (New York: Merrill, 1994).
50 Christine Sleeter and Peter McLaren, "Introduction: Exploring Connections to Build a Critical Multiculturalism," in *Multicultural Education, Critical Pedagogy, and the Politics of Difference*, ed. Christine Sleeter and Peter McLaren (New York: SUNY, 1995), pp. 5–32.
51 Wilma Longstreet, "Identity and Ethnicity in Multicultural Studies" (paper presented at the annual meeting of the American Educational Research Association, New York, April 1996).
52 See, for example, Diane Hoffman, "Culture and Self in Multicultural Education: Reflections on Discourse, Text, and Practice," *American Educational Research Journal* 33 (Fall 1996): 545–569; Terence Turner, "Anthropology and Multiculturalism: What Is Anthropology That Multiculturalists Should Be Mindful of It?" *Cultural Anthropology* 8 (November 1993): 411–429; Murray Wax, "How Culture Misdirects Multiculturalism," *Anthropology and Education Quarterly* 24 (June 1993): 99–115.
53 Nancy Fraser, "Equality, Difference, and Radical Pedagogy: The United States Feminist Debates Revisited," in *Radical Democracy: Identity, Citizenship, and the State*, ed. David Trend (New York: Routledge, 1996), pp. 197–208.
54 Ibid.
55 James Banks, ed., *Teaching Ethnic Studies: Concepts and Strategies* (Washington, DC: National Council for the Social Studies, 1973).

CHAPTER 21

DETRACKING (1997)

The social construction of ability, cultural politics, and resistance to reform

Jeannie Oakes, Amy Stuart Wells, Makeba Jones, and Amanda Datnow

> Detracking could fail because those coming from the innate intelligence perspective really believe that it's in the best interests of kids to be separated by some sort of perceived cognitive ability. We all know that that's been a masquerade sometimes for institutional racism and classism.
>
> —Educator at a detracking school

Educators attempting to detrack their schools and move from homogeneous to heterogeneous instructional groupings confront not only the logistical problems of restructuring but also the deeply held beliefs of colleagues, parents, and students about intelligence and privilege that legitimize tracking, especially in racially and socioeconomically mixed schools. In promoting detracking reform, educators cannot avoid normative and political struggles in which their critique of current power relations and distribution of opportunities clashes with traditional (and often racist) views of educational opportunity. The different world views, or standpoints, of educators who see the need for detracking and those who do not believe in such reform are culturally dissonant and politically conflictual because detracking butts up against fundamental issues of power and control played out in ideological battles over the meaning of intelligence, ability, and merit.

Some supporters of detracking, such as the educator cited above, are well aware of these normative and political dimensions of detracking reform. Many others are not. Most proceed as if support for their reforms will follow from a demonstration (either by research evidence or example) that the achievement of students from low-track classes will be enhanced while the achievement of students from high-track classes will not be harmed by detracking. Meanwhile, these educators are testing often unexplored technical tasks of teaching students in heterogeneous classrooms, often without the structural or institutional support needed to make their efforts successful. Thus, the chances that they will succeed in making wholesale and significant changes within their schools are diminished.

But those educators who deconstruct conventional conceptions of ability and confront detracking as a cultural and political struggle as well as a more technical challenge can never go back to feeling comfortable with traditional conceptions of students' ability or the segregated track structure of their schools. Because these educators do not see students' ability as a fixed variable over which they have virtually no control, they see themselves as powerful agents in students' learning and they will resist policies and practices that label and define students as failures (Oakes, 1996).

This article draws on data from our study of detracking schools and explores how conceptions of intelligence intervene in efforts to detrack schools. We are guided by three fundamental assumptions grounded in the sociology of knowledge: (1) that human knowledge of everyday social life is socially constructed, rather than objective scientific fact (Berger & Luckman, 1966); (2) that conceptions of intelligence are socially constructed rather than scientifically discovered; and (3) and that schools' responses to differences in intelligence (e.g., school structures and teaching practices) are themselves social constructions, rather than self-evident implications from established scientific knowledge.[1]

We begin with these premises, but the heart of our analysis goes considerably further. We argue that the process of knowledge construction proceeds from and is fundamentally shaped by the cultural and political context in which that process takes place. Specifically, historical and contemporary cultural norms about race and social class inform educators', parents', and students' conventional conceptions of intelligence, ability, and giftedness; these conceptions, in turn, interact with the local political context as schools attempt to implement detracking. We also argue that these prevailing conceptions of and responses to intelligence are grounded in ideologies that maintain race and class privilege through the structure as well as the content of schooling.

To demonstrate these connections, we provide a very brief history of the prevailing conceptions of inteligence and illustrative data from our recently concluded research. That research—Beyond Sorting and Stratification—consisted of a three-year longitudinal case study of ten racially and socioeconomically mixed secondary schools that have been undertaking detracking reforms.[2]

At each of these schools, virtually all the educators struggled to make sense of the individual differences they saw among their students, but they varied widely in how they dealt with these differences and which theories they drew on to help them do so. Furthermore, their varied views of student ability seemed to relate to their attitudes toward detracking. For instance, some teachers did not problematize conventional views of intelligence, which they saw as fixed—either innate or derived from students' cultural backgrounds. These educators thought that by the time students get to middle and high school, it is pretty clear which ones are "smart" and which belong in remedial classes. They did not see much if any need to meddle with the track structure.

Other educators had embraced new views of intelligence as plastic and multidimensional, views that are gaining public visibility and professional acceptance, and thus raised fundamental issues about tracking structures that rigidly compartmentalize students into separate classes for "slow" and "bright" students. Even though these conceptions of intelligence provide essential support for detracking reform, we found that most teachers had only superficial knowledge of these theories and, as in the larger society, the old views of intelligence had not gone away.

Yet there was also a small but critical mass of educators in each of the ten schools who had a powerful critique of more conventional views of ability and intelligence and the ideology that supports those views. These teachers and administrators fought the hardest and longest for detracking because the track structure no longer made any sense to them.

The normative and political connections between various conceptions of intelligence and cultural politics emerged strongly in our study, especially as parents and policymakers articulated their resistance to the schools' reforms. Many educators in the schools we studied struggled mightily to use their own sometimes tenuously altered normative perspectives as wedges to penetrate the fierce political opposition to detracking reforms and the beliefs about intelligence that support rigid track structures. By examining these more cultural and ideological aspects of detracking we reexamine common presumptions that resistance to policies providing greater opportunities to low-income, African-American, and Latino children are driven by so-called rational, self-interested estimates of the learning costs and benefits associated with such reforms (Sears & Funk, 1991).

The ideology of intelligence

According to Thompson (1990), ideology refers to the ways in which culturally based meanings serve, in particular circumstances, to establish and sustain relations of power that are systematically asymmetrical. Thus ideology, broadly speaking, is cultural meaning in the service of power. According to Gramsci (1971), insofar as ruling ideas are internalized by the majority of the people and become a defining motif of everyday life, they appear as "common sense"—that is, as the "traditional popular conception of the world" (Boggs, 1984, p. 161). And as Lewontin (1992) points out, these commonsense definitions are necessary, particularly in our society, to explain the contradiction between an espoused ideology of equality and meritocracy and the reality of extreme inequality.

From the turmoil in seventeenth-century Britain and eighteenth-century France and America there emerged a revolution-based ideology of liberty and equality that remains prevalent in our society today. But what also emerged was a society stratified in terms of wealth and power, along lines of race and gender. This inherent contradiction necessitated reconceptualizing the notion of equality, toward equality of opportunity rather than result. An ideology of equality of opportunity lends itself to a social system based on "meritocracy," or the belief that because the race for social rewards is fair, those who reach the finish line must be faster and thus more meritorious runners than those who came in last. This is a "natural" sorting process of who gets to be wealthy and powerful (Lewontin, 1992).

Not only does this view support the status quo of a few haves and many have-nots, but it creates a commonsense notion about difference, inferring that those without power cannot and will never acquire power because of their own innate deficiencies (inability to run fast). Lewontin argues that this "ideology of biological determinism" states that humans differ in fundamental abilities because of innate differences that are biologically inherited. Such biological principles are "meant to convince us that although we may not live in the best of all *conceivable* worlds, we live in the best of all *possible* worlds" (Lewontin, 1992, p. 21).

Measures of ability and intelligence have their root not in the tradition of scientific inquiry (as we often believe), but in the formation of this ideology of biological determinism, which guarantees the creation of a stratified society (haves and have-nots) and the legitimation of that stratification process. Definitions and understandings of intelligence, like all meanings, are sensitive to the cultural contexts in which they are constructed. In culturally diverse societies, the meanings that tend to dominate are those constructed by the actors with the most power within the social structure. Because of the political, economic, and social power of these actors, their world view is rarely challenged and their culturally based definition of intelligence becomes "common sense." In this way, the socially constructed, culturally embedded meaning of intelligence becomes an ideology (Mannheim, 1936).

Accordingly, the ideology of intelligence is enlisted to make the particular cultural capital (or ways of knowing) of the white and wealthy seem not only more valuable than others, but also the marker of biologically determined ability. This definition of intelligence is reified in the form of standardized tests that measure students' acquisition of this particular cultural capital. This measurement of "ability" provides students from white and wealthy families with considerable advantage, but under the guise of their "natural" abilities, not as a function of their social location (Bourdieu & Passeron, 1979).

Intelligence: the history of an ideology

Early in the twentieth century, American psychologists eagerly embraced Alfred Binet's (1913) "scientific" IQ tests as a more valid and reliable way to assess intelligence than earlier methods that relied on measuring head sizes and body types. Because the specific abilities that IQ tests measure are highly interrelated statistically—that is, the knowledge, speed, and accuracy required to successfully complete test items—British psychologist Charles Spearman conceptualized intelligence as a single, general attribute or entity (Spearman's g) that underlies all mental abilities (Spearman, 1904). The work of H. H. Goddard (1914), Lewis Terman (1916), and Robert Yerkes (1915) early in the century created standardized intelligence measures and scales that matched their belief that intelligence is innate, stable, and inherited. IQ tests administered to World War I army recruits and immigrants entering at Ellis Island proved to be a useful and socially important way to rank and sort individuals in terms of their perceived mental capacities.

From the inception of large-scale intelligence testing, psychologists found persistent racial group differences on IQ tests. Early intelligence test pioneers framed these measured differences as reflective of inherent biological differences among racial groups. Because intelligence was conceptualized as innate and hereditary, judgments about the moral character of various groups followed from their IQ scores. The views of Lewis M. Terman (1916) are bluntly illustrative:

> M. P. ["Boy, IQ 77"] represent[s] the level of intelligence which is very, very, common among Spanish-Indian and Mexican families of the Southwest and also among Negroes. Their dullness seems to be racial, or at least inherent in the family stocks from which they come. The fact that one meets this type with such extraordinary frequency among Indians, Mexicans, and Negroes suggests . . . enormously significant racial differences in general intelligence, differences which cannot be wiped out by any scheme of mental culture. Children of this group should be segregated in special classes and be given instruction which is concrete and practical. (pp. 91–92)

Some theorists go so far as to argue that the primary purpose of the early study of hereditary and biological intelligence, including craniology and craniometry, was to legitimize otherwise morally indefensible political and economic institutions such as slavery and colonialism (Gould, 1981). "Scientific" evidence proving that Africans, in particular, were feeble-minded by nature was essential to the ideology of biological determinism and helped to "rationalize" the inhuman actions of white Europeans and Americans. Obviously, the legacy of these institutions and the belief on which they stood are still with us today.

Some turn-of-the-century psychologists extended the concept of intelligence to include a wide range of human behaviors; in particular, undesirable social behaviors such as criminality were thought to reflect mental deficiency. Through this lens, human behavior was "decontextualized" from the unequal conditions of society and seen as predetermined and innate—for example, the "violent" gene. The bald sentiments of intelligence testing pioneer Lewis M. Terman, after nearly a century, are worth citing to reveal this side of our normative "heritage." He noted, for instance, that while not all criminals are feeble-minded, "all feeble-minded are at least potential criminals." He also wrote that hardly anyone would dispute that "every feeble-minded woman is a potential prostitute" (Terman, 1916, p. 11). Terman's link between intelligence and particular kinds of human behavior has proved to be an enduring theme in the ideology of intelligence.

By the middle of the twentieth century, straightforward biological or genetic explanations of intelligence had been opposed by researchers who argued that they were based on shaky empirical ground (Gould, 1981). Furthermore, with the rise of the civil rights movement and the beginning of the War on Poverty, genetic explanations of intelligence became somewhat less acceptable, although such beliefs are still very much with us and may be gaining more ground with the recent publication of *The Bell Curve* (Herrnstein & Murray, 1994).

Still, in the 1960s, education was increasingly seen as the solution to poverty, and thus arguments that intelligence was fixed became less popular in the public policy arena than arguments that intelligence is related to environment. Many liberals came to believe that the reason poor and black students were not achieving in school was because of the impoverished cultural environment in which they were being reared (Banfield, 1970; Lewis, 1968). Inherent in these culture-of-poverty arguments are understandings of intelligence that is culturally specific, and thus certain forms of behavior and style of life have been, consciously and unconsciously, equated with academic ability. In this way, a new ideology of intelligence emerged.

Conventional constructions of intelligence in detracking schools

As the quotations in the sections following reveal, many educators in the schools we studied held conceptions of students' learning ability that were reflective of the intelligence ideology discussed above.[3] They often accounted for students' school performance with references to stable, unidimensional, easily assessable traits that were beyond the ken of the school. They accepted as "normal" the fact that students fell along a predictable range, and many provided racial and/or cultural explanations for differences in students' ability to succeed at school learning. Many held that the ability differences among students were a legitimate basis for educational and social sorting, and thus they were the least likely supporters of detracking reform at their schools.

Intelligence as innate and fixed

Conceptions of learning ability as something inborn, stable, and unlikely to be altered by schooling were clearly evident among the educators we studied:

> Few of [the honors students] have a lot of *native intelligence*. Most of them are good kids—ones who will study without you telling them to.

> They try to put onto everybody else their *deficiencies that are coming from inside of them.*

He's a bright, achieving kid, but he's not *truly gifted*.

Once GT [gifted and talented], always GT. You don't become "ungifted" just because something happens in your life.

The school works best for those kids in the upper quartile who have the work ethic, and are not just *innately bright* and lazy.

Some kids have got it and some kids don't.

Intelligence as unidimensional

Also reflective of traditional conceptions of intelligence was the way in which some teachers saw students' ability along a single dimension. Most common was the tendency to equate intelligence with the *speed* at which students are able to accomplish school-like tasks. In all of the schools we studied, gifted students were contrasted with those "who don't get things quickly." Educators with more conventional understandings of intelligence often described students' ability to work quickly (as a proxy for intelligence) as distributed along a normal, bell-shaped curve, with those at the low-scoring end of the curve commonly referred to as "the slow end."

Intelligence as easily assessed

In addition to equating intelligence with speed, a number of teachers commented that students' intelligence was highly visible or *readily apparent*, and they noted with a high degree of confidence and certainty that teachers (and other students) can easily assess it.

I could have a kid in class for a week and talk with them two or three times, give them one written assignment, and tell you within a few points what their IQ is. You know intuitively when a person is smart and when they're not.

I can tell within four days what level kids are at.

Everyone knows who the gifted are.

The bell curve as "normal"

A number of teachers reiterated the conventional view that ability distributed along a bell curve is the "natural" order of things:

. . . a normal bell curve. Most students are one standard deviation away from the mean. I believe that is, indeed, how ability or intelligence or however you want to state it falls.

[lamenting the school's bimodal distribution of achievement] The school . . . has made little progress toward a bell-shaped curve even after all the desegregation money.

You know, the end of the bell curve . . .

Racial and cultural explanations

Beliefs that ability overlaps with race are salient in the schools. Many minority teachers worried that white teachers think that students of color are not as bright as whites. While these beliefs may often be "subliminal" rather than overt, some white teachers openly expressed such views:

> We're getting fewer honors kids, and that's just demographics.

> In terms of the percentage of academically capable kids—whatever that means ... that's a sweeping term that needs defining—the percentage of African-American students versus the percentage of white students is very disproportionate.

> They [Native American students] don't have the support at home, and they don't have the ability.

> [Regarding the need for vocational education] for kids from low-income and ethnic families ... not all kids are meant to go to school.

We found also that many teachers' conceptions of ability at detracking schools include a broad profile of culturally specific classroom behaviors or social deportment. Put bluntly, children who behaved in a manner that teachers approved of seemed to benefit from this broadened definition of ability.

> Smart students ... look like they're paying attention, turn in their homework, help classmates who don't understand something, and are good leaders.

> A lot of really smart kids are rote. They want to sit there and take notes and not be creative. Smart is taking notes and taking a test and getting a good grade.

> When it comes to ... my honors level, it's the most amazing thing because you've got these truly gifted children who are sitting there ... raised hands, no commotion.

> The bright child is too achievement oriented, and the slow child is not enough achievement oriented.

Many explanations of intelligence grounded in culture or social deportment inevitably break down along racial lines to the point that African-American, Latino, and Native-American students must literally "act white" in order to be perceived as intelligent by many of their teachers. Some educators in the schools we studied employ very race-specific understandings of culture as it relates to academic ability. In particular, Native-American children are perceived to be disadvantaged because they are too reserved; African-American children are perceived to disadvantage themselves because they are too forward. But rarely, if ever, is the culturally based standard against which students are measured questioned.

> [Regarding African-American students' avoidance of] asking questions, raising their hands, and waiting for answers. ... If it's not their age, then it's

certainly their culture where they're able to express themselves verbally at any and all times.

Let's face it, most Native kids are not highly verbal children. Their values are not competitive. They're not trying to get to the top of the pack. They're not trying to be noticed. It doesn't make sense to shove them into this [gifted] program and say, "Now we're meeting their needs." I'm really bothered by that.

[Regarding why identifying intelligence of Native-American minority students is difficult] because they are not verbally inclined [and testing] "shuts them down." [Evaluation is based on a] Western way of thinking.

[Regarding the low test scores of African-American students]. Personally, I believe that's a . . . that's a cultural situation . . . there's just a lot of things that they're . . . that they're deprived of, not because anyone is trying to deprive them, but because of their situation that they're born into.

Intelligence ideology rationalizing educational and social sorting

Much of teachers' resistance to detracking appears to stem from their belief that intelligence is so fundamental to students' school success and social futures that they could not create heterogeneous learning environments in which all students could benefit. Thus, this conventional understanding of intelligence lends itself to the process of ranking and sorting individuals, and for providing quite different opportunities to different groups.

But that's really been a problem as far as the grouping. . . . You know it looks good on paper. . . . It works pretty well if they're not too far apart, but there's some place there if the range gets too large, it doesn't work any more.

These bright kids are going to be in white-collar jobs, and they're going to have these so-called lower end kids as their employees.

For many who saw intelligence as constituting such profound educational and social differences among students, detracking not only seemed illogical; it seemed damaging to the more intelligent students. Some argued that the reform jeopardized the educational opportunities of "top" students in the hope of helping those at the bottom.

We do everything we can to help the low end of the scale. Why do we always want to punish the top end of the scale? I think everything should be done in the world for those kids to push them on, to stretch them. And that's what I plan to do.

It is not difficult to understand, given the history of intelligence and the voices of these educators, how tracking has become a systematic form of racial segregation within schools. Moreover, it is not surprising that those who teach in racially mixed schools and who hold these more conventional conceptions of ability as innate, fixed, unidimensional, and easy to measure are generally resistant to detracking reforms.

Newer constructions of intelligence

In recent years, cognitive and developmental psychologists have refined theories that support alternative constructions of intelligence and learning and challenge the prevailing ideology of intelligence. Such constructions emphasize intelligence as multidimensional, as contrasted with the traditional view of general intelligence as a single entity. These psychologists, like many culture-of-poverty theorists, stress that intelligence is developmental—that is, acquired as a product of experiences and social interactions over time, and alterable in social institutions such as school (Gardner, 1983a, 1983b, 1988; Sternberg, 1986)—in contrast with the view that it is inherited or the result of very early stimulation alone. Yet in this recent work, common patterns of cognitive development across individuals are more helpful for understanding learning than are individual and group differences espoused by those who hold traditional and fixed biological or cultural conceptions of intelligence. So too are the deep structures of cognitive processes more helpful for understanding and promoting learning than are more superficial variations across cultural groups in how these processes are displayed.

This new work views learning as unlimited, as opposed to the view that individuals' predetermined capacity—based on the testing of isolated skills—caps the extent of their development. Very recent thinking, in fact, suggests the possibility that children experience developmental "waves" of multiple, overlapping cognitive strategies of varying degrees of sophistication rather than discrete developmental stages of ability (Siegler, 1995). This hypothesis also suggests that the same child might simultaneously use cognitive strategies that are judged by adults as "smart" and "not smart."

Furthermore, some of these theories are now being written about and discussed in the popular press and by education scholars outside the field of psychology. Much of this interest has been spurred by the 1994 publication of Herrnstein and Murray's *The Bell Curve* and the considerable public response to it. Partially as a result of this discussion, more multidimensional and thus multicultural "ways of knowing" are gaining recognition and broader understanding. In his paper "Myths, Countermyths, and Truths about Intelligence," for example, Robert Sternberg (1996) presents a list of ideas about intelligence that illuminates for nonpsychologist education researchers how newer theories are quite at odds with traditional ones positing a hierarchical (if "normal") distribution of intelligence measured as a single dimensional entity.

Not surprisingly, the concept of genius, "superior ability," or giftedness has also shifted considerably with these new perspectives on intelligence. Sternberg and Davidson (1986) claim, for example, that "giftedness is something we invent, not something we discover" (p. 4). And considerably more attention has been focused on contrasting experts and novices, rather than geniuses and morons. This shift highlights the newer cultural emphasis on the alterability of human capacity with development and learning. If "giftedness" is socially constructed, then culture, or the highly subjective ways in which people make meaning of the world around them, must play a significant role in that construction. Recognition of the subjectivity of intelligence should help educators deconstruct the cultural hierarchies—with some cultural understandings highly valued and other completely devalued—that dictate whose knowledge is rewarded in the educational system.

A mix of old and newer constructions in detracking schools

Even as scholars begin to deconstruct old definitions and create new theories of intelligence, many people in our society, including educators, hang on to earlier understandings. In fact, while many of the teachers in the detracking schools we studied have broadened their understanding beyond the simple definition of intelligence as an IQ score, they still fall back on a narrower and more traditional concept of ability as something that is fixed. Thus, considerable ambiguity and confusion about the nature of intelligence permeate the culture of these schools, revealed both by disagreement among educators and by internal contradictions within the views of individual educators.

Grappling with newer theories

Most educators in detracking schools who have attempted to assimilate new meanings of intelligence have done so in an incomplete and somewhat superficial manner. Many who were eager to move away from the traditional intelligence ideology spoke vaguely about multidimensional and developmental conceptions of ability; perhaps these ideas have been popularized by staff developers who themselves may have only a shallow understanding of the implications of multiple intelligence theory as "learning styles" and "modalities." The following types of statements were quite common among some of the teachers at the ten schools who were wrestling with these theories:

> There's so many different learning styles. . . . I have a lot of honors kids that are frustrated with inferential reasoning because they like one right answer. Math people like one right answer . . . it's just different kinds of thinking.

> [Speaking of moving away from seeing students as "highs" or "lows."] Students are different and exhibit a variety of levels, styles, directions . . . in thinking, in the way information is absorbed, delivered by students, and students' responses.

> [Some students] have a particular talent . . . in terms of just being able to work through a situation from a commonsense standpoint, a realistic standpoint, a real world situation, . . . kids who have talent in speaking . . . in how they conduct themselves with their peers, their leadership roles.

> Being smart is being a good leader, sometimes physically fit and enthusiastic. There is interpersonally smart, physically smart, commonsense smart. . . . Students can be smart in different ways, including the smart that schools traditionally test.

> I may have to do an illustration on the chalkboard, trying to reach all the students that I have in my class, but with the honor roll students, sometimes I just use one type of illustration.

> Everybody is gifted in their own way.

The persistence of ranking and sorting

For many educators, moving away from a reliance on traditional intelligence seems not to have diminished the tendency to judge and rank, by whatever criteria, "smart" and "not smart" children. Some teachers suggest, for example, that multiple intelligences are distributed in much the same way as traditional IQ. Others have developed more elaborate classifications of students' ability.

> Different kids learn in different ways and at different rates . . . even my *bright* kids.

> [Explaining that there's more than one "bell curve" that students abilities fall along.] It's different for each curriculum content. . . . We have varying degrees of talent in each area of the curriculum.

> Honors is a slice of intelligence. When you talk about intelligence, it's that big picture. Some of those kids who would have been in Basic are really in Honors in this area of intelligence.

> [Explaining "brain modalities" to parents of low-achieving children.] This is how your child learns. . . . Your child is right-brained.

> Some kids can be straight-A students, but if they're concrete learners, that's not always viewed as high ability.

> Kids who are visual learners and oral learners can both pick up from this [notes on the chalkboard]. I also use colored chalk all the time, and that really gets to some kids . . . because I have a lot of either low level or average kids in my classes that are mixed. They've almost all responded, "Oh, I love that color" or "Cool design."

> Right-brained people learn from whole to part, and everyone else—left-brained—learns from the part to the whole, that goes with what I was saying about the honors kid.

Reinterpreting racial and cultural differences as "style"

We found educators in all ten schools who use the construct of the multidimensional nature of intelligence to explain and dignify racial and cultural differences in students' academic performance and school behavior. At many of the schools, explicit efforts had been made to help faculty acquire knowledge of how racial and cultural differences that are sometimes "mistaken" for low intelligence actually reflect different "learning styles." Some brought in "experts" on these topics to conduct professional development to assist with their detracking efforts. The impact of these efforts was clear in many teachers' discussions of race and ability.

> [It is important to encourage the] many different learning styles [because] different kids learn in different ways and at different rates. [However] an honors kid is put off by the loud kid, and often equates them with a nonproductive kid [even though some of the] loudest kids are B and A students. That's the way they learn. It's a cultural thing.

> We're not just dealing with modalities, we're dealing with culture. How children learn. . . . So, we are trying to deal with both. . . . Often we have people say, "We have African-American children, they are higher context, they talk more, they're busier." Most white Americans are generally more low context. So, if you're a low-context person and you've got a high-context person sitting in your class, you've got to adapt some—the same as I had to adapt to my low-context students.

Teachers' efforts to reconceptualize intelligence in ways that would allow them to expect that all students could learn, and prompt them to teach in ways that, in the words of one teacher, would allow students to "find the genius within them," were characteristic of the detracking advocates in the schools. Some of these teachers were further along in this process than others. However, the tentativeness of these new conceptions, the widespread tendency to accommodate (or even conflate) both conventional and unconventional views, and in many cases the broad misinterpretations of newer theories of intelligence made it extraordinarily difficult for reform-minded teachers to sustain the effort and commitment needed to deconstruct more powerful ideologies of intelligence that support tracking and ability-grouping structures, particularly when parents and others used the conventional ideologies to support the racial and cultural politics in local communities.

Cultural politics around intelligence and tracking

Educators do not live and work in a social vacuum. Their beliefs and understandings about intelligence and the ability of their students reflect in many ways the "commonsense" views of the society in general, and the dominant view in their community more specifically. Within a particular school community, certain voices are louder and more powerful than others, which means that some members of a given school community, particularly powerful parents, are better able to shape the meaning of ability than others. We found in our ten schools that parents of high-track students, who are more often than not white and relatively wealthy compared with others in their communities, benefit in significant ways when educators maintain more conventional views of intelligence (Wells & Serna, 1996). Because the cultural bias inherent in more traditional views is strongly skewed in their favor and because the track structure is built on those views, these powerful parents generally denounce detracking reform efforts and the more recent, multidimensional conceptions of intelligence on which they are based.

The more conventional and culturally and racially specific views of intelligence we heard from many teachers were echoed in the voices of parents and community members we interviewed at each of the ten schools. Thus, parental resistance to detracking reforms in these schools is often not about curriculum or instructional strategies but about whose culture and style of life is valued knowledge, and thus whose way of knowing is equated with "intelligence." In racially diverse schools, these cultural battles over the meaning of intelligence are often played out along race and social class lines because elite parents have internalized dominant, but often unspoken, beliefs about race, culture, and intelligence. In this way, race consistently plays a central, if not explicit, role in the resistance of powerful elite parents to detracking reform. Their ideology of merit and of deserving high-track students is often cloaked in symbolic politics that have clear racial implications. For example, these parents say they like the concept of a racially mixed school or classroom, as long as the African-American or Latino students act like white and middle-class children and their parents are involved in the school and buy in to the American Dream. This argument relates to the behavioral view of intelligence held by many educators.

The American Dream construction of the "deserving minority" also denies the value of nonwhite students' and parents' own culture or of their sometimes penetrating critique of the American creed (see Yonezawa, Williams, & Hirshberg, 1995). Only those students with the cultural capital and the ideology that supports it deserve to be rewarded in the educational system. Yet because the political arguments put forth by these powerful parents sound so benign, so "American," the cultural racism that guides their perspective is rarely exposed and thus the racial segregation within the schools is seen as natural.

For example, at Central High—a mostly Latino school on the West Coast with a 23 percent white student body—the local elite consists of a relatively small, mostly white middle class. The majority of Latino students come from very low-income families; many are recent immigrants to the United States. A white parent whose sons are taking honors classes explained her opposition to detracking efforts at Central, exposing her sense of entitlement this way:

> I think a lot of those Latinos come and they're still Mexicans at heart. They're not American. I don't care what color you are, we're in America here and we're going for this country. And I think their heart is in Mexico, and they're with that culture still. It's one thing to come over and bring your culture and to use it, but it's another thing to get into that . . . and I'm calling it the American ethic. They're not into it and that's why they end up so far behind. They get in school, and they are behind. That's one thing that irks my husband a lot is that we have to bring down the standards because that's where they're at. And that's what we were afraid . . . that the AP kids, that their education would be diluted because those kids just weren't up to where they're at.

For the most part, however, these powerful parents' resistance to detracking is cloaked in extremely rational and self-interested language about the quality of education their children will receive in tracked versus detracked classes. Yet these arguments are made even when reform-minded educators provide evidence that the curriculum and instruction in heterogeneous classes can be such that all students are challenged. While these political battles between parents and educators are publicly fought over which students—those labeled gifted under a more conventional conception of intelligence or those who are considered less than gifted by these standards—will have access to which curriculum and which teachers, the philosophical underpinnings of these debates are far more profound. At risk for the parents of high-track and gifted-labeled students is the entire system of meritocracy on which their privileged positions in society are based. The legitimation of inequality is called into question. As this system begins to crack with each effort on the part of educators to reconceptualize knowledge, ability, merit, and intelligence, these parents will, and understandably so, grasp at any rationale to support their commonsense understanding of what is fair. Such struggles, Bourdieu asserts, are not merely material conflicts over the distribution of social wealth, but are cultural conflicts between styles of life (Bourdieu & Wacquant, 1992; Harrison, 1993).

For instance, at one of the high schools in our study, the English teacher who created a heterogeneous American Studies class conducted some research on intelligence and decided that our society and educational system do not really understand what intelligence is or how to measure it. When the principal asked her to present her research to parents at an open house, her message was not well received, particularly by those parents whose children were in the advanced placement (AP) classes. According to the English teacher, "if you were raised under the system that said you were very intelligent and high achieving, you don't want anyone questioning that system, ok? That's just the way it is." She said that actually what some of the parents were most threatened by was how this research on intelligence was going to be used as part of the reform effort at the school.

A "gifted education" teacher at one of the middle schools in our study was severely criticized by parents of identified "gifted" students for not offering their children separate enrichment classes that were not available to other students. Instead the teacher had opted to offer extra "challenge" courses, which both gifted and "nongifted" students could choose to take. What upset this teacher most about the parents' anger was that it seemed to be based on whether their children were being singled out and treated differently and not on the content of the curriculum to which the children were being exposed:

> And they didn't ask, "Well what are our kids learning in your classes?" Nobody asked that. I just found that real dismaying, and I was prepared to tell them what we do in class, and here's an example. I had course outlines. I send objectives home with every class and goals and work requirements, and nobody asked me anything about that . . . to me it's like I'm dealing with their egos, more than what their kids really need educationally.

Similar examples, at other schools in our study, of powerful parents putting "manner over matter" or "form over function," as Bourdieu (1984) would explain it, lead us to question the instrumental "rationality" of the powerful parents' resistance to detracking. In fact, oftentimes we found the pedagogy in detracked classes far more creative and engaging than that in more traditional classes in which teachers basically lecture at the students and then test them on specific information.

Despite these curricular or pedagogical issues, efforts to alter within-school racial segregation via detracking are usually extremely threatening to elites and their position at the top of the hierarchy. The perceived stakes, from an elite parent's perspective, are quite high. And while these stakes are most frequently discussed in rational, academic terms—for example, the dumbing down of the curriculum for the smart students—the real stakes, we argue, are generally not academic at all.

Because traditional hierarchical track structures in schools have been validated, as they have so often, by the conflation of culture and intelligence, efforts to detrack schools will necessarily confront established culturally based "truths" about ability and merit. When the ideology of merit—of "deserving" high-track students—is challenged by educators who accept newer, less conventional views of intelligence and thus find that the rigid track structures no longer make sense, powerful parents must employ practices that make detracking reform politically impossible.

We have identified four prevalent practices[4] in the ten schools we studied:

1   *Threatening Flight*—In situations where local elite parents have several other viable public or private school options, the direct or indirect threat of elite flight can thwart detracking efforts.

2   *Co-opting the Institutional Elites*—When confronted with the threat of flight and the fear it creates in the hearts of educators, the "institutional elites"—that is, educators with power and authority within the educational system—are co-opted by the ideology of the local elites. We find that these institutional elites often see their roles as serving the needs and demands of the local elites. Indeed, in most situations, their

professional success and even job security depend on their ability to play these roles.

3   *Buy-in of the Not-quite-elite Parents*—Often the ideology of the local elite's entitlement is pervasive and powerful enough that the elites do not necessarily have to be directly involved in the decision-making processes at schools. Between the threats to flee, the ability to co-opt many of the institutional elites, and the ideology of their privilege as "common sense," greater parent involvement on the part of the not-quite-elite parents via more democratic school-site council and the like will not necessarily change the power structure (Beare, 1993). This is what Gramsci would refer to as the "consensual" basis of power or the consensual side of politics in a civil society (see Boggs, 1984; Gramsci, 1971).

4   *Detracking Bribes*—Powerful parents use their symbolic capital to bride the schools to give them some preferential treatment—for example, much smaller class sizes or the best teachers in the school—in return for their willingness to allow some small degree of detracking to take place. These detracking bribes tend to make detracking reforms very expensive and impossible to implement in a comprehensive fashion.

Educators' conceptions and local politics — a powerful combination

At the intersection of teachers' beliefs about intelligence and the political practices of parents in the local community we found consensus, co-optation, compromise, and conflict. For instance, we found that teachers holding conventional conceptions of ability pose the greatest threat to the implementation of detracking in part because they resist changes within the schools and in part because they seek political support for their cause among parents who want to maintain their children's place of privilege in school structured around inequality. Thus the school-based ideology of intelligence spills over to fuel the cultural politics of racially mixed communities and vice versa. But even when teachers have adopted new views of intelligence (however tentatively) and support detracking reforms, their efforts are shaped by what community elites will tolerate. In this way, the normative and political dimensions of detracking reforms are not only linked but mutually supportive.

In the previous section, we highlighted some of the political practices employed by powerful elite parents. In what follows, we describe how these political practices play themselves out as educators who have deconstructed traditional definitions of intelligence struggle to implement alternatives to tracking in the face of countervailing political forces. We have found it helpful to think about prevailing social constructions of ability, which are cultural-ideological, as operating in a reflexive relationship with school and social structures and with the actions of teachers and parents. By reflexive, we mean that they are mutually influencing, as opposed to one being determined by the other. That is, while educators may be active agents in shaping the reform efforts going on at their schools, their agency is involved in an interplay with actions of others and thus the structure and culture—at the local and the societal level—of which they are a part.[5] This larger context may both constrain and enable educators' actions (Datnow, 1995).

As Mehan (1992) has noted, cultural constructs—norms and ideologies—are not simply products of social structures over which individuals have no control.[6]

Neither are structures merely a result of unfettered individual actors making rational decisions about how to organize social life. Rather, social facts, such as intelligence, represent how people actively make sense of social life, and these conceptions are salient as educators decide how to organize teaching and learning at school.

Cultural politics empower resistant educators

A fierce political battle over the creation of a "custom calendar" at Central High School illustrates how this dynamic plays itself out in relation to the social construction of intelligence and resistance to detracking reform. Reform-minded teachers at Central who had deconstructed the notion that speed in learning is a proxy for intelligence advocated a new school calendar to complement the move toward detracking. As one teacher explained:

> The paradigm here is that it takes every student in California 180 days to learn algebra 1, and my question is, how valid could that be? Aren't there some students who might need a couple more days to do that? Now is it better to tell that student that they're a failure and can't learn, because they can't learn it in 180 days, or is it better to give them a few extra days to do it?

The calendar would have provided additional "intersession" days to allow lower-achieving students to make up work or get ahead. Despite support for the new calendar from a strong majority of the teachers, it was the cultural and political forces behind the minority of teachers who voted against it that ultimately won out when the school board voted against the calendar. These forces were marshaled through the actions of one particular teacher who rallied white, affluent parents against the custom calendar, touting what he believed to be its harmful effects, including increasing gang violence in the community when students were on their intersession breaks.

An assistant principal and long-time community resident noted that the custom calendar, although not intended as a redistributive policy, was seen as a symbol of policymaking aimed at helping students traditionally disadvantaged by the system and taking from those who benefit from the status quo. He felt the custom calendar was used as a symbol of a liberal ideology, an example of a larger movement to take away from the haves and give to the have-nots. Thus it was explicitly connected to parents' nonrational or culturally and symbolically based motives to maintain the traditional school structure and the conception of intelligence—for example, speed—that structure supports.

The failure of the custom calendar, which was seen by those with power as favoring those without it, is consistent with Apple's (1982) argument that schools help create the conditions necessary for the maintenance of ideological hegemony, the continued dominance of a particular set of values and norms supported by the policies of the local governing bodies. Similarly, Boyd (1976) found that superintendents and local school boards make policies in accordance with what they perceive as the predominant community values and expectations. Through their actions, the school board at Central reinforced the pro-tracking, racially biased ideology of intelligence and merit that is shared by the powerful affluent parents in the community.

The custom-calendar issue also provides a potent example of how educators interact with the larger structure and culture in which the school is embedded, particularly in their efforts to thwart reforms that challenge a prevailing ideology. Such interactions empower otherwise disempowered teachers when a powerful constituency of parents or community members support those educators who resist reform. The defeat of the custom calendar can be viewed as a case in which the culture (and political power) of affluent parents supported those teachers who held conventional views of intelligence and ability, and constrained the agency of teachers who wanted their school structure to acknowledge that such views are indefensible.

The reform-minded educators at Central High School faced a similar barrier when attempting to bring about detracking on a departmental level through the implementation of an integrated math curriculum. A math teacher explained her feelings about the program in which students are heterogeneously grouped: "Interactive math is good for a wide range of students. . . . I truly believe that Interactive Math will allow the honors kids that want to [excel] . . . to do so."

While four teachers teach integrated math, the traditional sequence still exists alongside this program, a compromise necessary to quell resistance from more traditional teachers. These teachers' cause to maintain the traditional math sequence, which includes an honors track, is bolstered by the support of parents of college prep and honors students who have fought to keep the traditional math sequence in place. Despite the assurance by integrated math program teachers that universities have approved the innovative program, these parents argued for separate classes for their children on the basis that universities favor the traditional math sequence. An educator at the school explained:

> Parents of the honors kids want things status quo. They want their kids in honors. They want it to look like it always worked. They don't want them in integrated math. They don't want them in anything different. They want it to look exactly like it looked twenty years ago when they did it. And they get very demanding about that. And that's something that we'll have to tackle. But it will be an out and out fight.

The efforts on the part of these parents to maintain honors classes reflect their decision (although often not conscious) to maintain the current social structure, in which people are stratified in terms of race and class. This hierarchical macro structure is supported by conventional conceptions of intelligence.

As these examples illustrate, we see patterns that reveal a reflexive relationship in the day-to-day life in detracking schools among culturally based ideologies about intelligence and learning; structural factors such as school schedules, grouping practices, grading systems, and so forth; and the political agency of educators and students to act on their beliefs to sustain or change the structures.

New conceptions as political wedges

As we have illustrated, newer, more democratic conceptions of intelligence and the ideal of detracking that follows from these conceptions compete with traditional beliefs about intelligence and a schooling structure that, for the better part of a century, has accommodated a hierarchical, "mass production" system. This competition is deeply entwined within the cultural stratification and the struggle for advantage in local communities. To the extent that cultural and political issues are unsettled or contested in the larger society, these conceptual ambiguities and political struggles are reflected inside the ten schools we studied and, most likely, in every school across the country. They will, more often than not, work against educators' efforts to detrack.

Yet we found in each of our schools some highly committed teachers and administrators who were able to use new conceptions of intelligence to bolster their efforts to interrupt patterns of race- and social-class privilege in schools. These visionary educators deconstructed the ideology that assures the privileged place of some students over others, and they committed themselves to creating new structures and practices based on still-contentious nonhierarchical views of intelligence. They engaged in normative and political struggles to develop flat opportunity structures (mixed-ability classes and a common curriculum) within an institution and a society still characterized by differentiated and hierarchical structures. In short, they expected to disrupt a rather smooth cultural fit of conventional beliefs about intelligence and tracking structures, and their interactions with students. Two types of circumstances seemed to spur these reformers forward. One was their use of powerful firsthand experiences with children to bolster their more abstract ideas about the nature of ability. A second was their sympathetic and politically savvy work with parents to create a safe space where a dialogue about their experiences could take place.

Firsthand experiences

Terri Jamison provides just one of several examples in our schools of teachers whose firsthand experiences—either personal or professional—challenged conceptions of ability and provided the impetus for reform. Jamison tells of how the experience of having her own daughter placed into the low track first led her to question the ideology of intelligence and tracking:

> You know you give them a test, they're all between here and here, great. You know exactly where to go, but it's not fair to the kids. In my opinion, it's not fair to the kids. My daughter was placed in a homogeneous grouping. She was stuck at the low end, in the lowest math class in the school. She is a bright little girl, but she's a divergent thinker so she doesn't focus. . . . So I have a real thing about it, because I have a bright little girl who would have been in the toilet, and I can see how destructive homogeneous grouping is. That's why I don't like it, because I saw it in action. And I had to fight, I mean fight hard, to keep my kid from believing what she was being taught in school, which was that she is incapable of doing math. And now this is the kid who wants to be an astrophysicist!

Because she was able to juxtapose her own "smart" daughter's experiences against the ideology of intelligence, Jamison became a strong advocate for heterogeneous grouping and designed new structures at her school to accommodate other "smart" children—including the school's considerable population of Latino students—who diverge from that ideology.

Other teachers found that their work with heterogeneous groups in classrooms had profound effects on their conceptions of intelligence and their dispositions about tracking. One teacher told us that she has learned over the years not to label students smart or dumb because they often end up surprising her:

> You get a lot of kids that may not . . . do well on a test, but you can tell they reason well, they think very quickly . . . and you know, I've learned . . . I mean

let's face it, you know kids can go through high school and make Cs and then go to college and make straight As, so I don't do a lot of labeling.

Like this teacher, others changed their conceptions of ability after realizing that a change in curricular and instructional strategies could create an environment in which all students could be "smart." One teacher told us, "Heterogeneous group-ing has made teachers think differently about all kids; they see more potential." Another told us, "The program has done amazing things for standard track kids because all of a sudden somebody says 'You can do this!' "

Olivia Jeffers, a senior high English teacher at a desegregated southern high school, developed an interdisciplinary course that she team-teaches with a teacher in social studies. The class attracts high- and low-track, white and black students who can choose the class to help satisfy college-entrance English requirements. Jeffers, in her interview with us, argued that this kind of heterogeneous grouping is essential to the learning process, and because she individualizes the curriculum for each student—letting them choose much of their own reading and work on research projects at their own pace—she does not feel that she is holding the high-achieving students back by having them in the same room with low-achieving students. In fact, she sees it as quite the opposite. She described the benefit of the detracked classroom for one of her high-achieving white students from a very wealthy suburban family:

> In class, when I have a discussion and she makes a statement, everybody else hears it, and we talk about it. She gets to pontificate, she gets to make a statement about something very important. She also gets insight from some-body who hasn't had her experience, or doesn't own a horse, or a place out in the country. A kid who gets on the bus everyday, and lives in two rooms. So when she defines self-reliance [the topic of recent class discussion on Emer-son] . . . it's from the perspective of the kid who has it—who has a family that has given it to her and the financial security to maintain it. But she's got to hear from a kid who's had to struggle his little buns or her little buns to get it. Now if that is not a learning experience, I don't know what is.

With independent student learning coupled with dynamic class discussions among students of very different backgrounds and academic strengths, Jeffers has created a learning environment in which she sees more students develop, as she explains it, insight into their own ways of knowing and learning. And when they do that, they become highly motivated "students" in the broader sense of the word, thirsty for a greater understanding of the world around them.

Work with parents

Some educators in our study also attempted to deal with countervailing political forces by convincing parents of white, high-achieving students that their children do not lose out in a detracked school because the school offers an enriched curric-ulum to all. These educators did not merely dismiss these parents as unthinking ideologues. They realized that there are very practical benefits for white and wealthy families in tracked schools—such as the currency that "honors" status has in college admissions. They respected these parents' concerns about the loss of these advantages, and attempted to engage and reassure them about reform.

For example, Sandi Wright, English teacher at Grant High School, led the formation of a parent advisory group to guide their detracking efforts. She invited parents who had expressed concern about tracking and detracking in the past to be members of this group, and then invited other parents to join in order to have a racially mixed group of parents of both high- and low-achieving students. Ms. Wright challenged the parents to become knowledgeable about the issues involved in tracking and detracking so that they could help the department plan its strategy.

> I said, "This is what we need. We need a parent group that is *as aware of* the problem as we are, who sees and knows it as well as we do. We don't need parents who are here to advocate for their student *or* for a group. We need parents who can say, *I'm* here for all students." (Emphasis in original)

Parents observed and compared regular and honors-level classes, and discussed their opinions at the monthly meetings. The advisory group suggested to Wright and her colleagues that if the detracked classes were to be successful, the faculty would have to create a curriculum that challenged everybody. The department listened carefully, and then spent a summer developing a flexible but rigorous curriculum to teach to both regular and honors classes. Detracking proceeded quite smoothly a year later. Politically savvy, Wright used the participation of powerful parents to help reassure others that their children were not being sacrificed by the reform.

In a middle school in our study, educators have attempted to deal with such countervailing political forces by helping parents of white, high-achieving students learn that their children do not lose out in a detracked program. The principal argued:

> To convince the parents of the strong students that heterogeneous grouping is a good idea, you really have to offer them a lot. You need parent education along with a rich program so that parents don't feel that their children are cheated. . . . Parents aren't going to allow academic integration anymore than they voluntarily do racial integration, unless it is something school led. So the school has got to be magnetic in some ways, and this school is.

The principal said she believes that parents are driven by cultural motives, as well as the rational, self-interested estimates of the costs and benefits of detracking. This urban middle school attracts its 50 percent white population by offering a wide variety of special programs and a large amount of resources (many funded by outside grants), all premised on the educational enrichment that is possible with diversity. Most teachers now believe that the only "hassle" with heterogeneous groupings is "educating" the parents, even as the school has implemented interdisciplinary curriculum, team teaching, and flexible scheduling, and almost complete detracking.

Conclusion

Our ten schools affirm the proposition that detracking includes far more than simply rearranging instructional grouping patterns in schools in ways that both boost and more evenly distribute learning. Detracking is also a highly normative and political endeavor that confronts deeply held cultural beliefs, ideologies, and fiercely protected arrangements of material and political advantage in local communities.

This normative and political view of reform supported by our detracking analysis suggests clear limitations in conventional approaches to school reform. As illustrated here, a conventional, primarily technical approach to reform runs into severe difficulty on two counts. First, it fails to render problematic commonsense, socially constructed conceptions that lie at the heart of the status quo of schooling, such as intelligence and merit. Second, it fails to account for how such conceptions support and are supported by the politics of culture in local communities that struggle over the distribution of power and privilege. These complex normative and political dynamics help us move beyond the commonplace assumption that resistance to detracking is rational—that its successful implementation hinges on the extent to which reformers demonstrate that low-ability students will learn more and high-ability students will learn just as much as in a tracked school.

Rethinking the meaning of children's capacity and reassessing how schools respond to individual and group differences are prerequisites to detracking reforms that do not simply replicate in heterogeneous learning environments the current distribution of school expectations, opportunities, and outcomes (Ball, 1981). So, too, is a consideration of how the politics of culture, reflected in parental attitudes about what children need and deserve, plays out in any particular community. Thus, the difficulties faced by schools attempting to detrack may be far better managed by educators and better understood by scholars as a simultaneous process of restructuring, of what Hargreaves (1994) calls "reculturing," and of what we might call "repoliticking."

Notes

1   A few scholars have made the connection between the socially constructed nature of knowledge and intelligence. Perhaps the examples most relevant to our work are found in the studies of Susan Rosenholtz (e.g., Rosenholtz & Simpson, 1984).

2   Our interdisciplinary research team, supported in part by a grant from the Lilly Endowment, used qualitative methods to examine changes in school organization, grouping practices, and classroom pedagogy—what we call the technical aspects of these reforms—in ten schools. We also investigated how the schools tackle well-established school and community norms and political practices that legitimize and support tracking as a "commonsense" approach to educating students. The ten schools in the study varied in size from more than 3,000 to fewer than 500 students. Geographically, they were widely dispersed across the United States with one in the Northeast, three in the Midwest, and one in the South, two in the Northwest, and three in various regions of California. Different schools included significant mixes of white, African-American, Latino, Native American/Alaska Native, and/or Asian students. We visited each of these ten schools three times between 1991 and 1994. Data collection during our site visits consisted of in-depth, semi-structured tape-recorded interviews with administrators, teachers, students, parents, and community leaders, including school board members. We also observed classrooms and faculty, PTA, and school board meetings. We reviewed documents and took field notes about our observations within the schools and the communities. Data have been compiled in extensive single-case studies that form the basis of cross-case analyses. For a full description of this study and its methodology, see Oakes & Wells, 1995. Comprehensive reports of the study's findings have been reported in papers presented at the annual meetings of the AERA and the ASA (see, for example, Oakes, Ray, & Hirshberg, 1995), and in Oakes & Wells, 1996.

3   The data presented here and elsewhere in this article are quotes that capture and illustrate themes throughout the data from the schools. For each category, many more statements underlie our confidence in asserting that what is presented here represents a theme across the schools.

4   A separate paper from this study (Wells & Serna, 1996) examines in more detail these four political practices employed by the powerful "elite" parents of the high-track students in their efforts to thwart detracking reforms.
5   Mehan (1992) argues, "Social actors no longer function as passive role players, shaped exclusively by structural forces beyond their control; they become active sensemakers, choosing among alternatives in often contradictory circumstances" (p. 3).
6   Note here the relevance of other theorists' work on the macro-micro problem in sociology, generally (Giddens, 1984) and, in the sociology of education, especially (Hargreaves, 1994).

References

Apple, M. W. (1982). *Cultural and economic reproduction in education.* London: Routledge & Kegan Paul.
Ball, S. (1981). *Beachside comprehensive,* Cambridge: Cambridge University Press.
Banfield, E. C. (1970). *The unheavenly city: The nature and future of our urban crisis.* Boston: Little, Brown.
Beare, H. (1993). Different ways of viewing school-site councils: Whose paradigm is in use here? In H. Beare and W. L. Boyd (Eds.), *Restructuring schools: An international perspective on the movement to transform the control and performance of schools* (pp. 200–214). Washington, DC: Falmer Press.
Berger, P. L., & Luckman, T. (1966) *The social construction of reality: A treatise in the sociology of knowledge.* New York: Doubleday.
Binet, A. (c. 1913). *A method of measuring the development of the intelligence of young children.* Chicago: Medical Book Company.
Boggs, C. (1984). *The two revolutions: Gramsci and the dilemmas of western Marxism.* Boston: South End Press.
Bourdieu, P. (1984). *Distinction: A social critique of the judgment of taste.* Cambridge: Harvard University Press.
Bourdieu, P., & Passeron, J. C. (1979). *The inheritors: French students and their relation to culture.* Chicago: University of Chicago Press.
Bourdieu, P., & Wacquant, L. D. (1992) (8th ed.). *Outline of a theory of practice.* Cambridge: Cambridge University Press.
Boyd, W. L. (1976). The public, the professionals, and educational policy-making: Who governs? *Teachers College Record, 77,* 539–577.
Datnow, A. (1995). *Making sense of teacher agency: Linking theory to school reform policy.* Unpublished doctoral dissertation, UCLA, Los Angeles, CA.
Gardner, H. (1983a). *Frames of mind: The theory of multiple intelligences.* New York: Basic Books.
Gardner, H. (1983b). *The mind's new science.* New York: Basic Books.
Gardner, H. (1988). Beyond IQ: Education and human development. *Harvard Educational Review, 57,* 187–193.
Giddens, A. (1979). *Central problems in social theory, action, structure, and contradiction in social analysis.* London: Macmillan.
Giddens, A. (1984). *The constitution of society.* Berkeley: University of California Press.
Goddard, H. H. (1914). *Feeblemindedness: Its causes and consequences.* New York: Macmillan.
Gould, S. J. (1981). *The mismeasure of man.* New York: W. W. Norton.
Gramsci, A. (1971). *Selections from the prison notebooks.* New York: International Publishers.
Hargreaves, A. (1994). *Changing teachers, changing times: Teachers' work and culture in the post-modern age.* New York: Teachers College Press.
Harrison, P. R. (1993). Bourdieu and the possibility of a postmodern sociology. *Thesis Eleven, 35,* 36–50.
Herrnstein, R., & Murray, C. (1994). *The bell curve.* New York: Free Press.
Lewis, O. (1968). The culture of poverty. In D. P. Moynihan (Ed.), *On understanding poverty: Perspectives from the social sciences* (pp. 187–200). New York: Basic Books.
Lewontin, R. C. (1992). *Biology as ideology: The doctrine of DNA.* New York: Harper Perennial.

Mannheim, K. (1936). *Ideology and utopia.* New York: Harcourt Brace.

Mehan, H. (1992). Understanding inequality in schools: The contribution of interpretive studies. *Sociology of Education, 65*(1), 1–20.

Oakes, J. (1996, July). *Mathematics & detracking in U.S. senior high schools: Technical, normative, and political dimensions.* Paper presented at the International Conference in Mathematics Education, Seville, Spain.

Oakes, J., Ray, K., & Hirshberg, D. (1995). *Access, press, and distributive justice: Technical, normative, and political changes in 10 detracking schools.* Paper presented at the annual meeting of the American Educational Research Association, San Francisco.

Oakes, J., & Wells, A. S. (1995). *Understanding the meaning of detracking in racially mixed schools: Overview of study methods and conceptual framework.* Paper presented at the annual meeting of the American Educational Research Association, San Francisco.

Oakes, J., & Wells, A. S. (1996). *Beyond the technicalities of school reform: Lessons from detracking schools.* Los Angeles: Center X, Graduate School of Education and Information Studies, UCLA.

Rosenholtz, S.J., & Simpson, C. (1984). The formation of ability conceptions: Developmental trend or social construction? *Review of Educational Research, 54,* 31–63.

Sears, D., & Funk, C. (1991). The role of self-interest in social and political attitudes. *Advances in experimental social psychology, 24,* 1–95.

Siegler, R. (1995). Paper presented at the Society for Research on Child Development, Indianapolis.

Spearman, C. (1904). General intelligence objectively determined and measured. *American Journal of Psychology, 15,* 201–293.

Sternberg, R. J. (1986). *Applied intelligence.* Boston: Harcourt Brace Jovanovich.

Sternberg, R. J. (1996). Myths, countermyths, and truths about intelligence. *Educational Researcher, 25*(2), 11–16.

Sternberg, R. J., & Davidson, J. E. (1986). Conceptions of giftedness: A map of the terrain. In R. J. Sternberg & J. E. Davidson (Eds.), *Conceptions of giftedness.* Cambridge: Cambridge University Press.

Terman, L. (1916). *The measurement of intelligence: An explanation and a complete guide for the use of the standard revision and extension of the Binet-Simon intelligence scale.* New York: Houghton Mifflin.

Thompson, J. B. (1990). *Ideology and modern culture.* Stanford, CA: Stanford University Press.

Wells, A., & Serna, I. (1996). The politics of culture: Understanding local political resistance to detracking in racially mixed schools. *Harvard Educational Review, 66*(1), 93–118.

Yerkes, R. (1915). *A point scale for measuring mental ability.* Baltimore: Warwick and York.

Yonezawa, S., Williams, E., & Hirshberg, D. (1995). *Seeking a new standard: Minority parent and community involvement in detracking schools.* Paper presented at the annual meeting of the American Educational Research Association, San Francisco.

CHAPTER 22

CHALLENGING THE MYTHS ABOUT MULTICULTURAL EDUCATION (1994)

Carl A. Grant

Multiculturalism is becoming pervasive in most aspects of our lives because of a significant shift in the sociological paradigm of the United States. This shift has been created by three major forces.

The foremost of these forces is the changing population demographics of our nation. The population of the United States has increased more than 10 percent since 1980: there are now nearly 250 million people living in this country. Forty percent of the increase is due to immigration, mainly from Asia, the Caribbean, and Latin America. In addition, the birth rate of women of color is on the rise. The Population Reference Bureau has projected that by the year 2080 the United States may well be 24 percent Latino, 15 percent African American, and 12 percent Asian American. In other words, within the next 90 years, the white population may become a "minority."

The face of the workforce is also changing. The ethnic breakdown of the workforce in 1988 was: 41 percent native white males; 33 percent native white females; 10 percent native males of color; 9 percent native females of color; 4 percent immigrant males; and 3 percent immigrant females. The projections for workers entering the workforce between 1989 and 2000 are: 28 percent native white females; 21 percent native females of color; 21 percent native males of color; 12 percent immigrant males; 9 percent immigrant females; and 9 percent native white males (National Association of State Boards of Education, 1993).

Finally, our national ethic is changing from "individual" centeredness to the acceptance and affirmation of both groups and individuals. The rugged hard-working individual since colonial times has been portrayed as the hero and the contributor to this country. The 1960s witnessed the rise and identification with groups—*e.g.*, ethnic/racial, women, lesbian and gay, physically challenged, and the poor. All of these groups demanded fairness and justice within and throughout all of society's formal and informal structures.

With the increasing pervasiveness of multicultural education have come myths, especially about what it is and what it isn't. These myths often serve to impede or halt the progress of multicultural education. Consequently, important to challenging and correcting these myths is first providing a definition of multicultural education that can frame and provide a context for espousing these myths.

Definition of multicultural education

Multicultural education is a philosophical concept and an educational process. It is a concept built upon the philosophical ideals of freedom, justice, equality, equity, and human dignity that are contained in United States documents such as the Constitution and the Declaration of Independence. It recognizes, however, that equality and equity are not the same thing: equal access does not necessarily guarantee fairness.

Multicultural education is a process that takes place in schools and other educational institutions and informs all academic disciplines and others aspects of the curriculum. It prepares all students to work actively toward structural equality in the organizations and institutions of the United States. It helps students to develop positive self-concepts and to discover who they are, particularly in terms of their multiple group memberships. Multicultural education does this by providing knowledge about the history, culture, and contributions of the diverse groups that have shaped the history, politics, and culture of the United States.

Multicultural education acknowledges that the strength and richness of the United States lies in its human diversity. It demands a school staff that is multiracial and multiculturally literate, and that includes staff members who are fluent in more than one language. It demands a curriculum that organizes concepts and content around the contributions, perspectives, and experiences of the myriad of groups that are part of United States society. It confronts and seeks to bring about change of current social issues involving race, ethnicity, socioeconomic class, gender, and disability. It accomplishes this by providing instruction in a context that students are familiar with, and builds upon students' diverse learning styles. It teaches critical-thinking skills, as well as democratic decision making, social action, and empowerment skills. Finally, multicultural education is a total process; it cannot be truncated: all components of its definition must be in place in order for multicultural education to be genuine and viable.

This definition, I believe, encapsulates the articulated and published ideas and beliefs of many multicultural scholars, and is not far removed from what many other multiculturalists believe multicultural education to be.

Six myths about multicultural education

There are numerous myths about multicultural education. The ones that are most frequently voiced are:

1   It is both divisive and so conceptually weak that it does little to eliminate structural inequalities;
2   It is unnecessary because the United States is a melting pot;
3   Multiculturalism—and by extension multicultural education—and political correctness are the same thing;
4   Multicultural education rejects the notion of a common culture;
5   Multicultural education is a "minority thing;" and
6   Multicultural education will impede learning the basic skills. These six myths will be the focus of my discussion.

Myth 1: multicultural education is divisive, and/or multicultural education is a weak educational concept that does not attempt to eliminate structural inequalities

As multicultural education has grown as a philosophy and a practice, critics representing both radical and conservatives ideologies have opposed it.

Radical critics argue that multicultural education emphasizes individual choice over collective solidarity (Olneck, 1990); that it neglects to critique systems of oppression like race or class (Mattai, 1992) and structural inequalities; that it emphasizes "culture" over "race" (Jan Mohamed & Lloyd, 1987). Radical critics also argue that multicultural education's major purpose is to advocate prejudice reduction as a solution to inequality. Therefore, they argue, its purpose is naive and misdirected.

Conservative critics of multicultural education argue that the United States has always been "multicultural" so there is, in fact, no controversy. Ravitch (1990) writes, "The real issue on campus and in the classroom is not whether there will be multiculturalism, but what kind of multiculturalism will there be" (p. A44). Ravitch is against "particularism," *i.e.*, multicultural education that is defined as African American-centric, Arab American-centric, Latino-centric, and/or gender-centric.

Similarly, E. D. Hirsh (1987) believes that there is value in multicultural education because it "inoculates tolerance and provides a perspective on our own traditions and values." However, he adds, "It should not be allowed to supplant or interfere with our schools' responsibility to insure our children's mastery of American literate culture" (p. 18).

Although these conservative critics believe in multicultural education, their vision of multicultural education is one that adheres to traditional Western thought and ideology and seeks to perpetuate institutions as they presently exist.

Also, since many conservative critics believe that there is already adequate attention given to race, class, and gender in American life, they have harsh criticisms for proponents of multicultural education. They argue that multicultural education is a movement by a "cult" (Siegel, 1991), or it is ideas from former radical protesters of the 1960s (D'Souza, 1991). Further, these conservative critics argue that multicultural education is divisive (Balch, 1992; D'Souza, 1991), and that too much attention is given to race and ethnicity. The multicultural education now being proposed, they argue, will "disunite America" (Schlesinger, 1991) and lead to "balkanization" or "tribalism."

Both radical and conservative critics of multicultural education often leave their research skills, scholarship, and willingness to conduct a thorough review of the educational literature at the academy door. Most radical critiques of multicultural education seem to be written after reading (not studying) a few limited selections from the multicultural literature. For example, some (*e.g.*, Olneck, 1990) claim that dominant versions of multicultural education are divorced from sociopolitical interests, and that multicultural scholars see ethnic conflict as the result of negative attitudes and ignorance about manifestations of difference, which can be resolved by cultivating empathy, appreciation, and understanding.

It is for certain that these critics have not examined the work of Nieto (1992), Banks (1991), Banks and Banks (1989), Gay (1986), Gollnick and Chinn (1994), Grant (1988), Sleeter and Grant (1988) and Sleeter (1993). These authors point out that people of color, women, the disabled, and the poor are oppressed by racism, sexism, and classism, and that one goal of multicultural education is to empower students so that they may have the courage, knowledge, and wisdom to control their life circumstances and transform society.

Some of the radical scholars (*e.g.*, McCarthy, 1990a) mainly quote from earlier publications on multicultural education, ignoring the context of time in which these publications were written, ignoring the conceptual evolution of multi-cultural education, and ignoring the more recent essays on multicultural education. Also, these critics seem to read what they wish into the writings on multicultural education. For example, McCarthy (1990b) compares the argument put forth in Sleeter and Grant's (1989) "Education That Is Multicultural and Social Reconstructionist" approach to one of crosscultural competence for enhancing minority negotiation with mainstream society (p. 49). This is difficult to understand, because a good deal of this approach is concerned with providing students with strategies for social action and developing self-empowerment (Sleeter & Grant, 1988, p. 201).

These misinterpretations of multicultural education by radical and conservative critics lead to continuous controversy, and undercut the influence that multicultural education can have on society Paul Robeson Jr. (1993) tells us:

> The controversy over multiculturalism is not, as many claim, merely a mani-festation of the politics of race and gender; rather, it is at the heart of a profound ideological struggle over the values of American culture and the nature of U. S. civilization. Above all it is a debate about whether the melting-pot culture, which is the foundation of the American way of life and imposes its Anglo-Saxon Protestant values on our society, should be replaced by a mosaic culture incorporating the values of the diverse groups that make up America's population. (p. 1)

This statement by Robeson provides an excellent response to the conservative critics, but I believe the radical critics have somewhat of a different problem. Their problem is one of a need to understand that many multicultural educators are not simply interested in an education that will lead to the assimilation of student into society as it presently exists. Many multicultural educators are inter-ested in changing the knowledge and power equation so that race, class, and gender groups that have previously been marginalized have equity and equality in all the structures of society.

Myth 2: the United States is a melting pot for all U.S. citizens

An increasing number of people are coming to the realization that the United States never was a melting pot. The argument they put forth is that people of color have not been able to "melt," and other groups, such as women, the physically challenged, lesbians and gay men, and the poor, have not been fully accepted into the mainstream of American society. Many realities—the glass ceiling in corpor-ate America that prevents women and people of color from reaching top leader-ship positions; inequities in pay between men and women and between people of color and white people; the lockout of women, people of color, and the poor from much of the political system; and the increasing slide of the United States into a two-class society of "haves and have nots"—invalidate the melting pot thesis.

Robeson explains that the melting-pot is based upon the denial of group rights and a one-sided emphasis on "radical individualism," whereas the mosaic culture affirms group rights along with individual rights and emphasizes a balance between individual liberty and individual responsibility to the community. Robeson further adds:

> This difference underlies the conflicts between the melting pot and the mosaic over the issue of race, ethnicity, gender, and class, since the melting pot has traditionally used the denial of group rights to subordinate non Anglo-Saxon White ethnic groups, non-White, White women, and those who do not own property (*i.e.*, people who do not belong to the middle or upper class). (p. 3)

Myth 3: multicultural education and political correctness are the same thing

Multicultural education is not a synonym for "political correctness." Many educators and other members of society unknowingly connect Political Correctness to multicultural education. Hughes (1993) states:

> Much mud has been stirred up by the linkage of multiculturalism with political correctness. This has turned what ought to be a generous recognition of cultural diversity into a worthless symbolic program, clogged with lumped-radical jargon. Its offshoot is the rhetoric of cultural separatism. (p. 83)

Political correctness, it is argued, is about doing the proper thing. Hughes (1993) also, says it is "political etiquette." Some conservative critics argue that political correctness is about speech repression. For example, penalizing students for using certain words on campus, that they would not be penalized for if they used these same words off campus. Cortes (1991), an observer of social history, explains:

> . . . some campuses have instituted ill-conceived speech codes that have reached ludicrous extremes of attempting to micro-manage the "unacceptable." Such action have had the unfortunate side effect of trivializing the critical issue of continuing campus bigotry, while at the same time casting a pall on the entire higher educational struggle against prejudice and for multicultural understanding. . . . (p. 13)

Repressing the use of speech, or limiting the books that make up the "canon," leads many—especially those who are opposed to multicultural education, or who are unsure about its meaning—to view multicultural education and political correctness as one in the same. An example may help to illuminate this point.

I was recently told that many P. C. advocates would probably ban or discourage the reading of *Huckleberry Finn*. I was then asked what would I, an advocate of multicultural education, do about the use of this American classic in schools. My reply was that *Huckleberry Finn*, or *Tom Sawyer*, can be read but in so doing needs to be read in a "context." By context, I mean the teacher leading the discussion should have experience teaching from a multicultural perspective. This would include having introduced the students (before the reading of *Huckleberry Finn*) to a variety of literature, some of which features African Americans as heroes and heroines; some of which has explained the historical meaning of words and terms; some of which included a rounded view of other ethnic groups, including whites. I would also add that the sequencing of *Huckleberry Finn* is important. It may not be wise to have it as the first book the class reads. It should be read after a positive climate is established, and students have developed an attitude of sensitivity and respect for each other within groups and across groups.

Garcia and Pugh (1992) claim that "political correctness" serves the purpose of defining a political and intellectual perspective as an aberrant ideology and then attacking it as indoctrination" (p. 216). When multicultural education is reduced to P. C., Garcia and Pugh (1992) argue, "[it] undercuts the validity of pluralism as a universally shared experience," and I would add it minimizes the importance of women, the poor, the physically challenged, and lesbians and gay men.

Myth 4: multicultural education reject a common culture

Multicultural education offers a way to achieve the **common** culture that doesn't presently exist. We all are aware that the United States is a land of many people, most of whose foreparents came from other countries, bringing different languages, customs, and religious beliefs. We are also aware that the United States' strength and humanity come from its diverse people. Additionally, we are aware that from this "diversity" it is important that we create a "oneness" or a common culture. Peter Erickson, using the canon as the context for his argument, offers four reasons why multiculturalism is not fraying America, and why it can help us the achieve a common culture.

First, Erickson (1991) argues that traditionalists view the canon as made up of diverse, inconsistent elements, but whole in the sense of being conceived as a single entity. He states, "The basic unit of organization is single authors, however diverse; their diversity is expressed through the framework of a single literary tradition" (p. B2). Multicultural education, on the other hand, supports the acceptance and affirmation of multiple traditions Erickson writes, "In a multicultural approach, the basic organizational component is not individual authors, but multiple traditions. Diversity is thus placed on a different conceptual foundation. This foundation implies that each minority tradition is a distinct cultural entity that cannot be dissolved into an overarching common tradition through the catalytic action of adding one or two minority authors to the established canon."

Second, multicultural education expands the idea of what constitutes "valid criticism." Criticism is not confined to the rules laid out by established classical authors. Erickson argues:

> Multicultural criticism . . . recognizes the possibility of a sharp criticism of Shakespeare that cuts through the mantle of his established position. Such criticism does not seek to eject Shakespeare from the canon, but proposes that Shakespeare no longer be viewed as an inviolable fixture. (p. B2)

Third, multiculturalists do not reject the idea of a common culture, as many opponents of multicultural education claim. Instead, "it [multiculturalism] opposes the traditionalist way of constructing a common culture through oversimplified appeals to a common heritage achieved by applying the principles of universalism and transcendence to peoples' differences" (p. B2). Erickson argues that for the multiculturalists, "common culture is not a given: it has to be created anew by engaging the cultural differences that are part of American Life" (p. B2).

Fourth, the common reader for the multiculturalist is shaped by "identity politics." In other words, the identity of the reader(s) needs to be taken into account if we are to understand the culture we hold in common. Similarly, race, class, and gender are active factors that must be acknowledged and deemed important to understanding and interpretations.

Myth 5: multicultural education is a "minority thing"

Many teachers and teacher educators see multicultural education as a "minority thing." They see it as mainly related to the school experiences of people of color. It is seen as an educational plan to help enhance the self-concept of students of color, especially African-American and Hispanic students, who many educators believe come to school with a negative self-image. Also, it is viewed as an educational plan to help manage the behavior of these same students. Additionally, it is regarded as a curriculum innovation that seeks to include the culture and history of under-represented groups in the American experience.

Conversely, multicultural education is not seen as important and necessary for whites. One reason for this is that many whites see the focus of multicultural as mainly race, and "race" is perceived narrowly as a "black or brown" problem—a problem that black and brown people need to overcome (Omi & Howard, 1986). Often forgotten is the United States' history of slavery and discrimination and the need for whites to understand how they contribute to everyday racism (Essed, 1990). Although the social science literature is replete with arguments that "race" (and racism) is very much the white man's problem, and that its evilness works against **all** of United States' society (Myrdal, 1944; Report of the National Advisory Commission on Civil Disorders, 1968; Tocqueville, 1969), this point is too often ignored (Omi & Winant, 1986; Ringer & Lawless, 1989).

Also ignored when race is seen as the only foundational pillar of multicultural education is the attention scholars of multicultural education gave to discussing socioeconomic class issues (*e.g.*, control of wealth in society, discussion of the causes of poverty and homelessness), gender (*e.g.*, the gender-based glass ceiling in corporate America, treatment of girls in math and science class), disability (*e.g.*, the isolation or absence of the physically challenged in the classroom and at school events).

Additionally, when multicultural education is seen as only a "minority thing" whites are mis-educated. They are inclined to develop ethnocentric and prejudicial attitudes towards people of color when they are deprived of the opportunity to learn about the sociocultural, economic, and psychological factors that produce conditions of ethnic polarization, racial unrest, and hate crimes. As a result, they do not understand their responsibility to participate in eliminating the "isms" (Miel, 1967; Suzuke, 1979).

Further, when multicultural education is seen as a minority thing, the importance of analyzing the impact of race, class, and gender interactions which are important to multicultural education research is ignored or understated. For example, Grant and Sleeter (1986) reported that studies of cooperative learning that mainly paid attention to one status group (race) oversimplified the behavior analysis, and this oversimplification could contribute to perpetuation of gender and class basis. Similarly, Bossard (1994) discusses the importance of studying the interaction effects of race, class, and gender over time in order to understand and break down the negative institutionalized patterns of social life in school.

Myth 6: multicultural education will impede the teaching of the basics and preparation of students to live in a global technological society

Learning the basics and being able to apply them to real life situations is essential to any quality educational program, and the purpose of multicultural education is to provide a high quality educational program for all students. Multicultural education includes curriculum and instructional approaches that place learning in a context that challenges students, while at the same time allowing them to have some familiarity with the learning context and the purpose for learning the content being taught (Gay, 1990; Trueba, 1991).

Much of the early multicultural curriculum in the 1970s and the early 1980s dealt with how to help teachers include or integrate multicultural education into the subject matter they teach daily. Reading and social studies especially received multicultural attention (Banks, 1979; Grant, 1977). More recently, beginning in the late 1980s, materials have been readily available to help teachers understand how to make their science and mathematics relate to their students' thinking and conceptual understanding (*e.g.*, Grant & Sleeter, 1989; Fennema & Franke, 1992).

The integration of multicultural education throughout the entire curriculum and instructional process is advocated to encourage students to learn the basics, understand that mathematics and science are tools that they can command, and that what they learn should give them greater control of their destiny.

Also important to multicultural education is developing the ability to listen to, appreciate, and critique different voices and stories. Development of these abilities, along with gaining an appreciation for differences, is essential to being able to successful live in the 21st century. Hughes (1993) reminds us:

> The future of America, in a globalized economy without a Cold War, will lie with people who can think and act with informed grace across ethnic, cultural, linguistic lines. (p. 26)

Finally, it is clear that multicultural education is being challenged, but we should not be dismayed or discouraged by this challenge. Just a few years ago, only a few people were seriously discussing multicultural education or paying attention to its potential and possibilities. Positive circumstances and events for multicultural education are happening all across the United States. For example, the State of Maryland has recently passed a law for education in the State entitled "Education That Is Multicultural."

Finally, it is important to remember the words of Frederick Douglass:

> If there is no struggle, there is no progress. Those who profess to favor freedom, and yet deprecate agitation, are men who want crops without plowing up the ground. They want rain without thunder and lighting. They want the ocean without the awful roar of its many waters. This struggle may be a moral one; or it may be both moral and physical; but it must be a struggle. Power concedes nothing without a demand.

References and resources

Balch, S. A. (Winter, 1992). Political correctness or public choice? *Educational Record*, 21–24.

Banks, J. A. (1991). Teaching strategies for ethnic studies (5th ed.) Boston, MA: Allyn & Bacon.

Banks J. A. & Banks, C. A. M. (1989). (Eds.) *Multicultural education: Issues and perspectives*. Boston: Allyn & Bacon.

Brossard, C. A. (1994). Why do we avoid class in this sig? Why do we fail to integrate two or more topics across race, class, and gender, in our paper? "Critical examination of race, ethnicity, class and gender in education." *AERA SIG Newsletter*, 9: 1 (March 1994)

Cortes, C. (September/October, 1991). Pluribus & unum: The quest for community amid diversity. *Change: The Magazine of Higher Learning*. 8–13.

D'Souza, D. (1991). *Illiberal education: The politics of race and sex on campus*. New York: The Free Press.

Erickson, P. (June 26, 1991). Rather than reject a common culture, multiculturalism advocates a more complicated route by which to achieve it. *The Chronicle of Higher Education*. 37 (41). B1-B3.

Hirsh, E. D. (1987). *Cultural literacy*. New York: Houghton Mifflin p. 18.

Essed, P. (1990). *Everyday racism*. Claremont, CA: Hunter House.

Fennema, E. & Franke, M. L. (1992). Teachers' knowledge and its impact. In D. A. Grouws (Ed.) *Handbook of research on mathematics teaching and learning*. New York: Macmillian.

Gay, G. (Winter, 1986). Another side of the educational apocalypse: Educating for being. *Journal of Educational Equity and Leadership*. 6 (4), 260–273.

Gay, G. (1990). "Achieving educational equality through curriculum desegregation," *Phi Delta Kappan*, 72(1).

Gollnick, D. M. & Chinn, P. C. (1994). *Multicultural education in a pluralistic society* (4th ed.) New York: Merrill/Macmillan.

Gracia, J. & Pugh, S. L. (1992). Multicultural education in teacher preparation Programs: A political or an educational concept. *Phi Delta Kappan* 75 (3), 214–219.

Grant, C. A. (1977). *Multicultural education: Commitments, issues, and applications*. Association for Supervision and Curriculum Development: Washington, D. C.

Grant, C. A. (1988). The persistent significance of race in schooling. *The Elementary School Journal*. 88 (5), 561–569.

Grant, C. A. & Sleeter, C. E. (1986). Race, class, and gender in education research: an argument for integrative analysis. *Review of Educational Research*. 56: 2, summer.

Hughes, R. (1993). *Culture of complaint the fraying of America*. New York: Oxford University Press.

JanMohamed, A. & Lloyd, D. (1987). Introduction: Toward a theory of minority discourse. *Cultural Critique* 6, 5–12.

Mattai, P. R. (1992). Rethinking multicultural education: Has it lost its focus or is it being misused? *Journal of Negro Education* 61 (1), 65–77.

McCarthy, C. (1990a). Race and Education in the United States: The multicultural solution. *Interchange*, 21 (3), 45–55.

McCarthy, C. (1990b). *Race and curriculum*. London: Falmer.

National Association of State Boards of Education (1993). *The American tapestry educating a nation*. Alexandria, Va.: The National Association of State Boards of Education.

Miel, A. (1967). The shortchanged children of suburbia. Institute of Human Relations Press, The America Jewish Committee. New York: Institute of Human Relations Press.

Myrdal, G. (1944) *An American dilemma*. New York: Harper and Brothers.

Nieto, S. (1992). *Affirming diversity*. New York: Longman.

Olneck, M. (1990). The recurring dream: Symbolism and ideology in intercultural and multicultural education. *American Journal of Education* 98 (2), 147–174.

Omi, M. & Winanat, H. (1986). *Racial formation in the United States: From the 1960s to the 1980s*. New York: Routledge.

Ravich, D. (1990). Multiculturalism yes, particularism no. *The Chronicle of Higher Education*, October 24, 1990, p. A44.

Ringer, B. B. & Lawless, E. R. (1989). *Race, ethnicity, and society*. London, England: Routledge.

Robeson, P., Jr. (1993). Paul Robeson, JR. speaks to America. New Brunswick, NJ: Rutgers University Press.

Schlesinger, A. Jr. (1991). *The disuniting of America*. Whittle Direct Books.

Siegel, F. (Feb. 18, 1991). The cult of multiculturalism. *The New Republic*.

Sleeter, C. E. (1992). *Keepers of the American dream: A study of staff development and multicultural education.* London, England: The Falmer Press.

Sleeter, C. E. & Grant, C. A. (1988). *Making choices for multicultural education.* New York: Merrill.

Suzuki, B. (1979). Multicultural education: What's it all about?" *Integrated Education.*

Tocqueville, A. de (1969) Democracy in America. Garden City, NY: Doubleday and Co.

Trueba, H. T. (1991). Learning needs of minority children: Contributions of ethnography to educational research. In L. M. Malave & G. Duquette (Eds.), *Language, culture & cognition.* Clevedon, England: Multilingual Matters Ltd.

U. S. National Advisory Commission on Civil Disorders Report (1968). New York: Bantam Books.

CHAPTER 23

THE CANON DEBATE, KNOWLEDGE CONSTRUCTION, AND MULTICULTURAL EDUCATION (1993)

James A. Banks

A heated and divisive national debate is taking place about what knowledge related to ethnic and cultural diversity should be taught in the school and university curriculum (Asante, 1991a; Asante & Ravitch, 1991; D'Souza, 1991; Glazer, 1991; Schlesinger, 1991; Woodward, 1991). This debate has heightened ethnic tension and confused many educators about the meaning of multicultural education. At least three different groups of scholars are participating in the canon debate: the Western traditionalists, the multiculturalists, and the Afrocentrists. Although there are a range of perspectives and views within each of these groups, all groups share a number of important assumptions and beliefs about the nature of diversity in the United States and about the role of educational institutions in a pluralistic society.

The Western traditionalists have initiated a national effort to defend the dominance of Western civilization in the school and university curriculum (Gray, 1991; Howe, 1991; Woodward, 1991). These scholars believe that Western history, literature, and culture are endangered in the school and university curriculum because of the push by feminists, ethnic minority scholars, and other multiculturalists for curriculum reform and transformation. The Western traditionalists have formed an organization called the National Association of Scholars to defend the dominance of Western civilization in the curriculum.

The multiculturalists believe that the school, college, and university curriculum marginalizes the experiences of people of color and of women (Butler & Walter, 1991; Gates, 1992; Grant, 1992; Sleeter, personal communication, October 26, 1991). They contend that the curriculum should be reformed so that it will more accurately reflect the histories and cultures of ethnic groups and women. Two organizations have been formed to promote issues related to ethnic and cultural diversity. Teachers for a Democratic Culture promotes ethnic studies and women studies at the university level. The National Association for Multicultural Education focuses on teacher education and multicultural education in the nation's schools.

The Afrocentrists maintain that African culture and history should be placed at the "center" of the curriculum in order to motivate African Americans students to learn and to help all students to understand the important role that Africa has played in the development of Western civilization (Asante, 1991a). Many mainstream multiculturalists are ambivalent about Afrocentrism, although few have publicly opposed it. This is in part because the Western traditionalists rarely distinguish the Afrocentrists from the multiculturalists and describe them as one group. Some multiculturalists may also perceive Afrocentric ideas as compatible with a broader concept of multicultural education.

The influence of the multiculturalists within schools and universities in the last 20 years has been substantial. Many school districts, state departments of education, local school districts, and private agencies have developed and implemented multicultural staff development programs, conferences, policies, and curricula (New York City Board of Education, 1990; New York State Department of Education, 1989, 1991; Sokol, 1990). Multicultural requirements, programs, and policies have also been implemented at many of the nation's leading research universities, including the University of California, Berkeley, Stanford University, The Pennsylvania State University, and the University of Wisconsin system. The success that the multiculturalists have had in implementing their ideas within schools and universities is probably a major reason that the Western traditionalists are trying to halt multicultural reforms in the nation's schools, colleges, and universities.

The debate between the Western traditionalists and the multiculturalists is consistent with the ideals of a democratic society. To date, however, it has resulted in little productive interaction between the Western traditionalists and the multiculturalists. Rather, each group has talked primarily to audiences it viewed as sympathetic to its ideologies and visions of the present and future (Franklin, 1991; Schlesinger, 1991). Because there has been little productive dialogue and exchange between the Western traditionalists and the multiculturalists, the debate has been polarized, and writers have frequently not conformed to the established rules of scholarship (D'Souza, 1991). A kind of forensic social science has developed (Rivlin, 1973), with each side stating briefs and then marshaling evidence to support its position. The debate has also taken place primarily in the popular press rather than in academic and scholarly journals.

Valuation and knowledge construction

I hope to make a positive contribution to the canon debate in this article by providing evidence for the claim that the positions of both the Western traditionalists and the multiculturalists reflect values, ideologies, political positions, and human interests. Each position also implies a kind of knowledge that should be taught in the school and university curriculum. I will present a typology of the kinds of knowledge that exist in society and in educational institutions. This typology is designed to help practicing educators and researchers to identify types of knowledge that reflect particular values, assumptions, perspectives, and ideological positions.

Teachers should help students to understand all types of knowledge. Students should be involved in the debates about knowledge construction and conflicting interpretations, such as the extent to which Egypt and Phoenicia influenced Greek civilization. Students should also be taught how to create their own interpretations of the past and present, as well as how to identify their own positions, interests, ideologies, and assumptions. Teachers should help students to become critical thinkers who have the knowledge, attitudes, skills, and commitments needed to participate in democratic action to help the nation close the gap between its ideals and its realities. Multicultural education is an education for functioning effectively in a pluralistic democratic society. Helping students to develop the knowledge, skills, and attitudes needed to participate in reflective civic action is one of its major goals (Banks, 1991).

I argue that students should study all five types of knowledge. However, my own work and philosophical position are within the transformative tradition in ethnic studies and multicultural education (Banks, 1988, 1991; Banks & Banks, 1989). This tradition links knowledge, social commitment, and action (Meier & Rudwick, 1986). A transformative, action-oriented curriculum, in my view, can best be implemented when students examine different types of knowledge in a democratic classroom where they can freely examine their perspectives and moral commitments.

The nature of knowledge

I am using knowledge in this article to mean the way a person explains or interprets reality. *The American Heritage Dictionary* (1983) defines knowledge as "familiarity, awareness, or understandings gained through experience or study. The sum or range of what has been perceived, discovered or inferred" (p. 384). My conceptualization of knowledge is broad and is used the way in which it is usually used in the sociology of knowledge literature to include ideas, values, and interpretations (Farganis, 1986). As postmodern theorists have pointed out, knowledge is socially constructed and reflects human interests, values, and action (Code, 1991; Foucault, 1972; S. Harding, 1991; Rorty, 1989). Although many complex factors influence the knowledge that is created by an individual or group, including the actuality of what occurred, the knowledge that people create is heavily influenced by their interpretations of their experiences and their positions within particular social, economic, and political systems and structures of a society.

In the Western empirical tradition, the ideal within each academic discipline is the formulation of knowledge without the influence of the researcher's personal or cultural characteristics (Greer, 1969; Kaplan, 1964). However, as critical and postmodern theorists have pointed out, personal, cultural, and social factors influence the formulation of knowledge even when objective knowledge is the ideal within a discipline (Cherryholmes, 1988; Foucault, 1972; Habermas, 1971; Rorty, 1989; Young, 1971). Often the researchers themselves are unaware of how their personal experiences and positions within society influence the knowledge they produce. Most mainstream historians were unaware of how their regional and cultural biases influenced their interpretation of the Reconstruction period until W. E. B. DuBois published a study that challenged the accepted and established interpretations of that historical period (DuBois, 1935/1962).

Positionality and knowledge construction

Positionality is an important concept that emerged out of feminist scholarship. Tetreault (1993) writes:

> Positionality means that important aspects of our identity, for example, our gender, our race, our class, our age . . . are markers of relational positions rather than essential qualities. Their effects and implications change according to context. Recently, feminist thinkers have seen knowledge as valid when it comes from an acknowledgment of the knower's specific position in any context, one always defined by gender, race, class and other variables. (p. 139)

Positionality reveals the importance of identifying the positions and frames of reference from which scholars and writers present their data, interpretations, analyses, and instruction (Anzaldúa, 1990; Ellsworth, 1989). The need for researchers and scholars to identify their ideological positions and normative assumptions in their works—an inherent part of feminist and ethnic studies scholarship—contrasts with the empirical paradigm that has dominated science and research in the United States (Code, 1991; S. Harding, 1991).

The assumption within the Western empirical paradigm is that the knowledge produced within it is neutral and objective and that its principles are universal. The effects of values, frames of references, and the normative positions of researchers and scholars are infrequently discussed within the traditional empirical paradigm that has dominated scholarship and teaching in American colleges and universities since the turn of the century. However, scholars such as Mydral (1944) and Clark (1965), prior to the feminist and ethnic studies movements, wrote about the need for scholars to recognize and state their normative positions and valuations and to become, in the apt words of Kenneth B. Clark, "involved observers." Myrdal stated that valuations are not just attached to research but permeate it. He wrote, "*There is no device for excluding biases in social sciences than to face the valuations and to introduce them as explicitly stated, specific, and sufficiently concretized value premises*" (p. 1043).

Postmodern and critical theorists such as Habermas (1971) and Giroux (1983), and feminist postmodern theorists such as Farganis (1986), Code (1991), and S. Harding (1991), have developed important critiques of empirical knowledge. They argue that despite its claims, modern science is not value-free but contains important human interests and normative assumptions that should be identified, discussed, and examined. Code (1991), a feminist epistemologist, states that academic knowledge is both subjective and objective and that both aspects should be recognized and discussed. Code states that we need to ask these kinds of questions: "Out of whose subjectivity has this ideal [of objectivity] grown? Whose standpoint, whose values does it represent?" (p. 70). She writes:

> The point of the questions is to discover how subjective and objective conditions together produce knowledge, values, and epistemology. It is neither to reject objectivity nor to glorify subjectivity in its stead. Knowledge is neither value-free nor value-neutral; the processes that produce it are themselves value-laden; and these values are open to evaluation. (p. 70)

In her book, *What Can She Know? Feminist Theory and the Construction of Knowledge*, Code (1991) raises the question, "Is the sex of the knower epistemologically significant?" (p. 7). She answers this question in the affirmative because of the ways in which gender influences how knowledge is constructed, interpreted, and institutionalized within U.S. society. The ethnic and cultural experiences of the knower are also epistemologically significant because these factors also influence knowledge construction, use, and interpretation in U.S. society.

Empirical scholarship has been limited by the assumptions and biases that are implicit within it (Code, 1991; Gordon, 1985; S. Harding, 1991). However, these biases and assumptions have been infrequently recognized by the scholars and researchers themselves and by the consumers of their works, such as other scholars, professors, teachers, and the general reader. The lack of recognition and identification of these biases, assumptions, perspectives, and points of view have frequently victimized people of color such as African Americans and American

Indians because of the stereotypes and misconceptions that have been perpetuated about them in the historical and social science literature (Ladner, 1973; Phillips, 1918).

Gordon, Miller, and Rollock (1990) call the bias that results in the negative depiction of minority groups by mainstream social scientists "communicentric bias." They point out that mainstream social scientists have often viewed diversity as deviance and differences as deficits. An important outcome of the revisionist and transformative interpretations that have been produced by scholars working in feminist and ethnic studies is that many misconceptions and partial truths about women and ethnic groups have been viewed from different and more complete perspectives (Acuña, 1988; Blassingame, 1972; V. Harding, 1981; King & Mitchell, 1990; Merton, 1972).

More complete perspectives result in a closer approximation to the actuality of what occurred. In an important and influential essay, Merton (1972) notes that the perspectives of both "insiders" and "outsiders" are needed to enable social scientists to gain a complete view of social reality. Anna Julia Cooper, the African American educator, made a point similar to Merton's when she wrote about how the perspectives of women enlarged our vision (Cooper, 1892/1969, cited in Minnich, 1990, p. viii).

> The world has had to limp along with the wobbling gait and the one-sided hesitancy of a man with one eye. Suddenly the bandage is removed from the other eye and the whole body is filled with light. It sees a circle where before it saw a segment.

A knowledge typology

A description of the major types of knowledge can help teachers and curriculum specialists to identify perspectives and content needed to make the curriculum multicultural. Each of the types of knowledge described below reflects particular purposes, perspectives, experiences, goals, and human interests. Teaching students various types of knowledge can help them to better understand the perspectives of different racial, ethnic, and cultural groups as well as to develop their own versions and interpretations of issues and events.

I identify and describe five types of knowledge (see Table 23.1): (a) personal/cultural knowledge; (b) popular knowledge; (c) mainstream academic knowledge; (d) transformative academic knowledge; and (e) school knowledge. This is an ideal-type typology in the Weberian sense. The five categories approximate, but do not describe, reality in its total complexity. The categories are useful conceptual tools for thinking about knowledge and planning multicultural teaching. For example, although the categories can be conceptually distinguished, in reality they overlap and are interrelated in a dynamic way.

Since the 1960s, some of the findings and insights from transformative academic knowledge have been incorporated into mainstream academic knowledge and scholarship. Traditionally, students were taught in schools and universities that the land that became North America was a thinly populated wilderness when the Europeans arrived in the 16th century and that African Americans had made few contributions to the development of American civilization (mainstream academic knowledge). Some of the findings from transformative academic knowledge that challenged these conceptions have influenced mainstream academic scholarship and have been incorporated into mainstream college and school

Table 23.1 Types of knowledge

Knowledge Type	Definition	Examples
Personal/cultural	The concepts, explanations, and interpretations that students derive from personal experiences in their homes, families, and community cultures.	Understandings by many African Americans and Hispanic students that highly individualistic behavior will be negatively sanctioned by many adults and peers in their cultural communities.
Popular	The facts, concepts, explanations, and interpretations that are institutionalized within the mass media and other institutions that are part of the popular culture.	Movies such as *Birth of a Nation, How the West Was Won,* and *Dances With Wolves.*
Mainstream academic	The concepts, paradigms, theories, and explanations that constitute traditional Western-centric knowledge in history and the behavioral and social sciences.	Ulrich B. Phillips, *American Negro Slavery*; Frederick Jackson Turner's frontier theory; Arthur R. Jensen's theory about Black and White intelligence.
Transformative academic	The facts, concepts, paradigms, themes, and explanations that challenge mainstream academic knowledge and expand and substantially revise established canons, paradigms, theories, explanations, and research methods. When transformative academic paradigms replace mainstream ones, a scientific revolution has occurred. What is more normal is that transformative academic paradigms coexist with established ones.	George Washington Williams, *History of the Negro Race in America*; W. E. B. DuBois, *Black Reconstruction*; Carter G. Woodson, *The Mis-education of the Negro*; Gerda Lerner, *The Majority Finds Its Past*; Rodolfo Acuña, *Occupied America: A History of Chicanos*; Herbert Gutman, *The Black Family in Slavery and Freedom 1750–1925.*
School	The facts, concepts, generalizations, and interpretations that are presented in textbooks, teacher's guides, other media forms, and lectures by teachers.	Lewis Paul Todd and Merle Curti, *Rise of the American Nation*; Richard C. Brown, Wilhelmena S. Robinson, & John Cunningham, *Let Freedom Ring: A United States History.*

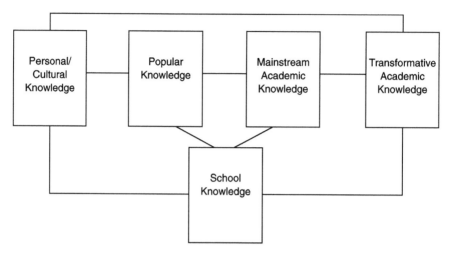

Figure 23.1 The interrelationship of the types of knowledge. This figure illustrates that although the five types of knowledge discussed in this article are conceptually distinct, they are highly interrelated in a complex and dynamic way.

textbooks (Hoxie, no date; Thornton, 1987). Consequently, the relationship between the five categories of knowledge is dynamic and interactive rather than static (see Figure 23.1).

The types of knowledge
Personal and cultural knowledge

The concepts, explanations, and interpretations that students derive from personal experiences in their homes, families, and community cultures constitute personal and cultural knowledge. The assumptions, perspectives, and insights that students derive from their experiences in their homes and community cultures are used as screens to view and interpret the knowledge and experiences that they encounter in the school and in other institutions within the larger society.

Research and theory by Fordham and Ogbu (1986) indicate that low-income African American students often experience academic difficulties in the school because of the ways that cultural knowledge within their community conflicts with school knowledge, norms, and expectations. Fordham and Ogbu also state that the culture of many low-income African American students is oppositional to the school culture. These students believe that if they master the knowledge taught in the schools they will violate fictive kinship norms and run the risk of "acting White." Fordham (1988, 1991) has suggested that African American students who become high academic achievers resolve the conflict caused by the interaction of their personal cultural knowledge with the knowledge and norms within the schools by becoming "raceless" or by "ad hocing a culture."

Delpit (1988) has stated that African American students are often unfamiliar with school cultural knowledge regarding power relationships. They consequently experience academic and behavioral problems because of their failure to conform to established norms, rules, and expectations. She recommends that teachers help African American students learn the rules of power in the school culture by explicitly teaching them to the students. The cultural knowledge that many African American, Latino, and American Indian students bring to school conflict with school norms and values, with school knowledge, and with the ways that teachers interpret and mediate school knowledge. Student cultural knowledge and school knowledge often conflict on variables related to the ways that the individual should relate to and interact with the group (Hale-Benson, 1982; Ramirez & Castañeda, 1974; Shade, 1989), normative communication styles and interactions (Heath, 1983, Labov, 1975; Philips, 1983; Smitherman, 1977), and perspectives on the nature of U.S. history.

Personal and cultural knowledge is problematic when it conflicts with scientific ways of validating knowledge, is oppositional to the culture of the school, or challenges the main tenets and assumptions of mainstream academic knowledge. Much of the knowledge about out-groups that students learn from their home and community cultures consists of misconceptions, stereotypes, and partial truths (Milner, 1983). Most students in the United States are socialized within communities that are segregated along racial, ethnic, and social-class lines. Consequently, most American youths have few opportunities to learn firsthand about the cultures of people from different racial, ethnic, cultural, religious, and social-class groups.

The challenge that teachers face is how to make effective instructional use of the personal and cultural knowledge of students while at the same time helping them to reach beyond their own cultural boundaries. Although the school should recognize, validate, and make effective use of student personal and cultural knowledge in instruction, an important goal of education is to free students from their cultural and ethnic boundaries and enable them to cross cultural borders freely (Banks, 1988, 1991/1992).

In the past, the school has paid scant attention to the personal and cultural knowledge of students and has concentrated on teaching them school knowledge (Sleeter & Grant, 1991a). This practice has had different results for most White middle-class students, for most low-income students, and for most African American and Latino students. Because school knowledge is more consistent with the cultural experiences of most White middle-class students than for most other groups of students, these students have generally found the school a more comfortable place than have low-income students and most students of color—the majority of whom are also low income. A number of writers have described the ways in which many African American, American Indian, and Latino students find the school culture alienating and inconsistent with their cultural experiences, hopes, dreams, and struggles (Hale-Benson, 1982; Heath, 1983; Ramirez & Castañeda, 1974; Shade, 1989).

It is important for teachers to be aware of the personal and cultural knowledge of students when designing the curriculum for today's multicultural schools. Teachers can use student personal cultural knowledge as a vehicle to motivate students and as a foundation for teaching school knowledge. When teaching a unit on the Westward Movement to Lakota Sioux students, for example, the teacher can ask the students to make a list of their views about the Westward Movement, to relate family stories about the coming of the Whites to Lakota Sioux homelands, and to interview parents and grandparents about their perceptions of what happened when the Whites first occupied Indian lands. When teachers begin a unit on the Westward Movement with student personal cultural knowledge, they can increase student motivation as well as deepen their understanding of the schoolbook version (Wiggington, 1991/1992).

Popular knowledge

Popular knowledge consists of the facts, interpretations, and beliefs that are institutionalized within television, movies, videos, records, and other forms of the mass media. Many of the tenets of popular knowledge are conveyed in subtle rather than obvious ways. Some examples of statements that constitute important themes in popular knowledge follow: (a) The United States is a powerful nation with unlimited opportunities for individuals who are willing to take advantage of them. (b) To succeed in the United States, an individual only has to work hard. You can realize your dreams in the United States if you are willing to work hard and pull yourself up by the bootstrap. (c) As a land of opportunity for all, the United States is a highly cohesive nation, whose ideals of equality and freedom are shared by all.

Most of the major tenets of American popular culture are widely shared and are deeply entrenched in U.S. society. However, they are rarely explicitly articulated. Rather, they are presented in the media and in other sources in the forms of stories, anecdotes, news stories, and interpretations of current events (Cortés, 1991a, 1991b; Greenfield & Cortés, 1991).

Commercial entertainment films both reflect and perpetuate popular knowledge (Bogle, 1989; Cortés, 1991a, 1991b; Greenfield & Cortés, 1991). While preparing to write this article, I viewed an important and influential film that was directed by John Ford and released by MGM in 1962, *How the West Was Won.* I selected this film for review because the settlement of the West is a major theme in American culture and society about which there are many popular images, beliefs, myths, and misconceptions. In viewing the film, I was particularly interested in the images it depicted about the settlement of the West, about the people who were already in the West, and about those who went West looking for new opportunities.

Ford uses the Prescotts, a White family from Missouri bound for California, to tell his story. The film tells the story of three generations of this family. It focuses on the family's struggle to settle in the West. Indians, African Americans, and Mexicans are largely invisible in the film. Indians appear in the story when they attack the Prescott family during their long and perilous journey. The Mexicans appearing in the film are bandits who rob a train and are killed. The several African Americans in the film are in the background silently rowing a boat. At various points in the film, Indians are referred to as *hostile Indians* and as *squaws.*

How the West Was Won is a masterpiece in American popular culture. It not only depicts some of the major themes in American culture about the winning of the West; it reinforces and perpetuates dominant societal attitudes about ethnic groups and gives credence to the notion that the West was won by liberty-loving, hard-working people who pursued freedom for all. The film narrator states near its end, "[The movement West] produced a people free to dream, free to act, and free to mold their own destiny."

Mainstream academic knowledge

Mainstream academic knowledge consists of the concepts, paradigms, theories, and explanations that constitute traditional and established knowledge in the behavioral and social sciences. An important tenet within the mainstream academic paradigm is that there is a set of objective truths that can be verified through rigorous and objective research procedures that are uninfluenced by human interests, values, and perspectives (Greer, 1969; Kaplan, 1964; Sleeter, 1991). This empirical knowledge, uninfluenced by human values and interests, constitute a body of objective truths that should constitute the core of the school and university curriculum. Much of this objective knowledge originated in the West but is considered universal in nature and application.

Mainstream academic knowledge is the knowledge that multicultural critics such as Ravitch and Finn (1987), Hirsch (1987), and Bloom (1987) claim is threatened by the addition of content about women and ethnic minorities to the school and university curriculum. This knowledge reflects the established, Western-oriented canon that has historically dominated university research and teaching in the United States. Mainstream academic knowledge consists of the theories and interpretations that are internalized and accepted by most university researchers, academic societies, and organizations such as the American Historical Association, the American Sociological Association, the American Psychological Association, and the National Academy of Sciences.

It is important to point out, however, that an increasing number of university scholars are critical theorists and postmodernists who question the empirical paradigm that dominates Western science (Cherryholmes, 1988; Giroux, 1983; Rosenau, 1992). Many of these individuals are members of national academic organizations, such as the American Historical Association and the American Sociological Association. In most of these professional organizations, the postmodern scholars—made up of significant numbers of scholars of color and feminists—have formed caucuses and interest groups within the mainstream professional organizations.

No claim is made here that there is a uniformity of beliefs among mainstream academic scholars, but rather that there are dominant canons, paradigms, and theories that are accepted by the community of mainstream academic scholars and researchers. These established canons and paradigms are occasionally challenged within the mainstream academic community itself. However, they receive their most serious challenges from academics outside the mainstream, such as scholars within the transformative academic community whom I will describe later.

Mainstream academic knowledge, like the other forms of knowledge discussed in this article, is not static, but is dynamic, complex, and changing. Challenges to the dominant canons and paradigms within mainstream academic knowledge come from both within and without. These challenges lead to changes, reinterpretations, debates, disagreements and ultimately to paradigm shifts, new theories, and interpretations. Kuhn (1970) states that a scientific revolution takes place when a new paradigm emerges and replaces an existing one. What is more typical in education and the social sciences is that competing paradigms coexist, although particular ones might be more influential during certain times or periods.

We can examine the treatment of slavery within the mainstream academic community over time, or the treatment of the American Indian, to identify ways that mainstream academic knowledge has changed in important ways since the late 19th and early 20th centuries. Ulrich B. Phillips's highly influential book, *American Negro Slavery*, published in 1918, dominated the way Black slavery was interpreted until his views were challenged by researchers in the 1950s (Stampp, 1956). Phillips was a respected authority on the antebellum South and on slavery. His book, which became a historical classic, is essentially an apology for Southern slaveholders. A new paradigm about slavery was developed in the

1970s that drew heavily upon the slaves' view of their own experiences (Blassingame, 1972; Genovese, 1972; Gutman, 1976).

During the late 19th and early 20th centuries, the American Indian was portrayed in mainstream academic knowledge as either a noble or a hostile savage (Hoxie, 1988). Other notions that became institutionalized within mainstream academic knowledge include the idea that Columbus discovered America and that America was a thinly populated frontier when the Europeans arrived in the late 15th century. Frederick Jackson Turner (Turner, 1894/1989) argued that the frontier, which he regarded as a wilderness, was the main source of American democracy. Although Turner's thesis is now being highly criticized by revisionist historians, his essay established a conception of the West that has been highly influential in American mainstream scholarship, in the popular culture, and in schoolbooks. The conception of the West he depicted is still influential today in the school curriculum and in textbooks (Sleeter & Grant, 1991b).

These ideas also became institutionalized within mainstream academic knowledge: The slaves were happy and contented; most of the important ideas that became a part of American civilization came from Western Europe; and the history of the United States has been one of constantly expanding progress and increasing democracy. African slaves were needed to transform the United States from an empty wilderness into an industrial democratic civilization. The American Indians had to be Christianized and removed to reservations in order for this to occur.

Transformative academic knowledge

Transformative academic knowledge consists of concepts, paradigms, themes, and explanations that challenge mainstream academic knowledge and that expand the historical and literary canon. Transformative academic knowledge challenges some of the key assumptions that mainstream scholars make about the nature of knowledge. Transformative and mainstream academic knowledge is based on different epistemological assumptions about the nature of knowledge, about the influence of human interests and values on knowledge construction, and about the purpose of knowledge.

An important tenet of mainstream academic knowledge is that it is neutral, objective, and was uninfluenced by human interests and values. Transformative academic knowledge reflects postmodern assumptions and goals about the nature and goals of knowledge (Foucault, 1972; Rorty, 1989; Rosenau, 1992). Transformative academic scholars assume that knowledge is not neutral but is influenced by human interests, that all knowledge reflects the power and social relationships within society, and that an important purpose of knowledge construction is to help people improve society (Code, 1991, S. Harding, 1991; hooks & West, 1991; King & Mitchell, 1990; Minnich, 1990). Write King and Mitchell: "Like other praxis-oriented Critical approaches, the Afrocentric method seeks to enable people to understand social reality in order to change it. But its additional imperative is to transform the society's basic ethos" (p. 95).

These statements reflect some of the main ideas and concepts in transformative academic knowledge: Columbus did not discover America. The Indians had been living in this land for about 40,000 years when the Europeans arrived. Concepts such as "The European Discovery of America" and "The Westward Movement" need to be reconceptualized and viewed from the perspectives of different cultural and ethnic groups. The Lakota Sioux's homeland was not the West to them; it was the center of the universe. It was not the West for the Alaskans; it was South. It was East for the Japanese and North for the people who lived in Mexico. The history of the United States has not been one of continuous progress toward democratic ideals. Rather, the nation's history has been characterized by a cyclic quest for democracy and by conflict, struggle, violence, and exclusion (Acuña, 1988; Zinn, 1980). A major challenge that faces the nation is how to make its democratic ideals a reality for all.

Transformative academic knowledge has a long history in the United States. In 1882 and 1883, George Washington Williams (1849–1891) published, in two volumes, the first comprehensive history of African Americans in the United States, *A History of the Negro Race in America From 1619 to 1880* (Williams, 1982–1983/1968). Williams, like other African American scholars after him, decided to research and write about the Black experience because of the neglect of African Americans by mainstream historians and social scientists and because of the stereotypes and misconceptions about African Americans that appeared in mainstream scholarship.

W. E. B. DuBois (1868–1963) is probably the most prolific African American scholar in U.S. history. His published writings constitute 38 volumes (Aptheker, 1973). DuBois devoted his long and prolific career to the formulation of new data, concepts, and paradigms that could be used to reinterpret the Black experience and reveal the role that African Americans had played in the development of American society. His seminal works include *The Suppression of the African Slave Trade to the United States of America, 1638–1870*, the first volume of the Harvard Historical Studies (DuBois, 1896/1969). Perhaps his most discussed book is *Black Reconstruction in America: An Essay Toward a History of the Part Which Black Folk Played in the Attempt to Reconstruct Democracy in America, 1860–1880*, published in 1935 (1935/1962). In this book, DuBois challenged the accepted, institutionalized interpretations of Reconstruction and emphasized the accomplishments of the Reconstruction governments and legislatures, especially the establishment of free public schools.

Carter G. Woodson (1875–1950), the historian and educator who founded the Association for the Study of Negro Life and History and the *Journal of Negro History*, also challenged established paradigms about the treatment of African Americans in a series of important publications, including *The Mis-education of the Negro*, published in 1933. Woodson and Wesley (1922) published a highly successful college textbook that described the contributions that African Americans have made to American life, *The Negro in Our History*. This book was issued in 10 editions.

Transformative scholarship since the 1970s

Many scholars have produced significant research and theories since the early 1970s that have challenged and modified institutionalized stereotypes and misconceptions about ethnic minorities, formulated new concepts and paradigms, and forced mainstream scholars to rethink established interpretations. Much of the transformative academic knowledge that has been produced since the 1970s is becoming institutionalized within mainstream scholarship and within the school, college, and university curricula. In time, much of this scholarship will become mainstream, thus reflecting the highly interrelated nature of the types of knowledge conceptualized and described in this article.

Only a few examples of this new, transformative scholarship will be mentioned here because of the limited scope of this article. Howard Zinn's *A People's History of the United States* (1980); *Red, White and Black: The Peoples of Early America* by Gary B. Nash (1982); *The Signifying Monkey: A Theory of African-American Literacy Criticism* by Henry Louis Gates, Jr. (1988); *Occupied America: A History of Chicanos* by Rodolfo Acuña (1988): *Iron Cages: Race and Culture in 19th-Century America* by Ronald T. Takaki (1979); and *The Sacred Hoop: Recovering the Feminine in American Indian Traditions* by Paul Gunn Allen (1986) are examples of important scholarship that has provided significant new perspectives on the experiences of ethnic groups in the United States and has helped us to transform our conceptions about the experiences of American ethnic groups. Readers acquainted with this scholarship will note that transformative scholarship has been produced by both European-American and ethnic minority scholars.

I will discuss two examples of how the new scholarship in ethnic studies has questioned traditional interpretations and stimulated a search for new explanations and paradigms since the 1950s. Since the pioneering work of E. Franklin Frazier (1939), social scientists had accepted the notion that the slave experience had destroyed the Black family and that the destruction of the African American family continued in the post-World War II period during Black migration to and settlement in northern cities. Moynihan (1965), in his controversial book, *The Negro Family in America: The Case for National Action*, used the broken Black family explanation in his analysis. Gutman (1976), in an important historical study of the African American family from 1750 to 1925, concluded that "despite a high rate of earlier involuntary marital breakup, large numbers of slave couples lived in long marriages, and most slaves lived in double-headed households" (p. xxii).

An important group of African and African American scholars have challenged established interpretations about the origin of Greek civilization and the extent to which Greek civilization was influenced by African cultures. These scholars include Diop (1974), Williams (1987), and Van Sertima (1988, 1989). Cheikh Anta Diop is one of the most influential African scholars who has challenged established interpretations about the origin of Greek civilization. In *Black Nations and Culture*, published in 1955 (summarized by Van Sertima, 1989), he sets forth an important thesis that states that Africa is an important root of Western civilization. Diop argues that Egypt "was the node and center of a vast web linking the strands of cultures and languages; that the light that crystallized at the center of this early world had been energized by the cultural electricity streaming from the heartland of Africa" (p. 8).

Since the work by Diop, Williams, and Van Sertima, traditional interpretations about the formation of Greek civilization has been challenged by Bernal (1987–1991), a professor of government at Cornell University. The earlier challenges to established interpretations by African and African Americans received little attention, except within the African American community. However, Bernal's work has received wide attention in the popular press and among classicists.

Bernal (1987–1991) argues that important aspects of Greek civilization originated in ancient Egypt and Phoenicia and that the ancient civilization of Egypt was essentially African. Bernal believes that the contributions of Egypt and Phoenicia to Greek civilization have been deliberately ignored by classical scholars because of their biased attitudes toward non-White peoples and Semites. Bernal has published two of four planned volumes of his study *Black Athena*. In Volume 2 he uses evidence from linguistics, archeology and ancient documents to substantiate his claim that "between 2100 and 1100 B.C., when Greek culture was born, the people of the Aegean borrowed, adapted or had thrust upon them deities and language, technologies and architectures, notions of justice and polis" from Egypt and Phoenicia (Begley, Chideya, & Wilson, 1991, p. 50). Because transformative academic knowledge, such as that constructed by Diop, Williams, Van Sertima, and Bernal, challenges the established paradigms as well as because of the tremendous gap between academic knowledge and school knowledge, it often has little influence on school knowledge.

School knowledge

School knowledge consists of the facts, concepts, and generalizations presented in textbooks, teachers' guides, and the other forms of media designed for school use. School knowledge also consists of the teacher's mediation and interpretation of that knowledge. The textbook is the main source of school knowledge in the United States (Apple & Christian-Smith, 1991; Goodlad, 1984; Shaver, Davis, & Helburn, 1979). Studies of textbooks indicate that these are some of the major themes in school knowledge (Anyon, 1979, 1981; Sleeter & Grant, 1991b): (a) America's founding fathers, such as Washington and Jefferson, were highly moral, liberty-loving men who championed equality and justice for all Americans; (b) the United States is a nation with justice, liberty, and freedom for all; (c) social class divisions are not significant issues in the United States; (d) there are no significant gender, class, or racial divisions within U.S. society; and (e) ethnic groups of color and Whites interact largely in harmony in the United States.

Studies of textbooks that have been conducted by researchers such as Anyon (1979, 1981) and Sleeter and Grant (1991b) indicate that textbooks present a highly selective view of social reality, give students the idea that knowledge is static rather than dynamic, and encourage students to master isolated facts rather than to develop complex understandings of social reality. These studies also indicate that textbooks reinforce the dominant social, economic, and power arrangements within society. Students are encouraged to accept rather than to question these arrangements.

In their examination of the treatment of race, class, gender, and disability in textbooks, Sleeter and Grant (1991b) concluded that although textbooks had largely eliminated sexist language and had incorporated images of ethnic minorities into them, they failed to help students to develop an understanding of the complex cultures of ethnic groups, an understanding of racism, sexism and classism in American society, and described the United States as a nation that had largely overcome its problems. Sleeter & Grant write:

> The vision of social relations that the textbooks we analyzed for the most part project is one of harmony and equal opportunity—anyone can do or become whatever he or she wants; problems among people are mainly individual in nature and in the end are resolved. (p. 99)

A number of powerful factors influence the development and production of school textbooks (Altbach, Kelly, Petrie, & Weis, 1991; FitzGerald, 1979). One of the most important is the publisher's perception of statements and images that might be controversial. When textbooks become controversial, school districts often refuse to adopt and to purchase them. When developing a textbook, the publisher and the authors must also consider the developmental and reading levels of the students, state and district guidelines about what subject matter textbooks should include, and recent trends and developments in a content field that teachers and administrators will expect the textbook to reflect and incorporate. Because of the number of constraints and influences on the development of textbooks, school knowledge often does not include in-depth discussions and analyses of some of the major problems in American society, such as racism, sexism, social-class stratification, and poverty (Anyon, 1979, 1981; Sleeter & Grant, 1991b). Consequently, school knowledge is influenced most heavily by mainstream academic knowledge and popular knowledge. Transformative academic knowledge usually has little direct influence on school knowledge. It usually affects school knowledge in a significant way only after it has become a part of mainstream and popular knowledge. Teachers must make special efforts to introduce transformative knowledge and perspectives to elementary and secondary school students.

Teaching implications

Multicultural education involves changes in the total school environment in order to create equal educational opportunities for all students (Banks, 1991; Banks & Banks, 1989; Sleeter & Grant, 1987). However, in this article I have focused on only one of the important dimensions of multicultural education—the kinds of *knowledge* that should be taught in the multicultural curriculum. The five types of knowledge described above have important implications for planning and teaching a multicultural curriculum.

An important goal of multicultural teaching is to help students to understand how knowledge is constructed. Students should be given opportunities to investigate and determine how cultural assumptions, frames of references, perspectives, and the biases within a discipline influence the ways the knowledge is constructed. Students should also be given opportunities to create knowledge themselves and identify ways in which the knowledge they construct is influenced and limited by their personal assumptions, positions, and experiences.

I will use a unit on the Westward Movement to illustrate how teachers can use the knowledge categories described above to teach from a multicultural perspective. When beginning the unit, teachers can draw upon the students' personal and cultural knowledge about the Westward Movement. They can ask the students to make a list of ideas that come to mind when they think of "The West." To enable the students to determine how the popular culture depicts the West, teachers can ask the students to view and analyze the film discussed above, *How the West Was Won.* They can also ask them to view videos of more recently made films about the West and to make a list of its major themes and images. Teachers can summarize Turner's frontier theory to give students an idea of how an influential mainstream historian described and interpreted the West in the late 19th century and how this theory influenced generations of historians.

Teachers can present a transformative perspective on the West by showing the students the film *How the West Was Won and Honor Lost*, narrated by Marlon Brando. This film describes how the European Americans who went West, with the use of broken treaties and deceptions, invaded the land of the Indians and displaced them. Teachers may also ask the students to view segments of the popular film *Dances With Wolves* and to discuss how the depiction of Indians in this film reflects both mainstream and transformative perspectives on Indians in U.S.

history and culture. Teachers can present the textbook account of the Westward Movement in the final part of the unit.

The main goals of presenting different kinds of knowledge are to help students understand how knowledge is constructed and how it reflects the social context in which it is created and to enable them to develop the understandings and skills needed to become knowledge builders themselves. An important goal of multicultural education is to transform the school curriculum so that students not only learn the knowledge that has been constructed by others, but learn how to critically analyze the knowledge they master and how to construct their own interpretations of the past, present, and future.

Several important factors related to teaching the types of knowledge have not been discussed in this article but need to be examined. One is the personal/cultural knowledge of the classroom teacher. The teachers, like the students, bring understandings, concepts, explanations, and interpretations to the classroom that result from their experiences in their homes, families, and community cultures. Most teachers in the United States are European American (87%) and female (72%) (Ordovensky, 1992). However, there is enormous diversity among European Americans that is mirrored in the backgrounds of the teacher population, including diversity related to religion, social class, region, and ethnic origin. The diversity within European Americans is rarely discussed in the social science literature (Alba, 1990) or within classrooms. However, the rich diversity among the cultures of teachers is an important factor that needs to be examined and discussed in the classroom. The 13% of U.S. teachers who are ethnic minorities can also enrich their classrooms by sharing their personal and cultural knowledge with their students and by helping them to understand how it mediates textbook knowledge. The multicultural classroom is a forum of multiple voices and perspectives. The voices of the teacher, of the textbook, of mainstream and transformative authors—and of the students—are important components of classroom discourse.

Teachers can share their cultural experiences and interpretations of events as a way to motivate students to share theirs. However, they should examine their racial and ethnic attitudes toward diverse groups before engaging in cultural sharing. A democratic classroom atmosphere must also be created. The students must view the classroom as a forum where multiple perspectives are valued. An open and democratic classroom will enable students to acquire the skills and abilities they need to examine conflicting knowledge claims and perspectives. Students must become critical consumers of knowledge as well as knowledge producers if they are to acquire the understandings and skills needed to function in the complex and diverse world of tomorrow. Only a broad and liberal multicultural education can prepare them for that world.

Notes

This article is adapted from a paper presented at the conference "Democracy and Education," sponsored by the Benton Center for Curriculum and Instruction, Department of Education, The University of Chicago, November 15–16, 1991, Chicago, Illinois. I am grateful to the following colleagues for helpful comments on an earlier draft of this article: Cherry A. McGee Banks, Carlos E. Cortés, Geneva Gay, Donna H. Kerr, Joyce E. King, Walter C. Parker, Pamela L. Grossman, and Christine E. Sleeter.

References

Acuña, R. (1988). *Occupied America: A history of Chicanos* (3rd ed.). New York: Harper & Row.

Alba, R. D. (1990). *Ethnic identity: The transformation of White America*. New Haven, CT: Yale University Press.

Allen, P. G. (1986). *The sacred hoop: Recovering the feminine in American Indian traditions*. Boston: Beacon Press.

Altbach, P. G., Kelly, G. P., Petrie, H. G., & Weis, L. (Eds.). (1991). *Textbooks in American Society*. Albany, NY: State University of New York Press.

The American heritage dictionary. (1983). New York: Dell.

Anyon, J. (1979). Ideology and United States history textbooks. *Harvard Educational Review, 49*, 361–386.

Anyon, J. (1981). Social class and school knowledge. *Curriculum Inquiry, 11*, 3–42.

Anzaldúa, G. (1990). Haciendo caras, una entrada: An introduction. In G. Anzaldúa (Ed.), *Making face, making soul: Haciendo caras* (pp. xv–xvii). San Francisco: Aunt Lute Foundation Books.

Apple, M. W., & Christian-Smith, L. K. (Eds.). (1991). *The politics of the textbook*, New York: Routledge.

Aptheker, H. (Ed.). (1973). *The collected published works of W. E. B. Dubois* (38 Vols.). Millwood, NY: Kraus.

Asante, M. K. (1991a). The Afrocentric idea in education. *The Journal of Negro Education, 60*, 170–180.

Asante, M. K. (1991b, September 23). Putting Africa at the center. *Newsweek, 118*, 46.

Asante, M. K., & Ravitch, D. (1991). Multiculturalism: An exchange. *The American Scholar, 60*, 267–275.

Banks, J. A. (1988). *Multiethnic education: Theory and practice* (2nd ed.). Boston: Allyn & Bacon.

Banks, J. A. (1991). *Teaching strategies for ethnic studies* (5th ed.). Boston: Allyn & Bacon.

Banks, J. A. (1991/1992). Multicultural education: For freedom's sake. *Educational Leadership, 49*, 32–36.

Banks, J. A., & Banks, C. A. M. (Eds.). (1989). *Multicultural education: Issues and perspectives*. Boston: Allyn & Bacon.

Begley, S., Chideya, F., & Wilson, L. (1991, September 23). Out of Egypt, Greece: Seeking the roots of Western civilization on the banks of the Nile. *Newsweek, 118*, 48–49.

Bernal, M. (1987–1991). *Black Athena: The Afroasiatic roots of classical civilization* (Vols. 1–2). London: Free Association Books.

Blassingame, J. W. (1972). *The slave community: Plantation life in the Antebellum South*. New York: Oxford University Press.

Bloom, A. (1987). *The closing of the American mind*. New York: Simon & Schuster.

Bogle, D. (1989). *Toms, coons, mulattoes, mammies & bucks: An interpretative history of Blacks in American films* (new expanded ed.). New York: Continuum.

Butler, J. E., & Walter, J. C. (1991). (Eds.). *Transforming the curriculum: Ethnic studies and women studies*. Albany, NY: State University of New York Press.

Cherryholmes, C. H. (1988). *Power and criticism: Poststructural investigations in education*. New York: Teachers College Press.

Clark, K. B. (1965). *Dark ghetto: Dilemmas of social power*. New York: Harper & Row.

Code, L. (1991). *What can she know? Feminist theory and the construction of knowledge*. Ithaca, NY: Cornell University Press.

Cooper, A. J. (1969). *A voice from the South*. New York: Negro Universities Press. (Original work published 1982)

Cortés, C. E. (1991a). Empowerment through media literacy. In C. E. Sleeter (Ed.), *Empowerment through multicultural education*. Albany: State University of New York Press.

Cortés, C. E. (1991b). Hollywood interracial love: Social taboo as screen titillation. In P. Loukides & L. K. Fuller (Eds.), *Beyond the stars II: Plot conventions in American popular film* (pp. 21–35). Bowling Green, OH: Bowling Green State University Press.

Delpit, L. D. (1988). The silenced dialogue: Power and pedagogy in educating other people's children. *Harvard Educational Review, 58*, 280–298.

Diop, C. A. (1974). *The African origin of civilization: Myth or reality?* New York: Lawrence Hill.

D'Souza, D. (1991). *Illiberal education: The politics of race and sex on campus.* New York: Free Press.

DuBois, W. E. B. (1962). *Black reconstruction in America 1860–1880: An essay toward a History of the part which Black folk played in the attempt to reconstruct democracy in America, 1860–1880.* New York: Atheneum. (Original work published 1935)

DuBois, W. E. B. (1969). *The suppression of the African slave trade to the United States of America, 1638–1870,* Baton Rouge, LA: Louisiana State University Press. (Original work published 1896)

Ellsworth, E. (1989). Why doesn't this feel empowering? Working through the repressive myths of critical pedagogy. *Harvard Educational Review, 59,* 297–324.

Farganis, S. (1986). *The social construction of the feminine character.* Totowa, NJ: Russell & Russell.

FitzGerald, F. (1979). *America revised: History schoolbooks in the twentieth century.* New York: Vintage.

Foucault, M. (1972). *The archaeology of knowledge and the discourse on language.* New York: Pantheon.

Fordham, S. (1988). Racelessness as a factor in Black students' school success: Pragmatic strategy or Pyrrhic victory? *Harvard Educational Review, 58,* 54–84.

Fordham, S. (1991). Racelessness in private schools: Should we deconstruct the racial and cultural identity of African-American adolescents? *Teachers College Record, 92,* 470–484.

Fordham, S., & Ogbu, J. (1986). Black students' school success: Coping with the burden of "acting White." *The Urban Review, 18,* 176–206.

Franklin, J. H. (1991, September 26). Illiberal education: An exchange. *New York Review of Books, 38,* 74–76.

Frazier, E. F. (1939). *The Negro family in the United States.* Chicago: University of Chicago Press.

Gates, H. L., Jr. (1988). *The signifying monkey: A theory of African-American literary criticism.* New York: Oxford University Press.

Gates, H. L., Jr. (1992). *Loose canons: Notes on the culture wars.* New York: Oxford University Press.

Genovese, E. D. (1972). *Roll Jordan roll: The world the slaves made.* New York: Pantheon.

Giroux, H. A. (1983). *Theory and resistance in education.* Boston: Bergin & Garvey.

Glazer, N. (1991, September 2). In defense of multiculturalism. *The New Republic,* 18–21.

Goodlad, J. I. (1984). *A place called school: Prospects for the future.* New York: McGraw-Hill.

Gordon, E. W. (1985). Social science knowledge production and minority experiences. *Journal of Negro Education, 54,* 117–132.

Gordon, E. W., Miller, F., & Rollock, D. (1990). Coping with communicentric bias in knowledge production in the social sciences. *Educational Researcher, 14*(3), 14–19.

Grant, C. A. (Ed.). (1992). *Research and multicultural education: From the margins to the mainstream.* Washington, DC: Falmer.

Gray, P. (1991, July 8). Whose America? *Time, 138,* 12–17.

Greenfield, G. M., & Cortés, C. E. (1991). Harmony and conflict of intercultural images: The treatment of Mexico in U.S. feature films and K-12 textbooks. *Mexican Studies/ Estudios Mexicanos, 7,* 283–301.

Greer, S. (1969). *The logic of social inquiry.* Chicago: Aldine.

Gutman, H. G. (1976). *The Black family in slavery and freedom 1750–1925.* New York: Vintage.

Habermas, J. (1971). *Knowledge and human interests.* Boston: Beacon.

Hale-Benson, J. E. (1982). *Black children: Their roots, culture, and learning styles* (rev. ed.). Baltimore: Johns Hopkins University Press.

Harding, S. (1991). *Whose science? Whose knowledge? Thinking from women's lives.* Ithaca, NY: Cornell University Press.

Harding, V. (1981). *There is a river: The Black struggle for freedom in America.* New York: Vintage.

Heath, S. B. (1983). *Ways with words: Language, life and work in communities and classrooms*. New York: Cambridge University Press.

Hirsch, E. D., Jr. (1987). *Cultural literacy: What every American needs to know*. Boston: Houghton Mifflin.

hooks, b., & West, C. (1991). *Breaking bread: Insurgent Black intellectual life*. Boston: South End Press.

Howe, I. (1991, February 18). The value of the canon. *The New Republic*, 40–47.

Hoxie, F. E. (Ed.). (1988). *Indians in American history*. Arlington Heights, IL: Harlan Davidson.

Hoxie, F. E. (no date). *The Indians versus the textbooks: Is there any way out?* Chicago: The Newberry Library, Center for the History of the American Indian.

Kaplan, A. (1964). *The conduct of inquiry: Methodology for behavioral science*. San Francisco: Chandler.

King, J. E., & Mitchell, C. A. (1990). *Black mothers to sons: Juxtaposing African American literature with social practice*. New York: Lang.

Kuhn, T. S. (1970). *The structure of scientific revolutions* (2nd ed.). Chicago: University of Chicago Press.

Labov, W. (1975). *The study of nonstandard English*. Washington, DC: Center for Applied Linguistics.

Ladner, J. A. (Ed.). (1973). *The death of White sociology*. New York: Vintage.

Meier, A., & Rudwick, E. (1986). *Black history and the historical profession 1915–1980*. Urbana, IL: University of Illinois Press.

Merton, R. K. (1972). Insiders and outsiders: A chapter in the sociology of knowledge. *The American Journal of Sociology, 78*, 9–47.

Milner, D. (1983). *Children and race*. Beverly Hills, CA: Sage.

Minnich, E. K. (1990). *Transforming knowledge*. Philadelphia: Temple University Press.

Moynihan, D. P. (1965). *The Negro family in America: A case for national action*. Washington, DC: U.S. Department of Labor.

Myrdal, G. (with the assistance of R. Sterner & A. Rose). (1944). *An American dilemma: The Negro problem in modern democracy*. New York: Harper.

Nash, G. B. (1982). *Red, White and Black: The peoples of early America*. Englewood Cliffs, NJ: Prentice-Hall.

New York City Board of Education. (1990). *Grade 7, United States and New York state history: A multicultural perspective*. New York: Author.

New York State Department of Education. (1989, July). *A curriculum of inclusion* (Report of the Commissioner's Task Force on Minorities: Equity and excellence). Albany, NY: The State Education Department.

New York State Department of Education. (1991, June). *One nation, many peoples: A declaration of cultural interdependence*. Albany, NY: The State Education Department.

Ordovensky, P. (1992, July 7). Teachers: 87% White, 72% women. *USA Today*, p. 1A.

Philips, S. U. (1983). *The invisible culture: Communication in classroom and community on the Warm Springs Indian Reservation*. New York: Longman.

Phillips, U. B. (1918). *American Negro slavery*. New York: Appleton.

Ramfrez, M., III, & Castañeda, A. (1974). *Cultural democracy, bicognitive development and education*. New York: Academic Press.

Ravitch, D., & Finn, C. E., Jr. (1987). *What do our 17-year-olds know? A report on the first national assessment of history and literature*. New York: Harper & Row.

Rivlin, A. M. (1973). Forensic social science. *Harvard Educational Review, 43*, 61–75.

Rorty, R. (1989). *Contingency, irony, and solidarity*. New York: Cambridge University Press.

Rosenau, P. M. (1992). *Post-modernism and the social sciences: Insights, inroads, and intrusions*. Princeton, NJ: Princeton University Press.

Schlesinger, A., Jr. (1991). *The disuniting of America: Reflections on a multicultural society*. Knoxville, TN: Whittle Direct Books.

Shade, B. J. R. (Ed.). (1989). *Culture, style and the educative process*. Springfield, IL: Thompson.

Shaver, J. P., Davis, O. L., Jr., & Helburn, S. W. (1979). The status of social studies education: Impressions from three NSF studies. *Social Education, 43*, 150–153.

Sleeter, C. E. (1991). (Ed.). *Empowerment through multicultural education.* Albany: State University of New York Press.

Sleeter, C. E., & Grant, C. A. (1987). An analysis of multicultural education in the United States. *Harvard Educational Review, 57,* 421–444.

Sleeter, C. E., & Grant, C. A. (1991a). Mapping terrains of power: Student cultural knowledge versus classroom knowledge. In C. E. Sleeter (Ed.), *Empowerment through multicultural education* (pp. 49–67). Albany: State University of New York Press.

Sleeter, C. E., & Grant, C. A. (1991b). Race, class, gender and disability in current textbooks. In M. W. Apple & L. K. Christian-Smith (Eds.), *The politics of textbooks* (pp. 78–110). New York: Routledge.

Smitherman, G. (1977). *Talkin and testifyin: The language of Black America.* Boston: Houghton Mifflin.

Sokol, E. (Ed.). (1990). *A world of difference: St. Louis metropolitan region, preschool through grade 6, teacher/student resource guide.* St. Louis: Anti-Defamation League of B'nai B'rith.

Stampp, K. M. (1956). *The peculiar institution: Slavery in the ante-bellum South.* New York: Vintage.

Takaki, R. T. (1979). *Iron cages: Race and culture in 19th-century America.* Seattle, WA: University of Washington Press.

Tetreault, M. K. T. (1993). Classrooms for diversity: Rethinking curriculum and pedagogy. In J. A. Banks & C. A. M. Banks (Eds.), *Multicultural education: Issues and perspectives* (2nd ed.) (pp. 129–148). Boston: Allyn & Bacon.

Thornton, R. (1987). *American Indian holocaust and survival: A population history since 1492.* Norman: University of Oklahoma Press.

Turner, F. J. (1989). The significance of the frontier in American history. In C. A. Milner II (Ed.), *Major problems in the history of the American West* (pp. 2–21). Lexington, MA: Heath. (Original work published 1894)

Van Sertima, I. V. (Ed.). (1988). *Great Black leaders: Ancient and modern.* New Brunswick, NJ: Rutgers University, Africana Studies Department.

Van Sertima, I. V. (Ed.). (1989). *Great African thinkers: Vol. 1. Cheikh Anta Diop.* New Brunswick, NJ: Transaction Books.

Wiggington, E. (1991/1992). Culture begins at home. *Educational Leadership, 49,* 60–64.

Williams, G. W. (1968). *History of the Negro Race in America from 1619 to 1880: Negroes as slaves, as soldiers, and as citizens* (2 vols.). New York: Arno Press. (Original work published 1892 & 1893)

Williams, C. (1987). *The destruction of Black civilization: Great issues of a race from 4500 B.C. to 2000 A.D.* Chicago: Third World Press.

Woodson, C. G. (1933). *The Mis-education of the Negro.* Washington, DC: Associated Publishers.

Woodson, C. G., & Wesley, C. H. (1922). *The Negro in our history.* Washington, DC: Associated Publishers.

Woodward, C. V. (1991, July 18). Freedom and the universities. *The New York Review of Books, 38,* 32–37.

Young, M. F. D. (1971). An approach to curricula as socially organized knowledge. In M. F. D. Young (Ed.), *Knowledge and control* (pp. 19–46). London: Collier-Macmillan.

Zinn, H. (1980). *A people's history of the United States.* New York: Harper & Row.

CHAPTER 24

THE PROGRESSIVE DEVELOPMENT OF MULTICULTURAL EDUCATION BEFORE AND AFTER THE 1960s (2000)

A theoretical framework

Charles R. Payne and Benjamin H. Welsh

The term "multicultural education" has come into vogue among educators to represent the type of education that many believe our young people should achieve. Although multicultural education represents a worthy goal for schools in the United States, multiculturalism has moved beyond the field of education. A multicultural perspective can help us to understand our place in both the present and the future. . . . It is a lens for viewing the motivations, beliefs, principles and imperatives that give rise to institutions and practices of people and their nations. (Kullen, 1994, p. vi)

> our place in both the present and the future. . . . It is a lens for viewing the motivations, beliefs, principles, and imperatives that give rise to institutions and practices of people and their nations. (Kullen, 1994, p. vi)

Multiculturalism has the potential to provide us with the means to get along in a time of rapid change.

Many people, including the critics of multicultural education, believe that multicultural education originated from the social unrest of the 1960s. Glazer (1995) stated:

> To its critics, multiculturalism looks like a very new thing in American education. In many respects, it is. However, viewed in the long stretch of the history of American public schooling, we can recognize it as a new word for an old problem: how public schools are to respond to and take account of the diversity of backgrounds of their students—religious, ethnic, racial. (p. 74)

In Banks's (1995) analysis of the development of multicultural education, he concluded that academic scholars developed the concept of multicultural education. Although scholars did, indeed, organize and research the content of multicultural education, the field was created ultimately in response to a desire for people from different segments of society to change their socioeconomic and political conditions. Furthermore, this desire was evident at certain points in history, starting centuries before the 1960s. Today, at the beginning of the twenty-first century, the concept of multicultural education represents the culmination of accomplishments and ideas resulting from 2,500 years of arduous struggles for dignity, duty, equality, freedom, and fundamental human rights.

The spirit of the struggle is found in such documents as the Hammurabi Code

(1750 B.C.), the Magna Carta (A.D. 1215), the British Bill of Rights (A.D. 1689); through every period in history, every revolution, every nationality, and every religion; and through philosophers such as John Locke, and Montesquieu. In more recent times this struggle has been revealed through the Russian and Chinese Revolutions; Women's Rights; the rise of the theory of rising expectations in Asia and Africa; and the rise of underdeveloped nations such as India and Africa.

Perhaps the acceptance in 1948 of the Universal Declaration of Human Rights by governments throughout the world will be considered one of the greatest displays of the universal determination for equality by the world's family of human beings. This agreement also gave many world governments the impetus to make human rights a priority. One of the most amazing human accomplishments of the past two millennia is that the concept of human equality was kept alive in the face of world slavery; extremely powerful, tyrannical, unethical political and religious leaders; and world wars. Miraculously, the idea of multicultural education is the culmination of all of the aforementioned historical struggles.

Human rights issues have always been at the core of the development of multicultural education. Although the issues of human rights are as old as human history, and no one country can claim a monopoly on them, why did the term "multicultural education" surface in the United States in the late 1960s? The answer to this question is similar to Lauren's (1998) explanation of how the British were able to end African slavery. Although people in other countries had a strong desire to see world slavery, particularly African slavery, come to an end, the political structure of Great Britain provided a vehicle for the "consideration articulation, and eventual implementation" (Lauren, 1998, pp. 38–39) of the idea. It was the established democratic political process, not hatred of slavery, that led to its abolition. So why was the concept of multicultural education created in the U.S. and not somewhere else? Since the adoption of the U.S. Constitution, the number one goal of the U.S. has been and continues to be the creation of a democracy—a more perfect union.

Multicultural education was a natural outgrowth of this process of democratization in the U.S. It was only in the U.S. that a process had been created by which the idea of multicultural education could receive full consideration, articulation, and implementation. But none of these three phases occur in a single step, especially in the U.S. All three are made up of two phases each that occur recursively and at times simultaneously. The two phases that make up consideration are consideration and reconsideration; the two phases that make up articulation are sociocultural and governmental; and, finally, the two phases that make up implementation are experimentation and institutionalization. Together the concepts form a heuristic with which to review the struggle that has led up to multicultural education.

Consideration

Phase one: consideration

To say that the concept of equality was given a full consideration in the U.S. does not mean that the deliberations were an organized debate in which everyone was sociable. Consideration of equality began in the struggle over slavery and through the signed, broken, and recently revisited treaties with Native Americans; the signing of the Bill of Rights; and the "employment" of Chinese and Irish individuals in building the Continental Railroad. Because decisions rendered by the courts were argued by lawyers and adjudicated by judges who were American citizens, their decisions must be treated as part of the consideration process even though they contributed to the creation of a segregated society. It was the same legal system that reversed these decisions in favor of a desegregated society within the next hundred years or so.

One legal decision that represents the consideration phase and serves as a landmark in the creation of a segregated American society is *Plessy v. Ferguson* (1896). This decision legalized segregation in all aspects of American society and culture and became known as the "separate but equal doctrine" (Zirkel, 1978, p. 76). Although this decision formally instituted what was a pre-existing oppressive condition for people of color, it is most ironic that the nation's high regard for equality was expressed in the statement "separate but *equal*." In fact it was the universal belief in equality that made reconsideration possible. Democracy is both a curse and a blessing in that America was blessed to have a process by which change of an unfavorable condition could occur.

Phase two: reconsideration

What is perceived to be the early developmental period of multicultural education is actually part of the second phase of consideration: reconsideration. Banks (1995) wrote that multicultural education is rooted in the work of earlier Black historians (e.g., Carter G. Woodson and W. E. B. Dubois). Banks's observations appear to be limited to Blacks. We must not forget that there were other groups concerned with getting their children an equal education before the emergence of these Black historians. Glazer (1995) wrote that Catholics and German-Americans argued for a more inclusive education as early as 1840. It was at this time that:

> ... the first of the "great school wars ... broke out." That first war centered on the demands of Catholic leaders for something like equal treatment for Catholic students in public schools whose principle aim was to socialize children into the Protestant moral and religious world of the mid-19th century. Catholic religious leaders objected in particular to readings from the Protestant King James Bible. Why not the Catholic Douay translation?
>
> ... In the 1880s, bitter public disputes broke out about the rights of the children of German immigrants to receive instruction in German. Teaching in German was widely established in Cincinnati, St. Louis, and elsewhere, to the discomfort of nativists and those concerned with the assimilation of immigrants. (pp. 74–75)

At the turn of the 20th century, John Dewey (as cited in Glazer, 1995) advocated for a new type of education by describing an American as being an amalgamation of Irish-Jewish-Greek-Pole-German-English Scandinavian.

> The point is to see to it that the hyphens connect instead of separate. And this means our public schools shall teach each factor to respect every other, and shall take pains to enlighten us all as to the great past contributions of every strain in our composite make-up. (p. 75)

Soon thereafter, Horace Kallen (as cited in Glazer, 1995), a student and follower of John Dewey, introduced the term "cultural pluralism." This term was coined to describe a new type of public education in which a variety of non-English cultures would receive a place in American public education. Here was another way to recognize cultural diversity as a central part of the American experience.

The human tragedies of World War II gave greater meaning to the term "human rights." The Jewish Holocaust, in particular, forced Americans to realize that inequality between races was inappropriate for American democracy. The well-documented human carnage clearly demonstrated to Americans and to the rest of the world what might happen in a society in which segregation and racism were institutionalized and sanctioned by law. Fear and concern that such atrocities happen in the U.S. led President Truman to appoint a Blue Ribbon Commission to study the condition of civil rights in the U.S. and to make recommendations for their amelioration. The report from the commission, "To Secure These Rights," paved the way for the elimination of legal segregation in military, in particular, and society, in general. Education was also addressed (Report of the President's Committee on Civil Rights, 1947). Reversal of the social direction of segregation in American society meant that a reconsideration of previous laws and policies had to be made. The following two Supreme Court Cases were pivotal in the early phase of reconsideration.

Although the decision in *Sweatt v. Painter* (1950) did not establish a direct value judgement against segregation, it did become the first decision to indicate that White Americans were recognizing the fact that separate could never mean equal:

> Rather than to allow Sweatt, a Black male, to attend the University Texas Law School the state of Texas had moved to create a new law school for Blacks. The decision that a new law school would not give him the preparation as that of a more established school, therefore he must be admitted to the University of Texas Law School, if qualified . . . (Zirkel, 1978, p. 79)

This was yet another example where the presence of the concept of "equal" worked, albeit unintentionally, in favor of a desegregated society. The Sweatt decision was limited in its reach because it applied only to the individual named in the case. It was not until four years later, with *Brown v. Board of Education*, 1954 (as cited in Zirkel, 1978, p. 80), that a decision was made that brought down the institution of segregation. The Court ruled that segregated schools were inherently inferior and that states operating dual school systems had to move toward a unified school system.

The Brown (1954) decision and others that favored educational equality over inequality brought the reconsideration phase to a close. The term "equal educational opportunity" emerged to reflect the shift. However, articulation, and implementation had yet to be accomplished. Strategies for transforming society, in general, and the educational system, in particular, from segregation to desegregation were needed.

Articulation

Phase one: sociocultural

Since before the Revolutionary War, ideas of democracy and equality originated within American culture and society. Governmental policy appeared only after sociocultural articulation had occurred. In fact, the government seems to require the language of public discourse in order to form its policies. The articulation of the vision of a desegregated society emergent in the late 1950s and early 1960s was no exception. Numerous people contributed to the articulation of this vision. When examining of the sociocultural articulation during this period, viewpoints of both sides of the issue, including the extremes, must be considered. Whereas the ideas of Martin Luther King are automatically included, the ideas of Huey Newton and Joe McCarthy must also be included.

Phase two: governmental

Several questions then emerged: How would the government articulate its vision of a desegregated society? And, what from the sociocultural articulation, if any, would be incorporated in the government's articulation? In the *Brown v. Board of Education*, 1954 decision (as cited in Zirkel, 1978), segregated schools were only declared to be unconstitutional. No reference was made to a time frame for ending the maintenance of legally segregated schools. However, a time frame of the vaguest sort was included in the *Brown v. Board of Education* decision of 1955 (as cited in Zirkel, 1978). The phrase "with all deliberate speed" (Zirkel, 1978, p. 81) was added. But this still was not a sufficient framework from which ordinary people who would be involved with implementation could develop a plan of action. State legislatures and school boards, in particular, could have used such a framework to better determine what they should do and when they should do it. A successful example of such a governmental framework is found in the Americans with Disabilities Act of 1990.

Another way to look at the governmental desegregation in America is that it went from consideration directly to implementation, bypassing governmental articulation altogether. However, there seems to have been logical reasons for this leap. First, the issue at hand was not an isolable problem that could be easily solved with a single legislative act. It involved the subtle, ubiquitous, and pernicious long-standing cultural practices of an entire society, from which no member of the dominant culture was entirely exempt. Second, in the late 1950s and early 1960s, many groups were at loggerheads, especially the minority-White liberal coalition that had pitted itself against powerful White Southerners for which segregation was an unquestioned fact of life. To articulate a plan would have taken time. Allowing more time would have been perceived by the minority-White liberal coalition as a stalling tactic. Further, conservatives might have taken advantage of additional time for articulation to develop more organized resistance. Stuck between the two were government leaders who were unable to speak with a single voice for they too were divided. Third, no other nation had ever done what the U.S. was trying to accomplish. There existed neither research nor model that reformers could look to for guidance. In short, the benefits for sidestepping articulation far outweighted the potential costs. Indeed, opening up discussion and taking the time necessary to come to consensus on desegregation might well have added to the existing strife, if not have triggered a second civil war.

Implementation

As the author Charles Payne experienced it in Mississippi, in the 10 years following the Brown (1954) decision, desegregation was attempted three times in three
different ways. With the first attempt, the most academically talented Black students were carefully selected and sent to White schools. In the second attempt,
Black students were allowed to transfer to the school they lived closest to, even if
it was a White school. Finally, after the other two had failed, desegregation was
forced through bussing Black students to White schools, whether it meant across
neighborhoods, across towns, or across counties. It is the legacy of forced bussing
that the Southern states are living with (and, in many places, reconsidering) today.

Although all three approaches to desegregation were based on the quest for
equality, decision makers at that time failed to recognize the vast cultural gulf that
existed between Blacks and Whites. This gulf was a result of a volatile combination of different cultural and ethnic origins, several centuries of slavery, and a
century of oppression under Jim Crow. Equality, however, was conceived of in
terms of sameness. Both Blacks and Whites believed that if Black students had the
same teachers and the same classrooms as Whites, they would do academically the
same as Whites. The concept of modifying the curriculum to account for cultural
differences was unheard of. Indeed many Blacks and White liberals might have
taken such a suggestion as an insult, for at that time "difference" was interpreted
as "inferior." Multiculturalists now recognize such thinking as erroneous, based
on the ethnocentric assumption embedded in the melting-pot metaphor.

One of the authors of this paper, Charles Payne, encountered this idea frequently, while growing up Black in a small Black community in Mississippi. He
writes:

> In 1952 when the Brown case was being argued, I was ten years old, in the 4th
> grade, and attending Booker T. Washington High School (Grades 1–12) in my
> home state of Mississippi. I recall vividly the nervous, reserved exuberance
> that was exhibited by my parents and teachers when they learned of the
> decision. From that very day they began telling me, "All you need is to be
> allowed in the room with little White chillun, you are jes' as smart." And they
> repeated that sentiment frequently throughout my schooling. But it was not
> until graduate school, almost 20 years later, that I first attended school with
> Whites. If adjusting to the new situation had required only academic
> adjustments, then perhaps they would have been closer to being correct in
> their thinking. In retrospect, the sociocultural differences, and the results of
> centuries of segregation of the races makes such a thought seem ludicrous.

In the minds of many Blacks and liberal White leaders, the entrance of highly
successful African Americans into the White world seemed to support the melting-
pot idea that Payne's role models expressed. In 1948, Jackie Robinson entered
White major league baseball, and rapidly became a superstar to both Blacks and
Whites. Mary McCloud Bethune, Leontyne Price, Marian Anderson, Nat King
Cole, George Washington Carver, Booker T. Washington, and other notable
African Americans seemed to represent the idea that for Black people to reach
equality with Whites, proximity with Whites was all that was needed.

But the success of these extraordinary individuals in the White world was not
without significant cost to each of them individually, and to the Black community
as a whole. Individually, they faced enormous struggles to maintain their

positions on a day-by-day, White person-by-White person, White institution-by-White institution basis. At the community level, they may have felt compelled to repudiate their ties to the Black community to maintain the appearance of (middle class) "respectability" to the White community, or they may have been rejected by the Black community for "selling out," or they may have had to endure some (often emotionally debilitating) combination of these two options.

Such struggles have become increasingly common in the Black community, particularly among middle-class Blacks who can now acquire their share of the American dream by buying homes in White neighborhoods and moving into them with legal impunity. The poorer (usually urban, inner city) community that is left behind finds itself isolated, with fewer role models to maintain the moral and ethical standards as was the case before desegregation. As a result, this poverty-stricken subculture or underclass is in the process of self-destructing through violence and drugs.

The White middle-class society's love-hate relationship with this underclass only exacerbates its problems. On the one hand, the White middle-class community approaches problems of this underclass as "Black problems" to be ignored and shunned. On the other hand, the White middle-class community embraces select representative members of this underclass as well as certain aspects of the creative and oppositional behaviors (e.g., dress, music, and slang expressions) that emerge from this underclass as being "cool" or "hip"—in other words, gold mines of insight and innovation waiting to be exploited by White culture industries. Jackie Robinson's story suggests that this pattern is not new nor are its unintended consequences.

White major league baseball embraced Robinson and Robinson, alone. It failed to embrace, or even recognize, the Negro League where he had been playing and where he had developed his celebrated skills. White major league baseball could have treated the teams within the Negro League as compatible expansion clubs, but it did not. Instead, it initially took one of the Negro League's best players. As a result, the Negro League died. Many Black players were robbed of the opportunity to earn a living by playing professional baseball. Young Black males' aspirations to become professional baseball players quickly faded. Lastly, the death of the Negro League deprived both the Black and White communities of significant economic opportunity and sociocultural exchange. It has been said that, "American baseball is a mirror of the American society." This model for desegregation is no exception.

The first court decision that produced in this "taking the best, leaving the rest" type of desegregation in the schools was *Cooper v. Aaron*, 1958. It forced the desegregation of Central High School in Little Rock, Arkansas (Zirkel, 1978, p. 82). The eight Black students who were allowed to attend Little Rock Central were chosen by the NAACP because they were considered the best prepared for the experience.

Many White Americans in Little Rock met this important test of the Brown (1955) decision with statewide resistance. Unfortunately, their behavior solidified White resistance to Supreme Court decisions related to the desegregation of schools. As a result of such resistance, extensive forced integration and forced bussing became necessary.

There is still a need for unified, singular governmental articulation of what the U.S. wants to accomplish and how it will accomplish it. Although an effort to articulate its goals at this time might appear to be going backwards, after nearly 50 years of uncertain experimentation it is still necessary. What has been accomplished is a plethora of legislative and legal decisions intended to move the nation in the direction of equality, a lessening of both heightened emotions and racist attitudes, and considerably more research from the social sciences. Multicultural education today can be seen as an attempt to make up for a lack of governmental articulation, to provide direction for future implementation, and to prepare individuals to participate in a culturally diverse, democratic society.

Post-implementation: the need for multicultural education today

The persistent problem of poor academic achievement by certain students, many of them minorities, has highlighted the need for the articulation of a plan and vital educational research to assist in reaching equality. The question of how to educate low-income students has long been an issue in American education. Ideas and information on how to teach the poor were available before the 1960s. But, in the 1960s, an additional concern for education became how to transform schools that indirectly taught segregation and racial hatred into schools that taught democracy and racial harmony, without favoring one race over the other academically. This transformational process was not possible through the existing implementation strategies. If the changes were to be effective and long lasting, then the rationale and benefits of such changes needed to be articulated and constantly taught to the citizenry as part of everyone's curriculum.

Fortunately, in the U.S., Americans have removed most, if not all, of the legal barriers to equality. Americans now have the arduous task of discovering what it means to become an even greater country on intercultural, intracultural, and interpersonal levels. Multicultural education aspires to move us in that direction.

Toward a curriculum for desegregation

Curricular content is not inconsequential. The curriculum that existed in schools under legal segregation did not teach the skills or attitudes that were essential for forming interdependent relationships between members of different ethnic groups. Although most graduates from the system would probably say that they were not taught to be prejudicial or racist toward any groups, prejudicial learning occurred indirectly by omission through what was not explicitly taught. The problems within schools today can be seen as results of the earlier system:

> America is made up of many cultures. The benefits of citizenship are distributed unevenly among these groups. Symptoms of inequity are easy to spot. For the poor and many ethnic or racial minorities, we educators see: abnormally high drop-out rates, extremely poor attendance at school, very limited participation in the curricular or co-curricular school programs, disproportionately higher representation in "educationally handicapped" programs, disproportionately lower representation in "gifted" programs, and strange phenomena such as a decrease in intelligence quotient with age for Black children who were at the same level as White children on measures of infant intelligent taken during the first 15 months of life. The list goes on, and it shows that some subgroups in our country are still in real trouble. (Hilliard, 1974, pp. 42–43)

If the nation is to become a better, more democratic society, then schools must develop environments and curricula that reflect the true ethnic, cultural, and religious diversity of our society. Omissions of the contributions of a variety of people convey messages of their worthiness. It is an indirect way of teaching disrespect of others. Throughout all disciplines, teachers must teach and model respect for human differences. Such teaching must go far beyond good manners and civil speech. Genuine respect can only occur when teachers incorporate the cultural experiences of all students as educational learning tools and when the curricular materials show the actual interconnectedness of different groups in the development of academic disciplines. Multicultural education is the label that is applied to this sort of teaching. It is a philosophy that teaches people the social and academic skills necessary for living in a culturally pluralistic world.

The critics of multicultural education

Many educators now approach multicultural education as if it were a moral imperative beyond criticism. Criticism nevertheless has its place in the restructuring of American education. As a national goal, developing a better democracy is too important for criticism not to be allowed. The dialogue that continues to occur between critics and proponents of multicultural education is an extension of the democratic process that has been created for bringing about change. If multicultural education is to have its maximum influence on American society, the national community must embrace it, and therefore, its proponents must answer the critics.

Arthur M. Schlesinger Jr. is one of the more prominent, early critics of multicultural education. His concern, as expressed in his book, *The Disuniting of America* (1992), is that multicultural education is causing polarization and separatism between ethnic groups. As an alternative to multicultural education, he seems to be arguing for a return to the melting-pot approach:

> The militants of ethnicity now contend that a main objective of public education should be the protection, strengthening, celebration, and perpetuation of ethnic origins and identities. Separatism, however, nourishes prejudices, magnifies differences, and stirs antagonisms. The consequent increase in ethnic and racial conflict lies behind the hullabaloo over "multiculturalism" and "political correctness," over the iniquities of the "Eurocentric" curriculum, and over the notion that history and literature should be taught not as intellectual disciplines but as therapies whose function is to raise minority self-esteem. (p. 17)

Schlesinger's (1992) comments related to the consequences of separatism cannot be argued with. However, separatism in this country predated multiculturalism and political correctness. Neither minorities nor multiculturalists instituted the *Plessy vs. Ferguson* (1896) decision, for example. As presented above, there has never been a time when the country was unified, so his argument is built upon a false premise. Perhaps a more honest title of Schlesinger's book would be: *Exposing the False Sense of Unity of America*, which is what multicultural education attempts to do.

Finally, a review of the multicultural literature reveals that its authors do not subscribe to the claims made by Schlesinger (1992). Although there is no one common set of goals espoused by all proponents of multicultural education, the following goals for multicultural education as expressed by Appleton (1983) and

Banks (1997) are representative. These goals point to a group of people trying to unite the country, not divide it.

In his own words, Appleton (1983) provided 10 principles for multicultural education. Among them are:

1 Multicultural education should help de-center people and thereby help depolarize interethnic hostility and conflict.
2 Implementation of multicultural education should be approached as a long-term process that will not produce dramatic, overnight changes in the schools.
3 Multicultural education should produce changes not only in the content of the curriculum but also in the teaching practices and social structure of the classroom.
4 Multicultural education must deal with the social and historical realities of American society and help students gain a better understanding of the causes of oppression and inequality and ways in which these social problems might be eliminated. (pp. 206–207)

More specifically, Banks (1997) provided us with the goals for multicultural curriculum:

1 A multicultural curriculum is to help students view events, concepts, issues, and problems from diverse cultural and ethnic perspectives.
2 A multicultural curriculum will contribute significantly to the development of a healthy nationalism and national identity.
3 The multicultural curriculum should help students develop the ability to make reflective decisions on issues related to ethnicity and to take personal, social, and civic actions to help solve the racial and ethnic problems in our national and world societies.
4 The multicultural curriculum should reduce ethnic and cultural encapsulation and enable students to understand their own cultures better.
5 The multicultural curriculum should help students to expand their conceptions of what it means to be human, to accept the fact that ethnic minority cultures are functional and valid.
6 The multicultural curriculum will help students master essential reading, writing, and computational skills. (pp. 25–28)

Perhaps what critics such as Schlesinger are really afraid of is that these goals will be reached, genuine equality will result, and White males will have to relinquish their hold on legislation and political discourse in this country.

In search of a new model for a new direction

Quite often discussions related to multicultural education have focused on racism, prejudice, and discrimination. It has even been referred to as "oppression studies" at times. Although these topics are unquestionably part of multicultural education, its major focus should be the examination of culture, including cultural similarities and differences, and how these differences and similarities have shaped the past and the present.

Effective education has long been thought of as a process by which an individual's life experiences become integrated with existing academic and social knowledge. Because culture and cultural differences are unavoidable and not limited to ethnicity, multicultural education as conceived of by Appleton (1983), Banks (1997), and others would be necessary whether or not it was called "multicultural education," or whether or not racism, slavery, the Holocaust, or American Indian reservations had ever existed. Multicultural education does not create or add anything new. It is simply "good teaching" and "good education" that acknowledges the actual contributions that members of different groups have made in the creation of our present world and the life experiences of all citizens. But, in order to implement this perspective and make it part of everyday educational practice, a new model must be created.

Equality is an American trademark. It is nowhere more evident than in the efforts to create an education system that fosters high student achievement, regardless of student background. However, as long as equality was viewed as sameness, earlier efforts by educators to address diversity were hampered. As Darling-Hammond, Wise, and Klein (1995) put it:

> The ongoing school reform movement of the last decade has riveted renewed attention on the capacities of teachers to teach a more demanding curriculum to the increasingly diverse groups of learners who are present—and who must become successful—in American schools. (p. 1)

A question that is frequently asked is "How do we know that multicultural education is the correct educational model?" We do not. What we do know is that the present model was not designed to teach racial harmony, and that its record of success is dismal, even among diverse groups of Whites, especially poor Whites. Why? Because the best teaching methods and the most resources have always been reserved for a very small segment of the dominant culture. Whatever negative things might be said about multicultural education, this much is clear: the present educational model is not withstanding the test of time. Once developed and fully implemented, multicultural education will be measured against that same test.

Institutionalization of multicultural education

An idea becomes institutionalized when it is incorporated into action without conscious thought or questioning, the way that standardized testing is accepted by almost everyone on every level of society. Laws and policies alone do not constitute full institutionalization. Full institutionalization does not occur until the idea is reflected in the practices of the people who make up the institution.

Many of the social and educational changes that people thought were accomplished in the 1960s and 1970s did not succeed over the long term because they did not become fully institutionalized. Forced desegregation through bussing is one example. Today, just over 30 years since its implementation, communities such as Charlotte-Mecklenburg, North Carolina, are rejecting bussing in favor of community-based schools, even if it means a return to an unequal distribution of resources.

In contrast, multicultural education seems to be well on its way to becoming institutionalized. Evidence, albeit circumstantial, of institutionalization is found in the growth of the use of the term and the number of books published on the subject. Figure 24.1 reveals the increase in the number of times the term "multicultural education" has appeared in a selection of professional education journals. Figure 24.2 reveals the increase in the number of library books with the

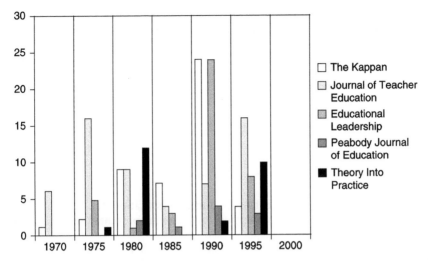

Figure 24.1 Frequency in using the term "multicultural education" in educational journal articles.

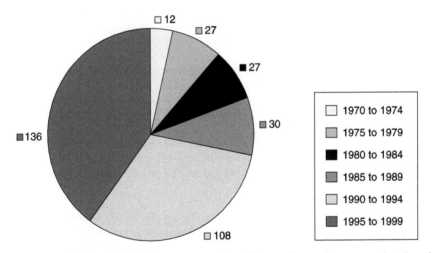

Figure 24.2 Number of books in university library that reference multicultural education (these numbers are approximations).

term "multicultural education" in their title since 1970 at a midwestern university with a teacher training program. From the above analyses it appears that the term "multicultural education" came into currency around 1970–1972 and is well on its way to becoming institutionalized at least within professional educational groups, an important step toward full institutionalization.

On the institutional and governmental side of the institutionalization equation, major nongovernmental organizations (e.g., the Anti-Defamation League, the National Council for Social Studies, and the National Council for Accreditation of Teacher Education) have instituted policies and practices related to equality. However, the National Education Association did not begin to address cultural diversity in schools until the 1970s. Noteworthy is the creation of the Interstate

New Teacher Assessment and Support Consortium (INTASC). By 1994, 9 of the 10 INTASC principles included attention to various aspects of diversity; and in 1992, 4 of the 18 NCATE standards included cultural diversity and multicultural education or both. It was expected that the revised NCATE standards of 1994 would be even more comprehensive (Gollnick, 1995, pp. 57–59).

Since 1965, federal initiatives that describe the course that the institutionalization of multicultural education or the ideas it represents have taken are:

1   The 1965 Elementary and Secondary Education Act (ESEA), Title I, was authorized as part of President Lyndon Johnson's War on Poverty to encourage schools with large concentrations of low-income students to improve their educational opportunities. Title I was replaced with Chapter 1 in 1988.
2   1968, Title VII of the ESEA, the Bilingual Education Act
3   1972, Title IX of the Education Amendments prevented discrimination based on gender.
4   The 1972–80 Ethnic Heritage Studies Act (Title IX of ESEA)
5   The 1975 Indian Self-Determination and Education Assistance Act (ESEA)
6   The 1980 Refugee Education Act (ESEA)
7   The 1988 Indian Education Act (ESEA) provided assistance to meet the special education and culturally related academic needs of Native American students in public schools. (Gollnick, 1995, pp. 45–48)

The above initiatives also point out the ongoing need for the articulation of mutually agreed upon goals for multicultural education.

The role of research

If multicultural education is to deliver its promise as an educational model, it must be based on the best, most current research available, which is being added to all the time. As a result, the multiculturalist has an obligation to be alert for any new research results. Payne (1993) wrote:

> Sound research is essential to guide us in our policies and educational practices. As professionals, we must have information which helps us to better understand the relationship between the Affective, Cognitive and Psychomotor Domains. We must approach educational research in a similar manner as that of nuclear physicist—a little at a time. Just as science, not technology, moves at a snail's pace so will knowledge in the field of education. (pp. 4–5)

In the absence of such research, human emotions will continue to play a significant role in pushing governments and school personnel into making decisions. In fact, in the U.S., many policies and practices related to education have been based on emotion, not research. Often, these emotionally appeasing policies and practices have been detrimental to the very groups that pushed for them.

Grant and Tate (1995) conducted an extensive review of the research literature on multicultural education. They began their report by reminding readers that "inquiry into education is a relatively new endeavor" (p. 145). Much of the research that has been conducted since the 1960s has focused on redressing the injustices of the past. Very little research has actually focused on the effect of cultural variables on student learning. It has focused on how minorities and women were represented in textbooks, with very little focus on how certain concepts and/or instructional strategies might influence the learning of students from different cultures. For example, to date there is very little research on the impact of culture on students when learning concepts and skills in mathematics and the biological and physical sciences as well as other areas except the social sciences and fine arts. Although we have come a long way, we clearly have a long way to go.

Ethnography

Since the early 1960s, a persistent concern for both multicultural educators and educational researchers has been the lack of achievement among students from certain minority cultures and among poor Whites. To address this lingering problem, a group of researchers are emerging who use ethnographic methods as both a research and teaching method in the creation of "culturally sensitive teaching." Their hope is the creation of instructional strategies that mesh with the culture of the students.

To accomplish the creation of culturally sensitive teaching, multiculturalists are beginning to incorporate the results of ethnographic research. Ethnographic research might prove to be what gives multicultural education its stability and credibility. Ethnography could possibly become the research arm of multicultural education, the source for evidence of the cultural factors that influence student achievement. In the future, such results could serve as a guide for teacher training and certification as well as educational policies at the local, state, and federal levels. However, such useful information might necessarily be slow in coming, because:

> Ethnographers learn about beliefs and behaviors of groups by becoming, to the extent possible, participants and observers of these groups. But as sites of ethnographers' studies, communities and families have been the most difficult social arenas for intense study. . . . [Furthermore] writing an ethnography requires long-term immersion, continuing involvement with community members, and some degree of comparative perspective that attempts to distinguish between what is common and what is unique across such groups. (Heath, 1995, p. 117)

To make ethnographic information practical, many such studies across time and distance will have to be conducted. But we may have no other choice.

Gains from focus on equality and diversity

Since before the 1960s equality and diversity have become a fixture in the American lexicon and social agenda. And, although the term "multicultural education" implies a focus on education alone, education is an important part of the total picture of the struggle toward equality. Because the American educational experience is considered the foundation for preparing Americans for full participation in U.S. society, it stands to reason that any measure of improvement in the behavior of the society at large is an indirect measure of the success of schools. In 1993, Payne stated that ". . . at this point in the United States we have not reached a destination with regards to diversity, but we have set a direction" (p. 5). Seven years later, in the year 2000, the process of articulating that direction and implementing the ideas generated from that articulation continues.

Author note

The authors wish to acknowledge Ms. Tyla Taneeka Turner, a graduate assistant, for her contribution in the preparation of the data for Figures 24.1 and 24.2 that represent the use of the term "multicultural education."

References

Americans with Disabilities Act of 1990 [On-line]. Available Internet: http://janweb.icdi. wvu.edu/kinder/pages/ada_statute.htm

Appleton, N. (1983). *Cultural pluralism in education: Theoretical foundations.* New York: Longman.

Banks, J. A. (1995). Multicultural education: Historical development, dimensions, and practice. In J. A. Banks & C. A. Mcgee Banks (Eds.), *Handbook of research on multicultural education* (pp. 3–24). New York: Macmillan.

Banks, J. A. (1997). *Teaching strategies for ethnic studies* (6th ed). Boston: Allyn and Bacon.

Darling-Hammond, L., Wise, A. E., & Klein, S. P. (1995). *A license to teach: Building a profession for 21st-century schools.* Boulder, CO: Westview Press.

Glazer, N. (1995). A new word for an old problem: Multicultural "school wars" date to the 1840s. *Annual Editions: Multicultural Education* (summer), 74–77.

Gollnick, D. M. (1995). National and state initiatives for multicultural education. In J. A. Banks & C. A. Mcgee Banks (Eds.), *Handbook of research on multicultural education* (pp. 44–64). New York: Macmillan.

Grant, C. A., & Tate, W. F. (1995). Multicultural education through the lens of the multi-cultural education research literature. In J. A. Banks & C. A. Mcgee Banks (Eds.), *Handbook of research on multicultural education* (pp. 145–166). New York: Macmillan.

Heath, S. B. (1995). Ethnography in communities: Learning the everyday life of America's subordinated youth. In J. A. Banks & C. A. Mcgee Banks (Eds.), *Handbook of research on multicultural education* (pp. 114–127). New York: Macmillan.

Hilliard, A. G. (1974). Restructuring teacher education for multicultural imperatives. In W. Hunter (Ed.), *Multicultural education through competency-based teacher education* (pp. 40–55). Washington, DC: American Association of Colleges for Teacher Education.

Kullen, A. S. (compli.). (1994). *The peopling of America: A timeline of event that helped shape our nation.* Beltsville, MD: Americans All, A National Program.

Lauren, P. G. (1998). *The evolution of international human rights: Visions seen.* Philadelphia: University of Pennsylvania Press.

Payne, C. R. (1993). Multi-cultural education as a process not a destination. *MEI Center Connection.* 2(1), 2–5. San Diego State University.

Report of the President's Committee on Civil Rights. (1947). *To secure these rights.* New York: Simon and Schuster.

Schlesinger, A. M., Jr. (1992). *The disuniting of America: Reflections on a multicultural society.* New York: Norton.

Zirkel, P. A. (1978). *A digest of supreme court decisions affecting education.* Bloomington, IN: Phi Delta Kappa.

APPENDIX 1: OTHER SUGGESTED READINGS

Apple, M. W. (1978). The new sociology of education: Analyzing cultural and economic reproduction. *Harvard Educational Review, 48*(4), 495–503.

Bacchus, M. K. (1969). Education, social change, and cultural pluralism. *Sociology of Education, 42*(4), 368–385.

Banks, J. A. (1995). The historical reconstruction of knowledge about race: implications for transformative teaching. *Educational Researcher, 24*(2), 15–25.

Berry, G. (1979). The multicultural principle: Missing from the seven cardinal principles of 1918 and 1978. *Phi Delta Kappan, 60*(9), 745.

Bigelow, W. (1989). Discovering Columbus: Rereading the past. *Language Arts, 66*(6), 635–643.

Hernandez, N. G. (1977). Another look at multicultural education. *Journal of Research and Development in Education, 11*(1), 4–9.

Olneck, M. R. (1989). Americanization and the education of immigrants, 1900–1925: An analysis of symbolic action. *American Journal of Education, 97*(4), 398–423.

Popkewitz, T. (1997). The production of reason and power. Curriculum history and intellectual traditions. *Journal of Curriculum Studies, 29*(2), 131–164.

Sizemore, B. A. (1979). The four M curriculum: A way to shape the future. *Journal of Negro Education, XLVIII*(3), 341–357.

Skinner, L. (1977). Multicultural education: A challenge for the future. *Educational Horizons, 55*(4), 189–201.

Tyack, D. (1993). Constructing difference: Historical reflections on schooling and social diversity. *Teachers College Record, 95*(1), 8–34.

APPENDIX 2: JOURNAL PUBLISHERS AND CONTACT INFORMATION

Action in Teacher Education
Association of Teacher Educators
1900 Association Drive, Suite ATE
Reston, VA 20191–1502
(703)620–2110; (703)620–9530
http://www.ate1.org

American Association of Colleges for Teacher Education
1307 New York Avenue, NW Suite 300
Washington, DC 20005–4701
(202)293–2450; (202)457–8096 (Fax)
www.aacte.org

American Educational Research Association
1230—17th Street NW
Washington, DC 20036
(202)223–9485, × 100; (202)775–1824
http://aera.net

American Journal of Education
University of Chicago Press
Permissions Department
1427 East 60th Street
Chicago, IL
(773)702–6096; (773)702–9756

American Sociological Association
1307 New York Avenue, NW Suite 700
Washington, DC 20005–4701
Jill Campbell
Publications Manager
(202)383–9005, × 303; (202)638–0882
www.asanet.org

Anthropology and Education
Anthropology and Education Quarterly
University of California Press
Journals and Digital Publishing Division
2000 Center Street, Suite 303
Berkeley, CA 94704

Association for Supervision and Curriculum Development
1703 N. Beauregard Street
Alexandria, VA 22311–1714
(703)578–9600; (703)575–5400 (Fax)
www.ascd.org

Banks, Cherry A. McGee
Professor, Education
University of Washington, Bothell
18115 Campus Way NE Room UW1 244
Bothell, WA 98011–8246

Banks, James A.
University of Washington
Box 353600, 110 Miller Hall
Seattle, WA 98195–3600
(206)543–3386; (206)542–4218 Fax
http://faculty.washington.edu/jbanks

Comparitive Education Review
University of Chicago Press
Permissions Department
1427 East 60th Street
Chicago, IL
(773)702–6096; (773)702–9756

Curriculum and Teaching
James Nicholas Publishers
PO Box 244
Albert Park, Australia, 3206

Education
Dr. George E. Uhlig
PO Box 8826
Spring Hill Station
Mobile, AL 36689

Education and Urban Society
Corwin Press, Inc.
2455 Teller Road
Thousand Oaks, CA 91320–2218
(805)499–9734; (805)499–0871 (Fax)
http://www.sagepub.com

Educational Horizons
National Association for Ethnic Studies, Inc. &
American Cultural Studies Department
Western Washington University
516 High Street—MS 9113
Bellingham, WA 98225–9113
(360)650–2349; (360)650–2690 (Fax)

Educational Leadership
Association for Supervision and Curriculum Development
PO Box 79760
Baltimore, MD 21279–0760
(703)578–9600; 1–800–933–2723; (703)575–5400 Fax
www.ascd.org

Educational Research Quarterly
113 Greenbriar Drive
West Monroe, LA 71291
(318)274–2355
hashway@alphagram.edu

Educators for Urban Minorities
Long Island University Press (No longer in operation)
Eugene E. Garcia, Ph.D.
Vice President Education Partnerships
Professor of Education
Arizona State University
Eugene.Garcia@asum.edu

English Journal
1111 W. Kenyon Road
Urbana, IL 61801–1096
(217)328–3870; (217)328–9645 (Fax)
http://www.ncte.org

Exceptional Children
Council for Exceptional Children
Permissions Department
1110 North Glebe Road Suite 300
Arlington, VA 22201–5704
(703)264–1637

FOCUS
Joint Center for Political Studies
1301 Pennsylvania Avenue, NW
Washington, DC 20004
(202)626–3500

Ford Foundation
320 East 43rd Street
New York, NY 10017

Gibson, Margaret A.
Professor of Education and Anthropology
Department of Education
University of California, Santa Cruz
1156 High Street
Santa Cruz, CA 95064
(831)459–4740; (831)459–4618 (Fax)

Harvard Educational Review
Harvard Graduate School of Education
8 Story Street, 1st Floor
Cambridge, MA 02138
(617)495–3432; (617)496–3584 (fax)
www.hepg.org
+
HarperCollins Publishers
10 East 53rd Street
New York, NY 10022
(212)207–7000

Interchange
Nel van der Werf
Assistant Rights and Permissions/Springer
Van Godewijckstraat 30
PO Box 17
3300 AA Dordrecht
The Netherlands
31 (0) 78 6576 298; 31 (0) 78 6576 323 (Fax)
Nel.vanderwerf@springer.com
www.springeronline.com

Journal of Curriculum Studies
Routledge (Taylor & Francis, Inc.)
4 Park Square, Milton Park
Abingdon, Oxon OX14 4RN United Kingdom
44–1235–828600; 44–1235–829000 (Fax)
http://www.routledge.co.uk

Journal of Curriculum and Supervision
Association for Supervision and Curriculum Development
1703 North Beauregard Street
Alexandria, VA 22311–1714
(703)578–9600/(800)933–2723; (703)575–3926 (Fax)
http://www.ascd.org

Journal of Teacher Education
American Association of Colleges for Teacher Education
1307 New York Avenue NW Suite 300
Washington, DC 20017–4701
(202)293–2450; (202)457–8095 (Fax)
www.aacte.org

Journal of Research and Development in Education
Julie P. Sartor, Editor
Office of the Associate Dean for Research,
Technology, & External Affairs
UGA College of Education
(706)542–4693; (706)542–8125 (Fax)
jsartor@uga.edu

Journal of Negro Education
Howard University Press
Marketing Department
2600 Sixth Street, NW
Washington, DC 20059
(202)806–8120; (202)806–8434 (Fax)

Journal of Literacy Research (formerly *Journal of Reading Behavior*)
Lawrence Erlbaum Associates, Inc.
10 Industrial Avenue
Mahwah, NJ 07430–2262
(201)258–2200; (201)236–0072 (Fax)

Journal of Educational Thought
University of Calgary
Faculty of Education – Publications Office
2500 University Drive N.W.
Education Tower, Room 1310
Calgary, Alberta, Canada T2N 1N4
(403)220–7499/5629; (403)284–4162 (Fax)
www.ucalgary.ca

Journal of Teacher Education
American Association of Colleges for Teacher Education
1307 New York Avenue NW 300
Washington, DC 20005–4701
(202)293–2450; (202)457–8095 (Fax)
www.aacte.org

Language Arts
The National Council of Teachers of English
1111 W. Kenyon Road
Urbana, IL 61801–1096
(217)278–3621
permissions@ncte.org

Momentum
National Catholic Educational Association
1077—30 Street, NW Suite 100
Washington, DC 2007
(202)337–6232; (202)333–6706 (Fax)
nceaadmin@ncea.org

Multicultural Education
Gaddo Gap Press
3145 Geary Boulevard PMB 275
San Francisco, CA 94118
(414)666–3012; (414)666–3552
http://www.caddogap.com

National Catholic Educational Association
1077—30 Street, NW Suite 100
Washington, DC 20007
(202)337–6232; (202)333–6706 (Fax)
nceaadmin@ncea.org

National Council for the Social Studies
8555 Sixteenth Street, Suite 500
Center for Multicultural Education
Silver Spring, MD 20910
(301)588–1800 × 122;
(301)588–2049 Fax

National Educational Service
1252 Loesch Road
PO Box 8 Department V2
Bloomington, IN 47402

Negro Educational Review
NER Editorial Offices
School of Education
1601 East Market Street
Greensboro, NC 27411
Alice M. Scales (scales@pitt.edu)
Shirley A. Biggs (biggs@pitt.edu)

Peabody Journal of Education
Lawrence Erlbaum Associates
10 Industrial Avenue
Mahwah, NJ 07430–2262

Phi Delta Kappan
Phi Delta Kappa International
408 N. Union Street
PO Box 789
(812)339–1156; 800–766–1156; (812)339–0018 fax

Race, Class, and Gender
Southern University at New Orleans (No Response)
Carl contact Jean Belkhir (jbelkhir@uno.edu)

Radical Teacher
Center for Critical Education
PO Box 382616
Cambridge, MA 02238
Saul Slapikoff, Permissions Editor
slap2@comcast.net

Researching Today's Youth: The Community Circle of Caring Journal
Dr. Carlos E. Cortes
Professor Emeritus
Department of History
University of California,
Riverside, CA 92521–0204
(951)827–1487
(951)827–5299 fax
carlos.cortes@ucr.edu

Review of Educational Research
American Educational Research Association
1230—17th Street NW
Washington, DC 20036–3078

Sage Publications, Inc.
Corwin Press, Inc
2455 Teller Road
Thousand Oaks, CA 91320
(805)410–7713; (805)376–9562 (Fax)
permissions@sagepub.com

Southeastern Association of Educational Opportunity Program Personnel (SAEOPP)
75 Piedmont Avenue NE
Suite 408
Atlanta, GA 30303–2518
(404)522–4642

Teachers College Record
Blackwell Publishing
PO Box 805
9600 Garsington Road
Oxford OX4 2ZG United Kingdom
44 (0) 1865 776868; 44 (0) 1865 714591 Fax
www.blackwellpublishing.com

Teacher Education and Special Education
Dr. Fred Spooner, Editor
Teacher Education and Special Education
SPCD/College of Education
University of North Carolina at Charlotte
Charlotte, NC 28223

(704)687–8851; (704)687–2916 Fax
fhspoone@email.uncc.edu

The American Scholar
1606 New Hampshire Avenue NW
Washington, DC 20009
(202)265–3808; (202)265–0083

The Educational Forum
Kappa Delta Pi
3707 Woodview Trace
Indianapolis, IN 46268–1158

The High School Journal
The University of North Carolina Press
PO Box 2288
Chapel Hill, NC 27515–2288
(919)966–3561; (919)966–3829
www.uncpress.unc.edu

The Journal of Educational Research
Heldref Publications
1319 Eighteenth Street, NW
Washington, DC 20036–1802
(202)296–6267; (202)296–5146 (Fax)
www.heldref.org

The New Advocate
Christopher-Gordon Publishers, Inc.
1502 Providence Hwy, Suite 12
Norwood, MA 02062–4643
(781)762–5577; (781)762–7261
http://www.christopher-gordon.com

The Social Studies
Heldref Publications
1319 Eighteenth Street, NW
Washington, DC 20038–1802
(202)296–6267; (202)296–5149 (Fax)
permissions@heldref.org

The Teacher Educator
Ball State University
Teachers College
TC 1008
Muncie, IN 47306
(765)285–5453; (765)285–5455

The Urban Review
Nel van der Werf
Assistant Rights and Permissions/Springer
Van Godewijckstraat 30
PO Box 17
3300 AA Dordrecht
The Netherlands
31 (0) 78 6576 298; 31 (0) 78 6576 323 (Fax)
Nel.vanderwerf@springer.com
www.springeronline.com

Theory into Practice
Lawrence Erlbaum Associates, Inc.
10 Industrial Avenue
Mahwah, NJ 07430–2262

Viewpoints in Teaching and Learning
Indiana University
School of Education
Education Building 109
Bloomington, IN 47405

Young Children
National Association for the Education of Young Children
1313 L Street, NW, Suite 500
Washington, DC 20036–1426
(202)232–8777; (202)328–1846 (Fax)
http://www.naeyc.org

PERMISSION CREDITS

Prophecy in Ghetto Education." *Harvard Educational Review,* 40:3 (August 1970), 411–451. Copyright © 1970 by the President and Fellows of Harvard College. Reprinted with permission.

Stephen S. Baratz and Joan C. Baratz, "Early Childhood Intervention: The Social Science Base of Institutional Racism." *Harvard Educational Review,* 40:1 (Winter 1970), 29–50. Copyright © 1970 by the President and Fellows of Harvard College. Reprinted with permission.

Daniel G. Solorzano and Tara J. Yosso, "From Racial Stereotyping and Deficit Discourse Toward a Critical Race Theory in Teacher Education." *Multicultural Education,* 9:1 (2001), 2–8. Copyright © 2001 by Caddo Gap Press. Reprinted with permission.

Part 3: Multicultural Education: 1980s

Michael W. Apple, "The Other Side of the Hidden Curriculum: Correspondence Theories and the Labor Process." *Interchange,* 11:3 (1980), 5–22. Copyright © 1980 by Springer. Reprinted with permission.

Michael Apple and Lois Weis, "Seeing Educational Relationally: The Stratification of Culture and People in the Sociology of School Knowledge." *Journal of Education,* 168:1 (1980), 7–34. Copyright © 1980 by Trustees of Boston University. Reprinted with permission.

Michelle Fine, "Silencing in Public Schools." *Language Arts,* 64:2 (1987), 157–173. Copyright © 1987 by the National Council of Teachers of English. Reprinted with permission.

Cameron McCarthy, "Rethinking Liberal and Radical Perspectives on Racial Inequality in Schooling: Making the Case for Nonsynchrony." *Harvard Educational Review,* 58:3 (August 1988), 265–279. Copyright © 1988 by the President and Fellows of Harvard College. Reprinted with permission.

Geneva Gay, "Multiethnic Education: Historical Developments and Future Prospects." *Phi Delta Kappan,* 64:8 (1983), 560–563. Copyright © 1983 by Phi Delta Kappa International. Reprinted with permission.

Kal Gezi, "Issues in Multicultural Education." *Educational Research Quarterly,* 6:3 (Fall 1981), 5–14. Copyright © 1981 by *Educational Research Quarterly.* Reprinted with permission.

Christine E. Sleeter and Carl A. Grant, "An Analysis of Multicultural Education in the United States." *Harvard Educational Review,* 57:4 (November 1987), 421–444. Copyright © 1987 by the President and Fellows of Harvard College. Reprinted with permission.

Christine E. Sleeter, "Learning Disabilities: The Social Construction of a Special Education Category." *Exceptional Children,* 53:1 (1986), 46–54. Copyright © 1986 by the Council for Exceptional Children. Reprinted with permission.

Part 4: Multicultural Education: 1990s

Jean Anyon, "Race, Social Class, and Educational Reform in an Inner City School." *Teachers College Record,* 97:1 (Fall 1995), 69–95. Copyright © 1995 by Teachers College, Columbia University. Reprinted with permission.

AUTHOR INDEX

SUBJECT INDEX